PEARSON   ALWAYS LEARNING

Keith D. Swim, Jr. • Leonard Bierman • Michael Pustay

Legal Environment of Business

Custom Edition for Texas A&M University

Pearson Learning Solutions, 501 Boylston Street, Suite 900, Boston, MA 02116
A Pearson Education Company
www.pearsoned.com

Printed in the United States of America

6 7 8 9 10 V0CR 18 17 16 15

000200010271777833

MP

ISBN 10: 1-269-39994-2
ISBN 13: 978-1-269-39994-4

CONTENTS

1

INTRODUCTION TO LAW AND SOURCE OF LAW

I. INTRODUCTION

A. Two Major Roles of Law in Business World

The law plays two major roles in the business world:

1. Dispute resolution
2. Regulation

In its **dispute resolution role**, the law gives people and business entities a forum to settle their differences whether it be through the enforcement of some legal issue, such as the enforcement of contracts, or the recognition of private property rights in eminent domain, both of which will be discussed in later chapters. Most of the related topics are the subject of a more narrowly defined business law class. However, we will have an introduction to this in Chapters 3–5. In its **regulatory role**, the law directs and standardizes activities that would otherwise be considered purely private interactions of individuals. In short, this involves government intervention. This regulatory role is typically justified on the grounds that society has some stake in the outcome of the regulated activity and that the well-being of society can and will be improved through the said government involvement. In essence, the government becomes an active third party by regulating the activity and is a potent force in the legal environment of business.

B. "Law" Definition

Since this is an introductory legal endeavor, it is important to have a working definition of law. "Law" is a very broad concept that hinders precise definition. It can mean different things to different people who find themselves in the same situation. One simple definition of **law** is as follows:

Law is the collection of rules and regulations that determines how the government will treat its citizens, as well as how, in turn, its citizens will treat the government; and, how those citizens will treat each other, and the enforcement there of.

In other words, this definition shows that law sets the parameters of acceptable and unacceptable behavior both between citizens and between citizens and the government. However, as stated, law can mean different things to different people in different situations. So, in essence, there is no set definition of law. Therefore, law is referred to as an abstract term where the meaning is fluid. For instance, *Black's Law Dictionary* lists law as follows.:

Law is that which is laid down, ordained, or established. A rule or method according to which phenomena or actions co-exist or follow each other. That which must be obeyed and followed by citizens, subject to sanctions or legal consequences, is a "law".

Irrespective of the definition of law being used, enforcement of the law is necessary. Without enforcement of a law, that law is useless. If a law is passed by the ruling governmental body, but is not enforced, then it ceases to serve any purpose. If, for instance, the Department of Public Safety in Texas (the State Police) announced that the legislature has passed traffic laws and lists penalty provisions for the violations of these laws, no one would drive within the speed limit or worry about following any of those laws unless they are enforced. Enforcement of the law leads to stability and predictability. If a law is enforced, then anyone who violates that law should know what is going to happen to him or her, thus predictability. If you speed through any police force's favorite speed trap, with enforcement of traffic laws, will you be pulled over and given a ticket? As for stability, does the fear of enforcement of law guide or force people into following the law? Again, think of traffic laws, if everyone ignores those laws what would your trip to campus entail? It would be a true adventure just to try to drive across town if no one followed speed limits or obeyed traffic lights or stop signs.

So, where do we get, "the Law"? There are several sources of law, as we will discuss below.

II. SOURCES OF LAW

A. Constitutional Law

Constitutional law is derived from the U.S. Constitution. The Constitution of the United States is the most important legal and political document in the country. If any other laws of whatsoever type are found to be unconstitutional, then those laws cannot exist. In short, the Constitution is the **supreme law** of the land and all laws must be found to be constitutional or they cannot exist or be enforced. Although states engage in considerable regulation of business, a legal environment of business course typically concentrates on federal regulatory law which will be the main emphasis of this text. However, we will also emphasize on Texas law. Constitutional law is very important and will be discussed in Chapter 2. However, remember this is meant to be an overview and therefore, the topics will not be covered in great depth, legally speaking.

B. Statutory Law

The second type of law is **statutory law** which is also called **legislative law**. Most of the legal environment of business and especially the regulatory role of the law will be defined by the U.S. Congress and the state legislatures. Subject to staying within the bounds of the law set forth in the Constitution which will be discussed in Chapter 2, the U.S. Congress has extensive power to pass laws (called **statutes**) that constrain businesses' behavior. The formal procedures for adopting statutes are set forth in the Constitution. Each bill must be approved in its final form by a majority of both Houses of Congress and the President must either sign the bill or have his veto overridden by a two-thirds vote of both Houses. Examples of federal regulatory statutes include the National Labor Relations Act of 1932, the Securities Act of 1933, the Consumer Product Safety Act of 1972, the Civil Rights Act of 1964, and several others which will be discussed later. However, do not forget that state legislatures and even municipal ruling bodies or other governmental entities can also pass statutory laws.

C. Executive

In addition to the requirement of presidential approval or veto of bills passed by Congress, the President, as head of the executive branch, is a major source of laws affecting the legal environment of business. Although the law-making authority of the President is limited by the Constitution, the President can independently create laws by issuing **executive orders** and controlling the policies of the executive branch. An example of the President's ability to create law through the issuing of executive orders is Executive Order No. 11246, which was issued by President Johnson in 1965. This order requires that all government contractors take "affirmative action" to ensure that their employment practices are not discriminatory. (We will discuss this more in depth in a later chapter.) President Clinton issued an executive order protecting federal homosexual workers. In effect, in the federal workplace, this executive order adds homosexuality to the list of categories for which discrimination is illegal. Then George W. Bush, a Republican, was elected President and he was not bound to follow President Clinton's executive orders and in fact dispensed with most but not all of them during the first few days of his administration. President Obama, a Democrat, recently overruled a Clinton executive order that President Bush had left in place which was commonly called the "Don't Ask, Don't Tell" policy, which meant that the military could not actively seek out and punish people for their sexual orientation. However, under that executive order, if the military learned that someone was gay or lesbian, they could be punished. However, the new Obama executive order allows gays and lesbians to openly serve in the military. However, remember that a law must be enforced to be effective and there are a lot of military people who are still hesitant to accept the new policy.

The President's exercise of official discretion in the control of some federal agencies such as department and bureaus by appointing the heads of those entities also affects the legal environment in a number of ways. For example, the enforcement policies of several regulatory agencies including the Antitrust Division of the Justice Department differ from administration to administration as does the membership of boards and commissions such as the National Labor Relations Board which can also influence their rulings and enforcement policies. Additionally, the negotiation of treaties with foreign governments, which is a Presidential duty, then become law when approved by the Senate, and trade agreements, which are also negotiated by the President but do not need Senate approval, are important sources of law for international business. This was seen during the George W. Bush administration with several trade agreements around the world, but especially with South American nations.

Also, the majority of the actual business of the federal government is conducted through the executive branch. Although Congress appropriates funds for governmental uses, it is the President who mostly through administrative agencies that actually spends the funds. Not only does the President appoint the heads of these administrative agencies as seen above, but there is also a great deal of administrative spending discretion. For instance, the Secretary of the Interior decides how government land is to be used. The Secretary of Housing and Urban Development (HUD) decides the qualifications for federal housing assistance.

As we shall see in the next section, federal courts make a great deal of federal law by interpreting federal statutes and the Constitution. The President appoints federal judges, from the very lowest federal trial judges to justices of the Supreme Court. Although the President cannot influence court decisions, the President can choose judges that have similar philosophies. For instance, if the President believes that economic efficiency should be taken into account in judicial decisions, nominees with a similar belief would be chosen. Appointments must be confirmed by a majority vote of the Senate and the process of presidential appointment of federal judges has become very political in recent years. Another area of debate is, once the position of the nominee is discussed and made known by the nominee, once he or she becomes a judge/justice, should he or she be required to follow that position? If a judge/justice changes his or her position on issues, should that be considered a misrepresentation and should he or she be subject to punishment or even impeachment? There are numerous examples of judges changing their liberal/conservative philosophies after they have been appointed to the federal bench. Should controls be put into place to force the judges to vote the way they had voted when they were selected to the federal bench? Hopefully, the answer to these questions is, and will remain, "No."

D. Judiciary (Courts)

1. Introduction

Judges have two basic functions in a trial which are as follows:

  1. Interpret the law.

2. Determine the facts, if there is no jury; if there is a jury, the jury does this. However, judges always interpret the law and thus, have the ability to create law.

2. The Common Law System

By interpreting the law and applying the law by determining the facts, judges create much of the law in the United States by a system known as **common law**. The heart of this system is the doctrine of stare decisis meaning that previously decided cases should be followed unless there is a good, legal reason to change the previous decision. When a court rules upon the facts of a particular controversy, it is said to be making a ruling and thereby setting **precedent**, which is the established answer to that set of facts. Normally an appellate court is the only type of court that can create precedent. (We will discuss the difference between trial and appellate courts in Chapter 2.) Then when the same facts appear before the court again, it normally follows the doctrine of *stare decisis* and rules in the same way, hence, following prior precedent. However, a judge does not have to follow precedent, and by showing good legal reasoning ithe or /she can change the precedent.

As stated, judges are not bound by precedent law. A judge is free to follow precedent or establish a new precedent. However, another factor that contributes to a judge following precedent is that if a judge radically changes prior precedent, the appeals courts will normally reverse that judge on appeal. Then a political opponent of the judge will make it look like the judge is incompetent to the voters and then they may not vote for that judge. Then the judge has to answer why he or she as a judge is being overruled by a higher court. Thus, the resulting reversal of the decision can and does often become a campaign issue in states where the judge is elected.

Judges are reluctant to change common law and under normal situations, a judge will follow precedent. Following the precedent leads to predictability and uniformity. You know that the judge will probably follow precedent and thereby treats everyone uniformly. Thus, if a prospective client goes in to an attorney and discusses a common law problem, upon asking about the outcome, the attorney can explain precedent and the common law system. If the client's issue is answered positively by precedent then the client will know that their chances in court are good. However, if their position is against the precedent, then the attorney can explain that they will probably have to take the case to court, appeal the case, and convince the appellate court or courts that precedent should in fact be changed. This is usually very expensive and the client needs to be aware of that before filing the lawsuit.

While precedent provides some clarity and consistency to the law, one often finds similar cases with different outcomes. One reason for this apparent inconsistency is that although the cases appear to be similar, there is usually at least one fact that distinguishes each case from other prior cases. The lawyer on each side of the issue tries to convince the court that the "significant" facts of the case are the same as those in prior cases that have been decided in their favor. Of course, the facts that one side considers significant are usually quite different from the ones that the other side views as significant. Thus, the parties often present different precedents in support of their respective positions.

Common law is often referred to as **judge-made law** since it is actually created by the court.

3. Interpretation of Constitutions, Statutes and Review of Agency Decisions

Judges and Supreme Court Justices interpret and apply the law and must be free to do so without the pressures of politics. As we will see in Chapter 3, most federal judges, called "Constitutional Judges," serve for life and they are free to make their own decisions independently of the President or the Congress. They have a major impact on the legal environment of business because their interpretations and applications influence the development of the law in many ways.

This interpretation of the law includes interpreting the meaning of state and federal statutes and constitutional provisions, both state and national. Statutes are typically written in general terms thereby giving the courts the flexibility to respond to unforeseen circumstances and to adapt to changing conditions over time. This flexibility is accomplished through **judicial interpretation** of the broad language when applied to specific individual circumstances. The legislative body expects the court to attempt interpreting statutes and constitutions according to the intent of the drafters, the legislative body. Therefore, courts look to the legislative histories of statutes for guidance in interpreting statutes according to **legislative intent**. This is called being **judicially passive**. A good example of judicial passivism was seen in the summer of 2012 when Chief Justice John Roberts of the U.S. Supreme Court voted in favor of the constitutionality of President Obama's health care program. It was obvious from his remarks that he personally disagreed with the health care program but chose to follow the intent of the Congress, against his own personal beliefs. He was vehemently criticized for doing so by the conservatives in this country.

However, judges are also free to "interpret" the law and this means that they do not always follow legislative intent. The judge or judges may feel that they can improve on the law or may just disagree with the legislative body. This can lead to a judge or judges changing, sometimes totally changing, the legislative intent. Of course, this is not the desire of the legislative body but can and often is done by courts. This is called being judicially active or **judicial activism**. Critics often refer to this as judges being legislators in black robes.

If Congress or state legislatures object to an interpretation of a statute by a court, the legislative body may resort to a new law or a constitutional amendment to mandate to the courts about how the law will be interpreted. While this is rarely successful, as seen below, it is a tool used by the legislative bodies to force courts to follow their views.

The judiciary also reviews or interprets agency decisions. As we shall see, the administrative agencies pass rules (laws) and regulations and also prosecute those individuals and companies that do not follow their rules. Such prosecution occurs in administrative law courts. Often, an appeal is taken from these administrative law courts to the judicial system, federal or state. That gives the judiciary the task of reviewing those administrative rules and regulations and interpreting them just as the courts do acts of Congress or state legislatures.

4. Judicial Review

As written, the Constitution does not give the courts the power to interpret the Constitution or statutes, but neither does it prohibit them from this action. The Supreme Court assumed that power in the landmark decision of Marbury v. Madison (**Marbury v. Madison 1 Cranch 137 (U.S. 1837)**). Since that time, the judiciary has been recognized as possessing the power of **judicial review**, the power to declare an act of Congress, or the President, unconstitutional and thus unenforceable. In exercising this power, there is traditionally a strong presumption by the court that a statute is constitutional. Moreover, courts cannot act on a constitutional issue unless an actual controversy is before that court. A court cannot simply issue a verdict saying an act is unconstitutional. An actual case must be filed in, or appealed to that court, by litigants seeking review of the law in some way. Finally, although the court is the final arbiter of what the Constitution means, the people have the ultimate voice on constitutional issues through the clearly specified amendment process in the U.S. Constitution. Therefore, if the judiciary interprets the Constitution to mean one thing, Congress can propose an amendment to the Constitution and thereby circumvent the judicial decision. This, however, is rarely attempted and even more rarely successful.

For an example of court review of laws, consider the flag burning issue: Can a person burn the American flag as a means of protest? When Ronald Reagan was President, the Republican Party chose to have its presidential nomination convention in Dallas, Texas, for what turned out to be President Reagan's second administration. An individual burned an American flag in protest to President Reagan's policies outside the convention hall in Dallas. The protester was promptly arrested and charged with violating a Texas law that prohibited the burning of the American flag. Eventually, the case went to the U.S. Supreme Court which declared the Texas law unconstitutional as being too restrictive on the First Amendment right of freedom of speech (**Texas v. Johnson 491 U.S.397 (1989)**).

Many people, including President George W. Bush, who by that time had succeeded Reagan as President, were very upset and expected dissidents and protesters throughout the country to start burning the American flag. President Bush called for a constitutional amendment forbidding the burning of the American flag, which is the ultimate way to overrule a court decision. Congress refused to pass President Bush's desired constitutional amendment. Instead, Congress in an effort to change the Court's ruling passed a federal law, the Flag Protection Act of 1989, prohibiting the burning of the American flag. The Supreme Court also declared the federal law unconstitutional on the same basis as they had declared the Texas law unconstitutional (**United States v. Eichman 496 U.S. 310 (1990)**). The President again demanded a constitutional amendment and Congress once again denied it saying that the government should not get involved in changing the Bill of Rights on this issue. However, politically, Congress changed since those times and Congress once again considering an anti–flag burning constitutional amendment and at that time, former President Bush has a strong advocate of his position in his now, President George W. Bush. In June of 2006, the Senate again tried to pass a constitutional amendment against flag burning and it failed by one (1) vote. Since then, in every session of Congress, the anti–flag burning amendment is filed in one form or another but the Congress has not taken any further action on a constitutional amendment.

Thus, the judiciary plays an important role in maintaining stability and flexibility in the legal environment of business. The ability of courts to change common law is stabilized through adherence to the principle of stare decisis, while the inherent rigidity of constitutional clauses and statutes is allowed to adapt to changes in society through judicial interpretations. It is important to note, however, that the proper role of the judiciary in constitutional interpretation has been the topic of heated debate throughout the twentieth and into the twenty-first century. The battle lines have traditionally been drawn between activist judges, who are often accused of rewriting the Constitution in accordance with their own personal agenda and strict constructionist judges, who are often accused of living in the past. This debate is always an issue in the Senate confirmation of federal judges.

E. Administrative Law

Perhaps the most important source, other than constitutional law, of laws affecting the legal environment of business is the collective law created by several federal administrative agencies. Because of the importance of these agencies, as well as the magnitude of frustration they tend to create for business executives, these agencies and their procedures will be studied in detail in later chapters in the text.

Although this text focuses on federal laws and regulations that affect businesses, the role of state law should not be overlooked. Each state has its own constitution and obviously state legislatures are free to pass statutory laws as long as these do not violate the U.S. Constitution. Furthermore, most states have administrative regulations that read much the same as federal regulations, but can be applied only within the state and only if they do not place an undue burden on interstate commerce.

The **police powers** of the state, the power of the state to place restraints on the personal freedom and property rights of persons for the protection of the public safety, health, and morals, or the promotion of the public convenience and general prosperity, are reserved to the individual states. This is specified in the Tenth Amendment of the U.S. Constitution. Police powers are also sometimes delegated to local governments. State legislatures have passed comprehensive statutes governing such subjects as corporations, commercial transactions, criminal law, motor vehicle law, and franchising contracts. These areas of state law will be covered when they have a major impact on the legal environment of business, but the primary focus of this course will be on federal, not state, regulatory law.

State and local governments are empowered to regulate business to protect the public health and safety and to promote the public welfare. These powers are part of the inherent police power reserved to the states, but given the broad definition of interstate commerce by the courts, many exercises of this power will impose a burden on interstate commerce. Normally, state regulation is not supposed to interfere with interstate regulation. This will be discussed in detail in Chapter 2.

Finally, municipal governments should not be overlooked as a source of rules governing business behavior. Municipalities have laws dealing with business hours, proper uses of property, and even garbage disposal. A good source for all city ordinances relating to business is the local Chamber of Commerce or City Secretary. However, under our federalist system, municipal governments are considered part of the state government.

III. CLASSIFICATIONS OF LAW

There are several different ways to classify laws. For example, as we already discussed, the law can be classified according to its source or type. Several other classifications of law are generally recognized and understood by the legal community.

A. Federal Law and State Law

Law may be classified according to the governmental unit that generates the law. The U.S. Constitution is based on the principle of **federalism.** As we have seen, this is based on our federal system, where the national government is given powers by the Constitution while reserving other powers to the states. Therefore, in the United States, both the national, or as it is often called, the federal government, and state governments can create law.

Federal law includes all laws developed under the authority of the Constitution by Congress, the President, or federal regulations. As we will learn in Chapter 2, the most important constitutional provision concerning the federal government's regulation of business is the Commerce Clause, specifically the Interstate Commerce Clause. Federal law also includes regulations created by federal agencies under the authority delegated to them by Congress. Likewise, the structure and procedures of federal agencies will be covered in a later chapter.

State law includes ordinances passed by local governments, laws passed by state legislatures, and the laws created by state regulatory agencies. It differs from state to state. This diversity of law sometimes seems beneficial in that it allows states to experiment with different aspects or versions of the law. In this regard, Justice Brandis referred to states as a "laboratory" for the law or more specifically as:

> It is one of the happy incidents of the federal system that a single courageous State may, if its citizens choose, serve as a laboratory: and try novel social and economic experiments without risk to the rest of the country. (**New State Ice Co. v. Leiberman 285 U.S. 262, 311 (1932)**)

Several times, as we shall see, the national government will largely copy state law whenever the national government chooses to act in that area. We will see several examples of this, such as in environmental law where the national government largely copied the pre-existing state of California law. Surprisingly, there is considerable uniformity across the states. Perhaps this is due to the ability of states to select the best law after a few years of "laboratory" work or experimentation. However, there are still areas of disagreement among the states and therefore, in several areas of the law you will have the **majority rule**, where a majority of states agree and the **minority rule**, where only a few states chose to follow that rule of law. For instance, due to the heavy influence of French law only being found in Louisiana, you will often find Louisiana following the minority rule or for that matter, their own law. In some areas of state law, uniform codes have been adopted by most states. The best-known example of this is the Uniform Commercial Code, which is a codification, making common law into statutory law, of the common law rules related to commercial activity.

B. Private Law and Public Law

The classification of law in terms of **public law** and **private law** looks to the type of parties that generate a legal controversy. If the controversy is based on rights and duties between litigants who are private parties, then it is called private law. Conversely, public law concerns controversies between private parties and the government. Therefore, the only difference is whether a governmental entity is involved in the controversy. If it is, then that is public law. If it is not, then it is private law. Keep in mind that this classification has nothing to do with the amount of publicity that the case generates.

C. Civil Law and Criminal Law

The government, or as it sometimes referred to, the "state," has an interest in preventing activities that upset social order, and it protects this interest through criminal law. **Criminal law** is designed to further society's interest in preventing crime and punishing criminals, not to provide remedies for victims of crime which often turn to civil law. Many of the rules of behavior whose violations lead to civil suits are derived from the common law, while criminal law is exclusively statutory in nature. However, the same facts can give rise to both civil and criminal violations. **Civil law**, on the other hand, is the law that provides remedies for individuals or entities that have been wronged by the other individual or entity such as in crimes. The primary purpose of civil law is reimbursement or restitution and not punishment, as in criminal law.

As stated above, in many types of antisocial behavior, both civil and criminal law is involved. For example, an automobile accident may lead to both a civil and a criminal suit. The harmed individual files a civil suit and criminal suits are filed by the state. In the automobile accident, if one driver brings suit against the other driver who caused the accident, this would be a civil suit. The remedy sought in a civil suit is compensation for the loss sustained. A criminal case could be filed arising out of the same facts, if the driver of the car that caused the accident broke a criminal law, such as driving while intoxicated. The remedy sought in a criminal suit is punishment in the form of fines, imprisonment, or both.

Unfortunately for many victims of crime, the perpetrators of crime, if caught, are often unable to pay the compensation (especially if they are in jail). The standard of proof necessary for the victim to win in a civil suit, preponderance of the evidence (more likely than not), is lower than the standard of proof necessary for conviction in a criminal suit. Our society places such a high value on liberty that it does not allow individuals to be deprived of their freedom unless the proof is beyond a reasonable doubt. For a difference in the impact of a criminal and civil case, which arose out of the same facts, think of a driving while intoxicated (DWI) case. Obviously, the driver can be charged with a criminal act of driving while intoxicated if he/ or she were driving under the influence but that same driver could also be sued civilly by the other driver if an accident occurred for the damages resulting from the accident. However, it takes more proof to convict the individual of the crime because the defendant's individual liberties can be denied such as being sent to jail. On the civil side, the legal system would only be taking money from the defendant and thus, the plaintiff would not need as much proof; hence, preponderance of the evidence or more likely than not is a sufficient burden of proof.

Although a few of the regulatory statutes studied in this textbook involve criminal sanctions (e.g., the Sherman Antitrust Act), most of the lawsuits encountered by the business community are civil suits. Many civil cases arise out of honest, good-faith disputes over the terms of a contract. Others involve lawsuits by government agencies against firms that are alleged to be violating regulatory law. One point to keep in mind is that firms do not like the adverse publicity that accompanies a lawsuit and will typically settle the suit out of court, unless they believe that they are being improperly or falsely accused of some activity. Moreover, the costly nature of the adverse publicity tends to give firms the incentive to play by the rules.

D. Substantive Law and Procedural Law

Another way of classifying law is in terms of whether the law defines rights and duties or describes the procedure through which rights and duties are enforced. **Substantive laws** define rights and duties. Substantive law is also seen as the meat of or heart of the law. **Procedural laws** define the procedural means through which violations of rights and duties are remedied. This very broad dichotomy of law results in the overlap of some areas of procedural and substantive law. Substantive law is the "meat of the law" while procedural law is the "how to of the law." For example, in Texas, if you murder someone and get caught you will be charged with murder which is defined in the Texas Penal Code, Chapter 19, Sec. 19.02(b) (1)., which defines murder as "intentionally or knowingly cases the death of an individual." This is the substantive law of murder. However, the steps you will go through in the prosecution and trial will be governed by the Texas Code of Criminal Procedure, which is procedural law.

E. Equitable and Legal Remedies

Equity is an area of the law separate from the traditional common law. It developed in England at the same time as the common law developed, and its primary purpose was to avoid unjust results occurring from strictly following the rules of the common law. For example, when the common law's refusal to enforce a contract due to some technical deficiency resulted in an unjust result, equity was used to save the contract and prevent the injustice. To illustrate, suppose the legal ownership of some timberland is in dispute. Before the issue can be settled, the alleged owner in possession may choose to cut the timber on the land against the wishes of the other alleged owner, thereby causing irreparable harm to the land because the timber is already cut. Then the only type of remedy available, if the court rules that it was not their property and thus, they cut the timber in error would be **legal remedies** or money. Under a strict interpretation of the common law of property, the alleged owner in possession can use the land for any legal purpose. So, if it was their property they could cut the timber if they so chose. However, in equity, the other (non-possessory) alleged owner could get a court order, an **equitable remedy**, known as an **injunction**, to prevent the cutting of the timber until the dispute is resolved. An injunction is an example of an action in equity or an equitable remedy. Unlike in England in the olden days, today, both common law and equity rules are administered by the same court in all federal and most state courts and so, the difference becomes apparent only in the types of remedies a court gives. Legal remedies usually involve the payment of money. On the other hand, equitable remedies involve a court order to do, or not do, something, such as the injunction in the illustration above. Furthermore, equitable remedies are generally only available where the monetary (legal) damage is too late or does no good. In other words, equitable remedies try to avoid the harm and legal remedies pay for the damages after the harm has been done.

CHAPTER SUMMARY

In this chapter, we have covered the sources of law that include constitutional, statutory, executive, judiciary, and administrative laws. Constitutional law is the highest law of the land and if any of the other types are not constitutional, then they do not survive the scrutiny of the courts. We also discussed that the courts are very important in law because they create common law, interpret other types of laws, and have judicial review. Of course, there is still statutory law, which is written down and available to the legal scholar. Administrative and constitutional laws will be the subjects of later chapters. Executive law is limited to indirect influence over the law or the enactment of executive orders or other limited, independent Presidential actions.

The last major category discussed in this chapter was that law could be classified into many categories such as state and federal laws. Public and private laws have as their distinction whether the government is involved or not. Civil and criminal laws are differentiated by whether the goal is to punish, which is criminal law, or to obtain restitution. Substantive law is the "meat" of the law while procedural law is the "how to" of the law. One last classification was common law and equitable law. Equitable law was a court order to do or not do something while common law normally involves monetary or legal damages.

2

CONSTITUTIONAL LAW

I. INTRODUCTION

In simple words, the Constitution is the supreme law of the United States and does several things. First, it establishes a federal system, commonly called **federalism**, in that the Constitution separates governing power among the various branches of the federal government and the states. Governmental power is split between a central governing body and local governments. This happens when local governments recognize the sovereignty of a central government and surrender certain powers to it, retaining other powers for themselves. Thus, the federal government's scope of activity is limited by the powers granted in the Constitution. All other powers are reserved to the states unless prohibited by the Constitution, as per the Tenth Amendment. This concept of federalism is very important to an understanding of the legal environment of business, as we will see later in this chapter. Second, the Constitution defines the relationship between the citizens of the United States and their government. Next, the Constitution limits the governing power of the national government by guaranteeing certain rights to individuals that are protected from infringement by those with governing power. Finally, and of particular interest for the study of the legal environment of business, is the constitutional power of the federal government to regulate business.

It must be understood that the nature and purpose of the Constitution is both to give power to the federal government and to limit the power of the federal government. This point is clearly underscored by a consideration of the historical context of its adoption. By doing so, the Constitution's organization and division of authority takes on added clarity and meaning.

II. HISTORY OF THE CONSTITUTION'S CREATION

A. Colonial Time Period

Colonists coming to the New World and particularly to the American colonies originally came as loyal British citizens who were given great latitude by the British to basically allow the American colonists the right to self-government. For instance, the Virginia colony had the House of Burgesses. The system worked for about 140 years but by the mid-1760s the ties to the crown were weakening mostly due to the repercussions of the French and Indian War which lasted from 1756 to 1763. The British Empire paid a huge price for protecting their interests from the French and the Indians in the New World and the British Parliament thought, who better to service that debt than the people who were being protected?

This was perceived as oppressive by the colonists. By this time, each colony had its own constitution providing that colony with fundamental law. The colonies fundamental laws not only tended to reject several of the oppressive British traditions such as feudalism, the rigid class system, the guild and craft system, but also included rejecting the absolute authority of the king and even the government mandated church including the compulsory tithing British requirement which was equivalent to a tax.

The British began to achieve their goal of trying to make the colonists pay for the war with a series of taxes such as the Sugar Act of 1764 which taxed sugar, wine, coffee and most of the products normally exported to the colonies by the British, the Stamp Act of 1765 which taxed all paper exported to the colonies, and the hated Quartering Act of 1765 that required the colonists to provide living quarters for the British soldiers at the colonists expense. Reaction was particularly harsh especially in the New England colonies with the opposition centered in Boston where the Sons of Liberty organized violent protests such as burning the British Colonial Governor's home, threatening the British stamp agents, and organizing a boycott of paper goods as well as other British imports.

This led to the first steps toward independence. However, in the 1770s, England (the British Empire) was the most powerful country in the world. Relations between Britain and her American colonies began to deteriorate rapidly. The colonists responded by convening the Stamp Act Congress in 1765. Of the 13 colonies, 9 of 13 sent representatives to New York City and drafted a detailed list of violations of the fundamental rights claimed by the colonists that were committed by the British. This was the first time that the colonists had acted in a unified manner but when the demands were given to the British government, they had little effect. The British followed up with the Townshend Acts which was yet another tax on the British imports to the colonies but this one included tea. The Colonists responded by boycotting tea.

Further, on March 5, 1770, the Boston Massacre occurred due to an unruly mob taunting and throwing snowballs probably containing rocks at the British troops outside the Boston Customs House. The British responded by shooting at the colonists killing five colonists. The British response was to lift all the taxes except the tax on tea. In 1772, the colonies created the Committees of Correspondence to form other colonies aware of British activities. This became a powerful tool to mold public colonists' public opinion against the British. The British responded with the Tea Act in 1773. This culminated in the Boston Tea Party where a group of American colonists dressed as Indians dumped tea into Boston Harbor. The colonists took this action in protest of the higher tax they had to pay on English tea based on a tax law passed by parliament. King George's response was "the colonists must either submit or triumph." The British responded with the Coercive Acts which the colonists called the Intolerable Acts which placed a naval blockade on Boston harbor and put more economic pressure on the colonists by denying the people of Boston the necessary food stuff and reinforcing the Quartering Act by sending 4,000 more troops to Boston. The colonists responded by forming the First Continental Congress to discuss future relations with the mother country which resulted in unity of the colonies since all of them had representatives present except Georgia. The colonists tried one more time to ask the King to recall the Coercive Acts. This was done by colonists as loyal British citizens but the King basically ignored their demands.

B. The Revolutionary War

War was just around the corner and on April 19, 1775, fight broke out at Lexington and Concord with what most historians call "the shot heard round the world." (April 19 is still celebrated in Boston with the running of the Boston Marathon on Patriots' Day which made the timing of the terror attack on Boston on April 19, 2013, even more devastating.) The colonists met in 1775 in Philadelphia in the Second Continental Congress in May of 1775 and asked the King to end the hostilities. The King rejected this and sent 20,000 more troops to Boston and labeled the delegates as traitors and subjected all of them to death. In January 1776, Thomas Paine published a pamphlet called *Common Sense* which was very popular and galvanized the colonist against reconciliation. Talk in the Second Continental Congress soon turned to talk of independence. By May of 1776, talk of independence was openly debated in the Second Continental Congress and on June 7, Richard Henry Lee of Virginia entered a resolution calling for independence. On July 2, the Continental Congress passed Lee's motion and on July 4, 1776, the Declaration of Independence, which had been prepared primarily by Thomas Jefferson, in anticipation of an independence vote, was adopted.

However, declaring independence and winning it were two different things. The colonists had no army or navy and had just declared independence from Britain, which had the finest army and navy in the world. The British had 400,000 troops in the colonies and the colonists, when they did form an army, rarely had one-eighth of the troops. An American navy was almost non-existent. Even so, the colonists prevailed and won independence in the Revolutionary War with the surrender of the British at Yorktown after a long and very destructive war.

C. Articles of Confederation

During, and after the Revolutionary War, the American colonies were organized by an idealistic, yet wholly dysfunctional document, known as the **Articles of Confederation**, which led to domination by the states and a very weak central (national) government which led to the Chaotic Period from 1781 to 1789. The states were viewed as independent entities that had joined together in a federation to achieve common goals as a band of friendly, mutually existing neighbors, and little more. A major problem with this approach was that the states often treated each other in an openly hostile manner. (Think how

13 brothers and sisters of varying ages would act when their parents left town and did not leave anyone in charge!) This was especially evident in economic relations as numerous trade barriers developed between the states. In general, whenever one state acted against the products of another state, the other state responded by adding a tax on a product of the first state. The result of this was that in many areas the states appeared to be anything but united and, at times, exhibited little friendship. Moreover, the central government did not have the power to tax. Instead, it relied on voluntary contributions from the states and, thus, was unable to finance an effective military force to defend the federation of friendly, mutually existing neighbors.

As far as government goes, there was just a one house Congress. There was no leader such as a President or a national judicial system to resolve border disputes or economic conflicts which were rampant. The chaotic economic relations between the states plus the inability of the federal government to conduct basic governmental functions led to a movement to change the central government. This was referred as the Chaotic Period.

This movement received a huge boost in the form of **Shay's Rebellion** in 1786. Daniel Shay was a farmer in Western Massachusetts. Farmers were especially hard hit by the post–Revolutionary War economic turmoil and depression. They were losing their farms to foreclosure and in an effort to stop the land foreclosures Shay led his approximately 1,500 men on a raid in Springfield, Massachusetts, to obtain weapons from the arsenal and then led armed attacks on the courthouses to prevent the creditors from foreclosing on the farms. While this was deemed to be a "little rebellion" by some leaders, other economic elites were shaken at the thought that their own citizens had turned to armed conflict. Since neither the central government nor the state governments would raise a militia to stop Shay, leaders of the country were justifiably very worried. Shay was eventually stopped by a privately paid force that had been put together solely for that purpose which ended Shay's rebellion on February 4, 1787.

This led to the realization that a change was mandatory. Therefore, in September of 1786 a few economic leaders met in Annapolis, Maryland, to discuss the weaknesses of the Articles of Confederation and to propose changes. However, the 12 representatives were from only 5 states and the only thing they accomplished was to request the Continental Congress to call a meeting of the states, which was granted and was to convene in May of 1787.

D. The Constitutional Convention

On May 25, 1787, 55 representatives of 12 of the states (Rhode Island did not send any representatives) met in Philadelphia to draft a new agreement to set forth the basic functions of a new government. We now call that historic meeting the **Constitutional Convention**, and the document that they eventually created is the Constitution of the United States of America. These delegates, the Founding Fathers, were relatively young, for the time, highly educated, and most were wealthy. However, they were also very different. For instance, 17 of them owned slaves and several Northern delegates believed in the abolishment of slavery. There were strong business, religious, and state loyalties as well as differences in current interests and issues. The convention was to be led by George Washington. It was evident on the first day that this was not going to be an easy process.

The lines were drawn between Virginia and some of the smaller states. The Virginia delegates introduced the Virginia Plan which had been written by James Madison. It called for a powerful central government with three branches, legislative, judicial, and executive. It called for a bicameral, two-house legislature, where one house was to be elected directly by the people with the other chosen by the state legislatures. This would lead to the national government being dominated by the larger states. Of course, the smaller states were against it. New Jersey introduced the New Jersey Plan which favored following the intent of the Articles of Confederation by strengthening the Articles and not replacing them. This plan favored the smaller states like New Jersey and called for one house in the legislature with one vote per state with the representatives chosen by the state legislatures. It also gave Congress the power to raise revenue from duties on imports and postal service fees and created a Supreme Court with the members chosen for life by the Congress.

Connecticut proposed a compromise which is now called the Connecticut Compromise or the Great Compromise. It called for a bicameral legislature, with one house called the House of Representatives where the representatives were to be elected by the people directly and based on population of the states and another called the Senate which would give each state an equal vote with members chosen by the state legislatures. It would take a vote of both houses to pass any legislation. National power would be supreme over state power. We now recognize this as the basic structure of the U.S. Congress.

The Founding Fathers were able to compromise for the good of the country because all of them agreed on one thing that the Articles of Confederation were not sufficient to serve the United States. Another example of compromise dealt with slavery. As stated above, several Northern delegates wanted to end slavery in the new government. The Southern delegates and especially the ones who owned slaves threaded to walk out of the convention. Therefore, slavery was an issue that could not be the subject of a compromise. There were several issues that the delegates could not work out and therefore, just ignored. Another example was who could vote, which was left up to the states. However, the slavery issue did come up again at the Constitutional Convention and that was about representatives in the House of Representatives. South Carolina felt that to determine population they should be allowed to count their slaves as well as the white citizens of South Carolina. The Northern delegates objected. However, the delegates did compromise on the issue and the result was the Three-Fifths Compromise where slave-owning states could count their slaves as three-fifths of a person but to get this provision, the Southern states had to agree to stop importing slaves in 20 years. Of course, this was overruled by the Civil War amendments but is still considered the most embarrassing section of the original Constitution. (However, it is important to learn that we must not judge people by our standards but by the standards that existed in their time.)

There were still other issues to decide and one of those unfinished business issues was the Executive Branch. The delegates had agreed to a one-person executive but not much else. They could not agree on the term of the executive nor how he would be selected. This was left to the Committee on Unfinished Portions which selected a four-year term and that the executive could serve more than one term. However, the executive would be elected by the Electoral College. They also addressed the issue of the removal of the executive by impeachment and conviction.

James Madison, who is generally regarded as the "author" of the Constitution, painstakingly recorded the proceedings of the Constitutional Convention of 1787, from its beginning until it closed in September 1787. He started the Constitution with "We the People" to show that it came from the people and "in order to form a more perfect Union" to show that it would improve upon the Articles of Confederation. He also stated the goals of the Founding Fathers, which was to "establish justice, insure domestic Tranquility, provide for the common defenses, promote the general Welfare and secure the Blessings of Liberty to ourselves and our Posterity." It also created a new government.

The primary ideological debate of the convention was over the need for a strong central government, *but not too strong of a central government*. Many of the participants agreed on the need for a central government but were very concerned over concentrating power in the hands of a few officials. After all, the abuses of King George III were still fresh in their minds. The drafters of the Constitution developed a framework of **limited government** in which the central government's power would be dispersed among three branches of the government (legislative, executive, and judicial) and where the power of each branch was limited by certain **checks and balances** from the other branches. The principle of **separation of powers** was designed to control the use of the powers granted by the states to the federal government. The Constitution also set up a structure based on federalism. This means that the powers would be divided between the national and state governments. However, prior to the Constitution, the states had all of the power and therefore they were going to lose power to the national government under the Constitution. The delegates adopted the document on September 17, 1787. However, as difficult as it had been to create the Constitution, another battle loomed. For the Constitution to become the supreme law of the United States of America, it still had to be ratified by the states which under the Constitution had to give up substantial powers to the national government and after all, who likes to give away power once you have it?

E. Ratification

The **ratification** process for the Constitution required that for the ratification of the Constitution to occur it would take nine states to ratify the Constitution or three-fourths of the states. An interesting point is that the Articles of Confederation required a unanimous vote of all 13 states, which of course would probably be impossible since Rhode Island did not even attend the Constitutional Convention. So the representatives to the Constitutional Convention simply ignored the requirement of the Articles of Confederation and just changed the rules. Delaware was the first state to ratify the Constitution. However, the debate over the ratification was intense. The most influential support in favor of adoption appeared in a series of newspaper articles written by James Madison, John Jay, and Alexander Hamilton. The collection of articles is known as the *Federalist Papers* and is often used as a guide by the courts in interpreting the Constitution. Those who supported the Constitution were called **Federalists**.

Several large states, in particular, Virginia and Pennsylvania, were hesitant to ratify without some additional limitations on governmental power. Those who opposed the proposed Constitution were called **Anti-Federalists** and were headed up by the very influential Virginian, Thomas Jefferson, who was generally known to the people as the creator of the Declaration of Independence, and was therefore held in high respect by large segments of the population. The Anti-Federalists opposed the Constitution because it took too much power from the states and that the Articles of Constitution provided the true federal system. They were also worried that the national government would have too much power through taxation, due to the Supreme Court's ability to invalidate state laws, and that the President could have too much power by being commander-in-chief of the military. However, the biggest fear was that the national government would deprive citizens of civil liberties. Although ratification did not require approval by all of the states, it was clear that the new Constitution would fail without the consent of the larger states, such as Jefferson's home state of Virginia. However, when the ninth state, New Hampshire, ratified the Constitution on June 21, 1788, the ratification of the Constitution was complete and it became official. However, the powerful states of Virginia and New York had still not approved the Constitution. Obviously, more work was needed.

F. The Bill of Rights Added

When Massachusetts ratified the Constitution, it called for a Bill of Rights to protect the civil liberties and personal freedoms of Americans. Thus, as part of the political negotiation that characterized much of the drafting and ratification process, yet another compromise was agreed to, whereby Virginia, New York, and the other hesitant states would hopefully ratify the Constitution if the new government would guarantee personal freedoms and state's rights. After all, at this time, Virginia and New York held 40 percent of the U.S. population. The Federalists agreed to propose, in the First Congress, amendments that would guarantee personal freedoms and state's rights thereby limiting the central government. Then the important states of Virginia and New York ratified the Constitution. However, the two remaining states, North Carolina and, of course, Rhode Island made the promise of the amendments their price to ratify the Constitution. North Carolina would not ratify the constitution until the amendments were introduced in Congress. Rhode Island did not ratify the Constitution until the Bill of Rights was a reality in 1790 after Washington had been President for a year.

Obviously, the Federalists kept their word and, in the First Congress, James Madison himself introduced 12 amendments, 10 of which were ratified in the next few years and became what we commonly call the **Bill of Rights**. The first 10 guarantee personal rights and freedoms as well as state's rights. An interesting historical point is that the last amendment to the Constitution, the 27th, is one of the two of the original 12 that did not become part of the Bill of Rights but was ratified in its original form, a mere 201 years later.

III. CONSTITUTIONAL INTERPRETATION

A. Structure of the Constitution

Although some provisions of the Constitution are clearly expressed, most of the Constitution is written in general terms or in terms that can be interpreted to have different meanings. This generality, or ambiguity, of some provisions was probably intentional because the framers were well aware of the fact that the Constitution would have to be flexible to deal with unanticipated circumstances. That is why some people refer to the Constitution as a Living Document. It can be interpreted in a different way by different people at different times. Most of the continuing body of constitutional law deals with judicial interpretation of the meaning of the Constitution as applied to specific circumstances. Two of those situations are discussed below.

B. Division of Authority

The Founding Fathers feared the central government that had too much power, but realized from the experience with the Articles of Confederation that a government that was too weak was as bad as one that was too strong. Their challenge was to create a government that was strong enough, yet not too strong. The solution devised was to separate the powers of the government into specific functions that together represented a strong central government, but would serve to operate as a system of **checks and balances**.

Three basic governmental units are created by the Constitution. First, the power to make law was vested in a **legislature**; second, the power to enforce law was granted to the **executive** branch, and third, the power to interpret and apply the law was placed in the **judiciary**. By exercising their powers, each of the branches of government keeps the others in control. Moreover, this separation of powers guarantees that no single branch is able to attain absolute power. Congress is the legislative body of the national government as per Article I of the U.S. Constitution and as such is given certain **enumerated powers** found in Article I, Section 8 which specify the powers of Congress. Congress is divided into the Senate and the House of Representatives. The executive branch is specified in Article II of the Constitution and is led by the President. The Judiciary is created in Article III of the Constitution which in turn creates the Supreme Court of the United States, which is the highest court in the country but gives Congress the authority to create other courts as Congress deems them necessary. The checks and balances of the three divisions are located throughout the Constitution. One example of checks and balances that cover all three divisions is in federal judges. Federal judges serve for life to make them independent of the other two branches. However, the President appoints federal court judges and they must be confirmed by the Senate before they take office for life.

The Supreme Court case of **Immigration and Naturalization Service v. Chadha 459 U.S. 1097 (1983)** also illustrates the functioning of the doctrine of separation of powers. Congress had passed an immigration statute, and the President had signed it into law. The statute granted an administrative agency certain powers, but also included a provision for a legislative veto that allowed either the Senate *or* the House of Representatives to overrule administrative decisions with a simple majority vote. The legislative veto did *not* require presidential signature in order to be effective. The Supreme Court declared the Act to be unconstitutional because the Constitution requires presidential approval before an act of Congress can become law. Moreover, both Houses of Congress must pass a bill before it is presented to the President.

C. Settlement of Conflicts of Authority

Occasionally, conflicts of authority can arise, particularly when the executive branch attempts to make law. The case of **Youngstown Sheet & Tube Co. v. Sawyer 343 U.S. 579 (1952)** gives us an example of the Supreme Court's check on the Executive Branch. Several steel mills were involved in a dispute concerning a collective bargaining agreement (see Labor Law) between Youngstown Sheet & Tube Co. and the union, the United Steelworkers of America, representing their employees. When an impartial settlement board failed to resolve the sides' differences, the union served notice that it planned to go on strike one week later. However, a few hours before the scheduled onset of the strike, President Truman, as Commander-in-Chief of the armed forces, decided that the armed forces needed steel production, and issued an **executive order**, which is an independent method to create law by the President which will be discussed later. This executive order instructed the Secretary of Commerce to seize the steel mills and keep them operating. The Secretary immediately complied with the President's order and directed the mill owners to continue producing steel. The steel mill owners obeyed the Secretary's directive but under protest. The owners then sued the Secretary (Sawyer) in federal district court, seeking to enjoin the government's actions and asking for a declaratory judgment on the executive order's constitutionality. The district court granted a preliminary injunction, a mandatory court order to do or not do something and a declaratory judgment or ruling in favor of the mill owners on the ground that the President did not have the power to take possession of the plant in the absence of an authorizing act of Congress or clear constitutional authority. The U.S. Court of Appeals for the District of Columbia stayed the execution of the judgment the same day. The U.S. Supreme Court, considering the situation urgent, granted an immediate writ of certiorari and heard the case the following week. The Court held that the seizure was illegal because it was not within the constitutional powers of the President. The President, who is bound to adhere to the Supreme Court's decisions, was forced to return control of the steel mills to their owners. Therefore, the Supreme Court "checked" the power of the President. We will see several other examples of the Supreme Court declaring an act of the President or Congress to be unconstitutional.

IV. MAJOR BUSINESS PROVISIONS OF THE CONSTITUTION

A. Introduction

Section 1, Article I of the Constitution endows Congress with the "legislative powers herein granted," not with unlimited legislative power. Any power of the national government must be authorized by the Constitution before it can be legally exercised. Thus, there must be a constitutional basis for any proposed action of Congress, including regulation of business. The most significant power to regulate business is found in Article 1, Section 8, which is called the Enumerated Powers Clause where several powers of the national government are specified. For instance, Article 1, Section 8, Clause 3 of the Constitution is usually referred to as the **Commerce Clause**. Other parts of the Constitution that are important in considering the regulatory power of Congress include the **Necessary and Proper Clause** and the **Supremacy Clause**. These clauses combine to allow Congress "To make all Laws which shall be necessary and proper for carrying into Execution" those specifically enumerated powers and to make federal law which is "the Supreme Law of the Land."

B. The Commerce Clause

1. Introduction

However, the most important clause in the Constitution for business is the Commerce Clause which states

> The Congress shall have the power ... to regulate Commerce with foreign Nations, and among the several States, and with Indian tribes

The language of the commerce clause has always been liberally construed or, in other words, broadly interpreted by the courts to allow Congress the power to regulate business. As noted above, the Commerce Clause is the chief source of congressional power to regulate business. It is likewise the major limitation on states' abilities to regulate business activities.

2. Gibbons v. Ogden

In the famous 1824 case of **Gibbons v. Ogden 22 U.S. 1 (1824)**, the Supreme Court determined that the Commerce Clause allowed Congress to legislate with respect to all "commerce which concerns more states than one." The case involved an attempt by the state of New York to grant monopolistic steamboat rights on the Hudson River between New York and New Jersey. Gibbons had licensed his boats under a federal statute but not under the New York statute. Ogden obtained a New York state court order that prohibited Gibbons from operating his boats without a state license. Gibbons appealed the court order. The question presented to the U.S. Supreme Court was whether the state of New York could grant licenses to boats that traveled between two states. Chief Justice John Marshall noted the distinction between **interstate commerce** (between states) and **intrastate commerce** (within a state), by analyzing the words of the Commerce Clause in determining the appropriate meaning of commerce:

> The subject to which the power is ... applied is to commerce "among the several States". The word "among" means intermingled with. A thing which is among others is intermingled

with them. Commerce among the States cannot stop at the external boundary line of each State, but may be introduced into the interior.

It is not intended to say that these words ["commerce among the states"] comprehend that commerce which is completely internal, which is carried on between man and man in a State, or between different parts of the same State, and which does not extend to or affect other States. Such a power would be inconvenient, and is certainly unnecessary.

Comprehensive as the word "among" is, it may very properly be restricted to that commerce which concerns more states than one. The phrase is not one which would probably have been selected to indicate the completely internal traffic (here, meaning business) of a state, because it is not an apt phrase for that purpose, and the enumeration of the particular classes of commerce to which the power was to be extended would not have been made had the intention been to extend the power to every description. The genius and character of the whole government seem to be that its action is to be applied to all the external concerns of the nation, and those internal. Concerns which affect the states generally, but not to those which are completely within a particular state, which do not affect other states, and with which it is not necessary to interfere for the purpose of execution some of the general powers of government. The completely internal commerce of a state, then, may be considered as reserved for the state itself.

However, in regulating commerce with foreign nations, the power of Congress does not stop at the jurisdictional lines of the several states. It would be a very useless power if it could not pass those lines. The commerce of the United States with foreign nations is that of the whole United States. Every district has a right to participate in it. The deep streams which penetrate the country in every direction pass through the interior of almost every state in the Union, and furnish the means of exercising this right. If Congress has the power to regulate it, that power must be exercised whenever the subject exists. If it exists within the states, if a foreign voyage may commence or terminate at a port within a state, then the power of Congress may be exercised within a State.

Commerce among the states must, necessarily, be commerce with the states. While recognizing the power of a state to regulate intrastate commerce, the Supreme Court in *Gibbons* says that the Congress has the power to regulate commerce or business that concerns more than one state. This interpretation of the Commerce Clause gives Congress immense power. However, this widespread power contained in the Commerce Clause was scarcely utilized by Congress until it passed the Interstate Commerce Act in 1887 and Sherman Antitrust Act in 1890.

3. *Further Defining Interstate Commerce*

In 1937, the Supreme Court restated the *Gibbons* position on interstate commerce in the landmark decision, **NLRB v. Jones & Laughlin Steel Corp 331 U.S. 461 (1937),** by holding that Congress could regulate labor relations at any manufacturing plant where a work stoppage "would have a most serious effect upon interstate commerce." Since 1937, the Supreme Court has chosen to defer to Congress in the determination of whether the required substantial economic effect is present. Over the years, the Court has extended the reach of Congress' legislative power to regulate interstate commerce even when it appears to be vital so long as the aggregate effect might reasonably be nationally significant. For example, in **Wickard v. Filburn 317 U.S. 111 (1942)**, the Court upheld congressional control of a farmer's production of wheat for home use because the cumulative effect of home consumption of wheat by *many* farmers would alter the interstate commodity market. This cumulative effect principle extends the bounds of Congressional control to activities that are confined to the internal commerce of a state. The Commerce Clause has more recently been used to impose the national government's standards on businesses involved in interstate commerce. Since 1980, it is well established that interstate commerce reaches local activities that "substantially affect interstate commerce," **McLain v. Real Estate Board of New Orleans, Inc. 444 U.S. 232 (1980)**.

In other words, with this expanded interpretation of the Commerce Clause, the national government is able to regulate areas, which are not specifically included in the delegated powers of the Constitution. This is very obvious in the way the national government has used the power of the Commerce Clause in that the door to regulation is often that a business is involved in interstate commerce and once the door is open, the national government can come roaring in with numerous regulations and requirements on the business which makes the Commerce Clause a very powerful tool of the national government.

4. Power of the Commerce Clause

The power of the Commerce Clause can be seen in many areas of the law but probably none more clearly than in the area of **State's Rights**. You will recall that this was a major issue to the Anti-Federalists and resulted in the Bill of Rights. The last of the amendments that comprise the Bill of Rights, the 10th Amendment, says:

> The powers not delegated to the United States by the Constitution, nor prohibited by it to the States, are reserved to the States respectively, or to the people.

This became the cornerstone of the argument for the state's rights advocates and is called the **Reserve Powers Clause**. The concept of State's Rights was an issue at the constitutional convention, during the ratification of the Constitution and continues to be so today. Historically, there have been three major events that have defined the struggle of state's rights v. national government rights. Remember the objective at the constitutional convention was to create a national government that was powerful enough, but not too powerful. The states had almost all of the power under the Article of Confederation, which meant that they would have to give power to the national government which of course, the states were reluctant to do. Therefore, there has always been a struggle between the states and the national government to define this power.

The first major historical showdown over power came in the form of a dispute over whether a state, Maryland, had the power to tax the national government. This came about in the case of **McCulloch v. Maryland 77 U.S. 316 (1819)**. The state of Maryland sent a tax statement to the U.S. bank that was operating in Baltimore. After all Maryland was taxing all of the banks in Maryland which of course, included the one owned and operated by the

U.S. government. The United States refused to pay the taxes. Maryland relied on the Tenth Amendment Reserved Powers Clause which basically says that anything not specifically given to the national government nor prohibited to the states was reserved to the states or the people individually. Maryland argued that the power to operate the bank did not include the power to operate the bank tax free. The United States argued that the Necessary and Proper Clause, the last power of the Enumerated Powers Clause, gave it the power to operate tax free because it was necessary and proper. The Supreme Court agreed with the United States and ruled that the Necessary and Proper Clause gave the national government the "inherent power" to operate the bank without interference from the state government. The Necessary and Proper Clause has been referred to as the Inherent Powers Clause, the Implied Powers Clause and the Elastic Clause since it stretches the power of the national government. The Court also relied on the Supremacy Clause which will be discussed later in this chapter.

The second major historical event defining state's rights was the American Civil War, which was fought primarily over state's rights with the major issue within the state's rights argument being slavery. The national government won the war and ended slavery thus expanding the power of the national government. However, this did not end the cry of state's rights.

The states, especially the Southern states, continued to advocate state's rights. One area in particular where the states flexed their muscles of state's rights was in how they treated their own residents. This was evident in a series of laws called "**Jim Crow Laws**" that were the states' efforts to keep minorities, primarily the African-Americans, as second class citizens. Early on, the national government actually gave its blessing to the laws in **Plessy v. Ferguson 163 U.S. 537 (1896)** when the Supreme Court created the doctrine of "**Separate but Equal**." In other words, as long as the races were treated equally, separation of the races was constitutional. There was no question that the races were treated separately, but equally was a different matter.

As an example of Jim Crow Laws, Texas utilized the "**white primary**." Early in the twentieth century, Texas only had one political party, the Democrats. No one in Texas would claim to belong to the Republican Party because they caused the Civil War! Well, if you only have one party on the ballot in the general election in November, then the real election is held in the primary election. So, having been forced to recognize the power of the national government due to the Civil War, Texas did nothing to interfere with the general election. However, since the states held the primaries, Texas felt it had state's rights to conduct the primary *as Texas deemed appropriate*. The law of the state of Texas allowed political parties to determine who could vote in its primaries. The Texas Democratic Party in 1927 adopted a resolution allowing only the white citizens, who were qualified to vote, to vote in the Democratic Primary. This action eliminated the minority vote, or at least postponed it until the general election, when there was one candidate who had been chosen by the white majority in the primary election. Was this separate? Yes, of course! Was this equal? In 1944, the U.S. Supreme Court decided that no, this practice was not equal and declared Texas' white primary unconstitutional in the case of **Smith v. Allwright 321 U.S. 649 (1944)**. Other examples of Jim Crow laws were "white only" and "colored only" facilities in areas such as water fountains and bathrooms and separate seating on buses, at eating establishments, and in movie theaters.

In 1948, President Truman, as Commander-in-Chief, ordered the armed forces of the United States to be integrated. In other words, no longer would the national government tolerate separate but equal treatment of the races, at least in the military. Gone were the "colored" divisions of the military that had existed through World War II. Of course, that did not mean that the military treated the "whites" and "coloreds" equally. Bigots in the military, as in other areas of society, continued to follow the separate but equal rule.

However, the big blow to Jim Crow laws and the beginning of the modern civil rights era came in 1954 when the U.S. Supreme Court overruled *Plessy* and declared its doctrine of separate but equal to be unconstitutional. This action was taken in **Brown v. Board of Education 347 U.S. 483 (1954)**. This is probably the defining moment of the beginning of the **Civil Rights Movement** which becomes the third major event in the struggle between state's rights and the power of the national government.

While this is not a civil rights topic, we can use the civil rights movement of the 1960s to illustrate the power of the national government through the Commerce Clause. In 1964, the U.S. Supreme Court handed down two major cases that not only further define the definition of interstate commerce, but also illustrate the power of the Commerce Clause to the business community. These two companion cases are **Katzenbach v. McClung 379 U.S. 294 (1964)** and **Heart of Atlanta Motel v. United States 379 U.S. 241 (1964)**.

Both of these cases dealt with the **Civil Rights Act of 1964**, a law passed by Congress to implement the decision in *Brown* and to guarantee civil rights to all peoples. However, it was not met with open arms by everyone. In fact, in the Deep South it was met with open resistance and was largely, if not totally, ignored by the southern state governments on the basis of state's rights. The national government opposed this position and filed suit against numerous businesses that were discriminating against people who were not of the ruling majority white race and therefore, were in violation of the Civil Rights Act of 1964, which forbids discrimination due to race. The constitutionality of the Civil Rights Act of 1964 became the issue. Was it constitutional for the national government to pass a law forbidding discrimination in virtually all areas due to race, color, religion, sex, and national origin? The legislative history of the Civil Rights Act of 1964 shows that Congress based the constitutionality of this law on the Fourteenth Amendment and on the Commerce Clause.

In *Heart of Atlanta Motel*, the Court was faced with a motel in Atlanta, Georgia, which had a "white's only" policy by only renting rooms to white people. The national government had found this exclusionary practice to be nationwide. They also argued that such restrictions had a qualitative as well as quantitative effect on interstate travel. In other words, if African-Americans could not be certain of finding overnight lodging at a decent place (the Court found that the "colored only" facilities were less than adequate), then they could not travel and that would hinder interstate travel.

The Supreme Court concluded that it was obvious that the Heart of Atlanta Motel was involved in a business effecting interstate travel since they rented rooms to interstate travelers and thus, were involved in interstate commerce. Congress was therefore within its constitutional power due to the Commerce Clause.

Katzenbach dealt with Ollie's Barbecue, a family-owned restaurant in Birmingham, Alabama. It had a seating capacity of 220 customers. However, Ollie's Barbecue refused to serve African-Americans in its dining rooms, a practice the owners had had since the restaurant opened in 1927, even though two-thirds of their employees were African-Americans. The restaurant sold food to the African-Americans, but only at the take-out window. Just because the Civil Rights Act of 1964 was passed making this practice illegal did not cause the owners of Ollie's Barbecue to change their policy. Keep in mind that the actions of the owners of Ollie's Barbecue represented the accepted behavior throughout at least the South and in reality, in most of the country prior to the Civil Rights Movement of the 1960s.

In the year prior to the enactment of the Civil Rights Act of 1964, Ollie's Barbecue purchased $150,000.00 worth of food, of which 46 percent was meat that was bought locally but from a supplier who had purchased it from out of state. The issue narrowed down to whether the purchase of about $70,000.00 worth of food that had moved in interstate commerce gave Congress sufficient exercise of the constitutional provisions of the Commerce Clause. Applying the rationale of the *Wickard* case, the Supreme Court held that

1. when you took the **cumulative effect** of not just Ollie's Barbecue, but all restaurants engaged in this activity, that there was a rational basis for finding that racial discrimination in restaurants had a direct and adverse effect on the free flow of interstate commerce,
2. that Ollie's Barbecue did not have to sell its product across state lines to violate the Commerce Clause, only **effect** interstate commerce, and
3. that the power of Congress in regulation interstate commerce is broad and sweeping. (Emphasis added)

Looking at these two cases, the history of the judicial interpretation of the Commerce Clause and knowing the position of the Supreme Court, it should be obvious that most, if not all, businesses are involved in interstate commerce. Therefore, the Commerce Clause applies and the national government can regulate that business in whatsoever way the national government deems to be appropriate. Hence, the Commerce Clause is the door through which the national government utilizes to open businesses to regulation by the national governments.

5. *Limitation on the Commerce Clause*

Simply put, does this mean that Congress can use this clause to regulate any business activity or for that matter, any activity by a business? After all, in almost every area of business, the business' activities have some *effect* on interstate commerce. So, is the reach of the Commerce Clause without limit? The answer is, no, the Commerce Clause still has some limits.

In 1995, the U.S. Supreme Court decided **United States v. Lopez 514 U.S. 549 (1995)**. Lopez was a 12th grade student who carried a gun into his high school. He was charged under federal law with violating the **Gun-Free School Zones Act of 1990** that made it illegal for anyone to knowingly possess a firearm at a place that he knew was a school zone.

In a 5-4 decision, the Court held that Mr. Lopez's charge had to be reversed because that law was unconstitutional. The Court found the Federal Gun-Free School Zones Act to be unconstitutional in that the law exceeded Congress' legislative power under the Commerce Clause. The Court went through the history of the expansion of the power of the Commerce Clause and concluded that the Commerce Clause allowed Congress three broad categories in which to assert its power to regulate interstate commerce. Those three categories are that (1) Congress may regulate the use of the channels of interstate commerce, (2) Congress can regulate and protect the instrumentalities of interstate commerce, or persons or things in interstate commerce, and (3) Congress' commerce authority includes the power to regulate those activities having a substantial relation to interstate commerce. The Court felt that Mr. Lopez's activities did not fall into either of the first two categories and so, carrying a gun on school property would have to have a substantial affect on interstate commerce. The Court refused to so rule and stated that the possession of a gun in a local school zone is in no sense an economic activity that substantially affected interstate commerce and that the firearm's possession in question had no requisite nexus with interstate commerce. The Court distinguished Lopez's activities from those of the farmer in *Wickard* by stating that the repetition of carrying a gun on school property in other situations would not compound the economic impact as that of the farmer in the *Wickard* case, thereby refusing to extend the cumulative effect principle of *Wickard*. Simply put, in Lopez, there was not sufficient economic activity to justify use of the Commerce Clause.

Therefore, there is a limit on the Commerce Clause in that its use must involve one of the three areas of interstate commerce and have a substantial affect on the interstate commerce. This is the first case to limit the use of the Commerce Clause.

Since *Lopez*, the Supreme Court has continued this trend of limiting Congress' use of the Commerce Clause in limiting or excluding several provisions of the Brady Handgun Violence Prevention Act of 1993. In **Printz v. United States 521 U.S. 898 (1997)**, the Court was faced with the question of whether the federal government could require the chief law enforcement officer of each local jurisdiction to conduct checks on prospective handgun purchasers' backgrounds. The Court held that this provision of the Brady Handgun Violence Prevention Act was unconstitutional because there was no basis for such action, and that the Commerce Clause did not apply. Furthermore, the Court specifically addressed the concerns of the dissenting justices by saying that the Brady Act's requirement of state executive officials, the chief law enforcement officers, was not constitutionally valid as a law necessary and proper to execution of Congress' Commerce Clause power since the law violated the state sovereignty principle. The vote again was 5-4 along the same lines as *Lopez*.

The Court then addressed the issue again in United States v. Morrison in a case concerning the legality of 42 U.S.C. Section 1391, the Violence Against Women Act 1994) (**United States v. Morrison 529 U.S.598 (2000)**). The Court followed the reasoning of *Lopez* and said that Congress had exceeded its constitutional bounds because once again they were dealing with a non-economic, criminal situation and that Congress could not regulate non-economic, violent criminal conduct based on its aggregate effect on interstate commerce. The vote again was 5-4, along the same lines as *Lopez* and *Printz*.

In 2005, the Court was faced with another Commerce Clause question. This issue was over California's Compassionate Use Act which allowed limited medicinal marijuana use. However, Federal Drug Enforcement Officers acting under the Federal Controlled Substances Act seized the medicinal marijuana from respondents Raich and Monson who sought relief prohibiting the enforcement of the Controlled Substances Act. However, the Court had no problem saying that the Commerce Clause *DID* authorize Congress to prohibit the local cultivation and use of marijuana based on the precedent of *Wickard*. The Court stated in Gonzales v. Raich that all that was needed was a "rational basis" test to determine if interstate commerce was affected and held, based on *Wickard* that it was affected in this case due to the commercial value of the marijuana and the government's interest in stopping it from being sold (**Gonzales v. Raich 545 U.S. 1 (2005)**). The Court distinguished *Lopez* and *Morrison* by saying that in those cases, the laws at issue had nothing to do with "commerce" or any sort of economic enterprise and prevention of marijuana did have an effect on interstate commerce.

Interestingly enough, since these cases have been decided, the Supreme Court has lost two members with the death of Chief Justice Rehnquist and the retirement of Justice O'Connor. These two justices have been replaced by Chief Justice Roberts and Justice Alito. What impact will Thomas and Alito have on this issue? Only time will tell but given their ideologies and those of Rehnquist and O'Connor on these issues, it will probably do no more than reinforce if not strengthen the previous views.

C. The Necessary and Proper Clause

The language of the **Necessary and Proper Clause** is simple. Congress is empowered:

> [To] make all laws which shall be necessary and proper for carrying into Execution the foregoing Powers, and all other Powers vested by this Constitution in the Government of the United States, or in any department or Officer thereof.

This clause is found immediately after the enumerated powers in Article I of the Constitution. The purpose of the Necessary and Proper Clause is to give Congress the ability to account for all contingencies. The founders were aware that Congress would need the added power of making laws necessary to carry out the enumerated powers. Herein lies another source of flexibility in the Constitution. The "foregoing powers" refers to the enumerated powers listed above the Necessary and Proper Clause of the Constitution. It should be understood that this clause only enhances the specified powers of Congress and cannot be used to increase the list of enumerated powers. For instance, Congress has the power to establish post offices. In order to do so, it is necessary to have the power to set the price of postage. However, it does not have from that specific enumerated power, the power to create any other, non-postal, related business.

The Necessary and Proper Clause has also been referred to as the **Elastic Clause** and the **Implied Powers Clause**. The case of McCulloch v. Maryland that was discussed earlier is a good example of the use of the Necessary and Proper Clause. Remember, in that case, the State of Maryland was attempting to tax the national government for property located in the state of Maryland. Maryland's argument was that the Necessary and Proper Clause only applied to restrict the power of Congress to that of making laws that were necessary and proper to implement the delegated or enumerated powers of the Constitution. The Supreme Court rejected this argument since the clause was listed with the powers of Congress and not among the limitations on Congress' power that the clause was meant to enlarge the powers given to the national government. Therefore, the Court enlarged the powers of the Necessary and Proper Clause and unanimously ruled that the clause allowed the national government to create a bank even though that power was not specifically given to them in the Enumerated Powers Clause of the Constitution. It further stated that the Maryland law allowing the state to tax the national government was unconstitutional as interfering with a right of the national government. The Court ruled that the state of Maryland had exceeded its authority. The implied powers of the national government were born and the national government continues to use this elastic clause to stretch their powers.

D. The Supremacy Clause

The **Supremacy Clause** is contained in Article VI, Clause 2, and provides:

> [t]his Constitution, and the Laws of the United States which shall be made in Pursuance thereof … shall be the supreme Law of the Land.

The essence of this clause is that whenever both state and federal laws cover the same subject, the federal law is supreme and the state law is preempted to the extent that it is in conflict with the federal law. However, this does not mean that federal law always preempts state law. As a general principle, the courts presume legislation to be constitutional whenever possible. There are numerous areas of **concurrent powers** where both the national and state governments can pass legislation. Congress can exclude or **preempt** state legislation when it chooses to act exclusively in a concurrent area. If a state attempts to pass laws in a preempted area, then there is a conflict with the Supremacy Clause.

Therefore, the issue often becomes, is a state acting in an area that is preempted by national law? It is not always easy to determine when Congress has chosen to act exclusively in a concurrent area. Congress very rarely says in a formal manner, "this is now a preempted area." Therefore, it is left to the courts to determine the preempted areas. There is no single issue or fact that will determine a preempted area and usually the courts determine the issue based on a case-by-case basis. Often, the determining factor will be whether the national law leaves the states with the ability to supplement the law and in turn, how the states supplement the existing national law.

Conflicts between federal powers and state powers are inevitable. Often these conflicts arise if the state's exercise of its police power directly or indirectly conflicts with federal regulation of the same subject matter. These regulatory conflicts are often resolved by the U.S. Supreme Court in its interpretation of the supremacy clause. Whether the state's interference in interstate commerce by the state law will be constitutional or not must be balanced with the state interest (that the state law is designed to protect) in determining if the state law is a valid exercise of the police power. The question is not whether an interference with, or a burden on interstate commerce exists, but whether there is a *substantial* interference or burden with interstate commerce.

The courts, in determining whether interference is substantial, first look to the interest the state law is trying to protect, whether it is a legitimate state interest and whether the law accomplishes the desired effect. Next, the courts analyze the interference or burden imposed and compare whether on balance, the accomplished goals of the state are worth the burdens imposed. Thus, a state's good intentions may not warrant the imposition of a burden. The courts usually decide the issue of whether there is a substantial interference with interstate commerce on a case-by-case basis. As a result, even though two state regulations appear to be similar, the results can vary. Consider the following two situations:

1. The State of Oklahoma had a law prohibiting residents from other states bringing minnows into the state of Oklahoma. (**Hughes v. Oklahoma 441 U.S. 3212 (1979)**)
2. The State of Maine had a law prohibiting residents from other states bringing bait into the state of Maine. (**Maine v. Taylor 477 U.S. 131 (1986)**)

Since both laws affect interstate commerce by controlling what crosses state lines, both could be declared unconstitutional for violating the Commerce Clause. In approaching the problem, the Supreme Court had to determine the interest the state law was trying to protect and whether it was a legitimate state interest. Maine proved to the Supreme Court that it had a legitimate state interest in that it was trying to protect its fishing industry. The economy of Maine depends heavily on fishing. After all, who has not heard of Maine lobsters? Maine went on to show that to protect its waters from contamination it required anyone fishing in Maine to buy the bait in Maine from a regulated bait shop. Hence, you could not bring bait in from out of state. The court felt that Maine did have a legitimate state interest to protect. Therefore, the next issue was whether the law accomplished the desired effect. The court held that it did since the Maine-regulated bait shops were plentiful and did not charge a price that was out of line with the other bait shops in the Northeast region. Next, the Court had to determine if the Maine law went too far to achieve the legitimate state interest. Since Maine proved that its regulated bait was plentiful and not excessively expensive as compared to other states' bait, the Court ruled that the Maine regulation did not go too far. Therefore, the Court upheld the Maine regulation.

However, the court had a problem with the alleged Oklahoma state interest. What part of the Oklahoma economy depended on fishing? Did Oklahoma have a state interest to protect such as Maine? The court could not find a legitimate state interest and declared the Oklahoma law unconstitutional.

One may ask why states go through the trouble of passing laws that read much like federal laws. The reason is that only the federal government can enforce federal laws. States do not want to depend upon the federal government to prevent behavior that wastes its resources or harms its citizens. In order to have authority to regulate activities of its residents, a state must have its own set of laws and regulations and in doing so, sometimes unintentionally gets into interstate areas.

V. MISCELLANEOUS CONSTITUTIONAL PROVISIONS

A. Power to Tax

Article I, Section 8 of the Constitution gives Congress the power to "lay and collect taxes," and Article I, Section 7 of the Constitution specifies that the taxing power of the federal government is vested in Congress and all revenue bills must originate in the House of Representatives. In practice, both the President and the Senate exercise considerable influence on tax policy. In fact, the President often proposes tax bills to members of both the House and Senate in an effort to influence the process.

It is true that the primary function of taxes is to raise funds for government functions that have been deemed necessary by the political process, but it should be recognized that taxes might also be used to alter behavior, that is, to regulate. In almost any taxing law, there is an element of regulation. At times, this regulatory intent is evident. This is particularly true of the corporate income tax system. As a general rule, businesses are entitled to recover the cost of their capital investments over time. Congress has made several changes in the speed with which the cost can be recovered in order to induce investment during times of slowing economic activity. As the economy heats up, Congress will change the recovery period to slow the expansion. Thus, the taxing laws are used to promote macroeconomic (economy-wide) policy.

The regulatory aspects of tax laws are also reflected in their impacts on specific industries. For example, interest paid on mortgages for personal residences is deductible to encourage the purchase of homes, which also represents a subsidy to the housing industry. Industry representatives spend considerable time lobbying on Capitol Hill attempting to make sure tax policies have a favorable impact, or at least do not have a negative impact, on their industries. Other tax laws are used to affect social policy. Tobacco products and alcoholic beverages are taxed at higher rates (sin taxes), in part, to discourage consumption. However, as evidence of the impact of politics on industry-specific tax regulation, the production of tobacco is also subsidized by federal crop limitations (which have the effect of driving up the market price).

Consider the legal drinking age. Several years ago the legal drinking age was 18 years. However, the national government decided that the minimum age to legally drink alcohol should be raised to 21. Therefore, using the taxing power and the resulting spending power, states were told to raise their legal drinking age to 21 or they would lose federal highway funds. Eventually every state changed the minimum age of legally drinking alcoholic beverages to 21. Recently, the national government has been threatening the same action unless states lower the legal level of intoxication to 0.08 from the 0.10 level that had been used in several states, such as Texas, for years. Given the history of regulation by the national government via the taxing power, you can expect all states to lower the standard of the level of intoxication to the 0.08 standard just as the Texas Legislature did during the 1999 legislative session.

B. The Contracts Clause

The Contracts Clause of Article I, Section 10 of the Constitution provides that:

No State shall … pass any … Law impairing the Obligations of Contracts.

The Supreme Court has not been consistent in its application of the Contracts Clause. During the middle and late 1800s, it appeared that the clause would be a formidable weapon of business against governmental regulations. However, the court changed its position and recognized the superior right of states to pass laws that impair contracts so long as the laws were consistent with the broad police powers of the states.

In spite of the preceding observations, the Contracts Clause does offer some protection to businesses in some instances. For example, in **United States Trust Company of New York v. New Jersey 431 U.S. (1977)**, the Supreme Court held a state statute that decreased the value of state guaranteed bonds which had been sold before passage of the statute by increasing their risk after the statute was passed, was unconstitutional under the Contracts Clause. Also, in **Allied Structural Steel v. Spannaus 483 U.S. 234 (1974)**, the Supreme Court declared a state law to be unconstitutional under the Contracts Clause because the state regulation of private pension funds altered significantly the contractual obligations of employers under previously existing private, unregulated pension funds.

Still, cases involving the Contract Clause are rarely seen.

VI. CONSTITUTIONAL PROTECTIONS AGAINST GOVERNMENT ACTIONS

A. The Bill of Rights

The first 10 amendments to the Constitution, known as the Bill of Rights, were adopted in 1791 as we have already discussed. The Bill of Rights guarantees certain rights, liberties, and freedoms from intrusion or abridgement by the federal government. Although generally thought of as protecting only individuals, the Bill of Rights is of considerable interest in the study of the legal environment of business. First, a business consists of individuals: owners, managers, and employees. Second, a business operated in the corporate form is considered a "person" for many purposes under the law but not all purposes as we will see. Thus, the Bill of Rights protects businesses in the context of the individuals who comprise the business and sometimes, even the business itself. Remember, originally the Bill of Rights was only intended to limit the power of the national government by limiting its activities. In **Barron v. Baltimore 32 U.S. 243 (1833)**, the U.S. Supreme Court held that the Bill of Rights did not apply to the states. However, with the adoption of the Fourteenth Amendment, the Bill of Rights has been increasingly applied to the state governments as well, through the **doctrine of incorporation**. This doctrine has been used over the years by the Supreme Court consistently holding that most of the rights contained in the Bill of Rights also apply to the state governments, thereby, also limiting the power of the state governments. Each of the following rights applies to both the national and state governments.

One of the first uses of the doctrine of incorporation was the case of **Gitlow v. New York 268 U.S. 652 (1925)**. Gitlow was a socialist who printed a manifesto urging workers to overthrow the government and was convicted under a New York law sedition law which limited his right to freedom of speech. Gitlow appealed his conviction to the U.S. Supreme Court where the Court held the New York sedition statute to be unconstitutional. Gitlow claimed that he had the right to due process by the Fourteenth Amendment, which of course he did. He then argued that the due process he was owed under the Fourteenth Amendment was the same due process that the national government owed citizens under the Fifth Amendment and since it was the same, he was entitled to the due process under both the Fifth and Fourteenth amendments. Also, under the Fifth Amendment due process he would also be entitled to freedom of speech under the First Amendment because the national government could only give him due process by also giving him freedom of speech. The Supreme Court held the New York statute to be unconstitutional. Thus, the doctrine of incorporation was born and the First Amendment was held to apply to the states.

There is a long line of cases that expand the doctrine of incorporation, with the latest being the cases of **District of Columbia v. Heller 554 U.S. 290 (2008)** and **McDonald v. City of Chicago 561 U.S. 3025 (2010)**, which held that the laws of the District of Columbia and Chicago that banned gun ownership were violations of the Second Amendment and thus made the Second Amendment applicable to the states.

There are only a few remaining portions of the Bill of Rights that do not apply to the states and those are the Third Amendment which is quartering of soldiers, the requirement for Grand Jury indictment in the Fifth Amendment and the right to a jury trial in civil cases in the Seventh Amendment. Otherwise, the Bill of Rights applies equally to the national government and the state governments.

B. Freedom of Speech

1. Introduction to General Speech Rights

Among the rights guaranteed by the **First Amendment** is the right of free speech. Although the First Amendment appears to be written in absolute terms, "Congress shall make no law," the constitutional guarantee is subject to certain limitations. It does not mean that individuals are free to say whatever they desire whenever they desire. Plainly put, the right of freedom of speech from the First Amendment is not absolute. This is best illustrated by the famous statement of Justice Holmes in **Schenck v. United States 249 U.S. 47 (1919)**: "The most stringent protection of free speech would not protect a man in falsely shouting fire in a theater and causing panic." Schenck held that Congress could restrict speech that created a "clear and present" danger. The crucial constitutional question, therefore, centers on what speech is protected and what speech may be controlled or even forbidden by the Constitution.

The Supreme Court has developed a "balancing of interests" approach that allows the state and federal governments to limit the right of free speech when other social values predominate. While the Supreme Court requires a high interest by the national and state governments to limit speech, there are areas of unprotected speech. The government can even forbid the speech before it is stated which is caused prior restraint or censorship.

The Supreme Court is generally very tough on censorship efforts by the government. One example was the Pentagon Papers in the **New York Times Co. v. United States 430 U.S. 713 (1971)** where it was held that the U.S. government could not block the publication of the Pentagon Papers which were secret papers about the Vietnam War that had been stolen from the Pentagon. The U.S. government did not want the papers published claiming that it would be detrimental to the foreign relations of several countries with the United States due to the content of the papers and violate the Espionage Act. However, the Supreme Court felt that it was wrong to prohibit the publication of the papers and allowed the publication due to the right of freedom of speech. This was followed up with another prior restraint case in 1976, **Nebraska Press Associate v. Stewart**, where the U.S. Supreme Court stated that there was a heavy presumption against the constitutionality of prior restraint.

Governmental limitations on the right of free speech exist in many areas such as symbolic speech, hate speech, obscenity and fighting words, and limitation on public advocacy of crime or revolution. Symbolic speech is when symbols or signs are used as a means of expression. The first case to recognize this as protected speech was **Stromberg v. California 283 U.S. 359 (1931)**, where the Supreme Court overruled the conviction of a communist for displaying a red flag as a symbol of opposition to the U.S. government. However, when this involved a school, the Supreme Court seems to be saying that the schools can prohibit the students' symbolic speech if it is a "sophomoric" way of expressing the speech. This was the 5-4 ruling in **Morse v. Frederick 561 U.S. 393 (2007)**, which is the case where students displayed a banner at a school function that said "Bong Hits 4 Jesus." This may be an indication that the Roberts Court, the current Supreme Court, might be willing to limit the rights of students in symbolic speech.

Hate speech is a relatively new area of limited speech. Hate speech is speech that occurs with intent of racial intimidation. In **Virginia v. Black 538 U.S. 343 (2003)**, a Klu Klux Klan leader, Barry Black, was convicted of burning a cross in Virginia and the Virginia hate crime law was upheld. Colleges and universities can limit hate speech by time, place, and manner of speech. Obscenity is a very difficult area and has proven to be difficult to define.

Obscenity limitation began in **Roth v. United States 354 U.S. 476 (1957)**, where it was determined by the Court that obscenity included speech that was utterly without redeeming social importance, and the test should be, was the dominant theme of the material as a whole appealing to the prurient interest? Obviously, the standard was difficult to understand and apply. Therefore, in 1973, the Court put forth a new test in **Miller v. California 413 U.S. 15 (1973)** which was, did the work taken as a whole lack serious literary, artistic, political, or scientific value? Today the Court has basically sent the issue back to the local authorities and leaves up to a community standard which can vary from community to community.

On the other hand, the Court has had a consistent standard on fighting words. This was established by **Chaplinsky v. New Hampshire 315 U.S. 568 (1942)**. Fighting words are words that by their very utterance inflict injury or tend to incite an immediate breach of the peace. Another recent speech issue is the Solomon Amendment. During the 2005–2006 term, the Supreme Court had to address the issue of the constitutionality of the Solomon Amendment, which provides that educational institutions will lose certain federal funds if they deny military recruiters equal access to other types of recruiters on campus. In other words, does the Solomon Amendment violate the First Amendment freedom of speech by forcing institutions to allow military recruiters to come on campus to recruit? In **Rumsfeld v. Forum for Academic and Institutional 547 U.S. 47 (2006)**, the Supreme Court said that Congress could require law schools to provide equal access to military recruiters without violating the schools' freedom of speech. The Court decided the issue 8-0 (Alito did not participate). Would the result have been the same if it was someone or something other than the military? If the Solomon Amendment had applied to other businesses, would the law schools have had to allow all business recruiters no matter what the business?

2. More Important Speech Rights to a Business

More important limitations from a business perspective include limitations on public employee speech, commercial speech, political speech by a business, and defamation, which will be taken up in more detail in the Chapter 5.

a. Public Employee Speech

In 2006, the Supreme Court decided **Garcetti et al. v. Ceballos 547 U.S. 410 (2006)**. In a 5-4 opinion the Court handed down a narrow decision distinguishing between official and private speech. The Court handed down a new method of determining when the First Amendment protects public employees' speech. The Court held that "when public employees make statements pursuant to their official duties, the employees are not speaking as citizens for First Amendment purposes, and the Constitution does no insulate their communications from employer discipline." The controlling factor is whether the statement is made pursuant to official duties and responsibilities. Restricting that type of speech does not infringe on any First Amendment rights, it simply allows the employer to have control over the employees' official duties and responsibilities. Thus, a government entity continues to have broader discretion to limit the speech of its employees in their official duties and responsibilities but now the government has even more control in limiting the said speech. The issue becomes, will this be interpreted narrowly or will the Court expand on this in the future and further limit public employees' speech? Could it be applied to private employees' speech on the same rational? Only time will tell; but one thing is clear, public employees do not have as much free speech protection as private employees have, for now.

b. Commercial Speech

A primary concern of the supporters of the First Amendment was that the new central government would become too powerful and that exercising that power would allow the government, or those in power, to abuse it. Because the control of the new government would be determined through democratic elections, it was viewed as essential that individuals in the minority be afforded certain guarantees that would protect their ability to voice their objections to the policies of the individuals in power. Thus, speech that includes some political content, **political speech**, is afforded the greatest protection under the First

Amendment. On the other hand, speech that does not contain a political message of any sort is sometimes subject to regulation with respect to both content and method. In fact, the Supreme Court has created a special classification, **commercial speech**, for such speech.

Advertising is perhaps the clearest example of commercial speech. In **Valentine v. Chrestensen 316 U.S. 52 (1942)**, the Supreme Court determined that "purely commercial speech" was not protected by the First Amendment. Subsequently, Justice Douglas, who joined in the unanimous *Chrestensen* decision, admitted that the ruling in the case had been "casual, almost offhand," and that it had not "survived reflection" (**Cammarano v. United States, 358 U.S. 498 (1959) (concurring opinion)**).

Numerous decisions involving advertising ensued in which the Supreme Court invalidated restrictions on advertising on the grounds that those elements other than pure commercial speech were involved. Finally, in **Virginia State Board of Pharmacy v. Virginia Consumer Council 425 U.S. 748 (1976)**, the Supreme Court overruled *Chrestensen* and declared a state statute prohibiting pharmacists from advertising prices of prescription drugs to be an invalid restriction on speech. The court determined that a purely economic reason for speech did not operate to remove it from constitutional protection. In addition, the court found it significant that "[t]hose whom the suppression of prescription drug price information hits the hardest are the poor, the sick, and particularly the aged" (**Virginia State Board of Pharmacy v. Virginia Consumer Council 425 U.S. 748, 763**).

Thus, the court balanced the interests of consumers in learning of lower prescription prices through advertisements with the state's interests in promoting professionalism, which was the stated purpose of the law. Under the court's approach, the state law unduly burdened the flow of valuable information to consumers.

Virginia Pharmacy is of significant interest because the court's analysis focuses on the effects of the restriction on the members of society receiving the information rather than the act of transmitting it. Moreover, the court also indicated that reasonable restrictions on time, place, and manner of commercial speech are justified where a "balancing of interests" reveals that such restrictions are justified by a significant governmental interest and by the availability of alternative means of conveying the information to consumers.

Central Hudson Gas and Electric Corp. v. Public Service Commission of New York 447 U.S. 557 (1980) illustrates that the constitutional analysis is composed of a four-part test to determine whether a restriction on commercial speech unduly burdens the flow of information. That four-prong test is as follows:

1. Is the speech legal?
2. Is the governmental interest substantial?
3. Does the regulation of speech directly advance that governmental interest?
4. Does the regulation of speech go too far than is necessary to advance that governmental interest?

Since the Supreme Court issued this four-prong test, there have been several cases where the Court has held that the First Amendment has been violated by restricting commercial speech. Most noticeable in this area has been the prohibition against governmental restrictions in lawyer and doctor advertising. More recently, in **Rubin v. Coors Brewing Co 514 U.S. 476 (1995)**, the Supreme Court struck down a federal restriction against beer companies putting the alcohol content of the beer on their labels. Coors had proposed to the Bureau of Alcohol, Tobacco and Firearms (BATF) to include the alcohol content of the beer on their labels. The BATF refused to allow Coors to put the alcohol content on the label based on a regulation that had been in existence for approximately 60 years. Coors brought suit and won in the District Court and the Court of Appeals. The Department of Treasury, being the department under which the BATF falls, through its head, Secretary of the Treasury Rubin, sought a *writ of certiorari* to the Supreme Court. Writ was granted and the Supreme Court ruled that the governmental regulation did not directly and materially advance the governmental interest and that the 60-year-old government regulation was declared unconstitutional.

c. Political Speech by a Business

It makes sense that if political speech were afforded the greatest protection, that political speech by a business would likewise be protected. However, this has not always been so obvious.

In **First National Bank of Boston v. Bellotti 435 U.S. 765 (1978)**, the Supreme Court struck down a Massachusetts's statute prohibiting corporate political speech. However, the Court has recognized that political speech by a business is not as protected as an individual's political speech and has held that there are legitimate restrictions in business political speech. For instance, in **Austin v. Michigan Chamber of Commerce 494 U.S. 452 (1990)** the Supreme Court upheld a Michigan law that prohibited corporations from using general corporate funds for independent expenditures in state political campaigns. The court found that Michigan did "burden the exercise of free speech" but that the state had a compelling state interest, which was to prevent corporate wealth from unfairly influencing elections. This action was taken by a much more conservative court than *Bellotti* and reverses a trend of allowing more political speech by corporations. Austin basically deferred this issue to the states and allowed the states to decide if a business had political speech.

The issue was again before the court in 2000 when a Christian student sued the University of Wisconsin because he was required to pay activities fees that the University then dispersed to student organizations including those that speak out in favor of gay rights. The Christian student felt that this was a violation of free speech since in essence he was forced to give financial support to some of the groups that he opposed. He argued a line of cases that due to free speech prohibited labor unions from using collected labor money for certain political activities. The District Court and the Seventh Circuit agreed with the student. However, the Supreme Court *unanimously* rejected this argument. The Supreme Court held that "the First Amendment permits a public university to charge its students an activity fee used to fund a program to facilitate extracurricular student speech, provided that the program is viewpoint neutral … If a University determines that its mission is well served if students have the means to engage in dynamic discussion on a broad range of issues, it may impose a mandatory fee to sustain such dialogue." The parties had stipulated that the University's program respected the principle of viewpoint neutrality; funds went to both sides of the argument (**Board of Regents of the University of Wisconsin v. Southworth 529 U.S. 217 (2000)**).

On January 21, 2010, the Supreme Court handed down **Citizens United v. Federal Election Commission 558 U.S. 310 (2010)** which changed just about everything about political speech by a business. Prior to this case, a national law, the **Bipartisan Campaign Reform Act of 2002 (BCRA)**, prohibited corporations and labor unions from donating funds to an "electioneering communication" which is any political communication or for speech that expressly advocates the election or defeat of a candidate for national office. The case was a 5-4 decision and ruled that corporations and labor unions have the same political speech as individuals under the First Amendment and struck down the BCRA and overruled Austin v. Michigan Chamber of Commerce which held that political speech could be banned based on the speaker's corporate identity and **McConnell v. Federal Election Commission 540 U.S. 93 (2003)** which had upheld a challenge to limits on electioneering communications. The Court also in a 8-1 decision ruled that the disclaimer/disclosure requirements associated with political speech in election communications was constitutional. So the statements like "I am Barack Obama and I approved this ad" are legal. Therefore, corporations and labor unions now have unlimited rights to political speech just like a normal citizen, which means they can donate money and run advertisements on behalf of candidates. President Obama took the unusual step of publicly chastising the Supreme Court for this decision in his 2010 State of the Union Address. This has in large part contributed to the large increase in spending during the 2010 Congressional election and the 2012 Presidential election.

C. Freedom of Religion

The First Amendment also contains two guarantees regarding the freedom of religion. The **Free Exercise Clause** protects the rights of individuals to free exercise of religion, and the **Establishment Clause** prohibits governmental establishment of an official religion. The right to exercise either of these rights is not absolute as held **in Reynolds v. United States 98 U.S. 145 (1878)** which prohibited polygamy by the Jesus Christ of Latter Day Saints religion. However, the right to believe a religion is absolute but to practice the religion is not as seen in **Cantwell v. Connecticut 310 U.S. 296 (1940)**. How to interpret the Establishment Clause has varied widely over the years. Normally the Court is against school prayer but has allowed funding to religious schools for books and computers (**Michell v. Helms 530 U.S. 793 (2000)**). The Court also allowed vouchers to be given to people to go to private schools (**Zelman v. Simmons-Harris 536 U.S. 639 (2002)**). Prayer in school continues to be an issue as well, where it appears the Supreme Court is continuing to not allow prayer in school. However, non-education establishment clause issues are often unclear. Recently, free exercise issues have centered on the legality of religious decorations and symbols displayed by governmental entities. In a much divided court, the Supreme Court decided **County of Allegheny v. American Civil Liberties Union, Greater Pittsburgh 492 U.S. 573 (1989)**. The case centered around two religious displays in Pittsburgh, Pennsylvania.

The County set up a manger scene donated to the County by a Catholic group that had an angel at its crest holding a banner which said "Glory to God in the Highest" in Latin. The city of Pittsburgh set up an 18-foot menorah next to the 45-foot decorated Christmas tree. The ACLU sued to have both removed as a violation of the Establishment Clause. The Court held that the Establishment Clause prohibits the government from appearing to take a position on questions of religious belief or from "making adherence to a religion relevant in any way to a person's standing in the political community." The Court felt that the manger scene failed this requirement due to the banner making it a declaration of a Christian holy day by suggesting that people praise God for the birth of Jesus rather than as just a cultural phenomenon. However, the Court ruled that simply displaying the menorah did not endorse a specific religion given its combination with other non-religious decorations like the Christmas tree with which it was displayed. This has not totally settled the issue and recently the display of the Ten Commandments by governmental entities has come into question as a violation of the Establishment Clause. On June 27, 2005, the Supreme Court decided two cases on the issue, **Van Orden v. Perry 545 U.S. 677 (2005)** and **McCreary County, Kentucky, et al. v. American Civil Liberties Union of Kentucky 545 U.S. 844 (2005)**. The Court allowed the Ten Commandments to remain in the Texas case (*Van Orden*) but not in the Kentucky case. The reason for the difference is that in the Texas case, the 6-foot high memorial to the Ten Commandments was among 21 historical markers and 17 monuments surrounding the Texas State Capitol. The Commandments monument had been given to the State by the Fraternal Order of Eagles. The Court agreed with the lower courts that Texas had a valid secular purpose in recognizing the Eagles for their civic efforts and that a reasonable observer of the monument would not think that the state was endorsing religion. In the Kentucky case, the Court was faced with a display in county courthouses entitled "The Foundations of American Law and Government Display" consisting of nine framed documents of equal size, one of which was the Ten Commandments identified as being the King James Version. The other documents also highlighted references to religion and to Christ. The Court felt that the counties acted with the ostensible and predominant purpose of advancing religion and therefore, violated the Establishment Clause. The Court felt that scrutinizing the purpose of the display was the proper test. The Court also found no secular purpose in display. Interestingly, both cases were 5-4 decisions with Justice Breyer being the swing vote. However, with Justice O'Conner, who was in the majority in the Kentucky case and the minority in the Texas case, the result in both cases could change with the addition of Justice Alito to the bench—again, only time will tell of the impact of the changes in the Supreme Court that occurred in 2006.

The two principal areas where freedom of religion affects business are in the prohibition of certain transactions on Sunday, known as "blue laws" or Sunday laws and when the employment relationship conflicts with an employee's right to the free exercise of religion. **Blue laws**, or **Sunday laws**, are state or local laws, which regulate the types of business activities that can be conducted on Sunday. Frequently blue laws involve such things as a prohibition on selling liquor or household implements that involve work on Sunday. Sunday blue laws have been held to be constitutional on the grounds that they serve the secular purpose of providing a uniform day of rest and recreation (for both employees and consumers).

Thomas Jefferson advocated that there should be a wall, a separation between government and religion. This is not the case and never has been in the United States. Instead, the First Amendment has been held to mandate accommodations of all religious beliefs. The issue then becomes to what extent one must go to accommodate religious beliefs. This is especially important to businesses. Not only does the First Amendment apply to this issue, but also so do other federal laws, such as the Civil Rights Act of 1964, which will be discussed in greater depth in a later chapter.

However, the Equal Employment Opportunity Commission has held that under Title VII of the Civil Rights Act of 1964, a business must make reasonable accommodations for the religious practices of its employees *unless* it causes undue hardship to the business. For instance, if a business has hundreds of employees, then the business is to schedule work times around someone's religion. In addition, if a person must perform a religious ceremony numerous times during each and every day, the business might have to allow the employee to take breaks to perform the religious ceremony. However, it does not have to build the employee a room to perform the religious ceremony.

Furthermore, the Court has upheld the law of the State of Oregon, which forbids the ingesting of peyote even when used in religious practices. The Court said that an employer who fired employees who violated the Oregon law and ingested peyote, even during religious practices, was justified. The Court found that the Oregon law burdening the use of peyote was constitutional and the workers' rights under the Free Exercise Clause were not violated. The Court held that the First Amendment's Free Exercise Clause does not require judges to engage in a case-by-case assessment of the religious burdens imposed by constitutional laws (**Employment Division, Department of Human Resources of the State of Oregon v. Smith 494 U.S. 872 (1990)**). Congress afterward in response to that decision passed the **Religious Freedom Restoration Act of 1993 (RFRA)**. RFRA prohibits the federal government from substantially burdening a person's exercise of religion except when the government can demonstrate that application of the burden to the person advances a compelling governmental interest and that it is the least restrictive means of furthering that governmental interest. Members of *O Centro Espirita Beneficente Unial Do Vegetal Church* (UDV) receive communion by drinking *hoasca*, a tea made with plants form the Amazon Rainforest that contains a hallucinogen that is banned by the Federal Controlled Substances Act. U.S. customs inspectors seized a *hoasca* shipment to the church and threatened prosecution. The church filed suit claiming that the Controlled Substances Act as enforced against the church violated RFRA. The government agreed that the church would substantially be burdened by the seizure since it was a sincere exercise of religion but argued that this burden did not violate FRFA because applying the Controlled Substances Act was the least restrictive means of advancing the substantial governmental interests. However, the U.S. Supreme Court ruled that the government did not demonstrate at the preliminary injunction stage a compelling interest in barring the church from sacramental use of *hoasca*. One of the major problems for the government that it could not overcome was that it's argument that this case was significantly different than the peyote use by American Indians which was an exception under the Controlled Substances Act. This peyote exception fatally undermined the government's contention that the Controlled Substances Act established a closed regulatory system that admitted no exception under FRFRA. The case was remanded for further deliberations but the church was allowed to use *hoasca* in religious practices.

D. Search and Seizure

It is well known that the **Fourth Amendment** prohibits **unreasonable search and seizure** without a warrant because people have the

> right to be secure in their persons, houses, papers and effects, against unreasonable searches and seizures, shall not be violated, and no Warrants shall issue, but upon probable cause, supported by Oath or affirmation, and particularly describing the place to be searched and the persons or things to be seized.

Of course, even though the Fourth Amendment seems to require a warrant, there are several situations where law enforcement does not need a warrant. Warrantless searches can be done when the search is for the arrested person's body and the immediate area around the arrested person which is places or things the arrested person could take or reach or have immediate control over, things in plain view or if a person is committing or about to commit a crime the police can stop and search them if the police have reasonable suspicion or obtain the consent of the accused or if the Open Fields Doctrine applies. This doctrine means that the police can search a field even if there are no trespassing signs because the accused cannot expect privacy in an open field (**Hester v. United States 265 U.S. 57 (1924)**).

Automobiles are mobile and hence, a unique problem and call for special rules and the Court is usually lenient on automobile searches due to the balance between public interest and the detained individual's right of security but public interest usually wins out. Also, law enforcement can now just have a reasonable suspicion of criminal activity to stop a car, whereas the Court used to require a higher standard called probable cause.

Furthermore, drivers do not have a right to object to drug testing if there is an accident. If the driver is arrested, he will be requested to give a specimen of his blood or breath and he can refuse but will face consequences. In Texas, you will more than likely lose your driver's license for up to six months and have to face a DWI charge. However, upon refusal, the driver can also be forced to give a specimen of blood or breath with a warrant that is requested by the officer and signed by a judge. On the issue of blood tests, keep in mind that student athletes and even students involved in any extracurricular activities can be required to undergo a drug test because they in essence give their permission by doing the extracurricular activity.

The **Exclusionary Rule** has held that any evidence seized improperly must be excluded from trial. However, the Rehnquist Court and it appears the Roberts Court have been limiting the Fourth Amendment prohibition against unreasonable search and seizure by creating exceptions to the Exclusionary Rule. For instance, during May and June of 2006 the Supreme Court has held that police officers have the right to enter a home without a warrant when they reasonably believe that an occupant is seriously injured or imminently threatened with a serious injury (**Brigham City v. Stuart 547 U.S. 398 (2006)**). Furthermore, the Supreme Court threw out the "knock-and-announce" rule that had required police to announce themselves and wait before entering or the evidence would be excluded (**Hudson v. Michigan 547 U.S. 586 (2006)**).

However, the Exclusionary Rule is not obsolete and does still have application as seen in **Georgia v. Randolph 547 U.S. 103 (2006)** where the Court recognized that warrantless entry and search was valid when police obtained the voluntary consent of an occupant who shares the common area with a co-occupant who later objected to the use of the evidence so obtained as set forth in **Illinois v. Rodriguez 497 U.S. 177 (1990)** but ruled that if the co-occupant was physically present and continually refused to permit entry, that the warrantless search as to the one denying the entry is invalid even if a co-occupant was consenting to the search. The Exclusionary Rule or what is left of it does apply to businesses, but, once again, as in speech, we will see that the businesses rights are not as protected as the individuals' rights of search and seizure.

Granted, in general, there is a constitutional protection for businesses against unreasonable search and seizure and normally this does require a warrant to search. However, the standard to obtain the warrant is much lower than probable cause (criminal standard) and sometimes renders obtaining a warrant merely a technicality. These warrants when required for inspection of business in regulatory situations are called **administrative warrants** and are normally easily obtained by the government regulators. Sometimes, no warrant is required to search a business, such as in highly regulated industries (liquor, guns, strip mining) or if health is an issue (food industry or meat packing plants).

However, one must keep in mind that employees of the business are persons and therefore fall under the strict requirements of the Fourth Amendment. This sometimes creates a dilemma as to which standard should apply at work.

E. Self-Incrimination

The **Fifth Amendment** promises that *no person* "shall be compelled in *any criminal case* to be a witness against himself" (emphasis added). However, the guarantee is only given to persons, and only applies in criminal cases. If the case is not a criminal case, there is no protection against **self-incrimination**. Since a business is usually involved in civil law, the Fifth Amendment right does not apply in most situations. Furthermore, person has been held to mean a natural person, which means someone who is a breathing, living human being. Therefore, the Fifth Amendment guarantee against self-incrimination does not apply to corporations and most partnerships and since most business is conducted in the corporate form, the Fifth Amendment guarantee against self-incrimination does not apply to a large percentage of businesses.

There is no Fifth Amendment guarantee if the statement or confession is voluntarily made by the accused. Also, **Miranda v. Arizona 384 U.S. 86 (1966)** is a Supreme Court case that attempts to prevent coerced confessions. Therefore, the police were supposed to read the accused his Miranda warnings which are, "you have the right to remain silent, any statement that you make can and will be used against you as evidence, you have the right to an attorney and if you cannot afford one, one will be appointed for you." However, Miranda has been substantially weakened since 1966.

F. Due Process

1. Introduction

Another right guaranteed by the Fifth Amendment by the national government is that of **due process**. The Fifth Amendment states that an individual shall not:

> be deprived of life, liberty, or property, without due process of law

Due Process by the state governments is guaranteed by the **Fourteenth Amendment**. The term "due process" is not defined in the Constitution but federal courts have defined it on a sliding scale depending upon the magnitude of the interests at stake. Due process for these two amendments results in a guarantee by governments of two types of due process: **substantive due process** and **procedural due process**.

2. Two Types of Due Process

a. Substantive Due Process

Substantive due process involves the content or meat of the law of governmental action. This is where the sliding scale is very obvious. If the issue is simply economic, such as restrictions on a business' activities, then the rational basis test is utilized. In other words, if the government can show a rational relation for the legislation to a legitimate governmental interest, then the legislation provides substantive due process. This test is easily satisfied and governments normally have no problem satisfying this test in the area of business regulation of wages, unfair competition, etc. However, if an individual's fundamental rights, for example, any of the First Amendment rights, are restricted, then the test changes and the government's action is closely scrutinized and the government must prove a compelling, overriding interest. Other fundamental rights include travel, privacy, and voting.

b. Procedural Due Process

Procedural due process applies when one reviews the steps the government uses to deprive anyone of life, liberty, or property. Again a sliding scale applies. Obviously, procedural due process protections are greatest when the government is taking an individual's life. Hence, the criminal trial procedural protections and right of appeal are greatest when capital punishment is at stake. Liberty refers to imprisonment and the criminal defendant is afforded the protection of a presumption of innocence until proven guilty beyond a reasonable doubt. Counsel is appointed for defendants who cannot afford an attorney. When the government is seeking to deprive someone of property, it is subject to a much lower level (standard) of procedural safeguards depending on the nature of the property and the potential for abuse of power by the government. Property has been defined as money, employment, pension funds, and licenses, to name just a few examples.

G. Eminent Domain

Eminent domain is the taking of private property by the government. It is another Fifth Amendment constitutional right of the people and of the government, but the government must have a reason to take the property and must give just compensation. Granted the government does not have to have much of a reason to take, simply having a legitimate governmental interest is sufficient. Also, keep in mind that just compensation does not mean fair market value. The gist of the procedural safeguards against the taking of property by the government involves the right to be notified before any taking and the right to be heard. The purpose of the right to notice is so that the owner of the property can prepare a defense to the taking and the right to be heard affords the owner an opportunity to present the defense to an impartial decision maker. Usually, the only issue is the amount of the payment.

In 2000, the city of New London, Connecticut, approved a development plan to create over 1,000 jobs and hopefully revitalize the Fort Trumbull area of the city. However, to do so, the city had to obtain the land, 90 acres, needed for the project. The city purchased most of the property from willing sellers and wanted to use its power of eminent domain to obtain the remaining land where the owners did not want to sell. When the city's negotiations with those remaining sellers failed, the city began condemnation proceedings under eminent domain. However, the owners who did not want to sell brought suit against the city to stop the condemnation proceedings. The issue was whether the city's proposed use of the property after the taking for economic development constituted a **"public use"** under the meaning of the Fifth Amendment. The Court held in Kelo v. City New London that it was citing a long line of cases that set forth the precedent that the meaning of "public purpose" was to be defined broadly. In **Kelo v. City of New London 545 U.S. 469 (2005)**, the Court held that "For more than a century, our public use jurisprudence has wisely eschewed rigid formulas and intrusive scrutiny in favor of affording legislatures broad latitude in determining what public needs justify the use of the takings power." The Court affirmed the city's authority to take the property but reminded the city that undue hardships could ensue to the people who did not want to sell. Furthermore, the Court could enact stricter "public use" requirements than the minimum set forth by the courts ruling. The Court even recognized that some states already had stricter requirements for "public use." Several states after this decision did enact tougher standards for "public use" to avoid what many people felt was an incorrect decision by the U.S. Supreme Court. Texas is one of those states.

H. Equal Protection

The Equal Protection Clause of the **Fourteenth Amendment**, passed shortly after the Civil War, prevents states from denying "equal protection of the laws." While its initial intent may have been to protect former slaves from discrimination, its use has been expanded to protect against other arbitrary government distinctions. While the Fourteenth Amendment originally applied to the states, the courts have held that it also applies to the national government due to the due process requirements of the Fifth Amendment. Therefore, we can read the Equal Protection Clause as no government can deny any person within its jurisdiction the equal protection of the laws.

Although various persons may be treated differently by the state and federal government, the distinctions between persons must be logically and rationally related to a valid objective. For instance, states may treat minors and adults differently with respect to the legal consumption of alcoholic beverages. The distinction on the basis of age and (presumably) maturity has been upheld because the courts felt it is logical and rational to accomplish the objective of reducing irresponsible and dangerous behavior such as driving while intoxicated.

The Supreme Court has struck down distinctions, however, that it deemed illogical. In **Skinner v. Oklahoma 316 U.S 535 (1942)**, a state statute provided for compulsory sterilization of habitual criminals who had been convicted two or more times of grand larceny but did not mandate compulsory sterilization of habitual criminals in embezzlement cases. The Court found the law unconstitutional because there was no logical basis for distinguishing between perpetrators of the two crimes.

The court has also invalidated state laws when the purpose of the distinction between persons was improper. In **Metropolitan Life Insurance Co. v. Ward 470 U.S. 869 (1985)**, the court struck down an Alabama tax law that taxed non-resident insurance companies at a higher rate than resident companies. The court held that the promotion of resident business by discriminating against non-resident competitors was not a legitimate state purpose.

The approach to an equal protection claim is similar to the sliding scale of a substantive due process claim seen above. However, under an equal protection claim, the courts are given the task of determining if classifications made by the law are justified. The courts have a three-tier sliding scale.

At the low end of the equal protection standards is the **rational basis test**. The rational basis test applies to laws concerned with economic or social classes. It is rare to see governmental activity declared unconstitutional based on this test. If, on the other hand, the classification involves gender or legitimacy, the government in creating this type of classification must have a **substantial governmental interest**. However, if the classification involves the exercise of some fundamental right or suspect classification such as race then to be justified a **compelling state interest** must be found.

Therefore, when faced with an equal protection claim, the court must determine which of the three equal protection tests apply. Federal courts and courts in numerous states have had to face these questions in several areas. One of those areas is state law mandating helmets for riders of motorcycles. This classification has been upheld under the rational basis test. Even so, due to a demand by motorcycle riders, these laws were repealed in Texas due to public demand.

I. Right of Privacy

The U.S. Constitution does not specifically guarantee a right of privacy and such a constitutional right was not recognized by the U.S. Supreme Court until the 1960s in the landmark case of **Griswold v. Connecticut 381 U.S. 479 (1965)**, which held that a Connecticut statue that forbid the use of contraceptives violated the rights of marital privacy under the Bill of Rights. Congress followed up on the right of privacy with the **Freedom of Information Act 1966**, the **Privacy Act 1974**, and more recently the **Health Insurance Portability and Accountability Act (HIPAA) 1996** and the **Uniting and Strengthening America by Providing Appropriate Tools Required to Intercept and Obstruct Terrorism Act (Patriot Act) 2001**. Congress has also been very active trying to ensure an individual and businesses right of privacy in cyberspace such as the **Electronic Communications Privacy Act of 1986 (ECPA)**, the **Children's Online Privacy Protection Act of 1998 (COPPA)**, and the **Financial Services Modernization Act of 1999 (FSMA)**. Of course, several of these statutory laws have been very controversial, especially the Patriot Act but the privacy issue has also been dominated by the opinion of several U.S. Supreme Court cases.

However, none has probably been more controversial than Roe v. Wade, which declared the Texas criminal laws prohibiting abortion in the first trimester of a woman's pregnancy a violation of the woman's right of privacy (**Roe v. Wade 410 U.S. 113 (1972)**). In other words, a woman had a right of privacy to decide whether to terminate a pregnancy in the first trimester. Of course, none of the justices who participated in that decision are still on the U.S. Supreme Court and the Court is constantly criticized and praised for its subsequent rulings on abortion.

Texas again had a law declared unconstitutional based on right of privacy in **Lawrence v. Texas Lawrence v. Texas 539 U.S. 558 (2003)**. In this case, the Texas statute making it a crime for two persons of the same sex to engage in certain sexual conduct was declared to be a violation of the Due Process Clause and right of privacy.

Privacy issues have always been and will remain controversial. Think of the political issue that the pro-life and pro-choice sides have made out of the abortion issue. Also, important in this area are the right to die laws as well as other controversial subjects.

CHAPTER SUMMARY

In this chapter we have reviewed the most important type of law in the U. S. constitutional law. After all, if a law of any type is not constitutional, it cannot stand. However, the United States was the first country to use such a system and we developed it from the Constitutional Convention until the present.

We examined the power of the Constitution and its importance to the business world primarily through an examination of the Commerce Clause and its importance not only in the Civil Rights area but in government regulation as a whole. We also examined the recent limitations on the Commerce Clause.

We also learned that constitutional protections against government actions basically had its origin in the Bill of Rights. Freedom of speech does apply to businesses but not to the extent that it does in private, non-business areas. However, that right has been expanded in political speech. As for religion, a business must give reasonable accommodation to its employee's religions. Search and seizure was also discussed and again a business does not have the degree of protection that an individual enjoys. Self-incrimination from the Fifth Amendment was also limited and did not apply in civil matters or to corporations. From the Fourteenth Amendment, we discussed due process and equal protection. In both due process and equal protection, we saw a sliding scale on the test for the extent of due process and equal protection to which one is entitled. Equal protection had three degrees of care and due process had two. We examined a right that is constitutional even though it is not in the Constitution with the Privacy Right. Lastly, we examined some miscellaneous constitutional provisions that are very important to the business world.

3

LITIGATION AND ALTERNATE DISPUTE RESOLUTION

PART ONE — LITIGATION

I. INTRODUCTION

Most business activity results in the satisfactory conclusion of mutually beneficial transactions between the parties. However, businesses also become involved in disputes with other firms, customers, or with the government. These disputes normally arise due to the belief by one party that the other party has committed a wrong or violated some law. If the disputes cannot be resolved through mutual agreement and compromise, a lawsuit may be filed in order to have the issues resolved by the courts in the process called **litigation**.

The reality is that in the business world, if you are a successful business, you are probably going to get sued because greedy people will want part of your success. On the other hand, if you are an unsuccessful business, you are probably going to be sued as well because of the problems that the demise of your business has caused. Therefore, litigation or at least the threat of litigation may be unavoidable for the business.

II. TYPES OF JUDICIAL SYSTEMS

A. Introduction

In litigation, there are three types of judicial systems in which businesses might become involved. The business would find itself in a criminal court if the state or federal government accused it of violating some criminal statute. It would be in a civil court if it had a dispute with another individual or business that could not otherwise be settled. Finally, it would be in an administrative court if a federal of state agency accused it of violating one of the regulations which one of the state or federal agencies are empowered to enforce.

These judicial systems operate separately. In business, the criminal system is probably utilized less than the other two systems and therefore, we will not concentrate on the criminal system. However, keep in mind that businesses can and do have criminal charges brought against them, but much more rarely than when a business gets involved in civil matters. The administrative court system is discussed in a later chapter. Therefore, this chapter will concentrate on the civil court system in which a business is likely to find itself as either a **plaintiff**, the party that begins the lawsuit or as a **defendant**, the party that is sued.

Civil courts have judges and juries like criminal courts, but the procedural safeguards required by the Constitution are somewhat less than in criminal courts. This is because loss of liberty is not a remedy that can be imposed by a civil court. Therefore, a civil court normally will not appoint an attorney for indigent parties because the Constitutional right to counsel only applies in criminal courts. Furthermore, the standard for proving the defendant responsible or liable in a civil court is by a **preponderance of the evidence** (more likely than not) while a much higher standard of proof is necessary in a criminal court (**beyond a reasonable doubt**). Finally, remember parties cannot refuse to testify against themselves in a civil trial as they can in a criminal trial because the Fifth Amendment only applies to criminal matters. Keep in mind that even in criminal cases, a corporation cannot rely on the Fifth Amendment. This is because in addition to only applying to criminal matters, the Fifth Amendment only protects individuals and individuals have been defined as being living, breathing human beings. However, even in a civil case, any individual can refuse to answer questions that he or she feels will incriminate them for a criminal act unless given the appropriate immunity by the proper authority.

B. The Civil Court System

All civil court systems are arranged in a sort of ladder of hierarchy. The **trial court**(s) is(are) the lowest rung on the ladder, meaning that this is where the case begins. However, it is very important because most of the trial courts develop the record of the case and this record will become the foundation for the appeal of the case to the higher court if an appeal is necessary. Some systems only have one trial court, whereas other systems have several. For example, the Federal Court only has one general trial court while the Texas state judicial system has six. All testimony, rulings by the judge, objections by the parties, admissible evidence, as well as other materials requested by the parties, become part of the record.

Appellate courts comprise the higher rungs of the ladder that lead to the highest court in the system. These courts are primarily concerned with whether or not error (mistakes) occurred at the lower court. To determine whether any error was committed or not, the appellate court relies on the record, the briefs of the parties, and oral argument. The procedure is as follows: (1) the **appellant**, appealing party, gives notice of appeal to the trial court and files a designation of the record which specifies all of the items from the trial that the party wants to include as part of the packet that is sent to the appellate court; (2) the appellant prepares a brief, a legal document citing precedent and proving error; (3) the **appellee**, the non-appealing party, files a response brief trying to show that the appellant is incorrect and; (4) **oral argument** which occurs before the appeals court where both parties have a limited time, usually 30 minutes each, to orally persuade the appellate judges that their position is correct; and (5) the decision of the appellate court which might be months after the oral argument phase took place.

There is a fundamental distinction between trial courts and appellate courts. As stated above, lawsuits are generally initiated in trial courts. The basic functions of the trial courts are to determine the facts in a case from the evidence presented by the parties involved in the lawsuit and then apply the law to the facts to reach a decision in the case. The judge determines the law and the jury, if there is one, or the judge (if there is no jury) decides the facts. Thus, trial courts decide issues of fact and issues of law. Issues of fact arise when the parties do not agree about what happened. If the testimony is conflicting and the evidence inconclusive, the trial court will determine which version to believe. Issues of law can be substantive (what law applies to a given case) or procedural (what evidence or testimony is admissible).

Appellate courts are normally only concerned with whether the trial court made a mistake in issues of fact or issues of law. It is rare to see an appellate court overturn a trial court on fact issues, that is, what are the facts. Instead, the appellate court is primarily concerned with mistakes in the application of the law to those facts.

There are 50 separate and distinct state court systems in the United States. The District of Columbia also has its own system. In addition to each state having its own system, there is also the federal system. All systems have somewhat different organizations and procedures but they are similar in more ways than they are different.

C. The Criminal Court System

The criminal court system is basically parallel to the civil court system and the average citizen may not see a difference. However, there are major differences between the two systems. The burden of proof is one example of this difference. In a criminal case, the government must prove the case beyond any reasonable doubt but in a civil case the victorious party only has to prove the case by a preponderance of the evidence which is a much lower burden of proof than beyond any reasonable doubt. In a criminal case, the burden of proving the case is always on the government's prosecutor. The person charged with a crime, the defendant, is always presumed innocent.

As we will see below, there may be specialized courts for either civil cases or criminal cases. Whether it is a specialized court for criminal cases or just a regular court that hears criminal cases, normally the jury is required to come to a unanimous decision in criminal cases and that may not be the case in a civil case. Also, in most situations a criminal case is a bifurcated trial which means that there are really two trials, one for guilt-innocence and one for punishment and different rules of evidence can exist for each of the situations. Referring to Chapter 2, a defendant has the constitutional right to a jury trial in a criminal case that can result in incarceration but civil courts do not guarantee a jury trial. Also, other constitutional rights apply to criminal cases but not to civil cases.

D. Administrative Court System

Regulation is a major part of the national and state government. Regulation will be accomplished by the bureaucracy and we will discuss several areas of regulation in later chapters.

These administrative agencies and/or regulatory agencies have their own courts and their own court system in part creating administrative law. We will discuss administrative courts in Chapter 6. Suffice to say, it is a very different system than any system discussed above.

III. TEXAS COURT SYSTEM

A. Introduction

A typical state court system has at least one tier of trial courts and usually at least two appellate courts. Most state court systems are patterned after the federal court system. However, some states like Texas vary significantly from the federal model.

The Texas court system is a complex system due in large part to the Texas Constitution which was written in 1876 after the Southern men, ex-Confederates regained control of the state. Furthermore, the Texas Constitution was written to insure that the radical, Republican, Yankees or anyone like them would ever rule Texas again. In their zeal to accomplish this goal, the delegates to the constitutional convention were guilty of overkill which has led to many problems in Texas. One of these problem areas is in the Texas court system. Like most states, the Texas legal system consists of trial courts and appellate courts. However, Texas has a rather complex court system, due in large part to the Texas Constitution.

B. Texas Trial Courts

1. First Tier of Texas Trial Courts

a. Municipal Courts

With several hundred municipal courts in Texas and with cities basically left to determine the specifics of the **municipal court**, obviously these courts are going to vary greatly from city to city. However, the judge of the municipal court is usually appointed by the ruling body of the city, which is ordinarily the city council. Normally, the city council also has removal power and can, therefore, remove the judge if he or she is not doing an adequate job as judge, as determined by the ruling members of the municipal government. The ruling body of the city also sets the qualifications for the municipal judge position, and while these requirements vary from city to city. This usually means that the municipal judge may or may not have to have a law degree.

The jurisdiction of municipal court is limited to violations of municipal ordinances, as well as criminal jurisdiction over minor state crimes (class C misdemeanors) that occur within the city limits of that municipality. Most municipal court dockets are dominated by traffic cases, loud noise violations, and minor alcohol infractions.

Furthermore, most municipal courts are not courts of record. In other words, no official record is kept of the proceedings. Therefore, any appeal to a higher court will be a trial *de novo*, the trial will start over, from the beginning, just like the trial never occurred in the municipal court. In essence, you will get two trials. However, recently the Texas legislature has, at the request of some cities, made those cities municipal courts to be "of record" to avoid this duplication of trials. However, this is only applicable in certain cities in Texas. Any appeal from municipal court goes to the appropriate county court or county court at law, depending upon in which county the municipal court is located.

b. Justice of the Peace Court

The Texas Constitution created the **justice of the peace court** which is the same level as the municipal court. Where the municipal court is limited to violations of municipal ordinances and violations of class C misdemeanors, the justice of the peace court, like the municipal court, has jurisdiction over criminal violations of class C misdemeanors but the justice of the peace court also has civil jurisdiction over low dollar amount civil cases. The amount was originally $200 as set by the Texas Constitution but has now been raised by the Texas Government Code to not more than $10,000.

The justice of the peace court only serves a part of a county and the number of justice of the peace courts in a county varies from county to county. The justice of the peace, the judge of the justice of the peace court, is elected in a partisan election, contested between political parties, by the people living in that geographic part of the county served by that justice of the peace. Originally, each county in Texas was divided into four equal parts, called precincts, by the ruling body of the county, the Commissioner's Court. This division is made according to population so that each justice of the peace serves the same number of people. Each one-fourth of the county can be served by more than one justice of the peace courts. However, in sparsely populated counties even the original four areas can be combined so that you have less than four justices of the peace in a county and a county can have as few as one justice of the peace court. Therefore, the number of justice of the peace courts per county varies throughout the state. There are over 800 justices of the peace in Texas.

The term of a justice of the peace is four years. A justice of the peace does not have to be a licensed attorney. In fact, the major qualifications to be a justice of the peace are to be 18 years old on the day they take office and have U.S. citizenship. In other words, they have to have about the same qualifications as a registered voter.

However, the justice of the peace can have other functions as well. For instance, in some counties the justice of the peace is also the coroner. In other words, it is up to the justice of the peace to pronounce someone to be dead. Justices of the peace can also perform weddings and serve as a magistrate and set bonds for criminal defendants.

Ordinarily the justice of the peace court is not a court of record and any appeal from the justice of the peace court is a trial *de novo* appeal to the appropriate county court or county court at law.

c. Small Claims Court

The **Small Claims Court** of Texas was a statutory court which means that these courts were created by the Texas legislature. These courts were the Texas equivalent to "People's Court". They were created so that the ordinary people of Texas would have a civil court in which they could present their case without the need of an attorney. The judge of the small claims court was the same judge as the justice of the peace court. Therefore, the term, method of election and people served were the same as the justice of the peace court. However, the small claims court only had jurisdiction over civil cases up to $10,000. It had NO jurisdiction over criminal matters. Again, the small claims court was ordinarily not a court of record and any appeal was a *de novo* appeal to county court or county court at law.

However, the courts that were know as the separate Small Claims Courts in Texas have recently been merged into the Justice of the Peace Courts. In other words, the Justice of the Peace Courts have assumed all of the duties of the Small Claims Courts thereby doing away with the Small Claims Courts as separate courts.

2. Second Tier Trial Courts

The next level of courts includes the county court, county court at law, and district court. Both the county court and the county courts at law are courts of record, where the judge is elected county wide to a four-year term, in partisan elections. They are also unique in that they are both trial court and appellate courts. (In the rest of the Texas system and the federal system, a court will either be a trial court or an appellate court but not both.) Since this is a county office, if there is a vacancy, that vacancy is filled by the County Commissioners. The district court is also a court of record where the judge is elected to a four-year term, in partisan elections. However, they can include more than one county and they are not appellate courts. The district court is a state position and any vacancies in an unexpired term are filed by appointment of the Governor of Texas.

a. County Court

The **County Court** is a constitutional court created by the Texas Constitution. The Constitution specifies that each of the 254 counties in Texas shall have only one county court. However, the jurisdiction of the county court now includes (1) appeals from municipal court, small claims court, and justice of the peace courts, as well as; (2) being a trial court for criminal cases of a higher nature (class B and A misdemeanors); (3) civil cases between $200 and $10,000; (4) juvenile matter; and (5) probate cases, according to the Texas Government Code. The county court also has numerous other non-judicial functions, such as being the head of the administrative arm of the courthouse.

The Texas Constitution specifies that this judge shall be elected in partisan elections by the voters of the county, which he or she serves for a four-year term. The qualifications as set forth by the Texas Constitution are that the prospective county judge be well informed in the laws of the state. This does not mean that they have to be a licensed attorney and in many counties the county judge is not an attorney.

b. County Court at Law

Due to the number of constitutional limitations placed on the county court; specifically the one-per-county limitation, the legislature created a second type of county courts which are named the **County Courts at Law**. Originally, the plan was that the county court at law would have the same jurisdiction as the county court. However, due to the expanding nature and population of Texas, the legislature has, from time to time, changed the jurisdiction of the county court at law. For instance, the civil jurisdiction of the county court at law has been raised to $100,000. Furthermore, jurisdiction from one county court at law may vary from Texas Government Code also makes special provisions for several counties. For instance, some county courts at law have jurisdiction over family law matters, while some others don't. (Note that a county court does not have jurisdiction over family law.)

Furthermore, the judge of the county court at law must have a law license and must be 25 years old, have lived in the county for 2 years, and practiced or served as a judge for the preceding 4 years. Otherwise, the county courts at law have the same criminal jurisdiction as a county court and also normally have the same probate jurisdiction. Some counties which have multiple county courts at law, the County Commissioners have determined that these county courts at law should be specialized and therefore, you will find county courts at law broken into civil, probate, and county criminal courts at law. For example, in Harris County, the county courts at law are specialized into all three types. An appeal from the county court or the county court at law goes to the Court of Appeals level.

c. District Court

The basic trial court that is only a trial court for the state of Texas is the **district court**. This court can either consist of one county or several counties. For instance, the district courts of Brazos County are only courts for the residents of that place. However, the 21st district court covers Washington, Lee, and Burleson counties. Originally, the district courts were created by the Texas Constitution, but more recently have been created by Texas statue. As of 2013, there are about 450 district courts in the state of Texas.

The district courts' jurisdiction includes original jurisdiction of all action, proceedings, and remedies unless exclusive jurisdiction is given to another court according to the Texas Constitution. This results in the district court having civil jurisdiction in cases beginning at $200 and going as high as necessary. (There is actually a disagreement between Court of Appeals as to whether the amount is $200 or $500.) In other words, multi-million dollar cases will be filed in district court. District courts also have jurisdiction over family law, which takes up a large percentage of the docket in most district courts. Additionally, the district court has jurisdiction over felony criminal cases, as well as, title to land cases, election contests as well as other areas of the law not given specifically to another court.

Approximately two-thirds of the cases filed in district courts are civil cases with the remaining one-third being criminal cases. District courts in some districts have been specialized to be either civil district courts, criminal district courts, or family district courts. For example, in Harris County, which makes up a single district, there are specialized district courts of all types. There is only one judge in each district court and the district court is *not* an appellate court. If the case is appealed from the district court, it is normally taken to the Court of Appeals. However, if the judgment of the district court is that the defendant receive the death penalty, that case is sent to the Court of Criminal Appeals of Texas, the state's highest criminal court.

The qualification to be a district judge are that the prospective judge must be at least 25 years of age, should have been a resident of the district for more than 2 years, be a citizen of the state of Texas (and therefore the United States), and be a licensed, practicing lawyer or judge for 4-year terms by the residents of the county or counties they serve.

3. *Appellate Courts, Third and Fourth Tier of Texas Courts*

a. Introduction

There are three types of true appellate courts in the Texas court system; Court of Appeals, Court of Criminal Appeals, and the Texas Supreme Court. The first level of appellate courts is the Court of Appeals.

As for the highest level of appellate courts, Texas and Oklahoma are the only two states in the union that have two highest courts of appellate jurisdiction. The Texas Supreme Court is the highest court of civil jurisdiction in the state, while the Texas Court of Criminal Appeals is the highest criminal appellate court in the state of Texas. In both the Court of Criminal Appeals and the Supreme Court, the decision of the court is final unless the case is reviewed by the U.S. Supreme Court.

b. Third Tier of Courts, First Tier of True Appellate Court, Texas Court of Appeals

There are 14 **Courts of Appeals** in Texas. These courts are located as follows:

- 1st Houston
- 2nd Fort Worth
- 3rd Austin
- 4th San Antonio
- 5th Dallas
- 6th Texarkana
- 7th Amarillo
- 8th El Paso
- 9th Beaumont
- 10th Waco
- 11th Eastland
- 12th Tyler
- 13th Corpus Christi
- 14th Houston

Note that these are in major metropolitan areas of the state, with the exception of Eastland. The number of judges in the Courts of Appeals varies from 3 in the 6th, 9th, 10th, 11th, and 12th Court of Appeals to 13 in the 5th Court of Appeal. The judges of the Court of Appeals are elected in six year overlapping terms, by all of the citizens of the counties which they serve. A Court of Appeals judge must be at least 35 years of age and have 10 years of experience as an attorney. Please note that a Court of Appeals judge does not have to have prior judicial experience.

These courts hear both civil and criminal appeals. In each court you have at least one chief justice while the rest of the appeals court justices are labeled associate justices. Justices on the Court of Appeals will either hear a case *en banc* which means the entire membership of the court will hear a case, or in panels, usually consisting of three judges per panel.

Any case from the district court, county court, or county court at law can be appealed to the Court of Appeals if it involves a fine of more than $100, imprisonment, or has a constitutional issue.

This usually is the final level of courts that an ordinary case will reach.

c. Fourth Tier, Highest Texas Courts

1) Introduction

Texas has another unusual fact in that it has two highest Courts of Appeals. The first is the Texas Court of Criminal Appeals for criminal cases and the second is the Texas Supreme Court for civil cases. These two courts are in essence equal to each other but hear different type of cases. They are both located in Austin by the State Capitol and both elected to office by statewide elections.

2) Court of Criminal Appeals

The **Court of Criminal Appeals** consists of nine members. This court only hears criminal cases. One is the chief justice and there are eight associate justices. The chief justice is the presiding justice and is elected as the presiding justice in a statewide partisan election. Likewise, the associate justices are elected in statewide elections. All the members of the Court of Criminal Appeals serve for six years. However, you only elect a part of the court every two years. In other words, they also serve staggered terms like the Court of Appeals. Qualifications are the same as the Court of Appeals and will be the same for the Texas Supreme Court.

3) Texas Supreme Court

The **Texas Supreme Court** also has nine members which are elected statewide in partisan elections for six-year terms. Every two years, three members of the Texas Supreme Court are elected for a six-year term. Qualifications are the same of the Court of Criminal Appeals and likewise it consists of eight associates and one chief justice. The Supreme Court of Texas is the final court for civil and juvenile cases unless they involve a constitutional issue which can be appealed to the federal court system. The court also has several non-judicial functions including determining the civil rules of procedure for attorneys in trial practice, as well as, licensing procedures for the State Bar of Texas. Like the Court of Criminal Appeals, the Supreme Court of Texas is in Austin.

4) Texas Court System Election Problems
a) Voter Confusion

Most counties are located in one Court of Appeals. However, Brazos County is located in three Courts of Appeals, the 1st, 10th, and 14th. Therefore, in Brazos County in any given election for county- and statewide office, you could, as a Brazos County voter, be voting for a justice of the peace, a county judge, as well as judge for county courts at law and district courts, three different Court of Appeals, as well as the Supreme Court and the Court of Criminal Appeals. (Of course, not all the judges will be running in every county or state election because these are held every two years in Texas and the judges either have four- or six-year terms.)

One of the many problems with the Texas Court System is that judges are elected and people do NOT know who they are voting for when it comes to the judges' selection. Most people do not research the judges and only vote by party or name identification or advertising claims of the candidate. The result is that often Texans have poor quality judges in office.

Another problem is the lack of pay. Most attorneys can make more money as an attorney than as an elected Texas judge and few want to give up a lucrative law practice to become a judge. Another problem is financing. A campaign is very expensive and a judge's campaign contributor might want to remind the judge about the contribution at the "appropriate" time during a trial.

b) Election of Judges

In the first place, all Texas judges are elected in partisan (Republicans vs. Democrats) elections, except for the judge of the municipal court which is usually an appointed position. This practice of electing judges had led to accusations from national television and news magazines, that Texas judges can be strongly influenced, if not bought, by political contributions. After all, some Texas judges must run a statewide election which is extremely expensive so they must take contributions and then the entity that made the contribution often feels that the judge then owes them. Therefore, candidates either have to be independently wealthy so that they do not have to take political contributions or accept political contributions from sources which may turn up in later months as those litigants who expect the judge to remember their political contributions, and return the favor by ruling for them. In June 2009, the U.S. Supreme Court addressed this issue in a case out of West Virginia, **Caperton v. Massey Coal Company, 556 U.S. 868 (2009)**. In *Caperton*, the Court ruled in a 5-4 decision that elected judges should not rule on cases involving their major backers. The Chief Justice of West Virginia's highest court, Justice Benjamin, had twice been the swing vote to throw out a $50 million verdict that a lower court had enacted against Massey Coal Company. In winning his highest court seat, Justice Benjamin in defeating the incumbent had accepted $3 million in campaign help from Massey Coal Company. Justice Benjamin was elected to a 12-year term and during that time period this case came to the highest court on appeal. The plaintiffs had requested a recusal, a request that Justice Benjamin step aside and not participate in the appeal. However, Benjamin refused and as stated became the deciding vote that resulted in the dismissal of the $50-million verdict. The Court held that the actions of Justice Benjamin in failing to recuse himself violated the Plaintiffs' due process under the Fourteenth Amendment. Justice Kennedy wrote the opinion for the Court and felt that this did not require judges/justices to recuse themselves in every case where they had received campaign contributions but that this case was so extreme that it required Justice Benjamin to have recused himself. Keep in mind there was no proof that Justice Benjamin was biased or influenced due to the campaign contributions but that this particular instance was extreme. The Supreme Court of Montana in Reichert v. State ex rel McCulloch 278 P.3d 455 followed in 2012 and quoted Caperton in saying that due process "requires recusal when the probability of actual bias on the part of the judge or decision-maker is too high to be constitutionally tolerable." Therefore, judges should recuse or step down when there is a probability of actual bias by the judge. However, do enough elected judges in Texas actually step down when they are biased and what about the litigant who challenges the judge on his bias and losses, would he have that judge continue as the litigant's judge in the trial?

Additionally, the voters of Texas tend to be extremely uninformed about the candidates they select as judges. The practice of relying solely on name recognition or political party affiliation has led to Texas voters electing judges who have legal, addictive problems or emotional problems, such as those elected who were under criminal indictment, are addicted to alcohol or drugs, who have mental problems, etc. This has led to great embarrassment and concern in Texas. Due to these concerns, as well as others, there have been numerous recent demands to change the selection process of judges in Texas. However, at present, the demands for changes have not been met and Texas judges, except municipal court judges, are still elected in the partisan elections that have caused the above referenced problems.

IV. THE FEDERAL COURT SYSTEM

A. Introduction

Article III of the Constitution of the United States created the Supreme Court and authorized Congress to create whatever lower courts it deemed necessary. The most important courts are the federal district courts, the Courts of Appeal, and the Supreme Court. Other specialized courts and administrative agencies are also part of the federal court system.

The Supreme Court and the courts created by Congress under Article III are called Constitutional Courts. The judges or justices in some cases of all of these courts are appointed by the President, confirmed by the Senate, and serve for life.

B. Federal District Courts

Federal district courts are the general trial courts for the federal court system. Each state has at least one federal district court. The districts for the federal district courts do not cross state boundaries. However, some states are divided into more than one district. Texas has four districts which are referred to as the Northern, Southern, Eastern, and Western Districts of Texas. Also, several judges may be appointed for each district, thus, creating more than one court per district.

A trial in federal district court is usually conducted by one judge. Because district courts are trial courts, juries may be used if the parties are entitled to a jury trial and if one of the parties requests one. If a jury is utilized, it usually consists of 12 jurors with two or more alternates. If both parties agree not to have a jury, then the judge performs the functions of a jury.

C. Federal Courts of Appeal

The **Federal Courts of Appeal** are divided into circuits and there are 13 circuits. Eleven of the courts are numbered 1 through 11 and cover different geographic regions of the nation,

1 is for the District of Columbia and the last Court of Appeals has nationwide but limited specialized jurisdiction over international trade, government contracts, intellectual property, etc.

The number of judges appointed to a circuit court differs from circuit to circuit depending in part on the case load. Courts of Appeals cases are normally heard by a panel of three judges, opinions issued by the panel of judges are referred to as a **panel decision**. Occasionally, controversial cases representing important public policy issues will be heard by all members of the court of appeals in a given circuit. The opinions issued in such cases are referred to as *en banc*.

An appeal from a federal district court goes to the Court of Appeals of the circuit in which the district court is geographically located. For instance, if you try your case in the Southern District of Texas and you want to appeal the case, you would appeal the case to the Fifth Circuit Court of Appeals because that is the court of appeals for Texas as well as Mississippi and Louisiana. Courts of Appeals precedent is binding upon all of the district courts within its circuit but is not necessarily binding upon those outside of the circuit. The Fifth Circuit has jurisdiction over all the federal district courts in the three states.

Therefore, it is not uncommon for federal law to vary from circuit to circuit. For instance, the law in the Ninth Circuit in which California is located is traditionally more liberal than the Fifth Circuit. Sometimes, but not always, the federal Supreme Court will accept an appeal from a case when the applicable law is different in several circuits in order to end the disparity since Supreme Court precedent is binding upon *all* federal courts. However, the Supreme Court is NOT required to settle these differences and does not have to take the appeals from the Circuit Courts when those courts are in disagreement.

Take for instance, **Hopwood v. Texas 236 F.3d 256 (5th Cir. 2000)** on rehearing from 84 F.3d 720 (1996) which was on rehearing from the original case 78 F.3d 932 (1996), where Cheryl Hopwood was one of four white students to be denied admission to the University of Texas Law School. The four white students claimed they were more qualified than some minority students who were chosen for admission over the four white students due to their minority status. Hopwood and the others filed a reverse discrimination case against the University of Texas. On August 14, 1994, the U.S. District Court, for the Western District of Texas in Austin, issued its ruling declaring that the admissions policy of the University of Texas Law School was in violation of the Fourteenth Amendment and that the four plaintiffs could re-apply without additional costs and awarded the plaintiff damages in the amount of $1. Any further relief was denied.

The plaintiffs were not satisfied and appealed to the Fifth Circuit Court of Appeals in New Orleans. In March of 1996, the Fifth Circuit issued a panel decision ruling that the University of Texas Law School violated the Fourteenth Amendment by giving substantial racial preferences to certain minority students specifically Blacks and Mexican-American, to the detriment of whites and other non-preferred minorities. The Fifth Circuit Court of Appeals further ordered the University of Texas Law School not to use race as a factor in law school admissions.

A motion filed by University of Texas Law School for a rehearing of the entire Fifth Circuit Court was denied and the school next filed a *writ of certiorari* to the U.S. Supreme

Court. On July 1, 1996, the U.S. Supreme Court refused to grant the petition for *writ of certiorari*. During the summer of 2001, the Supreme Court again refused to grant the *writ of certiorari*.

The refusal to grant the Writ simply means that the Fifth Circuit opinion stands. However, that opinion only applies to the Fifth Circuit and the rest of the nation is free to follow the previous court decisions. By refusing the writ, the U.S. Supreme Court did not overrule previous Supreme Court cases nor did it overrule other circuits' opinions, but it did allow the Fifth Circuit opinion in *Hopwood* to stand which has the effect of making the *Hopwood* case the law in the Fifth Circuit. However, the other circuits do not have to follow the Fifth Circuit opinion. In other words, in a state outside of the Fifth Circuit, colleges can still use race or ethnicity for admissions, financial aid, scholarships, fellowships, recruitment, and retention while in Texas, Louisiana, and Mississippi, the states within the Fifth Circuit, this is not the law. Simply put, the law in the Fifth Circuit is different from the law of the rest of the country in this one area.

However, in the summer of 2003, the Supreme Court issued two affirmative action cases from the University of Michigan. One case, **Grutter v. Bollinger**, 539 U.S. 306 (2003) dealt with the admission policy by the University of Michigan School of Law and the other, **Gratz v. Bollinger**, 539 U.S. 244 (2003), dealt with the University of Michigan's undergraduate admissions policy.

The Court made is very clear that the standards set forth by Justice Powell in **Regents of University of California v. Bakke**, 438 U.S. 265 (1978) were still in effect and would remain so, calling Justice Powell's opinion in *Bakke* the touchstone for constitutional analysis of race-conscious admissions policies. The Court made it clear that student body diversity is a compelling state interest that can justify using race in university admissions. This is important, because when racial discrimination is involved, the Court will apply strict judicial scrutiny, which means that the state has to prove a compelling state interest in support of the use of race. The state also had to show that use of race did not unduly burden disfavored groups.

The Court did recognize that universities cannot establish quotas for members of certain racial groups, *Bakke* at 315-316. Of course, this had been the downfall of the University of Texas School of Law case in Hopwood. It is fair to say that quotas could not be used.

The Court agreed that any University plan would have to be narrowly tailored to achieve diversity. In *Grutter*, the Court felt that the University of Michigan School of Law admissions standards met the *Bakke* test in that it was narrowly tailored in the proper manner. The plan did so because it did not "insulate each category of applicants with certain qualifications from competition with all other applicants" *Bakke* at 315. The court felt that the Law School gave individualized consideration to each applicant of that applicant's possible diversity contributions and thereby, did not harm non-minority students.

However, the Court did have a major problem with the undergraduate admission policy in *Gratz*. One problem was that the University required 100 points for admission. Underrepresented racial or ethnic minorities were automatically given 20 points. The Court found this to be unfair to the non-minorities in that it was not proper under individualized consideration. This was not properly used to narrowly tailor the admissions policy to achieve racial educational diversity. Therefore, the Court found that because of this practice, which the Law School did not use, but used by the undergraduate program, violated the Equal Protection Clause and therefore, the practice of the undergraduate program office was struck down. The Court made it clear that the University could use a race-conscious affirmative action program but in an individualized form.

Therefore, done properly, affirmative action is still legal. However, it is interesting to note that the justices in *Grutter* stated that race conscious admissions policies (affirmative action) must be limited in time and should be replaced with a race-neutral admissions policy as soon as possible. In fact, the Court predicted that in 25 years affirmative action would not be necessary.

One should note that there is a major affirmative action case pending before the Supreme Court involving the University of Texas (**Fisher v. University of Texas**). However, the Supreme Court has not issued a decision as of the publishing of this book. There is also a Michigan case, **Schuette v. Coalition to Defend Affirmative Action**, which the Supreme Court agreed to accept in March of 2013. It can be argued that these two cases involve different issues in affirmative action. Just how the Supreme Court decides these cases could have a major impact on affirmative action.

D. The U. S. Supreme Court

The **U.S. Supreme Court** is the court of last resort for all cases decided in the federal court system and all cases appealed from the state's highest courts. The Supreme Court consists of eight associate justices and a chief justice. All cases heard by the court are decided *en banc* by a vote of all of the justices. It must be kept in mind that even though the Constitution gives the Supreme Court original jurisdiction in some types of cases, these cases of original jurisdiction at the Supreme Court are extremely rare. Other than the original jurisdiction situations found in the Constitution, Supreme Court jurisdiction is determined by Congress.

Since 1988 and the passage of the **Supreme Court Selections Act**, Congress has given the Supreme Court almost total discretion over which cases will be accepted for review by the Supreme Court. Although thousands of cases try to reach the Supreme Court each year, on average only 100 to 150 cases per year actually reach the U.S. Supreme Court.

A party requests an appeal to the Supreme Court by filing a Petition for *Writ of Certiorari*. This petition is reviewed by the Supreme Court. If the petition is granted, a writ (order) is issued by the Supreme Court to the lower court, ordering the lower court to send the record of the case to the Supreme Court for review, and thereby grants the appeal to the Supreme Court. However, as we have already seen, the vast majority of these petitions are denied. Although the decision to grant certiorari is entirely at the discretion of the court, several generalizations about the process may be made. The writ is issued whenever four justices vote, in secret proceedings, to review the case. This is referred to as the "**Rule of Fours**."

The typical types of cases reviewed by the court may be divided into several categories. For example, the court often grants *certiorari* when a state Supreme Court has decided a substantial federal question that either has not been previously determined by the Supreme

Court or is in conflict with the trend of Supreme Court decisions on related matters. Another situation, in which the court regularly grants *certiorari*, as mentioned previously, is when there exists a conflict between the decisions of different federal circuit Courts of Appeal. The Court wants to avoid situations where different sets of rules are being applied in different regions of the nation.

E. Specialized Federal Courts and Administrative Agencies

The district courts, Courts of Appeals, and the Supreme Court represent the most important components of the federal judicial system. Other tribunals, such as specialized courts and even administrative agencies which create administrative law, also play important roles in the federal system. Specialized courts and administrative agencies have been created so that the judges will have a certain degree of expertise in handling certain types of cases. Perhaps the clearest example of the need for a specialized court is the Tax Court, which hears very technical and complicated cases involving the federal tax system. Other specialized courts include the U.S. Bankruptcy Courts, the Claims Court, and the Court of International Trade. The jurisdiction of the specialized courts is determined by subject matter, rather than by geographic location.

Administrative agencies, which are discussed in detail in a later chapter, include specialized courts that conduct proceedings brought by the agency against alleged violators of agency rules. The cases are heard by **administrative law judges (ALJ)**. The decisions in such cases may be appealed within the agency. The final decision of the agency then may be appealed to the Federal Circuit Court of Appeals.

V. THE SELECTION OF JUDGES

It should be obvious that judges have a great deal of power and influence in a common law system. Hence, no description of state and federal court systems would be complete without a discussion of the manner in which the judges are selected.

A. Federal Appointment

Article III of the Constitution provides that the President shall appoint judges subject to confirmation by the Senate and that such judges shall serve for life or for as long as they desire. Article III judges or justices have often been referred to as Constitutional Courts which include the district court, Court of Appeals and the U.S. Supreme Court. The requirement that federal judges serve for life is obviously intended to allow judges to act impartially without fear of political repercussions from their decisions. However, some federal judges, such as administrative law judges and Tax Court judges, do not have life tenure. The Article III requirement of life tenure is not necessary because the appointments for these courts are under Article I, which gives Congress the power to create these types of courts, rather than Article III, which requires the judges to have life tenure.

B. State Judges

As one might suspect from the discussion of the differences in the organization of state court systems, states also select judges in different ways. At least one state, Rhode Island, follows procedures that are essentially the same as the federal procedures, including life tenure. In other states, judges are elected for a specified term, in a manner very similar to the election of legislators. Still other states use a combination of the two approaches in which higher level judges are appointed and lower level judges, such as the justice of the peace, are elected. Some states like Texas are still seeking a better way of selecting judges.

VI. JURISDICTION

A. Introduction

Jurisdiction is the power of a court to hear and decide certain types of cases. Every court is not entitled to decide every kind of case. In order for a court to exercise its judicial functions, it must have jurisdiction over both (1) the subject matter of the dispute, **subject matter jurisdiction**, and (2) over the parties to the dispute, **territorial jurisdiction**. For a court to have jurisdiction, it must have both types of jurisdiction. Simply put, a court has subject matter jurisdiction if it has been given the power to hear that type of case. This normally comes from statute or constitutional law at the time the court is created.

B. Subject Matter Jurisdiction

1. Federal

The federal courts are courts of limited jurisdiction. They have subject matter jurisdiction over certain specified types of cases. If a dispute cannot be heard in the federal courts, then the parties to the suit must rely on the state courts.

Federal court subject matter jurisdiction may be established in two ways. First, the federal district courts are empowered to hear cases involving **federal questions**. This may involve important cases of constitutional interpretation as well as lawsuits filed pursuant to federal legislation or treaties. A large number of the cases in the business world are determined by federal courts because a large portion of the legal environment of business is shaped by federal regulatory legislation which necessarily involves federal questions.

The second method of establishing federal subject matter jurisdiction is through **diversity of citizenship**. The rationale for this means of access to the federal court system is embedded in the constitutional history of the United States.

As discussed in Chapter 2, prior to the adoption of the Constitution in 1787, the states were joined by the Articles of Confederation. Regional and state jealousies resulted in chaos in interstate affairs. The Constitution was intended to correct the problems associated with this rivalry. This intention is reflected in several constitutional provisions including the privileges and immunities clause, the contract clause and the commerce clause.

The requirement of Article III of the Constitution that allows the federal courts to hear disputes among citizens of different states also reflects the concern that citizens who use the courts of another state would not be treated impartially. That is, diversity of citizenship is designed to provide a neutral forum in the federal court system for the resolution of disputes among citizens of different states so that a citizen of one state will not get "homered" by a court of another state.

In order to establish federal subject matter jurisdiction through diversity of citizenship, the parties to the action must be both (1) citizens of different states, and (2) the amount in controversy must be greater than $75,000. For example, suppose a citizen of Virginia is vacationing in Colorado and has an automobile accident with a resident of Colorado. Assuming the jurisdictional amount is satisfied, the Virginia resident may sue the Colorado resident in federal district court. Moreover, if the Colorado resident attempts to sue the Virginia resident in the Colorado state courts, the Virginia resident has a right to have the case removed to a federal district court. This right is called the **Removal Doctrine**.

Corporations are discussed in detail later, but some background information is necessary at this time in order to understand how corporations satisfy the diversity of citizenship requirements for federal subject matter jurisdiction. Corporations are artificial legal entities, created by state statutes, and recognized by a state government through the granting of a corporate charter. Firms chartered in one state are allowed to operate in other states, subject to a certain procedural requirements. For purposes of establishing federal jurisdiction, corporations are considered citizens of their chartering state as well as citizens of the state that is their primary place of business (typically, where its headquarters is located). In many instances, the corporation is chartered and headquartered in the same state. Many large corporations are chartered in a state different than their primary place of business. For purposes of establishing federal jurisdiction, such corporations are citizens of both states. Thus, when a citizen of Delaware sues a corporation headquartered in New York, but chartered in Delaware, federal diversity of citizenship does not exist because Delaware is on both sides.

2. State

State courts also receive their jurisdiction when they are created. This is normally by the State Constitution or by statutory law if the court is created by statute. This can vary widely from state to state or even within a state, depending on the court and how, why and when the court was created.

Establishing subject matter jurisdiction completes only one-half of the jurisdictional requirements. The court must also have the ability to order the parties, specifically the defendants, to appear in the territory of the court and have the ability to bind those defendants' to the court's decisions. This is called territorial jurisdiction.

C. Territorial Jurisdiction

1. Introduction

Territorial jurisdiction is the ability of a court to have the power to require a litigant to physically come to court. The general rule is that you can always sue a defendant in his home state. However, there are a lot of reasons why you would not want to go to the defendant's home state. Instead, you would like for him to have to come to your state or at least meet him on neutral territory. This can be accomplished in any one of the following ways.

2. *In Personam Jurisdiction*

The most common way to establish territorial jurisdiction is by establishing jurisdiction over the parties to the lawsuit. This is accomplished by obtaining jurisdiction over the defendant. This is called in personam **jurisdiction** or jurisdiction over the person. This includes the power to order the defendant to show up in court and to bind the defendant to the court's decision. *In personam* jurisdiction is accomplished by serving the defendant physically with a **summons** which is also called a **citation**. This is a notice of a lawsuit, consisting of the actual lawsuit and instructions to the defendant of how to answer the lawsuit. This packet of papers is physically handed to the defendant while the defendant is actually within the state in which the court is located.

For instance, if you, a resident of Texas, want to sue a resident of Nevada who lives in Las Vegas but you do not want to try the case in Las Vegas, you could physically serve that resident of Nevada when he or she is voluntarily located in Texas. This is accomplished by the process server physically giving that summons or citation to the resident of Nevada in Texas. If this is accomplished, the state of Texas has jurisdiction over the resident of Nevada due to *in personam* jurisdiction.

3. *In Rem Jurisdiction*

Another way to obtain territorial jurisdiction over a non-resident defendant is by using *in rem* **jurisdiction**. This is where the state is given territorial jurisdiction over property located within that state and that property must also be the subject matter of that lawsuit. The property can either be tangible, property that can be touched such as land or automobile, or intangible, property that cannot be touched such as stocks and bonds.

Due to the subject matter property being located in the state, the state has territorial jurisdiction and the out-of-state defendant can be served with citation and be required to go to the jurisdiction of the state where the property is located because the property is the subject matter of the lawsuit and is located in that state.

4. *Quasi In Rem Jurisdiction*

A third type of territorial jurisdiction also involves ownership of property. However, in this situation, while jurisdiction arises due to the ownership of property in another state, that property is not the subject matter of the lawsuit. Historically, states abused the use of *quasi in rem* jurisdiction using it as a tool to obtain jurisdiction in situations, where to say the least, the state stretched its power. Due to this abuse, *quasi in rem* jurisdiction is subject to close scrutiny by the Federal Courts. This Federal involvement makes it extremely difficult, if not impossible, to establish *quasi in rem* jurisdiction. Therefore, it is very rare to see this type of territorial jurisdiction successfully used.

VII. VENUE

A court must also have **venue**, which involves the right of a defendant to be tried in a proper court within a specific geographic area. In other words, of all of the courts that have jurisdiction, the court that will hear the case is determined by venue. Venue is not a factor until jurisdiction has been established. Venue rules are set forth by statute.

Venue is usually based on the residence of the defendant and the general rule is that within a state, you can always sue the defendant where the defendant lives, but you might prefer the defendant to come to you rather than you going to the defendant. For instance, in Texas if you had to sue a defendant from El Paso and you are from Houston, you would rather force the defendant from El Paso to come to court in Houston rather than you traveling to El Paso for the trial. You might be able to accomplish this due to venue rules.

In a civil case, there are numerous statutory exceptions to the general venue rule of suing the defendant in his home location. For instance, if you are suing the defendant on a contract dispute for $250,000, then the district court of Texas has jurisdiction but the geographic location of the district court that will handle the case would normally be where the defendant lived. However, if the contract specified that the proper venue for any dispute under this contract was Harris County, Texas, then you would be able to file the case in district court in Harris County, Texas, and require the defendant to come to Houston rather than you going to El Paso.

Texas has many examples of how you can change venue because Texas has very liberal venue rules. Historically, some Texas counties earned a reputation for awarding very large civil judgments where other counties earning the reputation of being very stingy in awarding civil judgments. If in your case, the proper venue was in a county that was known to give low dollar amount awards, you might want to try using the venue rules and see if you could change venue to one of the counties with a reputation of being more generous. For instance, if you had a car/train accident in a county known to award low dollar amount judgments, you might want to search the venue rules and see if you could locate venue in another more generous county. In a car/train accident the Texas venue rules allow you to bring the lawsuit in the appropriate court in the county where the accident occurred or where the train company has its headquarters or in any county in Texas where the train company does business, meaning any county where the train operates. Therefore, if the train operates in a more generous county, you could file the lawsuit in that county.

However, due to the very liberal venue rules in Texas being abused by Texas attorneys just to find the appropriate jurisdiction, **Forum shopping**, steps have been taken in Texas and in other jurisdictions to limit the resulting venue shopping. These limitations are accomplished by requiring that the case should be tried in the proper court that is most convenient to all of the litigants. This is called the *forum non conveniens* **rule**. In other words, if you sued the defendant train company in a far away, but generous county's district court, expecting to receive millions of dollars, the defendant could file a motion with the court under the *forum non conveniens* rule claiming that the faraway county is not the most convenient court for all of the litigants and if the judge agreed, the case would be transferred to the district court in the county that was the most convenient court for all of the litigants.

VIII. BASIC TRIAL PROCEDURES

A. Introduction

The American courts operate through an **adversarial system** of justice. Courts will not decide lawsuits unless there is a true case or controversy between the parties to the action. Accordingly, a court will not decide hypothetical questions. The adversarial system is based on the belief that truth and justice can prevail only if both parties to the action have the incentive to win. The possibility of being harmed by the outcome of a case encourages the parties to strive to uncover and present all information supportive of their particular position. By having all of the information presented in the best manner, courts are in a good position to evaluate the relative merits of the parties' cases.

The case or controversy requirement is generally easy to meet in the business setting. The few exceptions would involve actions to have a law or regulation declared invalid where there is no showing that the business has been harmed in any way by the law or regulation. These exceptions involve the issue of "**standing**" and are very important in administrative agency law.

Obviously, the business can choose to go to court and occasionally, may be forced to go to court to enforce contracts, collect debts, etc. However, if you are a business, you can almost count on being sued over some business transaction, or due to the actions of your employees, or due to the products you make. Assuming an appropriate case or controversy exists, the proper court, in terms of jurisdiction and venue, is selected and the business firm's lawyers begin the steps necessary for the case to go to trial. Of course, sometimes it is in the best interest of the business to settle the lawsuit. Litigation is expensive, time consuming and public. There are phases to a trial and it all begins with the initial pleadings.

B. Pleadings

The natural starting point for a discussion of trial procedures is the **pleadings**, the papers that are filed with the court. The person instigating a civil lawsuit is called the **plaintiff**. The person being sued is called the **defendant**. There are several types of pleadings such as, the petition also called, the complaint that is filed by the plaintiff, the answer that is filed by the defendant, and motions which can be filed by any party to the lawsuit.

1. Complaint

A civil lawsuit begins when a plaintiff files a **complaint** which is also called a **petition**, or other names, but here we will refer to it as a complaint when it is filed with the clerk of the applicable court. The complaint must allege facts necessary to establish jurisdiction, and provide a short statement of the ultimate facts to be proved, the applicable law, and the remedy requested. In essence, the complaint tells the court "Here's what happened, this is why I should win, and this is the damage I have sustained."

The filing of the complaint is the beginning. The defendant must be notified that the action has been filed. This is accomplished by having a summons and a copy of the complaint served on the defendant. The summons is the order requiring the defendant to respond to the complaint. Generally, a sheriff/constable, U.S. Marshall, or professional process server will serve the summons and complaint on the defendant. This process is expensive and the courts have been experimenting with ways of reducing the cost. In particular, the federal courts allow service of the complaint by mail accompanied with an acknowledgment of service. The defendant can return the acknowledgment, and personal service will be unnecessary. If the defendant fails to return the acknowledgment, the defendant must be personally served, but the court may require the defendant to pay the costs of service unless it can be shown that the failure to return the acknowledgment was reasonable. Remember, the court must have subject matter jurisdiction to hear the case and territorial jurisdiction to be able to force the defendant to come to court.

2. Answer

The defendant must respond to the complaint by filing an **answer** within a statutory time period. The federal rule is usually 20 days. In Texas, the rule is somewhat different, in that the answer time is usually 20 days and you go to the court next Monday at 10:00 a.m. In other words, Texas takes the answer to the minute where the federal rules simply take it to a day. If the defendant in this required time period does nothing and thereby the answer time period passes, then the plaintiff is entitled to go to court and take a **default judgment** against the defendant. In plain terms, the plaintiff goes to court and gets everything they ask for.

Therefore, it is very important for the defendant to timely file his or her pleadings, which is usually an answer. The answer normally denies the allegations contained in the complaint. Ordinarily a defendant files a general denial which denies everything in the plaintiff's petition forcing the plaintiff to prove the whole case by a preponderance of the evidence. The defendant can also file specific denials armed at details of the plaintiff's complaint. The defendant has several options in answering the complaint in addition to the general or specific denials discussed above.

The defendant must include all **affirmative defenses** to the allegations in the complaint. Affirmative defenses are legal defenses that must be proven by the defendant. The defendant can also challenge the court's jurisdiction or venue. In addition, the defendant may want to set forth any cause of action that may exist against the plaintiff. This type of action would include anything that would allow the defendant to be a plaintiff in an independent suit against the plaintiff. This is called a **counterclaim**. Counterclaims allow parties with disputes to settle all of their claims at once. Since a counterclaim is like an original complaint, the original plaintiff is generally required to file a reply which is like an answer to a complaint. Finally, the defendant can file a **cross-action** and bring a third party into the lawsuit.

Obviously, like the petition, the answer can be amended as new information becomes available. That normally comes during the Discovery Phase.

3. Pretrial Motions

The third major type of pleading that is filed consists of **pretrial** motions which serve various purposes. Some motions are filed in response to the complaint, such as a motion to dismiss for failure to state a claim. Such a motion is designed to bring to issue, without admitting the facts alleged in the complaint, the proposition that even if the plaintiff is able to prove all facts alleged in the complaint, the plaintiff cannot win as a matter of law. Basically, such a motion is saying that the actions that the plaintiff is complaining about are not the type which gives rise to legal remedy. For example, suppose Smith sues Jones for damages because the shade tree in Jones' yard prevents Smith from sunbathing in his yard. Unless state law protects the right to sunbathe, it is likely that Smith has failed to state a claim for which the court can grant the relief sought.

Another common motion is a motion for summary judgment. In essence, this motion tells the court that both parties agree on the facts (or at least the operative facts) and the court can apply the law to those facts and enter a decision. The distinction between a motion for summary judgment and a motion to dismiss for failure to state a claim is that in the former, one party is saying to the court "We agree on the facts, make a decision" and in the latter, one party is saying "It doesn't matter if we agree, I win even if the facts alleged are true."

C. Discovery

1. Purpose of Discovery

Discovery is the pretrial process by which each party obtains information from the opposing party or some third party with relevant information. Stated purposes of discovery include preventing surprise at trial and allowing the parties to adequately prepare their case, both of which will increase the likelihood of settlement of the case without trial. Unfortunately, these noble purposes are not the ones most often accomplished. Often, discovery is used to harass the opposing party into submission. The use of discovery requires the opponent to expend resources in complying with the requests. Many lawyers refer to using discovery as "burying your opponent with paper." While this may force your opponent into settlement, it is not the type of settlement that discovery was designed to promote.

The four basic types of discovery are (1) depositions, (2) interrogatories, (3) requests for admissions, and (4) production of documents. Their names reflect the functions these procedures serve and each will be discussed briefly in turn.

2. Depositions

Depositions involve the oral testimony of witnesses before the attorneys for the parties and a court reporter. The function of the court reporter is to record the proceedings and subsequently to transcribe that testimony. Depositions have several functions. A principal function, as with all types of discovery, is to uncover all information "reasonably calculated to lead to discovery of admissible evidence." Questions can be asked and answered during depositions that would not be allowed at trial under the rules of evidence. For example, the rules of evidence generally do not allow testimony that is not firsthand knowledge to be introduced at trial. This type of evidence is called **hearsay**. However, questions involving hearsay responses are allowed in depositions because they may lead to the discovery of witnesses who have firsthand knowledge and would be allowed to testify at trial.

Another function of depositions is to preserve testimony. Litigation in complex suits can take many years. Witnesses can grow old and die between the filing of the action and actual trial. In such a case, a deposition can be used as evidence because the witness is no longer available.

Perhaps the most widely used function of depositions is to force one's opponent to take a position and stick to it. In developing the facts, the stories often change depending on which story is in your opponent's best interest at the time. A deposition of your opponent, or your opponent's expert witnesses, forces a stand to be taken. If the story changes at trial, the deposition can be introduced to show the change in testimony to **impeach** the credibility of your opponents or their witnesses. For instance, if the expert witness testifies one way in the deposition but changes his statement in trial you can ask that witness which time did they tell the truth and which time did they lie. Either way you have discredited their credibility.

3. Interrogatories

Interrogatories are simply written questions which are served on the opposing party. Unlike depositions, interrogatories cannot be used on third party witnesses. Interrogatories can only be sent to another party as is true of requests for admission and production of documents as well. The responses to interrogatories are in writing and sworn under oath. Interrogatories are very popular in the legal world because they are easier to use and less costly than depositions. However, they are often limited to the number of questions that can be asked, the number of answers sought or the number of times interrogatories can be sent to any one opposing party.

4. Requests for Admissions

A **request for admissions** is essentially a written set of facts that one party requests the other to admit as being true. The central purpose for such requests is to reduce the amount of evidence to be introduced at trial. Any facts that are admitted will not have to be proven at trial thus allowing the trial to concentrate on the facts which are in dispute.

5. Production of Documents

A **request for production** of documents is simply what the name implies, a request that the other side produce certain requested documents that are relevant to the dispute at hand. The normal procedure is to photocopy the documents and turn the copies over in response to the request. Sometimes, the documents may be so voluminous that the party seeking the documents is allowed access to view the documents at the other's place of business rather than being provided copies.

An obvious function of this discovery tool is to allow the parties to learn useful facts from the other party's records. Another function is to prevent the opponent from fabricating documents. If a document that should have been turned over in response to a proper request for production was not turned over, the court may in its discretion refuse to allow the document to be introduced into evidence.

Attorneys can also abuse the discovery process through requests for production by asking for information that they are not otherwise entitled to see such as trade secrets, e.g., formulas, customer lists, etc. If this happens, like in all discovery types, the other party can file a motion for an in-camera inspection which means the judge would look at the requested evidence and decide if it is relevant. If the judge finds no relevance, then the party does not have to show the opposing party the information.

D. Pretrial Phase

When these pretrial motions are filed, a judge must hear the pretrial motions. These hearings create the third phase of the trial, called the Pretrial Hearing Phase. At this phase, the judge obviously will decide the issues that were in the pretrial motions. Whereas discovery is used by the parties to ready the case for trial, the **pretrial conference** is the court's technique for pushing the case toward settlement or forcing the parties to prepare for trial. Many cases are filed and then stagnate. Neither side seems anxious to initiate discovery or otherwise prepare for trial. The court is able to arrange pretrial conferences at which the parties report to the court the progress that has been made in settlement negotiations and trial preparations. Being chastised by the court for failing to make progress will often force the parties to settle. There can be several pretrial hearings or conferences. The court can also send the parties to mediation to try to settle the case at this stage.

E. The Trial Phase

The actual trial is the culmination of the arduous dispute resolution process known as litigation. In a nutshell, a **trial** is the attempt by the plaintiff to prove the disputed facts which are necessary for the court to award the relief sought, and the attempt by the defendant to thwart the plaintiff.

After the plaintiff presents the evidence in the case-in-chief, the defendant may move for a **directed verdict**. In essence, the defendant is saying that the plaintiff has failed to sustain the burden of proof in proving the necessary facts. Thus, it would be a waste of the court's time for the defendant to present any evidence. The success rate for this type of motion is extremely low. The court generally requires the defendant to present evidence to make a complete record in the event of appeal, but allows the defendant to renew the motion after the presentation of the evidence. The plaintiff may also request a directed verdict after the defendant has finished presenting evidence on the ground that reasonable minds could not disagree on the outcome. In jury trials, the granting of directed verdicts is rare because judges would typically prefer the jury to make the finding of fact. If a directed verdict would have been warranted, the jury will almost invariably rule for the proper party.

In a civil case, the right to a jury is not absolute and normally you only get a jury in a civil case in a limited type of cases. In federal court, under the Seventh Amendment this is when there is an amount in controversy of over $20 that involves a common law claim. However, as we saw in Chapter 2, this provision of the Constitution has not been made applicable to the states. Federal courts also can receive a jury when federal statutory law gives it to the litigants. In state cases, whether you have a right to a jury depends on the state's constitution or statutory law but it is usually utilized less often that in federal court. Texas gives the litigants a very broad right to a jury, basically along the Seventh Amendment requirements as per the Texas Constitution.

If the litigants have a jury right, they still may decide not to utilize a jury. If the litigant does not use it, then it is as in the situation where there is no jury right; the judge of the court decides both the law, which the judge always does, and takes over the jury's duty and determines the facts as well. Whether you chose to utilize a jury right in a civil case often depends on who is the judge and what type of expertise does that judge possess. It can also depend on the jury and how they will handle the type of issues that are before them such as how emotional will the jury become. Juries are made up of either 6 or 12 jurors depending on the court and the verdict in a civil case does not usually have to be unanimous.

Jury selection is done through a process called *voir dire*, which literally means to speak the truth and that is what the litigants are seeking—fair and impartial jurors. Seating a jury is always important and attorneys in high-profile cases often use jury consultants. The attorneys conduct the *voir dire* questioning in Texas but in federal courts, the judge often does the actual questioning of the prospective jurors with questions submitted to the judge by the attorneys. Attorneys can use two different types of challenges to eliminate prospective jurors. The first is called a **challenge for cause** which is used when the attorney feels that the prospective juror cannot be fair and impartial in this type of case due to some bias or prejudice on the part of the prospective juror. However, the judge makes the decision on the challenge for cause. The other type of challenge is called a **peremptory challenge** and it can be used without the judge's permission. However, peremptory challenges are limited. The limit depends on the type of case. In Texas, this can range from 3 up to 15 peremptory challenges. The prospective jurors sit in order and the jury becomes the first 6 or 12 that were not excused by the judge for whatever reason.

Once the jury is seated and sworn in, the trial will begin with opening statements by the parties. During the opening statements, the attorney wants to tell the jury crucial facts and what to expect during the trial. Opening statements like the *voir dire* process are usually unlimited but sometimes the judge will place a time limit on either part of the trial. The party with the burden of proof which is normally the plaintiff goes first. After opening statements, the plaintiff begins their part of the case by calling their first witness. After all, the trial will be a succession of witnesses that tell part of a story and then the attorney hopes, the jury will put the parts together like you see a picture in a puzzle. In other words, the jury will see the picture as envisioned by the attorney. When it is a witness that an attorney calls as a witness, they must be the subject of **direct examination**. During direct examination, the attorney must ask direct questions such as: (1) What is your name? (2) Where do you live? Normally this means who, what, where, when, how, or why. Of course, an attorney should never use the why question unless he or she actually knows what the answer will be. When the direct questioning of a witness is over, the witness is passed to the other side who then gets to cross-examine the witness and also gets to ask leading questions such as "Isn't it true that …" It is at this stage that the defendant's attorney tries to discredit the witness, so the jury we disregard their testimony and if you will, not use that piece of the puzzle which will hopefully cloud the entire picture and the jury will not see the case like the plaintiff's attorney had envisioned.

After each of the plaintiff's witness have been cross-examined by the defendant's attorney, then the plaintiff gets to re-direct his or her witness to try to rehabilitate them by fixing whatever damage the defendant's attorney has done. After this, the defendant's attorney can again re-cross the witness to try to inflict more damage. Ultimately, there just are not any more questions to ask and the plaintiff's witness is excused. Then you go to the next plaintiff's witness and the whole procedure starts again. Once all of the plaintiff's witness have been through the process, the plaintiff will rest.

Normally, the defendant will ask for a Directed Verdict which is normally denied (see above). However, if the judge grants the motion, the trial is over. More often, the motion is denied and the case continues with the defendant's attorney putting his or her first witness on the stand. The defendant's witnesses go through direct examination and then cross-examination by the plaintiff's attorney. Once the defendant's attorney is finished, the defendant rests.

Then the plaintiff can present **rebuttal** witnesses but they can only rebut or try to fix the damage done by the defendant when he or she put on his case. The direct examination and cross-examination procedure applies at this stage as well. Once the plaintiff has finished with rebuttal, the defendant gets to do basically the same thing with his case only this is called **rejoinder**.

After all of the evidence has been introduced, both sides have rested and closed, then both sides have the opportunity to do closing arguments to the jury. The plaintiff has the power to go first and last with the defendant going in the middle. Like opening statements, closing statements are not considered evidence and can be limited in time. Before the case is submitted to the jury either side can present a Motion for Directed Verdict which is normally denied by the judge to allow the jury to make the decision.

Once the closing arguments are over, the jury gets the case and deliberates on the case using a **court's charge** explaining the law to the jury which the jury must follow. If the jury cannot decide the case, the jury is called **hung**. A judge will try to make the jury reach a verdict by issuing them a dynamite charge which is basically a message from the judge reminding the jury or the expense and time to retry the case and telling them to continue to deliberate. Sometimes this works and sometimes it does not. If it does not and the jury just cannot reach a verdict, then the judge has no choice but to dismiss the jury and at a later date, begin the case all over. Of course, this occurs rarely in civil cases since the verdict does not have to be unanimous. If the jury reaches a verdict, then the jury foreman reads the verdict in open court.

After the trial and before the appeal, either party can file post-trial motions. Occasionally, the jury will render a verdict against a party who had requested (and deserved) a directed verdict. Such a party can request the court to enter a **judgment notwithstanding the ver-**

dict or a **judgment n.o.v.** (*non obstante verdicto*). The judge can reverse the jury's verdict if he or she determines the moving party is entitled to judgment as a matter of law, or may grant a new trial if the verdict was against the great weight of the evidence. However, this rarely occurs, especially in Texas because judges are elected and the jury would basically take the judge's action as telling the jury they did not do their job!

Also, after the verdict, the losing party can also file a **Motion for New Trial**. However, the losing party will have to have a very good legal reason for the judge to set aside the verdict and start the trial all over again. Some examples of successful reasons for Motions for New Trial being granted are newly discovered evidence or finding a missing witness that either could not have been discovered or that the losing party used due diligence to find before the trial, jury tampering or proof that a material witness lied.

F. Appeal

If one of the parties is dissatisfied with the outcome of the case in the trial court, the unsatisfied party, whether they were the plaintiff or defendant, in the lower court normally has the right to have the decision reviewed by an appellate court. An appellate court is a higher court that has the authority to overturn the lower court decision. The purpose of **appeal** is to help guarantee that the parties to a lawsuit received a fair trial. In order to be successful on appeal, the appellant (the party appealing the case) must submit a list of alleged errors of law that were committed by the trial court in a legal document called a **brief** which includes legal precedent to prove your points of alleged errors. Such errors could include rulings on objections by attorneys, rulings on the admissibility of evidence, or failure by the trial court to follow procedural rules. The appellee (usually the winner in the trial court) tries to show the appellate court that the alleged errors were not errors or that even if they did occur; they had no effect on the outcome of the trial. The appellee does this in a response brief.

Then the parties are given a limited time, usually 30 minutes, to orally argue their points of error, or lack thereof, before the appellate court. The appeal is usually before a three-judge panel which then renders **a panel decision** but in some cases can be before the entire court which then renders an *en banc* decision.

Errors of law are always able to be appealed to at least one appellate court. At the appellate level, the court rules only on errors of law. The facts of the case as found by the trial court are not generally challenged and no new evidence is presented, or testimony heard. Errors in the findings of fact are not generally able to be appealed because the demeanor or presence of the witnesses determines in many instances which of the witnesses is most believable. Since appellate judges do not see evidence or hear testimony first hand (relying instead on a trial transcript), it would be difficult for them to determine the reliability of a witness. The exceptions to this general rule occur only if the appellate court determines that the announced findings of fact are not supported by the evidence submitted at trial. A finding of insufficiency of the evidence rarely occurs.

The appellate court's decision may be to **affirm** the lower court, **reverse** the lower court, or **remand** the case to the lower court for further proceedings on a matter that the court felt should have been addressed but was not. An appellate court decision affirming a lower court decision means that the appellate court agrees with the application of the law and the outcome of the case below. A reversal of a lower court decision generally means that the lower court applied an inappropriate rule of law and consequently reached an incorrect result. The court can also **modify** the decision which means that the majority wants to modify the lower court's rulings such as to lower the amount of the monetary award. Finally, a remand implies that an inappropriate law was applied below and that the lower court did not find the facts necessary to reach a decision using the appropriate legal rule. Occasionally, an appellate court's decision will encompass some combination of the three. The appellate court typically supports its decision with a written opinion which is usually printed and therefore available as precedent. If it is not published, there is no precedent value.

PART TWO—ALTERNATIVE DISPUTE RESOLUTION

I. INTRODUCTION TO ALTERNATE DISPUTE RESOLUTION

There are numerous problems associated with litigation. Litigation is expensive. Consider the situation of a private individual, who is by no means wealthy, filing suit against Ford Motor Company. Can Ford outspend you? Can they afford better experts? Then consider two mega-corporations in litigation against each other and you can see that the cost could be enormous. Another factor on cost is human work time and the resulting lost productivity. Even in the Ford example above, someone from Ford has to be at all of the trial procedures, and that takes them away from working on other business matters.

Furthermore, businesses sometimes have to worry about bias and prejudice from a jury or even a judge. A jury can be prejudiced against a business when they have the attitude that the business is worth millions so what will it hurt to give this defendant a few million dollars. Consider the recent case where McDonald's was sued by an elderly lady who had put hot coffee between her legs and sued them for her physical damages, the burns she suffered.

Another major factor to consider when facing litigation is the public nature of a trial. If a business is being sued for products liability and the business has sold thousands of those products, does the business want the public to hear all of the details every day over and over during the trial? Whether the allegations are true or not, can the adverse publicity lead to more, future litigation?

II. TYPES OF ALTERNATE DISPUTE RESOLUTION

A. Negotiation

A very simple and common alternative to litigation is **negotiation** which can be very informal. It can be done through the attorneys or sometimes it is more successful without the attorneys. For instance, it is possible that the plaintiff and defendant can meet each other for breakfast, review the case, discuss settlement options and work out a settlement after several cups of coffee. Granted it usually is not this easy but keep in mind that approximately 90 percent or more of civil cases settle prior to going to trial.

B. Mediation

Of course, a lot of times, animosity between the parties or the attorneys or simple pride, prevent negotiation from being successful. Often, it is necessary to have a third party come in and assist in the settlement. This is the type of situation where **mediation** can be helpful.

In mediation, the litigants turn to a third party to serve as the mediator, hoping that he or she can facilitate a settlement. Keep in mind that the mediator does NOT make a decision and is not to take sides. The job of the mediator is to point out weaknesses and problems as well as strengths to your claims, and using that push you toward a settlement. However, the litigants make the decision, not the mediator.

Mediation can be a difficult process and in some cases an impossible task for the mediator. After all, mediation is not for every case and it is by no means successful in every case. However, it gives you a chance to settle the case in a very informal setting, in much less time, without as much expense, and in private. Another advantage to mediation is that if it is successful, it usually does not result in the bitterness of a trial. After all, it is more likely that you will be able to preserve a business relationship if you have not gone into court and "fought it out" in front of a judge or jury.

However, mediation is not without its problems. First, who do you get as a mediator. That is usually done by the mutual agreement of the parties. Also, the mediator does not work for free, and normally the fee is split between the parties to avoid bias or prejudice associated with who is paying the mediator. Finally, since the mediator only facilitates in working out a settlement, the mediator cannot force a settlement, and therefore, the mediation can be unsuccessful and sometimes a waste of time.

C. Arbitration

If the parties are looking for someone to make a decision for them without going to court then **arbitration** is available. While arbitration is similar to mediation, in that a third party is involved, there are several differences between the two. Probably the most important difference is that in arbitration, the arbitrator makes a legally binding decision.

In many areas of the law, and in a growing number of other areas, arbitration is favored over litigation. This is true in the federal government and in more and more state governments. In 1925, Congress passed the Federal Arbitration Act[1] that requires courts to defer to all voluntary arbitration agreements in federal law cases. Once the parties agree to go to arbitration, the parties must go to and be bound by arbitration. In Shearson/American Express v. McMahon,[2] the U.S. Supreme Court ruled that, if the parties to a lawsuit had

---

1 United State Code Vol. 9, Sections 1-15 (9 U.S.C. Sections 1-15).
2 **Shearson/American Express, Inc. v. McMahon 482 U.S 220, 107 S.Ct. 2332, 96 L.Ed. 2d. 185 (1987).**

agreed, prior to the dispute arising, to go to arbitration rather than litigation, then the Federal Arbitration Act required them to go to arbitration. In other words, if you agree to go to arbitration, you give up your right to go to court and you are bound by the arbitration award. The Federal Arbitration Act however does not set forth the procedures for arbitration and the arbitrator is largely free to set forth his or her own procedures

Unlike court, you normally do not have the right to appeal the arbitrator's decision and as the *Shearson* case showed us, you do not have the option to go to litigation, which you would have if either negotiation or mediation were not successful. However, there is a very limited right to appeal an arbitrator's award. If an arbitrator's award mandates that a party violate the law then it can be set aside. An arbitrator's award can also be set aside if it is found that the arbitrator was biased or made the award based on corruption, fraud, or other "undue means," or the arbitrator exceeded his or her authority. However, under normal circumstances it is very difficult to set aside the award of an arbitrator. Therefore, the arbitrator's award is usually final.

CHAPTER SUMMARY

When it comes to litigation, there are several ways in which the business can and will become involved in the legal process. These include the civil courts, criminal courts and the administrative law courts. After all, if you are a successful business, you are going to get sued by people who want part of your success.

To sue someone or some business, the plaintiff must decide where to sue because there are 50 different state court systems as well as the District of Columbia and of course, the federal courts. Wherever the suit is filed, the plaintiff must establish jurisdiction and venue. To establish jurisdiction, the suit must be filed in the court that has subject jurisdiction over that type of case and territorial jurisdiction. To establish territorial jurisdiction, the court must have the power to make the defendant come to that particular court. This is established by *in personam*, *in rem* and maybe by *quasi in rem* jurisdiction. Once jurisdiction is established, the plaintiff must be sure that the suit is filed in the proper court that has jurisdiction and be the court with proper venue.

However, litigation is expensive and public. Therefore, a business might choose to pursue alternate dispute resolution. There are three major types of alternate dispute resolution (ADR). The most common is negotiation where the lawyers or the parties or a combination, meet and try to negotiate a settlement that is acceptable to all of the parties. Mediation is where the parties hire a third party to facilitate a decision. While the mediator does not make the decision, he or she, pushes the parties in the direction of settlement. If no agreement is reached, then just like if negotiations fail, the case goes to litigation. The third type of ADR is arbitration, which is where the parties hire a third person who makes a decision as to who wins and who loses. Normally, the decision of the arbitrator is binding. Furthermore, if you agreed to go to arbitration, the courts are clear, you have agreed to waive litigation and your only hope for a favorable outcome is to go to arbitration. If you waive litigation, you have given up your day in court.

Obviously, you have to operate your business as something and that choice will involve which type of business entity is best for you. There have been three major types of business entities for many years: the sole-proprietorship, the partnership, and the corporation. There are advantages and disadvantages of each. To try to create an even better business entity, limited liability companies where created in the 1990s. It appears that the only disadvantage to this new form is that it is so new that it is unknown if it is the answer to all the problems. Only time will tell.

4

CONTRACT AND AGENCY LAW

PART ONE—CONTRACT LAW

I. ECONOMIC ASPECTS OF CONTRACT LAW

A. The Nature of Contractual Exchange

Contract law is a system of rules for enforcing promises. It shows the extent to which our society allows people to make promises or commitments that are legally binding, and the consequences of failure by one party to perform as promised. It also shows what excuses our society will accept for breaking such promises. Contracts are developed by contract law.

Contracts are a fundamental part of our economic system and the legal environment of business. At the societal level, contracts and contract law serve a valuable social function in providing a legal environment conducive to voluntary exchanges, which tend to move resources to more valuable uses. From the individual's perspective, contracts serve several important economic functions including the facilitation of mutually beneficial exchange and the allocation of risk among the contracting parties. In this regard, contracts can be analyzed as two distinct agreements: one deals with performance, the other with risk allocation. Contract law provides a mechanism for the enforcement of both economic functions of contracts.

B. Mutually Beneficial Exchange

A fundamental purpose of the law of contracts is to facilitate beneficial exchanges. The most basic of exchanges requires little assistance from contract law to occur. The scenario can easily be altered to illustrate the potential for breakdown in the exchange process. One island native agrees to provide a second native with coconuts today in exchange for fish to be delivered tomorrow when the catch is in. Tomorrow's delivery is not forthcoming. What is the first native's remedy? Suppose instead that both sides of the transaction perform their promised duties in a timely fashion, but the purported first-rate coconuts have set in the sun too long and are spoiled. These are but two of the multitude of possible breakdowns in the process of exchange. Contract law serves to reduce the costs of these transactions by imposing external rules which create rights and duties in the parties to the exchange and provides remedies in the event the duties are breached.

It is important to emphasize that voluntary mutually beneficial exchanges will take place in the absence of contract law. Surely natives adept at gathering coconuts would find it advantageous to trade with natives skilled in fishing. Continued dealing with the same parties reduces negotiation costs and also increases the likelihood that the contract will be performed in good faith. One may seek to reduce transaction costs by limiting his trading partners to only those who have a reputation for honesty and fair dealing. In a sense, therefore, the market controls dishonest and unfair behavior by reducing the demand for the goods and services provided by dishonest and unfair traders. That is, market adjustments act as an enforcement mechanism.

In some instances, market adjustments may not be sufficient to enforce contracts. Herein lies the role for government enforcement mechanisms, including laws, in contractual exchange. On the Pacific island, societal customs may allow a party who has been cheated to exact retribution, thus effectively raising the costs of not completing the bargained-for exchange. Drug deals are not legally enforceable, but Colombian drug kingpins have clearly demonstrated their ability to "enforce" contracts and "execute" agreements. Contract law is simply another way of assuring the performance of the bargain reached by the parties. Thus, contracts are enforced by a number of market and non-market enforcement mechanisms.

C. The Allocation of Risk

The examples listed above suggest that contract law is most important in situations where the negotiations are not immediately followed by simultaneous performances on both sides of the transaction. Such contracts are referred to as executory contracts. An **executory contract** has not been fully performed by either party. Executory contracts "fix" future obligations, thus eliminating uncertainty and allocating the risk of future, unforeseen contingencies. An example of an executory contract is the agreement to repay a loan at some future date with a fixed rate of interest. During the interim between negotiation and performance (or execution) of the transaction, numerous events (contingencies) may occur that determine whether or not the parties have, in fact, engaged in a mutually beneficial contract. That is, an evaluation of the contract terms prior to performance may differ substantially from evaluations of the bargain at the time performance is due. Presumably, all contracts are mutually beneficial when negotiated. However, the mutually beneficial aspects of the exchange at the time the contract is made may change as a result of the occurrence of some unforeseen contingency prior to the execution of the contract (or even after the execution of the contract). The contract appears later to be one sided to the extent that the performance of the contract is not mutually beneficial. Nevertheless, contract law almost always requires the performance of such contracts, and this suggests that the law implicitly recognizes the importance of risk allocation through contract.

A straightforward example of how a mutually beneficial contract can appear to become one-sided as the result of the occurrence of a contingency during the period when the contract is executory is the farmer's contract to supply a certain quantity of grain to a grain dealer (wholesaler) at a certain price at a certain time. If the market price of grain falls substantially during the period, then the dealer will be stuck with the higher price even though grain is available at a lower price on the market. The situation is symmetric in that the farmer will be unhappy if the price rises considerably during the period. Such price changes are often the result of totally unforeseen events. For example, the Chernobyl nuclear reactor accident had an immediate impact on worldwide wheat markets in the form of higher prices because it was suspected that a large portion of the world's wheat supply had been contaminated. Obviously, the risk of such a contingency could not have been foreseen and thus was not reflected in the contract terms. Nevertheless, the courts routinely enforce such contracts because the purpose of such a contract is to allocate risk, no matter what the source of the risk.

Economic efficiency is enhanced not only by simple mutually beneficial exchanges (e.g., where there is simultaneous creation and performance and thus no risk), but also by contracts designed to allocate (or exchange) risk. As a starting point for the analysis of the efficiency of contractual risk allocation, it must be recognized that some parties in the economy are better (more productive) at minimizing the costs associated with risk than are other parties. Such parties are referred to as the "least-cost avoider of risk." Good examples of such people are grain dealers, like the one in the preceding example. In essence, grain dealers minimize risk by engaging in numerous buy and sell contracts so that an unexpected up or down fluctuation in the market price of grain will not be disastrous to them. Moreover, the grain dealers specialize in understanding the particular market and are able to hedge their risks on the basis of their specialized information. On the other hand, the individual farmer does not have the expertise to engage in the pooling of risks on his or her own, but may lock into a guaranteed price long before the market price at harvest is determined. The farmer clearly benefits from not exposing his or her entire income stream to a last-minute fluctuation in the market price of grain.

Understanding and appreciation of the risk allocation role of contracts will lead to richer analyses of various doctrines of contract law. In general, legal rules that enforce contracts when the risk is borne by the least-cost avoider of risk are efficient legal rules.

II. BASIC CONTRACT INFORMATION

A. Definition of Contract

Contracts consist of promises. A promise is a manifestation of intent to do or not do something. Of course, not all promises are legally enforceable because not all promises are contracts. Therefore, a contract consists of promises but a promise is not necessarily a contract. Thus, contracts require more elements than just the sky's promises. A contract is a legal agreement of the party or parties to do something that they are not already obligated to do or not do something that they have a legal right to do.

B. Standard

Contracts, and for that matter torts in Chapter 5, will be judged by the objective standard which means that the apparent intention of the parties to a contract is determined by what a reasonable person would have done in a similar situation. It is not the subjective standard of what did the individual person intend. Objective factors include the conduct of the party or parties, the words spoken or written by the party or parties and the circumstance surrounding the transactions. Texas courts have made this clear by stating that the objective standard is "what the parties said and did and not on their subjective state of mind."

III. TYPES OF CONTRACTS

Contracts may be classified in several ways, such as by the method of formation, content, and legal effect. Some standard classifications are express and implied contracts; conditional and unconditional contracts; bilateral and unilateral contracts; valid, void, voidable, and unenforceable contracts; and quasi contracts. Obviously, these classifications are not mutually exclusive. For example, a valid contract can be an express, bilateral contract.

A. Express vs. Implied Contracts

An **express contract** is one in which the terms of the agreement are fully and explicitly stated in words, written or oral. A signed lease for an apartment is an express written contract. If the girl next door offers to wash your car for $5 and you accept, an express oral contract has been made. Texas case law says that an express contract "arises when its terms are stated by the parties" (**Harrison v. Williams Dental Group, P.C. 140 S.W.3d 912 Tex. App. Dallas, 2004**).

A contract that is implied from the conduct of the parties is called an **implied-in-fact contract**, or simply an **implied contract**. An implied contract differs from an express contract in that the conduct of the parties, rather than their words, creates and defines the terms of the contract. When one takes a seat in a barber chair, it is implied that he or she is bargaining for a haircut for a reasonable price (unless the price is posted) even if no verbal obligations are exchanged. Again, Texas case law refers to an implied contract as one that "can arise from the acts and conduct of the parties" (Harrison).

Whether the contract is expressed or implied, if all of the elements to a contract are present, it is enforceable. Remember, the enforcement and interpretation of a contract is based on an objective standard of what would a reasonable person do in a similar situation. For instance, if you have an individual who is not from this country who stumbles into a cafeteria and thinks "America is truly a wonderful place, they give away food." Therefore, he loads up his tray. Of course, there is a person at the end of the food line who gives him a ticket. Would not a reasonable person in a similar situation have realized that the cafeteria expected for him to pay for the food since he was given a ticket and there is a cashier sitting in front of the only exit? In short, our immigrant cannot plead ignorance and be released from the contract because a reasonable person should have known that payment was expected. He is held to the objective standard of what a reasonable person would do and not the subjective standard of what he thought. We will see the objective standard, reasonable person test, throughout contract law and as discussed above in tort law in Chapter 5.

B. Quasi Contracts

There is another type of implied contract but in reality this is really not a contract. A **quasi contract** is "sort of" or almost a contract but there is something missing and it is therefore, not a true contract. However, one party is getting the benefit of the contract while the other is taken advantage of, so the aggrieved party can literally, throw him or herself on the mercy of the court and beg the court, to supply the missing element to the contract by law. In other words, the judge implies that the missing elements to the contract are by law present and then enforces the contract. As you might expect, this is done rarely and with little success.

Texas distinguishes between implied-in-fact and implied-in-law as follows:

A promise that is "implied in fact" is merely a tacit promise, one that is inferred in whole or in part from the expressions other than words by the promisor, and a promise "implied in law" in one that neither the words nor the conduct of the party involved are promissory in form or justify an inference of a promise, … A "quasi-contractual obligation is one made/created by law (Judge) for reasons of justice without any expression of assent and sometimes even against a a clear expression of dissent." (**Ferrous Products Co. v. Gulf States Trading Co. Tex. Civ. App. Houston, 1959**)

For example, if you enter into an agreement to do yard work at a professor's house, you have agreed to do certain types of yard work and the professor has agreed to pay you $10 per hour for the work. At the end of two weeks, you have done 75 hours of very difficult yard work and you have the blisters and ant bites to prove it! Furthermore, your work is very obvious since you have turned the professor's yard into a show place. The professor in fact is very pleased with your work. However, when you present your bill for payment, the professor asks to see your permit that allows you to do yard work in that city as required by the city code. You have no clue about any required permit. The professor explains that the city ordinance is very specific in that you must have the permit BEFORE doing the yard work. He tells you that if you do not have the permit, then you worked in violation of the law and that he cannot be a party to your illegal act by paying you. You are shocked, and think that the professor has taken advantage of you. The more you think about it the more you convince yourself that since you did the work, and since the professor got his yard work done, he should pay for that yard work. Therefore, you go to small claims court, fill out the forms and begin the lawsuit against your professor. However, the first rule of thumb of contracts law is, the courts do not bail you out of a dumb deal. Therefore, the court could easily throw you out of court and tell you that you have learned a very valuable lesson, the hard way. However, the court could also take mercy on you and since the professor did get the work done, feel that he should pay for the work. Therefore, the court could imply that you had the permit and declare by law that the court would pretend you had the permit and enforce the contract, thereby requiring the professor to pay you. Obviously, one does not count on the success of quasi contracts or as it is also called **implied-in-law contracts** but it is important to know that quasi contract is available, just in case!

C. Conditional vs. Unconditional Contracts

A duty of performance is absolute when the only occurrence necessary to require performance is the passage of time. Such a contract is an **unconditional contract**. The duty of performance is conditional if something other than the passage of time must occur before performance is required. For example, a travel agent may book a block of rooms at a ski resort for the weekend of February 15 so long as the snow pack is at least 80 inches. The agent has created a **conditional contract** under which there will be no duty to perform if the condition has not been met. Conditional contracts can be **condition subsequent**, **condition precedent**, or **condition concurrent**. The occurrence or non-occurrence of a condition will be discussed further in connection with the discharge of contractual obligations, later in the chapter.

D. Bilateral and Unilateral Contracts

All contracts involve at least two parties. The **offeror** is the party making the offer, and the **offeree** is the party to whom the offer is made. The offeror always promises to do or not to do something and thus is also a **promisor**. The party to whom a promise is made is the **promisee**. The classification of the contract as bilateral or unilateral depends on what the offeree must do to accept the offer. If a return promise is required, then the contract is a **bilateral contract** since both parties are promisors. For example, when the house painter offers to paint the owner's house for $1,000 and the owner promises to pay $1,000, there is an exchange of promises and the agreement gives rise to a bilateral contract. If the offer is phrased in such a way that the offeree can accept only by performance, then the contract is a **unilateral contract**. For example, if a home owner states that he will pay the painter $1,000 if the painter paints his house, then the painter can accept only by painting the promisor's house and the performance gives rise to a unilateral contract. Thus, a bilateral contract is a "promise for a promise" and a unilateral contract is a "promise for an act."

The difference between the two contracts becomes important in the enforcement of the contract. For instance, should the painter decide not to paint the house. If the contract was bilateral then the painter would be breaching the contract by breaking his promise. If the contract was unilateral the painter would *not* be breaching the contract since the contract did not exist until the painter painted the house.

E. Executory and Executed Contracts

We have already discussed executory contracts above (see the section on Allocation of Risks above). Keep in mind that an **executory contract** is a contract that has not been fully performed by both parties. On the other hand, an **executed contract** has been fully performed by all parties. According to Texas case law, "executed contracts exist where nothing remains to be done by either party while an executory contract is one which is still unperformed by both parties or one with respect to which something still remains to be done on both sides" (**B.L. Nelson & Associates, Inc. v. City of Argyle 535 S.W.2d 906 Tex. Civ. App. Ft. Worth, 1976**). You will also occasionally see the term **partially executed**. While this truly refers to an executory contract, it is also referring to the situation where one party has completed their part of the contract and the other has not. For example, if it is said that the contract is executed as to Michaela, it means that Michaela has performed her part of the contract and it is inferred that the other party to the contract has not or they would have said the contract was executed.

F. Valid, Void, Voidable, and Unenforceable Contracts

A **valid** contract is one with all of the elements necessary to entitle at least one of the parties to enforce it in court. A **void** contract is no contract at all; it is not recognized by law. A void contract produces no legal obligations by any of the parties. A contract to perform an illegal act such as hiring a hit man to kill someone is a void contract and cannot legally be enforced by either party to the contract even if both parties want to perform the contract. **Voidable** contracts are valid contracts, but one of the parties to the contract has the right to avoid his or her contractual obligations without incurring legal liability. In other words, at least one of the parties is able to void the contract. However, this is an option, it is not a requirement. A contract with a minor is often a voidable contract because the law gives minors the right to disaffirm most contracts. An **unenforceable** contract is a valid contract that cannot be enforced because of certain legal defenses. In this type of contract, there is a perfectly valid contract in place but then the law changes and the contract becomes unenforceable. For example, you come to college as an 18-year-old freshman; you enter into a contract with the local beer distributor for a keg of beer to be delivered to your apartment each and every Friday. This is a valid agreement for over a year. Then when you are 20, the law changes and that changed law requires you to be 21 to drink alcohol. This change makes the contract unenforceable and neither party can force the other party to perform under the contract. However, if money is still owed on the beer that was delivered prior to the law changing, that is still a valid contract obligation because at the time the debt arose the contract was enforceable.

IV. ENFORCEMENT OF CONTRACTS

A. Introduction

Breach of contract is the most common form of lawsuit filed in the American court system. Although most cases are dramatically different, the disputes are alike in a number of respects

The rules of contract law have evolved in order to make it easier for the court to resolve these issues. Although contract law is defined entirely by state common law and often supplemented with state statutory law, the law in all states is similar enough to make certain generalizations. The first step in this enforcement of contracts is to determine if there is a contract to enforce. To create a contract there are required elements to the contract.

B. Elements of a Contract

1. Introduction to the Elements to a Contract

At its simplest level, a contract is merely a special type of agreement between parties, one the law will enforce in some manner in the event of a breach. Not all agreements are elevated to the status of a contract, and thus, not all agreements are enforceable. In order for a party to enforce a contract, that party, usually the plaintiff must prove the existence of the contract.

Through decisions in individual cases, the common law of contracts has evolved a list of elements necessary to elevate a mere promise to the status of enforceable contract. These specified elements can vary by how they are listed. Normally, those elements include (1) mutual agreement between the parties, (2) consideration, (3) contractual capacity of the parties, (4) legal subject matter, (5) genuine and real assent to the contract, and (6) some contracts must be in writing. The person attempting to enforce the contract must prove the existence of the first two of these elements. The defendant, against whom the contract is sought to be enforced, can prove the non-existence of the contract by proving the lack of one of the last four elements. In other words, if the defendant can prove a lack of contractual capacity or that the subject matter is illegal, then no enforceable contract exists. (Of course, the defendant can also rebut evidence presented by the plaintiff with respect to mutual agreement and consideration and the plaintiff can rebut evidence presented by the defendant in the last four elements.)

Texas lists the elements as (1) offer; (2) acceptance; (3) meeting of the minds; (4) each party must consent to the terms; and (5) if it must be in writing, it must be executed and delivered with the intent that it be mutual and binding as determined by the objective standard (**Baroid Equipment, Inc. v. Odeco Drilling, Inc., 184 SW3d 1 Tex. App. Houston [1st District], 2005**). Of course, Texas still requires consideration (**Roman v. Roman 193 SW3d 40 Tex. App. Houston [1st District], 2006**) as well as legality and capacity (**TMC Worldwide, L.P. v. Gray 178 SW3d 29 Tex. App. Houston [1st District], 2005**) to have a legally enforceable contract. Texas is one of those states that looks as genuine and real assent as a defense to the contract.

2. Agreement

Fundamental to the formation of a contract is the mutual assent, or **agreement** of the parties. Because a contract involves a voluntary transaction, the courts will not enforce the transaction unless it is clear that the parties agreed and assented to the subject matter of the contract. That is, there must be a "meeting of the minds," a mutual understanding that is not mistaken. An agreement can be broken into two parts for purposes of analysis: the offer and the acceptance.

a. Offer

An **offer** is a promise that expresses the willingness of a party, known as the offeror, to enter into an enforceable agreement regarding a particular subject. The offer is made to the **offeree**.

1) Elements to an Offer

To have a valid offer there must be **intent, definite terms, and conditions** and the offer must be **communicated** to the offeree. These are the three elements to an offer.

a) Intent

The first principle of an offer is that the offeror must intend to create a legal obligation, or at least must appear to so intend, for the promise to constitute an offer. Intent is defined in Texas case law as "an expression of the terms (of the contract) with sufficient certainty so that there is no doubt regarding the parties' intentions" (**MG Bldg. Materials, Ltd. v. Moses Lopez Custom Homes, Inc. 179 S.W.3d 51 Tex. App. San Antonio, 2005**). A promise to do anything your friend asks if he or she will help you study for an exam does not satisfy the requirement that the offeror intend that the promise be a legal obligation. An offer made in jest or excitement is not binding because a reasonable person would not regard such an offer as indicating a willingness to enter into a binding agreement. The courts will scrutinize the events surrounding the offer to determine whether a reasonable person would have viewed the offer as intent to be bound.

Another situation often encountered in contract law involves whether the intent of an offer has been made is in the area of **preliminary negotiations**. The first statement from one of the two negotiating parties is not necessarily an offer. The question "Would you consider selling your business for one million dollars?" is not an offer to buy, but is an inquiry. It is the beginning of negotiations. It is common in commercial transactions for the parties to discuss a potential transaction in vague, general terms to determine whether an offer should be made. The test for an individual's intent in preliminary negotiations versus making an offer is the objective standard of whether a reasonable person would have believed that a binding offer had been made.

Another example of preliminary negotiation is an advertisement that appears in a newspaper. Advertisements, catalogs and circulars are construed as mere invitations to buyers to come in and negotiate with the seller. Of course, if the seller makes a habit of refusing to sell on advertised terms, customers will soon stop responding to the seller's advertisements. (Keep in mind that in some situations, state statutory laws requires advertisers to honor their advertisements.)

b) Definite Terms and Conditions

The second requirement for an offer is that its terms and conditions be definite. An offer whose terms are vague and indefinite cannot serve as the basis of a contract at common law. The terms of the offer must be sufficiently detailed so that the other party is reasonably certain of the terms of the contract. If two business people agree to form a joint venture "for as long as is reasonably profitable," the duration is too ambiguous for each party to clearly agree upon. Either party would be able to withdraw according to his or her understanding of "profitable" which was not defined in the agreement.

Not all offers with missing terms are too indefinite to be enforced. Courts will often supply the additional terms if they are minor or immaterial, so that the offer and the resulting contract will not be indefinite. For example, if Patsy agrees to buy Chris' car for $500, the contract will not fail simply because they have neglected to specify the method of payment. Because of the nature of the transaction, most courts would imply a term of cash on delivery. However, there is one term that the courts will not supply and that is the quantity term. Therefore, to be definite the offer must either state the quantity or the quantity must be readily ascertainable from the terms of the offer. For example, "I will pay you $400 for the items based on a price of $100 each," is obviously a contract offer where the quantity is four items.

c) Communication of the Offer

The third basic requirement of the offer is that it must be communicated. Until the offer is known to the offeree, he or she does not know that there is an offer that can be accepted. A frequently used example is the reward for return of an animal. The reward is typically an offer to pay money in return for the act of returning the animal. However, if the claimant returns the animal before learning of the reward, no acceptance takes place since the offer was never communicated to the claimant and the reward does not have to be paid.

2) Ways to Terminate an Offer
a) Termination by the Person
i) Revocation

An offer gives the offeree the power to bind the offeror to a contract. This power does not last forever and is terminated either through actions of the parties or through operation of law. The most obvious way for an offer to terminate is through **revocation** of the offer by the offeror. A revocation is where the offeror takes back or revokes his offer prior to the acceptance by the offeree and, like the offer, it must be communicated to the offeree and is not effective until it is communicated. However, no magic words are required. If the offeror tells the offeree "you'll be sorry you didn't accept my offer, because I sold the car to Joe yesterday," then this statement will serve to revoke the offer since the offeror told the offeree the car was in fact sold. Simply selling the car to Joe prior to the acceptance is revocation. The act of selling the car to Joe is notice that the offer to everyone else is revoked.

ii) Rejection

Rejection is when the offeree by words or actions does not accept the offer. If the offeree rejects the offer but then changes his mind and tries to accept then it is too late. A rejection terminates the offer. There is no resurrection of the offer. If the offeree then tries to accept the rejected offer, it is simply a new offer by the party that was the offeree but becomes the offeree. Under Texas law, once the offer is rejected, it is thereby terminated and consequently it cannot be accepted (**Harris v. Mickel 14 F.3d 428 (Ct of App. [5th Circuit] Texas, 1994)**).

iii) Lapse of Time

Often, an offer by its terms will allow the offeree a stated period of time to accept the contract. If the stated time expires without acceptance then the offer has terminated by **lapse of time**. If no time is stated in the offer, then the time period is a reasonable time under the circumstances. For example, Jim decides to sell his stereo in order to purchase a new one. He offers to sell it to Sally for $250 and agrees to give her two weeks to come up with the money. Three days later, Arnold offers to buy the stereo and has cash in hand. Jim accepts and tells Sally that the deal is off. Jim is allowed to revoke his offer to Sally before Sally accepts even though he expressly promised to keep it open. The offer was only good for two weeks and it is not a guarantee that it will not be revoked during those two weeks. However, there is an important exception to this rule under the common law of contracts. If Sally gave Jim something, say $5, in return for the right to have two weeks to decide, this is consideration and assuming all of the other required elements are present, Jim would not have the power to terminate the contract prior to the expiration of the two week period. In such a case, the exchange of $5 for two weeks' time is itself a binding contract, called an **option contract** and Jim must keep the offer open for the two-week time period as per the option contract with Sally. The option contract makes Jim's offer irrevocable for the two-week time period.

iv) Counteroffer

As noted, a rejection, which is where the offeree simply says "no," serves to terminate the offer. An important form of a rejection is the **counteroffer**. For example, Smith offers to rent Jones a three-bedroom house for $650 per month with a year's lease. If Jones counteroffers to rent at $700 per month with a six months lease, Jones has rejected the original offer, which she can no longer accept unless Smith is willing to renew the offer. Instead, Smith is now the offeree and he has the power to bind, if accepted by Jones, to a contract based on the terms of the counteroffer.

b) Termination by Law

Certain offers terminate through the operation of law. If the subject matter of the offer becomes illegal, the offer terminates. For example, Ben, the owner of the local liquor store, offers to supply a college fraternity with beer at wholesale prices for their parties after football games. The state subsequently passes a law making it illegal to sell alcoholic beverages at discounted prices. The offer terminates because of the changes in the law. The fraternity no longer has the power to bind Ben to a contract by accepting the offer. This is called an **intervening illegality**. The law also terminates other offers such as when the subject matter of the offer is destroyed or if the offeree or offeror goes insane or dies. As we will see later, parties to a contract must have capacity and dead people do not have capacity. Likewise, insane people lack a degree of capacity depending on the type of insane person.

b. Acceptance

After an offer has been made, an acceptance reflects the offeree's agreement to the terms of the contract. No particular form of words or method of expression is required by law but can be specified in the offer. In Texas, silence is normally not acceptance (**Thurmond v. Wieser 699 S.W.2d 680 Tex. App. Waco, 1985**). However, an acceptance must be **unconditional**, **unequivocal**, and **legally communicated**.

If the offeree adds terms through a purported acceptance, this operates as a counteroffer, which terminates the original offer as discussed above. Thus, the terms that are accepted must be the exact terms or the "**mirror image**" of the terms of the offer, nothing more or less. Further, the acceptance must be unequivocal and definite. If an offeree states that an offer "appears to be a very good bargain," there is no acceptance based on those words. However, if she states that it "appears to be a very good bargain and I accept," these words would constitute an acceptance. Texas courts say that the "offer and acceptance (must be) in strict compliance with offer's terms (and are) essential to creation of a binding contract (**Ishin Speed Sport, Inc. v. Rutherford 933 S.W. 2d 343 Tex. App. Ft. Worth, 1996**). Furthermore, the "acceptance must be identical with the offer in order to make a binding Contract" (**Gilbert v. Petliette 838 S.W.2d 890 Tex. App. Houston [1st Dist], 1992**).

Finally, the acceptance must be legally communicated through an acceptable mode or medium of communication. Whether the method chosen is acceptable depends on the facts and circumstances of each case. If the offer specifies acceptance by mail, then the offeree must accept by mail. However, if no means of acceptance are specified, then the offeree can use any reasonable method of acceptance. Normally, in this situation, the method used for communication of the offer to the offeree or any faster means of communication, is deemed to be reasonable.

Also note the time tables, if there is an offer it must be communicated to the offeree and is only valid when it is received by the offeree. Likewise, the revocation is only effective when the offeree receives it. In acceptance, the offeree is again the key person. However, the acceptance is valid when *dispatched* by the offeree if the acceptance is timely and properly dispatched. If it is improperly dispatched, such as being mailed with an incorrect address or sent in violation of the terms of the offer, then the acceptance is not valid until it is received by the offeror. This is called the **mailbox rule**. While it obviously is not a perfect rule, it does give us the rules to determine when the acceptance takes place.

In a unilateral offer, the only way for the offeree to accept is by performance of the offer. An interesting point is when does the acceptance occur? For years, common law has required complete performance before the acceptance occurred. This means that at *any* time prior to complete performance the offeror can change his or her mind and legally stop the offeree's performance and owe the offeree no legal obligation. However, there is a trend to allow acceptance by the offeree after either a substantial amount of the work has been completed or still require complete performance but force the offeror to pay the offeree for the work the offeree has performed prior to the offeror stopping the offeree from performing.

3. Consideration

a. Definition

A basic contract principle is that a promise, to be enforceable, must be supported by **consideration**. Consideration is something of value that is given up in return for the promise of the other party to the contract. Often, consideration for a promise is in the form of a return promise. Suppose that Billy, a neighborhood boy, offers to mow your lawn for $25. You agree. Billy has promised to mow your lawn and you have promised to pay Billy $25. Each of the promises is the consideration for the other.

The requirement of consideration is to assist the court in determining whether the parties intended to be bound by their promises, that is, whether they intended to enter into a contractual exchange. Ordinarily, a promise to make a gift to another is a gratuitous promise and is not enforceable because the promisor did not receive consideration in return for his or her promise. For instance, after a weekend at home, as you drive away, Mom yells "be good at school" and you in return promise her "I will." Since there is no stated consideration, you have only made a promise to Mom and when you get back to school and you are not "good," Mom has no legal action against you. However, if Mom, knowing contract law, says "Be good at school or I will not pay for school, nor provide you with that car and the gasoline for the car, and I will take all of my credit cards back from you," then, when you return to school and you are not "good," Mom has legal recourse due to your breach of contract.

Another way of looking at consideration is that one side must have a **legal detriment**, they are required to do something by the contract that they were not already previously obligated by law to do or they are agreeing to give up a legal right that they have. Meanwhile, the other party to the contract is receiving a **legal benefit** that they were not entitled to receive, but for the contract. Since there must be a mutual exchange of consideration, both parties will have legal detriment and both will receive legal benefit. Therefore, consideration is a present exchange bargained for in return for a promise. It consists of either a benefit to the promisor or detriment to the promise (**TMC Worldwide, L.P. v. Gray 178 S.W. 3d 29 Tex. App. Houston [1st Dist], 2005**).

As with most of common law, the doctrine of consideration is logically consistent with economic efficiency. The movement of resources to higher valued uses is not accomplished through enforcement of gratuitous promises. Thus, the benefits of enforcing such promises appear to be small. On the other hand, the costs of enforcing gratuitous promises appear large. If such promises were generally enforced, individuals would have to be very cautious about making any statement that could be construed as promissory. They would go to great lengths to disclaim any promissory intent when a statement is ambiguous. Lovers would have to refrain from promising the stars and the moon during moments of passion. In general, it would be inconsistent with economic efficiency to enforce promises that lack consideration.

b. Adequacy of Consideration

As a general rule, the courts do not interfere with the bargain of the parties. They do not inquire into the adequacy of consideration. If one of the parties bargained poorly, that party would generally be stuck with the bargain in the absence of fraud or other misconduct by the other party.

Furthermore, courts will not examine whether the consideration given by one party actually benefits the other party. All that is necessary is that each party agrees to do something that he or she is not already legally required to do or refrain from doing something he or she has a legal right to do. It is for the court to decide whether either party benefits from the actions of the other party or not. Simply put, *the courts do not bail you out of a dumb deal.*

c. Illusory Promises

An **illusory promise** is an expression cloaked in promissory terms that does not actually involve a commitment by the promisor. Texas courts define illusory promises as "when it creates no obligation whatsoever on part of purported promisor" (**Spacek v. Maritime Ass'n 134 F.3d 283 C.A. [5th Circuit] Texas, 1998**). This is a Fifth Circuit case out of New Orleans interpreting Texas law. For example, if a contract to supply raw materials at a specified price for a specified time contains a proviso that the price is subject to change without notice at the discretion of the supplier, then the supplier has not made a commitment to do anything. The doctrine of consideration requires that the promises of both parties to a bilateral contract be supported by consideration. However, if one of those promises is illusory, nor does not have to be done, then the entire contract fails. Either party to the contract may use the illusory promise as a basis for refusing to perform. On the other hand, for example, if the supplier promises to supply the materials subject to cancellation upon two weeks' notice, then the promise is not illusory and the contract will not fail for lack of consideration. In general, courts tend to find a binding promise whenever there is any type of constraint on the options available to the promisor, including a requirement that the discretion be exercised in good faith or for reasonable cause.

d. Promissory Estoppel (Detrimental Reliance)

Many courts will enforce certain promises that are not supported by consideration by applying the doctrine of **promissory estoppel**, which is also called **detrimental reliance**. If a person makes a promise under circumstances such that it is easy to foresee that a reasonable promisee would be induced to rely on the promise and if the promisee changes his position in reliance on the promise, and if the promisee will suffer a substantial loss if the promise is not kept, then promissory estoppel may be used to enforce the promise. Promissory estoppel differs from consideration in that the detrimental reliance is not a bargained for price of the contract. It is simply a result of the promise. In the evolution of contract law, the courts have viewed these types of promises to be enforceable as a matter of social policy. For example, Owens promises his alma mater $1 million to build a new alumni center knowing that the college will likely begin construction based upon his promise. The college begins construction in reliance on the promise, but Owens backs out and refuses to pay. As a matter of policy, this type of promise will be enforced.

4. Contractual Capacity

Contractual capacity refers to the ability of a contracting party to understand that a contract is being made and to understand its general nature. The presence of contractual capacity is normally assumed by the court, but a defendant that is desirous of avoiding contract obligations can attempt to prove that he or she lacked capacity to enter a contract at the time the contract was made. Texas states that "presumption exist in law that one possesses sufficient mental capacity to enter in to contracts" (**Buddy L, Inc. v. General Trailer Co., Inc., 672 S.W.2d 54 Tex. App. Dallas, 1984**). Therefore, the person claiming the lack of capacity has the burden of proving that they do not have capacity. All persons do not have the same legal capacity to make a contract. Limited capacity can render the contract void or voidable. This exists in several situations but it usually exists when one or both of the parties are either intoxicated, insane, or minors. These parties might have the legal capacity to enter into a valid contract but also have the ability to avoid liability under the contract under certain circumstances.

a. Minors

Under common law, any person under the age of 21 was a minor. This has been changed over the years in almost all situations to 18 (the obvious exception being the purchase of alcohol). Although minors can enter contracts in the same manner as adults, they have the right to disaffirm or void their contracts. This is the right of the minor, not the adult. If an adult enters into a contract with a minor and the minor wants to continue the contract and thereby ratifies the contract, the adult has no choice but to continue the contract. The lack of capacity on the part of the minor does not give the other party to the contract the right to disaffirm the contract.

A principal exception to this rule that a minor can disaffirm contracts is in contracts for necessities. Minors who are truly out on their own are liable for the reasonable value of necessities and therefore, cannot disaffirm contracts for necessities. However, the question of what is a necessity and for that matter what is "truly out on their own" is often a matter for the court to decide. Minors also do not have the right to void contracts under common law for the enlistment into the military and they cannot disaffirm marriage contracts. Also, by statute minors are bound to and cannot disaffirm contracts for insurance, some banking contracts, contracts for public transportation, and contracts for student loans.

In order to avoid a contract, a minor need only manifest an intention not to be bound by the contract. Words or conduct can manifest this intent to disaffirm the contract. If a minor disaffirms an executed contract, there may be a corresponding duty to return the object of the contract to the other party, which is called the duty of **restitution**. This duty is only required if the minor is able to make restitution. For example, Sarah, a minor, buys a stereo from Brenda, an adult. Sarah stops making payments on the stereo. (Her conduct evidences intent to disaffirm.) Assuming that the stereo is not a necessity, Brenda is unable to sue Sarah for the payments, but she can sue to require that Sarah return the stereo. However, if Sarah no longer has the stereo or it has been destroyed, she has no obligation to compensate Brenda.

After reaching the age of majority, an individual can ratify contracts formed as a minor, thus removing the ability to disaffirm. **Ratification** can be expressed through words, or may be implied from the individual's conduct. For example, if Sarah continued to make payments on the stereo after she reached the age of majority, then she would be held to have affirmed the contract and would be bound by its terms.

If a child misrepresents their age, most states still allow the child to disaffirm the contract. However, in a growing number of states, if the child lies about his or her age, they are bound by the resulting contract. However, evening though it is growing, it is still a minority approach to the problem of children misrepresenting their age.

Keep in mind this rule: *Do NOT do business with children.* If the contract is not beneficial to the child, the child will avoid the contract. If it is beneficial to the child, but not to the adult, the adult is bound by the contract and the child will choose not to disaffirm the contract since the child is the one benefiting from the contact. Therefore, the adult cannot win in a contract with a child.

b. Intoxicated People

If an individual is intoxicated when a contract is formed, the contract is potentially voidable. The simple fact that the contract was foolish does not in and of itself support the voiding of the contract, because sober individuals often sign foolish contracts. This may be evidence to support your claim of intoxication if you can prove that you normally would not do such a thing that is called for it the contract. Evidence that the sober party to the contract induced the person to become intoxicated in order to extract the favorable terms is definitely admissible and would go a long way in proving the case to disaffirm that contract due to the intoxication. With respect to the degree of intoxication necessary to make the contract voidable, the test is whether the individual was so intoxicated at the time that he or she did not understand the nature of the agreement. In this situation the drunker you are, the better. The burden of proof is on the party claiming that he is intoxicated. This is a very difficult burden because if you were too drunk to remember the contract terms, how do you remember being too drunk to remember? So, the issue becomes, how are you going to convince a judge or jury that you were so drunk that you did not understand the very nature of the agreement? The bartender has liability if he or she serves an intoxicated person, so he or she is not going to help you and in fact, would probably say that you were not intoxicated. In short, this is an easy defense to claim but it is a much more difficult defense to prove. Part of the crucial evidence is whether the individual attempts to disaffirm the contract when he or she sobers up and whether the individual attempting to disaffirm the contract did something totally out of character for him or her. However, the bottom line is, do not rely on the intoxication defense because you probably cannot prove it to the satisfaction of a jury or judge.

c. Insane People

Contracts formed by insane persons can be void, voidable, or valid. The distinction is based on whether the person is adjudged insane by a court or not and when they are adjudged insane. When a person is adjudged insane, there is a court declaration that he or she lacks contractual capacity. A contract with such a person is void. Insane persons not so adjudged by a court can enter a valid contract if they can understand the subject matter, nature, and consequences of the contract. If they do not understand the contract, it can be voidable. Typically the insane person voids the contract if they have a lucid period or even more likely, the insane person will be declared insane after entering into the contract. Then the administrator of the insane person's estate will go back and attempt to void out all of the contracts the insane person entered into while they were insane but before they were declared insane. However, it is not that easy. The administrator will have to prove that the person was insane when the person entered into the contract. Even if the administrator is successful, the insane person will be liable for restitution or damages to the other party. However, if the temporarily insane person affirms the contract during a lucid moment, then the contract becomes binding and cannot be disaffirmed. Obviously, such circumstances raise difficult questions of fact that must be resolved by the courts.

If you have a rich aunt and you are her favorite niece or nephew, then you would probably take the time to visit her if she lived in the same town or even close to where you are going to school. However, you have gotten busy and several weeks have passed since you have gone to visit. Therefore, you make a promise to your dad to visit his sister, Sharon, this weekend. When you get there you find several expensive cars parked in her driveway. You are about to leave thinking she has company until you notice that all of the cars still have paper license plates. You think this is strange and start to investigate. The BMW is marked sold to Benny, Aunt Sharon's parakeet. The Porsche is made out to Penny, the dog and the Lexus' plate says it belongs to "Tigger" your aunt's cat. Now you are understandably very worried. You go into the house and find that your aunt is totally delusional and thinks that you are with the animal shelter and there to take the pets away. She becomes violent and you have to flee for your life. You call your dad and he takes the next plane to town. Dad seeing the problem for himself has no choice but to have his sister committed after the court declares her to be insane. Dad then can go to all of the car dealers and, if he can prove Aunt Sharon was insane when she purchased the cars, void out the sales. However, Aunt Sharon is still responsible for restitution damages to the dealerships. Then, several months later Aunt Sharon escapes from the home for the insane, finds a new pet,and buys it a red Corvette. When she and the new pet are discovered driving the new Corvette, the aunt goes back to the home and the new Corvette is returned to the dealership where she bought it because the contract with that dealership is void. Furthermore, there is no duty of restitution owned to the dealership for the Corvette because of the void nature of that contract.

5. Legality

For a contract to be valid, its subject matter must be lawful. Unlawful agreements and agreements that violate public policy are not enforceable. A contract that violates a state or federal law is illegal and void. For example, an agreement to smuggle cocaine into the country is not an enforceable agreement. Likewise, an agreement to pay interest on a loan in excess of the statutory maximum (usury) will not be enforced. A court may reform the contract to reduce the interest rate to the statutory maximum, charge a fine or penalty to the party charging the usurious interest rate which can be up to three times the interest charged and even in extreme situations, forgive the principle of the debt.

In addition to being unenforceable because of illegality, some contracts are unenforceable because they violate public policy. In essence, the courts find that such contracts have a negative impact on society and refuse to enforce them. Two particular types of contracts that violate public policy are **unconscionable contracts** that are grossly unfair one-sided contracts where one person is taking advantage of the situation and exculpatory agreements.

An **exculpatory agreement** is one that releases one party from the consequences brought about by his or her wrongful acts or negligence. An example would be an airline that requires passengers to sign a release that relieves the airline of all liability for death or injury related to gross negligence of the airline. Such an agreement will not be enforced, and for good reason. The passenger has little choice but to sign the agreement if he or she wants to board the airline. Although exculpatory agreements are commonplace, they mainly serve to alert the signing parties of inherent dangers and possibly delude them into thinking they have no cause of action in the event of injury. However, in other cases, when a party has a reasonable choice of whether to engage in a dangerous activity, such exculpatory agreements have been upheld. For instance, if you pay to go hang gliding and are required to sign a waiver of liability, it will probably be upheld.

6. Genuine and Real Assent to the Contract

Once proof of agreement has been established, attention turns to the terms of the contract. The reason for requiring a specific offer before a contract can be made is because the terms of the offer are the terms of the contract. Since the offeree accepted the terms of the offer, those terms became the terms of the contract. However, there are a number of issues that arise even though the terms of the offer are clear. One of these is whether the contract was freely and voluntarily entered into. This usually centers on claims of **mistake**, **fraud**, **duress**, and **undue influence**.

a. Mistake

Obviously, if one or both of the parties were mistaken about the facts of the contract, the terms of their agreement are in doubt. However, there are several ways the parties can be mistaken about the contract. First, it is important to realize that **unilateral mistake**, which is mistake by only one party, gives no relief to the contract terms. Of course, if the other party caused the mistaken belief due to fraud then the situation changes and we will discuss that under fraud. Therefore, it must be a mutual mistake for there to be relief. However, there are two basic types of mutual mistake and since there is only relief from one of the two, it is important to know the differences between the two. The two types of mutual mistake are **mutual mistake of value** and **mutual mistake of a material fact**. There is no relief for mutual mistake of value. Therefore, if both parties thought the subject matter of the contract was a stone which they assumed was a diamond worth $30,000 and it turned out not to be a diamond but a rhinestone, then someone just bought a $30,000 rhinestone that is probably worth only a fraction of that price. On the other hand, if there is a mutual mistake of a material fact, there is relief. Either party to the contract can void the contract based on mutual mistake of material fact. So, if Bob agrees to sell Sue a tract of land believed to be 10 acres, but they learn that the tract is only 7 acres, then the terms of the contract have not been agreed upon and the contract is void.

b. Fraud

When an innocent party consents to a contract with fraudulent terms, the innocent party can normally avoid the contract because the terms of the contract were misrepresented. An innocent party has two basic options. First, the contract can be rescinded and the innocent party restored to his or her original position. Alternatively, the innocent party can seek to enforce the contract and sue for damages caused by the fraud.

The elements of **fraud** are (1) a misrepresentation has occurred; (2) there has been an attempt to deceive; (3) the innocent party has justifiably relied on the misrepresentation; and (4) the innocent party has been injured. Fraud only refers to misrepresentations of fact that are consciously intended to mislead another. Predictions or statements of opinion are not generally subject to a claim of fraud on the theory that the person hearing the statement recognizes or should recognize that it is merely the speaker's personal view and not a statement of fact. That is, reliance on an opinion is usually not justified.

The typical example of fraud is the con man that lies to you about a business transaction; you rely on his "facts" and are damaged legally by them. You, the innocent party have the right to rescind the contract or enforce the contract and sue for damages.

c. Duress

Duress is when someone forces another person to enter into a contract against his or her will. As long as the action that gives rise to the duress claim is wrongful or illegal, the innocent party can rescind the contract. If for instance, you borrow money and now cannot pay it back. The "loan company" then threatens to break your leg in seven places if you do not deed over your house to him and you are forced to do so, then you can set aside the transaction based on duress.

However, if the duress is simply economic in nature, there is no relief due to the "duress." For instance, you sell your car at a ridiculously low price to have the money for your child's operation. You made a choice freely and voluntarily to sell the car whether the child has to have the surgery or not. There is no relief due to the allegedly duress.

d. Undue Influence

Where duress involves threats of illegal or wrongful actions of a physical nature, **undue influence** is where someone mentally takes control of another person and substitutes their will for that of the victim. Elderly people are particularly susceptible to this type of action. Often TV ministers are only in the ministry for the money and they convince elderly people to send them thousands of dollars or even leave their entire estate to the TV evangelist who is sometimes no more than a crook. This can be a very real example of undue influence. Likewise, attorneys are often found to have exercised undue influence over clients, as well as parents over children and doctors over patients.

7. Statutes of Frauds

Even though the terms of the offer and acceptance are clear, certain contracts may not be enforceable unless the terms are in writing. Although it normally does not matter whether a contract is oral or written, most states require, by statute, that certain types of contracts be in writing in order to be enforceable. This is true even if all the elements of the contract are present. While this rule may seem harsh, the law is to prevent unscrupulous persons form making invalid claims against others based on an alleged oral contract.

Statutes of Frauds, which require certain contracts to be in writing, date back to early English law when parties to a suit could not testify in their own behalf. Certain morally deficient characters would hire third parties to give false testimony as to the existence of an oral contract with the defendant and plead for the court to enforce the contract. In order to deter this action, Parliament in 1677 passed the Statute of Frauds, which required certain important contracts to be in writing in order to be enforceable.

Of course, contracting parties can testify today, but the requirement of writing encourages parties to reduce important contracts to written form to insure agreement on the terms of the contract. The terms of the following types of contracts must be in writing and signed by the party against whom the contract is being enforced.

1. *Contracts incapable of being performed within one year.* A contract to work for someone "for life" could be completed within a year in the event of the death of the employee before the end of the year. Hence, such a contract need not be in writing to be enforceable. However, a contract to work for another for "five years" must be in writing because it could not possibly be completed within a year.

2. *A contract for the sale of goods over $500.* If the total purchase price of goods exceeds $500 the contract for the sale must be in writing to be enforceable. Suppose Lee offers to sell his car to Ralph for $1,000 and Ralph promises to pay $1,000 for Lee's car on delivery. This contract would not be enforceable unless it was in writing.

3. *Contracts for the sale on transfer of an interest in real property.* Real property is land and anything that is permanently attached to it and a contract to sell or transfer an interest in real property must be in writing.

4. *Promises to perform the obligations of others.* Since many gratuitous promises are made to perform the obligations of others, such as repaying another's debts, these must be in writing to assure the presence of consideration and for that matter, to prove there is agreement on the part of the party agreeing to pay the other party's debts.

5. Promises *made in contemplation of marriage.* In today's terms this usually refers to prenuptial agreements.

As a general rule, any other contracts may be either written or oral. The **parol evidence rule** prohibits the introduction of oral testimony, or extraneous writings that contradicts or varies from the terms of written contracts. At common law, the written contract is ordinarily assumed to be the complete embodiment of the parties' agreement. Courts are reluctant to recognize evidence of prior or contemporaneous agreements that conflict with the terms of the written contract because the courts assume all prior negotiations and oral agreements are embodied in the written contract.

There are several exceptions to this rule. First, when the parties modify an existing written agreement orally, evidence of the oral modification can be introduced into court. In essence, this is not an exception since the oral evidence does not reflect inconsistent terms at the time of the writing, but after the writing. The rationale is that the written contract fully reflects the parties' agreement at the time of the writing; however, any subsequent changes or modifications to the agreement would not be reflected in the writing. Thus, oral testimony about these changes and modifications can be presented. A second exception is that oral evidence can be introduced to show that the contract was void or voidable. For example, if the contract was induced by fraud, oral evidence attesting to the fraud can be introduced. A third exception occurs with written contracts that contain terms that are ambiguous or incomplete. Oral evidence can be presented to explain the terms. Similarly, if the written contract is incomplete, oral evidence can be used to fill in the gaps. Finally, a written contract may be subject to a written condition. Evidence of the condition does not alter or modify the terms, but instead, involves the enforceability of the written contract.

V. DISCHARGE OF CONTRACTS

Breach of contract cases are usually filed because one or both of the parties are alleged to have failed to live up to his or her promised performance. In legalese, it is said that the contract was not properly **discharged**. However, performance is but one way that contractual obligations can come to an end. Just as there are rules that determine when a legally enforceable contract exists, there are also rules for determining when the obligations are discharged. The legal environment of business requires the establishment of some point at which one or both of the parties can say, "I am now discharged from my obligations on this contract." This section discusses the ways in which contracts come to an end.

A. Discharge by Performance

The great majority of contracts are discharged by **complete performance**. The contract comes to an end when both parties have fulfilled their respective duties by performing the acts they have promised. Both parties are satisfied with the contract and the contract is terminated. Complete performance occurs when the performance is within the bounds of reasonable expectations. If both parties' performance is complete, the contract is discharged.

B. Discharge by Breach of Contract/Incomplete Performance

Sometimes the parties do not perform their complete obligations. The non-performance of the obligations promised in a contract is called a breach of contract. There are two types of breach of contract.

A party's reasonable expectations arising from the terms of the contract provide the test for determining into which category an attempted performance fits. Incomplete, but **substantial performance** involves performance that is only *slightly* below what is reasonably expected. Totally incomplete and insufficient performance occurs when the performance is well below what is reasonably expected and constitutes a **material breach of contract**.

If performance by one party is substantial, but not complete, there is a breach, albeit, a minor one. The non-breaching party is not excused from performance, although performance can sometimes be suspended. For example, you hire a painter to paint the entire interior of your house in specified colors while you are on vacation. When you return, you find that one of the rooms has been painted the wrong color. There is a breach of the contract, but it is one that can be corrected. You may be able to suspend payment until the room is repainted. If the room cannot be painted but you can live with a minor color difference, then you pay the painter for the job but not the full payment called for by the contract since he did not do the full job called for by the contract.

Substantial performance does not discharge the breaching party from the contract. The non-breaching party is still entitled to sue for any damages that may arise from the less than complete performance. When performance by one party is totally insufficient (i.e., materially breached), the non-breaching party is discharged from the contract. The non-breaching party is entitled to sue the breaching party for any damages sustained. For instance, suppose Betty pays Joe's Tire Co. $25 to fix a flat tire. Betty drives off with the "fixed" tire only to have it go flat again—this time ruining the tire. Not only can Betty get her money back but Joe must also reimburse her for the depreciated value of her tire or even replace the tire if it is destroyed.

C. Discharge of Conditional Contracts

One type of contract referred to earlier was the conditional contract. Under a conditional contract, a party's duty to perform is not always certain. The duty is dependent upon the occurrence or non-occurrence of some event. Contract law defines three types of conditions: conditions precedent, conditions subsequent, and concurrent conditions.

1. Condition Precedent

A **condition precedent** is a clause in a contract that identifies some condition or obligation-triggering event that must occur prior to the creation of an obligation under the contract. In the example given earlier, the travel agent would not be required to accept and pay for the rooms at the ski resort unless the snow pack reached 80 inches. The condition precedent of the snow pack reaching 80 inches must occur before the parties are obligated to perform. The non-occurrence of a condition precedent will relieve or discharge the parties of their duties under the contract.

2. Condition Subsequent

A **condition subsequent** is a condition that follows, or is subsequent to, the duty to perform. The occurrence of a condition subsequent operates to terminate a party's absolute promise to perform. For example, Alpha Company and Beta Company enter into a contract that has a provision that the contract will become null and void if either company becomes the subject of a hostile takeover. If Gigantic Corporation attempts a takeover of Beta Company, the obligations of the parties terminate.

The typical insurance contract includes both condition precedent and condition subsequent clauses that must be satisfied in order for the beneficiary to collect. For example, the typical life insurance policy requires the death of the insured (a condition precedent) before the obligation to pay is created and the filing of a claim within a specified period of time (a condition subsequent) in order to secure payment to the beneficiary from the insurer.

3. Concurrent Conditions

Where each party's absolute duty to perform is conditioned on the other party's absolute duty to perform, there are **concurrent conditions**. Concurrent conditions only occur when the parties expressly or impliedly are to perform their respective duties simultaneously. For example, in a cash transaction the seller's tender of goods is a concurrent condition to the buyer's duty to tender payment, and vice versa. A good example of concurrent conditions occurs in a house closing. Seller does not have to sign papers selling house to buyer until buyer sign papers buying the house and pays for the house.

D. Discharge by Agreement

1. Rescission

Any contract can be discharged by agreement. The agreement can be contained in the original contract, such as a contract for hotel reservations in which the hotel agrees to release the guest from the contract if notified before 5:00 p.m. Alternatively, the parties can form a new contract for the express purpose of discharging the original contract. It should be noted, however, that this type of contract, called a **rescission**, must be supported by consideration. In other words, if one party has completed his or her obligation and the other party has not, the non-performing party must give up some consideration to which the performing party is not otherwise entitled. Otherwise, the rescission contract is a gratuitous promise and is not enforceable. Other ways to discharge contractual obligations are through a novation or through an accord and satisfaction.

2. Novation

The process of **novation** substitutes a new party for one of the original parties. A substituted agreement is a new contract that expressly or impliedly revokes and discharges a prior contract. For example, Smith is the sole proprietor of a gravel pit and has contracted with Jones to supply 1,000 tons of gravel for a construction project to be delivered over a period of six weeks. Smith decides to sell the gravel pit to Johnson. A novation of the contract would release Smith from his duties and replace Smith with Johnson in a new contract.

3. Accord and Satisfaction

For a contract to be discharged through an **accord and satisfaction**, the parties must agree to accept performance that is different from the performance originally promised. An **accord** is the agreement between the parties for the different performance, and the **satisfaction** is the performance of the substituted obligation. An accord is not binding until the satisfaction is made. Accord and satisfaction is agreed partial performance and it is a total discharge only in an **unliquidated** debt. An unliquidated debt is a debt that is truly in dispute, neither party can prove the exact amount owed. Therefore, if Ashley feels that she only owes Sarah $1,000 but Sarah claims that Ashley owes her $1,500, and neither can prove with certainty that their claimed amount is correct. Since this is unliquidated debt, if Ashley offers to pay $1,250, that is an accord. If Sarah agrees to accept the $1,250, that is a satisfaction and the result is a complete discharge of the contract between the parties. In other words, Sarah cannot claim that Ashley still owes her $250. However, had this been a liquidated debt and Ashley paid $1,250 claiming that that was enough, then Sarah could rightfully treat that as a partial payment and take action to collect the remaining $250 of the debt.

E. Discharge by Impossibility

1. Subjective Impossibility

After a contract has been formed, performance may become impossible. This is known as impossibility of performance and, in some circumstances, may discharge a contract. In determining whether the parties to a contract are discharged from their duties, the courts distinguish between objective impossibility ("It can't be done.") and subjective impossibility ("I can't do it."). Examples of **subjective impossibility** are failure to deliver on time because of a shortage of trucks and failure to pay on time because the accounts receivable have not been paid. Normally, subjective impossibility will not relieve a party of duties under the contract, and the party will be liable for damages for the breach. In terms of the allocation of risk, the non-performing party clearly accepts the risk that it will be unable to perform. Moreover, this legal rule appears to promote efficiency because it places liability on the party who is in the best position to control whether or not performance is possible. For example, if breaching parties were relieved from liability under all cases of subjective impossibility, then the incentive to perform contracts under difficult circumstances would be lessened.

2. Objective Impossibility

There are four basic situations that will generally qualify for discharge of contractual obligations for objective impossibility where the law says "It can't be done":

1. Where one of the parties to a personal service contract dies prior to performance under the contract.
2. Where the specific subject matter of the contract is destroyed.
3. Where a change in the law renders performance illegal.
4. Where performance becomes commercially impractical.

The first type of impossibility would occur when an actress contracts to play the leading role in a movie, but becomes ill before production of the movie starts and dies. A lease of a building that is destroyed by fire can illustrate the second type of discharge for objective impossibility, destruction of the specific subject matter of the contract. If the contracting parties do not contemplate the possibility of the fire, then it cannot be said that the risk of fire has been allocated by the contract. Discharge for this type of impossibility of performance, however, is not appropriate where the parties include a clause specifying the obligations of the parties in the event of fire.

The parties do typically not contemplate the third type of objective impossibility, subsequent change of law which is also called **subsequent illegality** declaring the subject of the contract to be illegal. An example of this type of discharge would be a contract for the sale of asbestos where the sale of asbestos is declared illegal before the execution of the contract. The parties to the contract will be released from their obligations.

The fourth type of discharge by impossibility, the doctrine of **commercial impracticability**, allows parties to discharge contracts when the performance that was originally contemplated turns out to be *massively* more difficult or more expensive than could have been originally anticipated. This defense does not appear justified when at least one party to the contract is aware, or at least should have been aware, of the possibility that performance may be more difficult than expected. The party with the informational advantage about the risk should be held liable. The cases, however, do not always reflect this perspective. For example, in one case, the California Supreme Court held that a contract was discharged because to complete the contract would cost 10 times the original estimate to excavate a certain amount of gravel. This does not make sense in terms of the allocation of risk because one would expect that the excavator would be aware of the possibility that the work would be more expensive than preliminary studies suggested. Moreover, the excavator may have won the contract with the lower bid because he, but not the other bidders, failed to take that risk into account when calculating the bid. In general, the courts should encourage the parties best able to calculate a risk to bear that risk in the absence of a specific contract term.

This risk allocation perspective is reflected in other cases. For example, in a case involving the closing of the Suez Canal, a court determined that the closing did not discharge a carrier from its obligation to deliver wheat to a port in Iran. The court determined that the closing of the canal was foreseeable, and this is crucial in commercial impracticability cases. It is assumed that risks that are foreseeable are taken into account when agreeing on the price of the contract at the time of negotiations. Thus, the doctrine only applies (1) when the burden of complying is extreme; *and* (2) more importantly, when the additional burden was not recognizable when the contract was formed. The real conflict between the cases, therefore, turns on the question of whether the risks were recognized, or whether they should have been recognized by at least one of the parties. Rarely is a contract set aside for being commercially impractical.

F. Repudiation (Anticipatory Breach)

A contract can also be discharged by **repudiation** of one of the parties. This is also referred to as **anticipatory breach**. This is where one of the parties to the contract, prior to the required time of performance announces that he will not perform as required under the contract. Obviously, this is a material breach. However, the innocent party is discharged from the contract or he can simply wait and see if the breaching party changes his mind. If the breaching party realizes that he is in breach and does so prior to the non-breaching party treating it as a breach by finding someone else to perform the contract or otherwise canceling the contract, the breaching party who "sees the error of their ways" can still perform under the contract, *if allowed by the innocent party*, and if the contract is fully performed, there is no breach.

VI. REMEDIES FOR BREACH OF CONTRACT

A. Explanation of Remedies

When a breach of contract is established, the issue becomes one of determining the proper remedy. Essential to the policy of the law of remedies is the recognition that the goal is not to compel adherence to contracts, but to require each party to the contract to choose between performing in accordance with the contract and compensating the other party for any injury that results from a failure to perform. For this reason, damages that are designed to punish the defendant for breaching the contract, called **punitive damages**, are not awarded in breach of contract cases. Usually, a monetary award in the form of damages is sufficient to compensate the non-breaching party. When monetary damages, **legal remedy**, are insufficient to compensate the non-breaching party, several **equitable remedies** are available to provide more appropriate compensation.

B. Monetary Damages (Legal Damages)

1. Introduction
Monetary damages are the most common remedy awarded for breach of contract. The goal of monetary damages is to compensate the non-breaching party for the loss of the bargained-for exchange. Often, courts say that innocent parties are to be placed in the position they would have occupied had the contract been fully performed. There are three broad categories of monetary damages: (1) compensatory, (2) consequential, and (3) liquidated.

2. Compensatory Damages
Compensatory damages are designed to compensate the injured party for the loss of the bargain. These damages compensate the non-breaching party only for injuries actually sustained and proved to have arisen from the breach of contract. Lost profits, unless they can be calculated with reasonable certainty, are generally not recoverable. The method of measuring compensatory damages differs by type of contract.

As an example consider a construction contract. The measure of damages in a construction contract will vary depending upon which party breaches and at what stage of construction the breach occurs. The owner can breach at two different stages of construction, before performance is completed or after performance is completed. If the owner breach's before performance is completed, the measure of damages is the amount of time and effort expended plus the actual costs incurred by the builder up to the time the contract was breached by the owner. The contract price is the appropriate measure of damages when the breach occurs after the construction is completed. When the builder breaches a construction contract, the measure of damages is generally the cost of completing the contract when the builder fails to finish. If the builder substantially performs (i.e., the breach is minor), the cost of completion will be used to measure damages so long as there is no substantial economic waste in requiring completion. For example, if the contractor uses a lower grade pipe for plumbing than the contract called for, then there is a breach. However, the courts will not award damages in the amount required to tear out the plumbing and replace it. The damages will generally be measured by the difference in fair market value resulting from using the lower grade pipe.

Because the future is difficult to prove in the present, lost profits are generally not recoverable in breach of contract cases. Lost profits can be recovered only if they can be determined with reasonable certainty. For instance, suppose a retail lumber dealer had a contract with a wholesaler to buy a certain quantity of lumber to add to inventory for $1,000. If the wholesaler breaches the contract, the damages will not be lost profits because the court cannot determine the price for which the retailer would have actually sold the lumber. However, if the retailer had a contract to sell the same lumber to a particular buyer for $1,200 and lost the sale because of the breach by the wholesaler, the court could easily determine that the lost profits were $200. In the latter case, lost profits would probably be awarded because of the reasonable certainty in their calculation.

3. Consequential Damages

Consequential damages arise from the breach as a result of the special needs or unique position of the buyer. They differ from compensatory damages in that they are caused by special circumstances beyond the contract itself. Consequential damages flow from the results of the breach and are recoverable only if they are reasonably foreseeable and the non-breaching party tried to mitigate (or prevent) the damages.

In general, where the risk of loss of consequential damages is only known by one party to the contract, the other party is not liable for the consequential damages. The result of this legal rule is that the party with the special knowledge of the possibility of consequential damages has the incentive to make them known to the other party. Often, however, the value of the contract will change depending upon who bears the risk of the consequential damages. Thus, the law encourages the risk to be borne by the least cost avoider of the risk.

4. Liquidated Damages

The parties may stipulate in their contract that a certain amount shall be paid in the case of default. This amount is referred to as **liquidated damages.** Liquidated damage clauses are commonly used in construction contracts because it is difficult to determine the damage associated with a delay in completion. For example, a liquidated damage clause might stipulate that the contractor pays the owner $1,000 for every day beyond May 1, the deadline for completion of a construction project. If the amount specified is not excessive, and if the contract is of such a nature that determining actual damages would be difficult, then a liquidated damages provision will generally be enforced. On the other hand, if the provision calls for an unreasonably large sum that is unrelated to actual damages, the provision is called a penalty and the courts will not enforce it.

The distinction between enforceable and unenforceable penalty clauses is interesting from a policy perspective. A stipulated damage clause that amounts to a penalty may merely reflect the promisee's very strong desire to have the project finished on schedule. Moreover, it seems unreasonable to suspect that the inclusion of a penalty clause does not impact on other terms in the contract, including the negotiation of the completion date and the total value of the contract. Thus, the refusal of the common law courts to enforce penalty clauses appears to be based on some type of paternalistic notion. On the other hand, it has been suggested that the distinction between penalty clauses and reasonable damage clauses be justified on efficiency grounds because penalty clauses create perverse incentives for the beneficiary of the clauses to induce the breach of the contract in order to collect the penalty. For example, the owner might sabotage the construction project in order to collect the (excessive) damages upon delay in completion. Furthermore, penalty clauses increase the risk associated with events over which the parties have little control, such as weather. This increase in risk needlessly increases the cost of performance.

C. Equitable Remedies

1. Introduction

Occasionally, monetary damages are not sufficient to make the non-breaching party whole after a breach of contract. When the situation arises that monetary damages are insufficient, the injured party can seek **equitable remedies**, court-ordered action to do or not to do something. Equity may call for a remedy other than money damages. This section discusses remedies, called equitable or special, non-monetary remedies that are sometimes awarded in appropriate cases. Ordinarily, a party can only receive equitable damages in those situations where monetary damages do them no real good.

2. Rescission and Restitution

Rescission is essentially an action to undo or cancel a contract and return the parties to the position they occupied prior to forming the contract. Rescission is used most often where the court finds fraud, mistake, duress, or failure of consideration. For example, Baker signs a contract to purchase land in Florida that Meyer represents to be a prime building location on a recreational lake. Baker learns instead that the property is covered by floodwater for half of the year and that building on it is impossible. Money damages are inappropriate since Baker does not want to obtain the benefit of her bargain. The most efficient way to resolve the dispute is to return Baker to his pre-contract position by simply undoing the contract. Therefore, rescission is the appropriate remedy. If Baker had paid any amount to

Meyer, Baker would be entitled to **restitution** of that amount. Likewise, Baker would have to return title to the land if title had passed.

3. Reformation

Reformation is a remedy used to rewrite the contract to express the true agreement between the parties. It may be needed when there is a clerical error in a written contract that gives one of the parties an unbargained-for advantage. Another use of the reformation remedy is when a court finds a divisible portion of the contract to be invalid. Some courts will find the contract to be valid, but rewrite the invalid portion. For example, John sells Mick a bakery. In the sales contract, there is a provision called a covenant not to compete which prevents John from opening another bakery within the state. Based on state law such a broad limitation is invalid. Some courts will reform the covenant in such a way so as to protect both the buyer and seller, by providing, for example, that John will not open another bakery within five miles of the one he sold.

4. Specific Performance

Under special circumstances, the injured party may seek the equitable remedy of specific performance. **Specific performance** means that the court orders the breaching party to perform the exact bargain promised in the contract. This remedy is quite attractive to the non-breaching party. It also avoids problems associated with a money judgment such as collecting the judgment or finding another contracting partner, but is rarely the choice of the courts.

The courts are reluctant to order specific performance as a remedy because the courts would generally have to supervise the transaction to ensure that the breaching party performs as ordered. The court's position on this is reasonable, and probably efficient. The courts do not want to get involved in supervising employment contracts to make sure the party is performing as ordered. Specific performance will not be used so long as money damages provide an adequate remedy. Contracts for the sale of land are the principal type of contract where specific performance is an available remedy. Courts reason that individual tracts of land are unique, that is, one cannot be freely substituted for another. This is true because location plays a large part in determining the value of a tract of land and because the location of any particular tract is fixed. Consequently, money damages will not generally fully compensate the buyer for a seller's refusal to complete the transaction because that money cannot be used to obtain a substitute. Further, it is relatively easy for the court to monitor the sale of land.

D. Mitigation of Damages

The injured party is under a duty to mitigate the damages if reasonably possible. Damages must not be permitted to increase if they can be prevented by reasonable efforts. Whatever duty is owed depends on the nature of the contract. For example, some states require a lessor to use reasonable means to find a new tenant if the lessee abandons the premises and fails to pay rent. If an acceptable tenant becomes available, the landlord must accept the new tenant to mitigate the damages from the breach of the lease. Very simply, mitigation requires the non-breaching party to avoid running up the bill. This is efficient because it discourages the waste of valuable resources.

VII. ETHICAL CONSIDERATIONS

A. Why Prefer Written Contracts?

Many inexperienced members of the business community feel that requesting that an oral agreement be reduced to writing is tantamount to telling the other party that they are not worthy of being trusted. While this may be particularly difficult in face-to-face negotiations, if the other party is planning to keep his promises, he should want a written contract that will be easier to enforce. Perhaps it was once the case that a person's word was that person's bond, but in earlier times a person often dealt with the same parties on a continuing basis. Hence, breaking oral promises injured a person's reputation and increased the risk of doing business with that person. Today, contractual transactions are more frequent and are more often conducted between strangers. Hence, the value of a reputation is far less than it once was.

Written contracts are not only easier to enforce, but they also assist the parties in remembering the terms of their agreement. Think of families; family members bring suits against each other not because one member is trying to gain at the other's expense but because each sincerely believes a different version of an oral contract. Many family relationships could be saved by simply reducing oral agreements to writing.

When one's reputation for ethical conduct is an important factor in future transactions, market forces will eradicate unethical participants. If reputation is not important, the burden is upon the parties to protect themselves against the uncertain ethics of others. Wise businesspersons generally do not fault others for protecting themselves contractually as long as they receive similar protections. However, inexperienced businesspersons should beware of those who want protections for themselves but are not willing to give protection to the other party.

Also, it was discussed above that punitive damages are not available in contract law. The main reason is because you cannot force people to be good. Therefore, ethics is a choice and you cannot force people to be ethical so it is better to have a written contract.

PART TWO—AGENCY LAW

I. AGENCY LAW

A. Introduction

Agency law is an extension of contract law because an agency relationship is created when the agent agrees to act on behalf of and be under the control of a principal. They are simply entering into a voluntary agreement, which is usually a contract. Through this legal relationship the **agent** becomes a representative of the principal and can bind the **principal** to third parties in contracts and in tort law.

B. Types of Agencies

1. Agency by Agreement
An agency relationship is normally created by the agreement of the parties and is often a written agreement called a **power of attorney**. Keep in mind that unless the facts of the agency relationship cause the agreement to be under the Statute of Frauds, the contract does not have to be in writing. An agency by agreement gives express power which is whatever power is expressly given to the agent in the agreement. It also gives implied authority which is the power that is not expressly states but is necessary to carry out the expressed authority whatever it may be.

2. Agency by Ratification
A contract can also be created by **ratification**. In this situation, someone without the agreement of the "principal," which is in reality not a principal, acts on behalf of the "principal" and then after the fact, notifies the "principal of his actions." If the alleged "principal" agrees to the actions the agent has already done on his behalf, then an agency by ratification has occurred. The alleged "principal" thereby becomes a real principal. However, the principal could just as easily have told the "agent" that he does not agree to the "agent's" action. In that situation the "agent" has bound himself to the agreement with the third party and the "principal" has no liability. In other words, if the alleged principal does not ratify the agency, then the alleged principal is not bound to the agreement and the person who claimed to be an agent is bound to the agreement. However, the alleged principal must make it clear that they have not ratified the agreement or they could ratify by failing to disaffirm the agreement by giving the impression that the agent could in fact act on the principal's behalf.

3. Agency by Apparent Authority (Agency by Estoppel)
The principal's actions or in some cases, inaction, can also create an agency relationship. Again there is not an agreed agency relationship, but you have someone acting on behalf of someone else. There is no actual ratification by the principal after the fact. Instead, even though the "principal" knows the "agent" is acting as his agent and that this is well known to other people, the "principal" does nothing to stop the "agent" from acting like his representative. Since the "principal" has given the third parties the impression that the person is his agent since he knew of the agent's activities and did nothing to stop the agent, then the "principal" has allowed the impression that an agency relationship has in fact been established. Therefore, the principal is prevented, or estopped, from denying the agency relationship. This is creation of an **agency by estoppel** which is also called an **agency by apparent authority**. After all in this type of agency, the principal has made it appear to the third party that he has given the authority to act on his behalf to the agent.

4. Agency by Operation of Law

The final way an agency relationship can be created is by operation of law. There are several situations where, due to the facts, the law creates an agency relationship. This is normally in emergency situations such as medical emergencies when a decision must be made and the parents or legal guardian is not available to make the decision.

II. DUTIES OWED

A. Duties of Agents to Principals

By entering into an agency relationship both of the parties owe the other party certain duties. An agent owes the principal the following duties: (1) loyalty—the agent must put the principal's interest first, at all times; (2) obedience—the agent must follow the principal's instructions; (3) reasonable care—the agent must use reasonable care in the performance of his or her duties; (4) accounting—the agent must give an honest accounting of the property or money of the principal; and (5) notification—the agent must keep the principal informed of all necessary information.

B. Duties of Principal to Agent

Likewise, the principal owes certain duties to the agent such as: (1) cooperation with the agent so that the agent can do his duties; (2) payment, if the agent is to be compensated, if an agency is gratuitous then no payment is required; (3) reimbursement of the agent's reasonable expenses; (4) providing a safe work environment; and (5) indemnifying the agent for his or her losses suffered while acting within the scope of the agency relationship.

III. LIABILITIES

In addition to duties, the parties also incur liability due to their involvement in an agency relationship in both contracts and torts.

A. Contractual Liability

In contracts, the extent of the liability depends on whether the principal is disclosed, partially disclosed, or undisclosed to the third party. One of the major reasons for entering into an agency relationship is to hide the identity of the principal. This is called an **undisclosed agency**. Therefore, if an agent does not disclose the existence of a principal, the third party only knows that he is dealing with the agent. Therefore, the agent and the third party are bound to the contract. However, if the agent is acting within the scope of the agency, the principal, once he or she is disclosed is still liable to the third party. The principal also has a duty to reimburse or indemnify the agent for any losses he or she incurs within the scope of the agency relationship. If the agent discloses or partially discloses the principal, then only the principal is bound to the contract assuming of course that the agent was operating within the scope of his authority. A **disclosed agency** is when the agent tells the third party that he is only an agent and that there is a principal and the identity of the principal. A **partially disclosed agency** is when the agent tells the third party that he is just an agent and that there is a principal but does not disclose the identity of that principal. In both disclosed and partially disclosed agencies, the third party knows he is dealing with an agent and not the principal and therefore, only the principal is liable under the contract.

B. Tort Liability

In tort liability, the main issue is whether or not the agent acted within the scope of the agency. If the agent is doing what the principal instructed him to do, then the principal is liable. This is the legal status of **Respondeat Superior** and is based on employment law, the employer is liable if the employee acted within his scope of business. However, a principal can also be liable for the unauthorized torts of the agent. This is called **vicarious liability**. If an agent engages in unauthorized intentional or negligent torts, the principal is bound if the agent was acting within the **scope of the employment**. Employment here does not mean hired which or course would bind the principal but also to an agency where the agent is not paid. To determine whether the agent was within his or her scope of employment, the courts look to see if the act was similar to authorized acts of the agent, was the agent authorized to be where he was at the time the unauthorized act occurred and was the agent serving the needs of the principal when the agent did the unauthorized act. If the agent is acting outside the scope of his authority and committed unauthorized, intentional or negligent torts then only the agent is liable for those torts. Ordinarily, a principal is not liable for the crimes of the agent unless the principal knew or should have known of the criminal activity of the agent. This liability can also arise under the theory that the principal should have known due to the criminal background of the agent. Keep in mind that the courts are expanding this area of the law to make the principals more liable in criminal liability.

CHAPTER SUMMARY

The law of contracts reflects the extent to which society will bind a promisor to his or her promises. A contract is a special type of agreement that the law will enforce. The elements of a contract are mutual agreement of the parties, consideration, contractual capacity, and legal subject matter. If these elements all exist, the contract will generally be enforced.

Contracts take various forms. They may be either expressed through words or implied from the actions of the parties. Contracts may also be subject to conditions before performance is required or they may be unconditional. In a conditional contract, the occurrence or non-occurrence of the condition will often terminate the contract. Some contracts require a return promise for acceptance; others simply require that the offeree act to accept the contract.

The mutual agreement of the parties is generally evidenced through an offer and acceptance. An offer reflects the intention of the offeror to create a power in the offeree to create a legally binding agreement through acceptance. The offer is required to be definite, and it must be communicated to the offeree to be valid.

An offeror has the power to terminate the offer at any time under the common law unless consideration has been given to keep the offer open. The offer can also be terminated through rejection or counteroffer by the offeree. Offers will terminate whenever the subject matter of the offer becomes illegal, or with the passage of time. An offer can be accepted at any time prior to its termination. An acceptance has to be unconditional, unequivocal, and legally communicated to the offeror.

Consideration is the price of the contract. In keeping with its function to facilitate exchange, contract law will not enforce contracts where there is no consideration, because no exchange is taking place. As a general rule, the courts will not examine the bargain to determine whether the consideration is sufficient.

Once formed, a contract must eventually end. Contractual obligations end through performance or breach of the contract. When both parties have performed, the contract ends. When one party breaches the contract, the other is relieved from performing further. On the other hand, if one party substantially but not completely performs the contract, the other is not relieved from contractual duties, but does have remedies for the breach. Some contracts are ended without performance or breach. If a condition is required before performance is required, then the failure of the condition will terminate the contract. Alternatively, the parties can agree to terminate the contract at any time. Also, if performance of the contract becomes impossible, the courts can relieve the party who cannot perform from liability.

When one party breaches a contract, the non-breaching party is entitled to a remedy. The most common remedy is the awarding of monetary damages to compensate the innocent party—referred to as compensatory damages. Other types of damages are consequential, punitive, and liquidated. The innocent party is required to mitigate damages by seeking performance elsewhere. In the rare circumstances where money damages will not be sufficient to compensate the innocent party, several equitable remedies are available. These include rescission and restitution, reformation, and specific performance.

Agency law is often a type of contract. Agency relationships can be established by the expressed agreement of the principal and the agent, by ratification of the acts of another after he or she has acted on your parts, or by law. The parties owe each other duties. Either party is responsible to the other party for breach of those duties.

Another major concern in an agency relationship is liability. An agent can be liable under contract law depending on whether the agent disclosed his or her agency statues. If the agent discloses his status as an agent, it generally relieves his or her of contractual liability. However, if the agent does not reveal his status or only partially discloses it, then the agent can have contractual liability. Of course, he or she can look to the principal for indemnification.

An agent can also bind the principal due to a tort violation if the agent is acting within the scope of his or her employment. Here, if the act was unauthorized, the principal can look to the agent for indemnification or reimbursement.

5

TORTS AND PRODUCTS LIABILITY

I. INTRODUCTION TO THE LAW OF TORTS AND PRODUCTS LIABILITY

A. General Information

The preceding chapter was concerned with the rights and duties created in voluntary transactions. This chapter primarily concerns the rights and duties of parties to involuntary transactions, such as accidents, assaults, intentional interference with a contract, fraud, and many, many other situations. A tort can be defined as a civil wrong other than a breach of contract for which the courts will provide a remedy in the form of damages to compensate the injured party. There are three major types of torts and a business can be involved in all of them. These are intentional torts, negligence, and strict liability.

Crimes and torts are very similar. Both are wrongs. However, a crime is a wrong against society, and a tort is a wrong against a private party. Crimes are punished through fines or imprisonment. Torts, on the other hand, do punish defendants but are not primarily designed to punish defendants; rather, tort law is designed to compensate injured plaintiffs through an award of monetary damages. The standard of proof is also different. Torts are civil cases and thus only have to be proven by the more likely than not standard, whereas criminal cases must be proven by the beyond a reasonable doubt standard. The fundamental results of criminal law and tort law are the same: deterrence of activities considered to be wrong.

As stated above, the types of torts that are discussed in this chapter can be divided into three broad categories: intentional torts, negligent torts, and strict liability. An **intentional tort** involves a deliberate action, which results in an injury. The **tortfeasor**, party committing the tort, intends to do the acts that resulted in the harm. It does NOT mean that the tortfeasor intended to harm the innocent party. For example, a company commits an intentional tort when it knowingly makes false statements about the quality of a competitor's products. A negligent tort or **negligence** is an unintentional tort that arises from the failure to use reasonable care toward one, to whom a duty is owed, which results in injury. Unintentional torts occur in a variety of business settings that range from slip-and-fall accidents in a showroom to defectively designed products. **Strict liability** is liability without fault. You did the acts that resulted in the harm, therefore you are liable and it does not matter whether you intended to do the act or were negligent in doing the act. Usually, strict liability is reserved for abnormally dangerous activities such as building implosions or keeping a wild animal as a pet.

The law of torts provides a set of legal rules that allows parties injured as the result of the actions of others to collect damages under certain well-defined circumstances. Understanding the purpose for the existence of this body of law is necessary in order to evaluate its role in society. The purpose of the law of torts has been debated for centuries. Several possible justifications for the action for damages in tort are considered here. **Appeasement** as a goal of tort law means that the purpose of the law is to limit the negative impact of the infliction of injury to the event of the injury itself. Tort law provides a way to right the wrong without the injured party retaliating through some destructive means. That is, the victim's vengeance is bought off by imposing tort liability on the wrongdoer. The victim is appeased in two ways: (1) receipt of compensation and (2) knowledge of the fact that the transgressor is punished by being required to pay.

The law of torts is sometimes viewed as the expression of a moral principle: one who by his fault has caused damage to another ought to make compensation as a matter of **justice**. There are two views in support of this position, and either variant is simply a different way of saying the same thing. First, the principle of **ethical retribution** places emphasis upon the fact that the payment of compensation is harmful to the tortfeasor and that justice requires that the tortfeasor suffer the harm. Second, the principle of **ethical compensation** looks at the same situation from the point of view of the victim. It emphasizes the fact that the payment of compensation is a benefit to the victim of the wrong, and declares that justice requires that the victim should receive this compensation. Regardless of the perspective one chooses, the policy implications are the same.

Some legal scholars view tort law as a regime of prevention, thus the law is after **deterrence**. According to this perspective, the rules of tort law are designed to alter the incentives of interacting parties so as to control their future conduct in a manner that reduces losses due to accidents in the most efficient manner. This economic perspective has concentrated on developing legal rules that minimize the total costs associated with accidents. The two types of costs associated with accidents are the costs of preventing accidents and the actual costs of accidental injuries. When the costs of avoiding an accident are less than the costs of the injuries, an efficient legal rule would be one that imposes liability on the party that could have avoided the accident at the lowest possible cost. Thus, the deterrence view of the role of tort law not only concentrates on altering behavior so as to avoid accidents, but also generates public policy prescriptions based on efficiency: the party who is the "least-cost avoider" of an accident should be held liable. In practice, the identification of the "least-cost avoider" is not always obvious. Of course, the rule is intended to alter behavior so that the likelihood of accidents is decreased. Bearing the costs of injuries acts as an incentive to the liable parties to alter their behavior to reduce the risk of injury since the precedent set by such cases establishes liability rules for the future. For instance, many state courts have held that grocery storeowners are liable to customers that are mugged in unlit parking lots. Impliedly, courts are saying that it is cheaper for stores to light their parking lots to prevent muggings than for customers to hire bodyguards or provide some other form of personal security. The impact is to make the grocery stores install lights in the parking lot or pay damages to someone who is mugged in the dark parking lot. The deterrence perspective does not answer all of the questions about the proper liability rule, however. In some instances, the costs of preventing an accident may be greater than the cost of the accident. The liability rule will not alter the behavior of the parties because it is cheaper to pay for the cost associated with the accident rather than to try to prevent the accident.

Another approach to tort law is to consider it as a means of **social insurance**. According to this view, the party who is in the best position to spread the loss of the injury should be held liable. With respect to injuries resulting from products, for example, the manufacturer is often in the best position to cover the costs of compensation because the expected costs can be reflected in the price of the product (or, alternatively, they are borne by the share-holders of the company). All consumers, not just the unlucky few who happen to be injured by the product, bear some of the costs. This same theory is sometimes articulated as a deep-pocket theory: The business has greater wealth than the injured consumers do so the business should pay. This also leads to several seemingly frivolous lawsuits against busi-nesses. It must be recognized that all of tort law is not explained in terms of any single objective and that it is possible to attain several objectives under the same liability rules.

Most of the damages awarded in individual tort cases are intended to make the plaintiff whole again, at least financially. Such **compensatory damages** usually consist of three major types of loss. They are (1) past and future medical expenses, (2) past and future eco-nomic loss, and (3) past and future pain and suffering. The amount of damages suffered by the plaintiff is a jury determination and it is presented to jurors as an adversarial pro-ceeding. Testimony regarding damages is normally introduced only after the liability of the defendant has been established. There is no need to waste the court's time with damage evidence if the defendant is not responsible. The judge will carry out this function if there is no jury.

The plaintiff presents medical experts to testify to the level of medical care needed by the plaintiff for the rest of his or her expected life. The defendant may have experts to pres-ent contradictory evidence or cast doubt in the mind of the jurors as to the expertise of the plaintiff's experts. Damages with respect to loss of earnings and to future earnings capac-ity, if any, are presented in much the same way as medical expenses, except that economists are usually used as experts. In the case of physical injury, physical therapists may be called to establish the amount of recovery expected and the amount of time required for such recovery. In some cases, an attorney who specializes in pain and suffering awards may be called in to elicit the sympathy of the jury. Often, color photographs of the plaintiff imme-diately after the injury or in the hospital following the injury are used to give the jury a feel for what the plaintiff has experienced.

Courts also award punitive damages in some cases. **Punitive damages** are awards designed to punish individual defendants. The typical cases where punitive damages are awarded are for intentional torts and for negligence cases where the conduct was "gross negligence" or "willful and wanton" disregard for the plaintiff's safety. A number of appeals have asked that punitive damages imposed by juries in federal courts be reduced because such awards violate the Eighth Amendment protection against excessive fines. The Supreme Court has ruled that punitive damages awarded by civil juries are not "fines" within the historical context of the Eighth Amendment of the U.S. Constitution (**Browning-Ferris-Industries of Vermont, Inc. v. Kelco, 492 U.S. 257 (1989)**). However, this has led many state legislatures in recent years to impose statutory restrictions on punitive damages. Different states have used different forms of tort reform legislation. However, a common type of tort reform is to limit the punitive damages to a multiple of the actual compensatory damages. For instance, if a jury awards the plaintiff $1 million compensatory damages and $400 million punitive damages, then in a state which has enacted tort reform, the punitive damages would be reduced to probably three or four times the actual compensatory damages. States have imposed these limits in response to claims of injustice by the insurance companies as well as large donations made to numerous big businesses and insurance companies to politicians' re-election campaign. However, it must be mentioned that most large tort verdicts handed down by juries are sometimes reduced by the trial judge and almost certainly will be reduced or even thrown out by the appellate courts. This is especially true in states like Texas where judges are elected and have been bought and paid for by big businesses, particularly the insurance industries in legal campaign contributions.

A business normally becomes involved in a tort in one of three ways: (1) due to the actions of the business itself or its employees, (2) due to its own actions against another business, or (3) due to its products. If a business is successful, it is often a target for tort action. In addition to legitimate tort claims, there are people who abuse the system and stage torts. Our society has become "lawsuit happy."

When a tort is allegedly committed, the question is not "what did the victim think"? While the victim's state of mind is important in awarding the damages, it is not of paramount importance when trying to determine if a tort was committed. Rather the courts look to an objective standard of what would a reasonable person do in a like situation, under the same circumstances, or how would a reasonable person react in the case of defenses. This will be more fully explained as we discuss the intentional torts also. We have already discussed this objective standard in the previous chapter.

II. INTENTIONAL TORTS

A. Introduction

An intentional tort is based on the intentional invasion of a protected interest. It is not necessary that the wrongdoer intend to cause harm merely that an injury flows from the intentional act. For instance, if you intentionally pull a chair out from under someone as a joke without meaning to physically hurt them, but the person falls to the floor and breaks their hip, then you are responsible for their injuries. The interest harmed must be a legally protected interest, and not all wrongs are protected legally. Intentional torts can be classified as those interfering with personal rights and those interfering with property rights. This section concentrates on intentional torts.

B. Personal Intentional Torts

1. Assault and Battery

a. Assault

An **assault** is an intentional action that places a person in fear or apprehension of immediate bodily harm or offensive contact. An assault can be a threat, such as pulling a gun and pointing it at someone. Since the assault is the fear or apprehension that a reasonable person would have due to the intentional act, if a reasonable person would be afraid, there is a tort. Likewise, if a reasonable person would not be afraid, there is no tort. This is an example of the objective standard used in tort law that was described above. Using that objective standard, it does not matter whether the victim is easily scared or not. The question is "would a reasonable person be afraid?" The victim must know of the intentional act. Otherwise, there is no fear. However, in the gun example above, the gun would not have to be loaded because a jury would probably find that a reasonable person would be afraid if they knew a gun was pointed at them whether the gun was loaded or not. The gun could have even been a toy gun that looked real to a reasonable person.

A business can easily become involved in this tort if an employee of the business threatens or places a person in fear of harm. For instance, what if a security guard while at work at the mall and therefore, within the scope of his employment, told a female shopper at the mall that he would use his gun on her if she did not agree to go to a storage shed with him. He then proceeded to tell her all the horrible things that he planned to do to her in the storage shed. Would a reasonable woman in a like situation be afraid? Would the normal woman stop and think, well, he is not a real policeman and I would bet my life that the mall does not really let those "rent-a-cops" carry loaded weapons? Would he have to carry out the threatened action for an assault to occur? No, if the threat would cause a reasonable person to be afraid, it does not matter if the threat could actually have been carried out. Therefore, if the woman got away, she could still file suit for the assault even if the gun was not loaded, and yes, she can sue the employer because the employer is responsible for the action of their employees while on the job or within the scope of their employment.

An old case on this subject of reasonable fear and employer liability is **Hill v. Western Union Telegraph, 25 Ala. App. 540, 150 So. 709 (1933)**, where Mr. Sapp, an employee of Western Union Telegraph, was under contract to fix Mr. Hill's clock. Sapp called Mrs. Hill to come in to discuss an issue about the clock, which she did. When she got there, Sapp had been drinking and told Mrs. Hill "if you will come back here and let me love and pet you, I will fix your clock." Sapp was standing behind a counter and could not have gotten to Mrs. Hill on his own although there was conflicting testimony as to whether or not he tried. Mrs. Hill sued Western Union Telegraph for the assault. She did not sue Mr. Sapp individually probably because Western Union Telegraph had money and Mr. Sapp did not. The trial court ruled for Mrs. Hill and Western Union Telegraph appealed and won because Mr. Sapp was not acting within the scope of his employment. However, the Appellate Court made it clear that Mrs. Hill did have a case for assault against Mr. Sapp because she was placed in fear of an imminent battery by Mr. Sapp and that it was apparent to Mrs. Hill, a reasonable person, that he had the present ability to carry out the assault even though he could not have gotten to her due to the counter.

b. Battery

If the security guard in the above example does any unlawful touching or physical contact with the female shopper without her consent, a **battery** has also occurred. A battery is the intentional act of physical contact or offensive touching of someone else without his or her permission. This touching can include the clothes or other things identified as part of the person. Also, the touching does not have to be a direct but can be indirect such as someone throwing a rock and hitting another person or being shot by a gun.

It can be a battery if a person makes contact with someone else in any manner causing physical contact or offensive touching. Battery can be in any of the following situations: (1) a person hits another person in an offensive manner, (remember that the harm is being touched and where you are touched can be just as important as how much it physically hurts); (2) a person shoots another person and the bullet hits the person; (3) a person commands their dog to attack another person; or, (4) you throw a rock and hit someone. In summary, to have a battery, all you have to do is unlawfully or offensively touch someone without their permission and the harm does not have to be physical harm if it involves offensive touching. However, in both cases the physical contact is required. Also note that while we often hear the term "assault and battery" that can also be a combination of the torts or assault and battery but the two do not have to occur together.

Civil assault and even battery cases are rare because they are often handled under a criminal case and the victim gets court ordered restitution. Also, often the defendant does not have any money so there is no point in going to the trouble of a trial when you probably are not going to recover anything. However, there was a recent Texas case for assault that got a lot of media attention due to the wealthy women involved. This case did not involve a business but involved Victoria Osteen, co-founder and co-pastor along with her husband Joel Osteen of the very popular Lakewood Church in Houston. According to a Federal Aviation Administration (FAA) report, Mrs. Osteen got extremely upset over her dirty seat in the first-class section on a Continental flight from Houston to Vail on December 19, 2005. She complained about the seat and did not receive the attention she thought she deserved from the flight attendant and followed the flight attendant to the cockpit where she threw another flight attendant, Sharon Brown, the Plaintiff, against a bathroom door and elbowed her in the left breast. She was fined $3,000 by the FAA for interfering with a crew member during a flight. Mrs. Osteen then was sued by the flight attendant Sharon Brown for the push and elbowing, the assault. A jury trial was held in Houston in 2008 and even though Ms. Brown accused Mrs. Osteen of acting like a diva, the jury found for Mrs. Osteen some witnesses claiming that Mrs. Osteen never touched Ms. Brown. The jury obviously did not find that Ms. Brown was placed in fear or apprehension of immediate bodily harm or offensive contact. Later, people even criticized Ms. Brown for bringing the lawsuit and accused her of trying to force the Osteens into a settlement to avoid more adverse publicity. Of course, we were not on that plane but would this case have ever been filed if it were not someone who had money? Was it another example of celebrities allowed to do things that normal people cannot do simply because they do have money. (Keep in mind that insurance companies often have to pay these tort verdicts and thus have been strong advocates of tort reform as seen earlier.)

c. Defenses to Assault or Battery

Obviously, an assault and a battery can occur together or separately. For instance, if a mugger jumps out of the bushes, points a knife at you, and says "give me your money and jewelry or you are dead," then there is an assault. If you refuse and he just runs away, since there was no physical contact, there is no battery. Likewise, if someone hits you and knocks you unconscious and you never knew what hit you; there is a battery with no assault. Of course, the mugger could threaten you causing fear and then cut you with the knife when you refuse, and then, there would be both an assault and a battery. There is no question that assault and battery are related so it should come as no surprise that the defenses to one are also defenses to the other. See the Victoria Osteen case above. A **defense** is a legal justification to commit what otherwise would be a tort.

The first defense is consent. **Consent** can be expressed, as in signed releases or waivers or implied, as in most sporting events. However, if the **tortfeasor**, the person committing the tort, goes beyond the level of consent given, the appropriate tort would still occur. For instance, if a participant to a sporting event is frustrated because his or her team is losing, he or she does not have consent to intentionally break the leg of one of the other team's star players, during the sporting event anymore than he or she would have permission to take a gun and shoot the other player.

Another defense to assault and battery is **privilege**. This is a defense that allows the individual to commit the tort due to who he or she is, when they are acting within the scope of their official capacity. A good example of privilege is when a police officer responds to a call and finds burglars in someone's house. The police officer can pull his or her gun on them, which would normally be an assault. If the burglars give up, the police officer can also search them for weapons and handcuff them, which could be a battery. Of course, we have also seen in recent years examples of police brutality where officers allegedly went beyond the privilege and found themselves being prosecuted for violating a prisoner's civil rights. In those situations, the victim/alleged criminal also has a lawsuit against the city for which the police officers worked when the incident occurred. A business can find itself in the same position with night watchmen or other types of private security guards. The most famous case of alleged police brutality was Rodney King against the Los Angeles, California police where he was awarded $3.8 million by a jury, which was more than three times what the City of Los Angeles had offered when it accepted responsibility for the beating. However, there have been recent Texas allegations of police brutality as well, such as in San Antonio in March of 2011 where a San Antonio officer R. McDaniel pulled over a car on March 5 where the officer determined the driver, Diego Martinez, to be intoxicated. That is when the stories vary totally. Officer McDaniel says that both Martinez and his passenger got out of the car when McDaniel went to his police cruiser to run an identification check. McDaniel then states that he "tased" Martinez in the back when Martinez refused the officer's commands. McDaniel also states that

Martinez did fall from being "tased" and that he pulled Martinez from the traffic lane where he fell. Martinez filed a lawsuit in Federal District Court alleging police brutality in that the injuries did not come from a fall to the ground but from the "mercilessly beating" he took from McDaniel with his fists, a baton, and being kicked "throughout his face and body." Martinez claims that all of his teeth were knocked out and that he suffered "nasal fractures, trauma to his chest and abdomen, swelling in his brain, and numerous bruises and lacerations to his head, chest abdomen, and extremities." McDaniel and the City of San Antonio are the named defendants in the lawsuit. The City of San Antonio claims that the officer acted appropriately and that the lawsuit was without merit. Only time will tell if this is another Rodney King incident or someone hoping to recover damages at the expense of a public servant doing his job. The lawsuit was filed in 2013 and has yet to go to trial.

Another defense is that of **self-defense**. If someone is hitting you, do you just have to stand there and take it, or can you defend yourself? Of course, you can defend yourself and you can also go to the defense of others. The problem is usually the amount of force that you can use in self-defense and whether or not you exceeded that force. The victim can use a reasonable amount of force to defend himself or herself or others. This can even be deadly force if deadly force is first used against you and you have no other alternative, such as fleeing. However, in defending property you can use reasonable force, but under common law you cannot use deadly force to protect your property. However, several states have statutory laws that have changed common law that allow an individual to use deadly force in certain situations to protect themselves and their property. In Texas, this is popularly referred to as the "Castle Doctrine" or in Texas, Florida, and several other states, the "stand your ground law." The Texas laws are really two different laws. The so-called "Castle Doctrine" is found in the Texas Penal Code and makes it easier for homeowners to claim self-defense when shooting an intruder, but the Texas legislature has also joined Florida and other states with the "Stand your Ground" or "Shoot First" laws as have about half of the states. These laws have recently become the subject of much discussion due the George Zimmerman shooting of Trayvon Martin case in Florida. Was it self-defense or a murder of a young black man? Even under current Texas laws, a person cannot claim self-defense unless he or she was lawfully at a place, did not provoke the confrontation, and was in "reasonable fear" of his or her life, did not resist an arrest or search by a police officer, and cannot be the result of a verbal provocation alone. Of course, the reasonable fear is handled for homeowners in Texas by assuming that a person in their own home would be in reasonable fear if the other party has a weapon, so the home owner does not have to flee. However, the "provocation" and the "reasonable fear" aspects of this are usually where the self-defense claim is made or defeated. Texas law does not give you the right to use a gun in ANY situation and you cannot be seen as trigger happy even in Texas. Prosecutors must prove that the slaying was not self-defense. However, remember this is in criminal cases and we are talking about civil cases. These laws generally only apply to claims of self-defense in a criminal case, not in a civil case. Even in criminal cases, the right of self-defense is lost in Texas if the person is reckless in injuring or killing an innocent third person. If you are interested in this, these provisions in Texas are found in Chapter 9 of the

Texas Penal Code. Of course, reality also applies. If you live in Texas, can you get away with a lot more under self-defense? After all, Texas is a very conservative state and has some of the most far-reaching gun laws in the nation so who do you think a jury is going to side with in a self-defense case, criminal or civil?

Obviously, the facts of assault and battery also give rise to criminal charges. However, keep in mind that we are only concerned with the civil side of criminal activities. However, civil assault and battery are often seen when a victim of a crime is suing to recover from the criminal due to the criminal's actions in committing a crime, whether the "criminal" is convicted or not.

2. False Imprisonment

False imprisonment is defined as intentionally causing the confinement of another person without consent or legal justification. Confinement situations involve (1) physically restraining an individual, (2) using threatening force against an individual or his or her family members to restrain them, (3) using force or threat of force against an individual's property to restrain the victim, and (4) refusing to release a person from confinement when there is a duty to release.

One of the most common false imprisonment situations faced by the courts is the retail merchant detaining a customer suspected of shoplifting. In such a situation, the merchant may assert the common law defense of **"shopkeeper's privilege,"** alleging that the detention of the customer was justified. A merchant under common law has the right to detain a suspected shoplifter for a reasonable time period if the shopkeeper has reason to believe that the detained individual committed or attempted to commit a theft from the store. In most states "antishoplifting statutes" have been passed making the shopkeeper's privilege statutory. These laws usually require the merchant to show that he or she had a reasonable basis for suspecting the customer of shoplifting, and that the detention itself was reasonable. Texas does not have an anti-shoplifting statute. Texas simply relies on the Penal Code Theft Section 31, which defines theft and what the punishment for theft will be. In fact, in Dallas, Texas, the Dallas Police changed their policy making it harder for merchants to even report small-time (under $50) shoplifting cases. No longer do the Dallas police come to a call for minor shoplifting unless the alleged shoplifter will not identify themselves or other limited situations. The merchant instead must report the alleged crime by mail and even then, the police are not supposed to issue a citation or fill out a report. Evidently this was done to lower Dallas' crime rate. It is estimated that one-third of the 11 percent drop in crime that Dallas reported in 2012 can be attributed to this new policy. Keep in mind the merchants are still having the shoplifting occur but now they do not even have the police to help them and once this story was reported by the *Dallas Morning News* on March 23, 2013, in a story by Tanya Eiserer and Steve Thompson, it was probably a notice to thieves that they have *carte blanche* or a bland card to steal from businesses. Illinois does have a specific shoplifting statute, which basically codifies the common law privilege and also gives the merchant an affirmative defense on claims by the detained individual.

However, detaining shoplifters is a major problem for businesses involved in retail sales. For instance, a store employee sees what he thinks is a person who is in the process of shoplifting. The store employee follows the alleged shoplifter. If the alleged shoplifter realizes he is being followed, could he be afraid, especially if the store employee is undercover and does not look like a store employee? Continuing with the hypothetical, say that the store employee waits until the alleged shoplifter leaves the store, he then gives chase. Now the shopper is afraid and runs from what he thinks is a crazy person. This is a potential assault. Then, when the employee catches the shoplifter and tackles him in the parking lot there is a potential battery. Then, when the store employee takes the alleged shoplifter back into the store against his will there is potential false imprisonment. If the store can prove that their employee's actions were reasonable under the circumstances or that they acted within that state's statutes covering this area, if any, then the store is privileged in its actions. But, what if the alleged shoplifter either was not a shoplifter or the store could not prove its justification? Furthermore, what if the alleged shoplifter turned out to be the son of one of the most prominent businessmen or politician in town who just happens to be from the oldest and most powerful family in town? Then, what if the business is Wal-Mart or McDonald's? In that situation it is easy to see that a jury could have sympathy for the victim and after all, the business has lots of profits, so how much could it really hurt the business if the jury gave the poor accused shoplifter half a million dollars? Therefore, the result could be very bad for the business. Because of the potential damages in this type of situation, several businesses have a policy not to detain shoplifters. The business alone can make the decision on whether to be extremely tough on shoplifters or go to the other extreme and not even stop shoplifters. One compromise is to appear to be very tough on shoplifters by posting signs, have employees watch potential shoplifters, cameras, trained security, etc. and then decide on a case-by-case basis how aggressive they will in fact, actually be. Businesses need more than just the common law "shopkeeper's privilege" protection in this area.

3. Intentional Infliction of Mental or Emotional Distress

The **infliction of mental or emotional distress** is defined as the intentional or reckless causing of severe mental suffering in another by means of outrageous and extreme conduct or language that goes beyond the bounds of decency. Texas courts list the elements of intentional infliction of emotional distress as:

1. The defendant acted intentionally or recklessly
2. The defendant's conduct was extreme and outrageous
3. The actions of the defendant caused the plaintiff emotional distress, and
4. The emotional distress suffered by the plaintiff was severe.

Texas Farm Bureau Mut. Ins. Co. v. Sears 84 S.W.3d 604 (Texas 2002)
Keep in mind that we are talking about extreme, outrageous conduct that goes beyond the bounds of decency. This protects individuals from, among other things, harassing tactics by businesses to collect debts. For instance, collection agencies are prevented from calling a debtor in the middle of the night trying to collect a debt. If they do so in a repeated

and offensive manner, the debtor may have a cause of action for infliction of mental distress. The elements required for such an action to be successful are (1) outrageous and extreme conduct by the defendant, (2) which causes severe emotional and mental distress to the plaintiff, and (3) which is manifested by some form of physical injury to the plaintiff such as a heart attack, stroke, etc.

The courts are not inclined to find that obscene and abusive language, by itself, is sufficient for a cause of action for several reasons. First, freedom of speech is a highly protected interest. The courts will not tread on this interest lightly. Second, abusive and obscene language is a matter of definition and allowing suits on such a basis could give rise to trivial lawsuits. The citizen in today's society must be able to withstand a certain amount of insult, profanity, and discourtesy without legal redress. Since extreme and outrageous conduct is required for this tort, such conduct does not reach the level required for intentional infliction of mental distress.

Furthermore, the courts are hesitant to act in this area because mental suffering is not only difficult to measure, it also may be feigned in a fraudulent attempt to recover damages. The courts' skepticism is reflected in the requirement that the mental suffering must be severe. Hurt feelings are not sufficient. Various courts have awarded damages for infliction of fright, grief, shame, humiliation, embarrassment, anger, chagrin, and worry. Generally, the distress must be severe enough to manifest itself in some form of physical injury. However, an outward injury is not generally required. Tension headaches could suffice.

The Texas Supreme Court recently clarified the tort of Intentional Infliction of Emotional Distress by calling it a "gap filler" claim (p. 816) and cannot be used "to circumvent the limitations placed on the recovery of mental anguish damages under more established tort doctrines" (p. 180) (**Creditwatch, Inc. V. Jackson 157 S.W.3d 814 (Texas 2005)**). Furthermore, the Supreme Court of Texas has stated that the purpose of the tort of Intentional Infliction of Emotional Distress is "to supplement existing forms of recovery by providing a cause of action for egregious conduct that might otherwise go unremedied" and went on to say that "Where the gravamen of a plaintiff's complaint is really another tort, intentional infliction of emotional distress should not be available" (**Hoffman-La Roche Inc. v. Zeltwanger 144 S.W.3d 438 (Texas 2004)**). Therefore, it appears that the highest court in Texas is discouraging the use of this tort if it can be covered by another tort and that this is being followed by the lower appellate courts in Texas. In **Lewis Turner v. Linda Turner**, the court ruled that Lewis did not include evidence to sustain a claim of intentional infliction of emotional distress because he did not show any of the proof for that tort when showing the tort of assault and ruled that the trial court out of Montgomery County erred in awarding Lewis $50,000 for intentional infliction of emotional distress when another recognized tort, that is, assault existed (**Lewis Turner v. Linda Turner No. 09-06-570 CV ___ S.W.3d ___ (Tex. App. Beaumont 2008)**). Also note that the 14th Court of Appeal, upheld a lower-court verdict awarding Texas Children's Hospital and Baylor College of Medicine attorneys fees of $644,500.16 for Baylor and $766,000 for Texas Children's Hospital as sanctions against Dr. Nath because his claim for intentional infliction of emotional distress was in bad faith and harassing and lacked evidentiary support (**Rahul K. Nath, M.D. v. Texas Children's Hospital and Baylor College of Medicine 375 S.W.3d 403 (Tex. App. Houston [14th District] 2012)**). However, Texas does recognize the tort of Intentional Infliction of Emotional Distress, becoming the 47th state to do so in 1993 by action of the Texas Supreme Court in **Twyman v. Twyman 855 S.W.2d 619 (Texas 1993)**. However, it does appear that it is only recoverable in a very limited situation. One example where a Texas Court of Appeals did uphold a claim was in **Tidelands Automobile Club v. Walters 699 S.W.2d 939 (Tex. App. Beaumont 1985)**. In that case, Iva and Zibia Walters were members of the Tidelands Automobile Club and as part of that membership were to receive a life insurance policy through Legal Security Life Insurance Company. Mrs. Walters was killed in a one-vehicle accident and the life insurance company delayed paying claiming that alcohol was involved. Tidelands requested the autopsy report from a Justice of the Peace of Jefferson County, Harold P. Engstrom, who sent Tidelands a letter stating that the autopsy showed no alcohol use. Two months later, the daughter of the deceased contacted Tidelands asking why the policy had not been paid and received a letter, supposedly a copy of the Engstrom letter, saying that Mrs. Walters was intoxicated. The daughter took the letter to Judge Engstrom and compared the real letter to the copy of the letter she had received from Tidelands. Saying that his wife was intoxicated was taken by Mr. Walters as Intentional Infliction of Emotional Distress and he filed suit against Tidelands because someone had obviously altered the letter from Judge Engstrom. Of course, no one at Tidelands or the insurance company would confess to altering the letter and in fact, blamed each other both claiming they received the altered letter from the other. The jury awarded $10,000 actual damages for Intentional Infliction of Emotional Distress and $40,000 in punitive damages. The Court of Appeals upheld the verdict. Therefore, it is possible but not common to see a successful case on Intentional Infliction of Emotional Distress in Texas.

4. Invasion of Privacy

Generally, a person has the right to live his or her life privately without being subjected to unwarranted publicity. Note that unwarranted does not mean unwanted. However, the tort of invasion of privacy is when someone interferes with the right of someone else to be left alone unless there is a reasonable public interest. Texas lists the elements to the tort of Invasion of Privacy to be as follows:

1. The Defendant intentionally intruded on the plaintiff's solitude, seclusion, or private affairs, and
2. The intrusion would be highly offensive to a reasonable person.

Beaumont v. Basham 205 S.W.3d 609 (Tex. App. Waco 2006)

The tort of **invasion of privacy** usually occurs in one of four forms: (1) a person's name or likeness is used for business purposes without consent. The principal example is using a likeness or name for advertising purposes without consent. (2) There is an unreasonable intrusion upon an individual's physical solitude. Examples would include public disclosure of information obtained by illegal entry into one's home or an illegal wiretap. (3) Public disclosure about a person that is offensive and objectionable. For example, the publication of one's personal credit history would probably be actionable. (4) Publication of information that places an individual in a false light. For example, the publication that an individual possesses certain beliefs, when in fact, he or she does not. A necessary element for an action for the invasion of privacy is the public disclosure of a private fact. To be actionable, the disclosure must appear to be offensive to the "ordinary person of ordinary sensitivities." All that is required is that the fact be private and that the disclosure be objectionable even though the fact is truthful.

However, public figures such as actors and politicians relinquish the right to privacy to the extent that the public has a legitimate interest in their affairs, but public figures do retain their right to privacy to those matters that are not legitimate concerns of the public. For example, a few years ago when a very popular actor Brad Pitt was dating an equally popular starlet, they went on vacation together and in a very secluded, private area, evidently spent a large part of their vacation nude. A photographer took pictures of them in the nude through the windows of the condominium with the use of a very powerful telephoto lens. He then sold these pictures to a woman's magazine that specializes in male nudity. The young star found this to be an invasion of his privacy and sued the magazine. Even though he was a public figure the Court held that he did have a right of privacy that had been violated and forbade the magazine from selling any more issues with those pictures in the magazine. Of course, one must note that celebrities thrive on publicity and they themselves often stage publicity events.

However, just because you are a celebrity does not mean that your entire life is for public consumption. Take the example the case of **Galella v. Onassis 487 F.2d 986 (Court of App. [2nd Circuit] 1973)**, where Jacqueline Kennedy Onassis brought suit against a photographer, which we would call a member of the paparazzi today, because she felt that he was interfering with her life and the life of her children and even putting them in danger. (After all, think about what happened to Princess Diana.) The court established a three-prong test for celebrity right of privacy: (1) Was there a legitimate public interest being sought? (2) What about the right of the individual to be left alone? (3) What was the danger of continued surveillance without court intervention? The Court found for Mrs. Onassis and her children as to the details of the family's private life. However, few celebrities invoke this ruling due to the desire to have the publicity. After all, what would any of the Kardashians or Paris Hilton be without publicity?

These are the points to remember about invasion of privacy: (1) Unwarranted does not mean unwanted. For example, if a friend bets you that you cannot rollerblade nude around the outer perimeter of campus and you are stupid enough to take the bet. When you get caught by the campus police and arrested and have your name and picture in the nude printed in the school newspaper, there is no invasion of privacy. (2) If something is taken from public records, there is no invasion of privacy. So, when the school newspaper prints the arrest report of everyone arrested on campus and detained at the local jail for driving while intoxicated, there is no invasion of privacy since those records are available to the general public. (3) Public figures give up some, but not all of their rights of privacy.

5. *Defamation*

Defamation is generally defined as publication of a false statement that tends to injure a person's reputation or good name causing the public to hold that person up to hatred, contempt, or ridicule, or to cause him or her to be shunned or avoided. Defamation includes libel and slander. The difference between libel and slander has to do with the nature of the publication. **Libel** is defamation through some permanent form, in print or permanent recording (e.g., video tape). **Slander** is defamation through some transitory means such as unrecorded speech. The injury caused by defamation is the harm to a person's good name or reputation in the community. Examples of defamation would include statements that an individual had committed a crime, has a socially unacceptable disease, or has been cheating customers.

Keep in mind that for the tort of defamation to occur, the statement must be false. This does not mean that the person, in a normal situation, has to know that the statement was false. Ordinarily, simply making a statement that is false and that injures a person's reputation or good name is defamation. However, when the defamation is made about a public figure, the public figure must prove that the statement made was false *and* that the person making the statement knew it was false or should have known it was false. In short, the public figure has to prove that the statement was made with **malice**. This is a very high burden of proof and it is not easily attained. Therefore, scandal magazines flourish in spite of most of their stories being of a questionable nature because the stories are about public figures who either choose not to take action or who cannot meet the high burden of proof.

Also, to be defamation, the victim has to suffer harm, which means that someone else must hear the false statement. How could your reputation or good name be hurt if no one else hears or reads the statement? Therefore, the statement must be false and must be published or communicated to a third party for the victim to suffer a legal harm.

Truth and privilege are two defenses to defamation. If a statement is true, there has been no defamation. An action for invasion of privacy or intentional infliction of mental distress may exist based on publication of truths, but not an action for defamation. The defense of **privilege** is based upon the idea that the ability to publish some defamatory statements furthers certain social interests. Privileges may be conditional or absolute, which is sometimes called constitutional.

Absolute privilege applies in those situations where freedom of speech is required. It protects statements made in a civil or criminal action so long as the statements are relevant to an issue in the proceeding. Statements made by federal and state legislators and high-level public officials in performing their duties may also examples of absolute privilege but, these statements are sometimes referred to as **constitutional privileges**. Public policy dictates that such statements must be protected. However, this privilege is limited. In **Hutchinson v. Proxmire, 443 U.S. 111 (1979),** the Supreme Court determined that Senator Proxmire's famous "Golden Fleece Award" was not protected by the absolute privilege for legislators performing their duties when published in newsletters to constituents.

A **conditional** or **qualified privilege** is available when a defamatory statement is published in good faith and with proper motives. To avoid liability, a defendant would be required to show that the defamatory statement was published to protect some recognized interest and was published in good faith and without malice. "Recognized interests" include financial interests, membership in an organization, credit standing, and employment record.

Texas actually has codified Libel in the Texas Civil Practice and Remedies Code, Chapter 73 and lists the elements of Libel in Section 73.001 as:

A libel is a defamation expressed in written or other graphic form that tends to blacken the memory of the dead or that tends to injure a living person's reputation and thereby expose the person to public hatred, contempt or ridicule, or financial injury or to impeach any person's honesty, integrity, virtue, or reputation or to publish the natural defects of anyone and thereby expose the person to public hatred, ridicule, or financial injury.

It is interesting to note that Texas allows defamation for both dead and living people. In most common law jurisdictions, defamation does not apply to dead people due to the assumption that you cannot injure the dead. Texas also recognizes all of the common law defenses as well as statutory defenses to defamation and does add statutory defenses for newspapers and broadcasters.

6. Malicious Prosecution

Malicious prosecution is the wrong use of the legal proceedings, civil or criminal. This is a very difficult tort to win because you must first win the lawsuit or lawsuits against you. There can be no plea bargaining in a criminal case, there must be either a dismissal or a finding of not guilty. Likewise, in a civil case, you cannot settle the case. The opposing side must agree to dismiss the lawsuit or the judge or jury must enter a verdict for you after a trial.

Then in separate lawsuit, you have to prove by a preponderance of the evidence that the opposing party had no probable cause, no valid reason for the lawsuit. This means that you must show that the opposing party had no probable cause, but then, even though he knew he had no suit, brought the lawsuit anyway. It is difficult to prove that the opposing party acted in this type of a malicious manner and this step usually dooms malicious prosecution cases to failure. For instance, if you are arrested but you are innocent, then you would have to win the criminal case, and then prove that the government unit that brought the case against you had no probable cause and knowing that they had no probable cause, continued with the case. If the state had an eyewitness who identified you, the state has probable cause. Then, the only hope to win a malicious prosecution case would be to file a suit against the eyewitness and if they truly thought they were correct, you have little chance of winning because they thought they were correct. You would have to prove that the eyewitness lied and that they knew they were lying. This would be very difficult to do.

Texas does recognize the tort of malicious prosecution (**Texas Beef Cattle Co. v. Green 921 S.W.2d 203 (Texas 1996)**). Texas case law states that the elements to malicious prosecution are:

1. The institution or continuation of civil proceedings against the plaintiff
2. By or at the insistence of the defendant

3. With malice in the commencement of the proceeding
4. With lack of probable cause for the proceeding
5. Termination of the proceeding in the plaintiff's favor
6. Special damages or special injuries

Airgas-Southwest, Inc. v. IWS Gas and Supply of Texas, Ltd. 390 S.W.3d 472 (Tex. App. Houston [1st District] 2012)

If a plaintiff can prove the first five elements in Texas, it is often the requirement of special damages or special injuries that dooms a claim for malicious prosecution. Texas courts have long held that the special damages or special injury in a malicious prosecution claim must be interference with a person or his property in the form of an arrest, attachment, injunction, or sequestration (*Texas Beef Cattle* at 209). This is relatively unique to Texas. Texas adds this requirement to assure good-faith litigants access to the judicial system without fear of intimidation by a countersuit for malicious prosecution. The special damage requirement also prevents successful defendants in the initial proceeding from using their favorable judgment as a reason to institute a new suit based on malicious prosecution, resulting in needless and endless vexatious lawsuit. (*Texas Beef*, 921 S.W.2d at 209). Texas courts do not favor malicious prosecution cases because public policy favors the exposure of crimes without fear of the prosecutor being sued for malicious prosecution and allowing litigants in a civil case the right to have his or her issues settled in a court so proof in a malicious prosecution case in Texas must be to a higher degree than other lawsuits and said proof must be positive, clear, and satisfactory. (**Parker v. Dallas Hunting & Fishing Club 463 S.W.2d 496 (Civ. App. Dallas 1971)**).

Texas also recognizes a similar tort called abuse of process. This is where a party maliciously misuses or misapplies regularly issued civil or criminal process for a purpose and thereby obtains a result not lawfully warranted. The elements to this Texas tort are:

1. The defendant made an illegal, improper, or perverted use of the process, a use neither warranted nor authorized by the process
2. The defendant had an ulterior motive or purpose in exercising such illegal, perverted, or improper use of the process, and
3. Damage to the plaintiff as a result of such illegal act.

RRR Farms, Ltd. v. American Horse Protection Ass'n, Inc., 957 S.W.2d 121, 134 (Tex. App. Houston [14th District] 1997)

7. Fraudulent Misrepresentation (Fraud)
There are several elements to **fraudulent misrepresentation**, which you will also see called simply **fraud**. The elements to fraudulent misrepresentation are:

1. There must be misrepresentation of material facts (they are false).
2. The misrepresentation must be made knowing that it is false or with a reckless disregard for the truth.

3. There must be intent that the innocent party rely on the misrepresentation.
4. There must be justifiable reliance on the misrepresentations (the misrepresentations must be believable).
5. The innocent party must suffer damages.
6. There must be a causal connection between the misrepresentation and the damages suffered.

Ordinarily, when one thinks of this tort, you think of a "con man" at work. In a typical con, the con man sets up the innocent party with a series of lies, which the con man, of course, knows are untrue. The innocent party then relies on the lies and is taken in by the con man who then disappears with the innocent party's money before the innocent party discovers that he has been conned. (If you look closely you should be able to work through the elements of misrepresentation.)

Keep in mind that fraud is more than mere **puffery**, which is sometimes referred to as **seller's talk**. Puffery is usually an opinion and since fraudulent misrepresentation requires that the tortfeasor knows that the statement is untrue, this is not fraud. Most salesmen are well aware of the fine line between puffery and fraud and stay on the puffery side. However, in the case of an overzealous salesman who commits fraudulent misrepresentation, he can land his employer and/or himself into a fraudulent misrepresentation lawsuit.

Misrepresentations may occur through words, actions, or through concealment. Turning back the odometer on a car would be a misrepresentation through an action that would be concealed. Oral or written statements that an automobile had been trouble free for the past two years, when in fact it was constantly in need of repairs, would be a misrepresentation through words.

Sometimes, the failure to speak, silence, amounts to fraud. Some courts have found a duty to speak when one party to a transaction has knowledge of material facts of which the other does not, and the person with knowledge is aware that the other's decision would be affected if those facts were known. For example, Baker is the sole owner of the stock of a small corporation. The company is currently doing very well and as such, is very valuable. However, there is a potential lawsuit, which has not yet been filed, against the company that greatly reduces the expected value of the company. If Baker attempts to sell the company without disclosing the potential lawsuit, he is potentially liable in tort for fraud (among several other actions).

The element of falsity will obviously exist when a person makes a statement that he or she knows to be false. However, knowledge of falsity also exists when a person makes a statement without knowing whether it is true or false. Thus, when someone states, as fact, something that he or she does not know to be true, then he or she will have satisfied the requirement of recklessly making a false statement, if the statement turns out to be false.

Texas case law defines the elements of fraud as:

1. A material misrepresentation, falsehood, or untruth with the intent to deceive, was made
2. The representation was false

3. When the representation was made, the speaker knew it was false or made it recklessly without any knowledge of its truth
4. The speaker made the representation with the intent that it should be acted upon by the party
5. The party acted in reliance upon the representation, and
6. The party thereby suffered injury

In re D.E.H., 301 S.W.3d 825 (Tex. App. Fort Worth 2009)

Note that this is very similar to the normal common law elements listed above. Texas does not make the causal connection a separate element but does include the causal connection in the last element with the word "thereby." Texas also makes it clear that the statements must be false and that the speaker knew the statements were false or made the statement recklessly without any knowledge of its truth.

However, Texas has also statutorily defined civil fraud in special areas as:

Fraud in a transaction involving real estate or stock in a corporation or joint stock company consists of a:

1. False representation of a past or existing material fact, when the false representation is:
    a. Made to a person for the purpose of inducing that person to enter into a contract; and
    b. Relied on by that person in entering into that contract; or
2. False promise to do an act, when the false promise is:
    a. Material;
    b. Made with the intention of not fulfilling it;
    c. Made to a person for the purpose of inducing that person to enter into a contract; and
    d. Relied on by that person in entering into that contract

Texas Business and Commerce Code Section 27.01

C. Business Intentional Torts

1 Disparagement

An earlier section discussed defamation. **Disparagement** is a similar tort. The common law elements required to prove a case of product disparagement include:

1. The defendant published an untruth about the plaintif's property or products;
2. The defendant knew the statement was untrue;
3. The statement was made with malice with the intent to injure the plaintiff; and
4. Tht plaintiff suffered actual damages, (the loss of one customer or a general downturn in business after the statement was published).

Disparagement normally deals with property and can be found in two different types, **slander of title** and **slander of quality**. Slander of title is publishing false information about the legal ownership of property. Texas case law defines slander of title as defined as a false and malicious statement made in disparagement of a person's title to property, which causes him or her special damage. The elements in Texas are:

1. The uttering and publishing of the disparaging words
2. That they were false
3. That they were malicious
4. That the plaintiff sustained special damages thereby, and
5. That the plaintiff possessed an estate or interest in the property disparaged

Hill v. Heritage Resources, Inc., 964 S.W.2d 89, 110 (Tex. App. El Paso 1997)

An example of slander of title is when one used car dealer tells you that Old Joe of Old Joe's Used Cars can sell his cars at a reduced rate because they are stolen and the titles are all forgeries. Slander of quality is sometimes referred to as **trade libel** or in Texas it is called business disparagement. Slander of quality is publishing false information about the quality of the property of someone else, such as accusing another business of selling cheaper, inferior products from China when they are in reality selling the same products as the party that made the disparaging remark. Texas common law lists the elements of a business disparagement claim as:

1. The defendant published a false, defamatory statement of fact about the plaintiff
2. With malice
3. Without privilege
4. That resulted in special damages to the plaintiff

To prove special damages, the plaintiff must prove that the disparaging communication played a substantial part in inducing third parties not to deal with the plaintiff, resulting in a direct pecuniary loss that has been realized or liquidated, such as specific lost sales, loss of trade, or loss of other dealings (**Astoria Industries of Iowa, Inc. v. SNF, Inc., 223 S.W.3d 616, 628 (Tex. App. Fort Worth 2007)**).

Normally, both of these, slander of quality and slander of title, are said in an effort to get the innocent party not to purchase the products of a competitor, the victim of the disparagement.

2. False Advertising

The tort of **false advertising** is similar to product disparagement, but is different in that false statements are being made about the defendant's own products that give a false impression that the defendant's products are superior to plaintiffs. Section 43(a) of the **Lanham Act** establishes an action for damages for any false description or representation of one's goods or services, which may damage a competitor. Section 43(a) only applies to misrepresentations made about the defendant's own product, not the plaintiff's. False advertising will be discussed more fully in a later chapter.

3. *Intentional Interference with Contractual Relations*
a. *History*

A party to a contract, under some circumstances, can sue a third party for interfering with the performance of the contract. This tort was first established in an English common law case in the 1850s (**Lumley v. Gye, 119 Eng. Rep. 749 (Q.B.1853)**). In that case, the defendant had induced an opera singer to breach her contract, and thus, had intentionally interfered with the contract. Of course, a plaintiff would have a cause of action for breach of contract against the other party to the contract but the remedies available under the tort of intentional interference with contractual relations may offer some advantages. For example, damages for intentional torts often include punitive damages. Also, and occasionally more importantly, the tort allows for recovery from a party that may have more financial resources available to satisfy the damage award than does the contract breaching party.

The policy reason behind the tort of intentional interference with contracts is that contracts are voluntary transactions that reflect the agreement of the parties and that generally serve to move resources to their highest valued uses. Third-party interference with contracts that results in the breach of the contract would tend to diminish the value of contracts. If it is subsequently discovered that a more lucrative contract could have been formed with a third party, then it should be possible for the contracting parties, for a price, to relieve each other of their obligations under the contract so that resources can still flow to their highest valued uses.

b. *Elements of the Tort of Intentional Interference with Contractual Relations*

To establish that a tort of interference with a contract occurred, a plaintiff must show that (1) a valid contract with another party existed, (2) that the defendant knew about the contract, and (3) that the defendant interfered with the contract causing damage to the plaintiff. For example, Phyllis contracts to sell her car to Brenda for $1,000 with payment and delivery of the car to take place in 10 days. Before the car is delivered, Patsy, without knowledge of the contract, offers to buy the car for $1,200 and Phyllis accepts. Brenda does not have a cause of action against Patsy for interference with the contract; her only action is against Phyllis for breach of contract. Several areas of the tort of intentional interference with contractual relations are of special importance to the legal environment of business and thus deserve additional attention. The leading case in this area is a Texas case (**Texaco, Inc. v. Pennzoil, Co., 729 S.W.2d 768 (Tex. App. Houston [1st District] 1987)**) as we will see below.

c. *The Ten Billion Dollar Jury Award*

The largest award for damages ever granted by a jury was in an intentional interference with a contract case. Getty Oil Company agreed to a merger with Pennzoil. The deal was struck at a meeting of Getty's board of directors, at the conclusion of which parties from both sides shook hands, the classic signification of agreement. Gordon Getty, son of J. Paul Getty, even uncorked a bottle of champagne to celebrate the agreement with Pennzoil. However, the paperwork was not yet complete. Getty Oil announced the next morning that it had an "agreement in principle" to merge with Pennzoil and that the details of the merger would be worked out in a formal written agreement. No final writing of the terms of the agreement was ever executed, but as you have already learned, a contract does not need to be in writing to be enforceable.

Texaco's legal advisors were convinced that a contract between Getty and Pennzoil had not been consummated. Texaco proceeded to entice Getty Oil to hold off on the merger with Pennzoil and consider a merger with Texaco. At Texaco's request, Getty began stalling Pennzoil. Ultimately, Texaco convinced Getty Oil to merge with it rather than Pennzoil. As part of the agreement, Texaco agreed to indemnify Getty for any damages that Pennzoil might win in subsequent litigation. (Sounds like Getty knew there was a contract!)

During the trial of the case, Texaco did not present any evidence on the issue of damages. Apparently, they were overconfident of the outcome on the liability issue. Once the jury determined there was a contract, they only had evidence of damages that had been presented by Pennzoil. Punitive damages were awarded because this was a tort, not a contract, action. The jury awarded the full $7.53 billion in actual damages that Pennzoil had claimed with an additional $3 billion in punitive damages for an award in excess of $10 billion, all because of oral interference with a contract.

The case went from the Texas District Court through the Texas Court of Appeals and tried to go to the Texas Supreme Court without any of the Texas appeals courts finding any error. Even though the case was considered by the U.S. Supreme Court, there still was no error found and the verdict against Texaco was upheld. Texaco filed for bankruptcy protection and the case was eventually settled for $3 billion (**Texaco, Inc. v. Pennzoil, Co., 729 S.W.2d 768 (Tex. App. Houston [1st District] 1987)**).

d. Interfering with Employment

An employer–employee relationship is a contractual one and bears special mention. Well-trained and experienced employees are valuable assets to any business firm. It takes time and money to train employees properly. If such an employee is induced to quit and go to work for a competitor, the competitor gains a substantial advantage. The gain to a competitor is obvious, because a valuable employee that does not need much training is obtained, customers of the former employer may switch to the new employer, and the new employer may be able to learn the trade secrets and business operations of the former employer. Accordingly, an employment contract is a valuable property right that will be protected from third-party interference.

A key characteristic of the country's labor force is mobility. The question, then, is under what circumstances will a competitor be liable in tort for interference with an employment contract? A necessary condition is that there must be a contract for a specified period. If an employee is dischargeable at will, no tort will result if he or she quits taking another job. However, if a business entices employees from a competitor in order to injure the former employer, then an action in tort is possible even if the employment contracts were terminable at will.

Of course, the existence of a written contract would help define the conditions of employment. However, as we will see in a later chapter, Texas is an employment-at-will state and the employee often does not have a written contract or if they do it is very vague. Therefore, you may be dealing with an implied contract or no contract at all.

4. Interference with Prospective Economic Advantage

Some courts have expanded the tort of intentional interference with contracts to include interference with prospective economic advantages. This is broader because an agreement of the parties in the form of a contract is not required. This action could arise if a third party steals a competitor's customers during negotiations, but before a contract is made. However, the tortfeasor must intentionally interfere with someone else's business in an unreasonable and improper manner. This can include predatory behavior of unreasonably stealing a competitor's business. For instance, advertising is a permissible action as long as the advertising is truthful and fair. However, if a business paid someone to stand outside of its competitor's entrance and convince shoppers to go to your store by offering unreasonable incentives, a court could find you liable for interference with a prospective business advantage.

Likewise, if you went into business solely to drive a competitor out of business, then once the competitor was out of business you would have a monopoly and could control the market. As we will see later, this could also get you into antitrust problems. However, it is not predatory behavior if a large chain store comes into a town and just because it charges lower prices, drives the competition out of business. However, if the large chain store then raised its prices, it would have some explaining to do.

Texas does not recognize this tort.

D. Property Intentional Torts

1. Basic Property Law

Private property is a fundamental attribute of the free market economy. Various aspects of property law are discussed later, but it is important to realize that tort law protects many private property rights. Basically, tort law provides a set of **liability rules** intended to deter infringement upon private property rights by making the infringer pay. This is in contrast to property law, which provides a set of **property rules** involving an outright prohibition against interference with property rights. In this subsection, several tort actions that may be initiated when an individual or a business intentionally infringes upon the property rights of another are introduced.

However, to understand this more fully, some basic property law must be discussed. **Real property** is land or anything permanently attached to the land. On the other hand, **personal property** is anything else, such as your clothes, vehicle, money, etc. Personal property can include **tangible property**, which is property that you can touch, and **intan-**

gible property, which is property that you cannot touch such as stocks. While it is true that you can touch the stock certificate, you cannot touch the ownership interest in the corporation that the stock certificate represents.

2. *Trespass to Real Property/Trespass to Land/Trespass*

Trespass to land is any unauthorized physical intrusion or entry upon land where someone else has a superior right to the property. Note that someone with a superior right can be a non-owner such as the tenant under a lease agreement. The one in possession of the property simply has to have a superior right to the trespasser. This tort is often referred to as either **trespass to real property** or trespass to land or simply as **trespass**.

The elements can be broken down into the following:

1. A person
2. Who does not have permission to go on the land
3. Enters the land
   a. Onto
   b. Above
   c. Below the surface of the land, or
4. Causes anything to go onto, over, or under the land, or
5. Remains on the land after being told to leave

Therefore, trespass is when a person goes onto, under, or over the property of someone who has a superior right to that real property or causes anything under their control to go onto, under, or over the property of someone who has a superior right to the property. It can also be when the person was initially invited onto the property but was asked to leave and refused to leave. Intent is irrelevant to whether the trespass to land is actionable. Any unauthorized entry below, on, across, or above the land even in the absence of actual physical damage or physical contact is an actionable trespass to land. Thus, firing a bullet across a piece of property is actionable even if you thought you could fire the bullet across the property. An exception to this rule is that the flight of aircraft above the land is permissible so long as it is at a reasonable altitude and does not interfere with the proper use of the land. Also, note that the plaintiff does not have to show any harm. Harm is not a required element of trespass because the harm is inferred.

However, the owner or the person with the superior right to possession must implicitly or expressly establish that the trespasser cannot go onto the property. Express notice, actual notice is given in several ways such as telling a guest to leave and they refuse, post "No Trespassing" signs, or paint the outside perimeter of your property with a purplish, lavender paint, which was picked because even color-blind people can see it. The law is found in the Texas Penal Code Section 30.05 and the markings must be vertical, at least eight inches long and one inch wide and three to five feet above the ground. The makings have to be every 100 feet in timberland and 1,000 feet in open range and all makings must be in a place visible by those approaching the property. This section also makes trespassing a Class B misdemeanor unless the intruder is carrying a firearm, which is a Class A misdemeanor. Of course, there is also the common law civil trespass as well. Implicit is when it is obvious such as a closed door or locked window.

Generally speaking, the majority common law rule is that the property owner does not have any responsibility to a trespasser for damages the trespasser incurs while he or she is injured on your property. However, some states are determining that you even owe a trespasser the duty of reasonable care. Therefore, if you know of a danger, those states require you to warn the trespasser and take steps to see that the trespasser is not injured by a known hazard. If you do not do so, you will be liable to the trespasser. However, this is only the rule of law in a minority of states. On the other hand, it is almost a universal rule that if you have something on your property that you know attracts trespassers, then you must take whatever reasonable steps are necessary to protect the trespasser. This is called the **attractive nuisance doctrine** and applies to things like swimming pools and old abandoned refrigerators, which we saw is also the subject of consumer law when we discussed the CPSC.

If you discover a trespasser on your property, you have a right to use reasonable force to remove the trespasser. If you know that a trespasser is on your property and you do nothing, this may be inferred by the trespasser and ultimately by the courts, as implied permission. Therefore, any future such intrusions would not be recognized as a trespass.

It is a defense to a case of trespass that the trespasser went onto the property of another to protect the property or protect someone, even if that protected person is a trespasser, who is in danger. However, it is not a defense just because you thought that you had the right to be on the property. Likewise, it is not a defense if you go on the property of someone else and actually improve the property.

3. Trespass to Personal Property

Trespass to personal property is a wrongful invasion of ownership rights in property other than land. It is also sometimes referred to as **trespass to chattel**. The important element of this tort is interference by an individual or business with the property owner's right to exclusive use and possession of personal property. Trespass to personal property involves intentional meddling. In general, liability for damages on the theory of trespass to personal property is imposed in situations where the trespasser takes the property of another, slightly damages the property, or somehow deprives the owner of the use of the property. An example of a trespass to personal property is when one university takes the other universities' mascot before a game and then returns the mascot after the game. When the damage is intentional, the remedy is pecuniary damages to cover the actual damages and may also include punitive damages. In contrast to trespass to land, good faith is a defense to trespass to personal property such as when your neighbor's dog bites you and you take the dog and quarantine it to see if it has rabies. There is also a common law remedy called an artisan's lien which we will see in a later chapter. However, an artisan's lien allows a repairman to maintain possession of property of another until the owner pays for the repairs.

4. Conversion

The tort of conversion is similar to trespass to personal property. However, **conversion** occurs when personal property is taken by the wrongdoer and kept from its true owner or prior possessor. Conversion differs from trespass to personal property in that conversion represents the permanent disenfranchising of the owner from his or her personal property. Conversion is the civil side of crimes related to stealing. An example of a conversion is taking a new car for a test ride and never returning it to the automobile dealer's showroom. The civil remedy is to force payment for the car. It is also possible to have an equitable remedy such as a court order making the tortfeasor return the property. Acting in good faith or being mistaken about the ownership rights of the property does not constitute a defense to conversion. For example, the innocent buyer of stolen goods is liable for damages for converting them or may be forced to return the goods by equitable measures with a court order to return the goods. However, there are defenses to conversion such as the rabid dog example above. If you fail to return the dog that does have rabies, a conversion will have occurred but it is justified due to necessity. Another defense can be if the purported owner of the property does not in fact have title to the property such as when Mary accuses Joan of conversion of a ring when the ring is really owned by John.

5. Trespass to Personal Property or Conversion?

Obviously, somewhere along the way trespass to personal property becomes conversion. It is important to differentiate between the two due to the disparity of possible damages. Therefore, to try to differentiate between trespass to personal property and conversion, consider these questions:

1. What was the extent of dominion or control over the property?
2. How long did the interference with the property last?
3. What was the damage to the property?
4. What was the inconvenience or expense to the owner of the property?

The greater your answer to these questions is, the more likely you are dealing with conversion.

6. Nuisance

Individuals and businesses often engage in activities that affect either positively or negatively other individuals and businesses. Such third-party effects are referred to as **externalities**. In general, the law is not concerned with externalities that have a positive impact on third parties. Negative externalities, such as excessive noise especially, late at night, pollution, or emissions of noxious odors, are the subject of the common law tort of nuisance.

Any conduct that unreasonably and non-contractually interferes with the enjoyment or use of land is called a **nuisance**. The common law of torts recognizes two kinds of nuisance: private and public. A **private nuisance** is a nuisance that affects only one or a few people. A **public nuisance** is a nuisance that affects the community or the public at large.

All negative externalities are not considered nuisances. In determining whether an externality is to be considered a private nuisance, the courts will attempt to determine whether the interference with others is sufficiently great to be condemned as unreasonable. Some cases are easy to decide. For example, if a plant emits fumes that take the paint off the adjoining landowner's automobile, then a private nuisance will be found. The proper remedies for a private nuisance are damages and/or an injunction.

Many conflicts associated with private nuisances can be resolved through contractual negotiation between the parties. Of course, the adjoining homeowners have the right to have the paint stay on their automobile but the owners of the adjoining plant want to emit fumes that will continue to take the paint off the cars. Further, assume that all parties agree that the emission constitutes a nuisance and that an injunction could be ordered. That is, there is no disagreement about the relevant legal rights. If the number of landowners is small, which it is by definition a private nuisance, then it is conceivable that the owners of the plant will negotiate to purchase the right to emit the fumes from the homeowners. What must be considered is, the total amount that the plant would be willing to pay for that right determined by a number of factors, including the cost of abating the nuisance through some type of filtering, emissions control process, or the cost of shutting down the plant. The amount it would take to induce the homeowners to give up the right to keep the plant from ruining the paint on their automobiles is something totally subjective and must be determined by the individuals in the negotiations,

As was stated earlier, there are two different types of nuisance tort. The main difference between the two is the number of people affected by the nuisance. If it is a small number of people, then the nuisance is considered to be a private nuisance. If it affects the public as a whole then it will be considered a public nuisance. Texas also makes a difference between a temporary nuisance and a permanent nuisance. A temporary nuisance in normally reoccurring and thus the statue of limitations accrues anew upon each injury and can thus be ongoing and it then becomes subject to the Statute of Limitations, a time period in which the lawsuit must begin, which in Texas, in torts, is normally two years each time an injury occurs. However, if the nuisance is permanent the statute of limitations begins when the nuisance is discovered. This was the issue in **Schneider Nat. Carriers, Inc. v. Bates, 147 S.W.3d 264 (Texas 2004)**. In this case, Bates and 78 other people who lived close to the Houston Ship Channel brought suit for nuisance against Schneider National Carriers, Inc and others claiming that the plants which operated a trucking firm, a painting and sand-blasting firm, and firms that manufacture bleach, wood preservatives, polyesters, and other chemical products emitted air contaminants, noxious fumes, etc. The issue was, whether this was a temporary nuisance or a permanent nuisance. This case defined nuisance as "a condition that substantially interferes with the use and enjoyment of land by causing unreasonable discomfort or annoyance to persons of ordinary sensibilities" (*Schneider*, p. 269). The Texas Supreme Court recognized that the distinction between the two is an ongoing problem and a difficult issue to decide. However, the Court defined a permanent nuisance as one that involves "an activity of such a character and existing under such circumstances that it will be presumed to continue indefinitely." Therefore, a nuisance is permanent if it is "constant and continuous" and if "injury constantly and regularly recurs." On the other hand, a nuisance is temporary if it is of limited duration. Thus, a nuisance may be considered temporary if it is uncertain if any future injury will occur, or if future injury "is liable to occur only at long intervals." A nuisance is also temporary if it is "occasional, intermittent, or recurrent" or "sporadic and contingent upon some irregular force such as rain" (*Schneider*, p. 272) The Supreme Court held the problem to be ongoing and thus temporary and thus the statute of limitations had not run.

Another problem in the nuisance area that is very common is when a city declares a piece of property to be a public nuisance and then demolishes the property often sending the bill for the demolition of the owner's property to the owner. This public nuisance problem was seen in **City of Dallas v. Stewart, 361 S.W.3d 562 (Texas 2012)**. While the Texas Supreme Court recognized the right of cities to stop urban blight, deter crime and disease, and take the ultimate action of destroying property, it also recognized that the property owner has constitutional property rights and that the city must follow the Constitution prior to the destruction of the property. The City of Dallas had delegated that duty to an administrative board whose decisions were essentially conclusive and did not follow constitutional requirements. Therefore, the Supreme Court of Texas ruled that the City of Dallas had to reimburse Ms. Stewart for the destruction of her house. This was a 5-4 decision and has opened a whole new area of concern for Texas cities, many of which used the same type of system with an unelected administrative board having the final decision which means this could open the door for more lawsuits of this type.

III. INFRINGEMENT OF INTELLECTUAL PROPERTY

A. Introduction

Intellectual property is property created from the ideas or thought process of the creator. **Infringement** is when someone other than the owner uses those ideas without the owner's permission. There are several types of intellectual property, including copyrights, patents, trademarks and service marks, trade names, and trade secrets. Each of these will be discussed in the following sections.

Intellectual property is one of the most active areas of current law. There are many issues in intellectual property such as ownership rights, international rights, how to protect intellectual property on the internet and of course, infringement of intellectual property rights both in the conventional sense and with the use of electronic media. Infringement is the wrongful taking or use of intellectual property without permission or compensation to the rightful owner. Protection of intellectual property is a constitutional right because it is recognized in Article 1, Section 8 of the United States Constitution where the United States Congress is given the responsibility:

> To promote the Progress of Science and useful Arts, by securing for limited Times to Authors and Inventors the exclusive Right to their respective Writings and Discoveries

This, of course, includes the intellectual property rights in copyrights and patents. Therefore, the National Government is heavily involved in the regulation and protection of intellectual property. However, there are also areas of intellectual property in which we also see State involvement.

B. Copyright

Congress started enforcing their obligation on copyright protection with the Copyright Act of 1790 and has continued to exclusively do so with numerous amendments up until the present time. Copyright law is exclusively national or federal law; there is no state copyright law. A copyright is a form of protection for original works of authorship fixed in a tangible medium or that can be reduced to a tangible medium of expression and includes both published and unpublished works. A copyright gives the author the immediate, exclusive right to reproduce the copyrighted work; to create derivative works based on it, to distribute copies, to perform the work, or to display it in public. Any violation of this right gives the author a claim of copyright infringement. Of course, an author can sell the copyright to someone or something else such as a publisher. If a work was for hire, then the copyright belongs to the person or entity that hired or commissioned the work to be done. Work for hire includes a work prepared by an employee in the scope of his or her employment; the copyright belongs to the employer. A work for hire can also be designated by written contract.

Copyright law covers creative works including literary works, whether those works be fiction, non-fiction, prose, or poetry; musical works and lyrics; dramatic works and the accompanying music; choreographic works; photographs; paintings; sculpture; computer software; maps; architectural designs; recordings; motion pictures; and radio or television, whether it is dramatic, comedy, documentary productions, or reporting of the news. However, the actual news events, historical information, scientific information, ideas, processes, inventions, compilations of factual information, or trademarks can be copyrighted. Of course, several of these matters can be the subject of other intellectual property such as patents (ideas, processes, and inventions) or trademarks.

Obtaining a copyright is not a difficult situation. In fact, it is automatic for works created after January 1, 1978. All the author of the work has to do is claim the copyright by putting the work into a tangible medium and can, but is not required to, then designate the copyright such as "copyrighted 2013 by 'author' " or putting a "c" with a circle around it, the date and author. While giving notice is no longer required, it is still beneficial. The notice still, well, gives notice of the ownership, shows the year it was created, and makes proving an infringement easier because no weight will be given to a claim of innocence because how could you be innocent if you had notice. If you chose to give notice of copyright it must be done in a reasonable manner. However, even if you do not go to the trouble of doing this, the author still has the copyright as per the Copyright Act of 1976 as amended since copyright is automatic.

In any event it is better to register the copyright as set out in the Copyright Act. Registration is also simple; the author simply obtains the forms from the United States Copyright Office, Library of Congress, Washington D.C. 20559. The form that is required depends on the type of medium that is being copyrighted, for instance, magazines compared to sound recordings. The author simply specifies the type of medium to be copyrighted and the Copyright Office will send him or her the free packet. Once the packet is received, the author simply fills out the forms, pays the fees, and sends in the required number of copies of the work that is required. This can now be done online as well. Online registration is generally quicker, cheaper, can be tracked online, has faster processing times, has online payment facility, and the author can receive an email that the Copyright Office received the registration packet.

There are several advantages to registering the copyright rather than just claiming it. Once registered, the author can file suit against infringers. However, you cannot sue for infringement unless the copyright is registered. Registration also makes a public record of the copyright claim. If it has been registered for five years, the registration serves as *prima facie* evidence in any claim for copyright ownership. Registration can also have an impact on the damages you receive in a successful infringement case. It can also give you international protection if you take some additional steps past registration. To totally protect his or her rights, the author should register the copyright 90 days in advance of any type of publication but registration can be done after publication as well. If the registration is done 90 days prior to the publication or before the alleged infringement it will have an effect on the damages one can receive.

The remedies that are available to be used against the infringers include injunctions, impounding all of the pirated copies of the work, and disposition of the pirated works, damages and profits, costs, and attorney fees. If the work is not registered, the author forfeits the statutory damages and the attorney fees. These two remedies usually result in the highest monetary damages. For instance, in **Fogerty v. Fantasy, 510 U.S. 517 (1994)**, Fantasy filed suit against Fogerty for singing some of the songs that he had previously sung and which they claimed to own the copyright. Fantasy lost and was required to pay Fogerty $1,300,000 in attorney fees. Statutory damages are set by the Copyright Act in the normal range of $750 to $30,000 for each infringement, but this can be extended to a range of $300 for innocent infringements up to as high as $150,000 for flagrant, intentional infringements. Actual damages are limited to what the author can prove that they actually lost and the infringer's gross profit unless the infringer can prove his or her expense, in which case the expenses are deducted from the gross profit. The author who has a registered trademark can get either actual or statutory damages, they cannot get both. However, they are entitled to a jury to determine either the actual or statutory damages. Of course, given the choice, most copyright owners chose the statutory damages.

To prove an infringement, the copyright owner must prove that the alleged infringer had some access to the copyrighted work, that there is a substantial similarity between the copyrighted work and the pirated work and that the copyright owner has a valid copyright. To prove substantial similarity, the copyright owner normally utilizes expert witnesses to prove the similarity in the general ideas underlying the two works and in the copyrightable aspects of the expression of those ideas. The copyright owner must also show that the average person would see the new work as substantially similar to the original work. Of course, the author also has to prove that the infringer had access to the original work. This sounds simple but it is not always so simple to prove.

The duration of a copyright was extended when Congress passed the **Sonny Bono Copyright Term Extension Act in 1998**. The basic time period of an individual copyright owner is now the author's lifetime plus 70 years and for a publisher 95 years after the date of the publication or 120 years after the date of the creation of the work. With the publisher, it is the lesser of the two time periods. The Sonny Bono Copyright Term Extension Act basically extended the term limits of a copyright issued on or after January 1, 1978, by 20 years. The law does not restore any copyright rights to copyrights that had expired and are now in the public domain. The Disney Corporation was a big supporter of the Copyright Term Extension Act. So, now that the 20-year extension is almost over; that is, it will end in 2018, will there be more calls for extension? The constitutionality of the Sonny Bono Copyright Term Extension Act (CTEA) was challenged as being unconstitutionally broad but was upheld when the Court ruled: In placing existing and future copyrights in parity in the CTEA, Congress acted within its authority and did not transgress constitutional limitations (**Eldred v. Ashcroft 537 U.S. 186 (2003)**). So it appears that Congress can keep extended copyright protection whenever it needs to extend copyright protection. Keep in mind the 20-year extension will be up in 2018, so are more extensions coming? Will Disney once again push to save Mickey Mouse and Donald Duck?

Copyright owners have the exclusive right to reproduce their work, change their work, perform or not perform their work, or basically do anything that they want to do with the work. However, there are exceptions. One exception is called **compulsory licensing** and has to do with owners of sound recordings who under certain conditions must grant anyone permission to record their music once it has been distributed to the public. However, the subsequent performances must be done in essentially the same manner as it was written and the copyright owners are entitled to royalties as specified in the Copyright Act for these subsequent uses of their works. This prevents the copyright owners from choosing only one artist to perform their song. Compulsory licensing began with the 1909 Copyright Act and originally applied to a mechanical reproduction (known today as a **phonorecord**) of a musical composition. Originally, it came in to existence due to player pianos. The Copyright Act of 1976 was in part passed to clarify some of the problems that had developed in the compulsory licensing area over the previous years. It is now clear that a license is only available to someone whose primary intent is to distribute phonorecords to the public for private, not commercial use, the licensee cannot duplicate a sound recording embodying the musical work without the authorization of the copyright owner, there are limitations on the rearrangement of the copyrighted work and cannot change the basic melody or fundamental character of the work, the licensee must still serve the copyright owner of a notice to use the work before or within 30 days of using the work and the copyright owner is entitle to receive copyright royalties fees only if the work is registered and the compulsory license can be canceled if the licensee does not pay the royalties on a monthly basis. This area was further covered by the **Digital Performance Right in Sound Recordings Act of 1995**, which expanded compulsory licensing into the making and distribution of a digital phonorecord and changed the terminology to **digital phonorecord delivery (DPD)** and defined it as:

each individual delivery of a phonorecord by digital transmission of a sound recording which results in a specifically identifiable reproduction by or for any transmission recipient of a phonorecord of that sound recording, regardless of whether the digital transmission is also a public performance of the sound recording or any nondramatic musical work embodied therein. A digital phonorecord delivery does not result from a real-time, nonintegrated subscription transmission of a sound recording where no reproduction of the sound recording or the musical work embodied therein is made from the inception of the transmission through to its receipt by the transmission recipient in order to make the sound recording audible. (**17 U.S.C. Section 115(d)**)

Compulsory licensing and the resulting payment of royalties can get extremely complicated. Just determining royalties without the compulsory licensing can get very complicated. Simply put, several music-licensing organizations have been established to represent the composers, music lyricists, and music publishers. The two main music-licensing organizations are the American Society of Composers, Authors and Publishers (ASCAP), and Broadcast Music, Inc. (BMI). Keep in mind that these royalties go to the owners of the copyrights and not to the performers.

The major exception to the copyright rules set out by the Copyright Act is the **fair use doctrine**. This exception allows someone to use the copyright of someone else without permission when appropriate, depending on the following:

1. The purpose and character of the use being for a fair, appropriate purpose such as for a non-profit educational purpose
2. The nature of the copyrighted work
3. The percentage of the total work that is used
4. The effect the use will have on the value or profit-making potential of the original work

This four-prong test of the fair use doctrine is very vague and usually needs court intervention to actually determine its meaning. Therefore, litigation is often required in fair use cases. One of the main benefactors of the fair use doctrine is an educator but even this use is not without its limits. Basically, if the copying is spontaneous for class use and the number of copies is small, it is probably a protected use under the fair use doctrine. While there are other exceptions to copyright rules such as public's right to know where there is a legitimate public interest in the activities of celebrities, the major exception is the often-litigated fair use doctrine.

Furthermore, the Internet has created a lot of uncertainty in the copyright area. It is clear that a copyright is still a copyright whether it is on the Internet or in any other medium. Just because it is posted on the Internet does not mean that it has become part of the **public domain** and thereby belongs to everyone so anyone is free to use it. The copyright owner can still retain the copyright and grant others a license to use it even on the Internet. However, it is very difficult to enforce many aspects of copyright law on the Internet under today's laws. However, the laws are adapting and the technology to catch infringers on the Internet is getting better.

Another major problem in the area of copyright law is how to deal with international copyrights. As recently as the late 1800s, the United States was the world's leading infringer of other countries' copyrights and in such capacity did not join in with the world when most of the nations of the world signed an international treaty called the Berne Convention to protect the integrity of copyrights. Instead, the United States relied on reciprocal copyright agreements with other countries to protect American copyrights. By the time the United States signed the Berne Convention in 1989, it only added 24 countries that the United States did not already have reciprocal agreements in place with prior to signing the Berne Convention. However, not all countries of the world belong to the Berne Convention nor have reciprocal agreements with the United States on copyright infringement. Therefore, if one of those countries decides to infringe on U.S. copyrights, there is very little that the copyright owner can do to enforce their rights. This is a major trade problem with certain countries of the world and will be discussed in more depth in the chapters on international law.

C. Patents

Another area of exclusive national or federal law as found in the Constitution is the area of patents. The first Patent Act was passed by Congress in 1790. Congress more recently enacted the Federal Patent Statue of 1952 to overhaul patent law and to further the incentive to inventors to make their inventions public and to protect the patent holder from infringement. Furthermore, in 1982, the United States Court of Appeals for the Federal Circuit in Washington D.C. was created to hear patent appeals to try to make patent law more uniform throughout the country. The next change in patent law came in 1999 with the American Inventors Protection Act of 1999 (AIPA) to further revise patent law.

A **patent** is a grant from the federal government that gives the applicant the exclusive right to make, use, sell, or allow others to use an invention for 20 years from the date of the filing of the application for the patent. According to the statute, any person who invents or discovers any new and useful process, machine, manufacture, or composition of matter, or any new and useful improvement thereof, may obtain a patent. Each of the terms is further defined by the statute as follows:

> Process—a process, act or method, and primarily includes industrial or technical processes
> Manufacture—articles that are made, and includes all manufactured articles
> Composition of matter—relates to chemical compositions and may include mixtures of ingredients as well as new chemical compounds

The statute felt that machine did not need to be defined. If you think about it, these classes include practically everything that is made by humans and processes for making products, which is what is able to be patented. Patents do not cover mere ideas or suggestions. It also must be useful and new which excludes inventions known or used by others, or that are already patented either in the United States or a foreign country by someone else. One of the problems the patent office faces is determining what is "new." It is obvious that it must be substantially different to be considered "new," but how much different is often an issue.

A patent, unlike a copyright is not automatic. The applicant must be the inventor or his or her agent and must apply for the patent with the United States Patent and Trademark Office (USPTO). The USPTO was created in 1802 and applicants must prove to them that the applicant is in fact the original creator of the invention, discovery, process, or design and as stated above, that it is "new." There are about 6,500 employees of the USPTO and they receive almost half a million patent applications per year. Like copyright, the application for patents can be filed electronically via a system called EFS-Web and in 2011 about 93 percent of the applications were filed electronically probably because it is much cheaper to file for a patent electronically and it is expected that more and more applications will be done electronically due to what amounts to a penalty if the application is not made electronically.

The application process, unlike in copyrights, is expensive, time consuming, and very technical. For instance, you should be a registered e Filer to file a patent application due to the need to follow up on the filing and unregistered eFilers are not permitted to file follow-on correspondence with the EFS–Web. In short, you should not try to apply for a patent on your own for this reason but also because it is highly technical and you need to have someone who has the knowledge of patent law and the rules of the USPTO. You should go to a patent expert or patent attorney and of course, this can be expensive.

Obviously, the applicant must prove that the invention is genuine, novel, useful, and not obvious in light of current technology or as stated above "new." Application for patents can be non-provisional or provisional. A non-provisional application for a patent must include a written document which comprises a description and claims; drawings are sometimes required but not always; an oath or declaration, and filing, search, and examination fees. Description and claims are extensive and must be done according to and in the order specified by statute. Again, this is very complicated and tedious as are the rules for a drawing if required. The oath or declaration required in a non-provisional filing is an oath or declaration by the inventor that he or she is the inventor as well as other statements required by the USPTO and must be signed by the inventor or by his or her agent using their full name and the citizenship of each inventor. Forms for the required declarations are available at the USPTO. Fees change every October, but the fee schedule is posted on the USPTO website. Furthermore, all applications must be in English and if filed electronically even the processing program is specified, and must be either Microsoft® Word or Corel® WordPerfect and converted to PDF format. Any drawings or hand-signed declarations need to be scanned as a PDF file for filing on EFS-Web. Now, it should be obvious why you need to hire a professional to assist you in the patent application process!

A provisional application came into existence in 1995 and gives inventors the option of a lower cost first patent filing in the United States and to give U.S. applicants parity with foreign applicants. With provisional filing, you do not have to file claims and oath or declaration. It does allow the inventor to use the term "patent pending." However, a provisional application is not examined on the merits and will be considered abandoned if a non-provisional application is not made within one year of the filing of the provisional application. This 12-month pendency for a provisional application is not counted toward the 20-year term if a non-provisional patent is granted.

The patent office examiner then will research the invention to see if something similar has previously been patented. Once the patent office has completed its investigation, it will either grant the patent or reject it. The applicant will be notified in writing of the examiner's decision. If it is rejected, the notice will list the reasons for the adverse action. If the patent is rejected, the applicant must request reconsideration in writing and specify in detail responding to every ground of objection and rejection in the rejection notice and the reasons the applicant feels he or she should be allowed the patent by amending his or her application. Once the application is finally rejected, the applicant can appeal to the Board of Patent Appeals and Interferences in the United States Patent and Trademark Office. If the appeal is denied at this stage, the applicant can appeal to the Court of Appeals for the Federal Circuit or a civil action may be filed against the Director in the United States District Court for the District of Columbia. While the patent is pending, the applicant normally attaches the words "patent pending" to the article. Once the patent is granted, the owner of the patent must gives notice of the patent by placing on it the word "patent" plus the patent number of the patented item. From time to time you will see the terms "patent applied for" or "patent pending." Legally, these phrases have no effect and only give information that an application was filed with the USPTO. Patent protection does not begin until the actual grant of the patent and is normally of 20 years duration.

As stated, appropriate subject matter of patents include the creation or invention of machines, both new and improvements to existing machines; processes; designs used in manufacturing; and more recently, asexually reproduced plants and living materials that were "created" by humans. Furthermore, the patent must be applied for before the invention becomes part of the public domain. If the public has used the invention for more than one year prior to the filing of the patent application, the invention becomes public domain and once it becomes public domain it cannot be patented. Therefore, it is better to patent the invention before it is ever used by the public.

Once granted, the owner of the patent holds the exclusive right to use the patent. If someone or some business uses, makes or copies, offers to sell, or does sell any patented invention without the owner's permission in the United States or the U.S. territories, patent infringement has occurred. All patent infringement cases are private since the government does not enforce patents and the holder of the patent can sue in the appropriate federal court. Therefore, when the patent holder files suit in federal courts for the patent infringement, the successful patent holder can recover monetary damages equal to the royalties that they should have been paid by the infringer, any other damages caused by the infringement, an order for the infringer to destroy any infringing articles, and an injunction to prevent future infringement. If proven that the infringer acted intentionally, the courts have the discretion to award treble damages and interest. Any appeal from the Federal District Court goes to the Court of Appeals for the Federal Court.

Of course, the patent owner must also be prepared to defend their right to the patent from any challenges from others claiming that they do not have the right to have been granted the patent. Under the Declaratory Judgment Act, an alleged patent infringer may claim in court either as a defense or in an original case that the patent is invalid. There are at least 21 recognized defenses to patent infringement such as, expiry of the patent, misuse of the patent, fraud, abandonment, antitrust violation (see in a later chapter), etc. When such a challenge is made, the court has the right to review the entire application process for errors. Such a move often encourages settlement by the patent holder to avoid the chance of losing the patent if the review process might turn up to be an error. Also, patent infringement is a very costly lawsuit and so, often the owner of a patent will approach the infringer and offer to sell the infringer a license to use the patent. Due to the cost of patent infringement enforcement, some owners of patents cannot afford to defend their patent. This, of course, would render the patent virtually worthless.

Even if the U.S. Patent Office grants a patent, the patent is only recognized in the United States and the U.S. Territories. To be recognized in a foreign country, the holder of the United States patent must apply in each and every foreign country where patent infringement could occur for recognition of the patent in that country unless the patent falls under some international treaty or other agreement. Keep in mind that if that country requires a detailed schematic of the invention that is specific enough to allow an expert to reproduce the invention, like in the United States, the foreign country could deny the patent and then has the schematic to produce the invention itself.

D. Trademarks and Service Marks

Unlike copyrights and patents, trademark protection is not exclusively governed by federal or national law. This area of intellectual property has protection under both federal and state laws. The appropriate federal law is the **Lanham Act** that is also called the **Trademark Act of 1946, as amended, codified in 15 U.S.C. 1051** et. seq. The Lanham Act is non-exclusive and still allows state law as well. The purpose of trademark protection is to prevent customer confusion.

A **trademark** is any word, name, symbol or design, or any combination thereof, use in combination thereof, used in commerce to identify and distinguish the goods of one manufacturer or seller from those of another and to indicate the source of the goods (15 U.S.C. Section 1127). A **service mark** is basically the same thing as a trademark, only it is used to identify a service instead of a product. In the following paragraphs, a trademark and service mark will be used interchangeably as a trademark and product can also mean service.

There are generally four types of potential trademarks that can be registered: arbitrary or fanciful, descriptive, suggestive, and generic. First, to be a trademark and receive protection from infringement under the arbitrary or fanciful category, the mark must bear no rational or logical relationship with the product that it is to represent. After all, what does the actual word "Polaroid" mean to you? Does it give any hint as to the product used? Second, the mark can suggest a characteristic of the product, but cannot describe the underlying product with specificity. Third, the mark can also describe the product but not directly, it can only suggest a quality of the product and if it is too descriptive it will usually not receive trademark status. The fourth type, generic, is generally usually held to be too common and therefore is almost never allowed to receive trademark protection. These are more labels than categories and are sometimes difficult for a court to articulate and apply (**Soweco, Inc. V. Shell Oil Co. 617 F.2d 1178, 1183 [5th Circuit] 1980)**).

However, even in those categories that are not allowed to be trademarked under normal situations those marks may be trademarked if they acquire a secondary meaning, which means that it becomes the representation of the product. What do you think of when you see the Golden Arches? "The concept of secondary meaning recognizes that words with an ordinary and primary meaning of their own "may by long use with a particular product, come to be known by the public as specifically designating that product" (**Volkswagenwerk Aktiengesellschaft v. Rickard, 492 F.2d 474, 477 [5th Circuit] 1974)**). "Factors such as amount and manner of advertising, volume of sales, and length and manner of use may serve as circumstantial evidence relevant to the issue of secondary meaning" (**Zatarai's, Inc. v. Oak Grove Smokehouse, Inc., 698 F.2d 786 [5th Circuit] 1983)**). Normally, the plaintiff who is trying to establish the trademark has the burden of proving secondary meaning. Generic terms are not allowed to be trademarked even if they have secondary meaning. Of course, some of these problems can be avoided by registering the trademark but the owner of the mark does not have to register the mark to receive the state common law protection.

The federal law, the Lanham Act, allows for a nationwide registration system for trademarks. The USPTO is the national office in charge of trademarks just as we saw in patents. However, trademark is a totally different process than patent. Probably, the first question a person or entity that is seeking trademark protection should ask is, do I need legal help with this process. While it is not required and definitely not as necessary as in obtaining a patent, it is suggested by the USPTO that an applicant may use a private trademark attorney for help in the application process or to decide if the individual or entity even needs to register the trademark. An attorney can also assist in helping the potential registrant to identify your mark. Once the registrant has determined what the mark will actually be, the registrant then must be sure that they can identify the goods to which the mark will apply in a clear and precise manner; the exact specificity of this identification depends on the type of goods.

Any applicant that is thinking about choosing to register a trademark must conduct a search to see if any competitors are using a word, name, symbol, or design that is similar to the trademark that the applicant wants to register. USPTO does not conduct the searches. This can be done by the applicant itself by using the USPTO database. This search is free via the Trademark Electronic Search System, TESS. This search engine allows the registrant to avoid a finding that the proposed trademark will create confusion with another previously registered trademark. The USPTO gives guidance on how to use TESS on their website with a Design Search Code Manual.

After conducting the search, if the registrant is convinced that their trademark is clear and can be registered, the registrant should then specify the proper basis for the filing, which is the "use in commerce" of the trademark if it is currently in use or the "intent to use" the said trademark in the future if it is not in current use. If the registrant chooses the "use in commerce" option, then they must prove that they have used the mark on all of the goods they will identify in their application, in commerce which can be interstate, territorial (with U.S. Territories), or with a foreign country. The applicant will need to provide date of first use and submit an example of how it was previously used in commerce. If the mark has not been used in commerce, then the applicant must file under the "intent to use" process and the registrant has to have a true intent to use the mark in the near future. This form of filing also requires an additional fee and an additional form prior to the registration.

The actual filing of the trademark application can be done in writing, but online filing with the Trademark Electronic Application System (TEAS) is the preferred method. However, this process can be complex and there are definite time requirements so once again, the applicant might want to consider an attorney to help with the process. Keep in mind that anything you file will be able to be viewed by the public and will remain public even if the registration is abandoned or any registration is surrendered, canceled, or allowed to expire. Any required forms are available on the USPTO website, uspto.gov. Of course, the registrant also must pay the required fees, which are based on three distinct factors. First, you can only file one trademark per application; so, a separate fee must be paid for each mark to be registered. Second, the fee will depend on the number of classes that you wish to register under. There are several classes, such as Class 18, which is leather and imitations of leather, and Class 25, which is clothing, footwear, and headgear. So, if you are combining leather with clothing you have at least two classes. The third factor to consider is the version of the form being used. For example, the application filing fee is normally $275 but if you choose the TEA Plus version, the fee goes to $325 per class. Also, fees are non-refundable.

Once the application is submitted, any competition can then object to the proposed trademark. Remember, at filing the information becomes public and the representation of the mark will be filed in the USPTO search records and will be printed in the *Official Gazette* (OG), a weekly online publication that gives notice to the public that the USPTO plans to register that mark, what classes it will be issued under. The OG also publishes issued registration certificates and the date they are effective. When the OG publishes the Marks Published for Opposition, any opposition must be made within 30 days. If no opposition, then the OG publishes the registration certificate.

Under Lanham, certain marks cannot be registered as trademarks. If you are registering you trademark, it must have been or will be used in interstate commerce. Also, Lanham does not allow registration of any mark that:

a. Consists of or comprises immoral, deceptive, or scandalous matter; or matter which may disparage or falsely suggest a connection with persons, living or dead, institutions, beliefs, or national symbols, or bring them into contempt or disrepute.

b. Consists of or comprises the flag or coat of arms or other insignia of the United States, or of any State or municipality, or of any foreign nation, or any simulation thereof.

c. Consists of or comprises a name, portrait, or signature identifying a particular living individual except by his written consent, or the name, signature, or portrait of a deceased President of the United States during the life of his widow, if any, except by the written consent of the widow.

   d. Consists of or comprises a mark which so resembles [another] mark ... as to be likely, when used on or in connection with the goods of the applicant, to cause confusion, or to cause mistake, or to deceive.

   e. Consists of a mark which, (1) when used on or in connection with the goods of the applicant is merely descriptive or deceptively misdescriptive of them, or (2) when used on or in connection with the goods of the applicant is primarily geographically descriptive, or (3) deceptively misdescriptive of them, except as indications of regional origin may be registrable or is primarily merely a surname. (15 U.S.C. Section 1052)

Just because these cannot be registered under Lanham, it does not mean that they cannot be trademarked. These may be protected and available for registration under statue common law or depending on the state, state statutory law.

However, you must keep in mind that it is easier to obtain a registered trademark under Lanham. However, it can still take months or years to get the registration certificate.

Once a trademark is registered under federal law, the owner of the trademark must give notice of the trademark. This can only be accomplished by use of the letter "r" circled, "®" and cannot be used during the registration process. If you are simply claiming the trademark, "TM" can be used or "SM" for a service mark to notify the public of your claimed ownership through common law of the trademark or service mark. A trademark registration is valid for 10 years if you file all of the post-registration documents to maintain the trademark and can be renewed for another 10 years. However, the "Declaration of Use," which is one of those required post-registration documents, must be filed between the fifth and sixth year after registration and you must file a "Declaration of Use and Application for Renewal" between the ninth and tenth year and every 10 years thereafter. If you do not file these documents in a timely manner, you will lose the trademark protection under Lanham. Renewal is required every 10 years and there is no limit on the number of renewals as long as the trademark is still being used "in commerce." Therefore, the time period for a trademark can be indefinite as long as the trademark is still being used and the proper post-registration documents are timely filed.

So, a trademark can be lost by failing to keep the registration current. A trademark can also be lost when it is abandoned by a business. Abandonment of a trademark occurs if the trademark is not used for a period of three years. This makes sense when you think that a trademark is supposed to be for products used in commerce. In **Major League Baseball Properties, Inc. v. Sed Non Olet Denarius, Ltd., 817 F. Supp. 1103 (S.D.N.Y. 1993)**, the court held that the Los Angeles Dogers had abandoned the trademark and thus the rights to the Brooklyn Dodgers trademark. An owner of a trademark can also lose the trademark if they allow other entities to use the trademark because it would then be deemed generic. Therefore, once granted, a business must aggressively defend its right to trademark protection. For instance, the following trademarks have been lost by the business that originally had the trademark protection: thermos, cornflakes, raisin bran, escalator, trampoline, and cellophane. Probably the most well-known case of losing a trademark to it becoming generic was about Bayer Aspirin where the Bayer Company lost the trademark rights to the word "aspirin" (**Bayer Co. v. United Drug Co., 272 F.505 (S.D.N.Y. 1921)**). To protect the trademark, a business should aggressively sue infringers, advertise its trademark, inform journalists in magazines and publications how to use the trademark, correct journalists who use the trademark incorrectly, and demand a retraction or correction in the next issue. The best way to protect your trademark is to find a way to get people to use the trademark as an adjective followed by a generic name for the product such as in the phrase "a Chevrolet Tahoe all terrain vehicle." A company that is strenuously fighting to keep its trademark is Xerox.

What if you fail to register your trademark or Lanham is not appropriate because you only use your trademark in the local market and not throughout the nation? Most states have registration systems for purely local trademarks. Of course, registration under neither Lanham nor state law is required to achieve trademark protection. If the trademark is not registered, then it is up to the entity claiming the trademark to prove that that the logo, word, phrases, etc. have acquired a "**secondary meaning**," which we briefly discussed above. Secondary meaning is achieved if a substantial number of people feel that there is a secondary meaning from the logo, word, etc. If you can prove that your unregistered trademark has acquired a secondary meaning, then a newcomer is prevented from fraudulently trading on the goodwill of an established business. An interesting secondary meaning case is **Fruit of the Loom v. Girouard, 994 F.2d 1359 [9th Circuit] 1993**, which is a case where Fruit of the Loom claimed that *Girouard* was infringing on its trademark phrase "Fruit of the Loom" that they had owned since 1871 by using fruit to advertise underwear. Of course, *Girouard* was using fruit in a sexually suggestive way to advertise its, shall we say, exotic underwear. The 9th Circuit ruled that fruit had NOT acquired a secondary meaning sufficient enough to ban *Girouard* from using the fruity names for its exotic underwear. In other words the court did not feel that *Girouard* had infringed upon the phrase "Fruit of the Loom" by simply using fruity names for its underwear.

Colors and sounds can also be trademarked. Interesting color cases have been (1) UPS has trademarked the color brown in transportation and delivery services, Registration 2091090, and (2) Tiffany's Jewelry Company has trademarked the blue color used in their bags, boxes, etc. with several registrations on the individual items. A recent case was about the use of the color red on the soles of women's shoes and it was held that red could be registered in that context (**Christian Louboutin S.A. v. Yves Saint Laurent America, Inc. ___ F.3d ____ [2nd Circuit] 2012**) on rehearing March 8, 2013. However, it should be noted that the courts have been reluctant to give colors trademark status and so you will only see this in some but certainly not all (universal) situations. As for sounds, cases have held that the roar of the MGM lion at the beginning of movie is a sufficiently distinctive sound to be trademarked, as was the familiar musical sound of NBC's three-note chime. However, the courts would not go so far as to state that the sound of a Harley–Davidson V-twin engine could be trademarked.

There have been several recent revisions of the Trademark Law. In 1988, Congress passed the Trademark Law Revision Act. This Law made two major changes in trademark law. First, it gave business owners the right to seek treble (triple) damages in false comparative advertising situations. This had long been available in most state trademark laws and simply brought federal trademark law into agreement with state law. However, this treble damage provision is only available to businesses and does not apply to the average consumer. The second thing that the Trademark Law Revision Act did was to make it possible to apply for a trademark ahead of actually using the trademark as discussed above. Prior to this, the trademark right had to be earned by using the trademark prior to applying for registration. This is the "intent to use" filing.

Congress also passed the Federal Trademark Dilution Act of 1995, which allows trademark holders to sue even non-competitors for blurring and tarnishing a trademark. Blurring is the situation were someone makes a totally unrelated product and uses a famous name, for example, using Xerox as the name of a baby oil treatment. Tarnishing is using a word or phrase to create a negative association with an established trademark such as creating a poster that looks like the Coca-Cola Santa Claus but instead of drinking a Coke, he is snorting cocaine and the caption says "enjoy cocaine"(**Coca-Cola Co. v. Gemini Rising, Inc., 346 F. Supp. 1183 (E.D.N.Y. 1972)**) (Coke did not see the humor on this poster!).

There are two basic types of defenses in trademark infringement: fair use and parody. Fair use is usually found in the descriptive mark type of trademarks and is where the trademark is used in good faith for the primary meaning as opposed to interfering with its secondary meaning. In *Zatarain's*, the court held that using the term "fish fry" by the defendant in describing a batter coating for fish did not infringe upon Zatarain's trademark of "Fish-Fri." As for parody, the courts seem to say that certain parodies are permissible under the First Amendment protection when they are not tied to closely to the commercial use. However, sometimes this has to be ascertained on a case-by-case basis. Consider the case of **L.L. Bean, Inc. v. Drake Publishers, Inc., 811 F.2d 26, 28 [1st Circuit] 1987**, where the parody of an L.L. Bean magazine advertisement that was risqué was found not to be an infringement and the parody was allowed. But, in **Toys "R" Us v. Akkaoui, 40 U.S.P.Q.2d (BNA) 1836 (N.D. Cal. Oct. 29, 1996)**, where the defendant Akkaoui and others were using the phrase "Adults "R" Us for a variety of sexually related products, the Court found for Toys "R" Us due to tarnishing and did not think this was an allowable parody.

Like other forms of intellectual property, the Internet has brought new problems to the area of trademark law. Recently, there was a rush of people claiming Internet domain names and in doing so actually violated trademark protection. These people were called cybersquatters because they would register the domain name that should have belonged to a legitimate trademark holder and then try to hold the name ransom while "offering" the domain name to the legitimate trademark holder for an exorbitant price. This practice was stopped by the **Anticybersquatting Consumer Protection Act of 1999** that bans and even criminalizes cybersquatting. It defines cybersquatting as registering someone else's trademark or a famous person's name as an Internet domain name in bad faith, hoping to make a profit by selling the name to its rightful owner. The fines for violation of the Anticybersquatting Consumer Protection Act are up to $100,000 per violation and cancellation of the Internet names registered in bad faith. Furthermore, this law applied to names already registered or that were to be registered in the future. Of course, other Internet issues still exist and like other areas of the law when the Internet is concerned, it will take some time for the law to sort out the remaining issues as well as new ones that are constantly arising. However, you might think that cybersquatting is pretty much a thing of the past but there were more cybersquatting cases in 2012 than ever before. Google just recently won the rights to over 750 domain names that had been registered by the defendant Chris Gillespie between February 29 and March 10 of 2012, such as googlechevron.com., by the National Arbitration Forum (NAF) in 2012. Gillespie's reaction was to file a petition with the USPTO to void all Google trademarks in the United States as being generic.

A form of trademark that still needs to be discussed is **Trade Dress,** which is where an infringer steals the entire inherent distinctive look of a competitor. One of the leading cases in this area is **Two Pesos v. Taco Cabana, 505 U.S. 763 (1992).** Taco Cabana claimed that Two Pesos imitated the appearance and décor of their restaurants. Truly the two Mexican food chains were very similar. The setup for ordering, the placement of the menu board, and the location of the serve-yourself drinks and condiments were the same and the general look of the buildings were very similar except that Two Pesos was turquoise and Taco Cabana was pink. The Supreme Court ruled that Two Pesos had indeed violated Lanham by taking the inherent distinctive look of Taco Cabana. The Court, however, did not define inherent distinctiveness.

However, in **Wal-Mart v. Samara Brothers, 529 U.S. 205 (2000),** the Supreme Court did state that the public had to so strongly associate the two entities in a trade dress situation so as to be confused with the source of the product and not just with the product itself. This case dealt with a clothing designer of expensive children's wear suing Wal-Mart for trade dress due to the similarities between their expensive clothing and that sold at Wal-Mart, which was extremely similar (as in almost exact) in appearance. However, the Court found that the public did not confuse the source of the product—they knew they were not getting designer clothes at Wal-Mart and therefore, there was no trade dress infringement. The result was that Wal-Mart was allowed to sell the designer look-alike clothes.

E. Trade Names

Where general trademarks apply to products, **Trade Names** apply to a part or all of a business name. A trade name is a type of trademark. The trade name is usually directly related to the goodwill and the good name of a business. Unless the trade name is also the name of the product, trade names cannot be registered under the Lanham Act and instead must look wholly to state law for protection. Normally, state law requires a business to earn a trade name. Trade name protection is not automatic. Just as in trademarks, a trade name must be unique to the business and be unusual or fanciful.

Often the trade name of the business is not the actual name of the business, so the trade name is the name the business uses to identify the business to the public. For instance, the business may be incorporated as ABC, Inc. but do business as Freaky Fright's Paintball Haven. This is when you will see the abbreviation ABC, Inc. d/b/a Freaky Fright's Paintball Haven. Most states require ABC, Inc. to file an assumed name certificate with the appropriate state authority. This is required to disclose the name of the real owner to the public thereby stopping a business from hiding behind its trade name for legal reasons.

However, more often, the business will probably find itself having to protect its trade name in court. After all, if you operate a successful business under a certain trade name, other people will want to benefit from the goodwill and good name of your business. Since there is no federal protection for trade names and the protection is only local in nature, several businesses make their trade name a part of their trademark and thereby register it as a trademark under Lanham.

F. Trade Secrets

Trade secrets are anything that the business wants to keep secret. Because you want to keep this information secret, you do not want to use any of the intellectual property protection schemes that make you file the secret, such as patents or copyrights. Trade secrets can include formulas, customer lists, price lists, research, and plans for future development, marketing techniques, or any other information that would give your competitor an advantage over you in the market.

To be protected under state law, trade secrets must be both original and secret. Of course having a secret and keeping it secret are two different matters entirely. Industrial espionage is a major problem in trade secrets. This can include actual breaking into a business to steal the trade secrets, computer hacking, or hiring a key employee away from the business in order to learn what secrets that employee knows about the business. This is one of the main reasons why companies use employment contracts that forbid key employees from divulging information that they learn under one employer when they leave to work for a second employer. Until 1979, this was the only effective way that businesses had to try to protect their trade secrets unless the theft of the trade secrets fell under some criminal provision such as burglary or theft.

In *1979*, a model act, the Uniform Trade Secrets Act was presented to the states for adoption. Over 40 states and the District of Columbia have adopted at least part of the Uniform Trade Secrets Act, but often the adopting states have only adopted the parts of the uniform law that were already present in that state's common law. Therefore, in reality, trade protection is still largely left up to common law. Under common law, the owner of a trade secret can bring a lawsuit for **misappropriation**, taking or stealing the secret, and using it without the owner's permission, against anyone who obtains the trade secret in an unlawful manner. However, if the competitor independently develops the same trade "secret," then there is no action. This even includes reverse engineering where a competitor buys your product and then takes it apart to see what makes it work, thereby discovering the "secret." (Of course, this would be a violation of patent law if you had patented the "secret.")

The owner of a trade secret must take whatever precautions are possible to protect the trade secret. It should be obvious that the more sensitive and important the secret the more protection it deserves. One of the most protected trade secrets in the world is the formula for Coca-Cola. Very few people know all of the formula for the syrup to make Coca-Cola.

Of course, Coke's competitors can analyze the ingredients and try to determine how Coca-Cola is made but so far they have been unsuccessful. What do you think the value of that trade secret would be to the competitors of Coca-Cola? At least one man thinks it is valued at $15 million. An antique dealer found what he thought was the formula for Coca-Cola and posted it on eBay in May 2013 for sale at a "buy it now" listing on eBay for $15 million. It was purchased for $15 million but it turns out that it was purchased by a 15-year-old and the chances of the young person having $15 million are slim. However, the antique dealer vows to relist the item. It will be interesting to see what if any steps Coca-Cola takes in this latest claim of having the formula for Coca-Cola.

Generally, if a misappropriation of trade secret does occur, the owner of the trade secret can receive damages. Those damages can include the profits that were made due to stealing the trade secret by the company that stole the trade secret. The owner of the trade secret can also obtain an injunction to stop the appropriating business from using the trade secret in the future. Of course, if criminal laws were broken, like the **Federal Espionage Act of 1996**, the person or entity that stole the trade secrets also will be facing criminal liability and the owner of the trade secret might be entitled to restitution from the criminal courts. However, remember the purpose of criminal law is to punish the wrongdoer and not to compensate the victim.

One must always remember, it is better to keep it secret than have to retrieve it. This is the old adage that "once the cat is out of the bag it is hard to put him back." Furthermore, you are usually on your own to protect your trade secrets.

IV. BUSINESS NEGLIGENCE

A. Introduction

Negligence deals with careless or reckless conduct rather than intentional conduct like was discussed in intentional torts. There are four basic elements to a negligence claim. The four elements, which are required for a cause of action for negligence to arise, are:

1. Defendant has a duty to the plaintiff against unreasonable risks—Duty
2. Defendant fails to perform this duty—Breach
3. There is actual loss or damage to the plaintiff—Harm
4. A reasonably close connection between the defendant's conduct and the plaintiff's injury—Causation

All four of the elements are important since a cause of action would fail if any one of the elements were lacking. Each of these elements will be discussed in turn below. An acceptable definition for our purposes is that negligence is the failure to exercise due care when there is a foreseeable risk of harm to others. The failure to exercise due care can be either an act or a failure to act. The standard imposed is that of a reasonable person. That is, how would a reasonable person have acted under the circumstances?

B. Elements of Negligence

1. Duty of Care—Duty

The first element of negligence is commonly called a duty of care. A simplistic definition is that a duty of care arises whenever a person should foresee that his or her conduct would create an unreasonable risk of harm to others. Everyone owes everyone else a duty of reasonable care. For example, target practicing in an urban area would create an unreasonable risk of harm to others and would create a duty of care to all whose injury could have been foreseen. On the other hand, a rancher target practicing in the middle of his five-mile-wide ranch is not creating an unreasonable risk of harm to others and the practicing may not create a duty of care to others.

2. Failure to Exercise Care—Breach

Once it is determined that a duty exists, a plaintiff in a negligence action is required to show that the defendant failed to exercise due care or breached his or her duty of care. The courts have established a standard of care known as the "**reasonable person of ordinary prudence**." Negligence is often described as the failure to do what the ordinarily prudent person would do under the same or similar circumstances. The problem is how we differentiate reasonable behavior from unreasonable behavior. A dangerous activity that has a high probability of causing very serious injuries to many people would require great expenditures in order to avoid a judgment of negligence. On the other hand, if the activity is "safe," that is, an accident is unlikely, and if the expected injuries were small, then more than small expenditures would be required to avoid a judgment of negligence.

Normally, it is not negligence if an injury occurs for which the expenditure to prevent the injury exceeds the benefits derived from the expenditures. All injuries from flying baseballs can be prevented only at a great cost, whereas the likelihood of injury in certain areas of the stands may be quite low and the severity of injury small. Failure to protect against the risk of a fan being hit by a baseball behind home plate where the risk of injury is great may be negligence, whereas failure to protect fans on the right field may not.

Simply put, everyone owes a duty of care to everyone else and the failure to live up to that duty is a failure to exercise due care. For instance, if you are late for a test that the professor has told you that there will be no late admittance into the room to take the exam. You obviously have a need to hurry but can that need excuse you for running people off the road and resulting in damages that they incur simply due to your need to get to campus on time? Obviously your actions would breach the required reasonable duty of care.

Some individuals are not held to the ordinarily prudent person standard. A person possessing (or perhaps merely claiming to possess) special knowledge or skill is held to a higher standard of care. Doctors, lawyers, accountants, engineers, and other professionals must meet a higher standard of care. If sued for professional malpractice, professionals are judged by a standard of skill and learning possessed by members of the profession in good standing in the community. Failure to possess the presumed level of skill and knowledge is strong evidence of negligence.

3. Injury or Harm

If an individual owes a duty and fails to exercise reasonable care, but there is no injury, a negligence cause of action will fail. The required injury can take several forms. Physical harm to the person or to property is always sufficient. In addition, mental harm such as fright, humiliation, or emotional distress may be sufficient in limited, proper situations.

4. Causation

Causation is the most basic element of negligence. As discussed previously, there must be a duty that has been breached by negligence and there must be an injury. However, there must also be a causal connection between the breached duty (failure to exercise reasonable care) and the injury. Two types of causation are generally required to maintain an action for negligence: cause in fact and proximate cause.

Cause in fact is established by evidence showing that the complained-of act is the cause of the event that caused the injury. That is, the injury would not have occurred but for the conduct of the wrongdoer. Cause in fact can be illustrated by thinking of a demonstration where someone has set up thousands of dominoes so that one will cause the next to hit the next and so on, until several thousand dominoes have fallen in order, which results in the last domino falling. Cause in fact is sometimes looked at as the "but for" test. The last domino would not have fallen over but for the next-to-the last domino hitting it and it would not have fallen but for the previous domino falling and so forth, all the way back to the first domino. However, cause in fact is not sufficient standing alone to find negligence. This can be illustrated by the following example. Marshall runs a stop sign causing a minor fender bender. It ties up traffic and causes Linda to be delayed for five minutes. The delay results in Linda driving on a mountain road at the precise moment that a landslide engulfs her car and she is injured. But for Marshall's running of the stop sign, Linda would not have been injured. However, she does not have a cause of action because Marshall's actions were not the proximate cause of her injuries.

Proximate cause is a judicial limitation of cause in fact. Proximate cause is most often defined in terms of foreseeable risks. The responsibility for one's actions is limited to consequences that bear a reasonable relationship to the conduct. If the consequences are too remote or too far removed from the conduct, no liability will result even if the conduct was the cause in fact of the injuries. A landmark case in the area of proximate cause is **Palsgraf v. Long Island Railroad Co. 162 N.E. 99, 248 N.Y. 339 (1928)**. In this case a man was carrying a package and jumped onto a slowly moving train of the Long Island Railroad Company. When he landed on the train's platform, he wavered, as if about to fall. Two of the railroad's guards grabbed the man in an attempt to keep him from falling. In so doing, they dislodged the man's small package. The package though harmless in appearance contained fireworks (note the age of the case, fireworks used to be much more powerful), and upon falling to the ground it exploded. The shock of the explosion caused the ground to shake causing the platform that was some distance away to shake, which caused a scale on the railroad platform to topple over, injuring the plaintiff, Mrs. Palsgraf. The railroad argued that they owed no duty to Mrs. Palsgraf because they owned no duty to her since the injuries were too remote from the act that was claimed to be negligent, helping the man onto the train. The court agreed with the railroad and thus added a second type of required causation, proximate cause. Proximate cause means that the harm must be foreseeable by the actor when he committed the negligent act. In other words, he had to know of the danger and that the injuries or harm would result. Mrs. Palsgraf received nothing. Some states have their own version of proximate cause, but proximate cause is an essential element to a negligence case. Texas says the defendant must know or should have known that the harm would result. California and other states say that the defendant's act must be a substantial factor in bringing about the harm.

C. Defenses to Negligence

Proving the elements of negligence does not end the inquiry in a negligence action. There are defenses a defendant can use to reduce, or even eliminate, liability for the negligence. The two principal defenses are the assumption of the risk by the plaintiff and the plaintiff's own negligence, which has two types of defenses. A third defense is that of superseding cause, which will also be discussed.

The defense of **assumption of risk** may be defined as voluntary exposure to a known risk. Suppose, for example, that two electric drills are available in the hardware store priced at $20 and $50. It was explicitly stated on the package of the lower-priced drill that it was not safe to use to drill through concrete. A purchaser of the lower-priced drill who plans to drill through concrete does so because the added protection of the more expensive drill is not worth the added cost. Thus, the purchaser assumes the risk of injury that may occur when drilling through concrete. The purchaser may not recover damages from the manufacturer.

A person can only assume known risks. An example often given is that of a spectator at a baseball game who assumes a certain amount of risk that he or she will be injured if hit by a baseball. A spectator probably assumes the risk of being hit by a baseball in areas that are not protected by screens because most can appreciate the risk they are taking. However, spectators do not assume the risk that a ball will penetrate a protective screen and cause them harm since it is difficult to assess the risk of such an event. However, if you turn your ticket to just about any baseball game over it will say that the baseball club is not liable for your injuries and you are assuming the risk by going to the game. How far that assumption of the risk will actually go is determined by courts.

Contributory and comparative negligence are important when the plaintiff and the defendant are both at least partially responsible for his or her own injuries. The defense of **contributory negligence** is the failure of the plaintiff, the injured party, to exercise reasonable care, which contributes to the injury. Traditionally, contributory negligence would completely bar recovery of damages for any injuries suffered by either party. They were both negligent; since they both caused the injuries, no one is responsible for the other party's injuries. This rule had harsh consequences that often were unintended and led to a rule called the "Last Clear Chance Doctrine" where the court would ask who had the last clear chance to avoid the incident and did not. Once that question was answered it was determined that the party with the last clear chance to avoid the incident but chose not to was the party held responsible. However, even with the last clear chance rule the results could still be harsh or totally wrong. The defense of contributory negligence has largely been replaced by the defense of comparative negligence. Therefore, the defense of contributory negligence is a minority rule only followed by a minority of states.

The result of the harshness of contributory negligence has been the adoption by most states of the doctrine of **comparative negligence**, which allows a proration of the damages resulting from the combined negligence of the parties. If a plaintiff's injuries amount to $100,000 and are 40 percent the result of plaintiff's negligence and 60 percent the result of defendant's negligence, then the plaintiff's recovery would be limited to only $60,000. In other words, the plaintiff recovers, but only for the damages the defendant caused. Some states provide that if plaintiff's negligence is greater than 50 percent, then recovery is barred.

The economic justification for the contributory negligence defense is that it provides an incentive for the plaintiff to take care when it is efficient for the plaintiff or both parties to avoid the loss. The concern is that under a simple negligence standard those at risk do not have the incentive to take self-protective or loss-avoidance measures. This problem is referred to as **moral hazard**. The absolute defense of contributory negligence controls moral hazard. Many argue that comparative negligence controls moral hazard in a more equitable manner.

1. Superseding Cause

A third type of defense is a superseding cause. This is when something occurs that breaks the causal connection required to have a negligence case. For instance, in the *Palsgraf* case, if the defendant had proven that at the same time the box fell there had been an earthquake and that it was the earthquake that had really caused Mrs. Palsgraf's injuries, then the earthquake would have been a superseding cause of the injuries and the defendant would not be found negligent.

Likewise, in the domino example, change the facts to show that Johnny, a boy out of the crowd of spectators, who had gotten bored watching the thousands of dominoes fall, came out of the crowd and started another chain of dominoes toppling over by knocking over one much closer to the last one. Then, it would have been Johnny's action that caused the last domino to fall. Therefore, Johnny would have been the cause of the last domino falling over thereby making Johnny's actions the superseding cause of the last domino falling over.

V. STRICT LIABILITY IN TORT

A. History

Strict liability in tort, or liability without fault, had its origins in the early English case of **Rylands v. Fletcher, L.R. 3 H.L. 330 (1868)**. In that case, the defendants constructed a reservoir upon their property. The water from the reservoir broke through into the shaft of an abandoned coal mine and then filled up the plaintiff's active mine. It appeared that the plaintiff would not be able to recover against the owner of the reservoir for the damages because the defendants' acts did not fit into any conventional torts such as trespass or nuisance. Moreover, the plaintiff could not sue on the basis of an intentional tort because the defendant did not know of the abandoned mine. The court, however, held the defendant liable for damages and in doing so introduced the concept of strict liability for cases involving "abnormal" or "ultra-hazardous" activities.

B. Application of Strict Liability in Tort

In general, strict liability has been applied to activities that are recognized as hazardous or dangerous, but are not so unreasonable as to be prohibited altogether. The early applications of *Rylands* imposed strict liability on hazardous activities such as keeping wild animals or blasting with dynamite. Strict liability theory began to be applied to sellers of food and drink in the early part of the twentieth century. Today, strict liability theory has been expanded to apply to manufacturers who sell defective products, products liability. However, not all areas of products liability are governed by strict liability.

VI. PRODUCT LIABILITY

A. Introduction

Every year, thousands of consumers are injured by unsafe products and the National Government recognized the need in the consumer product area with the creation of the Consumer Product Safety Commission (CPSC). There is little disagreement with the proposition that many injuries due to unsafe products could be avoided through greater expenditures for safety. However, because such expenditures would most likely lead to higher prices, consumer and producer behaviors reveal that absolute safety is not valued by either individuals or the market. On the other hand, it is clear that consumers are not willing to accept the risks of unreasonably unsafe products. Thus, the difficult and important policy issue becomes the determination of the proper or appropriate level of safety.

The legal aspects of product safety are discussed in this chapter. Product safety has been primarily governed by private law, which allows for the compensation of parties injured by unsafe products, and through market adjustments to unsafe products. The government's role has been relatively passive. The federal government has begun to play an active role in consumer product safety with the CPSC. For example, rather than allowing tort and contract law to compensate individuals injured by unsafe products, some federal laws actually prohibit the sale of certain products or in some circumstances regulate the product's design. Thus, there has been a gradual shift from common law to direct regulation. These legal developments are discussed in detail in this chapter.

Traditionally, the primary means of controlling product safety, other than market adjustments, was through lawsuits based on the common law of tort (and to a lesser extent contract law) that allowed consumers injured by an unsafe product to be compensated for their losses and injuries. Although the federal government has begun to play a more active role in regulating product safety, the common law is still the most important parameter of this aspect of the legal environment of business and in compensation for the injuries received by those products. Once a product has hurt someone, the issue becomes who should be responsible for the damages.

B. Historical Aspect of Product Safety Law

Originally in the very early 1900s and before, the relationship between consumers and producers regarding product quality and product safety was properly described as *"caveat emptor"* in Latin for let the buyer beware." Under "caveat emptor," the purchaser of a product simply bore all the risks as to its use; there was no product liability on the part of the product's manufacturer, the store where it was sold, or anyone else. If a consumer bought any product, and the product turned out to be dangerous and caused the purchaser of the product harm then, that was just the purchaser's problem. The purchaser war required to inspect the product and otherwise gather all necessary information before making the purchase. Once the purchaser paid for the product, there was no further recourse against anyone else. In other words, the purchaser assumed all the risks. However, this began to change in the food and drug area, as we will see in a later chapter. However, that change came about due to two historical events, the Spanish American War and the publication of a book called *The Jungle* by Upton Sinclair. The Spanish American War was important in this area because it exposed problems in canned goods. There was a major problem with the canned goods that were supplied to the troops during the war because they made the soldiers ill. *The Jungle* was an expose on the meat-packing industry in Chicago. These two events led to major changes in the food and drug area, which will be discussed in a later chapter. However, the other industries were largely unchanged and the doctrine of "let the buyer beware" continued into the next decade in other products. However, the public was aware of the problems and the demanded change was about to occur in common law. Therefore, we will see a series of cases that will develop products liability principles.

C. Products Liability Based on Negligence

In 1916, the New York Court of Appeals forged new ground in products liability and began products liability based on a negligence theory. This occurred in the case of **MacPherson v. Buick Motor Company, New York Court of Appeals, 217 N.Y. 382, 111 N.E. 1050 (1916),** by stating that a person who bought a car which had a defective wheel could sue the car's manufacturer for "**negligence**." Briefly, the facts of this case were that Donald MacPherson bought a Buick automobile. Of course, Buick was the manufacturer and seller of the automobile. MacPherson was injured when the wooden spoke wheel on the Buick that he had purchased collapsed, and he was thrown from the automobile while he was driving the automobile at 8 miles per hour. However, Buick had bought the wooden spoke wheels from a separate manufacturer. The defect in the wooden spoke wheel could have been easily found had it been inspected by Buick. MacPherson sued for his damages. This lawsuit was permitted even though there was no direct relationship between the consumer and the auto company, that is, the consumer bought the car in 1909 from a local dealership, Close Brothers of Schenectady who had purchased the automobile from Buick, and it was the local dealership (and not the consumer) that was the purchaser from the manufacturer and furthermore, the manufacturer had bought the wooden spoke wheel from another manufacturer, the Imperial Wheel Company. Therefore, Buick tried to argue they had no responsibility to MacPherson. The Court held that the manufacturer Buick of a finished product, here the automobile, had a duty to the consumer if the product was negligently placed on the market in a defective condition knowing that the product would be used without inspection and when the product reached the consumer in the same condition it was in when it left the manufacturer's possession. This was a big departure from the only theory that once the purchase was made the purchaser assumed all the liability for any damages from the product. Since the Court used a theory based on negligence, all of the requirements for a negligence case must also be in a products liability case based on negligence. Therefore, there must be a duty that is breached causing harm to the purchaser. The *Macpherson* case and later cases have held that manufacturers generally owe a duty of care for their products to all persons in a "foreseeable zone of danger." This duty applies to the buyer of a product, the buyer's household, and even innocent bystanders such as pedestrians injured by a defective car with defective brakes which hits the pedestrians due to the brake failure. We have already seen in this chapter that breach of duty turns in large measure on reasonableness. Similarly, a manufacturer is not required to produce a "perfect" product. A manufacturer is, however, required to "reasonably" design the product in such a way as to prevent injury from its use. The standard of "reasonable design" is established and based on the current knowledge and technology at the time.

Even if a duty exists in a case and this duty has been breached, a plaintiff can only recover in a negligence case if he or she proves causation. In essence, the plaintiff needs to show that the defendant's actions actually caused the harm. Causation, which generally is not a big problem to prove, simply involves showing that the given action was the actual cause of the harm to the plaintiff, cause in fact and also the proximate cause, which as we have seen turns on the issue, was the harm foreseeable. The court felt that causation existed of both types in MacPherson and therefore, caused Mr. MacPherson's harm.

Once a plaintiff has proven duty of care, breach of duty, and causation, and has proven his or her harm, he or she has established a basic or "prima facie" case of negligence. The product manufacturer or other defendant can then only overcome this case if proper defenses are offered. The primary defenses to negligence actions are **contributory** or **comparative negligence** and **assumption of risk**. Manufacturers of products are clearly able to defend themselves if there was an **assumption of risk** on the part of the product user/plaintiff. In such cases, the plaintiff was fully aware of the risk, the possibility of injury occurring, and voluntarily proceeded to use the product, in spite of such risk. Contributory or comparative negligence is a related but somewhat more difficult defense. At its essence, the theory of negligence is asserting that the defendant; for example, the product manufacturer, had not acted "reasonably." In cases of contributory or comparative negligence, the manufacturer then comes back and asserts that the product user also had not acted "reasonably" and that this should allow the manufacturer to be off the hook. Traditionally, any contributory negligence on the part of a plaintiff completely barred or prohibited that plaintiff from any recovery. Because of the purported unfairness of any contributory negligence acting as a complete bar to recovery, a majority of states in the United States today permit some form of comparative negligence. There is also another defense, which is intervening cause. If something comes in and breaks the causal connection then there is no negligence. For instance, the town of West, Texas, in April 2013 was rocked with a massive explosion at the local fertilizer plant. If the explosion was due to a negligent act on the part of the fertilizer plant, the plant would be liable. But what if something else caused the explosion? For instance, what if it was a criminal act? That would be an intervening cause and could release the plant from liability.

Texas has long held that the "general rule is that one who manufactures or supplies a product has a duty of reasonable care to users, and to those in the foreseeable zone of danger of such use, to prevent physical harm that he should reasonably foresee could result from the use of the product for its intended purpose. The obligation of such manufacturer or supplier is to exercise reasonable care to discover the dangerous propensities of the product and to warn those whom he should expect to use it." (**Starr v. Koppers Co., 398 S.W.2d 827, 830–831 (Tex. Civ. App. San Antonio 1965)**). Texas also recognizes third-party liability in products liability based on negligence when there is no privity. Likewise, a manufacturer will be held liable if they negligently make the product in an unreasonable manner to those individuals that the manufacturer should have expected to have been harmed. However, the product must be used a lawful way and in the way it was intended to be used. Manufacturer also has the negligence defenses in Texas, except assumption of the risk unless there was "knowing express consent" (**Farley v. M M Cattle Co., 529 S.W. 2d 751, 758 (1975)**). If there is knowing express consent, assumption of the risk can still be used in Texas with these elements present: (1) the plaintiff had knowledge of the facts making up the dangerous condition, (2) making the plaintiff aware that the situation was dangerous, (3) the plaintiff understood the nature and extent of the danger, and (4) voluntarily undertook the dangerous activity (**Duncan v. Cessna Aircraft Co.665 S.W.3d 414 (Texas 1984)**).

D. Product Liability Based on Breach of Warranty

1. Express Warranty

The next step in products liability was to make the manufacturers liable for **express warranty**. Express warranty can occur based on the statements of the manufacturer in advertising, sales literature, statements of their representatives, etc. One of the first cases in this area was **Baxter v. Ford Motor Co 168 Wash. 456, 12 P.2d 409 (1932)**. The brief facts were that Baxter bought a Model A Ford Town Sedan in 1930 from St. John Motors. St. John Motors was a Ford dealer and had bought the automobile from Ford Motor Corp. Baxter claimed that the dealer and the manufacturer had made express warranties to him that the automobile had a glass called Triplex that would not shatter. The literature did say that the glass would not break, fly, or shatter. These claims were found in catalogs printed by Ford and distributed at St. John Motors. However, the glass was not shatter proof. A rock hit the window and caused glass to get into Baxter's eye causing him lose his sight in his left eye and injuries to his right eye. The court ruled that Ford was responsible for their material statements if they were false, if someone relied on them, and acted upon them and then was injured thereby. Furthermore, since Baxter had read the brochures, which claimed to have Triplex non-shatterable glass, he bought the Ford relying on the statements that turned out to be false and was injured by the glass, then Ford could be liable. Note that again the privity of contact between Ford and Baxter was not required.

Texas does not require privity of contract between the manufacturer and the purchaser even in an express warranty case. The Texas Supreme Court came to that conclusion based on the Texas Business and Commerce Code, **Tex. Bus. & Com. Code Sections 2.203** which defines a seller as "a person who sells or contracts to sell goods" and the Texas Supreme Court further said that that could mean anyone and if privity was still allowed then corporations would simply set up sham corporations to sell the goods they manufactured to avoid liability (**Nobility Homes of Texas, Inc. v. Shivers, 557 S.W.2d 77 (Texas 1977)**). Texas also recognizes that express warranty can be by sample. In **Indust-Ri-Chem Laboratory, Inc. v. Par-Pak Co., Inc., 602 S.W.2d 282 (Tex. Civ. App. Dallas 1980)**, the manufacturer was held liable for changing the specifics of a sample they had given the purchaser.

Texas also recognizes express warrant statutorily in the Texas Business and Commerce Code.

Section 2.313. EXPRESS WARRANTIES BY AFFIRMATION, PROMISE, DESCRIPTION, SAMPLE.

a. Express warranties by the seller are created as follows:
   1. Any affirmation of fact or promise made by the seller to the buyer, which relates to the goods and becomes part of the basis of the bargain, creates an express warranty that the goods shall conform to the affirmation or promise.
   2. Any description of the goods which is made part of the basis of the bargain creates an express warranty that the goods shall conform to the description.
   3. Any sample or model which is made part of the basis of the bargain creates an express warranty that the whole of the goods shall conform to the sample or model.
b. It is not necessary to the creation of an express warranty that the seller use formal words such as "warrant" or "guarantee" or that he have a specific intention to make a warranty, but an affirmation merely of the value of the goods or a statement purporting to be merely the seller's opinion or commendation of the goods does not create a warranty. (Tex. Bus. & Com. Code. Section 2.313)

2. Implied Warranty

A manufacturer can also be held liable for the product due to implied warranties. As the name implies, these are not express warranties but warranties that arise due to the facts and situations of the case. A leading case in this area is **Henningsen v. Bloomfield Motors, Inc., 151 A.2d 69 (1960)**. Claus Henningsen purchased a 1955 Plymouth, Plaza "6" Club Sedan as a Mother's Day gift to his wife. Ten days after purchase, Helen Henningsen was driving the car when she said she heard a loud noise under the hood and felt as if something cracked, the steering wheel spun in her hands, and the car veered sharply hitting a high-way sign and a brick wall. It was a one-vehicle accident. The damage to the front of the car was so extensive that no proof of defects could be found. However, the court held "under modern marketing conditions, when a manufacturer puts a new automobile in the stream of trade and promotes its purchase by the public, an implied warranty that it is reasonably suitable for use as such accompanies it into the hands of the ultimate purchaser. Absence of agency between the manufacturer and the dealer who makes the ultimate sale is imma-terial" (*Henningsen*, p. 384). The court in this case is the Supreme Court of New Jersey and thereby recognized the implied warranty of merchantability, which means that the product conforms to the expected standard of care of a similar product. The only issue was, was there breach of the implied warranty of merchantability and the court found that it was due to facts in the case and ruled for the Henningsens.

Texas also recognizes liability for implied warranties in statute. Texas bases this on the Uniform Commercial Code, which in Texas is found in the Business and Commerce Code, Sections 2.314 and 2.315 (**Tex. Bus. & Com. Code Sections2.314 and 2.315**). These are implied warranty of merchantability, Section 2.314, and implied warranty of fitness for a particular purpose, Section 2.315.

Section 2.314. IMPLIED WARRANTY: MERCHANTABILITY; USAGE OF TRADE.

a. Unless excluded or modified (Section 2.316), a warranty that the goods shall be mer-chantable is implied in a contract for their sale if the seller is a merchant with respect to goods of that kind. Under this section the serving for value of food or drink to be consumed either on the premises or elsewhere is a sale.

b. Goods to be merchantable must be at least such as:
   1. pass without objection in the trade under the contract description; and
   2. in the case of fungible goods, are of fair average quality within the description; and
   3. are fit for the ordinary purposes for which such goods are used; and
   4. run, within the variations permitted by the agreement, of even kind, quality and quantity within each unit and among all units involved; and
   5. are adequately contained, packaged, and labeled as the agreement may require; and
   6. conform to the promises or affirmations of fact made on the container or label if any.

c. Unless excluded or modified (Section 2.316), other implied warranties may arise from course of dealing or usage of trade. (Tex. Bus. & Com. Code Section 2.314)

This has also been used in common law to further explain and perhaps expand the implied warranty of merchantability in practical usage (**Nobility Homes of Texas, Inc. v. Shivers, 557 S.W.2d 77, 80 (Texas 1977)**).

Texas also recognizes an implied warranty for fitness in Tex. Bus. & Com. Code Section 2.315 as follows:

Section 2.315. IMPLIED WARRANTY: FITNESS FOR PARTICULAR PURPOSE. Where the seller at the time of contracting has reason to know any particular purpose for which the goods are required and that the buyer is relying on the seller's skill or judgment to select or furnish suitable goods, there is unless excluded or modified under the next section an implied warranty that the goods shall be fit for such purpose. (Tex. Bus. & Com. Code Section 2.316)

Note the seller must be aware of the time of the sale that the buyer needs the goods for a particular purpose and then seller warrants that the product will meet those needs. This does not have to be communicated directly between the parties. For instance, a buyer goes to a store looking for the paint that will cover a tin roof and reads on the label that the seller's product will indeed cover metal and thus fit his or her particular purpose, but it does not. This could also give rise to an implied warranty for fitness for a particular purpose.

E. Strict Liability

1. Overview

The theory of **strict liability** differs considerably from that of negligence. For example, let's suppose an eccentric entertainer decides to have dangerous wild animals such as tigers in his 20-acre backyard. The entertainer, though, has plenty of money and builds an elaborate $50-million security system and hires 50 full-time security personnel to make sure the animals don't get loose. Despite all this, however, one of the tigers somehow breaks out the backyard and ends up seriously mauling/injuring a neighbor. The entertainer had acted very reasonably in terms of spending a tremendous amount on security. The entertainer would be liable, however, under the legal theory of **strict liability**. In the product safety area, almost all states in the United States including Texas follow the doctrine of strict liability as enunciated in Section **402(A) of the Second Restatement of Torts**, which is a legal treatise that summarizes the general principles of tort law in the United States as set forth below:

1. One who sells any product in a defective condition unreasonably dangerous to the user or consumer or to his property is subject to liability for physical harm thereby caused to the ultimate user or consumer, or to his property if
   a. the seller is engaged in the business of selling such a product, and
   b. it is expected to and does reach the user or consumer without substantial change in the condition in which it is sold.
2. The rule stated in Subsection (1) applies although
   a. the seller has exercised all possible care in the preparation and sale of his product, and
   b. the user or consumer has not bought the product from or entered into any contractual arrangement with the seller.

Restatement Section 402(A) basically sets forth a **consumer expectations test**, that is, when consumers buy a product they have the right to expect that it is safe. As such, the basic rule of *"caveat emptor"* has been almost completely transformed into a doctrine of *"caveat venditor"*: "let the seller beware."

2. Elements Necessary to Establish Strict Liability

The basic elements that a plaintiff must establish in order to recover from a manufacturer under strict liability are relatively straightforward. To prove a strict liability case, the Plaintiff must show that (1) there was a sale, identifying the seller who must be engaged in the business of selling the product and the relationship between the product and the plaintiff's injury; (2) the product was defective and the defect was a substantial factor in plaintiff's harm; (3) that there was unreasonable danger; and (4) that the defect existed when it left the manufacturer. It is important to recognize and remember that strict liability means, in essence, liability without fault. This point is illustrated by the facts and legal result in **Cunningham v. MacNeal Memorial Hospital 47 Ill. 2d 443, 266 N.E. 2d 897 (1970)**. Cunningham, while a patient in the defendant hospital, contracted serum hepatitis from blood transfusions administered by the hospital. She sued in tort on both strict liability and negligence theories. The hospital claimed that it was without fault, and therefore not liable, because there is no way to tell the presence of serum hepatitis virus in whole blood. In a decision that has been followed in many other states, the Illinois Supreme Court held for the plaintiff stating that under strict liability "the defendant is liable whether or not he was at fault in creating that condition or in failing to discover and eliminate it. ... Thus, the test for imposing strict liability is whether the product is unreasonably dangerous, to use the words of the Restatement. ..."

3. Strict Liability Defenses

Application of the rule of strict liability holds producers to a high standard of product safety. However, in some instances, producers of defective products may escape liability if the plaintiff has engaged in some activity that actually increased the risk that the plaintiff would be injured. Strict liability does not mean absolute liability. **Abuse or misuse** of the product is a bar to recovery when the misuse is a proximate cause of the injury. For example, a person who uses a lawn mower to trim a hedge cannot recover for the loss of an arm even if the lawn mower was defective. However, if such misuse can be foreseen by the seller, the seller should take care to label the product advising against such use. Similarly, **assumption of the risk** also bars recovery. A person who recognizes a manufacturing defect in an electric knife, but (voluntarily) uses the knife anyway, is said to have assumed the risk of injury resulting from the defect and will not be allowed to recover. For obvious dangers like a knife there is normally no duty to warn. Likewise, if it is a commonly known danger in that industry, there is no duty to warn, hence, there can be no assumption of the risk. However, most states do not allow the defense of contributory negligence because it is seen as inconsistent with the purposes of strict liability. However, comparative negligence can be a defense and most jurisdictions will reduce plaintiff's recovery based on whether the plaintiff's activities caused part of his or her damages. Obviously, if the statute of limitations has run, there can be no recovery.

4. Rationale for Strict Liability

As the name suggests, strict liability imposes a very strict standard of producer conduct. Producers are required to pay full compensation to consumers injured by defective products, even though the producer exercised all reasonable care in the design and manufacture of the product. Legal commentators and the courts have advanced several arguments to justify the use of the rule of strict liability.

First, it is often suggested that, as a matter of public policy, consumers ought to be given the maximum possible protection from dangerous defects in products. Part of this rationale is based on a belief that consumers are helpless to protect themselves against products that they must buy. This rationale clearly does not recognize the importance to firms of reputation in competitive markets. However, when the market for a particular product is not a competitive one, then this rationale may be justified on the grounds that consumers do not have choices of alternative brands.

Second, it is often asserted that strict liability is justified because only the producer can prevent dangerous and defective products, and that the rule encourages producers to make safer products. This rationale has some validity, subject to several caveats. First, it is important to recognize that in many instances the producer could also be held liable for injuries under a negligence theory. Second, consumers often play an important role in accidents and the rule of strict liability may discourage them from being as cautious as they might otherwise be under a rule of negligence with contributory or comparative defenses. Finally, it should be remembered that absolute safety is very costly to obtain, and it is not clear that all consumers would be willing to pay the price necessary to reduce the risk to the absolute lowest possible level.

Third, strict liability is often justified on the ground of judicial economy because it is alleged that the rule simplifies what could often be obtained through the more costly legal procedures associated with a negligence trial. For example, the relative certainty of a strict liability rule (relative to a negligence rule) increases the likelihood that the parties to the lawsuit will settle out of court because the probable outcome of the lawsuit is recognized by both sides. Thus, the legal costs and attorneys' fees are reduced. Perhaps the most telling criticism of this rationale is that the adoption of the strict liability rules for defective products is often credited with creating the current "explosion" in products liability cases. Another side to the judicial economy argument is that strict liability is preferred to other rules because it reduces the need for numerous duplicative lawsuits against retailers, distributors, and manufacturers, by permitting the injured party to skip over the middlemen and sue the manufacturer directly. A major problem with this rationale, however, is that it relates to judicial procedure rather than the substantive products liability rule. That is, the duplicative lawsuit problem could be solved under a negligence standard by simply allowing consumers to sue the manufacturer directly. Thus, it appears that the judicial economy argument offers little support for the imposition of a rule of strict liability.

A fourth justification for the strict products liability rule argues that manufacturers receive the benefit of the sale of the product and ought to bear the burdens (such as products liability payments) as well. This argument portrays a fundamental misunderstanding of markets and exchange. Market exchange involves mutually beneficial transactions. Consumers do not engage in a transaction unless they expect to benefit from it. Thus, consistency in this rationale for a rule of strict liability suggests that consumers should also bear some of the burdens since they also benefit from the sale.

A fifth rationale for the adoption of a rule of strict liability is the so-called "social insurance" theory. The basic observation underlying this theory is that the manufacturer is financially better able to bear the burdens of the cost of injuries than are consumers, since the costs can be passed along in the form of higher prices. Adherents to this rationale recognize that strict liability may increase manufacturers' costs and, thus, increase product prices, but this is merely another way of stating that the financial cost of the defect should be spread out among all consumers rather than merely being borne totally by the innocent individuals that are unlucky enough to be the ones injured by the defective product. Cast in this light, strict liability is a form of compulsory insurance where the premiums are paid by higher prices of the products. Of course, we could allow all individuals to make their own decisions regarding how they deal with their injuries resulting from defective products. For example, consumers could be allowed to purchase their own insurance from an independent insurance company. In fact, most individuals' health insurance would pay for most of their medical expenses resulting from an accident. Apparently, some supporters of the social insurance theory do not have faith in the individual's ability to handle risks.

F. Effect of the Restatement (Third) of Torts on Products Liability

The **Restatement (Third) of Torts** was published in 1998 and suggests major changes in products liability. For instance, it suggests doing away with any distinctions between negligence, warranty, or strict liability in the products liability area and replacing with one term of products liability. It then divides the liability rules based on the type of products, liability in design or manufacturing, or inadequate instructions on warnings. Whether the states or for that matter the courts adopt this change will only be seen with the passage of time. So far, it appears that Texas courts and the Texas Legislature are not willing to make the wholesale changes suggested in Restatement (Third) of Torts.

G. Market Share Liability

One interesting and developing area of strict liability has been the so-called **market share liability**. The leading case in this area is **Sindell v. Abbott Laboratiories 607 P.2d 924 (1980)**. This case deals with an antimiscarriage drug called DES, resulting in cancer and sterility in the children of the mothers who took the DES. The FDA approved DES in 1947 as an experimental drug requiring a warning label. The FDA revoked approval of DES in 1971. Before 1971, the defendant manufacturers marketed DES as safe in spite of the fact that they knew of its adverse side effects, failed to test the drug properly, and, in violation of FDA policy, marketed it in a widespread manner without any warning whatsoever. DES victims experienced great difficulty proving that any specific manufacturer was negligent because pharmacists generally sold the drug under its generic name with no indication of its maker. The main question for consideration was whether the manufacturers could be held jointly liable for damages to DES victims who cannot positively identify which manufacturer was actually responsible. The Supreme Court of California established a novel remedy of market share liability. Drug companies will thus be liable based on the percentage of the overall production of DES for miscarriage for which they were responsible. For example, a given drug company with a historical 15-percent share of this DES market will be responsible for 15 percent of the monetary damages for the DES victims.

Keep in mind that DES was identical no matter which manufacturer made the product and that is a requirement of market share liability, the products must be exactly the same no matter which manufacturer makes the product. Market share liability is very limited and has only been used in a handful of cases since its creation in *Sindell*.

H. Absolute Liability?

Asbestos was a form of insulation used in several areas for decades. It came in many forms, but one way it was utilized was to be sprayed in as a liquid and when it became hard, forming a very effective insulation material. It was extensively used in construction, ship building, and other areas where traditional insulation was hard to place. However, it was determined that after time the asbestos fibers began to flake off and when exposed to the asbestos a person could develop a form of cancer called asbestosis or mesothelioma. Asbestosis is an irreversible thickening of the lung linings and eventually suffocates the victim. Mesothelioma is a cancer of the lining of the lungs caused by exposure to asbestos and is usually fatal. Asbestosis exposure can lead to other problems as well. However, asbestos problems are not new. The first known case of asbestos exposure was written about in 68 A.D. by Phiny the Younger. Anyone exposed to the fibers could become a victim.

The first lawsuit for asbestos exposure in the United States was brought in 1969. By 1982, one manufacturer of asbestos was facing 11,000 lawsuits. Many courts began to lower the legal standards required in asbestos-related injury claims even allowing recovery where no medically recognized asbestos-related injury was proven to exist. Courts also lowered the procedural rules giving rise to even more lawsuits on asbestos, which led to a large number of frivolous lawsuits. This led to mass tort attorneys taking to the television and soliciting clients by the thousands. This led to bankruptcy by many of the asbestos manufacturers, which led to layoffs in thousands. The insurance industry was also hard hit by the amounts that it was paying in claims. This forced attorneys to find new sources of defendants.

In an effort to stop the increase in frivolous asbestos litigation, the Senate proposed the **Asbestos Claims Criteria and Compensation Act of 2003** aimed at "providing for the fair and efficient judicial consideration of personal injury and wrongful death claims arising out of asbestos exposure, to ensure that individuals who suffer harm, now or in the future,

from illnesses caused by exposure to asbestos receive compensation for their injuries ..."
(S.B. 413 in the 108th Congress, 1st Session). However, the Bill died in committee. Congress
did not give up and proposed the Fairness in Asbestos Injury Resolution Act of 2005 proposing a $140-billion national trust fund for victims and a 5 percent cap on attorney's fees.
It also failed to become law. However, courts have ordered private trust funds to be set up
by companies that made asbestos for compensation to the victims. It is estimated that these
trust funds totaled $30 billion.

One of the newest areas of asbestos litigation is against property owners. The courts and
state legislatures seem to be mixed on the issue of liability in this area. Some courts have
held the property owners liable and others have not. Some state legislatures have statutorily given property owners a defense against litigation. However, the fear of asbestos continues to grow creating a whole new industry for asbestos removal.

This makes asbestos one of the costliest and longest running torts in history. If you are
diagnosed with asbestosis or mesothelioma, it is established that it was due to asbestos
exposure. By some estimates, 1 in every 125 deaths in the United States of Americans over
the age of 50 is related to asbestos exposure. It can take 10–20 years after exposure for the
problems to develop. Therefore, by the time you are sick, you probably have no way of
knowing how you were exposed to asbestos and certainly do not know who made the
asbestos that you were exposed to, but you can still recover from the trusts or sue on your
own such as the employer who made you use the asbestos or the building owner.

Therefore, have we entered into an era of absolute liability for the manufacturers of
asbestos? After all, they made it and anyone who is claiming to be exposed to any asbestos
is suing to recover from any source. Today it is asbestos, but what product will it be next?

I. Summary of Products Liability

Products liability can arise in negligence; warranties both expressed and implied, strict
liability, market share liability, and perhaps absolute liability in asbestos. However, what
are the applications in today's legal world?

Products liability in negligence can still be seen in cases relating to design defects in the
product, due to selection of materials used in the product, problems in the production process such as the product being made incorrectly, and in the testing of the product as well
as not placing adequate warnings for the purchaser, done in a negligent manner with the
necessary duty, breach, causation, and harm required.

Express warranty can still be used if the manufacturer gives you any express warranties. Obviously, the manufacturer can avoid these claims by not giving any express warranties. For instance, if you will watch, you will see that most television advertisements do not
give you any express warranties. Manufacturers also will normally tell the purchaser that
"no express warranties are given" to avoid express warranty claims.

Implied warranties can still be used if factually present. Implied warranty of merchantability and fitness for a particular purpose are still very real legal principles today.
However, again, the manufacturer can try to avoid these claims by selling a product "as is"
or even "no warranties given, expressed, or implied."

However, when dealing with an unreasonably dangerous product, strict liability dominates. Of course, not all products are unreasonably dangerous; hence, negligence and the warranties still exist to deal with the products that are not deemed to be unreasonably dangerous. Strict liability deals with manufacturing problems in unreasonably dangerous products such as design defects, failing to exercise due care in the manufacturing of the product thereby creating those defects and inadequate warning as well. Therefore, at first glance it seems that strict liability covers basically the same problems as the negligence products liability cases. However, you must remember that strict liability only covers unreasonably dangerous products and if the product is not unreasonably dangerous it is not covered by strict liability. Unreasonably dangerous usually means that the product is so defective so as to cause extreme health and safety risks. Market share liability only exists when the products are identical and therefore is rarely seen. Asbestos, so far, is in a category of its own that may be absolute liability. Therefore, all the theories of products liability still exist and are being currently litigated.

CHAPTER SUMMARY

The law of torts concerns the legal rights and duties of parties to involuntary transactions that have resulted in injury to one of the parties. There are several different perspectives on the purposes of tort law. An efficiency perspective concentrates on the use of tort law to alter incentive structures so that the minimum amount of resources will be devoted to accidents (both prevention and compensation). In general, the law of torts tends to reflect this view. However, the impact of the law of torts is also consistent with other views of the purpose of tort law, such as compensation or risk spreading.

An intentional tort is the intentional invasion of some legally protected interest. Examples of intentional torts include: intentional infliction of mental distress, invasion of privacy, defamation, assault, battery, false imprisonment, product disparagement, false advertising, intentional interference with contractual relations, trespass, conversion, nuisance, and fraud. In effect, tort law strengthens many property interests. For example, nuisance law provides a means for enforcing the right to exclusive use and enjoyment of real property.

Intellectual property rights are also protected under tort law. Therefore, when someone uses the intellectual property of another, the innocent party can bring an infringement lawsuit against the liable party. This is true in copyrights, patents, trademarks and service marks, trade names, and other areas of intellectual property.

Negligence law deals with accidents, which are unintentional torts. The elements of a cause of action based on negligence are duty, breach of duty, injury, and causation. The Hand formula provides an economic guide to determining when the defendant in a negligence action has breached the duty to exercise reasonable care. In general, the least cost avoider of an accident should be liable. The defenses to a negligence action are assumption of risk, contributory negligence, and comparative negligence. The Hand formula also provides an economic rationale for allowing certain defenses to a showing of negligence when the plaintiff's conduct could have reduced the likelihood of an accident.

Strict liability, or liability without fault, applies to activities that are recognized as hazardous, but are not so unreasonably risky as to justify a prohibition. Strict liability is the modern standard for holding manufacturers liable for injuries resulting from defective products.

The world is not free of risk, and reducing risk is costly. Many injuries that result from unsafe products could be avoided through greater expenditures on safety measures. Consumers are well aware of this basic fact, and it is reasonable to state that much consumer behavior indicates that they are not willing to incur the costs associated with lowering risk below some reasonable level. The basic public policy goal in this regard is to formulate a legal environment that tends to generate the amount of safety that corresponds to society's preferences for risk. Product safety is governed by market adjustments to risk and legal rules and regulations at both the state and federal levels. Market adjustment to risk means that when firms sell products that are riskier than most consumers or employees find acceptable, then the appropriate market adjustments will be reflected in lower prices. Thus, the business firm that imposes risks through voluntary transactions pays for such behavior through lower profits that result from lower revenues. Of course, the firm is also free to attempt to increase its profits by investing more in safety measures. A major problem with complete reliance on market incentives to generate the optimal level of safety is that consumers often do *not* have adequate information to judge the risks associated with certain products. Moreover, even in circumstances where the information is known to the relevant economic actors, some policy makers are concerned that the poor financial circumstances of some consumers will encourage them to take risks that the policy makers think are not warranted. The legal system, however, offers additional protections for consumers.

Products liability law deals with compensating consumers who have been injured as a result of a defective or otherwise unsafe product. Common law liability rules, which are the product of the state court systems, have evolved to reflect the development of the consumer economy. The old common law rules resulted in a legal environment characterized as *caveat emptor*, but the twentieth century has seen an evolution toward *caveat venditor*. Today, strict liability in tort is the most common theory of recovery in actions against producers of products that result in injuries.

6

ADMINISTRATIVE LAW FOOD AND DRUG ADMINISTRATION CONSUMER PRODUCT SAFETY COMMISSION

PART ONE

I. INTRODUCTION TO ADMINISTRATIVE AGENCIES

A. Primary Tool for Regulation by Government

Administrative agencies are the primary vehicles for imposing federal regulatory law on business and society. Administrative agencies are often referred to as the fourth branch of government because they exercise broad authority through the use of powers that were divided among the three branches of the federal government by the Constitution. Although this creates some potential for abuse, procedural safeguards have been developed to control agency power. In reality, administrative agencies supplement the three branches of government in their various functions rather than acting as a fourth branch of the federal government.

Administrative agencies exert a major influence on the shape of the legal environment of business because almost every major piece of federal regulatory legislation provides for some role for administrative agencies in its implementation and enforcement. Examples of the regulatory activities engaged in by administrative agencies that may affect the behavior of business firms include product safety regulations, pollution control standards, information disclosure for the sale of securities, workplace safety, union-organizing activities, employee hiring and promotion practices, and the antitrust treatment of contractual relationships between manufacturers and their distributors. In short, administrative agencies have a major influence on the behavior of American business.

B. Overview

The substantive laws promulgated by federal regulatory agencies are covered throughout this textbook. In order to understand the power of administrative agencies, one must know something of the procedural aspects of these agencies. However, the potential difficulty of this task is lessened considerably by the fact that all agencies follow similar procedures. This chapter considers the history or creation, structure, powers, and procedures of administrative agencies. The final sections consider some policy issues related to the costs and benefits of administrative agencies as well as some regulatory reform measures and proposals.

II. HISTORY OR CREATION

A. Why Created? Result Is to Usurp Other Branches' Powers and Functions

In evaluating the impact of administrative agencies on the legal environment of business, it is important to consider initially why administrative agencies developed, and why the other branches allowed their powers and functions to be usurped. As the country developed from an agrarian to an industrial economy, social and economic interrelationships and transactions grew more complicated and complex. In light of these changes, it became impossible for Congress to legislate in sufficient detail to regulate all activities that needed attention. Initially, Congress simply passed a law and allowed the courts to apply it to specific situations. Eventually, however, it became clear that the courts did not have the time or the expertise to handle even some of the more routine matters. Congress responded by **delegating** certain activities to specialized administrative agencies.

B. Creation

Administrative agencies are created by, and receive their powers from, an **enabling statute** in which Congress specifies the agencies' regulatory mission, organizational structure, procedures, and enforcement powers. Operationally, Congress paints with a very broad brush in enacting general statutes that set forth the purposes of the laws, and leaves the filling in of details to the agencies created to administer the laws. If an agency enacts rules or regulations that conflict with Congressional views, Congress has the power to alter the statutory language to clarify the purposes of the statute. The administrative process is also subject to review by the courts, as is discussed later in this chapter.

The first federal administrative agency, the Interstate Commerce Commission, was created by Congress in 1887. Over the past century, Congress has created dozens of other agencies. This history of federal regulatory activity may be divided into three eras: the first involved the passage of regulations aimed at specific industries such as railroads, drug companies, and securities. The second came during the administration of President Franklin D. Roosevelt and had the main goal of getting the country out of the Great Depression and protecting people from another similar economic situation. Roosevelt used many different types of regulatory agencies to accomplish his goal and several of them, once they achieved their goal, were allowed to expire. The third period, the Socially Conscious Era of the 1960s and 1970s, involved the passage of legislation aimed at particular activities that could be identified with many industries, such as pollution control, workplace safety, product safety, and hiring and firing practices in employment. The differing types of agencies created during these eras are examined below.

III. STRUCTURE

A. Types of Agencies Based on the Industry Regulated

The Interstate Commerce Commission was created by Congress to regulate railroad rates. In other words, the regulatory agency was meant to regulate one business. These are called **Industry-Specific Regulatory Agencies**. Other industry-specific agencies created by Congress include the Securities and Exchange Commission (SEC) and the Federal Communications Commission (FCC). A major criticism of such agencies is that they tend to lose sight of their public-interest mission over time. That is, although an agency may be created to control a particular industry, which suggests that it is to somehow constrain the industry, experience reveals that most agencies eventually adopt the perspective of the members of the regulated industry. This is often referred to as "regulatory capture." Thus, the regulated industry, which is supposed to being regulated or told what to do, is in essence frequently benefiting from the regulation and ends up telling the regulators how the regulation will be done. Therefore, it is not unusual for administrative agencies to act in the interest of the industry rather than in the so-called public interest or operating for the people. One explanation that has often been given is that the selection of board or commission members is biased toward choosing individuals from the industry. This is accomplished by the targeted industry donating money to the presidential campaign and then when the candidate is elected as President of the United States, reminding him that the industry helped him get elected. The result is likened to hiring the fox to guard the henhouse.

On the other hand, the hiring of industry insiders may be necessary because such current participants in the industry may be the only individuals who have the special knowledge of the industry that is required to make a meaningful contribution to the agency. Such knowledge is not often found in "outsiders" who would be more public interest oriented. Further, it is not clear that selecting board and commission members from outside the industry would change the result. There are other reasons why the regulated industries will tend to have relatively more impact on the regulations than representatives of the public at large. The industry has the greatest interest in the rules and regulations to be promulgated by the agency, thus, their side is likely to be better represented through lobbyists and expert testimony than the public at large. This imbalance is not surprising because individual citizens usually do not have the incentive to lobby for their positions on public policy issues nor the funds. From the perspective of the individual, active participation in the political process involves real and immediate costs with little expected direct benefit from the participation. The expected benefit is small because there is only a small likelihood that the individual's actions will influence the outcome and even if they do, an individual taxpayer's share of increased societal efficiency is not likely to amount to much. The rational individual may decide to "free ride" on the efforts of other citizens to promote the public good and not participate in the process. The more citizens that free ride on each other, the less represented are their views in the administrative process. While there may be consumer-advocate groups that oppose special interest groups, funding for salaries, expert testimony, and lobbying efforts is limited.

Industry-specific regulations were the predominant form of administrative regulation throughout the first half of the twentieth century during the Historical Era and also into the New Deal Era. For example, President Franklin Roosevelt's New Deal legislation of the 1930s includes several examples of industry-specific regulations, including the SEC (1934), the FCC (1934), and the Civil Aeronautics Board (1938), which has since been abolished.

Economy-wide regulatory agencies regulate problems that are not isolated in one particular industry. In other words, they regulate across industry lines. These have mostly been used during the Socially Conscience Era. However, the Federal Trade Commission (FTC) (1914), which is charged with preventing anticompetitive, unfair, and deceptive practices, was created during the Historical Era. Only a few economy-wide agencies were created with the passage of the New Deal legislation of the early 1930s. One example of these is the National Labor Relations Board (1935), which governs the organizing and bargaining rights of labor unions in virtually all industries.

The 1960s and 1970s were marked by an explosion of legislation designed to correct economy-wide economic and social problems. Examples of administrative agencies created during this era include the Environmental Protection Agency, the Consumer Product Safety Commission, the Equal Employment Opportunity Commission, and the Occupational Safety and Health Administration. These agencies are concerned with activities that involve all industries. For example, the Consumer Product Safety Commission regulates the safety of all consumer products.

As a result, it is less likely that one particular industry will have such a vested interest that it will dominate the decision-making process of the agency. Administrative agencies that implement economy-wide regulations have the greatest impact on the overall legal environment of business. Most of this text is devoted to understanding the impact of the substantive rules imposed on business by such agencies.

B. Types of Agencies Based on Control

The Federal Bureaucracy is divided into (1) Executive Agencies that are also called Dependent Agencies, (2) Independent Executive Agencies, (3) Independent Agencies, and (4) Government Corporations. **Executive Agencies** are part of the executive branch, and they usually are placed within the hierarchy of an executive department (such as the Department of Labor) headed by a cabinet member (the Secretary of Labor), but can also have several subparts such as the Wage and Hour Division of the Department of Labor. They can often be identified by the terms "departments" or "administrations," but can also be called by other names such as division in the example above. Executive Agencies, although often initially created by an executive order of the President, receive most of their powers from Congress in an enabling statute. There is normally one person in charge of an Executive Agency. These heads of Executive Agencies are appointed by the President and normally confirmed by the Senate, but they can be removed by the President for any reason. Therefore, much of the President's policy can be implemented through these agencies. This results in them being under the direct control of the President of the United States.

Independent Executive Agencies are basically created like an Executive Agency, but are not placed under a cabinet. However, they are dependent in that the President appoints their head and can remove him or her. These were normally created to be "independent" in that they are not under a cabinet level, but they are still "Executive" in that the President can appoint and remove their head. These were created to be independent so as not to be tied to a cabinet. Sometimes, this was for political reasons such as the National Air and Space Administration (NASA). NASA was created to develop the United States space program, but the United States did not want the world to feel that it was to have a military or weapons purpose. Therefore, it was created to be an Independent Executive Agency and was not placed under the Department of Defense nor under military control. However, it is still under presidential control since the President can appoint and remove the head of NASA. The Environmental Protection Agency is also an Independent Executive Agency and not under the Department of the Interior but is still answerable directly to the President. Other examples of Independent Executive Agencies are the Central Intelligence Agency (CIA), Board of Governors of the Federal Reserve System (the Fed), and the General Services Administration (GSA). Sometimes, they are truly administrative and sometimes they have other purposes including regulation.

Independent Agencies are created by Congress and given broad powers over regulation in a particular area. The typical independent agency is headed by a board or commission whose members are appointed by the President, but normally requires confirmation by the Senate. The members are generally appointed for staggered terms and can only be removed for cause. Note, the President does NOT have removal power over these positions, which means that, the President cannot fire the preceding President's appointees and must wait until those appointees' terms expire to replace them. The purpose for this requirement is to maintain some stability and continuity in policies during changes in presidential administrations. Generally, there is a restriction that the makeup of the board or commission can only contain a bare majority from the same political party. For example, the five-member SEC cannot have more than three members from one political party. This is also an effort to insulate the agencies from political pressure. Furthermore, since members can only be removed for cause, that is, failure to perform the duties of the office or crimes involving moral turpitude, they are generally insulated from the influence of Congress or the President. Nevertheless, Congressional control over the budgets of independent agencies means that such agencies will never be completely independent because Congress will always have ultimate control over them. However, they are acting independently on a day-to-day basis and do not answer directly to anyone.

C. Constitutional Status of Administrative Agencies

The Constitution separates the power of government into three distinct branches. As noted earlier, agencies possess powers of each of the three branches of government. When Congress creates an administrative agency, it typically delegates to that agency the power to promulgate certain rules and regulations that have the force of law. The delegation of this legislative function to agencies has led to numerous constitutional challenges during the development of the administrative agency as an element of the federal regulatory scheme. The basic constitutional question concerns the conditions under which it is permissible to allow some government body other than the Congress to make laws.

The most important early case involved a challenge to the authority of regulatory boards established pursuant to the National Industrial Recovery Act (NIRA), a key piece of New Deal legislation. The NIRA was designed to stabilize the falling prices and deter the cut-throat competition that was present in almost all industries during the Great Depression. The NIRA established price-setting boards for every major industry (the members of the boards were representatives of the leading firms). The essentially private boards were empowered to set prices for the entire industry, and violators of the set prices were subject to prosecution and fines. The boards amounted to legalized cartels. An individual charged with violating the price schedule challenged the constitutional status of the delegation. In 1935, in the famous case of **Schechter Poultry Corp. v. U.S., 295 U.S. 495 (1935)**, the Supreme Court ruled that the law was invalid as an unconstitutional delegation of legislative authority. Thus, the effectiveness of administrative agencies in producing specialized regulations was in doubt.

President Roosevelt was to say the least disappointed with the ruling and began to publically show his dissatisfaction with the makeup of the Supreme Court by proposing that the Supreme Court needed to be expanded. The NIRA was not the only piece of New Deal legislation that was overruled by the Supreme Court and most of these decisions were 5-4. This occurred during Roosevelt's first administration. Shortly after he was elected to a second term by 10,000,000 votes, he appealed to the Supreme Court to follow the will of the people. Roosevelt also suggested that the age of the Supreme Court Justices was a problem since six of the seven justices appointed by a Republican were over the age of 70. Therefore, he proposed to Congress that Congress give the President the authority to appoint one new justice, up to six for each justice over 70. Of course, the current Supreme Court Justices fought this move by Roosevelt. However, that changed in 1937 when Justice Owen Roberts, who had been appointed to the Supreme Court by President Herbert Hoover and normally voted against Roosevelt's New Deal, changed his vote and voted for the New Deal Program calling for a minimum wage, which he had voted against in 1936. Also, Justice Charles Hughes, another Republican appointee, also reversed his opinion on the Social Security Act and the National Labor Relations Act. Another Conservative Justice, Willis Van Devanter, announced his resignation from the Court paving the way for a Roosevelt appointee. The Senate overwhelmingly defeated Roosevelt's Court Reorganization Bill 70-20, but Roosevelt still won because some of the conservatives started voting for his New Deal programs. Therefore, the phrase a "stitch in time saves nine" was born, meaning that that shift of the conservative judges voting for the New Deal saved nine justices on the United States Supreme Court. So the issue became, did the Supreme Court bow to the political pressure or change its philosophy? Either way Roosevelt won.

The continued use of administrative agencies as an arm of the legislature was assured, however, as the Supreme Court's position on delegation evolved. The leading case on this point is **Yakus v. United States, 321 U.S. 414 (1944),** a 1944 Supreme Court case that involved the federal government's efforts to control the inflationary pressures that accompanied shortages of consumer goods in domestic markets during World War II. Congress had created the Office of Price Administration to set maximum rents and commodity prices. Congress directed that, in setting prices, the agency be guided by prices prevailing on a particular date and listed the factors to be considered when deviating from those prices. The Court determined that the act "conferred no greater reach for administrative determination" than previously acceptable, and upheld the delegation of legislative power. Thereafter, the Supreme Court would uphold the delegation of rule-making authority if sufficient standards were set forth and the powers were limited. In particular, it was permissible for administrative agencies to ascertain facts and fill in the details of the legislation as long as they complied with the standards and guidelines set forth by Congress.

Today, the Congressional delegation of broad powers to the President and administrative agencies is recognized as essential to effective regulation because of the greater complexity of economic relationships. Although powers must be given and constrained to some extent, they are often expressed in broad terms such as promoting "public convenience" or the "public interest." Nevertheless, an agency must remain within the confines of its delegated power.

IV. STRUCTURE OF REGULATORY AGENCIES

A. Organizational Structure

The organizational structure of an administrative agency is provided for in the enabling statute that creates the agency, which comes from an act of Congress or in the President's executive order or whatever the manner of creation of the regulatory agency. An agency's structure, or bureaucratic hierarchy, differs with the functions and size of the agency. In general, there is little difference between the structure of Independent Agencies and Executive Agencies; the primary difference is that the head of an Executive Agency is usually directly accountable to a cabinet member. The organizational structure of FTC, an independent agency, is headed by five commissioners, one of which is the chairman. The FTC is responsible for the regulation of many of the substantive areas of the legal environment of business, including antitrust (some duties are shared with the Department of Justice), unfair, and deceptive trade practices, and product safety (some duties are shared with the Consumer Product Safety Commission). The functional area of the bureaucracy is divided into three bureaus: the Bureau of Consumer Protection, the Bureau of Competition, and the Bureau of Economics. The Bureau of Consumer Protection concentrates on product safety issues as well as deceptive and unfair practices. The Bureau of Competition attempts to maintain competition through the enforcement of the antitrust laws. The Bureau of Economics provides support for the other two bureaus by conducting economic studies of areas targeted by the FTC. Of course, the actual structure can vary between agencies of any type due to the flexible nature of their structure.

B. History of the Structure

It was once the case that each administrative agency was allowed to establish its own procedures for carrying out its powers that were authorized by Congress. Each agency developed its own procedures through trial and error, which spawned a great deal of litigation concerning whether due process protections guaranteed by the Constitution were being violated. In 1947, Congress passed the **Administrative Procedures Act** (APA) which has become the rulebook for administrative agencies. The procedural requirements in this chapter draw heavily from the APA. Although powers differ from agency to agency, it is possible to make accurate generalizations about the powers of the typical administrative agency. As noted earlier, administrative agencies enjoy powers similar to the three branches of government. The next section discusses the most important of these powers: legislative, enforcement, and adjudicatory.

V. POWERS AND PROCEDURES OF ADMINISTRATIVE AGENCIES

A. Source

All of the powers of an administrative agency are granted to the agency by Congress. The enabling statute that creates the agency also defines the purpose of the agency and empowers the agency to promulgate rules and regulations to accomplish its purpose. Often the purpose is stated in broad terms such as to prevent the use of "unfair or deceptive trade practices." This gives great flexibility to the agency to determine behavior that is unfair or deceptive and gives it broad authority. However, all are now under the APA as seen above.

B. Legislative (or Rule-Making) Powers and Procedures

The enabling statute generally commands the agency to take actions necessary to achieve the stated public-interest goals of the legislation. Because the statute is broadly written, the agency is usually authorized to adopt rules and regulations to further the purposes of the statute through a delegation of legislative power, which was the subject of concern as seen above in the *Schechter Poultry* and *Yakus* cases seen above. Rule making is simply the process of promulgating rules and regulations that have the force of Congressional statutes.

    A primary goal of the APA is to allow interested parties the opportunity to be heard when agencies are proposing to adopt rules that will have an impact on their lives. Thus, the APA procedures require notice to interested parties and in some cases the holding of public hearings. Such hearings are analogous to Congressional hearings on proposed legislation. In both instances, the purpose is to add legitimacy to the process by allowing greater citizen participation.

The APA provides for both informal and formal rule-making procedures. The type of procedure used may be proscribed by Congress or determined by the agency depending upon the consequences of the rule. The following is a stepwise description of the typical use of these procedures. The first type of rule making is called **informal rule making**, which is a much simpler form of rule making than the formal rule making which will be discussed later. The steps to informal rule making are as follows.

The agency first identifies the need for a rule or regulation, perhaps through correspondence from the public, a Congressional subcommittee, industry spokespersons, or members of the agency who deal with the subject of the regulation. The agency then drafts the proposed regulation in comprehensive language to induce commentary from the public. The APA, pursuant to the Constitution's requirement of procedural due process, requires that proper notice be given to all interested parties to enable them to be heard before the regulation becomes law. This notice requirement is satisfied by the agency publishing a "Notice of Proposed Rule Making" in the *Federal Register*, a daily government publication. The notice contains information regarding the legal authority under which the rule is proposed and either the terms of the proposed regulation or a description of the issues and subjects involved.

With the exception of wholly internal procedural rules and in the case of emergencies, publication in the *Federal Register* must occur at least 30 days prior to the date the final draft is written. During this period, the public is invited to send written comments to the agency for it to consider before enacting the proposed regulation. Informal rule making is often called "notice and comment" because written commentary is usually the only method through which the public will be heard. The comments do not have the status of testimony because the commentators are not sworn and their comments do not generally become part of any record used to generate the final draft of the regulation. In other words, the agency can completely ignore the comments and proceed as it wishes or rewrite the regulation in response to comments. No hearing or meeting within the agency is required for informal rule making although hearings are sometimes held with proper notice to interested parties. The last step is that the final draft of the regulation must be published in the *Federal Register* at least 30 days prior to its effective date.

The second type of rule making is called **formal rule making** and begins just like the informal method with a "Notice of Proposed Rule Making" published in the *Federal Register* after the agency determines that it needs the rule and promulgates the rule. Unlike the informal process, the notice contains information regarding the time, place, and nature of the proceedings; the legal authority under which the rule making is proposed; and a description of the issues and subjects involved. The notice must be at least 30 days prior to the proceedings. It is not unusual for the notice period to be several months to allow proper preparation for the proceedings. The next step is that a formal trial-like hearing is held and a record made of oral testimony and documentary evidence. Interested parties can introduce exhibits and call expert witnesses who are subject to examination and cross-examination. Obviously, a party opposing a regulation can delay the proposed regulation by calling numerous witnesses and introducing voluminous documentary evidence which must be reviewed. In some cases, the final proposal has been delayed by such tactics for as much as a decade. The agency then writes the final draft of the regulation giving due deference to the evidence contained in the record. The regulation is then published and becomes effective no less than 30 days later unless enjoined by a federal court.

Given the time and expense consumed by formal rule-making procedure, it is not surprising that the vast majority of rule making is accomplished through the informal process. In fact, the difference in expenditure of resources is so extensive one may inquire why the formal procedure is ever used. The answer is simple: the APA mandates the different rule-making procedures. The APA requires that substantive rules be created by the formal procedure while the procedural rules and regulations can be done informally. Formal rule making is mandated by the APA in the interests of society, in order to allow the agency to develop a thorough record of information based on oral and written testimony and cross-examination. For instance, Congress requires the approval of new drugs by the Food and Drug Administration to follow the formal procedure. The formal procedure is also used when an adversarial proceeding is expected to generate information that the agency could not otherwise assemble. Another factor that determines the level of procedural due process is the property interests at stake. The greater is the impact of a regulation on a specific group the more formal the procedure. For instance, a regulation mandating retirement of airline pilots at age 40 would require a more formal procedure than a regulation requiring a medical examination at age 40.

C. Enforcement (Investigatory) Powers and Procedures

In order to fulfill its powers, an administrative agency must be able to gather information. The enforcement powers of agencies allow them to gather information by requesting the voluntary submission of information by companies. Companies usually comply with such requests in order to avoid the cost of more formal means of information collection, an exercise that would ultimately lead to the submission of the information anyway. Since there is potential for misuse of private information by the government and there may be Fifth Amendment self-incrimination issues, agencies are generally not permitted to exchange information gathered through self-reporting. For example, the law requires taxpayers to disclose the source of income on their income tax returns but the Internal Revenue Service is not permitted to share such information with the Justice Department. This restriction does not apply to information obtained from corporations because they are not protected against self-incrimination. Other methods of gathering information include holding hearings, using subpoena power, and the physical inspection of businesses. A subpoena is a legal instrument that orders a business to appear to give testimony or produce documents. If a business fails to comply with a legal subpoena, representatives of the business can be imprisoned until they do comply. Physical inspection of the business can be due to a warrant, due to the business being open to the public, or because the business agrees to the inspection. If a warrant is necessary it is an administrative warrant, which simply requires the agency to go by the administrative law judge and get a warrant. It does not require probable cause under the Fourth Amendment. However, no warrant is required if the business is open to the public, the business is considered "open field," or if the business consents. This open field exception was seen in **Dow Chemical Co. v. United States 476 U.S. 227 (1986)**. In this case, the United States was the Environmental Protection Agency (EPA). The EPA had requested an onsite inspection of Dow's 2,000-acre chemical plant that consisted of several buildings with outdoor manufacturing equipment and piping conduits between the various buildings. Dow did not have a warrant and refused the request. So, the EPA hired a commercial aerial photographer to take photos of the Dow plant using enhanced techniques for better accuracy. Once they found out about the photos, Dow claimed that its Fourth Amendment rights had been violated and objected to the photos being used in the investigation. The case reached the Supreme Court and the Court ruled that Dow's Fourth Amendment rights had NOT been violated because the Dow plant was an "open field" and Dow could not claim a privacy right. Furthermore, the government had not used any sensory devices that were not available to the public and that it had simply enhanced human vision by using the commercial pilot's photo equipment.

However, this does not mean that the investigative techniques are unlimited. The investigative techniques of administrative agencies are subject to other constitutional limitations such as the Fourth Amendment protection against unreasonable searches and seizures. Therefore, the Fourth Amendment does apply when an administrative agency believes it needs to search or seize and thus most administrative inspections are considered searches within the meaning of the Fourth Amendment's reasonable expectation of privacy. Although a search warrant must be obtained prior to such searches, the requirement of probable cause is somewhat relaxed because the stakes are not as high as in a criminal investigation. The purpose of requiring such warrants is to prevent agencies from using their search power to harass businesses into complying with agency directives. The basis for a warrant in administrative law basically refers to reasonable cause to search and the government can usually obtain the warrant if it can show that it has a legitimate governmental interest. Therefore, specific evidence of the violation of an administrative rule or law will justify the issuance of an administrative warrant as will a showing that there is a reasonable plan supported by a valid public interest. Furthermore, there are exceptions in search and seizure law. For instance, in closely regulated industries, such as liquor and firearms, a warrant is not required to conduct an administrative search. This is because the industry is subject to close supervision and inspection and does not have the same reasonable expectation of privacy that most individuals and businesses share (**Colonnade Corp. v. United States, 397 U.S. 72 (1970)**). Such businesses must accept searches as part of the privilege of doing business. This is also true if the business is part of a hazardous industry and a statute expressly provides for warrantless searches, thereby putting members of the industry on notice that they have less expectation of privacy (**Donovan v. Dewey 452 U.S. 594 (1981)**). Exigent or emergency circumstance will also justify a warrantless search. This has recently been seen in the emergency situations where human life is at risk in searches of drug-compounding companies in Massachusetts and in meat-packing companies thought to be selling *E. coli*-tainted beef.

In addition to the gathering of information, agencies have the power to force businesses to comply with its rules and regulations. The enabling statutes typically specify the penalties that may be imposed by an agency. Agencies employ several tactics in enforcing their rules, including the use of threats, fines, and court action. In some instances, the mere threat of public exposure of a business firm's misconduct will entice the company to comply. For example, exceeding pollution abatement standards and subsequent loss of goodwill in the eyes of consumers may be enough to force the firm to comply. This form of informal enforcement is used in areas where it is easy for a business to inadvertently violate a regulation. In other instances, the agency may have to resort to more punitive enforcement measures, which are designed to deter future violations. Although agencies typically have the power to fine violators without a trial, they do not have the power to imprison violators. The Supreme Court has held that procedural due process in the levying of a penalty does not require a pre-determinative hearing in an administrative setting (**Dixon v. Love, 95 S.Ct. 1723 (1977)**). Of course, the alleged violator may seek agency and judicial reviews. If violators refuse to obey agency remedial orders, the agency can petition the appropriate federal district court to get an order forcing the violator to comply. Failure to comply with the court order is a separate offense and, possibly, a criminal one. Of course, agencies often also have to file complaints in their own administrative courts as is seen in the next section. Furthermore, we will see other types of enforcement tools used as well, and usually an agency will rely on a combination of enforcement tools to force businesses to comply with its rules and regulations.

D. Adjudicatory Powers and Procedures

Perhaps the most controversial power delegated to administrative agencies is the power to adjudicate the disputes within their jurisdiction. Not only do the agencies make and enforce the rules, but an agency employee, an **administrative law judge** (ALJ), also adjudicates the controversies. Thus, when an enforcement action is brought by the agency, it results in the agency acting as both prosecutor and judge. Furthermore, there is usually no jury right in administrative law. In practice, this dual role does not seem to cause problems because ALJs take pride in their independence and ability to render unbiased opinions and the agencies typically separate their prosecutorial and judicial functions. However, ALJs can also be replaced or reassigned; after all, they are employees of the agency. The potential conflict of interest is also minimized by the imposition of certain required procedures in administrative law.

The typical adjudicative action begins with the filing of a complaint by the agency or by a private party alleging that an individual or business has violated an agency regulation. The alleged violator is notified of the complaint, and the agency's staff investigates the allegations in the complaint. After the investigation, the agency decides whether or not to continue the action. If the agency dismisses the complaint for lack of supporting evidence, then the process is usually over. If the agency decides to pursue the matter, and if a compromise remedy cannot be reached with the alleged violator, then the next step is to hold a hearing before an ALJ.

In administrative agency adjudications, the defendant is entitled to certain rights. In particular, the adjudication must conform to the procedural due process as guaranteed by the Constitution. This requires that notice of the allegations or charges be given to the defendant, and that the defendant be allowed to present evidence on the matter. Generally, this evidence-presenting requirement is satisfied by a hearing before an administrative law judge where witnesses are called, examined, and cross-examined under oath, and a record of testimony is produced.

Although adjudicatory hearings are similar to trials in federal court, there are a number of differences. Defendants are permitted counsel, but attorneys will not be appointed for those who cannot afford them. Unlike federal trial courts, defendants are not entitled to a trial by jury. In **Atlas Roofing Company, Inc. v. Occupational Safety and Health Review Commission, 430 U.S. 442 (1977)**, where the petitioner was fined $600 for having unsafe working conditions, the Supreme Court ruled that the Seventh Amendment's requirement that jury trial is to be "preserved" in "suits at common law" did not extend to statutory proceedings such as administrative adjudications. Since the ALJ is the fact finder and an expert in the field, the rules of evidence, which are designed to prevent juries from giving too much weight to unreliable evidence, are somewhat relaxed. The burden of proof necessary to sustain the charges against the defendant depend upon the sanctions imposed by the ALJ. For instance, a greater degree of proof would be required to revoke a permit than would be necessary to fine a holder of a permit for violation of a regulation.

The ALJ's written decision includes the findings of fact, conclusions of law, and recommended disposition. The losing party may appeal to the review board of the agency. Agency decisions have value as precedent for other cases heard within the agency, but they typically are interpreted narrowly so as to apply to cases only with very similar facts. The APA provides that the losing party can appeal to the Circuit Court of Appeals after all appeals within the agency are exhausted.

Since the decision by the ALJ theoretically sets a precedent that has the same force as a regulation, the agency often has the choice of promulgating a regulation or charging an alleged violator and setting a precedent. For instance, suppose the FTC wanted service-station operators to place the octane ratings of gasses on their pumps. The agency has the choice of making a regulation requiring such disclosure or bringing suit against an operator, who had not posted octane ratings, for committing an unfair or deceptive trade practice. By finding the operator guilty, the agency could set precedent without having a formal rule-making hearing. From the typical agency's perspective, APA rule-making proceedings are something that must be put up with before the agency can give its stamp of approval to regulations that it supports. Because of this fact of bureaucratic life, agency employees often attempt to minimize the time and effort devoted to rule-making hearings. In fact, for a time, the agencies used to end-run around the rule-making procedures by attempting to make rules through adjudicative hearings. This expansive use of precedent saved the agency the inconvenience of complying with the rule-making provisions, but denied other interested parties the opportunity to be heard. This clearly violated the spirit of the APA, and the courts no longer give such rulings the broad force of regulations promulgated through the rule-making hearings.

As stated above, the APA sets forth the requirements for a party dissatisfied with the outcome of an administrative procedure, either adjudicatory or investigatory, to challenge the outcome by appeal to the appropriate Circuit Court of Appeals. Such an appeal is referred to as **judicial review**. The most important aspects of judicial review concern who has the right to a review and what is the scope of the review.

In general, unless Congress specifies otherwise, just about any party injured by an agency action can appeal to the federal courts subject to meeting specific requirements of **timeliness** and **standing**. Timeliness means that the aggrieved party cannot appeal the case until all remedies within the agency have been exhausted, which includes the appeal to the review board within the agency. Standing relates to the constitutional requirement in Article III that limits the jurisdiction of the federal courts to actual "cases and controversies." In the present context, the obvious reason for the standing requirement is to assure that the parties challenging the administrative action are in a true adversarial relationship to the agency. In order to satisfy this requirement, parties must show that they are members of the class that are affected by the agency action and that they are aggrieved by such action. This requirement assures that the parties will pursue the case to the best of their abilities and provide the court with the most complete record upon which to make its decision. Courts will not involve themselves in declaratory judgments before someone actually suffers harm. Otherwise, courts would be inundated with hypothetical controversies that may never occur, while true controversies wait in line to be settled. A party that has a *real* dispute with the agency is said to have **standing to sue**.

After all administrative remedies have been exhausted and the aggrieved party has established the right to judicial review, the Circuit Court of Appeals is then called upon to review the administrative agency's actions. As with other forms of appellate review, the typical judicial review of administrative actions involves only questions of law. Thus, the scope of judicial review is limited. In rare instances, a *de novo* review will be made by the court, which means the court will examine the issue as if the agency had not yet acted. Thus, the court is not bound by the agency's findings of fact. Such review is possible only in a few instances.

The typical questions of law involved in judicial review concern agency procedures, sufficient justification for agency actions, erroneous interpretation of the enabling statute, and whether the action was within the authority of the enabling statute. For example, agency procedures are mandated by the Constitution, the APA, and the enabling statute. If the agency has not followed the correct procedures, then the agency's action may be reversed. Also, the agency's action may be reversed if the reviewing court finds that it is premised on an erroneous interpretation of the enabling statute. Finally, the agency's actions may be challenged on the ground that the agency exceeded its authority granted by the enabling statute.

In some situations, the agency is called upon to justify the promulgation of a regulation. The level of proof necessary to sustain a regulation depends upon the procedure used in the decision-making process. When informal rule-making procedure is used, no record is made of the evidence. Appellate courts cannot examine the evidence as a whole to determine if the correct decision was made by the agency. Therefore, the Court of Appeals is going to require that the agency follow its own rules and regulations. The standard for appeal used in such a circumstance is whether the decision of the agency was "**arbitrary or capricious**." In other words, is there any rational reason for the agency decision?

However, the burden on whether the rule or regulation is fair is usually high since the rules and regulations were forced on the business. When formal rule-making procedure is used, a record is made of testimony and documentary evidence so that appellate courts have a record to review. The standard for appeal is the **"substantial evidence"** test. This means that the agency decision must be based on a substantial piece of evidence. The Courts of Appeal normally yield to the agency's judgment in technical or scientific matters if they have met the substantial evidence test. However, as to whether the rule itself is fair, the companies already had their day in hearings to object and therefore, those violations are given the lowest amount of review as opposed to the procedural rules and regulations, which receive the higher amount of review since the business did not have a chance to object to them.

Judicial review is not the only means of controlling the activities of administrative agencies. In practice, both Congress and the President keep a close eye on the activities of the agencies and exert considerable control over agency policies. The President appoints the heads of almost all agencies, both executive and independent, and definitely makes an effort to appoint persons who will adopt policies consistent with the President's beliefs. Congress also exerts considerable control over both executive and independent agencies. Each house of Congress has committees designated to oversee the activities of agencies operating within the particular expertise of the committee. For example, the House Committee on the Judiciary oversees the antitrust activities of the FTC. The oversight committees review the work of the agencies, hold hearings, and propose changes in the enabling legislation if they find that an agency is interpreting its purposes differently from the intent of Congress. An additional control is through "the power of the purse." Wayward agencies often find their budgets cut. Congress occasionally dictates that appropriations be used for certain purposes.

A final limitation on agency power should be noted. Interest groups monitor the activities of administrative agencies that may affect their interests. Such groups are prepared to put their lobbyists into action both on Capitol Hill and at the White House in order to influence the outcome of the administrative process.

VI. POLICY ISSUES—THE BENEFITS AND COSTS OF REGULATION

A. Introduction

Increased attention directed toward the federal budget deficit has fueled the debate over the role of federal administrative agencies in the allocation of society's resources. Some commentators argue that one way to trim the federal budget deficit is to reduce the size of the government and one way to do that is to reduce the number of administrative agencies or greatly reduce their budgets. Opponents of this view argue that because of certain market problems, reduction of administrative agencies would cause a reduction in the efficiency with which our resources are being used, hence, the direct savings would be overwhelmed by the indirect losses though inefficiency. They also argue that this would ultimately result in harm to the general public. In early 2013, Congress battled President Obama over what cuts to make in the federal budget. When the sequestration came in March that resulted in painful, mandatory cuts to the federal budget, President Obama argued that if Congress did not do something about these cuts it would harm the American public in numerous ways. This has resulted in severe cuts to several agencies and only time will tell if President Obama is correct or if the cuts will be a positive step toward reducing the deficit of the United States.

B. Benefits of Regulation

If the market system operated perfectly, then the well-being of society would be maximized with little need for government. However, the market system is not perfect. One argument in favor of administrative agencies is that they can correct certain imperfections in the market system and make the allocation of resources more efficient. Here are a few examples of market imperfections. Competition, which causes producers to be efficient, also causes producers to overpollute in order to keep their prices low. In some areas, the presence of high transactions costs reduces the number of productive transactions that can potentially occur. Sometimes, the costs of information are so great that individuals make costly errors that more and cheaper information could have prevented. Often, if competition is not present, prices will be artificially higher than the true value of resources, thereby causing a misallocation of the related resources. In still other cases, profit-seeking activities will cause some individuals to invade the property rights of others, which will decrease the real value of such property. Administrative agencies that can improve upon the allocations of resources that are the result of imperfections in the market system clearly benefit society, provided that they do not impose greater costs on society than the benefits they create.

Administrative agencies have proliferated because they provide certain other easily identified benefits to Congress. One such benefit is the relief of some of the duties traditionally handled by the three branches of government, which were unable to adequately handle the details required by the increasing complexity of the changing economic and social environments. Furthermore, many of the duties performed by agencies are politically sensitive issues that are difficult for members of Congress to publicly vote upon for fear of losing voters who cast their votes according to a candidate's stand on that issue alone. Approval of prescription drugs, defense policy, aid to foreign nations, Social Security and health care benefits, and employment discrimination are but a few such issues, handled by administrative agencies, and for which members of Congress are only indirectly responsible.

Another well-recognized benefit of the use of administrative agencies is that they employ experts with specialized knowledge in the fields they regulate. The EPA and the Food and Drug Administration (FDA) hire biologists and chemists, the FTC hires economists, and the FAA hires aeronautical engineers. Over time, an agency develops expertise in making rules in a certain subject area and the agency's ALJs also acquire a level of expertise not found in federal district courts. Thus, administrative agencies confer obvious benefits by supplementing the functioning of the three branches of government.

C. The Costs of Regulation

These benefits, however, are not free. In recent years, administrative agencies have come under attack for creating too many rules and regulations with which businesses must comply. The most damaging criticism of administrative agencies is that the costs of complying with their rules and regulations bear no relationship to the benefits to be gained from compliance. Here, the benefits of compliance refer to the benefits associated with the correction of some problem in the market system that Congress has targeted. These societal benefits must be compared with the aggregation of total costs imposed on individuals and businesses by the regulations in order to evaluate the desirability of the government intervention. In regulating any given activity, Congress is well aware of the fact that it is imposing costs on some parties. That is, all regulations constrain behavior, and to the extent a constraint alters behavior away from the least-cost way of conducting business, it imposes costs. For example, Occupational Safety and Health Administration (OSHA) proposes a regulation making employers responsible for providing ergonomic office equipment for employees who work at home which is often the most efficient place for them to work. Employers responded that they would prohibit employees from working at home in order to avoid the cost of providing and monitoring the use of ergonomic office equipment. OSHA would have to back off from its proposed rule or live with the unintended consequences.

Assuming that Congress is motivated by the goal of enhancing the public interest when it authorizes a certain type of regulation, then the effectiveness of the legislation can be evaluated by comparing the benefits and costs of the legislation as implemented by the appropriate administrative agency. However, although the trend is changing and may continue to do so with the new budget talks in Congress, Congress has not generally required agencies to consider the costs and benefits of the rules they promulgate. Moreover, in instances where Congress does not explicitly require a cost-benefit analysis, the courts will uphold agency rules and regulations without a showing that costs are worth the benefits. For example, in **American Textile Manufacturers Institute, Inc. v. Donovan, 452 U.S. 488 (1981)**, the Supreme Court held that the statutory language requiring OSHA to promulgate standards necessary to control health hazards "to the extent feasible" did not mean that OSHA was required to conduct a cost-benefit analysis prior to the imposition of such a regulation. Thus, in order to get agencies to perform cost-benefit analysis, Congress must be explicit in its language.

There is a tendency among some commentators to condemn many regulations simply because they impose costs. This is unfortunate because it ignores the reason for the imposition of the regulations and the conscious decision of Congress to impose costs in order to achieve the desired goals. However, it is easy to see why the benefits of some regulations are sometimes ignored. Costs of regulatory compliance are more easily identified than benefits which may be diffused throughout the country. That is, the financial burden on business is often very high and very visible because the rules and regulations will often require expenditures on new equipment or additional personnel, but the benefits are not immediately apparent. For example, compliance with environmental protection laws imposes enormous costs on business firms, and the benefits, while extensive, do not inure to any well-defined group. The real problem, therefore, is to quantify the benefits so that the regulation can be evaluated in terms of its net benefit to society. However, we are not a very patient society.

When agency regulations impose costs on businesses, they respond by finding ways around the regulations. As a result, agencies must continue to pass rules that constrain this new conduct. This requires additional costs for the agency and sometimes they go to such an extreme that it borders on ridiculous. For example, the Civil Aeronautics Board once regulated the airline industry. One of its goals was to prevent competition between airlines because it feared that one airline would emerge to dominate the industry and charge monopoly fares. In order to prevent competition, the board regulated fares and routes that airlines were permitted to fly. Since they could not compete on fares or routes, airlines attempted to attract customers by offering better in-flight meals. In one instance, such competition caused the board to issue a 7,000-word rule specifying what constituted a "sandwich" on designated sandwich flights. It is not surprising that the *Code of Federal Regulations* is requiring more and more shelf space. Given the sheer volume of rules and regulations produced by administrative agencies, it is costly for members of the business community to stay abreast of the current law. Therefore, the more the business tries to avoid the rule, the more rules are necessary and more costs to businesses resulting in a vicious cycle. However, reasonable ignorance of a government regulation is not a defense to an agency action (**Federal Crop Insurance Corporation v. Merrill 332 U.S. 380 (1947)**).

VII. ADMINISTRATIVE AGENCIES AND REGULATORY REFORM

A. Continual Calls for Reform of Regulatory Agencies

There are continual calls for reform in the agency process. As suggested above, much of this activity may be attributed to the high visibility of costs relative to the visibility of benefits. The criticisms range from dissatisfaction with unnecessary delays in the decision process to complaints about perceived weaknesses in enforcement. Depending upon the critic, agencies are too slow or too fast, or they act too weakly or too strongly. Other criticisms charge that administrative agencies almost always outlive their usefulness, or that they are pawns of the industries they are supposed to regulate. Another form of criticism focuses on bureaucratic behavior and suggests that many of the problems with agencies are due to incompetent or lazy personnel who care only about making sure their jobs are secure. Therefore it is easy to put the blame on the Federal Bureaucracy.

Therefore, over the years, numerous proposals for reforming the administrative process and improving its output have been made. Some proposals, which have been adopted at either the federal or state level or both, are worthy of discussion.

B. Types of Reform

Some critics of the administrative process think that the process will tend to produce better regulations if it is conducted in a manner that allows for monitoring by the general public.

The basic theory is that better regulations will result from increased accountability of bureaucrats. Two federal statutes reflect this approach: the **Freedom of Information Act** (FOIA) of 1966 and the **Government in the Sunshine Act** of 1976. Both Acts are amendments to the APA. The former Act deals with the availability of records after an administrative action has taken place, and the latter involves attendance at administrative agency hearings.

The FOIA requires federal agencies to make agency information available to "any person." Requests for records must be directed to the agency that produced the records, and the agency must respond to the request. The agency bears the burden of showing that the records may not be released due to one of the several exceptions to the Act, such as exceptions for records containing trade secrets or pertaining to matters of national security. If the agency fails to cooperate with a legitimate request, the Act provides for court actions to force the agency to produce the records.

The Government in the Sunshine Act requires that agencies headed by two or more people appointed by the President hold "every portion of every meeting" in the open and subject to public observation. The agency, by majority vote, may decide to close the meeting if it qualifies for one of the enumerated exceptions to public meetings. Day-to-day activities of agency personnel are not subject to the Act and it applies only to deliberations of agency members when official agency business is conducted or decided. The exceptions enumerated in the Act are similar to the justification for not releasing information under the FOIA. Decisions by agencies to close their meetings are subject to review by the appropriate United States District Court.

Another regular concern is the effect of administrative rules and regulations on small businesses. This concern of Congress over the effects of new regulations on small businesses led to the passage of the **Regulatory Flexibility Act** in 1980. Whenever a new regulation will have a "substantial impact upon a substantial number of small entities," the agency must conduct a flexibility analysis. The agency must measure the costs that the rule will impose on small businesses and must consider less burdensome alternatives. The agency must alert small businesses about forthcoming regulations by appropriate methods.

The **Small Business Regulatory Enforcement Fairness Act** (SBREFA) of 1996 permits Congress to review federal regulations for at least 60 days prior to their effective date. This gives additional time and an additional forum for opponents to present their arguments. It also requires agencies to prepare guides that explain the requirements imposed on small businesses in "plain English." Importantly, the Act permits small businesses to recover their legal expenses from the government when an agency imposes fines or penalties that the court considers excessive.

The Act created the National Enforcement Ombudsman within the Small Business Administration to serve as a clearinghouse for comments from small businesses concerning their dealings with federal agencies. Based on these comments, agencies are rated and the results are published.

As we discussed above, one of the criticisms of government regulations is that they tend to outlive their usefulness, which means they continue to impose costs long after they have stopped producing benefits. In order to remove such regulations, many states have adopted **sunset laws**, which require periodic review of many laws and regulations. If the laws are not extended by new legislation, then the law expires. Sunset laws typically call for the reevaluation of laws and regulations every five to ten years. In Texas, most are given a "death date," which is an expiration date built into the administrative agency. If the Texas Legislature does not extend the administrative agency with a new piece of legislation, the agency ceases to exist on the death date. Therefore, it is up to the agency to prove to the Texas Legislature that it is doing the job it was designed to do and deserves to be extended. Otherwise, it dies on the stated "death day." While some federal laws provide for periodic review, but there is no general federal sunset law applicable to agency regulations.

In contrast with those who say that better regulations or regulators are the solutions to the problems with government regulation, many critics of the administrative agency process suggest extensive deregulation is the best means of regulatory reform. **Deregulation** simply means to do away with the regulation. Therefore, these critics believe that the market functions more efficiently without regulation than with regulation, so it is better to have no regulation at all. Those that adhere to this free market philosophy claim that administrative agencies create more problems than they solve. The cure is worse than the disease.

Deregulation of certain types of activities began during the Nixon Administration and continued into the Reagan and Bush Administrations. Most of the deregulation activity has concentrated on industry-specific regulations such as the airlines, trucking, banking, and telecommunications. As with all changes in legal rules, there have been winners and losers as industries were deregulated. In general, the previously regulated industries, or at least some segments of them, have suffered, while consumers have been greeted with lower prices and greater variety. However, this was not the case during the Clinton Administration and does not seem to be the case during the Obama Administration. Therefore, deregulation seems to be more popular with Republicans than with Democrats.

As for the future reform efforts, on January 18, 2011, President Barack Obama issues Executive Order 13563 titled Improving Regulation and Regulatory Review. This executive order requires a limited form of cost justification for a new regulation, a requirement that a new regulation must impose the least burden on society and where practical consider costs, select the approach that maximizes net benefits, specify performance objectives, and identify and assess available alternatives to direct regulation. Agencies are to use best available techniques to quantify the present and future benefits and costs. Furthermore, the public is expected to participate in regulation adoption and be notified of the proposed rule or regulation and post the proposed or final rule online and then the public is to be given the opportunity to comment online. The Agency is also required to include the relevant scientific and technical findings online and available for download to the general public. The executive order also calls for agencies to work together to avoid redundant, inconsistent, or overlapping regulatory requirements. Agencies were also ordered to conduct a retrospective analysis of existing rules to reduce outdated, ineffective, and overly burdensome rules and regulations. President Obama has also called for consolidation of some agencies to save costs. However, that call does not include any of the agencies we will discuss in this course.

C. Ethical Considerations

The businesspersons have a number of ethical dilemmas with respect to administrative agencies. First, is it unethical for special interest groups to lobby for legislation or regulations that favor themselves at the expense of the public interest? For instance, if it were known that dairy price supports were actually contrary to the public interest because they increased prices of dairy products to consumers more than they increased profits to the dairy industry, would it be unethical for the dairy industry to lobby in favor of increasing price supports? Most would agree that it would be unethical and illegal to offer payoffs or other forms of bribery to decision makers in return for favorable treatment. But, many also feel that the federal budget is a vast resource that exists in perpetuity and that competition with other interest groups for a share of that resource is part of our economic system. If their group does not get the funds, so they say, the budget will not be reduced, but the funds will go to some other use that is similarly contrary to the public interest.

Many feel that lobbying for favoritism is a form of profit seeking that they did not create, but in which they are simply participating. They feel that if they do not participate, others will obtain favoritism that operates to their disadvantage. Hence, it is not just a matter of profitability, but survival. Proponents of this view argue that the general public has an opportunity to oppose favoritism through the rule-making process and the fact that special interests win is a sign that the public interest has been served. Unfortunately, such a view ignores the fact that individual members of the public do not have much incentive to oppose favoritism since interests are much less concentrated among individuals.

A second dilemma facing members of the business community is a result of many regulations that are difficult or impossible to enforce but impose substantial costs on firms that do comply with them. If one's competitors are cutting costs by ignoring regulations, it may be difficult for a law-abiding firm to survive. For instance, if some firms are disposing of wastes in violation of a law that is difficult to enforce, which enables them to charge lower prices than their law-abiding competitors, they may drive the latter from the market. In such cases, it is very costly for individual firms to behave ethically.

PART TWO

I. THE FEDERAL FOOD AND DRUG ADMINISTRATION

A. History

The monitoring of food and drug safety has long been considered a legitimate governmental activity. Federal regulation began with the passage of the **Federal Pure Food and Drug Act of 1906**. However, the fight for federal food regulation began long before 1906.

The first national law actually came about in 1848 during the Mexican War and was centered on the importation of adulterated drugs. The meaning of adulterated is adding something to the product that diminishes the quality of the product. Congress was asked to criminalize adulteration of food and drugs in 1879, but it failed to gain any real, serious interest. In 1886, the question became natural foods versus the newly created artificial substitute, specifically butter versus oleomargarine. This obviously had economic effects but also the argument was whether public health was being affected, not to mention if the federal government even had the authority to get involved in the controversy. You have to remember that this was a time of great change in the United States due to the country changing into an industrial, urban society. Also, there were major scientific discoveries leading to not only new food products but also new synthetic medicines. Even transportation changes had made it easier to deliver new products to the consumers.

Basically we were moving from a society where you grew and then preserved what you would eat to a time of processed food. After all, in the past you had prepared the food and now it was being done for you. Of course, this led to more complex problems about deceptive claims, adulterated products, and hazards in the food and drug supply. Adulterated products are products that are unsafe or impure. Furthermore, other countries such as Britain were passing regulations and if we wanted to export our products to those countries we were going to have to have our products up to their mandated standards. Competition proved to also be a problem in that adulterated foods that were improperly prepared could be sold cheaper but could also cause huge problems. This led to what was deemed unfair competition by the producers who were willing to sell adulterated foods as opposed to the honest producers who refused to cut costs and sold the safe, pure food.

In short, people were losing their faith in commercial integrity as stated in an 1890 Senate report and thereby undermining the "very foundation of trade." Therefore, the states started passing laws to restore the public's faith, which led to different regulations in different states. Of course, farmers and dairy producers fought for natural food and not the newer synthetic products and also called for a national standard. In short, a national standard was needed. During the Populist movement, in 1892, the farmers got one bill passed by the Senate but it failed in the House of Representatives. Numerous individuals and organizations began to crusade for pure food such as, the National Consumer League, the General Federation of Women's Clubs, and Harvey W. Wiley who was the chief chemist of the Department of Agriculture who crusaded for a national law touring throughout the country. Wiley had been appointed the head of the Division of Chemistry, which became the Bureau of Chemistry in 1901. Wiley also united other chemists, state officials, women's groups, doctors, journalists, and even the reform-minded businessmen. Even then, the fight was going to be long and difficult. However, more rigorous crusading began from the American Medical Association, scientists, and journalists about patent medicine abuses and adulterated products and this led to the public to become more involved. Congress still resisted.

Then catastrophe concerning the meat industry came in the form of the Spanish-American War where the meat packers were accused of shipping "embalmed beef" to the troops that sickened the troops in the war. Then, in 1906, Upton Sinclair published his expose on the Chicago meat-packing industry called *The Jungle*. The public and thus the politicians joined the move to have pure food, and the Pure Food and Drug Act of 1906 was passed and signed by President Roosevelt after the House of Representatives finally agreed and approved the bill.

B. The Pure Food and Drug Act of 1906 (The Wiley Act)

The Pure Food and Drug Act forbid interstate and foreign commerce in adulterated and misbranded food and drugs. Misbranding was making false or misleading label claims in food or drugs. If a producer violated the law they could be fined and even jailed. Furthermore, drugs had to abide by standards of purity and quality as set forth by committees of physicians and pharmacists in the United States Pharmacopoeia and the National Formulary. Any variation such as standards set by the industry had to be plainly stated on the label. Both sides claimed victory; business for the fact that the law was not more stringent than it was and Wiley and his coalition that they actually finally got a pure food and drug law passed. The Food and Drugs Act of 1906 is also known as the Wiley Act due to Wiley's work. Wiley was the head of the Department of Agriculture, Bureau of Chemistry. Therefore, it was the Department of Agriculture which was given the task of enforcing the Pure Food and Drug Act of 1906. However, for Wiley and the proponents of regulation, the battle had just begun. When Wiley tried to enforce the law, his efforts were met in court by the opposition. This led to protracted court battles.

C. The Food and Drug Administration

Wiley's Bureau of Chemistry's name was changed in 1927 to the Food, Drug, and Insecticide Administration and continued to administer the 1906 Act. In July of 1930, the name was shortened to the **Food and Drug Administration**. However, the FDA remained under the Department of Agriculture until June of 1940 when it was moved to the Federal Security Agency. It was then transferred to the Department of Health, Education and Welfare (HEW) in 1953. In 1980, HEW was changed to the Department of Health and Human Services, the FDA's current home.

Originally, Wiley's main emphasis was on foods since he felt that they led to a greater public health problem. He concentrated on chemical additives to food to avoid unnecessary adulterants. This caused Wiley political problems with the Secretary of Agriculture and even President Roosevelt, and Wiley's personal administrative authority started to be diluted early after 1906 and he resigned in 1912. Then, the emphasis was on drug regulation. The court battles continued and resulted in the loss of several cases in the U.S. Supreme Court. However, the seizures of misbranded and adulterated drugs increased into the 1920s and 1930s. In 1930, much of the 1906 law expired fueling the debate for a new law to replace it. However, Congress was reluctant to move. Again, the journalists and consumer protection organizations fought. However, one of the most effective measures was done in an exhibit by the FDA itself with what one reporter dubbed the "American Chamber of Horrors." This exhibit included several products that were legal under the 1906 law but caused numerous problems such as Banbar, which was advertised as a cure for diabetes when in fact it was worthless and Radithor, which was a tonic that was laced with radium that led to a slow and very painful death by those who used it. However, the bill to replace the 1906 was stalled in Congress for five years. Again, a catastrophic event led to action.

In 1937, a Tennessee company drug called Elixir Sulfanilamide was marketed as a new sulfa wonder drug for children. However, the solvent in the drug was basically antifreeze and over 100 people died, many children. The public was outraged and the result was the **Food, Drug, and Cosmetic Act of 1938** signed by President Franklin D. Roosevelt on June 25, 1938.

D. The Food, Drug, and Cosmetic Act of 1938

1. New Powers of the FDA in Drugs and Subsequent History of Drug Regulation
The Food, Drug, and Cosmetic Act of 1938 gave the FDA new powers and they wasted no time in utilizing those powers, going after those sulfa drugs that could not be labeled for safe use and required those types of drugs and others only to be dispensed with a doctor's prescription and only after the manufacturer proved it was safe and had the drug approved by the FDA. However, there was still a debate over what constituted an over-the-counter drug as opposed to a prescription drug. This was answered with the Durham–Humphrey Amendment in 1951. At this time, from the 1940s to the 1960s, the misuse and abuse of amphetamines and barbiturates led to more regulation that all other drugs combined. To try to curb the illegal sales of these drugs, the FDA resorted to undercover tactics to try to catch the illegal drug dealers. Also, it was a period of great increase in new drug applications to the FDA. One such drug that was never approved for sale in this country led to yet another potential catastrophe in the drug world.

Thalidomide was a sedative that resulted in thousands of grossly deformed babies being born outside the United States. While we dodged the problem in the United States, again the public was worried and again Congress responded with the Kefauver-Harris Amendments of 1962, so named after Senator Estes Kefauver who held hearings looking into the drug situation in the Senate. The Kefauver-Harris Amendments require that a drug in addition to being safe also had to yield the maximum response achievable. Therefore, drugs had to give the best results that were possible in addition to being safe to receive FDA approval and be legal for sale in the United States. This led the FDA to require stricter control over drug approval, thus over drug trials. This was achieved by giving the control of false advertising in prescription drugs to the FDA, from the FTC, forced better manufacturing practices by the drug industry, and gave the FDA even greater powers over drug company production and practices and even inspection of the drug companies' records to prove such was in fact being done.

Furthermore, amphetamines and barbiturates were still a problem as noted above. Therefore, in 1965, Congress passed the Drug Abuse Control Amendments giving the FDA new controls over amphetamines, barbiturates, hallucinogens, and other drugs felt to be subject to considerable potential abuse. This led to the creation of the Drug Enforcement Administration in 1968.

In the next 20 years during the 1970s and 1980s, the FDA had to deal with new situations such as Acquired Immune Deficiency Syndrome (AIDS) where the public demanded accelerated drug approval to try to help the people infected with AIDS and more importantly to the general public, to stop the spread of the deadly disease. It was also during this time period that Congress passed several beneficial laws in the drug area such as allowing for the approval of generic drugs, creating procedures for the drug industry to reimburse the FDA for the speedier approval of drugs, and giving the FDA the authority to recall medical devices.

2. *New Powers of the FDA in Drugs and Subsequent History of Food Regulation*

In Section 341 of the 1938 Act, it is clear that the Secretary was to take such action to promulgate regulations fixing and establishing for any food, thereby expanding the regulation of foods to all foods, not just canned goods as in the Pure Food and Drug Act of 1906. Furthermore, each food was to be referred to by its common or unusual name, given a reasonable definition and standard of identity as well as a reasonable standard of quality and reasonable standard as to the fill of the container. Of course, as always there were exceptions such as fresh or dried fruit or vegetables.

In addition, food producers started adding nutrients to their products to enhance their sales. For example, this product is fortified with Vitamin D. This led to new FDA controls over food additives. Furthermore, the FDA developed recipes for foods that included the ingredients that producers could lawfully use in the product. If the producer varied from the approved ingredients the product had to be labeled as "imitation." This led to the Delaney Clause named after Representative James Delaney who had held hearings in the 1950s addressing food additives. The FDA, with the Delaney Clause, assumed more control over any food additive and banned any carcinogenic additive with a zero-risk standard.

The late 1960s and 1970s saw changes for the FDA as well. The FDA became a part of the Public Health Service within the Department of Health, Education, and Welfare and picked up new responsibilities such as being responsible for control over unnecessary radiation from both consumer and professional electronic products, but it also lost some of its duties such as the FDA control over some products such as potential poisons, hazardous toys, and flammable fabrics that were transferred to the Consumer Product Safety Commission, which we will discuss in Part Three of this chapter. Furthermore, in the 1970s, the FDA showed great interest in the vitamin industry and the claims made by that industry.

In the food area during this time, the FDA had to deal with the battle over saccharin, an artificial sweetener banned by the Delaney Clause for causing cancer. Congress, however, interfered and stopped the FDA from banning saccharin. Had Congress not done so, saccharin or anything containing saccharin would have had to carry a warning that it caused cancer. This led to the 1990 **Nutrition Labeling and Education Act**, which revolutionized how the FDA would list basic nutritional information. After intense lobbying by the dietary supplement industry, Congress in 1994 allowed such supplements to make substantiated claims about the role of these products in health but they also had to issue a statement that the FDA had not evaluated the said statements and required the FDA to have the burden to prove that the dietary supplement was in fact misbranded or adulterated.

3. *General Powers of the 1938 Food, Drug, and Cosmetic Act*

While most of the Food, Drug, and Cosmetic Act of 1938 dealt with Food and Drug Regulation and as outlined above, did in fact greatly expand the regulatory power in that area. It also extended FDA control to include cosmetics and therapeutic devices. It added new enforcement provisions including court injunctions to the previous penalties under the Pure Food and Drug Act of 1906 of seizures and prosecutions.

It should be kept in mind that meats and meat products are exempt from the Food, Drug, and Cosmetic Act and are still under the control of the United States Department of Agriculture.

E. Structure of the Food and Drug Administration

1. Introduction

As stated above, the FDA is a subdivision of the Department of Health and Human Services. The FDA is organized into the Office of the Commissioner and four subparts covering (1) Medical Products and Tobacco, (2) Foods, (3) Global Regulatory Operations and Policy, and (4) Operations. The head of the FDA is the Commissioner and there are several offices that answer to the Commissioner such as the Chief Counsel, the attorney for the FDA, the Office of the Chief Scientist who gives his/her expertise to scientific excellence, the Office of the Counselor to the Commissioner who provides leadership in emergency and crisis situations as well as at least six other offices with other duties. The Food and Drug Administration regulates (1) Foods; (2) Dietary Supplements; (3) Human Drugs; (4) Vaccines, Blood Products, and other Biologics; (5) Medical Devices; (6) Electronic Products; (7) Cosmetics; (8) Veterinary Products; and (9) Tobacco Products. The FDA shares the regulation of pesticides with the United States Department of Agriculture (USDA) as well as the EPA and relating to water, the FDA only regulates labeling and safety of bottled water while the EPA sets the national standards for drinking water as we will see in a later chapter. We will deal with foods, dietary supplements, human drugs, and a certain type of medical devices, silicone breast implants.

2. Reporting

Reporting a problem can be done voluntarily by consumers, health professionals or, by the industry member themselves, which can also be a mandatory requirement from the FDA when the industry member discovers a problem. Each situation requires filing a complaint with a different entity of the FDA. For instance, if a consumer has a complaint they should contact a Complaint Coordinator. Complaint Coordinators are located in the FDA district offices across the country. In Texas, this can actually be done by Skype with a toll-free number. However, an industry member that must file a Mandatory Adverse Report about Dietary Supplements must complete a form called a Mandatory MedWatch Form and file it with the FDA. Of course, to report a problem to the FDA you must know what the FDA actually regulates, as seen above. Keep in mind meat and poultry is regulated by USDA. Once the complaint is reported, the FDA normally acts immediately but what they do is dependent on the seriousness of the alleged problem. Usually, an FDA investigator will begin the investigation by contacting the person or entity that made the complaint. Next, the investigator will personally go to the company for observation, interview the company's staff, review some documents, and personally examine the different aspects of the product from raw materials to finished product and then collect samples. The FDA provides inspectors with a detailed operations manual as well as inspection guides for several areas such as drugs, food, and medical devices. At the conclusion of the inspections, the FDA investigator creates a report that is subject to public disclosure under the Freedom of Information Act. This report can lead to (1) no action being indicated, which is a favorable outcome for the company because no objectionable practices were found in the inspection; (2) objectionable conditions found, but were not serious to require any type of regulatory action (this normally results in voluntary action by the company) which results in an untitled letter; or (3) serious objectionable conditions found, which results in official action in the form of a warning letter to the company. The warning letter, of course, is the most serious of the three and lists the FDA's position backed up by statute or FDA rules. This is basically a warning that possible enforcement steps will be taken. The company is then given a chance to respond to the allegations of the warning letter, which is usually 15 days. Enforcement can include recalls, an injunction, the seizure of the subject product, fines, a consent decree, or even criminal investigations.

3. Recent Recalls, Outbreaks, and Emergencies

When an FDA-regulated product is defective or potentially harmful, the FDA can recall that product. Recall simply means that the product is removed from the market and hopefully, thereby correcting the problem or stopping the emergency. Recalls are usually voluntarily done by the company to avoid further liability. The company can do so on its' own or after an FDA inspection determines that a problem exists. The FDA rarely has to order a recall but does have the power to do so if necessary. The FDA normally uses the media to alert the public of the recall. Two of the most recent recalls in the food industry resulted due to outbreaks of salmonella in the nut industry with Sunland, Inc. and due to a potential health risk in broccoli produced by Taylor Farms Pacific out of California.

On September 24, 2012, the FDA issued a press release stating that Sunland, Inc., a New Mexico company, had initiated a voluntary limited recall of its almond butter and peanut butter products manufactured between May 1, 2012, and the date of the announcement due to potential salmonella outbreak that could result in serious and sometimes fatal infections. This voluntary recall came about as a result of 29 people reporting problems in 18 states. The recall included products sold under several different product names including Trader Joe's, Archer Farms, Sprouts as well as Sunland and others, which included over 100 products. The recall was later expanded to all peanut products manufactured by Sunland after March 1, 2010, which included an additional 139 products, due to a report by the Centers for Disease Control and Prevention (CDC) and the FDA. This addition recall occurred on October 4, 2012, and was followed with yet another recall on October 12, 2012, to include raw and roasted peanuts distributed primarily under the Sunland name. The company also announced that it was ceasing the production and distribution of all of its products from its peanut butter plant as well as its peanut processing plant.

On February 24, 2011, Taylor Farms Pacific voluntarily recalled its products containing broccoli out of an abundance of caution due to a risk of health problems from listeria monocytogenes even though no illnesses had been reported. Listeria monocytogenes is a bacterium that causes high fever, muscle aches, and gastrointestinal problems such as diarrhea and nausea. These products had primarily been sold in the western states at Safeway, Vons, and other western grocery stores.

Of course, recalls can be as a result of problems in the drug area as well as other areas covered by the FDA such as medical devices and cosmetics. Recently, the United States suffered a deadly meningitis outbreak due to a Massachusetts compounding pharmacy, the New England Compounding Center (NECC) which produced tainted pain injections that killed over 50 and sickened over 700 Americans. This was one of the deadliest medical outbreaks in U.S. history. The compounding industry had resisted FDA jurisdiction since the 1990s and regulation had been slowed by conflicting laws and court decisions. The compounding industry mixed customized medications based on doctors' prescriptions. These had traditionally been overseen by state pharmacy boards. Due to the outrage of the public and the resulting pressure, the FDA began to crack down on these compounding pharmacies within their current limits in April 2013. Furthermore, the FDA Commissioner Margaret Hamburg responded by asking Congress to give them more authority to act in this area. In conclusion, only with the passage of time will we know how these compounding pharmacies will be regulated and by what agency or agencies.

F. Food

1. Past and Future

As seen in the historical section above, impure food was a major problem in the United States as recently as the early 1900s, and federal regulation (along with major technological innovations in processing, preserving, and distributing food) certainly deserves a great deal of credit for the fact that impure food is not a major public concern in America today. However, that does not mean that the FDA is not involved in monitoring food production in today's world, as seen from the recalls detailed above in the nut and broccoli products. The FDA's food regulation activity ranges from complaints and discovery of food-related products that lead to those recalls, as well as to food defense in helping to reduce the risk of attacks from whatever source on the United States food supply; that is, **bioterrorism**. The FDA is still highly involved in the long-term, or latent, effects of the consumption of various food additives and nutritional labeling, which is now required for all processed foods and nutrition as well. The nutrition information must include caloric, protein, carbohydrate, and fat content, and the percent of the U.S. Recommended Daily Dietary Allowance for protein and 19 vitamins and minerals.

However, a major change in the manner in which the FDA acts in food came about with the signing into law of the FDA **Food Safety Modernization Act (FSMA)** by President Obama on January 4, 2011. The main goal of this law is to shift the focus of making sure that United States food supply is safe and then responding to any contamination of the food supply to preventing the contamination of the food supply in the beginning. Of course, this is another law related to the terrorists and the threat that those individuals might attack the U.S. food supply. Since the law's passage, the FDA, as required by FSMA, has conducted vulnerability assessments on over 50 products or processes and has identified areas of highest concern and potential ways to avoid vulnerability in the food supply. FSMA sets the framework for the FDA in four areas: human food, safety of produce, imports, and animal food. The FDA has two proposed rules on this subject that as of April 2013 are still in the proposed stage. These proposed rules were originally published on January 16, 2013, in the Federal Register. These proposed rules were amended and a corrected version filed with the Federal Register on March 20, 2013. The first of these proposed rules, Current Good Manufacturing Practice and Hazard Analysis and Risk-Based Preventive Controls for Human Food will govern facilities that produce food and the other entitled Standards for Growing, Harvesting, Packing, and Holding of Consumption concerns the safety of produce. This will be an ongoing area of concern in the future for the FDA.

2. Food Additives

As seen above, in 1950, Rep. James Delaney of New York formed a committee in the House of Representatives called the Delaney Committee that investigated the safety of food additives. Very simply put, a food additive is any ingredient that is added to food that was not naturally occurring in the food or that was naturally occurring but was lost during the preparation of the food production process. This led in 1958 to the Food Additives Amendment to the Food, Drug, and Cosmetic Act of 1938 that is commonly called the Delaney Clause. This prevents the approval of ANY food additive shown to cause cancer. Food manufacturers of any new food additives had to prove to the FDA that there were no food additives that could cause cancer in their products before the particular food additive could be used. GRAS, a food substance generally recognized as safe by qualified experts, was excluded from the definition of a food additive and a list of about 200 GRAS substances, which included ascorbic acid and other common additives, was included. In 1960, the Color Additive Amendments were enacted regulating color additives that required food color additives to be proven to be safe before they could be used as well as regular food additives. This led to a zero-risk standard for any additives that could cause cancer.

For example, in the 1970s, Soviet scientists published a report claiming that Red Dye No. 2 caused cancer in lab rats. This caused a panic of "red" products in the United Sates after the FDA concluded that Red Dye No. 2 could cause cancer in high doses and pulled Red Dye No. 2 products from the United States market in 1976 even though it was never proven harmful to humans and was still legal in Canada and Europe. One such example of this panic was red M&Ms made by the Mars candy company. *Even though red M&Ms never contained Red Dye No. 2,* due to the panic over red products, Mars decided to pull the red M&Ms from the product and a bag of M&Ms no longer contained red M&Ms. Years later, Mars test marketed red M&Ms in special holiday packages of green and red M&Ms. After the public accepted them, Mars put the red M&Ms back in the package some 10 years later! However, Mars also learned the value of the colors of the M&Ms and has been using the colors in advertising, special promotions, and contests ever since. While Red Dye No. 2 is still banned in the United States, its successor Red No. 40 is legal in the United States and Canada but still is not readily used in Europe which still uses Red Dye No. 2.

During the Clinton Administration, Congress passed and President Clinton signed the **Food Quality Protection Act (FQPA)** on August 3, 1996. The FQPA added pesticides to the jurisdiction of the FDA, and also ended the zero-risk standards in food additives that are as a result of the use of pesticides in the food. The zero-risk standards were replaced with a reasonable certainty of no-harm standards. In other words, a food additive due to pesticides can be used unless the FDA can show that there is a reasonable certainty that it is harmful to humans. However, the Delaney Clause still exists for the regulation of normal, non-pesticide-related food additives.

3. Nutritional Labeling

The only nutritional labeling that actually existed from 1941 to 1966 was some information on calorie or sodium (salt) content that was required by the FDA in "special dietary uses" such as diet product. After all, consider the times in a historical context; consumers did not purchase pre-prepared foods. At that time, most consumers prepared their own means at home from "scratch" in the beginning so there was little demand for nutritional labeling. In 1966, **the Fair Packaging and Labeling Act** required retail products sold to consumers in interstate commerce to be honestly and informatively labeled. Consumers were supposed to be able to get accurate information about the quantity of the contents and guide them in comparing value. However, the need for consistent, understandable, and generally usable nutrition information was not met by this law. There was not a consistent serving size so the consumer really was not clear on the total calories or how much protein, carbohydrates, and fat that the product actually contained. This was increasingly inadequate for consumers concerned about their diet for health reasons or simply to lose weight. In 1972, the FDA proposed voluntary food labeling of nutritional information on packaged food labels. These were mandatory when the producer made nutritional claims on the labels or in advertising, or if there was a food additive included in the product. The final rules of the FDA came out in 1973 and required or used voluntarily by the company then the labeling was to include the following information:

1. Number of calories
2. Grams of protein, carbohydrate, and fat
3. The percentage of the U.S. Recommended Daily Allowance (RDA) of protein, vitamins A and C, thiamin, riboflavin, niacin, calcium, and iron, and could include other information at the manufacturers' discretion.

Furthermore, all of this reporting was to be based on an average or usual serving size. The RDAs were determined by the National Academy of Sciences (NAS). The USDA used similar standards in the nutritional labeling of meat and poultry products. However, consumers demanded more nutritional information on labels. Manufacturers responded to the demand but not in a uniform manner. The terminology was not uniform and led to the proliferation of claims that were at least ambiguous if not deceptive. However, in most situations the information contained in nutritional labeling was very confusing to the consumer and even dangerous because manufacturers started making health claims in nutritional labeling that was also questionable at best if not false.

The FDA in August 1987 proposed a new rule to allow health claims on labeling if certain criteria were met. This received criticism from several fronts and led to Congressional hearing in December 1987. The proposed rule was withdrawn, but the consumer interest was not. In fact, the consumer interest grew in large part to recent scientific studies that showed the relationship between diet and death caused by heart disease, diabetes, heart problems, and cancer. This leads to major changes in nutritional labeling.

The result was the **Nutrition Labeling and Education Act (NLEA)**, which was passed in 1990 to allow consumers to use the latest advances in nutrition by having the information on the label of food products. The NLEA amended the Food, Drug, and Cosmetic Act of 1938 to give the FDA explicit authority to require mandatory nutritional labeling on almost all food products and specified the nutrients that had to be listed on the label. The main goals of the NLEA were to make labels easier to read and understand by the consumer, make standardized serving sizes, list the amount of servings per package and the number of calories, fats, saturated fats, and cholesterol per serving, standardize the language used in food the level of nutrients, and make manufacturers prove health claims. Examples of standardizing the language used in food production can be seen with the uniform standards for fresh or raw food, which cannot be processed, frozen, or preserved; low fat (three or less grams of fat per serving per 100 grams of food); few calorie (fewer than 40 calories per serving and per 100 grams of food); and the terms light or lite (has one-third fewer calories than a comparable product). The NLEA only covers products regulated by the FDA. However, the USDA has also implemented these changes. The NLEA then left it to the FDA to publish proposed regulations to implement the provisions of the Act.

However, Congress passed the **Dietary Supplement Act of 1992** that instructed the FDA to hold off for one year on regulations based on RDAs. Final regulations from the FDA and the USDA came in 1993 and required nutritional labels on most products in the form of a Nutrition Facts panel. However, there was still a lot of criticism of the new regulations based on the RDAs so the FDA asked NAS to provide scientific data on new Dietary Reference Intakes from the NSA and to update the nutrient reference values on the Nutrition Facts panel. It was determined that Daily Reference Values (DRVs) would be used in reporting values of fat, saturated fatty acids, cholesterol, total carbohydrate, dietary fiber, sodium, potassium, and fiber. The DRVs were based largely on recommendations from several sources. However, DRVs were not available for all nutrients so it was determined by the FDA that in nutrition labeling they would use a consistent system of percentages, which would make it possible for virtually all nutrients on the label to be provided in equivalent units as a percentage of the appropriate RDI or DRV and simply called the "Percent of Daily Value," which is based on a 2,000-calorie diet.

Another issue was the serving size. Obviously, the serving size would affect almost every number in the Nutrition Facts panel and so how to determine the serving size is of major concern. The NLEA had stated that serving size had to be based on a single serving normally eaten in one sitting. According to the Code of Federal Regulations (CFR) Section 101.9(4)(b)(1):

> The term serving or serving size means an amount of food customarily consumed per eating occasion by persons 4 years of age or older which is expressed in a common household measure that is appropriate to the food.

The FDA issued a Food Labeling Guide for United States manufacturers of food products and for foreign food products to be sold in the United States in 2009. Manufacturers are responsible for the accuracy of the content and information; and, must act in good faith when preparing the Nutrition Facts panel. Ordinarily, the FDA's rules determine the serving size. However, in some cases determining the actual serving size is largely left to the manufacturer and therefore, the serving size can still be confusing to the average consumer. For instance, let's examine the serving size in the breakfast cereal industry, which FDA rules do not determine. Instead, density of the cereal is the determining fact so in essence weight is the determining factor. Therefore, heavy or more dense cereals have one serving size and lighter or less dense cereals have yet another serving size. As an example, consider the following General Mills cereals and their serving sizes:

Rice Chex	1 cup	27 grams
Corn Chex	1 cup	31 grams
Wheat Chex	¾ cup	47 grams
Apple Cinnamon Chex	¾ cup	31 grams
Chocolate Chex	¾ cup	32 grams
Honey Nut Chex	¾ cup	32 grams

If you will note, both Corn Chex and Apple Cinnamon Chex by weight determine a serving size to be 31 grams, but a Corn Chex serving size is 1 cup and an Apple Cinnamon Chex serving size is ¾ cup. Is this not confusing to the customer?

Another area that probably needs revision is the serving size itself. After all, how many of people eat either ¾ cup or 1 cup of cereal in a "normal" sitting? Or, how many people eat ½ cup of ice cream or five saltine crackers as a serving size? It would seem that there either needs to be a realistic determination of serving size that is consistent throughout the industry or re-educate the masses or what is actually determined to be the serving size and why it is different in different products such as cereals.

4. Genetically Engineered Foods

While the FDA has received numerous inquiries into a requirement concerning the labeling of foods as genetically engineered, as of April 2013, the FDA has chosen to encourage voluntary notice by the manufacturers of genetically engineered foods but not to require that a manufacturer disclose to the consumer that the food was genetically engineered. The FDA has even issued drafts of the voluntary labeling, which would indicate whether foods have or have not been developed using bioengineering. The FDA has gone on record reminding consumers of the fact that foods, all food, genetically engineered or not have to go through the same inspection process. However, this issue is still under consideration by the FDA.

G. Drugs

The history of drug safety regulation in the United States, as we saw in the historical section above, like so many other areas of regulation, was greatly influenced by dramatic or even tragic events. In 1938, approximately 100 deaths resulted from the marketing of a new drug, Elixir Sulfanilamide. Congress responded with the passage of the Food, Drug, and Cosmetic Act of 1938, which provided the FDA with additional powers to regulate the quality of drugs and prohibited the marketing of new drugs until granted FDA approval. Drugs had to be proven to be safe before they could be sold. It also required that sulfanilamide and other dangerous drugs had to be given only under the direction of a medical expert, which began the requirement for prescription-only drugs. However, in 1941, there were almost 300 deaths due to the use of Sulfathiazole tablets, which was an antibiotic tainted with Phenobarbital, a sedative. This led the FDA to develop good manufacturing practices (GMPs). In 1951, Congress passed the Durham-Humphrey Amendment which defines the kinds of drugs that must be prescription only and if the drug was not on the list, it could remain non-prescription or "over the counter." In 1962, Thalidomide, a newly developed sleeping pill, was found to cause major birth defects such as missing limbs in Western Europe. However, due to an FDA medical officer named Dr. Frances Kelsey, Thalidomide did not receive approval of the FDA in the United States. However, the public was afraid and demanded stronger drug laws.

Congress responded with a major change in the FDA approval procedures in the **Kefauver-Harris Amendment of 1962**. Thereafter, the FDA was required to approve drugs, not only on the basis of their safety, but also on the basis of their proven effectiveness for the purpose sold; in other words, they had to work. Pharmaceutical companies must apply to the FDA for approval of human clinical testing of drugs and the FDA may specify the testing format. The FDA regulations concerning the development, testing, and adoption of new drugs reflect a strict interpretation of the amendment's provisions. This required FDA process became very expensive with an average cost of $250 million to the company and 12 years for approval.

Some critics charge that the FDA is too cautious in its approval procedures and that it often caused, unnecessary, delays in the approval of the use of new, more effective drugs that could save or prolong lives, cure or treat diseases, and reduce pain. In some instances, desperately ill Americans have sought treatment in foreign countries where they could legally use drugs not yet approved by the FDA. Thus, the FDA could be viewed as another example of a federal agency limiting the ability of informed consumers to take risks. Of course, the opposite side of this issue is the primary concern of the FDA. The FDA believes that FDA approval of risky drugs will suggest to consumers that the drugs are not really risky. It seems that the FDA's action regarding Thalidomide would have swayed public opinion to the FDA; however, remember the public often has a short memory.

Furthermore, from 1966 through 1968, studies were done by the National Academy of Sciences and the National Research Council to study the effectiveness of thousands of drugs approved between 1938 and 1962. The findings of these studies were implemented by the FDA in the Drug Efficacy Study Implementation (DESI) in 1968. 1970 saw the requirement of patient-package inserts to provide the consumer with information about the risks and benefits of the drug. The FDA began Over-the-Counter Drug Reviews in 1972. After the Tylenol scare in Chicago where bottles of Tylenol were laced with the poison cyanide, the FDA issued Tamper-resistant Packaging Regulations that led to Congress passing the **Federal Anti-Tampering Act** in 1983.

In 1984, Congress passed the **Hatch-Waxman Act**, also called the **Drug Price Competition and Patent Term Restoration Act**, which allowed the FDA to approve of generic versions of brand-name drugs without the formal investigation of the generics that had been done with the original name brand. After all, the generics were supposed to be the same drugs as the originals. This also allowed the brand-name companies to apply for up to five years of additional patent protection for the time lost in the FDA approval process.

In the next few years, the FDA sought to protect elderly people as well as children, and people used in research, by setting up a system called MedWatch that collects reports from health professionals on problems with drugs, which was computerized with the Adverse Event Reporting System (AERS) in 1998. In 1999, the FDA exercised power to regulate drug labeling in "over-the-counter" drugs with the Drug Facts Label Rule. In 2005, the FDA established the Drug Safety Board consisting of FDA staff and representatives from the NIH and Veterans Administration (VA) to advise the FDA on drug safety issues.

H. Medical Devices

The FDA also has jurisdiction over medical devices and one such medical device that the FDA dealt with was silicone breast implants. Silicone breast implants were developed by two Texas doctors and the first known silicone breast implant occurred in the early 1960s. Dow Corning introduced the first silicone implants in 1963. By the 1970s, the Dow Corning product accounted for about 83 percent of all silicone breast implants.

In 1976, Congress enacted the Medical Devices Amendment to the 1938 Act giving the FDA the power over medical devices, which would have included silicone breast implants. However, since the silicone breast implants had already been on the market they did not fall under this new amendment and did not have to get approval to sell the implants. In 1977, the first of the silicone breast implant lawsuits where women who had the implants sued due to the implants rupturing and spilling the silicone into their bodies requiring subsequent operations, pain, and suffering, etc.

In the 1980s, the Ralph Nader's Public Citizen Health Research Group sent out warnings that silicone breast implants caused cancer. It was at this time that the FDA was flooded with complaints about silicone breast implants by women who had had the implants. In 1982, the FDA attempted to require silicone breast implant manufacturers to prove the safety of the implants. The lawsuits followed as did television exposes about the danger of silicone breast implants. In 1988, The FDA re-classified silicone breast implants and required premarket approval.

In 1990, a House of Representatives subcommittee began conducting hearings on the FDA's regulation of silicone breast implants due to the publicity generated by the lawsuits and the television stories. Several witnesses testified both for and against the implants, including at least one of the six manufacturers, Dow Corning. It was determined that about 1 million American women had had the breast implants at the rate of about 100,000 per year, mostly for breast enhancement purposes, but about 20 percent were for breast reconstruction after mastectomies or some type of breast deformity. Most of the questionable implants had been sold between 1980 and 1990. The committee found that the FDA had determined that the leakage of the silicone could possibly cause breast deformities, ulcers, a burning sensation or pain, enlarged lymph nodes, palpable masses, and respiratory distress as well as other problems such as surgery to replace the leaking implants and problems with cancer screening in women with breast implants. There were also concerns that the implants themselves could cause cancer. It was determined that the FDA had ignored warning signs from several sources for more than 12 years, including their own scientists' advice. Furthermore, it was determined that the manufacturers had never provided proof of safety to the FDA.

In 1991, the FDA Advisory Panel met and unanimously recommended that the FDA continue to allow the implants to remain on the market. The lawsuits continued and the verdicts became larger. However, in early 1992, the FDA held a second Advisory Panel that called for a voluntary moratorium on the distribution and use of the silicone breast implants until further research could be conducted. The manufacturers agreed and, if they stayed in the market, normally switched to saline-filled implants. Since no manufacturers submitted proof of safety, the silicone breast implants effectively were off the market except for breast reconstruction surgery and those would be considered a clinical study and the women who received them would continue as a part of a clinical study after the surgery.

Almost immediately thereafter, a class action lawsuit was filed on behalf of the affected women. The FDA did conduct hearings beginning the next month and found no causal link between the silicone breast implants and the medical problems the women were claiming to have suffered. However, most of the major manufacturers of the silicone breast implants pulled out of the market and did not sell the devices anymore.

However, the lawsuits continued and in December of 1992 a Houston jury awarded a woman $5 million in actual damages and $20 million in punitive damages even though the expert witnesses had testified that her symptoms were like having a bad case of flu. The lawsuits continued and the class action lawsuit that had been filed was settled in 1994. It was the largest class action settlement in history even though the manufacturers still maintained that there was no scientific evidence of the claimed damages. The class action settlement allowed women to claim against a fund set up by the leading manufacturers and get a set payout. Leading scientific studies by the Mayo Clinic, the New England Journal of Medicine, the American Academy of Neurology, and the American College of Rheumatology backed the claims of the manufacturers that there was no evidence that the implants caused the claimed problems.

In 1995, the main distributor and manufacturer of the silicone breast implants, Dow Corning, filed for Chapter 11 bankruptcy (reorganization) since it was facing almost a half-million lawsuit claims. By the late 1990s, the scientific evidence started to overwhelm the women's claims and courts started dismissing the claims in favor of the scientific evidence and by 1997 the New York Times reported that the manufacturers were winning 80 percent of the cases against them. The scientific studies from the United States such as the National Cancer Institute and major European studies continued to side with the manufactures. Even so, Dow Corning offered $3.2 billion to settle in an effort to emerge from bankruptcy. However, there was still no medical evidence to support the claims as concluded by the Institute of Medicine, a part of the National Academy of Sciences when requested by Congress to investigate the silicone breast implant controversy.

By 2000, at least two companies were submitting proposals to the FDA to prove the safety of silicone breast implants and asking for approval to sell their devices and by 2006 the FDA had approved the sale by both companies of the silicone breast implants with conditions including continued monitoring of the women receiving the implants. One of the companies, Allergan, improved their product and in February of 2013, Allergan was allowed to sell the newer product but again was required to do post-approval studies to continue to monitor and prove the safety and effectiveness of their product. Therefore, silicone breast implants are back on the market, but the FDA continues to require proof of safety and effectiveness.

I. Tobacco

The FDA also regulated tobacco products. This is based on public health standards and trying to reduce the damage done to people by tobacco. On June 22, 2009, President Obama signed into law the **Family Smoking Prevention and Tobacco Control Act of 2009**, which gives the FDA new sweeping powers over tobacco. This FDA-Tobacco Bill was designed to be an antismoking law and will give the FDA the power to ban certain labels such as those claiming to be low tar or low nicotine and will also outlaw flavoring that the government feels has been used to lure teenagers into smoking and orders the tobacco companies to lower the nicotine levels in their products. It will also allow the government to regulate what goes into cigarettes and require the manufacturers to make those ingredients public. Furthermore, it will also allow the FDA to regulate the advertising of the cigarettes, par-ticularly those advertising campaigns directed at children and teenagers. In signing the Bill into law, President Obama reflected on his own smoking habit and how difficult it has been to quit and reminded those in attendance how he had begun smoking at a young age as a teenager. This law could prevent the addition of new cigarette brands since the manu-facturers will have to have FDA approval before introducing new tobacco products. This is a far-reaching law directly aimed at the tobacco industry and will undoubtedly bring major changes to the tobacco industry.

One of these changes seen recently is in labeling. The FDA has issued new rules on a variety of tobacco products, but we are going to concentrate on warning labels on cigarettes and the newer smokeless tobacco products. In September of 2011, the FDA issued what they call the "most significant change to cigarette warnings in 25 years." They are requiring larger and more prominent cigarette health warnings on all packages and advertising. This also includes restrictions on tobacco products that chose to label their product as "light," "low," "mild," etc. Finally, they also require larger and more visible warnings on packages and advertisements in the smokeless tobacco industry. Plain and simple, these warnings are very graphic and by their use, the FDA is hoping to scare people into quitting or never starting to use tobacco products and hope to have many people become more aware of the specific health risks associated with tobacco product use such as death, cancer, lung disease, stroke and heart disease, and addiction to tobacco products. This is also targeted at young people and designed to give children the strength to resist the temptation of tobacco use.

II. THE CONSUMER PRODUCT SAFETY COMMISSION

A. History

In 1967, the bipartisan National Commission on Product Safety was established to investigate the adequacy of state law in protecting consumers from unreasonable risks caused by "hazardous household products." In its report to the President and the Congress, the Commission estimated that 20 million Americans were injured each year as a result of defective or otherwise dangerous products, and that those incidents resulted in 30,000 fatalities, 11,000 permanent injuries, and an annual economic loss of $5.5 billion. It is interesting and important to note, however, that the Commission concluded that only 20 percent of those injuries were preventable.

In response to the Commission's report, Congress enacted in 1972 the **Consumer Product Safety Act (CPSA),** the first direct control of product safety by the federal government. The CPSA applies only to "consumer products," which are defined as products produced or distributed for "personal use, consumption, or enjoyment, in a household, in school, or in recreation." Obviously, the desired goal was to prevent those deaths, permanent injuries, and economic losses. The CPSA specifically excluded products intended for use primarily for industrial purposes, as well as consumer products already covered by other regulatory agencies, such as tobacco, drugs, cosmetics, food, motor vehicles, insecticides, and boats. However, thousands of products including baby products such as cribs, children's toys, household products such as furniture, and even household chemicals were covered.

The CPSA also established an independent regulatory agency, the **Consumer Product Safety Commission (CPSC).** The CPSC consists of five members appointed by the President for staggered seven-year terms. Not more than three commissioners may belong to the same political party. Normally, there must be at least three commissioners to conduct business and often two of the commissioner positions are vacant. The CPSC is structured like most independent agencies and its procedures are regulated by the Administrative Procedures Act. The CPSC engages in many activities, but most activities fall under one of two areas: (1) information collection and dissemination, and (2) setting and enforcement of product safety standards. In the last 40 years, the CPSC has contributed to a steady decline in the rate of deaths and injuries due to the use of the products that are covered by the CPSC.

In 2007, the CPSC required more recalls that ever before and resulted in Congress passing the **Consumer Product Safety Improvement Act (CPSIA)** of 2008, which requires nearly all children's products to comply with all children's product safety rules, be tested for compliance by a CPSC-accepted laboratory, have a written Children's Product Certificate proving the product is in compliance, and have permanent tracking information affixed to the product. The CPSIA also requires all domestic manufacturers or importers of non-children's products, which are governed by a consumer product safety rule, to issue a General Certificate of Conformity (GCC) that is based on a test of each product.

There are also several other laws enforced by the CPSC such as the **Children's Gasoline Burn Prevention Act (CGCPA)** which concerned portable gasoline containers, the **Federal Hazardous Substances Act (FHSA)** which requires warning labels on certain hazardous household products such as electric toys, several baby goods, bicycles, and children's bunk beds, the **Child Safety Protection Act (CSPA)** to try to better protect young children from choking, the **Labeling of Hazardous Art Materials Act (LHAMA)** to regulate art supplies, and the **Flammable Fabrics Act (FFA)** to regulate flammable clothing and interior furnishings. There is also the **Poison Prevention Packaging Act (PPPA)**, which requires several household substances to contain child-resistant packaging and the **Refrigerator Safety Act (RSA)**, which requires refrigerators to be able to be opened from the inside to prevent accidental suffocations. The most recent is the **Virginia Graeme Baker Pool & Spa Safety Act (P&SS Act)** so named in memory of Virginia Graeme Baker, granddaughter of the former Secretary of State James Baker III. The child had become trapped to the drain of a hot tub and was unable to pull herself free and even her mother was unable to pull her free due to the suction. Two men eventually were able to pull her free by breaking the drain. However, the child died. The P&SS Act requires public pools to install equipment to avoid drain problems.

B. Major Activities of the CPSC

1. Information Collection and Dissemination

One of the main problems is informing the consumer. If the consumers have information about the dangers of the product, then they would be more likely NOT to purchase that product. The market failure with defective or unsafe products, of course, comes from the observation that consumers do not have full and complete information about the safety of products. The market does not adjust completely, and it is not correct to state that consumers are voluntarily accepting a risk if they are not aware of it.

The CPSC engages in several different activities in its effort to correct this information problem in the market. The CPSC has established and maintains an Injury Information Clearinghouse to collect and analyze consumer product injury reports. This is supplemented by the National Electronic Injury Surveillance System, which is a computerized record compilation system that accumulates consumer product injury data from hospitals across the nation. The information-gathering function is also facilitated by CPSC's authority to require manufactures to keep records, supply the CPSC with information regarding safety, and furnish the CPSC with notice and description of any new consumer products before making them available to the public. Finally, the CPSC may conduct hearings regarding consumer product safety and can eventually ban the sale of the product.

The CPSC uses the information it gathers to detect products that present a higher risk of injury. In some instances, the CPSC will disseminate the information to the public to help consumers make better decisions. The expected result of such dissemination is a fall in the price of the product. This dissemination is clearly an effort to correct the market imperfection by correcting the source of the imperfection. That is, it reinforces the market incentives and common-law liability rules that were already in place. Another strategy used by the CPSC when the data reveal that a product presents an unacceptably high risk of injury involves taking action to force the correction of the problem or to remove the product from the market. The CPSA contains adequate enforcement powers for exercising this role. This response is closely related to the CPSC's setting of product safety standards.

2. Product Safety Standards

The CPSC is authorized to develop and issue consumer product safety standards for all products covered by the CPSA. Product safety research may be performed by the CPSC or by outside consultants who specialize in such testing. If the testing reveals that there is a hazard of injury, illness, or death, then the CPSC is required to issue a standard. The CPSC is empowered to issue two types of product safety standards. **Performance standards** specify minimum performance criteria, such as the minimum amount of weight that a tow bar can safely pull. **Labeling standards** typically require the placement of warning labels on products, such as "Not suitable for children under the age of 6." Manufacturers are required to test and certify that their products meet the standards.

The CPSC's procedures for issuing a product safety standard must comply with the Administrative Procedures Act's rule-making procedures, including formulating the rule, notice in the Federal Register, and the opportunity for interested parties to be heard. As mentioned above, in some instances, the CPSC has the authority to ban the product completely. For example, if the CPSC determines that a currently marketed product is an "imminently hazardous consumer product," the CPSC may petition the appropriate federal district court for an order to seize the product and call for recall, repair, replacement, or refund. All interested persons may petition the CPSC to issue, amend, or revoke a product safety standard. All CPSC rule-making activities are subject to judicial review under the APA. The basic test for judicial review of a CPSC mandatory product safety standard is that the standard must be "reasonably necessary" to eliminate the unreasonable risk identified by the fact-finding process. To make this determination, the CPSC and then the reviewing court often engage in a type of cost-benefit analysis, which includes a consideration of the marginal benefits expected to result from the standard and the marginal costs in terms of the expected costs of compliance to the producer or impact on the price paid by consumers.

The setting of product safety standards by the CPSC is the first area of government intervention to correct the market failure caused by information problems where the solution has involved government intervention to such an extent that it does not allow consumers to make a choice. That is, unlike federal securities regulation which we will see later, the CPSC prevents consumers from taking certain risks and can even remove the risk totally in a recall of the product. If a product is recalled, any person is banned from selling the product and this applies to voluntary recalls or CPSC-mandated recalls. Of course, in a manner similar to securities regulation, the CPSC also helps the market adjust to risk by collecting and mandating the disclosure of certain types of information. This more intrusive type of regulation illustrated by the product safety standards is also present in food and drug safety regulations.

C. Major CPSC Recalls

1. Lawn Darts

Lawn darts are thought by some people and consumer groups to be the most dangerous toys of all time. A lawn dart is just what the name implies, a dart complete with colorful fins and a pointed, weighted end, but much larger than the traditional darts thrown at a dart board. The purpose was to throw it into a target into the lawn. It came with a target or plastic hoops to throw the darts into. Of course, children being children threw them at each other or up in the air and hit another child or themselves. Lawn darts caused at least three deaths and 700 injuries requiring attention at an emergency room since their introduction in the 1970s. Before they were banned by the CPSC, the manufacturers of lawn darts previously had voluntarily agreed to stricter advertising and labeling to avoid the recall. However, these agreed steps were not having the desired effect. The CPSC also uncovered violations of the lawn dart regulations that had previously been imposed by at least two American manufactures of lawn darts and even brought civil contempt charges against one of the companies. The CPSC then began the Congressionally mandated process to ban law darts by (1) developing a lawn dart ban in May of 1988, (2) publishing the proposed rule banning lawn darts in the Federal Register in July 1988, and (3) allowing public comment about the proposed rule banning the lawn darts. In October 1988, the Commission voted to ban lawn darts. (Incidentally, Congress had already banned lawn darts on its own one week before the CPSC's Congressionally mandated process was completed.)

2. Various Thomas & Friends Wooden Railway Toys

As stated earlier, 2007 was the year of recalls and lead to the passage of the CPSIA. One of these recalls involved various Thomas & Friends Wooden Railway Toys, which were manufactured in China due to lead paint on the wooden toys. Lead can be toxic to children or at least make them very ill. It is estimated that about 1.5 million of these toys were sold prior to the recall. It should be noted that there were no reports of injuries to children from these wooden toys. These toys had been sold from 2005 to June of 2007. Consumers were urged to take the recalled toys away from children and contact the importer RC2 Corp. of

Oak Brook, Illinois, for a replacement product. This was just one of several recalls of products from China during this period.

3. Buckyballs and Buckycubes

On April 12, 2013, the CPSC announced a voluntary recall of all Buckyballs and Buckcubes. These are high-powered magnet sets and are a series of several small magnetized balls (Buckyballs) or cubes (Buckycubes) that are about 5 millimeters in diameter. You can make them into chains or other designs. The CPSC felt that there were defects in the design, warnings, and instructions of this product, all of which posed a substantial risk of injury or death to children. It is estimated that 3 million of the sets of these products have been sold in stores and online in the United States since 2010. The consumers who purchased these products were encouraged to contact the retailer from which they bought the product to obtain instructions on how to receive their remedy. So far, the voluntary recall is only by the stores that sold the products. The importer of the products, Maxfield & Oberton Holding LLC of New York, has refused to cooperate in the recall. The CPSC has filed an administrative complaint against the importer. However, as of April 2013, this complaint had not been resolved.

CHAPTER SUMMARY

Administrative agencies perform many functions that are normally associated with the three branches of government. Administrative agencies were created to supplement the three branches of government and accordingly perform similar functions. By using administrative agencies, Congress can write laws in more general terms, with the administrative agency filling in the details. They also provide specialized adjudication of disputes that are too numerous and complex for federal courts to handle. And, they assist the executive branch in the enforcement of laws.

The delegation of legislative and judicial powers to agencies has led to challenges that the delegation is unconstitutional. In general, the delegation is upheld only if the statute contained specific standards and guidelines for agency activity. The current approach allows the statutory standards to be broadly stated.

The two basic types of agencies are Independent and Executive Agencies. Independent Agencies are created by Congress and given broad powers over regulation in a given area. The President has some control through the appointment of the members of the agency's board or commission. Executive Agencies are part of the executive branch and are generally part of an executive department headed by a cabinet member.

Agencies have the power to make rules, to investigate whether statutes or rules have been broken, to enforce rules and statutes, and to adjudicate controversies concerning enforcement. There are limitations on these powers. Congress can change the enabling statute if the agency's rules go outside the scope intended by Congress. The investigatory powers are limited by constitutional rights. For example, inspections of business premises without a warrant are not generally allowed unless there are special circumstances. The adjudicatory power is limited by the courts' review of agency decisions.

The Administrative Procedures Act (APA) is a Congressional response to the vast discretion and power given to administrative agencies. The APA sets forth uniform procedures that all agencies must follow in formulating rules, conducting adjudications, and for judicial review of agency action.

The use of administrative agencies provides substantial benefits by supplementing the functions of the three branches of government. Principal benefits are derived from the specialized rule making and the specialized administrative law judges. However, agencies have been criticized because of needless and excessive costs they impose on businesses, including burdensome paperwork and a disregard of whether the costs of complying with a regulation are justified by the benefits.

There is a trend toward regulatory reform in administrative agencies. The Freedom of Information Act provides for public access to agency records, except for when an statutory exception exists. The Sunshine Act requires agency meetings to be public unless a majority of the agency's board or commission votes to close the meeting for an enumerated reason contained in the Act. Deregulation is also considered a valuable tool in regulatory reform.

Dissatisfaction with the results of the state regulation of product safety led to the creation of a federal administrative agency, the Consumer Product Safety Commission (CPSC), designed to prevent the marketing of unsafe products and to collect and disseminate information about unsafe products. The CPSC issues standards and rules governing the safety of certain categories of products. Producers are not allowed to deviate from such standards. As a result, the costs of such standards are reflected in product prices even if consumers do not value the CPSC-approved level of safety. Similar, but even stricter, regulations are applied to the development of drugs, which is regulated by the Food and Drug Administration (FDA). In order for drugs to be approved by the FDA they NOT only must be safe, but also be proven effective for the purpose sold; that is, they must "work."

7

ANTITRUST LAW IN THE ENVIRONMENT OF BUSINESS

I. INTRODUCTION

A. Competition

Competition is the lifeblood of capitalism. The most highly valued principles of capitalism—efficiency, opportunity, individual liberty, and others—all rely upon the maintenance of a healthy state of competition within the economy. Indeed, the basis for promoting competition throughout the economy is that it delivers the best set of rules and outcomes for society as a whole. By offering a wide range of choices, competitive markets permit consumers to reward those firms that most closely match their individual tastes. In turn, these individual choices channel resources to the most efficient and responsive firms creating a dynamic reward system that promotes entrepreneurship, efficiency, and risk taking—all the things an economy needs to continually create wealth. Clearly then, competitive markets are in the best interests of the economy.

However, competition is not always in the best interests of individual firms within the economy. Indeed, competition in some markets reduces profits for individual firms and forces costly change upon them. Consequently, individual firms frequently use their resources to reduce competition in their markets by "unfairly" cooperating with or eliminating their competitors. For example, a company that is able to eliminate all its competitors and have a monopoly in a market where it's the only seller of a product has helped itself but clearly reduced "free market" competition in its market.

B. Smithian Model

Adam Smith was an economist in the late 1700s whose fundamental point was that individual choice and self-organized firms rather than governmental authorities could make the best use of society's scarce resources. Moreover, by relying upon self-interest and profits to motivate entrepreneurs and businesses, capitalism would bring about the fastest possible pace of technological advance and wealth creation. In Smith's view, the automatic self-corrective force of competition replaces and improves upon the parental role of government in protecting consumers. This reduced role for government is one of the hall-marks of capitalism and the reason many react negatively to any government involvement in business. However, it is important to remember that the rationale for eliminating gov-ernmental involvement is predicated on the presence of "competition." When competition is not present, for whatever reasons, governmental intervention is warranted in the inter-est of protecting consumers and promoting wealth creation. Antitrust law has grown out of the belief in protecting consumers whenever competition cannot do so by reversing anticompetitive outcomes and eliminating anticompetitive practices.

C. What Is Anticompetitive?

It is worth spending some time discussing the word, "anticompetitive," before diving into the remainder of the chapter. Doing so will allow us to distinguish actions and outcomes that run counter to competition from those that do not. It is common to regard competition between firms as best when it is the fiercest. This "no holds barred" view is partly true but should not be taken to mean that anything goes. Extreme efforts to better one's competitors do go hand in hand with efficiency and wealth creation but only when those efforts lead to better products or more efficient production methods. In other words, the means of com-petition matter just as much as the ends. Means of beating one's competitors that do not lead to better products or enhanced efficiency are anticompetitive, meaning they go against the perpetuation of healthy competition.

We'll explore many anticompetitive practices and the laws that apply to them throughout the chapter. Generally, anticompetitive practices take the form of deliberate actions by firms to outperform their competitors by harming them rather than by improving their own products and services. Antitrust laws work to prevent and punish such anticompetitive actions. It is quite a bit like sports. In baseball or tennis, for example, competitors are permitted and indeed encouraged to increase their chances of winning by training harder, improving their strategies, and adding superior players to their teams. All of these actions make it harder for some of the competitors to win but this is okay since these actions simultaneously raise the level of perfor-mance and skill brought to the competition. On the other hand, competitors are generally not permitted to deliberately injure each other, bribe referees, use unlawful performance-related drugs, steal or damage the other teams' equipment or cooperate with each other to "fix" the outcome. These actions can improve a given competitor's chances of winning but only by low-ering the level of performance and skill brought to the competition by one of, if not all, the competitors. In business, as in sports, there are rules and referees whose purpose it is to define and enforce the set of activities that remove the benefits of competition.

II. ORIGINS OF ANTITRUST LAW

A. Powerful Trusts Created

The federal government's efforts to preserve competitive markets began in earnest during the last quarter of the 1800s. In good measure, these efforts were in response to John D.

Rockefeller's creation of the Standard Oil Trust. Standard Oil grew into a behemoth by absorbing various competitors through stock transfers and using its near-monopoly power to squeeze the remaining competitors out of the market. The absorbed companies transferred their stock to Standard Oil, the trustee, in exchange for stock certificates. Standard Oil then administered the activities of the entire group of companies free of the limitations of competition. Rockefeller's original company, Standard Oil, basically controlled the flow of almost all U.S. oil products from producer to consumer by 1870. By 1882, he controlled much of the world's oil trade. However, Rockefeller made a lot of enemies in the process of creating the Standard Oil Trust and this led to the Ohio Supreme Court dissolving the Standard Oil Trust in 1892. At that point in time, the overall Standard Oil Trust began to be broken down into various geographically based companies such as Standard Oil Company of New Jersey, Standard Oil Company of California, Standard Oil Company of Indiana, etc. Somewhat amazingly, many of these companies still exist well over a century later, albeit under new names. For example, the Standard Oil Company of New Jersey is today known as the Exxon-Mobil Corporation and the Standard Oil Company of California is known as the Chevron Oil Company.

B. Railroads Trusts

The railroads in the late 1800s were also dominated by trusts and like Standard Oil used their market power to increase prices almost at will. The public and state reaction to these trusts was understandably negative, and in 1887 Congress passed the **Interstate Commerce Act** to regulate the railroads. This was the first large step towards protecting consumers and small businesses by preserving competitive markets, but dealt only with the railroads. Consequently, Congress shortly thereafter addressed the broader problem of trusts in the **Sherman Antitrust Act of 1890.**

III. MAJOR ANTITRUST LEGISLATION

The Sherman Act essentially outlawed trusts in the United States and empowered the federal government to break up an existing trust as it saw fit. However, the Sherman Act fell short of protecting consumers from all anticompetitive practices and at times was even ineffective at dismantling well-established trusts due to a reluctant Supreme Court that narrowly interpreted the law. The public's dissatisfaction over inaction in this area was a major political issue in the 1912 Presidential campaign. Congress attempted to address many of the holes left by the Sherman Act and those created by the courts in interpreting it, by passing the **Clayton Antitrust Act** in 1914. The biggest step forward in the Clayton Act was that it directly outlawed "anticompetitive practices"—those acts that tended to *lead* to monopolization. Thus, while the Sherman Act addressed mainly outcomes, trusts, or monopolies themselves, the Clayton Act addressed activities that could lead to such outcomes. Congress passed another antitrust law in 1914, called the **Federal Trade Commission Act**. This Act created the **Federal Trade Commission** and regulated unfair methods of competition and deceptive acts or practices of competition.

A. The Sherman Antitrust Act of 1890

1. Introduction

The **Sherman Act** is primarily directed at trusts like Standard Oil in which groups of companies agree to eliminate competition among them. The Sherman Act is also referred to as the **Trust Buster Act**. It is written in very broad terms and has very severe penalties.

The most important provisions of the Sherman Act are contained in Sections 1 and 2. Section 1 of the Sherman Act outlaws contracts and concerted actions between two or more parties to restrain trade.

2. Section 1 of the Sherman Act

Section 1: Restraints of Trade—*Every contract, combination in the form of trust or otherwise, or conspiracy, in restraint of trade or commerce among the several States, or with foreign nations is declared to be illegal.*

Essentially, Section 1 of the Sherman Act makes it a criminal offense (a felony punishable by a fine or imprisonment) to engage in any contract, combinations, and conspiracies that unreasonably restrains trade. A **restraint of trade** is any agreement between two or more parties that substantially reduces competition in the marketplace. In other words, rival firms must compete and cannot enter into any agreement to eliminate competition unreasonably. For example, two firms cannot contractually agree to fix prices on their products so as to exclude competition.

An important feature of Section 1 though is that it does require a contract on behalf of the involved parties. A contract requires an agreement, express or implied, between two or more persons. Unilateral actions to restrain trade are not covered by Section 1 of the Sherman Act.

The federal courts initially interpreted Section 1 quite narrowly and were generally reluctant to undo many contracts that clearly restrained trade. The principal reason behind the hesitation was that some agreements restraining trade seemed unharmful to society.

Because of the ambiguity regarding contracts to restrain trade, the courts divided Section 1 violations into two distinct categories. Some contracts to restrain trade are deemed blatantly anticompetitive and are always considered violations of Section 1. These automatic violations, called *per se* **violations**, include price fixing (as noted above), group boycotts, refusal to deal, and some division of markets. When a court finds that two or more parties have entered into an agreement that is a *per se* violation of Section 1, it must find them guilty of violating the Sherman Act and address the violation. *Per se* violations are strong and relatively efficient deterrents of the most egregious anticompetitive actions.

Other contracts that work to restrain trade but do not fall under the per se categories discussed above are labeled **Rule of Reason** violations. Agreements in this category do restrain trade and may lessen competition to some degree but they may also create benefits that arguably outweigh the damage they do to market competition. In these cases, the courts reserve the right to weigh the evidence and determine whether the agreement in question is defensible on the grounds of its overall benefits to society.

3. Section 2 of the Sherman Act

Section 2: Monopolization (Anticompetitive Behavior)—*Every person who shall monopolize, or attempt to monopolize or combine or conspire with any other person or persons to monopolize any part of trade or commerce among the several states, or with foreign nations shall be deemed guilty of a felony.*

Most people wrongly believe that the fundamental purpose of antitrust law is to outlaw all monopolies, but Section 2 only outlaws *attempts to monopolize* not the existence of monopolies. The distinction between popular perceptions and the actual language of Section 2 may seem slight but it is vitally important to an understanding of U.S. antitrust law.

Section 2 does not outlaw *all* monopolies, it outlaws anticompetitive means of achieving a monopoly or attempting to use anticompetitive means to create a monopoly, and there is a big difference between the two. If in fact a firm becomes the market's sole provider of a given good, not because it shut-out or undermined its competitors but because its superior products won the loyalty of all customers, that firm has not violated the Sherman Act. In most cases, such a monopolist does not subvert the benefits of market competition. So long as this type of monopolist refrains from maintaining its position through anticompetitive means and competitors can readily enter the market, it poses no real harm to society.

In order to differentiate monopolies that violate Section 2 from those that do not, the courts look for the **intent to monopolize** a market—that is, the willful acquisition of and/or maintenance of monopoly power. Actions by one firm that make it harder for rival firms to compete but do not attempt to improve product quality or production efficiency are the hallmark of Section 2 violations of the Sherman Act.

Proof of predatory behavior or similar anticompetitive action is, for example, sufficient to find a firm in violation of Section 2. However, Section 2 also requires the courts to show that the alleged violator has monopolistic power in the relevant market. As mentioned above, Section 2 outlaws anticompetitive attempts to monopolize not just monopolies themselves. Nevertheless, a firm must be shown to have acquired monopolistic power and to have engaged in willful attempts to acquire or maintain that monopolistic power to be in found in violation of Section 2. Thus, Section 2 is not a legal tool for preventing monopolies before they arise. Instead, it is a means of punishing successful, anticompetitive attempts to create and sustain them.

No part of the Sherman Act defines monopolistic power but it is clear that the Act's definition of monopoly was not meant to be synonymous with "the sole provider" of a good or service. Consequently, the courts have relied upon a wide and evolving series of economic tests to determine the presence and strength of monopolistic power. Despite the significant changes in economic tests for monopolistic power, the courts have more or less consistently required the test to (1) define the relevant market, and (2) show that the alleged monopolist has the ability to price above the competitive level for a significant period of time.

The first of the requirements to show that a firm has monopolistic power in a given market is straightforward and essential. Without a definition of the relevant market, there is no possibility of determining whether a firm has the ability to reduce competition. The second requirement is just as important but can present significant problems in application. How does one determine just how high a firm can raise prices and how long it can keep them high if the firm hasn't already done so? Who can say whether a high price would result in a rush of new competitors or remain unchallenged?

In practice, such a determination is made through a combination of methods that typically include actual pricing history, econometric testing, expert testimony, and comparisons to similar cases. In addition, the courts have frequently used market share tests as rules of thumb in determining whether a firm could price above competitive levels for a prolonged period. For example, a firm whose sales represent more than 80 percent of purchases of a given product, in a given market, would be expected to have market power to price over competitive levels. Through whatever combination of methods it is achieved, the determination of market power for Section 2 violations is a difficult one to prove.

B. The Clayton Antitrust Act of 1914

1. Introduction

As stated, the public's frustration with the usefulness, power, and judicial interpretation of the Sherman Act grew steadily in the two decades after its passage. For a variety of reasons, the Sherman Act was arguably ineffective at punishing even some of the most egregious anticompetitive actions. Scholars blame undue lenience; political beliefs and pressure; and even corruption in federal courts, for the Sherman Act's lackluster early start. In response to rising public dissatisfaction with the Sherman Act, Congress passed the Clayton Act in 1914 to supplement the Sherman Act and close some of the gaps in its administration and application.

The Clayton Act is specific and preventative whereas the Sherman Act is broad and punitive after the fact. One important difference between the two acts is that the Clayton Act only requires that actions have a significant probability of reducing competition, whereas the Sherman Act requires that competition has already been reduced. Since the Clayton Act deals primarily with probable harms to competition, there is no criminal liability for violations. Instead, violations of the Clayton Act lead only to civil or monetary damages. The Clayton Act aims at specific practices that may lead to monopolistic behavior or are anticompetitive but are not covered in the Sherman Act. This Act is administered by the Department of Justice in both civil and criminal enforcement and can be utilized by private citizens in civil suits. The Clayton Act can be enforced by the Federal Trade Commission (FTC) or the Department of Justice, but in either situation, it only deals with civil violations. There are four major provisions of the Clayton Act.

2. Clayton Act Violation Areas
a. Price Discrimination
Section 2 of the Clayton Act forbids firms from **price discrimination**. Because businesses often circumvent Section 2, Congress strengthened this part of the Clayton Act with an amendment to Section 2 with the passage of the Robinson-Patman Act of 1936. Price discrimination occurs when firms charge different buyers different prices for the same good

and the differences in prices cannot be explained by differences in cost justifications. At first glance, it may seem illogical to prevent firms from charging whatever price they like. Furthermore, it may seem reasonable to question why and under what circumstances firms would want to charge different prices to their customers. However, in fact, charging different prices in different markets is one way to initiate a monopoly and the ability to charge different prices often depends on monopolistic power. Furthermore, the ability to price discriminate between buyers can only be present when markets are not perfectly competitive. Only then will buyers actually pay a higher price than is available elsewhere.

Often times, firms attempt to drive their competitors out of the market by charging above market prices where they have market power (e.g., where they are the only supplier) and consumers of course, have little choice but to buy the over-priced product. Then, using the profits from those overly inflated prices, the manufacturer offsets the losses suffered in markets where they compete with rival firms when they set prices far lower, perhaps even below cost, to gain an advantage over their competition. In this way, firms may use price discrimination to eliminate competition.

b. Exclusionary Practices

Section 3 of the Clayton Act prohibits exclusionary practices, where one firm is given the exclusive right to the exclusion of others, to buy, sell, or trade another's product, if the effect is "to substantially lessen competition or tend to create a monopoly." Exclusive dealing contracts are contractual attempts by a seller to prevent a buyer from considering competitive bids from other sellers. For example, an auto parts store may agree to an exclusive dealing contract whereby it agrees to only sell the products of a particular parts manufacturer. The contract may only apply to a particular item but typically requires that the buyer not consider purchases of rival products for the duration of the arrangement. The potential harm of such an arrangement is that it prevents other auto parts manufacturers from competing for the buyer's purchases. In other words, exclusive dealing arrangements forestall competition and are therefore anticompetitive.

However, there are also good reasons why manufacturers may want to prevent the firms that sell their products from selling the products of rival manufacturers. The courts now recognize that some exclusive dealing arrangements help firms reduce selling and advertising costs. Furthermore, exclusive dealing arrangements are a threat to market competition only when the arrangement applies to a substantial share of the products in a particular market

c. Tying Arrangements (Tie-in Sales Agreements)

Like exclusive dealing contracts, **tying arrangements or tie-in sales agreements** tend to forestall competition and may facilitate the spread of monopoly power from one market to another. Tying arrangements are also violations of Section 3 of the Clayton Act. Tying arrangements occur when a seller requires buyers to purchase a "tied" product as a condition of purchasing another, typically more desirable, "tying" product. Forcing buyers to make such an all-or-nothing purchase decision would never work in competitive markets.

Buyers would simply exercise their ability to purchase only those products they truly desired. However, a seller can compel buyers to purchase a less desirable product in order to acquire a more desirable product over which it has market power. In this way, a seller can use its market power over one product to prevent competition over another product over which it has little or no market power. Under the Clayton Act, tying arrangements apply only to the exchange of goods, not services or land.

d. Mergers

Perhaps the best-known antitrust activity of the Department of Justice and the FTC is the review and prevention of some mergers. **Mergers** refer to the joining of two or more companies into one. A merger can be accomplished by having one firm acquire another firm directly or by having the component firms combine their assets into a new firm. In either case, Section 7 of the Clayton Act charges the Department of Justice and FTC to prevent mergers when they *"substantially lessen competition"* or *"tend to create a monopoly"* in *"any line of commerce in any section of the country."*

Clearly, many mergers do not tend to create monopolies and do not promise to substantially forestall the forces of competition. But others do, and like other anticompetitive practices, mergers that lessen competition reduce consumer choice and the efficiency of markets for the sake of profits. The essential challenge of administering this section of the Clayton Act is deciding which mergers lessen or at least threaten to lessen competition and which do not. Typically, examining firm concentration and barriers to entry in the relevant market makes the distinction between lawful and unlawful mergers.

1) Firm Concentration

Firm concentration refers to the proportion of the relevant market served by the largest firms in the market. For example, most courts would agree that if two firms accounted for 80 percent of the sales in a given market, a merger between these two firms would lessen competition and tend to lead to a monopoly. Concentration of market share in the hands of a few firms is a precondition for mergers that violate Section 7. Nevertheless, market concentration is not always an appropriate basis for determining that a potential merger will lessen competition.

2) Barriers to Entry

In recent years, the courts have begun to consider more complex criteria for determining whether a proposed merger reduces competition. The availability of substitute products and the ability of new firms to enter concentrated markets are also important considerations when evaluating the effects of mergers on competition. More generally, courts consider whether any barriers to entry exist in the markets in which the merging firms operate. **Barriers to entry** refer to any characteristics of the relevant market that make it particularly difficult for new firms to enter and thereby compete with established firms. If barriers to entry are substantial, reducing the number of existing competitors through a merger is all the more likely to appreciably lessen competition.

Some of the more common barriers to entry are licensing requirements, large-scale investments like manufacturing plant development and construction costs, and access to scarce resources. Whatever the barrier, if potential competitors cannot offer their products to buyers, the market may be made substantially less competitive by a merger between existing firms.

3) Types of Mergers

The Clayton Act applies to four distinct types of mergers: **horizontal mergers**, **vertical mergers**, **market extension mergers** and **conglomerate mergers**. A merger between firms that compete in the same market is a **horizontal merger**. A strict interpretation of the Clayton Act implies that the court can deem illegal any horizontal merger that significantly raises market concentration. Thus, a merger between two firms each with 25 percent of the sales in a given market would likely be prevented. However, as mentioned above, the courts now recognize that an increase in market concentration is not a sufficient basis upon which to solely conclude that a merger reduces competition.

Vertical mergers occur when two firms in the same chain of production and distribution combine into a single firm. In other words, a vertical merger is a supplier-customer merger. By grouping a broader array of operations into a single firm, a vertical merger may substantially increase the efficiency of production. However, vertical mergers may also exclude competitors from a market where they once competed. For example, if an apparel manufacturer merges with a department store, it may exclude other apparel manufacturers from selling their products to that department store. In essence, such a vertical merger removes some of the existing competitors from the market in much the same way that horizontal mergers do.

The third general category of mergers, **market extension mergers**, comes in two types: (1) geographic market extension mergers and (2) product market extension mergers. Market extension mergers are mergers between two firms in similar fields of business but not in the exact business field. A geographic market extension is when two firms in the same product market, but not in the same geographic market, decide to merge. For example, a bank with operations in South Dakota merging with a bank having operations in North Dakota would represent a merger of this kind. A product market extension merger, however, is where one company merges with another company that makes a similar, but not exactly the same, product as the first company.

Conglomerate mergers, or **diversification mergers**, are neither horizontal nor vertical, rather they involve mergers between firms that operate in distinct and unrelated markets. It may appear that no damage could arise from a merger of firms in different markets since such a merger will not reduce the number of competitors in either market. However, a merger between firms in related markets can substantially reduce the threat of competition, and that may be enough to harm consumers. Some experts consider market extension mergers to be types of conglomerate mergers.

Preventing mergers that reduce the mere threat of competition but not actual competition may seem to be overreaching and unnecessary, but the rationale is actually consistent the intent of the Clayton Act. Two of the principal benefits of competitive markets are that they prevent suppliers from charging exorbitant prices and encourage them to constantly improve their products. If barriers to entry are not prohibitive, the mere threat of competition can confer these same benefits. If an existing firm with no competitors begins charging high prices and stagnating, potential competitors will enter the market, drive prices down towards competitive levels and prod an improvement in products. Thus, a conglomerate merger between firms in unrelated, distinct markets can eliminate the benefits of competition in much the same way that horizontal or vertical mergers can.

4) Interlocking Directorates

Section 8 of Clayton restricts **interlocking directorates**, having the same people or a controlling interest of the same people sit on competing corporations' board of directors. People are forbidden from creating interlocking directorates based on the profits of the competing companies or on the competitive sales totals of the two companies. These amounts are set by the Federal Trade Commission and are normally adjusted upward.

C. Federal Trade Commission Act (1914)

Congress passed the Federal Trade Commission Act in 1914. The most important section is Section 5 and it prohibits "unfair methods of competition in or affecting commerce, and unfair or deceptive acts or practices in or affecting commerce." Therefore, any business activity that may tend to create a monopoly by unfairly eliminating or excluding competitors from the marketplace is condemned. This literally can be used to regulate all forms of anticompetitive behavior that not covered by the Sherman or Clayton Acts. For this reason, the FTC Act has been referred to as a "catch-all law." The FTC Act also created the FTC, one of the key regulatory agencies used to regulate antitrust law.

IV. ENFORCEMENT AND PENALTIES

A. Enforcement

There are two federal regulatory agencies that enforce antitrust law. These are the U.S. Department of Justice and the FTC. Furthermore, private parties can enforce most provisions of the Sherman and Clayton Acts. However, only the DOJ can enforce the criminal penalties of the Sherman Act.

1. Private Parties

Remember that "private" means non-governmental entities and can include individuals or businesses. If an individual brings an antitrust act lawsuit under Sherman or Clayton Act they are generally entitled to treble damages plus attorney fees and court costs if the case is successful. Private parties cannot file suit under the FTC Act. The majority, sometimes up to 90 percent of antitrust cases, in recent years, have been initiated by private parties.

2. Criminal Sanctions

If criminal sanctions are being sought, then the case must be brought by the DOJ under the Sherman Act. Criminal penalties for Sherman Act cases brought by the DOJ, Antitrust Division, can result in a prison term of up to three years and/or a fine of up to $350,000 per violation for individuals. Corporations can have up to a $10 million fine per violation levied against them. Private individuals cannot bring criminal actions.

3. Civil Action by the Government

Under the Sherman Act, the government can seek an equitable remedy, an injunction. If granted it is basically a court order stopping some alleged antitrust violations. The FTC and DOJ can also seek civil damages and if successful, just like individuals, can receive treble damages. The FTC can also investigate suspected business dealings, hold hearings, and issue cease and desist orders to discontinue or modify certain business acts. The FTC under the FTC Act can prevent mergers and assess substantial civil penalties. Civil actions can be sought by either individuals or by the government under the Sherman or Clayton Act and both individuals and the government can receive treble damages.

B. Remedies Available

In addition to injunctions and monetary damages, there are other remedies in civil antitrust. For example, a targeted company can be ordered to divest, or get rid of, a given subsidiary if continuing to own that subsidiary creates antitrust legal problems.

V. THE COURTS AND ANTITRUST ANALYSIS

A. Antitrust Law is Dynamic

Just as businesses and society change, so does antitrust law. As more is learned about the costs and benefits to society from different business agreements, arrangements, and activities, attitudes about antitrust law also change. As we have discussed, there are two basic rules of antitrust law (i.e., "*per se*" and "rule of reason") and on occasion, the courts might change from one to the other or carve out an exception in some area of antitrust law due to business or societal changes.

B. The Two Rules

1. Per Se Rule

If the Supreme Court has adopted a *per se* **rule**, then all the government has to prove is that the company violated antitrust law. There is no chance for the company to defend its action. It violated antitrust law by whatever its action was and no defense or justification can explain the violation. Therefore, the Supreme Court has only found violations to be *per se* in antitrust areas that are considered inherently anticompetitive. In short, the basis for the company's antitrust activities is irrelevant, if it violates an area of antitrust law that is handled by the *per se* rule, once the violation is found, the only remaining issue is the type and amount of damages.

2. *Rule of Reason*

The **rule of reason** is a much more flexible standard. Basically the rule of reason allows some contracts that restrain trade, but they cannot reach an unreasonable level. To determine whether an "unreasonable level" of restraint exists, courts examine a wide range of factors.

VI. HORIZONTAL RESTRAINT OF TRADE V. VERTICAL RESTRAINT OF TRADE

A. Horizontal Restraint of Trade

Horizontal Restraint of Trade occurs when businesses operate at the same level of competition and generally in the same market. An example of horizontal restraint of trade would be if Ford, Chrysler, and General Motors entered into a horizontal scheme to fix the prices of their automobiles. Horizontal means that you are on the same plane in the product market and are, in fact, competitors. A gross example of an illegal horizontal restraint of trade is a **cartel** where rival firms come together to purposely restrain trade. A good international example of a cartel is OPEC, that is, the oil producing countries' price fixing arrangement, that would obviously be illegal in the United States. Many types of horizontal restraint of trade are per se illegal, but others fall under the rule of reason.

B. Vertical Restraint of Trade

A vertical restraint of trade occurs when two or more firms in the distribution chain enter into a contract or conspire to restrain trade. An example of a vertical chain of businesses is a manufacturer to a distributor to a wholesaler to a retailer to the customer. Again, the Supreme Court has applied both of the basic antitrust rules in determining the legality of different types of vertical restrains of trade. It can depend on given circumstances.

VII. PRICE FIXING

A. Introduction

The Sherman Act prohibits "every contract, combination in the form of trust or otherwise, or conspiracy, in restraint of trade or commerce among the several states, or with foreign nations" (Section 1). When firms selling the same product agree to fix prices, it is almost certain to be a violation of Section 1 of Sherman. The issue becomes, is it a *per se* or rule of reason violation?

B. Horizontal Price Fixing

1. *United States v. Socony-Vacuum Oil Co. 310 U.S. 150 (1940)*

In this case, independent Texas and Louisiana oilmen were accused of fixing prices. The oil industry was in the midst of an oil glut brought on by lack of sales during the depression and newly discovered oil fields. Therefore, they entered into an agreement with major refining companies to limit production in the market and thereby raise prices. The Supreme Court held the *"per se"* rule applied, elaborating in the case's very famous footnote 59 which states in part:

> A conspiracy to fix prices violates Section 1 of the (Sherman) Act though no overt act is shown, though it is not established that the conspirators had the means available for accomplishment of their objective, and though the conspiracy embraced but a part of the interstate or foreign commerce in the commodity. Whatever may have been the status of price-fixing agreements at common law, the Sherman Act has a broader application to them that the common law prohibitions or sanctions. Price-fixing agreements may or may not be aimed at complete elimination of price competition. The group making those agreements may or may not have power to control the market. But the fact that the group cannot control the market prices does not necessarily mean that the agreement as to prices has no utility to the members of the combination. The effectiveness of price-fixing agreements is dependent on many factors, such as competitive tactics, position in the industry, the formula underlying price policies, Whatever economic justification price-fixing agreements may be thought to have, the law does not permit an inquiry into their reasonableness. They are all banned because of their actual or potential threat to the central nervous system of the economy.

Therefore, the Court ruled that horizontal price fixing is per se illegal even if the parties to the agreement do not have the actual market power to affect market price. (Of course, as important as this is, it is usually irrelevant because most defendants who enter into these price fixing schemes *have* the power to control the market. However, footnote 59 is still of major importance in antitrust law.)

2. *Arizona v. Maricopa County Medical Society 457 U.S. 332 (1982)*

In this case two Arizona counties had formed two foundations for medical care as an alternative to existing health insurance plans. The doctors who joined the medical foundations had to agree not to charge more than the maximum fees set by the foundation. The fee schedules were set by a vote of the members of the foundations. However, non-member physicians were only reimbursed to the maximum amount allowed by the fee schedules to be paid to the member physicians. The Attorney General for the State of Arizona filed suit alleging horizontal price fixing. The U.S. Supreme Court granted *certiorari* and held that the fee arrangements were a *per se* violation of Sherman, Section 1.

3. *Federal Trade Commission v. Superior Court Trial Lawyers Association 493 U.S. 411 (1990)*

In the District of Columbia, the District's Criminal Justice Act (CJA) set the fees for court-appointed attorneys. The attorneys who regularly took court appointed cases belonged to a professional organization that was not a labor union called the Superior Court Trial Lawyers Association (SCTLA). The SCTLA tried to persuade the CJA to raise the court appointed attorney fees but was unsuccessful. The result was that most of the attorneys who regularly took court appointed cases in the District of Columbia refused to take the cases. This had the anticipated adverse impact of turmoil on the court system in the District of Columbia, and the FTC filed a complaint against SCTLA claiming an unreasonable restraint on trade. The FTC ruled against the SCTLA but on appeal the Court of Appeals reversed the FTC. The FTC applied for *writ of certiorari* to the U.S. Supreme Court. The Court ruled that the SCTLA's agreement was in fact horizontal price fixing and was a *per se* violation of Section 1 of Sherman in that by refusing to serve the only customer (CJA), the attorneys constricted the supply of available attorneys and that was the essence of price fixing. The Supreme Court put it as follows: "The horizontal arrangement among these competitors was unquestionably a 'naked restraint' on price and output. No matter how altruistic the motive of respondents may have been, it is undisputed that their immediate objective was to increase the price that they would be paid for their services."

C. Vertical Price Fixing

1. Dr. Miles Medical Co. v. John D. Park & Sons Co. 220 U.S. 373 (1911)

This case was one of the first Supreme Court cases on **resale price maintenance** (RPM) which is when the manufacturer of a product tells the buyer that they must sell the product for a stated amount. Normally RPMs are where the manufacturer requires the buyer to agree not to sell their product below a certain price and they are utilized to protect the integrity of the product. In *Dr. Miles* the producer of patented medicines sold its product to wholesalers and required the wholesalers to agree not to sell the product below a certain price. The Supreme Court said that once the manufacturer sold the product, it was no longer the manufacturer's to control and therefore, it had no control over the price once it was sold and to attempt to do so was *per se* illegal.

2. Problem with the Per Se Approach

It is argued by small businesses that RPM schemes help small businesses to compete with larger businesses. Often large discount stores do not provide the customer with the services that smaller stores provide. The argument of the smaller stores is that this additional service is a major benefit to the consumer. However, due to possible volume discounts, the smaller stores cannot compete with the large discount stores and a large number of them have been forced to go out of business. These smaller stores argue that if a reasonable RPM scheme could be set, that they could compete with the larger discount chains and provide the services that the customer needs as well.

For instance, consider the hypothetical Joe's TV and Repair store in a town of approximately 5,000 people. Joe ordinarily purchases only three of model X7G TVs from Zenith each year. On the other hand, Wal-Mart buys thousands of model X7G TVs from Zenith each year and negotiates a much lower price due to volume discounts than Joe is able to do. In fact, Wal-Mart can sell the model X7G TV to a customer cheaper than Joe can purchase the same TV from Zenith. Of course, when the model X7G TV breaks and a customer takes it back to Wal-Mart, Wal-Mart has no service department and the customer is left with a broken TV or the option of taking it to Joe to have it fixed. Of course, if Joe's TV and Repair has gone out of business because it had no business, then the customer is left with a broken TV or the prospect of loading up the TV and taking it to another town to have it repaired. Joe's argument is that if small stores, like Joe's, and Wal-Mart both bought the TV for the same price under a reasonable RPM that Joe could still compete and the customer would not be harmed because he would still get a "low" priced TV (although, maybe not as low priced), and still have the business around to repair his TV. In the recent Texas-based case of **Leegin Creative Leather Products**, the U.S. Supreme Court changed the rules of the game in the RPM area.

3. *Leegin Creative Leather Products, Inc. v. PSKS, Inc., dba Kay's Kloset U Kay's Shoes 551 U.S. 877 (2007)*

In June of 2007, the U.S. Supreme Court decided the case of Leegin Creative Leather Products, Inc. v. PSKS, Inc., dba Kay's Kloset U Kay's Shoes, hereinafter called *Leegin*. In this case, it specifically overruled *Dr. Miles* and replaced the *per se* rule on vertical price fixing also called **vertical price restraints** with the rule of reason, at least for minimum price fixing.

In *Leegin*, Kay's Kloset, a women's apparel store in Lewisville, Texas, sold Brighton Leather Goods which were made by Leegin Creative Leather Products, Inc. beginning in 1997 and at one point, the Brighton line, accounted for 40–50 percent of the profits of Kay's Kloset. In 1997 Leegin distributed its "Brighton Retail Pricing and Promotion Policy" to its retailers. If a retailer would not follow the said policy, and sold Brighton below the suggested price, Leegin would not sell Brighton to the retail establishment, except that the retail establishment could put items that were not selling and the retailer did not plan to reorder, on sale. Kay's Kloset pledged to follow the price suggestions. However, in 2002, Leegin learned that Kay's Kloset had been discounting the entire Brighton line by 20 percent. Leegin requested Kay's Kloset to stop discounting Brighton which Kay's Kloset refused to do and Leegin stopped selling Brighton to Kay's Kloset. Kay's Kloset filed a suit against Leegin claiming that the price guidelines were in fact vertical price-fixing agreements between Leegin and its retailers in violation of the long-standing *Dr. Miles* precedent. The U.S. District Court, ruled for Kay's Kloset and awarded damages of $1.2 million and then trebled the amount to around $3.6 million. The Court of Appeals, Fifth Circuit, affirmed the district court judgment.

Leegin took the case to the U.S. Supreme Court and the issue became whether the Court should overrule *Dr. Miles's per se* rule and allow price maintenance agreements to be reviewed under the rule of reason? The Supreme Court reversed the Court of Appeals and therefore, specifically overruled *Dr. Miles* with the result being that vertical price restraints are to now be judged by the rule of reason.

Adopting various of the arguments discussed above with respect to Joe's TV and Repair store, the Supreme Court felt that resale price maintenance agreements could potentially have pro-competitive effects, meaning that resale price maintenance agreements could enhance the marketplace. Thus, it, ruled that in minimum vertical price restraints or vertical price fixing cases the rule of reason should replace the *per se* rule. The Supreme

Court's decision in Leegin though, was 5-4 in nature, with all five votes coming from the more conservative wing (justices appointed by Republican Presidents) of the Court. It clearly signaled a more "relaxed"/"rule of reason"—type approach to antitrust law by the U.S. Supreme Court's more conservative justices (i.e., Chief Justice Roberts, and Justices Scalia, Thomas, Alito, and Kennedy). Should there be any changes to this conservative high court judicial majority, there could be the potential for the return to a "stricter"/more "per se" scope of regulation in this antitrust law area.

VIII. HORIZONTAL EXCHANGES OF INFORMATION

A. Is Trading Information between Businesses Good or Bad?

The obvious answer to this question is that it depends on what information is exchanged and for what purpose. In other words, is the consumer harmed or benefited with better products, or, reduction of wasted or inefficiency? Does the information shared help the businesses to violate the spirit of the antitrust laws?

B. Conspiracy to Restrain Information

A leading case in this area is **FTC v. Indiana Federation of Dentist 476 U.S. 447 (1986)**. An Indiana dentists' association had a rule that dentists could not share information with insurance companies. Sometimes the insurance companies wanted to look at the X-rays to see if the dental work was necessary. The Supreme Court ruled that the Indiana Federation of Dentists practice to bar the sharing of information was illegal based on a rule of reason approach. The Court found that there was no pro-competitive reason for the ban on sharing information.

IX. MARKET DIVISIONS

A. Horizontal Market Divisions

A horizontal market division is when competitors divide up the different markets based on geography, product, or some other term. The Court is concerned with competitors effectively eliminating competition within divided areas. For example, what if three automobile manufacturers divided up the country and said that Company S should take west of the Mississippi River; Company A should take south of the Mason-Dixon Line; and Company M should take the area that is left. Can you see how that would be unfair and create monopolies in each of the three areas?

Keep in mind that this can be geographic as in the example above, or it can be functional. A functional division is to divide up customers such as Company A agrees to sell only to retailers and Company M agrees to sell only to wholesalers. The courts are clear on either type of horizontal market divisions it is per se illegal so long as it involves more than one company.

1. *United States v. Suntar Roofing, Inc. 897 F.2d 460 (1990)*

Suntar Roofing, Inc. and Ronan's Roofing, Inc. agreed to a customer allocation plan dividing roofing customers in Kansas City, Kansas between the two roofing companies. The government brought criminal charges against them under Section 1 of the Sherman Act. The district court found the defendants guilty and they appealed to the 10th Court of Appeals. The issue was, should the trial judge have considered evidence of reasonableness in the contract between the two companies? The 10th Circuit Court held that the issue of horizontal market divisions had long been decided by the per se approach and that the government had met its burden of proof. Therefore, the district court acted properly in excluding evidence to consider why the defendants had violated the antitrust laws. In other words, there was no rule of reason approach so the district court was correct in excluding the evidence of reasonableness.

2. *Rule*

A single company cannot be involved in territorial allocation antitrust activities due to the nature of allocating territory; there must be two or more companies. However, if two or more companies are involved in territorial allocation, whether it is by customer, product, or geographic allocations, it will be per se illegal.

B. Vertical Market Divisions

1. *Types of Vertical Market Divisions*

Vertical market divisions can be territorial restraints where a manufacturer tells a retailer where they can sell a product such as in a distributorship. If the distributor sells the product outside of the allotted territory, that is grounds for the manufacturer to revoke the distributor's franchise. There can also be vertical customer restrictions where the manufacturer limits who the distributor will sell to, such as to wholesalers only.

2. *Case Law*

a. *White Motor Co. v. United States 373 U.S. 253 (1963)*

A truck company required its dealers to sell trucks only in an exclusive territory around their dealerships. However, White Motor Co. retained the right to sell to governmental entities throughout the country. The government attacked the scheme as a violation of Section 1 of the Sherman Act. However, White argued that it was a small company in an industry dominated by large firms and that White's restrictive practices were necessary to force its dealers to concentrate on the competition with other types of trucks and not with each other. The Court agreed based on a rule of reason approach.

b. *Continental T.V. v. GTE Sylvania, Inc. 433. U.S. 36 (1977)*

Sylvania had terminated Continental as a dealer and Continental sued based on its claim that Sylvania was trying to monopolize the market. Sylvania had decided to sell TVs directly to franchise retailers and to give them territorial restrictions. The U.S. Supreme Court upheld Sylvania's actions based on a rule of reason approach.

c. Business Electronic Corporation v. Sharp Electronic Corporation 485 U.S. 717 (1988)
The Sharp case clearly gives manufacturers the freedom to have wide control in selecting dealers that will distribute their product to retail distributors. It firmly established the rule of reason in this area. However, Sharp does warn of conspiracies to fix retail prices. However, it is clear that in the absence of any price fixing, vertical market divisions are handled by the rule of reason.

X. HORIZONTAL GROUP BOYCOTTS

A group boycott is a refusal to deal. It becomes a horizontal group boycott if you have two competitors who agree not to deal with other competitors on the same level of competition. The purpose is to eliminate or discipline a competitor of the boycotting group who violates the agreement. The U.S. Supreme Court is clear; any boycott that involves horizontal agreements among direct competitors is per se illegal.

XI. PRICE DISCRIMINATION

A. Introduction

Clayton Act, Section 2 always restricted price discrimination but it was unclear in its application due to several major loopholes. To clear up any ambiguities, Congress passed the Robinson-Patman Act in 1936 to read:

> it shall be unlawful for any person engaged in commerce, either directly or indirectly, to discriminate in price between different purchasers of commodities of like grade and quality, where either or any of the purchases involved in such discrimination are in commerce, where the effect of such discrimination may be substantially to lessen competition or tend to create a monopoly in any line of commerce, or to injure, destroy, or prevent competition with any person who either grants or knowingly receives the benefit of such discrimination, or with customers of either of them. (Section 2a)

Basically this is saying that a manufacturer cannot sell the same product to different purchasers for different prices without justification. Section 2a is one of the most controversial areas of antitrust law because its original intent was to prevent the large chain stores from exerting their bargaining power in dealing with suppliers so that the chain stores would have lower costs and therefore, lower prices than smaller independent competitors. The government has been generally reluctant to enforce Section 2a, and therefore, most of the cases in price discrimination are private cases.

B. Predatory Pricing

One of the major types of price discrimination is **predatory pricing** which is when a manufacturer sells its product for a lower price in one geographic area to drive the competition out of business in that geographic area, and then raises the price once the competition is removed from the market. The cases on predatory pricing can be brought under either Section 2a of the Clayton Act (Robinson-Patman) or Section 2 of the Sherman Act. However, the cases are difficult to win because the issue always becomes whether the given action is indeed "predatory" or just "aggressive competition"? The plaintiff in an allegation of price discrimination must prove (1) that the defendant priced the product below cost; (2) that the defendant was then able to monopolize the market; and (3) that the monopoly would last long enough for the defendant to recoup losses suffered during the price war when the defendant was trying to remove the competition from the market place.

C. Defenses

There are several defenses to price discrimination. The first of these is also one of the most common and one of the most controversial. Volume discounts are allowed as an exception to price discrimination. Therefore, when one business, say Wal-Mart, can afford to buy thousands of the same model of TVs and another smaller business will only need a few and therefore, only buys a few, Wal-Mart can legally demand and receive a "better deal" due to volume discounts. Should this be legal?

A defense that is obvious is cost justification, such as more differences in transportation costs. This is sometimes difficult to prove because it is virtually an accounting and economic impossibility to assign specific costs of production to most individual products.

Changing conditions can also give rise to legal price discrimination. This can include deterioration of perishable goods, such as the grocery store putting bananas on sale when they start to turn black, or selling day-old bread at reduced prices. This can also involve disposing of seasonal goods such as selling winter coats at reduced prices in early spring or plants at a lower price in the heat of summer. Another defense is meeting the competition's price. If one competitor puts its product on sale, then the other competitor can meet the price so long as it is done in good faith. Of course, the second seller is only supposed to meet, not beat, the competitor's price but this is also a good way for a price war to get started.

XII. EXCLUSIONARY PRACTICES

A. Introduction

The principal concern of antitrust law is to be sure that firms with market power cannot control the markets in which they do business. The statutory provisions in this area are Section 1 of the Sherman Act for exclusionary practices dealing with both products and services due to illegal restraint of trade and Section 3 of the Clayton Act dealing with products and attempts to lessen competition.

There are three major types of exclusionary practices: (1) tying arrangements or tie-in sales, (2) exclusive dealing contracts, and (3) boycotts. Each will be dealt with in detail in the following paragraphs.

B. Tying Arrangements (Tie-in Sales)

1. Introduction

A **tying arrangement** is also called a **tie-in sale**. A tying arrangement is where a seller sells one product conditioned upon the requirement that the buyer also purchase another product. There are legal tying arrangements that are often used in the business world as advertising techniques such as "buy one, get one free" or "buy one, get the next one for half price," etc. There is also a justification to a tying arrangement if there are technological reasons that make the tying arrangement necessary. However, in many cases this technological justification is over-used and really does not apply. That was the situation in the IBM case that follows.

2. Case Law

a. International Business Machines Corporation (IBM) v. United States 298 U.S. 131 (1936)

IBM leased automated tabulation machines to customers and then required the customers to purchase cards to run the machines from IBM. IBM did have competition in this area, Remington Rand, which was also a co-defendant in the lawsuit, for doing the same tying arrangement. The Supreme Court held the tie-in sale to be a violation of Section 3 of the Clayton Act. IBM tried to claim the technology requirements defense but the Court did not accept that argument because the card was not of such a requirement that someone other than IBM or Remington Rand could not have made it. The Supreme Court felt that both defendants each possessed market power sufficient to "substantially lessen competition through their respective tying arrangements."

b. Northern Pacific Railway Company v. United States 356 U.S. 1 (1958)

In this case, Northern Pacific, the Railroad, was selling land to individuals at a below market price and in exchange required the individual purchasers to agree to ship any goods that they produced on the land via the railroad, unless the purchasers could find a cheaper way to ship the goods. The Supreme Court defined the tie-in sale as "an agreement by a party to sell one product (the tying product) but only on the condition that the buyer also purchase a different (complimentary or tied) product, or at least agrees that he will not purchase that product from any other supplier." In this case, the tying product was the land, and the tied product was the shipment of the goods on the Railroad. The Railroad argued that this was not an illegal tying arrangement because the purchaser was not required to "buy" the tied product-if they could find a cheaper way they could use the cheaper method to ship their goods. Of course, the Railroad established a monopoly by using this tying arrangement and no one could come in and compete with the Railroad on a grand scale and so the Railroad would almost always have the cheapest method of shipment. The Supreme Court felt that this was a violation of Section 1 of the Sherman Act since the tie-in sale tended to exploit the Railroad's monopoly.

c. Datagate, Inc. v. Hewlett-Packard Co. 60 F.3d 1421 (1995)

Hewlett-Packard (HP) had a tie-in contract with one company, Rockwell International, Inc. worth $100,000 per year. The issue was whether having only one contract enough to be an antitrust violation? The U.S. Court of Appeals (Ninth Circuit) said it was because the tying arrangement affected a not insubstantial volume of commerce and that one contract represented a "not-insubstantial" dollar-volume of sales.

C. Exclusive Dealing Contracts

Contracts under which a seller stops a buyer from purchasing the seller's competitors products are **exclusive dealing** contracts which are restricted by Section 3 of the Clayton Act. Exclusive dealing contracts are generally prohibited if the effect of the contract is to "substantially lessen competition or tend to create a monopoly."

The leading decision in this area is still the classic 1949 Supreme Court decision in **Standard Oil Co. of California v. United States 337 U.S. 293 (1949)**. The issue there was did the then largest gasoline seller in the United States make exclusive-dealing contracts with independent stations that were illegal under Section 3 of the Clayton Act? Was this to the point of having the effect of restricting entry into the market? The Supreme Court answered both questions in the affirmative. Standard Oil had entered into contracts with independent stations in several western states to supply gasoline to the independents. The independents constituted 16 percent of all the retail outlets and 7 percent of all retail gas sales in the area. The Court also noted that the other biggest competitors of Standard Oil also used the same arrangement so that taken as a whole they controlled 65 percent of the market with these exclusive-dealing contracts. The Court found that these were illegal exclusive dealing contracts and did violate Section 3 because competition was "foreclosed in a substantial share" of the relevant market.

D. Boycotts

A **boycott** is when a group conspires to prevent the carrying on of business or to harm a business. The group can include basically anyone including consumers, union members, retailers, wholesalers, and suppliers. Boycotts are often associated with price fixing schemes or other restraint of trade situations. If the group possesses market power and the boycott is intended to restrict or exclude a competitor, the *per se* rule will be imposed. This has been a long-standing rule in antitrust law.

One of the first cases was **Eastern States Retail Lumber Dealers Association v. United States 193 U.S. 38 (1904)**. In Eastern States, lumber retailers would turn in the name of wholesalers who sold lumber to the public to the Eastern States Retail Lumber Dealers Association. The Association would then send the names of those wholesalers to other retailers hoping that those retailers would boycott the wholesalers who sold directly to the public. The Supreme Court held that this was a *per se* violation of the Sherman Act.

As we have already seen in *FTC v. Superior Court Trial Lawyers Association*, this is still the rule today. Both *Eastern States* and *Superior Court Trial Lawyers* hold that when horizontal competitors use a boycott to force a change in the nature of a vertical relationship, there is a *per se* violation. Therefore, there is no question that boycotts are handled by the *per se* rule.

XIII. MERGERS

A. Introduction

A merger is when two or more firms come together to form a new firm. There are several types of mergers. A **horizontal merger** is when firms that were previously competitors merge such as United and Continental Airlines. A **vertical merger** combines two firms up and down the business chain such as a retailer and a wholesaler. A **market extension merger** is a merger between two firms in similar fields but not in the same exact field. There are two types of market extension mergers. The first type of market extension merger is a **geographic market extension merger** where a company merges with another company that sells the same product but in a totally different geographic region of the country where they had no contract prior to the merger. An example of a geographic market extension merger is when two ice cream makers, Blue Bell Creamery out of Brenham, Texas, and Purple Rabbit Ice Cream out of Charleston, West Virginia, merge. The other type of market extension merger is a **product extension merger**. This is when a company merges with another company that makes a similar product to that made by the first company, for example, if Blue Bell Creamery mergers with an ice-cream cone manufacturer. The last type of merger is a **conglomerate merger** or **diversification merger** that is a merger of at least two firms outside the first three types of merger. It is normally a merger of two totally unrelated businesses.

B. Pre-Merger Notification

The Hart-Scott-Rodino Antitrust Improvement Act of 1976 requires pre-merger notification to the Federal Trade Commission and the Department of Justice. This is required to give the government time to decide if it opposes the proposed merger on antitrust grounds. This rule applies only to fairly large mergers (over at least $70 million in value). In such cases, though, the parties must file the notification form and wait 30 days before proceeding any further with the merger. If the government sues to stop the merger during this time period, the suit is entitled to an expedited hearing in the courts.

C. Government Response to Pre-Merger Notification

If the government files suit during the waiting period, it normally files suit under Section 7 of Clayton which was amended in 1950 by the Celler-Kefauver Act. Section 7 now applies to virtually all methods of external expansion. It states in relevant part that a person or business cannot hold stock or assets in another business "where in any line of commerce or in any activity affecting commerce in any section of the country, the effect of such acquisition may be to substantially lessen competition." The key factor is to determine the concentration of market power.

D. Determining Market Power

The FTC and the DOJ have established merger guidelines that give businesses advance notice of when mergers will probably be challenged. These guidelines are updated on a regular basis. The guidelines discuss factors that will be used by the government in deciding if a merger should be allowed. The first factor to consider is the concentration of market power. This is done by the Herfindahl-Hirschman Index (HHI). The HHI is determined by adding the squares of the percentage market shares in the relevant market. For example, if there are four firms with shares of 10 percent, 20 percent, 30 percent, and 40 percent, then the HHI equals 3,000 (100 + 400 + 900 + 1600 = 3,000). Normally, if the pre-merger HHI is less than 1,000 then the market is deemed to not be concentrated and the merger is unlikely be challenged. If the HHI is between 1,000 and 1,800, the government considers the industry moderately concentrated and the merger may be challenged depending on the circumstances. If the HHI is greater than 1,800, the market is highly concentrated and the merger will probably be challenged.

It is important to note that the guidelines are only a starting point and the FTC and DOJ will look at numerous other factors when deciding whether to challenge a proposed merger. Some of these factors are ease of entry into the market place, economic efficiency, the financial condition of the merging firms, politics, etc.

To further understand this concept, it is important to define some applicable terms. **Market power** is the ability of one or more firms to profitably maintain prices above competitive levels for a significant period of time. **Market share** is the percentage of the relevant market controlled by the firm. **Product market** is the market of inter-changeable products. The desire is to have enough producers so that one firm cannot affect the market for the products. Then if one firm does raise prices, the consumer can simply switch brands to a cheaper product. However, if you only have one firm producing a product and there is no good substitute, then you have a monopoly. The **geographic market** is where the product is sold. It can be local, state, regional, national or even international. The geographic market is also influenced by the price of the product. Generally speaking, the more expensive the product is, the larger the geographic area, because people will be more likely to search further to compare prices. The **relevant market** is the product market plus the geographic market.

E. Once a Section 7 Prima Facia Case Is Made by the Government

If the government meets its burden of proof under Section 7, then the defendant must convince the court that the proposed merger does not have anticompetitive effects or that there is a defense that will otherwise allow the merger. General attempts to prove that the merger does not have anticompetitive effects are hard to establish. A merger is more likely to be allowed if the parties who desire to merge can show a specific defense to the merger. There are several specific defenses used to try to permit mergers.

The **failing firm defense** is a defense that allows a merger even if the HHI might otherwise prevent the merger. The failing firm defense applies if the firm being acquired is not likely to survive anyway; there are no other potential buyers or at this point, this is the potential buyer that affects the competition the least; and all other alternatives to save the business have failed. The government is more likely to allow the merger because the consumer is going to lose the competitive benefits anyway because the firm is going to go out of business.

Another defense is the **lack of power in the industry**. This was seen in 1974 in **United States v. General Dynamics 415 U.S. 486 (1974)** where the government attempted to block General Dynamics from acquiring a strip-mining coal-producing company. General Dynamics already owned a deep-mining coal operation and the government felt that the acquisition of the strip-mining coal producing company would give it too much power in the coal industry in that region. General Dynamics argued that a strip-mining operation and coal in general was consistently losing market share in the energy industry. Therefore, the demand for coal was going down, so it should not matter who bought the one strip-mining operation because there was no other demand for the coal. The merger was allowed.

XIV. EXCEPTIONS TO MAJOR ANTITRUST LAWS

A. Introduction

Without question, the Sherman Act and the Clayton Act are the two most important pieces of antitrust legislation in the United States. In part, the prominence of these two acts derives from their rather broad proscriptions. Taken together, these two acts cover a wide range of attempts to reduce competition and punish many of the harmful outcomes of those attempts. In addition, the FTC Act also serves to fill in gaps left out of Sherman and Clayton. Moreover, these acts have been enforced to varying degrees for over 100 years. Nevertheless, another area of discussion remains in our examination—the diverse and sometimes seemingly illogical assortment of exceptions to major antitrust laws.

B. Natural Monopolies

Conventional wisdom tells us that there are exceptions to just about every rule and so it is with the application of antitrust laws. For example, antitrust laws are not applied to natural monopolies. Local utility providers like gas and electric companies are the best examples of natural monopolies. A natural monopoly exists when total production costs for a single firm serving a market are lower than total production costs for a group of competitive firms serving that same market. When this is true, a monopoly can sustain itself by simply charging lower prices than its competitors, not by excluding them through anticompetitive practices. Therefore, some monopolies may offer lower rather than higher prices and serve just as many consumers as a competitive market can. Logically then, antitrust laws should not be applied to natural monopolies.

Paradoxically, breaking-up natural monopolies would violate the underlying intent of antitrust laws, which is to improve the lot of consumers. Nevertheless, it is not enough to leave natural monopolies alone. With the threat of competition eliminated, the natural monopolist has a powerful incentive to raise profits by raising prices. Therefore, various governmental/public utility commissions set prices in this area to ensure that the benefits of lower production costs are passed along to consumers.

C. Individual Exemptions

For a wide variety of reasons, not all of which are arguably consistent with the spirit of consumer protection, a number of key industries are exempt from antitrust laws.

1. Labor Unions

The exemption of labor unions from antitrust laws is one of the most significant parts of the Clayton Act. Labor unions may organize and collectively bargain without violating these laws. Similarly, the Clayton Act permits labor unions to strike and boycott firms or entire industries. To qualify for these exemptions, labor unions must act solely in the interest of their membership, which cannot include any non-labor affiliates. Labor unions are primarily regulated through the National Labor Relations Act.

2. Agricultural Cooperatives or Associations

The Clayton Act specifically exempts agricultural cooperatives from antitrust laws. Agricultural cooperatives are not–for–profit organizations that work to assist farmers by providing them with loans, price supports, and a pool of mutually provided resources. The Clayton Act's exemption of agricultural cooperatives was later augmented by the Capper-Volstead Act of 1992, which exempted from antitrust laws *"persons engaged in the production of agricultural products."* These acts broadly apply to farmers and other agricultural producers like commercial fisherman. Fisheries are also exempt due to the Fisheries Cooperative Marketing Act of 1976 that allows the fishing industry to set prices.

3. State Action Exemptions

Sometimes, states restrain or regulate trade in ways that create monopolies or other non-competitive industrial structures. Examples include the granting of liquor licenses, logging rights, and firearms dealerships to a small group of firms. These and other such state-directed anticompetitive activities are exempt from antitrust laws via the "state action" exemption to the Sherman Act. The U.S. Supreme Court has recognized that actions by a state government are exempt if the state clearly articulates and actively supervises the policy behind its action. This was established by **Parker v. Brown 317 U.S. 341 (1943)** and is normally referred to as the Parker Doctrine or the Parker v. Brown doctrine.

XV. EUROPEAN/INTERNATIONAL REGULATION

U.S. businesses today frequently have operations globally and thus may be subject to international antitrust regulation, in addition to regulation under just U.S. law. The European Union (EU) has in recent years been a quite aggressive antitrust regulator of U.S. business.

For example, the EU in 1991 quite prominently blocked, on antitrust grants, the merger of two U.S. companies, General Electric and Honeywell. (The EU had jurisdiction here because of the European operations of both companies.) More recently, in 2013, the EU blocked U.S.-based United Parcel Service (UPS)'s planned takeover of the Netherlands package delivery service company "TNT Express." Today, companies need to be increasingly mindful of global antitrust regulatory schemes.

CHAPTER SUMMARY

In the United States, as in most other economies, antitrust law attempts to preserve competition in markets and prevent the consolidation and maintenance of market power through anticompetitive practices. Originally designed to eliminate and undo the problems associated with trusts, antitrust law has developed into far-reaching efforts to ensure that consumers are not harmed by the lack of choice and inefficiency that typically results from a lack of competition.

The most important antitrust laws in the United States are the Sherman Antitrust Act of 1890 and the Clayton Act of 1914. The Sherman Act was designed to break up existing trusts and punish individuals and firms that deliberately try to monopolize markets. Violators of the Sherman Act are guilty of felonies and may also be subject to civil trials and their resulting judgments. The Clayton Act was designed to address some of the anticompetitive activities not proscribed by the Sherman Act. The Clayton Act is more directly aimed at preserving competitive markets than is the Sherman Act and only requires that anticompetitive practices are likely to substantially lessen competition. The Clayton Act also prohibits mergers in certain circumstances. Because the Clayton Act covers acts that may not have already resulted in the acquisition of monopoly power, violators of the Act are not guilty of felonies: only civil monetary damages may result from violations of the Clayton Act.

Not all anticompetitive practices and outcomes are proscribed by the Clayton and Sherman Acts. Various exceptions to antitrust legislation exist. Natural monopolies, state-supported anticompetitive arrangements, and agricultural cooperatives are, for example, exempt from federal antitrust legislation. Today, global regulation of antitrust, particularly regulation in this regard by the EU, is also an important consideration for U.S. businesses.

8

LABOR-MANAGEMENT RELATIONS

I. CHAPTER OVERVIEW

A. Introduction

This book has two chapters analyzing legal and governmental regulation of the workplace. The chapters follow in somewhat historical order. In the present chapter, we discuss the growth and general decline of labor unions and governmental regulation of these unions. Today in the private employment sector only about 8 percent of the workforce belongs to a labor union. In the public/governmental sector, however, close to 38 percent of employees belong to a union. Moreover, in certain sectors of the economy, a relatively large percentage of the workforce still belongs to a labor union (or is covered by a collective bargaining agreement, which we will discuss later). In addition, the ongoing threat of unionization has had a considerable continued impact on human resource management/employment regulation even in non-unionized sectors of the economy, and legislation potentially increasing the power of unions continues to be introduced in the U.S. Congress. Understanding labor-management relations is thus important from a number of different perspectives.

B. Historical Overview: Early History

The "free market"/laissez-faire economic climate of the United States in the nineteenth century and early twentieth century was generally not a particularly hospitable one for labor unions. America was a land of rugged individualism and a great frontier. The basic legal rule was one of "employment-at-will," that is, an employee could quit his or her job at any time for any reason, and likewise an employer could fire an employee at any time for any reason. Should an employee lose his or her job, many new jobs were found in the American frontier. Many Americans simply did not see the need for collective action via unionization during this period of free market rugged individualism.

That said, around the mid-nineteenth century the American economy started changing, that is, moving away from simple master/apprentice manufacturing production and its general agrarian roots. The growth of the railroad played a major role in this, and thus it was not surprising that a number of the country's first unions were formed by railway workers. In addition, thousands and thousands of immigrants were coming to America's shores, many from European countries where labor unions were already flourishing and where unions also frequently played a large role in politics and social activism generally. In Great Britain, for example, one of the two major political parties has historically been the "Labor Party" (indeed various British Prime Ministers such as Tony Blair have been members of this party).

The history of American labor political parties such as Eugene V. Deb's Socialist Labor Party was a relatively short one. American employers fought union organizations of this kind bitterly going to court to establish the principle that unionization efforts were "criminal conspiracies against trade." Pursuant to such theories, police and even the U.S. Army were brought in to break up a variety of union strikes such as the Haymarket Square strike and the Pullman strike, with criminal charges being brought against the striking workers.

As a result, as the twentieth century approached, American unions began to take a different tack. In 1886, Samuel Gompers was elected to the presidency of the American Federation of Labor (AFL), a union focused more on the business of winning its members increased wages and benefits than on social/political goals per se. The AFL primarily tried to organize skilled workers (e.g., cigar makers) and got involved with politics primarily only as a means of helping its organizing/bargaining efforts. The AFL was thus involved more with what is called "business unionism" as opposed to what is known as "social unionism" When asked once what he wanted, Samuel Gompers famously replied "more" (in terms of wages, benefits etc. for its union employees)! However, while the business community did not go to the extreme of trying to get Gompers' activities declared "criminal," it still fought his activities in the courts. In particular, the business community argued that union efforts represented attempts to monopolize or restrain trade in violation of the **Sherman Antitrust Act of 1890**. In 1914 Samuel Gompers and others got the U.S. Congress to enact the **Clayton Antitrust Act** which specifically excluded labor unions from U.S. antitrust laws.

Even with this exemption from antitrust laws, though, labor unions continued to face both employer resistance and relative worker apathy. The economy in the "roaring" 1920s was very good, and employees saw no particular need to join a labor union. Many employers were able to get employees to sign what are known as **"yellow dog contracts"** or contracts whereby an employee as a condition of taking a job with a certain employer agreed not to join a union or engage in any union organizing activities while working for the given company. Courts during this period of time regularly upheld such contracts pursuant to the doctrine of "freedom of contract." A laissez-faire contractual parity between employees and employers was presumed to exist.

C. The Great Depression and the New Deal

The above dynamics changed considerably with the stock market crash of 1929 and the ensuing Great Depression which resulted in massive (about 30 percent of the workforce) structural unemployment in the United States. With millions of individuals unable to find any sort of work, laissez-faire parity between employers and employees no longer seemed appropriate. If employees were to have any sort of power they needed to group together, to form "unions." President Franklin D. Roosevelt's New Deal Administration thus immediately asked Congress to pass a variety of pro-union measures. In essence, Congress stepped in and passed regulations to redress a so-called economic "market failure," that is, a breakdown or failure in the general free market economic system. The first key new law passed in this area was the **Norris-La Guardia Act of 1932**. This legislation outlawed "yellow dog contracts," specifically noting that free market freedom of contact between employers and employees no longer existed, that is, an employee would sign just about anything to get a job in an economic environment of 30 percent unemployment. The Norris La-Guardia Act also made it much more difficult for employers to get court orders or injunctions stopping labor union activity activities. The Norris-La Guardia Act helped labor unions by making it more difficult for employers to stop their activities. It did not, however, directly sanction the development of labor unions in the United States. Such legislation, though, came three years later in the **Wagner Act of 1935** otherwise known as the original **National Labor Relations Act (NLRA)**. Section 7 of this new law explicitly stated that American "[e]mployees shall have the right to self-organization, to form, join, or assist labor organizations, to bargain collectively through representatives of their own choosing, and to engage in other concerted activities for the purpose of collective bargaining or other mutual aid or protection." Moreover, Section 1 of the NLRA stated that because of the "inequality of bargaining power" between employees and employers it was the "policy of the United States" to encourage employee collective action and bargaining. In short, the Wagner Act of 1935 made labor unions clearly lawful in the United States, and indeed adopted a governmental policy of encouraging workers to join unions and engage in collective bargaining. The Wagner Act of 1935 was called the Magna Carta of the American Labor Movement. What follows is a discussion of various key provisions of the Wagner Act of 1935, the original NLRA.

II. PROVISIONS OF WAGNER ACT OF 1935—ORIGINAL NATIONAL LABOR RELATIONS ACT

A. Defining "Employer" and "Employee"—Section 2

Not all employers and employees in the United States are covered by the National Labor Relations Act, and Section 2 of the NLRA spells out the specific scope of the law's coverage. The NLRA, for example, excludes from its coverage virtually all government employers—federal, state, and local. As noted above, a high percentage of government workers belong to labor unions, but they do so pursuant to separate federal and state laws independent of the NLRA. Moreover, because of the historical importance of railroads (they were they key means of interstate transportation when the NLRA was enacted), railroad employers are excluded from the NLRA and instead covered by a different law called the **Railway Labor Act** which makes it more difficult for unions to go on strike. Airlines today are also covered under the Railway Labor Act.

Numerous "employees" are also excluded from the coverage of the NLRA. Employees in the "domestic service of any family or person at his home," that is, butlers, maids, etc., and any "individual employed by his parent or spouse" are directly excluded from the law's coverage under Section 2. These provisions make fairly obvious sense, for example, it would be rather awkward for children in a family business to form a union and go on strike against their parents!

Other exclusions are somewhat less obvious. For example, the law excludes all "agricultural laborers" from its coverage, even though in some parts of the country agricultural labor represents a significant part of the workforce. Any thoughts on why agricultural labor might have been excluded from the law?

Section 2 also directly excludes "supervisors" from the coverage of the NLRA and gives a rather specific definition of what kind of employee is a "**supervisor**." According to the NLRA, a supervisor is any "individual having authority, in the interest of the employer, to hire, transfer, suspend, lay off, recall, promote, discharge, assign, reward, or discipline other employees" if their authority to do so "is not of a merely routine or clerical nature, but requires the use of independent judgment." Can you think of any "supervisory" employees at places you've worked that might not be deemed supervisors under the NLRA's definition?

Finally, Section 2 excludes from the NLRA's coverage all individuals having the status of an "independent contractor." There are currently a number of arguments being made by unions throughout the country that certain types of "employees" are not really "independent contractors" and that they thus should be able to organize in unions under the NLRA. The most prominent of these arguments involves drivers at the Fed Ex Corporation, that is, they are currently legally independent contractors, but various unions have argued that they are really "employees" of the company subject to NLRA coverage.

B. Company Unions—Sections 2 and 8

One of the major concerns when the NLRA was enacted was that employers would force employees interested in unions into so-called "**company unions**" or unions essentially run by the employer. As a result, the NLRA in Section 8(a)(2) makes it unlawful for an employer "to dominate or interfere with the formation or administration of any labor organization or contribute financial or other support to it." Moreover, Section 2(5) defines the term "labor organization" quite broadly to mean "any organization of any kind, or any agency or employee representation committee or plan, in which employees participate and which exists for the purpose, in whole or in part, of dealing with employers concerning grievances, labor disputes, wages, rates of pay, hours of employment, or conditions of work." Under Section 2(5), it seems clear that an employee committee formed to organize a summer softball team would *not* be deemed a "labor organization." Why not? What about an employee committee formed by the company to process employee complaints? Would such a committee be legal under Section 8 of the NLRA?

C. National Labor Relations Board—Section 3

The NLRA mandated the creation of an administrative agency, the **National Labor Relations Board**, to administer the law. Members of the NLRB are appointed by the President and confirmed by the U.S. Senate. The NLRB has broad administrative powers under the NLRA. Its General Counsel's office prosecutes alleged violations under the law, while the members of the Board function somewhat like a court hearing and deciding cases involving alleged violations. Appeals from NLRB decisions are made directly to the federal courts of appeals throughout the country.

D. Union and Non-Union Employee Rights—Section 7

As noted above, Section 7 of the NLRA gives employees broad protected rights to form labor organizations and engage in collective labor bargaining. Although often over-looked, Section 7 of the NLRA also gives employees the clear right to "engage in other concerted activities" for the purpose of "mutual aid or protection." This provision has interestingly been interpreted to protect the rights of non-unionized employees to engage in certain kinds of concerted or collective activities. Thus, in the classic case of **NLRB v. Washington Aluminum Co., 370 U.S. 9 (1962)**, a group of non-unionized manufacturing employees walked off the job to protest the lack of adequate heating in the plant where they worked. The U.S. Supreme Court ultimately ruled that the employer's discharge of these employees was illegal under the NLRA because that law protected non-unionized employee **concerted activity** when such activity was for "mutual aid or protection" (which the court found to exist there).

More recent applications of this provision have occurred with respect to employee usage of social media such as Facebook and Twitter to comment about conditions at their work-places. The NLRB, in a variety of cases, has held that such employee usage of social media represents "concerted activity … for mutual aid or protection," particularly where the employee is using such social media to directly complain about pay inequities, workplace safety, and other fairly clear workplace conditions. Employers are thus increasingly faced with issues of how they can possibly discipline employees for saying derogatory things about the employer on Facebook and other social media without violating the NLRA. Labor unions are also increasingly using the Internet in labor organizing drives, something the writers of the Wagner Act in 1935 wouldn't have even dreamed about! Are you surprised that the NLRA potentially so widely protects non-union employee activities of this kind? Why are so relatively few employees aware of this protection? Why are so many employers surprised about the scope of the NLRA in this regard?

E. Employer Unfair Labor Practices—Section 8

As noted above, Section 7 of the NLRA protects, among other things, the right of employees to form labor unions and engage in collective bargaining. Section 8 then makes it unlawful, or what the law calls an "**unfair labor practice**" or **ulp** or for an employer to "interfere with, restrain, or coerce employees" in the exercise of these rights. Section 8(a)(3) specifically states that employers can not discriminate in hiring or rewarding employees based on their union membership/affiliation, while Section 8(a)(5) says it's an "ulp" for an employer to refuse to bargain collectively with duly chosen employee representatives. Thus, for example, it would be clearly unlawful for an employer to directly tell an employee that he or she is being fired for union activity. It would also be explicitly unlawful for an employer to completely refuse to bargain with employee representatives, for example, a duly elected labor union.

Life, though, is rarely so simplistic. Today employers facing employee unionization efforts often have sophisticated legal/human resource management advice, and it would thus be extremely unusual for an employer to directly tell an employee expressing an interest in unions that she or he was being fired for union activity. Instead, the employer might tell the employee that they are being fired for poor job performance. The burden would then shift to the employee to prove to the NLRB that the real reason for his or her discharge is protected union activity. Similarly, an employer will almost never completely refuse to bargain with a duly elected union. However, what happens if the employer has no real intention of agreeing on anything and is simply going through the motions of collective bargaining, that is, engaging in so-called "surface bargaining"? How does a union successfully prove the absence any real "good faith" employer bargaining to the NLRB? Moreover, what remedies do employees/unions have if employers are found to be committing unfair labor acts pursuant to Section 8 of the NLRA? Finally, what happens in so-called "mixed motive" situations where perhaps a given employee is being fired in part *both* for poor performance issues and because he or she is a union activist? Does the NLRA still protect such an employee, and if so what standards should be applied?

F. Collective Bargaining—Section 8

The NLRA mandates that employers must bargain collectively in "good faith" with duly elected employee unions regarding wages, hours, and other terms and conditions of employment. Defining exactly what constitutes **good faith bargaining** is, as noted above, not always that easy. Moreover, the NLRA in Section 8(d) does state that neither side is ever "compelled" to reach an agreement.

In addition, Section 8(d) mandates that good faith bargaining must occur with respect to "wages, hours, and other conditions of employment." These three areas constitute the **mandatory subjects** for collective bargaining. In the collective bargaining process, a key first step is to determine which issues fall within the statutory definition of mandatory subjects. When bargaining about such mandatory subjects does not result in an agreement, either party may attempt to impose its proposal on the other through a strike or a lockout. However, strikes and lockouts in support of proposals not included under mandatory subjects are considered unfair labor practices. Accordingly, this makes the classification of issues within the statutory definition very important.

The classification of mandatory subjects has been interpreted rather broadly. Wages are defined to include all forms of compensation including pensions, fringe benefits, profit sharing, and stock purchase incentives. Hours include seniority, work-loads, and disciplinary measures. "Other conditions of employment," easily the most controversial and difficult aspect of the mandatory subjects classification, may include such matters as union status, job security, subcontracting, volume of production, plant closings, and other responses to technological change. The following U.S. Supreme Court case illustrates the outer limits of the lists of mandatory bargaining subjects.

First National Maintenance Corp. v. NLRB Supreme Court of the United States 452 U.S. 666 (1981)

Facts: First National Maintenance Corporation (FNM) supplies its customers a contracted-for maintenance labor force and supervision for a fee plus costs. The relationship with one customer, Greenpark Care Center, was not very remunerative or smooth. FNM decided to terminate its contract with Greenpark.

While FNM was experiencing the difficulties which led to the contract termination, its employees at Greenpark selected a union as their bargaining agent. The employees were terminated when the contract terminated and a complaint was filed with the NLRB, and the NLRB held that FNM had a duty to bargain under Sections 8(a)(5) and 8(d) with the union over the decision to close the Greenpark operation. The Court of Appeals enforced the order and the Supreme Court granted certiorari.

Holding: Management decisions of the kind here involving the scope and direction of the enterprise should *not* be subject to collective bargaining. The Supreme Court said that management must be free from the constraints of the bargaining process to the extent essential for the running a profitable business.

G. Election of Labor Unions—Section 9

Suppose the employees of a local grocery store express an interest in unionization. The NLRB must first determine the relevant and appropriate **bargaining unit** at issue. For example, all the employees of the store may constitute the relevant bargaining unit or perhaps just the employees of a certain department of the store might be deemed the appropriate unit. Thus, for instance, the 13 employees of the store's pharmacy department might be deemed the relevant and appropriate unit in a given situation.

For a labor union representation election to be held by the NLRB to determine whether employees in a given unit truly want a union, at least 30 percent of said employees must sign **authorization cards** expressing their interest in unionization. More specifically, if the 13 employees of the grocery store's pharmacy are found to be an appropriate bargaining unit at least four of these employees must sign cards authorizing union representation in order to trigger an NLRB representation election. If the requisite number of employees does sign such cards the NLRB will schedule a secret ballot election to be held in the relatively near future.

In the NLRB representation election itself, the 13 pharmacy grocery store employees will either vote "yes" for the union, or "no" against having the union. The NLRB makes special efforts to assure that electoral ballot process is not only 100 percent secret in nature but also completely free from any fraud or abuse. NLRB labor representation elections are conducted on a **majority rule basis**, that is, if a majority of employees vote for the union it comes into power and is the employee's exclusive or only representative. Conversely, however, if less than a majority of employees in the given unit vote for the union, its election effort is a complete loss, and it is prohibited from even attempting to organize the given employees again for at least a year. The United States, unlike some European countries, has no legal provision for minority unions or unions that represent less than a majority of employees.

For example, suppose in the above pharmacy example, 7 of the 13 employees vote for the union. The union will then come into power and represent *all* 13 employees in the bargaining unit, and under the Wagner Act, all 13 employees were essentially required to become members of the union (as we'll see later subsequent laws have changed these dynamics.) The union will then start bargaining with the employer (and remember the employer will be required to bargain in "good faith") with the goal of reaching a collective bargaining agreement or labor contract. However, if only 6 of the 13 employees vote for the union, the union will completely lose the election and have no bargaining or other rights. The "winner takes all"/majority rule construct of NLRB labor representation elections thus, mimics the model in the U.S. political elections, for example, in a given race for a state governorship the person that wins even a slight majority of votes becomes the governor and the person who garners 49.9 percent of the vote is essentially a complete loser.

H. Collective Bargaining Agreements—Contract Administration

Upon coming into power, a union will attempt to negotiate a **collective bargaining agreement** or labor contract with the employer covering the employees in the given bargaining unit. Collective bargaining agreements are typically of three years duration and set forth in specific detail the employment relationship governing the given employees during this time period. For example, a typical labor contract/collective bargaining agreement will set forth rates of pay for given workers including contracted pay increases and/or bonuses during the three-year period. Provisions in the contract will likely also deal with vacation rights, rights to overtime work, rights of seniority in case of layoffs, etc.

Virtually all collective bargaining agreements have a **grievance procedure** whereby employees with complaints during the three-year contractual period have a process by which they can air their concerns. Most labor contract grievance procedures have various "steps" (e.g., step one—talk to your immediate supervisor about your grievance) ultimately culminating in **labor arbitration**. Labor arbitration involves having an outside third party such as a minister, professor, etc. hear evidence regarding the grievance and then rendering a binding decision. Virtually all labor contract grievance procedures have as a "quid pro quo" a union agreed to "**no strike clause**." Pursuant to such a clause the union which is party to the labor agreement agrees not to strike during the (typically three year) term of the contract. In essence, the union waives its right to strike during the contract term in return for the ability to air its concerns via the grievance procedure culminating in arbitration. Finally, it should be noted that most labor contract grievance procedures provide that employees can only be fired for "**just cause**." Such "just cause" provisions basically overrule the doctrine of employment-at-will in that employers cannot simply fire employees "at will," that is, they have to show "cause" for the discharge and often prove such "cause" to an outside arbitrator. Thus, an employee caught stealing or clearly not meeting his/her sales quota can relatively easily be fired since demonstrable "cause" exists. An employer under a labor contract, however, probably can't fire an employee because he simple doesn't like them or their social/political views since it'd be hard to show demonstrable "cause" for the discharge. Do you know of anybody that's ever been fired without clear "cause" because there was no union/labor contract at their place of employment?

I. The Right to Strike

Labor contracts prevent union strikes (and generally employer lockouts) during the term of the labor contract. Once the contract has expired, though, unions are free to go on strike over mandatory bargaining issues. Can you recall the issues that have led to any important recent labor strikes? If the union goes on strike, though, the classic U.S. Supreme Court case of **NLRB v. Mackay Radio & Telegraph Co. 304 U.S. 333 (1938)**, makes it clear that the employer is free to hire permanent or temporary replacement workers/striker replacements (unions pejoratively call such individuals "scabs") for the striking workers. What are some of the pros and cons involved with an employer deciding whether or not to hire replacement workers for striking employees? (Hint: the controversial hiring of purportedly "unqualified" replacement referees during a Fall, 2012 National Football League [NFL] labor dispute led to an arguable "bad" touchdown call during a September 25, 2012 Seattle Seahawks-Green Bay Packers football game, costing Green Bay a victory. The NFL quickly agreed to a new labor contract with the permanent referees after this game.)

J. Remedies—Section 10

A very important question arises regarding what happens if an employer/union commits an unfair labor practice or otherwise violates the NLRA, that is, what remedies are afforded to aggrieved individuals/entities under the law? At its heart, it should be noted that the NLRA is a "remedial" rather than a "punitive" statute. Consequently, the goal of NLRA Section 10's remedial provisions is to simply "remedy" a given statutory violation by putting the aggrieved party in the status they would've been in absent the violation. For example, if an employee is unlawfully fired for union activity, the NLRA's traditional remedy will be to reinstate the employee to his/her old job with lost wages plus interest (minus any wages the employee earned elsewhere in the interim). The law does not, for instance, provide for triple/treble damages as in antitrust law, whereby an unlawfully discharged employee might be reinstated to his old job with three times his lost wages. Some observers, though, have argued that the NLRA's current "make whole" remedial scheme does not effectively deter ulps, and that a treble damages kind of punitive remedy might act as a more effective determent. Indeed some legislative proposals have been advanced in this regard. What are your thoughts on this matter?

III. THE TAFT-HARTLEY ACT

A. Overview

The very pro-union nature of the Wagner Act led to a very sharp increase in unionization in the United States during the period of 1935–1941. The advent of World War II in 1941 further accelerated the growth in unionization and union power since from a macro-economic perspective the war brought about a tremendous growth in the demand for labor coupled with a decrease in the supply of labor (most able-bodied males were overseas fighting). Some unions though, unduly flaunted their power during World War II by having workers go on strike and engage in other activities despite the existence of clear special war-time regulations preventing strike or related activity. To cut the long story short, by the end of World War II, there was considerable public backlash against unions, with many Americans feeling that the Wagner Act was too pro-union, and that the power of American labor unions needed to be cut-back. In 1947 a Republican Congress, over the veto of President Harry S. Truman enacted the **Taft-Hartley Act,** which achieved the goal demanded by the people to cut-back union power.

B. Section 7 and 14 Right-to-Work Laws

While the union movement's categorization of the Taft-Hartley Act as the "Slave Labor Act" may have been a little extreme, the law in many ways represented the beginning of the long decline in private sector unionism in the United States. The Taft-Hartley Act technically constituted various provisions amending the NLRA, that is, the NLRA now comprised the language of both the Wagner and the Taft-Hartley Acts. The most significant amendatory language in Taft-Hartley was its addition of a provision to Section 7 that employees not only had the right to form unions, but they also now had the *"right to refrain"* from joining unions or engaging in other forms of self-organization. While the Wagner Act had been unabashedly pro-union/collective action, the NLRA as now amended by Taft-Hartley was essentially *neutral* on the question, that is, be federal government took no position either way on the issue of unionization (or put another way, the economy had rebounded to the extent that employee unionization was not seen as being absolutely necessary to correct a "market failure"). One of the most important ways the new law's neutral posture was made operational was in its new Section 14 provisions allowing states to enact **rights to work laws**.

As noted above, when a labor union wins an NLRB representation election in a given bargaining unit it then represents *all* the employees in the bargaining unit, for example, it cannot discriminate and win wage increases for or process the grievances of only its election supporters. This is called the union's **duty of fair representation.** For example, in the aforementioned grocery store pharmacy bargaining unit of 13 employees, the union must fairly represent all 13 employees in collective bargaining/contract administration even if only 7 of the employees (a bare majority) voted for it in the NLRB election. An important ongoing issue, though, has been what kind of relationship the six employees that voted against the union have to have with it.

Under the Wagner Act, the law basically mandated that all employees in a given bargaining unit (including in the above example the six that voted against it) must join the union. Since the union had the duty to represent all of them, all workers in given bargaining units had to join the union and pay union dues, etc.

In cutting back on unions' power, however, the Taft-Hartley Act permitted individual states to pass right-to-work laws or laws that gave employees the "right to work" without joining a union, even where a union had won an NLRB representation election and was representing said workers. To date about one-half of the states in the United States have passed right-to-work laws. Most of the "right to work" states are more generally conservative southern and western U.S. states such as Alabama, Texas, and Utah. On December 11, 2012, however, a Republican Governor and State Legislature enacted a right-to-work law in the State of Michigan, a traditionally very pro-union mid-western U.S. state. The passage of right-to-work legislation in Michigan was widely seen as further evidence of the decline of private sector unions in the United States.

Right-to-work laws tend to deter union organizing efforts in those states because unions winning labor elections in those states can find themselves in the situation where they are paying monies to represent employees, but those employees are not paying any union dues. Unions have argued that employee **free-ridership** of this kind is unfair, and that Congress needs to repeal Section 14 of the Taft-Hartley Act in this regard. Congress, however, has steadfastly refused to repeal Section 14 of the Taft-Hartley law.

C. Free Speech

Under the Wagner Act, the NLRB and the courts broadly found employer anti-union campaign and other speech to be unlawful under Section 8 of the law since such speech was interpreted as unlawfully interfering with employee's Section 7 rights to self-organization. In essence, it was very difficult for employers to speak out against unions—a result consistent with the law's clear goal of encouraging unionization.

By 1947, though, Congress had problems with this approach, particularly since the U.S. Supreme Court has raised some First Amendment concerns regarding NLRB decisions in this area. Consequently, it enacted as part of its Taft-Hartley amendments an explicit *"free speech"* provision, Section 8(c). Section 8(c) states that both employers and unions are free to speak out during labor election campaigns and otherwise so long as such speech does not contain any "threat of reprisal or force or promise of benefit." Thus, under Section 8(c) an employer could tell employees that unions were bad because they (in non-right-to-work states) can charge you a lot of dues and give you very little back, but he or she could not directly threaten to fire all employees if they vote for a union. However, what if an employer in Texas during a labor representation campaign simply passes out to all employees a pamphlet discussing the pros and cons of doing business in Mexico? Determining whether such pamphlets represent an unlawful "threat" would likely ultimately be a question for the NLRB and federal courts to decide, and may depend to some extent on the overall context of the given situation.

D. Union Unfair Labor Practices

Under the Wagner Act, unions essentially could do no wrong. While Section 8(a) of the Wagner Act set forth a wide variety of possible ulps by employers, no similar provision existed with respect to possible unlawful acts by unions. The Taft-Hartley Act changed this by enacting Section 8(b) which set forth a number of potential union unfair labor practices/ulp's. Thus, now under the amended NLRA (including both the Wagner Act and the Taft-

Hartley Act) Section 8(a)(5) makes it an unfair labor practice for an employer to refuse to bargain fairly with a union, but conversely Section 8(b)(3) also makes it an unfair labor practice for a union to refuse to bargain fairly with an employer. The enactment of Section 8(b), of free speech Section 8(c), of Section 14 allowing states to pass right-to-work laws, and other provisions of the Taft-Hartley law all cut back on the power of unions in the United States. As noted above, the NLRA after the enactment of the Taft-Hartley amendments essentially put the federal government in something of a neutral posture regarding whether or not employees should join labor unions.

IV. LANDRUM-GRIFFIN ACT OF 1959

The U.S. Congress even further regulated and cut back on the power of U.S. labor unions with its enactment, 12 years after Taft-Hartley, of the **Landrum-Griffin Act of 1959**. Once again, labor unions to some extent brought additional governmental regulation on themselves. During the 1950s, some labor unions (particularly Jimmy Hoffa and the Teamsters Union) began purportedly forming alliances with the Mafia as a way to further gain/regain power (and as they argued to offset the power of large employers to hire "scabs" etc.). During important congressional hearings in the 1950s this and other forms of union corruption came to light leading Congress to pass the comprehensive Landrum-Griffin legis-lation (which further amends the NLRA) regulating the internal affairs of U.S. labor unions. Today, the financial affairs of unions as well as the election of union officers and other activities are strictly overseen by the U.S. Department of Labor. Labor unions today are among the most highly regulated private organizations in the country. Why should labor unions be regulated by the federal government while other private organizations, like sororities and fraternities on your campus, are not so regulated?

V. THE FUTURE OF PRIVATE SECTOR UNIONISM

During the 1970s and early 1980s strong attempts were made by pro-union supporters in Congress to amend the NLRA in ways that would make union organizing easier (e.g., increasing the penalties employers faced for firing union supporters). After bitter debates, though, these legislative proposals failed, and the inexorable decline in private sector unionism continued. The increasing loss of U.S. manufacturing jobs to countries like China and Mexico has in many respects added fuel to this fire, as has internal squabbling within the union movement itself (e.g., the split-off of some unions from the umbrella AFL-CIO labor organization). That said, while American labor unions are "down," they are not completely "out," with a number of unions experiencing recent successes in organizing lower-wage service workers. Along these lines, the nation's largest private sector employer, the Wal-Mart Corporation, has in the early twenty-first century become a major union organizing target. Moreover, President Barack Obama was elected with strong union support, and possible pro-union congressional legislation being considered by Congress has his support. Thus, the NLRA and its regulation of private sector unionism continue to be an important part of the legal environment of business.

VI. PUBLIC SECTOR UNIONISM

While the NLRA has declined in importance, most states in the country have enacted special state laws allowing school teachers, sanitation workers, librarians, and other state and local government employees (even state university professors!) in their given states to join unions and engage in collective bargaining. The federal government has also enacted more limited federal legislation allowing federal government workers to unionize. One major area of controversy with respect to public employee unionization has been the right to strike. In general, it is unlawful for federal, state, and local governmental employees to go on strike. Some states, however, have laws that permit "non-essential" employees (e.g., librarians) to go on strike. Moreover, as state and local government budgets have come under increasing pressure in today's economy, there have been calls to cut back on the power of public sector unions—somewhat similar to the 1947 Taft-Hartley concerns with respect to unions in the private sector. Most notably, in 2012 controversial legislation was enacted in the State of Wisconsin reducing the rights of public employee unions in that state.

CHAPTER SUMMARY

The National Labor Relations Act comprehensively regulates the ability of American workers to join and be members of labor unions. The NLRA as currently amended (the original 1935 law was amended in major ways in both 1947 and 1959), however, very much puts the federal government in a "neutral" posture regarding the unionization question. This shift in governmental policy coupled with macro-economic trends (such as the movement of U.S. manufacturing jobs overseas) has led to a steady decline in the percentage of U.S. private sector employees that are unionized. That said, private sector unions have had recent success in some sectors of the economy, and they played a major role in helping Barack Obama get elected and re-elected as President of the United States. Moreover, most of the largest states in the country (e.g., California, New York, Florida, and Illinois) have passed special state laws permitting unionization by state and local governmental workers in those states. This has generally in recent decades been a growth area for unions.

9

BUSINESS ENTITIES

I. INTRODUCTION

A. Factors in Deciding Type of Business Entity

One of the first decisions someone has to make when going into business is in what capacity should the business operate? Picking the appropriate form of business entity depends on several factors, such as the following: (1) ease of operation—set up costs and difficulty of operation, (2) desired length of existence of the business, (3) personal liability, (4) taxation, (5) ease of sale of business, and (6) ease of raising capital.

B. Major Types of Business Entities

Historically, there are three major types of business entities: (1) sole proprietorship, (2) partnership, and (3) corporation. There is also a relatively new form of business entity that is becoming very popular called a limited liability company.

II. HISTORICAL BUSINESS ORGANIZATIONS

A. Sole Proprietorship

The oldest and simplest business entity is a **sole proprietorship**. There are no formalities to creating a sole proprietorship assuming you have the legal right to open that type of business, which can include having certain degrees, permits, or other requirements. Once created, there are no special rules or regulations to follow on the operation of the sole proprietorship. In a sole proprietorship, the owner is the business and vice versa. The major disadvantages of a sole proprietorship are unlimited liability, difficulty of selling the business and difficulty in raising capital. Since the owner is the business and the business is the owner, the owner has unlimited liability if the business gets sued. In other words, the owner, sole proprietor will be personally responsible for all of the debts of the business. Since sole proprietorship only has one owner and because that owner has unlimited liability, it is very difficult to get investors to invest in a business of this kind. Also, there is a limit to the amount of credit that one owner can have and this can make it difficult for the owner to borrow money. Once that one owner has reached their credit limit, the sole proprietorship has usually reached its credit limit. As far as taxes go, the owner is the business and thus claims all of the income and/or loss on her personal tax forms.

B. Partnership

One way for a sole proprietor to raise additional capital is to abandon the sole proprietorship entity and form a **partnership** with other partners. However, by doing so, the owner becomes one of several owners. This makes management of the partnership a joint operation. Granted, a partnership can technically operate with no formalities, but that is not the suggested way to create a partnership. Partners have unlimited liability in the partnership which means each partner is liable for all of the partnership's debts. It is difficult enough for partners to get along and make group decisions for the business, but when you throw unlimited liability into the partnership mix that gives you a potentially explosive situation that dooms most partnerships. Therefore, it is a good practice to have a very detailed *written* partnership agreement specifying the relationship of the partners to each other prior to entering into a partnership. This agreement should enumerate partnership duties, responsibilities and profit divisions, as well as the duration of the partnership and any other vital information necessary to operate the partnership. Even written partnership agreements don't solve many of the problems and it should not come as a surprise that the partnership form is the least favorite of the three major historical forms of business entities.

C. Corporation

The third of the three major historical types of business entities is the corporate form. It is the most popular form of business entities for large businesses. Therefore, while by number there are more sole proprietorships; on a dollar volume basis most of the business in the United States is conducted by corporations.

A **corporation** is a separate legal entity and is created by state statute. Since is it a separate legal entity, it is taxed separately. In addition, any income that is dispersed to the owners of the corporation, the shareholders, is also taxed. This is a disadvantage of the corporate form—there is **double taxation**. However, the corporate form also has at least one major advantage and that is **limited liability**. In the sole proprietorship and partnerships, the owners are liable for all of the debt of the respective business entity. This is not the case with a corporation. The owners of the corporation have limited liability, limited to the extent of their investment and only to the extent of the investment. This makes it much easier to raise capital when using the corporate form. Therefore, ease of raising capital and limited liability are two of the reasons for the popularity of the corporate form. However, there is still the problem of double taxation. A further, discussion of corporations will be found in the chapter on corporate governance.

III. MISCELLANEOUS FORMS OF BUSINESS ENTITIES

A. Limited Partnership

Since none of the major three types of businesses entities gives the business owners limited liability without double taxation another form of business entity is often desired by businesses. One such business entity is called a **Limited Partnership (LP)**. An LP like a corporation is created by state statute and requires a filing of documents to create the limited partnership. Partners must file a **Certificate of Limited Partnership**, which is similar to the filing in a corporation with the appropriate state official. A limited partnership is in part like a partnership and in part like a corporation. There must be two classes of partners, **general partners** and **limited partners**. An LP must have at least one general partner and at least one limited partner. Of course, it can have several of each but it must have at least one of each at all time. A general partner has unlimited liability. In other words, he or she is responsible for the debts and obligations of the limited partnership whether he or she incurred the debts or obligation, just like a partner is in a regular partnership. A limited partner on the other hand is only an investor. The limited partner is prohibited from taking part in the management of the limited partnership; for instance, the limited partner is normally not allowed the right of access to the LP books. Of course, this does not give general partners *carte blanche* to do whatever they please. The general partners have a fiduciary duty to the LP and to the limited partners. The limited partner is only liable for the limited partnership debts and obligations up to the amount of his investment, like a shareholder in a corporation. However, if the limited partner does involve him or herself in the management of the limited partnership, then he or she becomes a general partner and has unlimited joint and severable liability. Upon dissolution of the LP, the limited partner is normally paid after the creditors and before the general partners. For the investor who does not and will not take part in any of the management of the business, the LP will work. It is also a good way for general partners to raise capital by taking in a limited partner.

B. Closely Held Corporations

Closely held corporations are referred to by several names, **family corporations, close corporations,** or even **privately held corporations**. Compare these to **publicly held corporations** whose stock is traded on one of the stock exchanges. A closely held corporation, no matter what the name, is a corporation, created under state corporate statutes. However, the shares of a closely held corporation are normally held by a small number of people that are personally known to each other or by one family. Closely held corporations are not traded in the public market and are generally operated like a sole proprietorship or partnership that utilizes the corporate form to take advantage of the limited liability of the corporate form.

A closely held corporation can be owned by as few as one shareholder. However, the closely held corporation must follow all of the steps of the sometimes complicated corporate structure. Hence, this is the major disadvantage of closely held corporations. Normally, transfer of shares in a closely held corporation is severely limited as set forth by the closely held corporation when it was created. This is normally a limitation placed on the closely held corporation by Articles of Incorporation.

However, if the owners of the closely held corporation act as required by corporations in general, for example, having the required meetings and structure, then the owners receive limited liability. (Some states due to the normally small, personal nature of the closely held corporations, give these types of corporations special structure provisions that allow them to depart from some of these requirements.) However, the closely held corporation is still a corporation and still subject to double taxation.

C. S Corporation

However, the IRS will allow closely held corporations that meet the requirements of an **S Corporation** to avoid double taxation and still have limited liability. To qualify a closely held corporation as an S corporation the following qualifications must be present:

1. The corporation must be a domestic, organized under the laws of the states or territories of the United States, corporation.
2. The shareholders can only be individuals with certain very limited exceptions like estates or some trusts.
3. The corporation can have no more than 100 shareholders and all of the shareholders must agree on the S Corporation status.
4. There can only be one class of shareholders.
5. Shareholders must not be non-resident aliens.

If a corporation elects to be an S Corporation, profits are passed directly to its shareholders and the shareholders pay personal income taxes on these distributions. The S Corporation itself does not pay tax and thereby avoids double taxation.

Today, however, the advantages of the S Corporation structure are being overshadowed by the Limited Liability Company (LLC) and the Limited Liability Partnership (LLP) structures for doing business, which we will discuss below.

D. Professional Corporations

Another type of closely held corporation utilized to some degree to take advantage of the corporate limited liability is **professional corporation (PC)**. PCs are normally used by professionals like attorneys, doctors, dentists, and accountants. The major advantage of the PC has to do with limited liability. Normally, professionals such as attorneys are not allowed to avoid liability for the malpractice of other professionals in their professional organization. This is true even in PCs. However, the shareholders of a PC can be insulated from liability based on the tortious acts of their fellow professionals if malpractice is not involved, and from liabilities arising from the contractual obligations of their fellow professionals. Again, the use of the PC form is largely overshadowed by the development of the LLC and the LLP forms to be discussed next.

IV. LIMITED LIABILITY ENTITIES

A. Limited Liabilitiy Company

1. *History and Purpose of Limited Liability Companies*

The county of Germany is generally given credit for creating the first **LLC** in the late 1800s. It is well known that LLCs were used in Europe and Latin America long before they became accepted in the United States. The LLC is a very appealing business form because it combines the positive aspects of traditional corporations (e.g., limited personal liability) with those of partnerships (e.g., flow-through taxation/no double taxation). Moreover, LLCs generally involve less recordkeeping, start-up costs/registration fees than some other possible alternative business structures such as S corporations.

In 1991, the State of Texas became one of the first states in the United States to enact LLC legislation. The Texas Limited Liability Company Act was passed by the Texas Legislature in May of 1991 and became effective on August 26, 1991. By the end of 1991, though, only five other U.S. states had passed similar legislation. Over the next five years, however, the trend set in Texas and elsewhere caught on, and by the end of 1996 all 50 states in the country and the District of Columbia had enacted limited liability company statutes.

Despite the tremendous advantages of the LLC as originally permitted by U.S. state legislation during the 1991–1996 period, there were still a number of practical problems with businesses using this governance form. For example, in many states (including Texas) when one member of the LLC died or otherwise left the organization (e.g., one senior accountant in an accounting LLC passed away) the LLC technically "dissolved." To continue in business, the remaining members of the LLC literally had to form a new company. In addition, while the U.S. Internal Revenue Service made clear that LLC distributions to given members flowed directly through to the individual for federal income tax purposes (i.e., there was no double taxation) the rules were less clear in certain states with respect to state taxes (e.g., those that, unlike Texas, imposed state income taxes). Thus, in recent years there have been efforts in many states to clarify and amend their LLC statutes, especially with respect to the issue of permitting them to continue in existence even, for instance, when one LLC member dies. To assist in these efforts, in 2006 the U.S. National Conference of Commissioners on Uniform Laws passed a revised LLC law.

Along these lines, in 2006, the State of Texas passed a new limited liabilities companies law, and effective January 1, 2010, *all* LLCs in the state became governed by this new (this includes both LLCs established in recent years and those under the old 1991 act). The new Texas law expressly permits LLCs to continue in business even if there is a "terminating event" involving one member, so long as other members of the LLC still remain with the firm.

2. Creation of the LLC

An LLC is created by filing **Articles of Organization** with the proper state official. In Texas, this is called **Articles of Formation** and is filed with the Secretary of State in Texas. The Articles of Organization must contain the following:

1. The name of the LLC, which normally has to include the words "Limited Liability Company," "Limited Company" or the abbreviations "L.L.C.", "LLC," "LC" or "L.C.". Likewise, the word limited can be abbreviated to "LTD" or "Ltd." and company can be abbreviated to "Co."
2. The period of duration, which can be perpetual
3. The purpose of the LLC, which can be for all lawful business purposes
4. The address and name of the registered agent
5. If the LLC is to have manager(s), a statement to that effect and the name(s) and address(es) of the manager(s) or if the LLC will not have managers, a statement that there will be no managers and the names and addresses of the initial members (owners), and
6. Name and address of each **organizer** of an LLC. (Organizers are literally the people who organize the LLC and can be future members or professionals hired to organize the LLC.)

Once the Articles of Organization are filed, the state official will issue a **Certificate of Organization**, attach it to the Articles of Organization, and return it to the organizers of the LLC. Once the Certificate of Organization is issued, the LLC's existence begins.

3. Structure of the LLC

The owners of the LLC are called members. An LLC may have one or more members, since the number of permitted members is unlimited. (This differentiates an LLC from an S Corporation which has a limited number of permissible members.) Members can be individuals, corporations, or other LLCs. The members of an LLC may enter into an **operating agreement** or it is sometimes called by other names like **company agreement**, as in Texas, or Company Regulations. The operating agreement which can be oral or a few states require it to be in writing, governs the internal affairs of the LLC and the relations among members, managers and officers of the company. It can usually only be amended with the consent of all of the members of the LLC. The operating agreement should specify to the LLC the division of the income of the members, how a membership is transferred, what happens upon dissolution of the LLC, and other important matters.

4. Governance of the LLC

An LLC can be governed by the members of the LLC. This is called a **member-managed** LLC. However, upon creation of the LLC, the organizers can instead choose to have managers. This is referred to as a **manager-managed** LLC. If an LLC has managers, they can designate one or more persons who may or may not be members as officers to do whatever the managers direct them to do as long as it is within the parameters of the operating agreement and applicable state law. The managers are the agents for the LLC and the members no longer have the responsibility/right to govern the LLC. The managers can be members or non-members. In fact, a manager does not even have to be a legal "person," it can be a corporation or another LLC. Whoever the governing authority is, he or they shall manage the LLC as provided by the operating agreement and applicable state law since they have a fiduciary duty to the owners of the LLC.

If the organizers of the LLC choose to create a member-managed LLC, the structure and operation of the LLC will more closely resemble the partnership structure. In the member-managed LLC, each member (e.g., each accountant-member in an accounting LLC) gets one vote in the firm's business decisions and the members are agents of the LLC. However, remember that the members still have limited liability and do not have individual personal liability for LLC debts or debts incurred by other members. This is in stark contrast with the partnership, where each partner has joint and severable liability.

5. Dissolution of the LLC

Dissolution of the LLC occurs due to the following:

1. At the end of the fixed period, if any, when the duration of the LLC expires. However, the period of and LLC can now be perpetual and most LLC will in fact be perpetual
2. The occurrence of specified events in the operation agreement or Articles of Incorporation
3. Action of the members to dissolve the LLC
4. When the LLC has no members
5. Entry of a decree of judicial dissolution

Note that given recent legal amendments, as pointed out above, LLCs can generally continue as long as they still have at least one continuing member. (The 2006 amendments to the Texas LLC law specifically permit this.) Upon dissolution and the resulting **winding up** of the LLC, the creditors of the LLC are to be paid first and then the members. Once the winding up process is over, **Articles of Dissolution** are to be filed and then the state official shall issue a **Certificate of Dissolution** which terminates the LLC.

6. Advantages of the LLC

The advantages of the LLC of business entity include the following:

1. Limited liability for the members
2. An LLC is easier to operate than a corporation (or arguably even than an S corporation)
3. Shareholder meetings, board meetings, and the required minutes of a corporation are generally not required in an LLC
4. The LLC can be taxed like a partnership, thereby no double taxation or the LLC can opt to be taxed like a corporation if that is more advantageous to the LLC
5. Flexibility in management, member-managed or manager-managed

6. No limit on the number or who/what can be members
7. Disadvantages of the LLC

Granted there are some disadvantages to the LLC form. They are established pursuant to state law, and as noted above, LLC laws are not necessarily uniform among the different states. There are also some types of business under some state and IRS rules that are barred from using the LLC business form such as state banks that are insured by the FDIC, joint stock associations, certain foreign entities and insurance companies. Furthermore, LLCs are potentially the victim of the "unknown" in that the body of court decisions dealing with LLCs is relatively limited due to their newness.

However, many experts feel that given recent changes in the area, for example, the 2006 reforms to the Texas LLC law, the LLC form's advantages clearly outweigh its disadvantages. Therefore, it seems like an almost certainty that LLCs will continue to grow in popularity in the years to come. In other words, we will continue to see more and more LLCs created both in Texas and throughout the United States.

B. Limited Liability Partnerships

Another relatively new form of business entity is a **Limited Liability Partnership (LLP)**. Texas was the first state to create an LLP also in 1991 and other states quickly followed suit. An LLP is a form of business entity that was first used only by professionals. In fact, initially several states, including Texas, limited the use of LLPs to professionals like accountants, attorneys, etc. However, in most states, LLPs are today open to almost any type of business but since they were tailor-made for attorneys and accountants, those industries still dominate in the LLP structure.

LLPs are creatures of state law, and were created to avoid some of the earlier problems of the LLCs, which have now generally been done away with. However, there are still some advantages to an LLP. The organization is created more like a partnership than an LLC, but it clearly limits the personal liability of the partners. While the limits to personal liability vary from state to state, normally partners are not responsible for the errors, omissions, negligence, incompetence, or malfeasance of their fellow partners arising in tort, contract, or otherwise. However, a partner does sometimes still have potential liability if another partner is directly involved in a wrongful activity or she had notice or knowledge of the wrongful activity and failed to take reasonable steps to correct the wrongful activity.

An LLP is created by registering with the appropriate state official. The LLP must file annual reports with the state to maintain its status as an LLP. Since this is a partnership, a fee must be paid each year by each partner but the partners do not have to be listed on the registration as were the organizers in an LLC.

The LLP itself is a separate entity and can be sued for the actions of one or more of its partners. The partnership assets can be reached to satisfy any judgment against the partnership. Therefore, state law normally requires the partnership to maintain liability insurance or have separate funds available for that purpose. The amount of this insurance or set aside varies from state to state but can be in the seven figure amount. However, each individual partner of the LLP can, as pointed out above, generally avoid personal unlimited liability. Remember, this is not the case in a regular partnership where each partner has joint and severable liability. An LLP also differs from a limited partnership in that the LLP gives ALL the partners' limited liability whereas in the limited partnership only the *limited partners* have such limited liability. Also, in the LLP, all of the partners can take part in the management without incurring unlimited liability, unlike the limited partners in a limited partnership.

As stated earlier, LLPs are today somewhat overshadowed by LLCs now that some of the problems involving LLCs seem to have been cleared up. However, LLPs are still advantageous in certain situations.

C. Limited Liability Limited Partnership (LLLP)

A **Limited Liability Limited Partnership (LLLP)** is a type of limited partnership that tries to combine the LP form with the LLP form. In the LLLP, the general partner has the same liability as the limited partner. In other words, the general partner in the LLLP has limited liability. So far, the use of LLLPs has been rather limited, and for the most part untested.

CHAPTER SUMMARY

Obviously, you have to operate your business under some sort of legal form and thus choose which type of business entity form is best for you. There have traditionally been three major types of business entities. These are: the sole proprietorship, the partnership and the corporation. There are advantages and disadvantages to each. To try to create an even better business entity form, there have over the years been several other types of entities created such as closely held corporations, and limited partnerships. However, these still had problems and so a new hybrid structure called the LLC began to evolve in the 1990s. The LLC, particularly with some recent (post 2006) changes to its structure, has become an increasingly popular form of business entity. Today, it appears that the only real disadvantage to this new form is that it is still relatively new. Furthermore, there are some other forms that are also relatively new and can be used to help structure businesses such as the LLP and the LLLP.

10

CORPORATE GOVERNANCE

I. INTRODUCTION

A. Corporate Overview

The corporate form of organization is the dominant means by which business activity is organized in the United States and most other developed countries. Almost all of the largest businesses in United States are organized as corporations, as are many smaller firms. Many of the features that have made the corporate form so successful stem from the corporation's status as a separate legal entity, which we discussed in the previous chapter. In particular, a corporate entity is responsible for its own debts, which implies that shareholders are not personally liable for the debts of the corporation. The limited liability granted shareholders makes it easier for corporations to tap the public capital market for funds needed to expand their operations, which is another benefit of the corporate form.

B. Chapter Focus on Publicly Owned and Traded Corporations

This chapter focuses on publicly owned, publicly traded corporation. The existence of such corporations allows individuals with no managerial expertise to participate in the profits and growth of corporations as owners by purchasing shares of stock. The corporate form also allows specialization of management functions through the hiring of professional managers. In particular, the corporate form allows individuals with little financial capital, but considerable managerial talents, to specialize as professional managers of corporations. The talents of such individuals would be much more difficult to tap in the absence of the corporate form of business organization, which conveniently allows for the separation of ownership and management functions.

Limited liability clearly facilitates this specialization, for it allows shareholders to be "rationally ignorant" of managerial practices. Because their risk is limited to their initial investment, shareholders need spend less time trying to monitor managerial behavior than would be the case if their liability were unlimited. Investors are thus able to diversify their holdings by owning interests in several different firms at the same time, reducing the riskiness of their investment portfolios. Unfortunately, the separation of ownership and control creates potential disincentives on the part of the managers. Corporate governance, the focus of this chapter, involves constraining and controlling these managerial disincentives so that the corporation is governed in the best interests of its owners, the shareholders.

Shares of stock in large corporations are typically sold in organized securities markets, such as the New York Stock Exchange, the American Stock Exchange, and the NASDAQ. A major advantage of the publicly traded corporation is that the investors' ownership interests can be transferred without the permission of fellow owners and without the expense of locating buyers. If a shareholder becomes dissatisfied with the operations or profitability of a corporation in which he or she owns stock, the shareholder can sell the shares rather than become involved in the corporation's decision-making process. The transfer of shares is facilitated by limited liability, which allows buyers to purchase shares without incurring more risk than the potential loss of the purchase price. The role of securities markets in the success of the modern corporation is addressed in detail in this chapter as well.

II. THE GROWTH OF THE CORPORATE FORM OF BUSINESS

A. First Major Corporations

Although the corporate form of organization dominates American business today, for most of recorded history sole proprietorships and partnerships were far more important for legal and technological reasons. The first major corporations were trading companies established by the larger European colonial powers to exploit the wealth of far-off lands, such as the East India Company (chartered in 1600) or the Hudson Bay Company (1670). Because corporate charters had to be granted by an act of the legislature during this era, it was difficult to form corporations. Moreover, these charters typically limited the organization to explicit and narrowly defined business purposes. Accordingly, most large enterprises were organized as unincorporated joint stock companies—essentially limited partnerships.

B. First General Incorporation Law

The first general incorporation law was passed by the Connecticut Legislature in 1837, giving anyone who met certain basic requirements the right to incorporate for "any lawful purpose." Most states soon passed similar legislation.

C. Late 1800's

Only later in the nineteenth century did corporations begin to dominate commercial activity. Once the legal obstacle to their easy formation was removed with the passage of general incorporation laws, the two most important factors motivating the growth of the corporate form of organization were the invention of the steam engine and its application to a new technology, the railroad. Until the advent of the railroad, high transportation costs often limited the size of the market that a factory could serve. This in turn implied that factory sizes were small, and thus the need for capital was limited.

To better see the connection between transportation, factory size, the need for capital, and organizational form, let's go back to simpler times when the only way of transporting goods over land was using a cart pulled by horses or oxen and power to factories was delivered by wind or water. Because of the high costs and slowness of such transportation, most factories served a small, localized market. Moreover, each factory's output was limited by the inadequacies of the power supply—wind or water. Each town would have its own baker, barrel maker, carriage maker, etc. Because they served such a small market, these businesses were organized as sole proprietorships. Typically the proprietor supplied all of the capital needed to run the business, supplemented perhaps with bank loans for which he was personally responsible.

In 1764, James Watt began a series of experiments that culminated in the creation of an efficient steam engine. In the beginning of the nineteenth century, Watt's invention was used to develop the steam-powered railroad locomotive, and during the rest of the century railroad networks spread throughout the Americas, Africa, Europe, Asia, and Australia. Railroads lowered the cost of land transportation dramatically. This had the effect of increasing the market area that a factory could serve and thus the optimum size of a factory. Watt's engineering breakthroughs also implied that factory size was no longer limited by the power generated by waterwheels or windmills. As the efficient size of factories increased, the need for capital to outfit those factories also increased, often beyond the means of one individual. However, as we noted earlier, the corporate form of organization is well suited to raise large amounts of capital from investors. By the end of the nineteenth century, the corporation had become the dominant form of business organization due to the advent of general incorporation laws and these technological changes.

III. THE CORPORATE ENTITY

A. Corporate Law is State Law

In the United States, each corporation is organized under the general incorporation law of a state, which grants the organization a corporate charter once it has complied with simple filing procedures and paid any required fees. The charter is similar to a birth certificate; it recognizes the legal existence of a separate entity. A firm incorporated in one state may operate in any other state (subject to a few minor regulations such as registration requirements). The law of the chartering state governs the internal relations of the firm regardless of which state the firm operates in or the physical location of its headquarters. For example, many major corporations are incorporated in Delaware and thus governed by its laws, although most are headquartered and do most of their business elsewhere.

The corporation is governed by its articles of incorporation and its bylaws, which are normally submitted when the organization files its initial incorporation papers. The articles of incorporation perform a function analogous to that of a private constitution. The bylaws are rules or private laws that regulate and govern the operations of the corporation. Normally the articles of incorporation and the bylaws describe the procedures by which they may be amended or deleted.

B. Rights of Shareholders

Shareholders, as the owners of the corporation, possess certain well-established rights. The two most important rights are the right to vote in the election of directors as well as on certain corporate decisions and the right to file derivative lawsuits against the management of the corporation on behalf of the corporation.

1. Shareholder Voting

The right to vote is inherent in common stock ownership. Shareholders elect the board of directors, and also vote on their approval or disapproval of fundamental corporate changes such as mergers and amendments of the articles of incorporation. Elections take place at shareholder meetings, which typically must be called at least once a year. In addition to their voting rights, shareholders may question directors at annual meetings to influence corporate policy further. Shareholders who are unable to attend the meeting are able to vote by proxy. A **proxy** is a written authorization by the shareholder, on a form typically provided by the corporation, designating an agent to vote on the shareholder's behalf at the shareholders' meeting. Proxy solicitation is one of the few areas of internal corporate affairs regulated by the federal securities laws.

2. Proxy Solicitation

The principal method of voting corporate shares in the United States is the proxy. As shareholders are scattered around the country, it is rarely worth their time and expense to travel long distances to vote at annual shareholder meetings. The **Securities Exchange Act of 1934** regulates the manner in which proxies are solicited. The concern that prompted the federal intervention in this area is related to Berle and Means' assertion that corporate managers, that is, the officers and directors, use the proxy machinery to maintain control that rightly belongs in the hands of the shareholders. Evidently, Congress felt that the state laws were inadequate in this area.

The 1934 Act and Securities and Exchange Commission (SEC) regulations require the disclosure of specified information in the form of a proxy statement whenever proxies are being solicited. Proxy statements contain information about the nominees for the board of directors when an election of the board is scheduled. When a contested matter is being put to a shareholder vote, the proxy statement must explain the consequences of the vote and, in some circumstances, identify the interest of the party soliciting the proxy.

Proxy contests are a means for outsiders, that is, individuals not connected with the incumbent management team, to take control of the corporation by convincing shareholders to vote for their slate of directors. In order to mount an effective campaign, the insurgents need to know the names and addresses of the shareholders. SEC rules require that the incumbents either mail the insurgents' proxy solicitation for them or provide the insurgents with the shareholder mailing list. Insurgents are held to the same standards of truthfulness in their proxy statements as those of the managers. It is unlawful for either side in a proxy contest to submit a proxy statement that contains a false or misleading material fact. A violation of the proxy solicitation rules gives rise to a private cause of action to remedy the violation.

Even if proxies are not solicited, SEC rules require the corporation to send shareholders notification of the shareholders' meeting and an agenda of the meeting. In essence, the information statement forces the disclosure of information that would have been required in a proxy statement. Thus, the incumbent managers cannot avoid sending information by simply not using the proxy mechanism.

3. Shareholder Proposals

There have been numerous proposals to make the corporation more democratic. One manifestation of the reform movement in corporation law is the requirement under the 1934 Act that shareholders have the right to make proposals at shareholders' meetings. Shareholders also have the right to have shareholder proposals included in the proxy materials so that all shareholders may vote on them. Under some conditions, most of which are designed to prevent frivolous or repetitious proposals, the incumbent managers may exclude a shareholder proposal from consideration. Some courts have also held that managers can exclude shareholder proposals that deal with the "ordinary course of business." In general, shareholder proposals are rarely successful.

4. Derivative Actions

In some instances, the corporation may choose not to bring suit against someone who has injured the corporation. For example, directors may be reluctant to sue a fellow director who has profited at the expense of the corporation. In such a case, shareholders may file a **derivative action** on behalf of the corporation that permits the corporation to recover damages if liability can be established. A major prerequisite for a derivative suit is that the shareholders first make a formal demand upon the directors that the corporation pursue remedies available to it. If the directors refuse, their reasons become a matter of record, and the shareholders may pursue the derivative action. Some states further require that a majority vote of all outstanding voting shares first be obtained. If the suit is successful, damages are awarded to the corporation and the shareholders recover only to the extent the corporation increases in value.

The law with respect to derivative actions is somewhat confused because of attempts to balance the conflicting purposes of derivative suits. On one hand, suits can serve as a check on the behavior of corporate managers; on the other, unscrupulous shareholders and their lawyers can use them in an attempt to extort a settlement from managers whose time is very valuable. Accordingly, some states require that a shareholder filing a derivative action first post a security-for-expenses bond which can be used to pay the legal expenses of the defendants if they should prevail in the suit. Other states permit the dismissal of derivative action suits if it can be demonstrated that the judgment not to bring suit was made in good faith and for a legitimate business purpose. In order to prevent dismissal before the merits of the case are heard, some states require the court to delegate the authority to dismiss the case to a special litigation committee composed of "disinterested" directors of the corporation, a requirement which unfortunately often creates obvious conflicts of interest.

IV. CORPORATE GOVERNANCE

A. Introduction

Corporate governance involves formulating, overseeing, and monitoring the processes by which a corporation is governed in order to shape its strategic direction and performance, define its mission and scope, and assess its interactions with affected groups. It also involves formulating and implementing the rights, responsibilities, and accountability of three distinct groups within the corporation—its stockholders, its board of directors, and its managers. (We will also refer to this last group as officers or executive officers.) The question of corporate governance has become more important as corporations have grown larger and their shareholders have become more numerous. Public perceptions of abusive corporate behavior have also raised the visibility of this concern.

B. Basic Corporate Structure

Corporations are owned by their shareholders, each of whom own one or more shares of the corporation's common stock. Ownership carries the right to vote for the board of directors of the company. In most corporations, each share of stock has one vote, so that those who have more investment in the company have a larger voice in its governance. The board of directors is elected by shareholders to oversee the running of the firm and shape its overall strategy. The board, in turn, employs officers and other subordinate employees to manage the daily affairs of the corporation. In general, the managers have the power and authority to engage in all legal activities necessary for conducting the firm's business. Corporate officers often serve on the board of directors, in order to allow the board to benefit from their intimate knowledge of the corporation's business. Such directors are known as **inside directors**. Directors who are not executives of the corporation are known as **outside directors**.

The obligations, responsibilities, and relationships among these three groups are of particular importance in large, publicly owned corporations. The governance of such corporations is particularly susceptible to principal–agent problems.

C. The Principal–Agent Problem

An important relationship in all organizations is that existing between principals and agents. In a typical business situation, one party (the principal) empowers a second party (the agent) to act on his or her behalf to accomplish certain tasks or objectives. By agreeing to this arrangement, the agent assumes a fiduciary responsibility: The agent has a duty to act loyally and in the best interests of the principal in carrying out the tasks assigned by the principal. Moreover, an agent acting with due authority may bind the principal to a course of action and subject the principal to legal action should contract disputes or liabilities arise. For example, a salesperson employed by a computer manufacturer may commit the firm to shipping 50 laptop computers within 30 days for a price of $1,199 per unit by signing a contract with a customer. In this case, the salesperson (the agent) has legally bound the manufacturer (the principal) to a course of action (ship 50 computers within 30 days).

Such occurrences are normal in businesses. Indeed, in this situation the salesperson was probably doing what he or she was hired to do. However, it may be that the salesperson receives a 10 percent commission on sales, has a big MasterCard payment due next month, and thus has chosen to cut the sales price below the firm's normal price in order to generate a large order and a large commission. From such behavior arises the **principal–agent problem**, which can be summarized by the following question: Since the principal and the agent are two different people, how can the principal ensure that the agent will always act in the principal's best interests rather than in the agent's best interests? The company in fact has several ways it can eliminate, or at least reduce, the salesperson's tendency to act in his or her best interest instead of the firm's best interest:

- The firm may directly monitor the salesperson's behavior.
- The firm may impose control systems to audit the salesperson after the fact.
- The firm may develop a system of rewards and punishments.
- The firm may utilize legal remedies and sue the salesperson for damages.

Depending upon the circumstances, these approaches may or may not be successful. However, regardless of their efficacy, the firm incurs costs in implementing and utilizing each of these approaches.

Corporate governance is based upon a pair of principal–agent relationships. The ultimate owners of the corporation are its shareholders. The shareholders as principals elect the board of directors to act as their agents and to govern the corporation in the shareholders' best interests. The board of directors acting as a principal in turn hires the corporation's officers as its agents to run the corporation.

These two principal–agent relationships create major problems in many older, publicly owned corporations. A company like General Motors, General Electric, or Boeing is owned by hundreds of thousands (if not millions) of shareholders, each of which owns a very small percentage of the corporation's shares. This ownership structure creates a problem known as the **separation of ownership and control**. Because of fractured ownership, no one shareholder finds it in his or her self-interest to monitor actively the performance of the company. Rather, most simply look at the stock price and decide if the company is still a good investment. If the answer is yes, the shareholder holds on to her stock or perhaps buys more. If the answer is no, the shareholder sells her stock. The implication of this behavior is that the owners have lost control of the firm; instead, the firm's officers and its board of directors are free to do as they please. In such circumstances, implementing programs and policies to encourage officers and board members to act as faithful agents becomes very important. (Note that this problem may be less important in corporations where the founder or the founder's family still controls significant blocks of stock. Paul

Allen (one of the co-founders of and a major shareholder in Microsoft), for example, closely follows the company's performance even though he gave up an active management role years ago. Similarly, the Ford family has actively monitored the Ford Motor Company for decades.)

The control of management is solidified further because most shareholders do not directly vote their shares themselves. In practice, because of the expense of traveling to the firm's annual meeting where the board of directors is to be elected, most shareholders exercise their voting rights by delegating their proxy—the right to vote their shares—to another person. Typically that person is a corporate officer, who will normally vote the shares in support of the corporation's management. Indeed, these proxies are routinely solicited by the corporation's managers in a packet of information mailed to shareholders annually. Only rarely do third parties solicit shareholders proxies. Usually such solicitations occur in the midst of a takeover battle in which another corporation is trying to take over the firm, and chooses to do so by staging a proxy fight in an attempt to oust the existing board of directors and the management team that they have hired.

D. Conflicting Interests of Shareholders, Board Members, and Executive Officers

As owners, the shareholders expect the corporation to be run in their interest. Presumably the shareholders want the board of directors and the corporate officers to adopt strategies and policies that maximize the expected long-run present discounted value of the after-tax stream of profits earned by the corporation, which, according to finance theory, equals the price of a company's stock. Thus, simply put, the goal of the shareholders is to maximize the value (price) of their shares of stock in the company.

However, the executive officers of the company have different goals. Among other things, they would like to maximize the financial compensation that they receive from the corporation, their quality of life, and the status they achieve in their corporate positions. Accordingly, they might prefer to be paid above-market salaries, to hire numerous assistants who will continually sing their praises, to have corporate aircraft on call to jet them and their families to the south of France for holidays, and to give lots of corporate donations to highly visible charities so that they can get their names in the newspaper.

Similarly, the goals of the members of the board of directors may differ from those of the shareholders. Corporate directorships can be very cushy sinecures: they are very prestigious, may not entail much work, and are often very well paid. (Most board members of a Fortune 500 firms earn at least $100,000–200,000 a year as a director, and many board directors serve on multiple corporate boards.) Thus, some board members may decide that their self-interest is promoted by staying on the board. In the case of a proposed merger, for example, board members may prefer not to sell the company for fear that they may lose their directorships and the benefits associated with the position even if the sale is in the best interests of shareholders. This conflict is even greater for inside directors, for they may lose their jobs, their benefits, and their opportunity to advance up the corporate ladder as well as their seat on the board if the company is sold to another.

This problem is worsened in those corporations that rely on the CEO to suggest to the board the names of potential new members of the board. In such instances, the new board members may feel beholden to the CEO for their positions, and less likely to vote against the CEO should a crisis arise. Moreover, in many U.S. companies the CEO and the board chairperson is the same person. (This is not the case in Europe, however.) This concentration of power has obvious benefits and dangers. Communication between the board and the management team is facilitated by this arrangement. However, giving one person such vast power can prove troublesome should that person no longer be up to the job. Moreover, it makes it more difficult to solve the principal–agent problem should the CEO/board chairperson not act in the best interests of the shareholders.

V. PRIVATE SOLUTIONS TO THE CORPORATE GOVERNANCE PROBLEM

A. Introduction

Because of the enormous benefits of the corporate form of organization and the significant corporate governance problems created by the separation of ownership and control, consultants, business persons, regulators, public policy makers, and various other interested parties have developed a variety of techniques to address, if not solve, the principal–agent problem in corporate governance. We will first discuss the private solutions to this problem; in the next section, we will assess public solutions.

B. Alignment of Financial Interests

One approach to addressing the principal–agent problem in corporate governance is to align the financial interests of the executive officers and the board members with those of the shareholders. If shareholders are interested in maximizing stock value, why not compensate officers and board members with stock, rather than salary? By so doing, the officers and board members will have a greater incentive to act in ways that further the interests of the shareholders, for they now have an increased self-interest in raising the value of the company's stock. Accordingly, many corporations are changing the compensation packages offered their executives by increasing the importance of stock, stock options, stock appreciation rights, stock warrants, and other equity-based instruments in that package. Similarly, many corporations now compensate board members with a combination of salary and stock or stock options. Pharmaceutical giant Merck & Co., for example, pays its outside directors an annual retainer of $100,000 plus small stipends for chairing key board committees. Additionally, each outside director is granted $150,000 of Merck common stock annually at the then existing market price.

Note that this approach lessens, but does not eliminate, the principal–agent problem. Executive officers and board member may still be motivated by factors other than the stock price. Moreover, if an executive transfers a dollar from the corporation for some purpose (such as a higher salary or a plusher office), his share of the cost as an equity owner is only a small fraction of that dollar. Presumably the gains he will capture from the transfer will be higher than his small share of the costs.

C. Outside Directors

In some corporations insider directors may outnumber outside directors, the CEO may serve as board chairperson, or the outside directors may feel beholden to the CEO for their positions. If so, the board of directors is likely to be ineffective in its role of overseeing the corporation's officers. Accordingly, another approach for improving corporate governance and lessening the principal–agent problem is to increase the number, power, and independence of outside directors on the company's board of directors. This objective can be accomplished through adopting any or all of the following options:

- *Separate the role of board chairperson and the company's CEO*: The role of the board of directors is to oversee the decisions and policies adopted by the firm's executive officers. Having one person serve in this dual capacity is like having the fox guard the chicken coop. Nonetheless, many corporations combine the two jobs. For example, Merck's CEO, Kenneth Frazier, also serves as its board chairman.
- *Increase the number of outside directors on the board relative to inside directors*: Inside directors have valuable working knowledge of the firm, which is often of use to the board in shaping its decisions. For example, as noted in Merck's 2000 proxy statement, its "Board of Directors is strengthened by the presence of senior Merck officers, who provide strategic, operational, and technical expertise and context for the matters considered by the Board."[1] However, inside directors have inherent conflicts of interest in their dual roles as executive officers and board members. Moreover, because of their position in the corporate hierarchy, non-CEO inside directors are highly likely to vote for whatever position the CEO-inside director favors. If outside directors constitute a majority of the board, the board is more likely to exercise independent judgment and to effectively oversee the performance of the executive officers than if they are in the minority. In Merck's case, 11 of its 12 board members are outside directors.
- *Increase the independence and power of the board*: One important reform is to reduce the power of the CEO in the selection of new board members. A board member personally recruited by the CEO or with strong ties to the CEO is less likely to exercise his or her independent judgment than one recruited by others. Conversely, appointing business executives from other industries with no existing ties to the firm or to the CEO often brings new insights and fresh ideas to the firm. Merck's board includes the CEOs or former CEOs of such major corporations as J.P. Morgan Chase & Co., Corning, Alcatel-Lucent, and Ogilvy & Mather Worldwide. Key committees of Merck's board of directors, including its audit committee (which oversees the company's financial controls), its compensation committee (which establishes executive salaries), and its committee on directors (which establishes board policies and procedures and nominates new board members), are composed solely of outside directors in order to minimize corporate officers' influence on their decision making.

---

1. Merck & Co, Inc., Proxy Statement dated March 16, 2000 at p. 24.

As a result of these policies, Merck's board of directors was ranked among the top fifteen "best boards" in the country in a recent analysis by *Business Week*.

D. Institutional Investors and Corporate Democracy

One increasingly important counterweight to the problem of separation of ownership and control and the lack of concentrated ownership is the growing role of institutional investors in corporate governance. The term **institutional investor** is used to describe a large, professionally managed provider of capital, such as a pension fund, insurance company or mutual fund. Although each of these investors may own a small portion of a company's stock, cumulatively they are major shareholders in most publicly owned companies. By some estimates, institutional investors own 60 percent of the typical company listed on the New York Stock Exchange. In 1986, a group of institutional investors banded together to create the Council of Institutional Investors (CII) to promote accountability by corporate executives. One way the CII promotes this objective is by monitoring the governance of publicly traded corporations to ensure that their governance structure promotes the interest of shareholders. For example, the CII has lobbied against corporations adopting takeover defenses such as "poison pills" without the formal approval of their shareholders.

One of the primary leaders in this movement is the California Public Employees Retirement System (CalPERS). CalPERS has focused on changing corporate charters to promote the interests of shareholders. Exercising its rights as a shareholder, it has sponsored a variety of reform proposals to be voted on by shareholders at the annual meetings of companies whose corporate governance it believes inadequate. Most of the proposals it has filed have dealt with three goals:

- Outside directors should constitute a majority of the board of directors
- The chairperson of the board of directors should be an outside director
- The audit committee should be composed only of outside directors.

CalPERS has not won many of these votes; indeed, more often than not it has withdrawn its petition for a vote amending the way the corporation is governed prior to the vote being taken. The reason for this outcome is simple. Corporate officials typically dislike having to have these shareholder votes and the attendant publicity they create. Accordingly, they often negotiate with CalPERS and promise to adopt governance reforms if CalPERS withdraws its request for a formal vote by the shareholders. Thus CalPERS—and its goal of improving corporate governance—wins, while the corporate officers save face. Other important CalPERS allies include the Florida State Board of Administration, TIAA-CREF, and the State of Wisconsin Investment Board.

E. Product Market Competition

The product market may also provide constraints on the corporation's executive officers' ability to act in their own interests rather than in the shareholders' best interests. A firm must remain competitive with its rivals. If the market for its products is highly competitive and/or constantly changing, the corporation's officers must continually strive to develop new products, reduce costs, and eliminate waste. In such circumstances, corporate officers have less ability to act as faithless agents. Conversely, if the industry environment is non-competitive, then corporate officers have more ability to run the company in their own interests than in those of the shareholders.

F. The Market for Executive Talent

The labor market—the market for executive talent—may also induce the corporation's executive officers to act as faithful agents for the shareholders. If managers believe that their talents will be recognized and rewarded for performing their duties successfully, they will have strong incentives to work in the corporation's (and its shareholder's) best interests. This incentive is magnified if executives believe that if they distinguish themselves at one company they may be wooed by other firms and offered higher salaries and more prestigious positions to work for them.

G. The Market for Corporate Control

Another mechanism for encouraging a corporation's executive officers to act as faithful agents on behalf of the shareholders is the **market for corporate control**. Suppose the executives of a corporation are acting in their own best interests, rather than in the share-holders' interest. The market value of the corporation will thus be less than it would otherwise be. The poor stock market performance of the corporation may then attract the attention of other potential teams of managers, who believe that if they ran the corporation they could do a better job. Often this hypothetical "other team of managers" is another corporation. For simplicity, we'll call the corporation in question the **target company** and the company who wishes to take over the target company the **acquiring company**.

Suppose that the market price of the target company's stock is currently $50. Assume further that the acquiring company believes that if it were in control, it could raise the target company's value to $75 a share. In that case, the acquiring company may offer to buy up the shares of the target at a price of say, $60 a share. (Any price above $50 but less than $75 can be used in this example). This offer is known as a **tender offer**, as the acquiring company is technically asking the target's shareholders to tender their shares for purchase. If the acquiring company is right in its assumption that it can manage the target company better than its current executives, then the acquirer will make a profit based on the difference between the $60 tender price and what the target's shares are worth once the acquirer takes control of the target. If the acquirer is wrong, it suffers the consequences. Note that the market for corporate control does not depend on people making promises that "we're better than them." Rather, it works because they put their money where their mouths are.

The board of directors often plays an important role in a tender offer. Normally the acquiring company asks the target's board of directors to endorse the tender offer and recommend its acceptance by the shareholders. If the board concurs, the tender offer is called a **friendly offer**. If the board rejects the offer, it is called an unfriendly offer. Many times, however, the board chooses to reject the initial offer but signals it might accept a higher offer. Oftentimes, the acquiring company amends its tender offer by raising the tender price in order to get the target board of directors' approval. In most cases, once the board of directors accepts a tender offer, the target's shareholders also agree to it and tender their shares.

The market for corporate control can create strong incentives for the existing team of corporate executives to operate the company efficiently. If they fail to do so, they are vulnerable to having the company taken over by others and losing their jobs in the aftermath. Institutional investors like CalPERS believe that a well-functioning market for corporate control is of vital concern to the shareholders. That is one of the reasons why CalPERS insists that a majority of the board of directors be outside directors. CalPERS believes that inside directors might reject a tender offer for fear of losing their jobs, while outside directors are more likely to focus on the interests of the shareholders.

VI. PUBLIC SOLUTIONS TO THE CORPORATE GOVERNANCE PROBLEM

A. Introduction

The corporate governance problem is also subject to several public sector solutions and constraints. We will discuss two of these: (1) the legal responsibilities imposed on board of directors and executive officers by common law and statutory law, and (2) regulatory constraints impose by the Securities and Exchange Commission.

B. Legal Duties of Directors and Officers

The directors and the officers have a fiduciary relationship with the corporation and its shareholders. As fiduciaries, the directors and officers have a duty to act on behalf of the corporation and its shareholders with the highest standard of good faith. The law of fiduciary duties, which has been defined through common law decisions rather than statutes, specifies standards of care and loyalty. The primary enforcement mechanism is to hold directors and officers liable for the losses to the corporation that result from their failure to fulfill their fiduciary duties. Shareholders often attempt to enforce fiduciary duties by filing derivative suits on behalf of the corporation against directors and officers.

1. Duty of Care

As part of their fiduciary obligations, directors and officers assume a **duty of due care and diligence**. This duty has been interpreted to mean that they must act in good faith and exercise a level of care that an ordinary prudent person would under similar circumstances. The obligation to exercise due care and diligence is also important for what it does not entail. It does not require officers and directors to make the "right" decision—whatever that means. The courts have recognized that corporate officers and directors are continually forced to make difficult decisions involving large sums of money with imperfect information in a constantly changing business environment. The courts have also recognized that they are in no position to second-guess corporate officers. They further recognized that both the court system and the decision-making process of publicly owned corporations would bog down if directors and managers could be sued everyvtime some shareholder or other affected party disagreed with a corporate decision. Accordingly, the judicial system has developed the **business judgment rule** to assess such conflicts. This rule states that corporate officers and directors are held harmless for any decisions they make in good faith, after prudently exercising due care and diligence, even if those decisions later prove to have been in error. In order to avail themselves of the rule, managers must prove the following elements:

1. The action taken was an informed decision.
2. There were no conflicts of interest between the decision maker and the corporation.
3. There was a rational basis for the decision.

The decision does not need to be the correct one or even be supported by the weight of available information. As long as it was made on some rational basis, the court will not substitute its judgment for that of professional managers.

An example of the impact of the business judgment rule is the decision by the Delaware Chancery Court (a special court established in that state to adjudicate corporate governance issues) in 2005 regarding the highly publicized $140 million severance package paid Michael Ovitz by the Walt Disney Corporation. Ovitz was hired by his erstwhile friend, Disney CEO Michael Eisner, to serve as his second-in-command. Ovitz' hiring proved to be a mistake, and 14 months later he was fired. His employment contract, however, entitled him to a severance package worth $140 million. A group of shareholders filed a derivative suit against the company's board of directors, arguing that they should be held personally liable for this payment because they failed in their fiduciary duty to the shareholders—that is, they failed to carefully consider whether Ovitz was the right person for the job and they agreed to an outrageous, expensive, and wasteful severance package. While the judge was highly critical of the state of corporate governance in the Disney Corporation, he found that as long as the directors believed that they were acting in the best interests of the company and were not grossly negligent, the court should defer to the directors' decision under the business judgment rule.

There are at least two major policy reasons in support of the business judgment rule. First, holding directors personally liable in situations where hindsight reveals that they made a mistake would make it difficult to attract top quality individuals to serve on boards of directors. Second, without a business judgment rule, those who agreed to serve might be unwilling to approve any venture, even one that appeared to be in the best interests of the corporation, because they would be worried about being held personally liable if even the surest gamble failed. In recognition of the adverse impact of holding directors and officers liable when they acted in good faith, several states' corporation laws authorize corporations to indemnify (reimburse) directors for liability payments or for expenses incurred in defending themselves against unwarranted suits.

2. *Duty of Loyalty*

In contrast to duty of care, courts are much less tolerant of deviations from the fiduciary duty of loyalty. Judicial intolerance of disloyalty is illustrated by the classic language of the Delaware Supreme Court in the 1939 case of *Guth v. Loft, Inc.*:

> A public policy, existing through the years, and derived from a profound knowledge of human characteristics and motives, has established a rule that demands of a corporate officer or director, peremptorily and inexorably, the most scrupulous observance of his duty, not only affirmatively to protect the interest of the corporation committed to his charge, but also to refrain from doing anything that would work injury to the corporation, or to deprive it of profit or advantage which his skill and ability might properly bring to it, or to enable it to make in the reasonable and lawful exercise of its powers. The rule that requires an undivided and unselfish loyalty to the corporation demands that there shall be no conflict between duty and self-interest.

The concern in this area of corporation law is that directors and officers will use their corporate positions to benefit themselves at the expense of the corporation. The duty of loyalty addresses conflicts of interest that may arise from time to time in the performance of the manager's duties. The **corporate opportunity doctrine** represents one form of fiduciary loyalty owed by the officers and directors to the corporation. This doctrine mandates that should an officer or a director discover a business opportunity, he or she must first present it to the corporation. For example, an executive of a commercial real estate development company who discovers a plot of land suitable for a strip mall must present his findings to his corporation. He cannot develop it on his own through a second corporation that he controls, for example.

Conflicts of interest may also develop in self-dealing transactions. Under modern common law principles, self-dealing transactions are not necessarily violations of the duty of loyalty. Self-dealing cases involve two basic types of situations. The first type includes transactions between a director or officer of a corporation and the corporation. Examples of this include the sale of property by the director to the corporation at a price greater than the market price, or the payment to a director/officer of an exorbitant salary. The second type includes transactions between corporations with common directors. The basic fear here is that one of the corporations will not be treated fairly in the transaction.

It is difficult to state a clear rule for how self-dealing cases are handled by the courts, but the following statement is an accurate reflection of the overall trend of decisions:

1. If the court feels the transaction to be fair to the corporation, it will be upheld;
2. If the court feels that the transaction involves fraud, undue overreaching or waste of corporate assets (e.g., a director using assets for personal purposes without paying for them), the transaction will be set aside;

and

3. If the court feels that the transaction does not involve fraud, overreaching or waste of corporate assets, but is not convinced that the transaction is fair, the transaction

will be upheld only where the interested director can convincingly show that the transaction was approved (or ratified) by a disinterested majority of the board of directors without participation by the interested director, or by a majority of the shareholders after full disclosure of all relevant facts.[2]

Thus, the fiduciary obligations of corporate directors and officers do not bar them from entering into contracts with the corporation. However, any such contracts must be fully disclosed and the burden of demonstrating that the contract is fair to the corporation rests with the officer or director.

Another important aspect of officers and directors' fiduciary duties involves their obligation not to profit from trading in the company's stock based upon information they have acquired as agents of the shareholders. Such activities are known as **insider trading**. An insider is defined as any person who has access to confidential corporate information. These include employees, officers, directors, and outside experts such as lawyers, accountants, or investment bankers who may learn about such information in the course of their dealings with the corporation. Insiders are not allowed to profit from this information, as it is deemed a breach of their fiduciary duties to the corporation. More importantly, insider trading is believed to undermine the public's confidence in the integrity of the public capital market. As a result, corporate directors and officers face liability under the federal securities regulations should they utilize insider information to profit from stock transactions, a topic we will discuss in more detail in the next section of the chapter.

C. Regulatory Controls

1. Statutory History

Federal laws and federal regulators provide another important set of constraints on publicly owned corporations. The initial federal laws regulating the issuance of securities were passed during Franklin Roosevelt's New Deal—the Securities Act of 1933 and the Securities Exchange Act of 1934. Their passage reflected the nation's distrust of the securities market subsequent to the Great Crash of 1929 and the concerns that corporate insiders were abusing their possession of non-public information to the detriment of the general investor. Both laws are designed to promote public confidence in the public capital market by ensuring that investors are provided with necessary and accurate information designed to allow them to make informed investment decisions.

The Securities Act of 1933 regulates the initial sale of securities to the public. It requires that sellers of securities—bonds, common stock, preferred stock, etc.—to the public must file a registration statement with the Securities and Exchange Commission (SEC). The term *security* has been defined very broadly as a result of the 1946 *Howey* case. In this case, the Supreme Court decided that a security is any "contract, transaction or scheme whereby a person invests his money in a common enterprise and is led to expect profits solely from

---

2. Robert W. Hamilton, *The Law of Corporations* 243 (St. Paul, Minnesota: West Publishing Co., 1980).

the efforts of a promoter or third party."[3] The SEC requires any issuer of a security to provide detailed information about the issuer and the terms of the security being issued in the registration statement.

The goal of the statement is to provide potential investors with all relevant information necessary to make informed investment decisions. The SEC does not offer its own independent assessment about the risks and rewards borne by the purchaser of a security, however. That task is left to the investor. Rather, the SEC focuses on ensuring that the registration statement fully discloses all relevant information, such as the terms of the security, audited financial statements of the issuer, short biographies of the corporation's top management team, discussions of their financial interests in the issuer (such as stock holdings and stock options), any potential conflicts of interest they may have, an enumeration of the potential risks facing the issuer, the status of any pending lawsuits, etc. Should the registration statement contain a material misrepresentation, an investor who suffers a loss may sue any underwriter, corporate director, or corporate officer who signed the document for statutory fraud. Outside experts (such as accountants, engineers, geologists, attorneys, etc.) who helped provide misleading information may also be sued. Additionally, violators may be subject to fine of $10,000 and/or prison sentences of as much as five years.

The Securities Exchange Act of 1934 focuses on regulating the sale of previously issued securities on secondary markets, such as the New York Stock Exchange or NASDAQ. One portion of this Act regulates the activities of stock exchanges, stockbrokers, stock dealers, and other market professionals to ensure that they do not engage in fraudulent, deceptive, or unfair practices. For example, brokers are required by the **know thy customer rule** to ascertain whether particular investments are appropriate for a client before recommending it to him or her. A highly speculative "dot.com" stock selling at a price–earnings ratio of 150 might not be appropriate for an 86-year-old widow dependent on Social Security, for example.

The 1934 Act also deals with the securities themselves. All securities traded on public exchanges must be registered with the SEC, and their issuers must file periodic reports to the SEC detailing their financial performance on a timely basis. Companies are also compelled to disclose any "material" item—mergers, unexpected changes in earnings, significant new contracts, key personnel changes, loss of important customers, etc.—as such events occur. The goal of these requirements is to ensure that investors are provided any and all information that may be relevant to their investment decisions.

2. Liability for "Short-Swing" Profits

The SEC also imposes special restrictions on the ability of certain corporate officials and investors to take advantage of inside information known only to corporate insiders when buying or selling shares of the company's stock. These regulations are designed to promote investors' faith in the integrity of the public capital market.

---

3. **SEC v. W.J. Howey, Co., 328 U.S. 293 (1946).** Some types of investments are exempt from the SEC's filing requirements, such as purely intrastate investments, private offerings, many insurance products, commercial paper, securities issued by the U.S. government, states, and municipalities, and certain small investments.

Inside information refers to any information that is not yet publicly available. Persons with access to inside information could use such information to make favorable stock transactions. For example, a corporate director may learn that the corporation's research and development division has discovered a cure for the common cold. Before the information about the discovery becomes publicly available, the director purchases a large number of shares in the corporation. After the disclosure of the information, the company's stock soars and the director sells the shares for a large profit. The director receives an almost risk-free windfall. This activity could be considered a violation of the fiduciary duty of loyalty under state corporation law, but such trading is also regulated by federal securities law.

The Securities Exchange Act of 1934 takes a very strong stand against the use of inside information in stock transactions. Section 16(b) prohibits corporate insiders from profiting on short-term investments in their own company. Section 10(b), which is the general anti-fraud provision of the Securities Exchange Act of 1934, is also aimed at the prohibition of insider trading.

Section 16(b) applies to all securities registered under the 1934 Act. This section defines corporate insiders as all directors, all officers, and any shareholders that own 10 percent or more of the corporation's shares. The statute presumes that these officials, as well as any 10-percent shareholder, have access to inside information. Insiders are prohibited from gaining from short-term investments in their corporation; should corporate insiders enjoy any **short-swing profits**—a capital gain made by buying and selling the company stock within any six-month period—the gain must be returned to the company's treasury. The actual reason for the purchase and sale by the inside investor is irrelevant: short-swing profits are presumed to be the result of inside information. There are no defenses to this provision. The corporation is supposed to bring suit against any inside investor to recapture any short-swing profits earned by them. Shareholders may file a derivative action lawsuit for the recovery of profits in the event the corporation refuses to sue one of its officers.

Enforcement of Section 16(b) is facilitated by registration and disclosure requirements for insiders. The insiders are required to disclose their holdings in the corporation. Directors and officers cannot avoid liability by resigning their position with the corporation. For example, a director cannot avoid short-swing liability by purchasing shares in a corporation, resigning from the board, and then selling the shares at a profit within the six-month period. As long as either the purchase or the sale takes place while the person is an officer or director, Section 16(b) applies.

Similar rules apply to 10-percent shareholders. A 10-percent shareholder is liable for short-swing profits only if both the sale and purchase take place while the owner owns at least 10 percent of the shares. A purchase that makes an owner a 10-percent shareholder does not trigger the short-swing provision. For example, if an offeror acquires 51 percent of a company in a tender offer and then sells the shares for a profit within six months after the purchase, the offeror is not liable for the short-swing profits. In calculating the liability for short-term profits, the profits may not be offset by losses from trading in the same corporation's stock during the same period. This is a very harsh penalty.

3. Insider Trading

Insider trading is another form of self-dealing that is prohibited by federal statute. The Securities Exchange Act of 1934 prohibits insider trading under the general anti-fraud provisions of Section 10(b) and provides for criminal penalties. The Securities Exchange Commission, which is charged with enforcement of the Act, has since issued Rule 10b-5 pursuant to its power to regulate the trading of securities. Rule 10b-5 declares:

> It shall be unlawful for any person, directly or indirectly, by the use of any means or instrumentality of interstate commerce, or of the mails, or of any facility of any national securities exchange,
> 1. to employ any device, scheme, or artifice to defraud,
> 2. to make any untrue statement of a material fact or to omit to state a material fact necessary in order to make the statements made, in the light of the circumstances under which they were made, not misleading, or
> 3. to engage in any act, practice, or course of business which operates or would operate as a fraud or deceit upon any person, in connection with the purchase or sale of any security.

Rule 10b-5 is worded as a prohibition, but the courts have interpreted it as allowing for civil liability and private actions for damages.[4] Over the years, Rule 10b-5 has been applied to many different types of activities.

Rule 10b-5 supplements the Section 16(b) prohibition of short-swing trading. Its definition of insiders extends beyond the 16(b) statutory definition of insiders—officers, directors, and 10-percent shareholders—to include almost anyone who gains access to material non-public information through their relationship to the corporation and trades on it without first making disclosure. Insider trading should not be confused with short-swing trading. There is no six-month term after which trades are legitimate. Trading on inside information becomes legal only after a reasonable time elapses after the information becomes public. Of course, the price of the stock then reflects the information, and the opportunity to profit from inside information has ended.

No federal statute or regulation contains a formal definition of insider trading. Rather, they contain a broad prohibition of certain behavior and allow the federal courts to determine whether insider trading has occurred on a case-by-case basis. A general definition based upon federal courts' interpretation of federal statutes is the misappropriation of material inside information for profit. The term misappropriation means the misuse of information in violation of one's duty. Inside information is non-public information obtained through one's relationship to the corporation either as an employee, lawyer, accountant, banker, or even janitor. Material means that the information is likely to affect the price of the stock. Profit is any expected benefit, whether it is tangible (such as money or information) or intangible (such as love or promises of sexual favors).

---

4. **Kardon v. National Gypsum Co., 69 F. Supp. 512 (E.D.Pa. 1946)**.

Tippees who receive inside information from insiders also inherit their liability. If the act of an insider giving a friend, relative, or acquaintance constitutes a misappropriation of material inside information for profit, then the tippee who profits from the information will be liable as will anyone further down the line.

The Insider Trading Sanctions Act passed by Congress in 1984 provides both civil and criminal penalties in federal court for anyone who buys or sells securities while possessing material non-public information. The Act has some advantages over Rule 10b-5 in prose-cuting inside traders in that it provides for treble damages and includes aiders and abettors as potential defendants. Securities firms, however, are not liable without knowledge of illegal transactions by their employees. The statute of limitations is five years under the Act. The Act is conspicuously silent on the definitions of insider trading and non-public information, which means that the Act did little to change current substantive law.

The SEC has been able to convince district and appellate courts that a person should be criminally liable for violation of Rule 10b-5 if that person conveys nonpublic information which was intended to be kept confidential, even if shareholders of the employer corpora-tion are not injured. This is known as the misappropriation theory of insider trading.

It is also clear that the SEC places high priority in curbing insider trading. It wants to maintain the integrity of the public capital markets and make sure that the investing public is not disadvantaged by insiders or by those who benefit from insider information. The most publicized insider trading case of the past decade involved Martha Stewart, who was warned by her friend Samuel Waksal, founder of ImClone, that the Food and Drug Administration was not going to approve one of the company's experimental drugs. Stewart, Waksal and several members of his family, and other company executives sold some of their stock prior to the public announcement of the FDA's decision. Waksal was sentenced to more than seven years in federal prison and fined $4 million, while Stewart was sentenced to five months in prison, five months house arrest, and two years probation and fined $30,000.

The ImClone defendants are but one example of the SEC's efforts to control insider trad-ing; other examples include:

- Affiliates of SAC Capital Advisors, a $15 billion hedge fund controlled by Stephen Cohen, agreed to pay $616 million to settle an insider trading complaint filed by the SEC; the SEC alleged that SAC obtained confidential details about an Alzheimer's drug trial from a participating doctor and advance information about earnings of technology companies from other insiders.
- Raj Rajaratnam, founder of the hedge fund Galleon Group, paid $157 million to settle SEC claims that he benefited from insider tips from a network of corporate insiders that he had cultivated. He was also sentenced to an 11-year federal prison sentence.
- Scott London, a partner at KPMG, passed along secrets he learned from auditing five KPMG clients to a friend in return for $50,000 in gifts. (This case has not yet been settled.)
- Thomas Conradt, a stock broker received information about details of IBM's plans to acquire SPSS, Inc. from a friend of a lawyer working on the acquisition. (This case has not yet been settled.)

All told, in 2012 the SEC instituted 58 insider trading enforcement actions against 131 individuals and firms

4. Reporting Requirements for Insiders

Finally, the Securities Exchange Act of 1934 requires that corporate officers, directors, and large shareholders (those with ten percent of more of a company's stock) must inform the SEC on a timely basis regarding any purchase or sale of stock made by them, as well as the source of the funds made to purchase the stock and the person's reason for purchasing the stock. As we noted earlier, these persons are presumed to benefit from inside information owing to their position. The logic of the reporting requirement is that public investors (ones not privy to the inside information) should be made aware of what the insiders are doing—that is, "What do they know that I don't know?" and "If they're dumping their stock, shouldn't I do the same?" Financial media, such as the *Wall Street Journal*, routinely publish changes in the stock holdings of corporate insiders. Financial analysts use such information in deciding whether to recommend the sale or purchase of a given stock to their clients.

D. The SEC's Role in the Market for Corporate Control

The SEC also plays an important role in regulating the market for corporate control. Its regulations are designed to ensure that investors are provided with necessary and accurate information regarding the terms and implications of any takeover. It also tries to ensure that small investors receive the same treatment and terms as larger investors in any corporate takeover.

Much of the SEC's control over takeovers is derived from the Williams Act of 1968. It compels any prospective purchaser of more than five percent of a public company's stock to file a tender offer with the SEC. The prospective purchaser must also inform the target company and its shareholders about the terms of the proposed purchase. If the target company's board of directors opposes the proposed purchase, it too must file statements before the SEC. Under the Williams Act, all takeover offers must be put on the table for at least 20 days, and shareholders who agreed to sell their shares have seven days after the offer expires to withdraw their shares from sale. Should the acquiring company sweeten the deal by raising its offer price, shareholders who tendered their shares at the lower price are given the opportunity to obtain the higher price by first withdrawing and then re-tendering their shares. These requirements are designed to prevent the acquiring company from pressuring small shareholders to sell their shares with quick deadlines or coercive "now or never" threats and to allow shareholders sufficient time to judge the attractiveness of the tender offer.

E. The Impact of the SEC on U.S. Competitiveness in World Markets

One clear message runs through U.S. public policy toward the capital market, as manifested in the SEC's regulations—information rules! The SEC's policies are designed to ensure that investors are provided accurate and complete information on which to base their investment decisions. The SEC also plays a major role in the formulation of the Generally Accepted Accounting Principles (GAAP) that U.S. firms must utilize in their accounting statements. The GAAP are designed to promote consistency and transparency. Because of these features of the GAAP, outsiders—that is, you, me, and the rest of the public—can study a U.S. firm's accounting records and make a reasonable assessment of how well it is performing in an absolute sense and relative to its peers. This is not the case in many other developed countries, however. Company accounts in Germany, Japan, and France, for example, are much more opaque—they are much harder for an outsider to "see through" (i.e., to understand and analyze). Companies in these countries, not coincidently, have historically relied on bank loans rather than the public capital market for new capital.

Conversely, U.S. companies rely on the public capital market to raise much of their new capital. Many foreign companies now believe that they are at a substantial competitive disadvantage vis-à-vis U.S. firms because of the efficiency of the U.S. public capital market in providing capital to growing firms at low cost. An increasing number of European and Asian companies are utilizing the U.S. GAAP in creating their accounting statements and complying with SEC reporting requirements so that they can better access the U.S. capital market. Lenders also find the U.S. rules helpful. Many foreign bankers, for example, believe that the SEC's disclosure requirements and the GAAP make the United States the easiest place in which to conduct their lending operations. SEC rules and the GAAP together ensure that the firm's lending officers have reliable numbers on which to assess the riskiness of extending funds to potential borrowers.

F. The Enron Debacle and the Sarbanes-Oxley Act of 2002

The public capital market's faith in the SEC and in the U.S. accounting system was severely shaken in the beginning of the new millennium by a series of accounting and corporate governance scandals engulfing major American corporations, including Enron, WorldCom, Tyco, and Adelphia Communications. The Congress recognized that if investors were to lose faith in the public capital markets, it could negatively affect the competitiveness of U.S. firms by raising their cost of acquiring new capital. To restore trust in the capital market, Congress passed the Public Company Accounting Reform and Investor Protection Act of 2002, more commonly known as the Sarbanes-Oxley Act.

This Act has several important goals. First, it seeks to strengthen corporate governance of publicly traded corporations by imposing new requirements on auditors, member of the company's board of directors, and corporate executives. The Act requires that the audit committee of a company's board of directors oversee the hiring and performance of its outside auditors, not the company's managers. The auditors must report to the audit committee any disagreements they have had with the company's managers over the accounting treatment of corporate financial transactions. Only outside directors can serve on the audit committee. Additionally, the chief executive officer (CEO) and chief financial officer (CFO) must certify that certain financial statements issued by the corporation (such as its annual report) "fairly present, in all material respects, the operations and financial condition" of the corporation. This requirement effectively eliminates the "I didn't know" defense used by corporate officers in several recent high-profile court cases. A publicly traded corporation is also required to include an internal controls report in the annual report it issues to its shareholders. The internal control report must assess the effectiveness of the firm's internal controls overseeing its financial reporting, and the firm's auditor must then assess the accuracy of management's assessment of its internal controls. Finally, it eliminates most company loans to officers and directors, a practice that played a prominent role in the WorldCom case.

Second, the Sarbanes-Oxley Act addresses perceived problems within the public accounting profession. It created the Public Company Accounting Oversight Board, a five person committee that is charged with establishing and enforcing ethical and auditing standards for auditors of public companies. Auditors are required to keep work papers associated with their audits of public companies for five years. To reduce conflicts of interest, accounting firms are forbidden to provide certain types of consulting services to firms that they are serving as auditors. This requirement is a direct response to a problem uncovered in the Arthur Andersen–Enron relationship. The revenues that Arthur Andersen earned by providing consulting services to Enron far outweighed the fees it charged Enron for auditing its financial statements. Many critics believed that auditors from Arthur Andersen approved dubious accounting entries by Enron's financial officers for fear of jeopardizing Andersen's lucrative consulting contracts with Enron.

The Sarbanes-Oxley Act has proven to be highly controversial. Some critics argue that it offers only modest improvements in corporate governance and that Enron-like scandals will continue unabated. Other critics claim that compliance with the Act is too expensive, particularly for smaller firms, and believe that in the future new firms will chose not to "go public"—that is, offer their stock to public investors—rather subject themselves to the requirements of Sarbanes-Oxley. Only time will tell whether these criticisms are justified or are not justified.

CHAPTER SUMMARY

The corporate form is the dominant form of business organization in the United States and most developed market economies. The limited liability that is granted to corporate shareholders makes it easier for corporations to tap the public capital market for funds to expand their operations.

A corporation is organized under the laws of an individual state and is regarded as a separate legal entity. The laws of the state, as well as the corporation's articles of incorporation and its bylaws, dictate how the corporation will be governed. Shareholders, as owners of the corporation, possess certain rights, including the right to vote for the corporation's board of directors.

The principal–agent problem is an important issue that corporations must address. Corporate governance rests on two principal–agent relations, that between the shareholders and the board of directors and that between the board of directors and the managers of the corporation. A variety of private and public solutions have been developed to curb the principal–agent problem, including alignment of financial incentives, the use of outside directors, expansion of the influence of institutional investors, encouragement of corporate democracy, product market competition, the market for executive talent, the market for corporate control, and the common law obligations of duty of due care and diligence. The Securities and Exchange Commission plays an important role in corporate governance. Its regulations detail the rules under which proxy solicitations and proxy contests occur. The SEC has also imposed numerous regulations to reduce misappropriation of insider information and insider trading.

11

ADVERTISING

Consumption of goods and services is a driving force of the American economy. American consumers' demands for goods and services result in the production of a wide variety of products. This chapter considers some of the regulations involved in the selling of goods and services to consumers. Specifically, the chapter addresses the federal regulation of the content of advertisements.

Some aspects of the regulation of advertising deal with the correction of an information-problem type of market failure. For many products, inexperienced, unknowing, or unsophisticated consumers have a difficult time determining the nature and quality of the product. Producers can increase the demand for their products by informing consumers of the relevant virtues of the product. However, in some instances, producers can increase their profits by using their huge informational advantage to distort consumers' demand for products by portraying their products in a false light. Government regulations are intended to prevent sellers from creating chaos in consumer goods markets by generating false information and to equalize knowledge about various products so that competition will be heightened.

I. THE ROLE OF ADVERTISING IN MARKETS

Advertising is defined as any communication that businesses offer customers in an effort to increase demand for their products. Few subjects in the economics of market structure or industrial organization economics have been debated as vigorously as advertising. Some economists consider advertising to be wasteful or "self-canceling," while others consider it to be evidence of the presence of vigorous competition.

One of the primary sources of debate among economists has been over the informational content of advertising. Critics of advertising argue that most ads are tasteless and wasteful assaults on consumers' senses. Advertising is criticized on the ground that it creates illusory differences between products that are actually very close substitutes for each other; advertising is not productive because it merely allocates demand among competing firms producing goods that are fundamentally alike. Critics also charge that high advertising expenditures can create barriers to entry that ultimately reduce competition. For example, the millions of dollars that Procter & Gamble, Unilever, and Colgate–Palmolive pour into advertising their soaps and detergents may make it harder for small firms to crack these markets.

On the other hand, defenders of advertising argue that it offers real information on products and their characteristics (including their prices). The provision of such information lowers the consumers' cost of searching for goods, and permits them to make a rational choice among competing goods. Support for this interpretation of the value of advertising is found in the market: If it were not cheaper for sellers to provide the information in lieu of having consumers search for it, some sellers would cease to advertise and lower their prices to consumers by more than the cost of getting the information. Sellers not relying on advertising could then drive out of the market those sellers who continued to advertise. This, of course, has not happened. Moreover, in situations where consumers do not have perfect information, unsatisfactory products are simply not purchased again.

In response to the critics' claims that advertising is tasteless, defenders of advertising argue that the critics are merely trying to substitute their own subjective judgments for consumer sovereignty. In essence, the critics do not have faith in the intelligence of the average consumer, and the defenders do.

Regardless of one's position on the value of non-fraudulent information, almost all economists would accept the proposition that false advertising is socially wasteful. It harms consumers by inducing them to purchase goods and services that they might otherwise not purchase. Moreover, it harms competing producers who lose potential customers to the fraudulent advertiser.

Similar problems occur with deceptive advertising. Newspapers around the country, for example, have carried stories on people who have flown to corporate headquarters to claim the grand prize from a magazine seller, which annually sends millions of letters to Americans. These letters proclaim, in essence, "You are the winner of our $10 million prize" and then in much smaller print comes the disclaimer—"if your number is selected." While tens of millions of people are not fooled by the small print, what should be done about the dozen or so poor souls who show up at company headquarters each year to claim their prize? Should the government impose new restrictions on such advertisements? Or is such intervention necessary, since the vast majority of people are not misled by them?

II. PRIVATE REMEDIES FOR FALSE ADVERTISING

False advertising can injure both consumers and competitors. It is useful therefore to discuss the private remedies for false advertising according to the party suffering the economic injury. Consumer and competitor remedies are provided for under the common law and certain statutes.

A. Consumer Remedies

Most of the remedies for consumers injured by false advertising are based upon contract law and tort law. The common law provides remedies for breach of contract; statutory remedies for breach of express warranty exist as part of the *Uniform Commercial Code* (UCC). In practice, however, the common law of contracts affords very little protection to consumers injured by false advertising. In order to have an enforceable agreement, the common law of contracts requires an offer and acceptance. An advertisement is viewed as the solicitation of an offer from the consumer by the seller, not an offer to sell by the advertiser. Thus, because the seller is free to reject the consumer's offer on the advertised terms, the common law of contracts provides a remedy to consumers injured by false or deceptive advertising under only very limited circumstances.

The statutory remedy for breach of express warranty is also of only limited value to consumers harmed by false advertisements. Section 2-313 of the UCC provides that any statement, sample, or model of a product may constitute an express warranty, if such representation is the basis of the bargain between the consumer and the seller. Advertising claims may create express warranties, and if the representations turn out to be false, the consumer may sue for breach of warranty. However, UCC Section 2-313 is of little practical value because the courts require that the consumer reasonably rely on the advertising claims and often it can be shown that the consumer would have purchased the good at the same price even in the absence of the advertisement. Moreover, sellers are able to avoid liability for false or deceptive advertising by disclaiming the creation of an express warranty under the UCC. Thus, the UCC does not provide consumers with a great deal of protection against false advertising.

The common law of torts also provides limited protection to consumers from false advertising. The common law tort of **deceit** is available to consumers when an advertiser misrepresents the quality of goods and services. However, the tort is of little value because it is difficult for consumers to prove all of the following elements, which are necessary for them to win their cases:

- A misrepresentation of a material fact
- Knowledge by the seller that the information is false
- The sellers' intent that the consumer rely on the misrepresentation
- The consumer's justified reliance on the misrepresentation
- Damage to the consumer

It is not difficult to see how a seller's attorney can defend against an action based on the tort of deceit by attacking one or more of these elements. For example, statements made in convincing the consumer to purchase the product are often viewed by the courts as the seller's opinion, not fact. Or, it may be argued that such statements were merely "puffing," and that no consumer would reasonably rely on them. Consumers have a very difficult time recovering from an action based on the tort of deceit.

B. Competitor Remedies

False, fraudulent, or misleading advertising injures the advertiser's competitors as well as its customers. Three basic types of injuries to competitors may result from this type of advertising. First, the competitor may be injured when the false advertising attracts customers to the advertiser and away from the competitor. Second, if the advertiser falsely represents that the goods are those of the competitor, when in fact the goods are produced by another firm and are inferior, then the competitor is injured through lost sales as well as lost consumer goodwill. Third, the advertiser may harm its competitors by making false statements about the competitor.

False advertising messages can concern two subjects: (1) the products of the advertiser's competitors and (2) the advertiser's own products. The common law of torts provides competitors with a remedy for the first type of false message through the tort of disparagement. This tort is similar to the tort of defamation, except that the injury is to one's products or business rather than to one's reputation.

Protection from false statements concerning the advertiser's own products is found in a federal statute, the **Lanham Trademark Act**, passed by Congress in 1946. The most important provision of the Act dealing with false advertising is Section 43(a): "Any person who shall use in connection with any goods or services a false description or representation shall be liable … ." The Act also creates a private cause of action for any competitor likely to be injured by the false representation. Although the Act was initially interpreted very narrowly, most federal circuit courts now recognize the right of competitors to sue another false-advertising competitor for any possible injuries resulting from false advertising. For example, Gillette successfully sued Wilkinson Sword, Inc. after Wilkinson's ads falsely implied that users of Wilkinson razor blades would receive a shave that was "six times smoother" than users of other razor blades. Similarly, Coca-Cola, the producer of Minute Maid orange juice, successfully sued rival Tropicana Products under the provisions of the Lanham Act. Tropicana had falsely described its product as "pure, pasteurized juice as it comes from the orange," suggesting that its orange juice was fresher and more natural than that of Minute Maid. Coca-Cola's attorneys convinced the court that juice straight from the orange is not pasteurized; as such, Tropicana's advertising claim was false. Tropicana was forced to discontinue its advertisements that made this claim.

III. THE FEDERAL TRADE COMMISSION AND CONSUMER PROTECTION

Prior to the enactment of federal laws regulating advertising, the prevailing attitude among policymakers and advertisers was that consumers were responsible for what they bought. This doctrine was known as *caveat emptor*, or let the buyer beware. Advertisers freely and flagrantly exaggerated the qualities of their products, relying on the gullibility of their customers to believe even most outrageous claims about their products' benefits—an opportunity captured in the popular nineteenth-century phrase, "There's a sucker born every minute." While the common law theoretically allowed injured consumers to sue a seller for fraudulent advertisements, such lawsuits were expensive and difficult to win as discussed above.

The **Federal Trade Commission (FTC)** was established by Congress with the enactment into law of the Federal Trade Commission Act of 1914 (FTC Act). The FTC is headed by five commissioners appointed by the President of the United States and approved by the Senate.

It is an independent federal regulatory agency with a staff of 1,200 and a budget of $300 million. The FTC is charged with the enforcement of the Clayton Antitrust Act of 1914 and the FTC Act, which prohibits "unfair methods of competition." Initially, the FTC's efforts were focused on prosecuting unfair methods of competition as they affected businesses. The 1938 Wheeler-Lea Amendment to the FTC Act broadened the FTC's mandate to protect consumers from "unfair or deceptive practices." In 1975, the FTC powers were again expanded by the Magnuson-Moss Act, which gave FTC the power to act against all fraudulent practices and granted FTC power to regulate industry-wide behavior by formulating trade regulation rules.

A. FTC Structure and Procedure

FTC's Bureau of Consumer Protection is charged with regulating unfair and deceptive advertising. In response to consumer complaints and Congressional concerns, as well as its own experience, the FTC staff investigates a variety of practices that it believes may violate the deceptive advertising provisions of the law and of FTC regulations. The FTC's investigation is often informal at first, and frequently is quickly terminated if the target of the investigation agrees to stop engaging in the allegedly unfair or deceptive practice. More formal settlement procedures are available if and as the investigation continues. If the FTC determines during its investigation that there is an adequate basis for bringing a complaint, the defendant often settles the dispute with the FTC by agreeing to the terms of a **consent decree**. The advertiser may determine that FTC is right or that, while FTC is wrong, battling it in court is not worth the time, effort, or money. Consent decrees are similar to a contract between the accused and the FTC. Typically, they detail the terms of the settlement, and may include an agreement to discontinue the advertisement at least in its present state, redress for injured consumers, payment of penalties, and/or prohibitions of certain practices. However, the advertiser does not have to admit to any violations of the law. The consent decree is published in the *Federal Register* and the public and any affected parties have 60 days to challenge its terms. After hearing these public comments, the FTC then typically issues a consent order, which gives the consent decree the force of law.

If the defendant and the FTC cannot agree to a settlement, then the matter goes to trial before an administrative law judge (ALJ). The ALJ may dismiss the complaint or issue a **cease and desist order**, an order from the ALJ stating that the advertisement has indeed been found to be deceptive. If either the advertiser defendant or the FTC is not satisfied with the ALJ's ruling, that ruling can then be appealed by either party to the five FTC commissioners. If appealed, the ALJ's findings of fact and legal opinion are reviewed by the FTC commissioners. The commissioners can affirm, modify, or reverse ALJ's ruling. The Administrative Procedures Act provides for judicial review of the commissioners' decision by the U.S. Court of Appeals if the defendant advertiser chooses to challenge their decision.

However, these formal procedures take time. Since many advertising campaigns are over in a few months, the offending advertisements might have ended before the FTC can complete its formal proceedings. Therefore, in some instances—particularly when the FTC believes that an ad campaign is especially harmful to the public—the FTC will file a lawsuit in federal district court seeking an injunction to immediately discontinue an advertisement while it is being challenged in FTC proceedings.

To reduce the prevalence of false or fraudulent advertisements and reduce the costs of litigation, the FTC publishes information for advertisers that explains how the FTC interprets and enforces its advertising regulations. (This information is available on the FTC's website, www.ftc.gov.) Alternatively, advertisers can request an **advisory opinion** from the FTC as to whether a proposed advertisement will meet FTC standards.

Another approach used by the FTC is the issuance of **trade regulation rules** that are aimed at governing business practices in specific industries, such as used car dealers, telemarketers, or funeral homes. The FTC often utilizes this approach in industries where history suggests the probability of unfair or deceptive acts by a business is high or where consumers are particularly vulnerable if such practices occur. Trade regulation rules currently in place can be viewed on the FTC's website as well.

B. Remedies Available to the FTC

The FTC has broad powers in attacking and correcting deceptive and false advertising through issuing consent decrees and cease and desist orders. Another remedy available to the FTC is the issuance of an **affirmative disclosure order**, which requires an advertiser to disclose all relevant information about a product, both positive and negative. For instance, the makers of Geritol were forced to advertise that Geritol did little to cure anemia, despite previous advertisements that they had run claiming that the tonic helped "tired blood" **J.B. Williams Co. v. FTC**.[1] The effects of affirmative disclosure orders can be seen in many advertisements, such as those of banks marketing Certificates of Deposit ("there is a substantial penalty for early withdrawal"), manufacturers of diet products ("these results are not typical of the normal use of this product"), and automobile companies ("your actual mileage may differ from EPA estimates"). Obviously many businesses only take this action when forced to do so by the FTC, and affirmative disclosure orders are very unpopular among advertisers and businesspersons.

However, even more controversial is corrective advertising. **Corrective advertising** is an FTC remedy that requires the affirmative disclosure by the defendant that past advertising claims were misleading. In one famous case, the FTC ordered Warner-Lambert, the maker of Listerine mouth wash, to include in its advertisements the message "Listerine will not prevent colds or sore throats or lessen their severity" after determining that years of Listerine commercials asserted, without evidence, that Listerine was effective against the common cold.

Other products/manufacturers that have had to engage in corrective advertising include STP, Exxon, Volvo, and Doan's. In the case of STP, this manufacturer of a popular engine oil additive was forced to undertake corrective advertising stating that its advertised claims that the use of STP would reduce oil consumption were based on studies that were unreliable. Exxon was required to issue corrective advertisements acknowledging that its

---

1. **J.B. Williams Co. v. FTC 381 F2d 884 (1967).**

premium gasoline did not lower maintenance expenses or clean automobile engines better than its normal grades of gasoline, since they all contained the same amount of engine-cleaning additives. Volvo incurred the wrath of the FTC by running an advertisement purporting to demonstrate that Volvos were safer than other cars by showing a big-wheeled truck run over various models of cars and flatten them. The Volvo did not flatten like the other expensive cars. After investigating complaints filed by rival car manufacturers, the FTC discovered that Volvo had modified the Volvo depicted in the TV commercial by building extra supports in it. Volvo had to run corrective advertisements admitting that they had, in essence, rigged the demonstration. Similarly, Doan's was forced to run corrective ads admitting that the company's back pain medicine was no more effective than other pain relievers, despite two decades of advertisements claiming its product's pain-relieving abilities were superior to those of competitors.

IV. FTC REGULATION OF UNFAIR OR DECEPTIVE ACTS OR PRACTICES

The FTC's implementation of its consumer protection mandate to prevent unfair or deceptive acts or practices is illustrated by its activities in three related areas: deceptive price advertising, deceptive quality advertising, and unfair advertising. An important first step in studying this area is to consider the meaning of "**deceptive**." In general, the FTC will hold a particular act or practice to be deceptive if it finds that there is a representation, omission, or practice that is likely to mislead a reasonable consumer and result in material harm to the consumer. It is important to keep this definition in mind when considering the FTC's treatment of specific practices.

A. Deceptive Price Advertising

Price advertising is potentially one of the most informative types of advertising. This is especially evident when competing stores advertise the price of the same brand of the same product. Of course, when products differ in terms of quality, price is not the only dimension that influences consumer choices. Nevertheless, even when goods are of equal quality, it is possible for sellers to distort relative price comparisons and, in doing so, violate Section 5 of the FTC Act.

Deceptive price advertising typically involves situations where the seller is attempting to make a sale price look more attractive than it really is. For example, if a merchant offers a product for sale at "two for one," but the presale price of one unit was less than one half of the sale price, then the advertisement would be deceptive under Section 5. Similarly, an advertisement that states that the sale price is 50 percent off the regular price violates Section 5 if the advertised price is not reduced from a former regular price. Thus, for example, pre-ticketing of merchandise at a higher than regular retail price and then marking it down by 50 percent is a violation of Section 5.

In addition to such false price comparisons, Section 5 is also used to attack a similar deceptive pricing practice called "bait and switch." The "bait" of the bait and switch is an advertisement of a product at a very low price in an attempt to lure (pun intended) customers into the store. The "switch" occurs when the advertiser refuses to sell the advertised product and attempts to get the customer purchase a higher-priced substitute product. The FTC has investigated numerous bait and switch pricing schemes.

In 2004, the FTC filed a complaint against PWR Processing, Inc. and a group of affiliated Colorado mortgage brokers in what can be described as a sophisticated variation of bait and switch. The defendants promised consumers that they could provide them with "no fee," low interest rate mortgages on their homes. They enticed home owners to apply for two loans, one carrying a high, above-market interest rate and the second a lower, competitive interest rate. PWR claimed it would rebate to the consumers payments it received from lenders issuing the high-interest-rate loans. The consumers could then use the rebates to pay the fees associated with the low-interest-rate loan and use the low-interest-rate loan to pay off the higher interest rate loan. Often, however, consumers were granted the loan carrying the higher interest rate but not the one carrying the lower interest rate, leaving them to pay both the fees and the higher interest rate.

B. Deceptive Quality Claims

As suggested above, consumer demand for a particular product is dependent upon both the price and perceived quality of the product. Thus, deceptive quality claims can be as harmful to consumers as deceptive price advertising. There are two basic steps to the legal analysis of deceptive quality claims. First, it must be determined what claim, if any, is being made by the advertisement. Second, the identified claim must be shown to be deceptive.

In determining whether a particular claim is being made implicitly or explicitly by an advertisement, the standard applied is that of a reasonable consumer. The advertisement is viewed in its entirety and in a reasonable context. For example, a gasoline company's claim that its gasoline will "put a tiger in your tank" is not literally construed. The FTC sometimes relies on consumer surveys to determine the reasonableness of charges that implicit quality claims are being made in advertisements. In other instances, it is clear that the advertiser is making a claim about the quality of its product. For example, if the advertisement says that a certain bleach product will get shirts whiter than other bleaches, then the advertiser has made an explicit statement about the quality of the product in a manner that suggests that the statement is to be believed. Such statements can be tested for their truthfulness, which brings us to the second step in the analysis of deceptive quality claims. When an advertiser makes a claim about the quality of its product, the FTC requires that the advertiser have a reasonable basis for that claim. Businesses need to be careful to be sure that they are able to substantiate any claims made in their advertising.

Regulating deceptive advertising has been a high priority of the FTC because it interferes with the ability of consumers to spend their incomes wisely. For instance, in 1993, the FTC filed deceptive advertising complaints against five large marketers of weight-loss programs. The FTC argued that these companies made unsubstantiated claims about the efficacy of their products and that the testimonials featured in their ads were not indicative of the actual weight loss experienced by the typical users of their products. Although two of the five (Weight Watchers International and Jenny Craig, Inc.) initially resisted, by 1997 all five companies signed consent decrees, promising to have scientific data supporting any weight loss claims they made; any testimonials offered by users in advertisements would have to be typical of the experience of product users, unless accompanied by a statement proclaiming "This result is not typical; other users may be less successful"; and all of the advertisements would include the disclaimer, "For many dieters, weight loss is temporary."

In more recent cases involving deceptive advertising, in 2013, the FTC barred the marketers of POM Wonderful 100% Pomegranate Juice from making any claim that its products are "effective in the diagnosis, cure, mitigation, treatment, or prevention of any disease" without supporting evidence from two separate scientifically valid human clinical trials. The FTC found that the company's claims that pomegranate juice was effective in treating heart disease, prostate cancer, and erectile dysfunction lacked any competent and scientific evidence. Similarly, the FTC negotiated $40 million in consumer refunds with Skechers USA, after determining that the Skechers' claims that its toning shoes would facilitate weight loss, improve cardiovascular health, and strengthen and tone muscles were unfounded. As part of its complaint, the FTC noted that some of Skechers' advertisements featured an endorsement by Dr. Steven Gautreau, a chiropractor who conducted an "independent" clinical study of the benefits of wearing Skechers footwear. The FTC's analysis of this clinical study found that it did not support the claims made in the advertising campaign, nor did Skechers mention that Gatreau was married to a Skechers marketing executive and that Skechers failed to disclose that it funded his clinical study.

The FTC is kept very busy simply pursuing false claims made by marketers of diet products and dietary supplements. In 2005, for example, FTC alleged that Body Wise International failed to substantiate advertisements that claimed that its AG-immune dietary supplement prevented or cured asthma, cancer, and HIV/AIDS. The company agreed to pay $3.5 million in fines to settle the case. That same year, Enforma Natural Products was banned from marketing or advertising weight-reduction products after the FTC found that claims for many of its products, including Fat Trapper, Fat Trapper Plus, and Exercise in a Bottle were unsubstantiated. Similarly, Sagee U.S.A. Group, Inc. was fined $10,000 after the FTC found that the company's claims for its dietary supplements, which were targeted to Californians of Chinese and Vietnamese ethnicity, were unsubstantiated. Among the illnesses purported to be cured by Sagee's products were insomnia, migraine headaches, cerebral embolisms, cerebral hemorrhages, strokes, epilepsy, Parkinson's disease, tinnitus, autism, Alzheimer, and senile dementia.

C. FTC Regulation of Unfair Advertising

In addition to prohibiting deceptive acts or practices, Section 5 of the Federal Trade Commission Act also prohibits "unfair ... acts or practices affecting commerce." The FTC thus regulates advertising practices that it finds to be unfair, even though they might not be deceptive or fraudulent. Although it recognizes that it is difficult to find a definition of "unfair" upon which everyone can agree, the FTC has developed the following test for determining when it will prosecute alleged unfair practices:

> To justify a finding of unfairness, the injury must satisfy three tests. It must be substantial; it must not be outweighed by any countervailing benefits to consumers or competition that the practice produces; and it must be an injury that consumers themselves could not reasonably have avoided. (FTC Statement on Unfairness, p. 3)

The first test focuses on economic harm or unreasonable risks to health and safety. The cumulative size of the harm determines whether it meets the "substantial" test. The harm may be substantial if a few people suffer large damages or a large number of people each suffer small damages. The second test focuses on the net benefit to consumers and/or the marketplace of a practice. As noted by the FTC,

> A seller's failure to present complex technical data on his product may lessen a consumer's ability to choose, for example, but may also reduce the initial price he must pay for the article. The Commission is aware of these tradeoffs and will not find that a practice unfairly injures consumers unless it is injurious in its net effects.

Thus, for example, the FTC does not require a maker of alarm clock radios to provide a 200-page technical manual to each consumer detailing how the clock is made or the failure rates of the parts that go into it. The cost of such a manual will be large, and the value to most consumers small. Moreover, requiring such a manual might allow alarm clock manufacturers to steal each other's technology and trade secrets, thereby reducing innovation and investment in this industry.

The third test has proven to be the most controversial. Much of U.S. public policy dealing with economic affairs revolves around the concept of consumer sovereignty. Consumer sovereignty assumes that individual consumers are the ones best able to decide how to spend their money. Indeed, the concept is generally sound: Mary is the one who is best able to decide whether she should spend $50 on a fancy dinner or buying a new skirt. As noted by the FTC policy statement, "We anticipate that consumers will survey the available alternatives, choose those that are most desirable, and avoid those that are inadequate or unsatisfactory" (FTC Statement on Unfairness, p. 3). The third test suggests, however, that there are certain situations or certain sales techniques that may make it difficult for consumers to make decisions effectively. In those cases, the FTC believes it is appropriate "to halt some form of seller behavior that unreasonably creates or takes advantage of an obstacle to the free exercise of consumer decision-making" (p. 4). A hypothetical example offered by the FTC is a dishwasher repair person who disassembles the appliance and then refuses to put it back together unless the consumer signs an expensive service contract.

The FTC's enforcement of unfair advertising has often proven to be very controversial. In 1978, the Commission launched an investigation into advertisements targeted at children. It proposed to ban all TV commercials aimed at young children and severely restrict commercials for heavily sugared food aimed at older children. The logic was that these audiences would be unduly swayed by the commercials and, because of their age, would not be able to carefully weigh the costs and benefits of consuming such products. The FTC also proposed trade regulation rules to govern funeral directors that would have required them to provide consumers with detailed information on different services offered by them, as well as specific prices for each service. Similarly, the FTC proposed trade regulation rules to govern the business practices of used car dealers. These proposed regulations created an enormous political backlash against the FTC by affected businesses. In response, in 1980, the Congress temporarily refused to appropriate any funds to operate the FTC. It then passed the Federal Trade Commission Improvements Act, which ordered the FTC to focus its energies on regulating deceptive or misleading advertising, rather than on truthful advertising that might be unfair. After a few years, however, Congress revisited the issue and decided that once again the FTC should regulate unfair advertising, as well as deceptive or misleading advertising. The FTC's actions in the mid-1990s to halt the "Old Joe Camel" advertising campaign provide an example of its renewed attacks on unfair advertising. In this case, the FTC accused the R.J. Reynolds Tobacco Company of promoting a dangerous and addictive product to consumers who were in fact too young to legally purchase it and too unsophisticated to assess the benefits and costs of consuming the product. In 1997, the FTC in a 3-2 vote banned the Joe Camel commercials and mandated that the company run corrective ads educating teenagers on the dangers of smoking. The FTC's actions were reinforced by the 1999 settlement of a $206-billion lawsuit filed by the attorneys general of 46 states, in which the tobacco companies agreed to end all billboard advertising and terminate the use of cartoon characters in their ads.

V. POLICY ANALYSIS

The FTC's regulation of deceptive advertising is based on the assumption that an information-problem type of market failure results in consumer abuse. Thus, it is appropriate that a policy analysis of the case for government regulation of advertising begin with an identification of the alleged market failure. Proponents of government intervention argue that, in the absence of government intervention, consumers would not have available accurate and necessary information on either the quality of many products (including relatively simple products like light bulbs, gasoline, and cigarettes) or the price of complicated bundles of goods and services (such as funeral services, insurance contracts, and legal services). As a result, under some circumstances, consumers may make decisions that consistently end up reducing their welfare.

Critics of the FTC's regulation of deceptive advertising argue that there are adequate market mechanisms to regulate deceptive advertising. At least three such mechanisms can be identified. First, consumers (as a group) are not dumb and are not gullible. Much deceptive advertising has little impact on consumers. This view of consumer sovereignty is illustrated by a poster in many U.S. Post Offices, designed to reduce mail fraud, which states "If it sounds too good to be true, it probably isn't." Of course, some consumers can be consistently fooled, but this raises the question of whether they can ever be protected by government regulations. Moreover, fraud is less likely to occur with major ticket purchases than with small sales because consumers have greater incentive to invest in information on the quality of the goods or services when more is at stake. Thus, the fraud that occurs is not likely to be of significant magnitude.

Second, the market encourages firms to develop reputations for honest and fair dealing with consumers (goodwill) and discourages firms from engaging in behavior that reduces such goodwill. The penalty for making false claims is that a firm will develop a reputation for dishonesty. Eventually, the seller's false claims will be detected and the demand for the firm's products will decline. If the firm sells a product that typically leads to repeat sales, then the cost in terms of fraudulent or deceptive advertising will show up with the failure of customers to return.

These observations on goodwill also help identify situations where fraud is most likely to occur. In one class of such situations, the quality of a product or service is difficult to ascertain even after it has been consumed. A good example of this is medical care. In another situation where one would expect fraud to occur, the seller's profitability is not dependent on repeat purchases. A good example of this is a gasoline service station along an interstate highway in the middle of West Texas. One would expect that such a service station would provide better service to its local customers than to travelers with engine trouble. In fact, the service station example encompasses both types of situations because tourists are notoriously vulnerable to false diagnoses of problems with their automobiles (e.g., fixing things that are not broken). In these situations, however, government regulations will likely be ignored. For example, even if a tourist has been swindled, it is unlikely that the tourist will go to the trouble of reporting the fraud (i.e., the service station gets away with it).

The role of consumers in this situation should not be forgotten. Tourists driving through West Texas are aware of the risks of fraud should they encounter automobile problems and many of them take steps to protect themselves. Automobile clubs, such as the American Automobile Association, provide a nationwide network of certified service stations whose quality is signaled to club members (and, indeed, to the general public) by its affiliation with the club. Other examples of such market-generated private regulatory systems include Consumer Reports, the Better Business Bureau, and Underwriters Laboratory.

A third market constraint on false advertising is competition. If a business firm is attracting customers by engaging in false advertising, competing firms have the expertise to detect the fraud and the incentive to expose it to the public through their own advertising programs. Presumably the false advertiser would lose customers as a result of such exposure, or, perhaps more likely, would not engage in the fraud in the first place for fear of exposure by its competitors. This market constraint is subject to at least two caveats, both of which relate to the competitive structure of the particular market. If the firm engaged in false advertising is a monopolist, then there are no competitors to expose the fraud and consumers cannot purchase close substitute products because, by definition, there are no close substitutes for the monopoly product. On the other hand, if the firm is in a competitive industry where the costs of entry and exit by competing firms are relatively low, then the firm may simply exit the industry when it is discovered to be dishonest.

These three market mechanisms will not reduce the amount of deceptive advertising to zero; on the other hand, even the FTC agrees that its regulations cannot attain such an ideal state. Thus, the relevant comparison in deciding whether the FTC regulations are cost justified is balancing the costs saved as a result of a reduction in deceptive advertising resulting from the regulation against the costs of administering and complying with the FTC regulations. Clearly, if the regulations do not result in less deceptive advertising than would occur in an unregulated market, then the costs of implementing the program cannot be justified. This debate promises to continue for years.

CHAPTER SUMMARY

Many of the regulations governing advertising attempt to correct an information-problem type of market failure. Advertising regulations are designed to make sure the information given to the public is correct, allowing them adequate information for engaging in comparison shopping.

Economists disagree over the productive value of advertising. The basic disagreement centers on the information content of advertising. Some economists argue that advertising conveys valuable information on products, while others argue that advertising does not convey any valuable information and is wasteful. Nevertheless, all economists agree that fraudulent advertising is socially wasteful, harming both consumers and rival producers.

False advertising can injure both consumers and competitors. The common law provides little protection for either group. The primary protection for competitors injured by false advertising is found in the Lanham Trademark Protection Act. The Federal Trade Commission (FTC) exercises an important role in consumer protection through its regulation of "unfair and deceptive" practices. The FTC's regulation of deceptive advertising is based on the belief that an information-type of market failure results in consumer abuse. Critics of the FTC's policies argue that there are adequate market mechanisms to regulate deceptive advertising.

12

EMPLOYMENT REGULATION

Employment relationship today is one that is highly regulated by the federal government. This chapter deals with the general construct of employment regulation in the United States in the twenty-first century. Chapter 8 dealt with a more specific aspect of the said regulation—the labor union—management relationship.

Before we proceed, one important question to ask is why there should be *any* government intervention in the employment relationship? Can't "free markets" be counted on so that employers will always hire the best employee regardless of race, creed, religion, sex, etc.—that is, that employers will not engage in employment discrimination? Can't "free markets" be counted on to make sure employers will treat employees "fairly," paying them a fair wage, etc.—, that is, if the employer doesn't pay a fair wage how can he or she ever attract good employees? This chapter will attempt to answer some of these questions and to analyze situations in the employment context that might arise so as to cause "market failures" justifying government intervention, along the same lines as our earlier discussion in Chapter 8 of the "market failure" of the Great Depression and how it led to the enactment of the Norris LaGuardia and Wagner Acts.

I. UNREGULATED MARKETS—"GLOW BOYS AND GLOW GIRLS"/WORKER SAFETY

A number of years ago there was a feature article in a leading newspaper about people who had jobs inside nuclear reactors. The newspaper dubbed these employees to be "glow boys" and "glow girls"! The nuclear reactor jobs were extremely well paying and involved only a few minutes of work (you had to go inside the reactor and turn some screws—during which time you got "zapped" with radiation) per month. Would you take a job in a nuclear reactor earning about $100,000 per month and involving only 15 minutes a month of work? Would you take such a job if it paid $1 million per month? What if it paid $25 million per month and you only had to work one (15 minute) month (and probably never had to work again?!)

Should the government regulate this type of employment? Should the government prevent people from taking these jobs because they are too "dangerous"?

To these questions, most of us would probably answer "no." In this situation, the folks are *clearly aware* of all the risks involved in their job, and indeed are required to sign special waiver forms stating that they will not sue their employer should they encounter health problems due to their work. Obviously, an employer is not paying these people $100,000 for 15 minutes of work because this is a risk-free job. These employees, however, are openly willing to *trade off* health risks for the money. What business does the government have in intervening in this "free market" decision?

The problem, though, is that people don't always *know* the full risks involved in their jobs. This causes something known as a "market failure"—which means that "free markets" don't always work perfectly. A good example of this occurred during World War II. After the Japanese destroyed our Navy at Pearl Harbor, considerable efforts were devoted during the war to building ships. An important component of virtually all the ships being built was a substance called *asbestos*, which was the best fire-retardant of that day. Thousands of workers helped build these ships and worked with asbestos everyday. These workers all received "average" wages—no one had any idea working with asbestos would present any health or other problems. A few decades later, though, it was found that asbestos was *extremely* harmful to workers' health—gradually eating away their lungs. Thus, there was a *"market failure."* Workers at the time did not have full knowledge of the danger of asbestos, and consequently did not demand any sort of wage premium for working with the substance. "Market failures" of this kind ultimately led to the passage of the federal **Occupational Safety and Health Act (OSHA)** whereby the federal government now plays a major role in monitoring workplace safety and providing workers with information on workplace health risks.

II. FAIR LABOR STANDARDS ACT

In 1938, the U.S. Congress enacted the **Fair Labor Standards Act (FLSA)**. The most significant aspect of this legislation is that it provides for a **minimum wage** for most all American workers. The minimum wage started out very low (25 cents per hour) and has risen over the years to around 30 times this level. The FLSA also mandates that employees working over 40 hours per week be paid overtime (at the rate of 1½ times their basic wage), and has some restrictions on the usage of child labor.

Why do we have the FLSA? Why does the federal government get at all involved in wage setting? Shouldn't this be a matter solely for the employee and employer; for example, if an employee is willing to work for $4.00 per hour (significantly below the minimum wage) why should the federal government prevent such employment (perhaps the employee really wants the experience, etc.)?

The answers to this again turn on the concept of "market failure." The FLSA was passed during the Great Depression during which (as was discussed in previous chapters) there was a 30 percent unemployment rate and individual employees had virtually no bargaining power. The FLSA assured that employees would receive a "fair" wage for their work and not be unduly "exploited" by employers who during this period had tremendous power over their workers. This obviously poses the interesting question of whether in today's economy the FLSA should be repealed? What are the arguments in favor of maintaining the FLSA even in today's economic environment? Is an unemployment rate of seven or eight percent "low"?

Another goal of the FLSA when it was enacted was to make sure that everyone who worked full time would earn enough to stay above the poverty line. Today, however, the approximately $15,000 per year an individual would earn working full time at the minimum wage is *not* enough to keep above the poverty line in many areas of the United States. Consequently, there have been pushes in Congress to even further raise the minimum wage to provide a clear "**living wage**," and many individual cities (e.g., the City of Boston) have already done this with regard to people working in their jurisdictions. (The FLSA provides a federal/national minimum wage, but does not prevent individual states or cities from mandating higher minimum wages in their jurisdictions.)

Do you think the federal minimum wage should be significantly raised to say $15 per hour to provide a clear "living wage" (around $600 per week)? Is not it better having folks out working at this wage than being on social assistance programs or welfare? What are some of the possible *negatives* of dramatically raising the minimum wage? Would employers be more or less likely to invest in technological substitutes for labor? How might a dramatic increase in the minimum wage affect labor unions?

III. EMPLOYMENT-AT-WILL

A. Overview

The classic rule of "**employment-at-will**" was expressed in 1884 by the Tennessee Supreme Court in the statement:

> Men must be left, without interference to buy and sell where they please, and to discharge or retain employees-at-will for good cause or for no cause, or even for bad cause without thereby being guilty of an unlawful act. ... all may dismiss their employees at-will, be they many or few, for good cause, for no cause or even for cause morally wrong, without being guilty of legal wrong. (**Payne v.. Western & Atl. R. R.**)[1]

Under the "laissez faire" capitalistic approach of employment-at-will, employers are free to set virtually any personal or other standard for employment and employees that don't abide by that standard can be fired. These standards do *not* have to have anything directly to do with the given job or its performance. For example, one major corporation (headed by a later-to-become politically prominent CEO) believed strongly in "traditional family values" and for many years fired any employee that got a *divorce*. Courts have also, pursuant to the doctrine of employment-at-will, upheld employee discharges based on the fact that their employer did not like the charity where they were volunteering during their spare time. In an interesting case in the Fall of 2012, the Iowa Supreme Court upheld, under the

---

1. **Payne v. Western & Atl. R. R. 81 Tenn. 507 (1884).**

doctrine of employment-at-will, a dentist's firing of a dental assistant that worked for him because she was too "attractive"/"irresistible" and a "threat" to his marriage.

The flip side of the employment-at-will doctrine's "laissez faire" approach, of course, is that employees are (unlike in many foreign countries) free to quit their job at any time for any reason. Employees are generally not legally required to provide any "notice" to the employer before they quit a job.

B. State Court Intervention

Over the past two decades, however, state courts throughout the country have been chipping away at the doctrine of employment-at-will. The most prominent basis for state court intervention is where the discharge is deemed to contravene "public policy." For example, numerous courts have intervened where employers have fired employees for being out on jury duty. In essence, these courts have held that the public policy in favor of jury trials outweighs the employer's right to fire an employee for missing work. Similarly, courts have overturned the discharge of employees who were fired because they refused to disobey the law (e.g., refused to perjure themselves at the employer's request). In a classic 1985 case, for example, the Texas Supreme Court held that an employee in Texas cannot be fired for refusing to perform a criminally illegal act ordered by his employer.[2] The Supreme Court of Minnesota issued a similar ruling two years later in the *Phipps* case below.

Phipps v. Clark Oil & Refining Corporation
Supreme Court of Minnesota
408 N.W. 2d 569 (1987)

FACTS: Mark A. Phipps worked at a full service gas station owned by Clark Oil & Refining Corporation. A customer pulled up and requested her car gas tank be filled with leaded gas, even though her vehicle was clearly designed to take unleaded gas only. Phipps refused to dispense the leaded gas maintaining it was against federal law to do so. Phipps was then fired by the gas station manager. Phipps brought a lawsuit, but the trial court dismissed his suit and upheld the right of Minnesota employers to hire and fire employees "at will." A state appeals court, however, reversed this decision, and the employer now appealed this decision to the state supreme court.

HOLDING: The Supreme Court of Minnesota held that Phipps' discharge violated important "public policy" as enunciated in laws like the federal Clean Air Act. Consequently, his discharge was illegal.

C. Montana Statute

While some states (like Minnesota) have passed laws preventing the discharge of employees for refusal to violate state/federal law or similar things, the state of Montana is the only

---

2. **Sabine Pilot Service Inc. v. Hauck, 687 S.W. 2d 733 (Texas 1985).**

state in the United States to provide all employees comprehensive protection from employ-ment-at-will. Under the Montana law, an employee's discharge is unlawful if it is against "public policy," in violation of an employer-written personnel policy, or "not for good cause," assuming that the employee has passed the employer's probationary period. In return for this protection, however, the Montana law generally limits the amount of dam-ages an employee can recover for a "wrongful discharge" to a period of four years plus interest. Relevant portions of the **Montana Wrongful Discharge From Employment Act** are set forth below.

State of Montana
Wrongful Discharge From Employment Act

39-2-901. Short title. This part may be cited as the "Wrongful Discharge From Employ-ment Act."

39-2-902. Purpose. This part sets forth certain rights and remedies with respect to wrongful discharge. Except as limited in this part, employment having no specified term may be terminated at the will of either the employer or the employee on notice to the other for any reason considered sufficient by the terminating party. Except as provided in 39-2-2912, this part provides the exclusive remedy for a wrongful discharge from employment.

39-2-903. Definitions. In this part, the following definitions apply:

(1) "Good cause" means reasonable job-related grounds for dismissal based on a failure to satisfactorily perform job duties, disruption of the employer's operation, or other legitimate business reason. The legal use of a lawful product by an individual off the employer's premises during non-working hours is not a legitimate business rea-son, unless the employer acts within the provisions of 39-2-313(3) or (4).
(2) "Lost wages" means the gross amount of wages that would have been reported to the internal revenue service as gross income on Form W-2 and includes additional compensation deferred at the option of the employee.
(3) "Public policy" means a policy in effect at the time of the discharge concerning the public health, safety, or welfare established by constitutional provision, statute, or administrative rule.

39-2-904. Elements of wrongful discharge. A discharge is wrongful only if:

(1) It was in retaliation for the employee's refusal to violate public policy or for report-ing a violation of public policy;
(2) The discharge was not for good cause and the employee had completed the employ-er's probationary period of employment; or
(3) The employer violated the express provisions of its own written personnel policy.

39-2-905. Remedies. (1) If an employer has committed a wrongful discharge, the employee may be awarded lost wages and fringe benefits for a period not to exceed 4 years from the date of discharge, together with interest thereon. Interim earnings, including amounts the employee could have earned with reasonable diligence, must be deducted from the amount awarded for lost wages. Before interim earnings are deducted from lost wages, there must be deducted from the interim earning any reasonable amounts expended by the employee in searching for, obtaining, or relocating to new employment.

(1) The employee may recover punitive damages otherwise allowed by law if it is established by clear and convincing evidence that the employer engaged in actual fraud or actual malice in the discharge of the employee in violation of 39-2-904(1).
(2) There is no right under any legal theory to damages for wrongful discharge under this part for pain and suffering, emotional distress, compensatory damages, punitive damages, or any other form of damages, except as provided for in subsections (1) and (2).

D. Off-Duty Conduct Statutes

One very interesting part of the "good cause" definition in the Montana statute contained in Section 39-2-903 (5) above deals with the use of "lawful" products during non-working hours. More specifically, the provision states that the "legal use of a lawful product by an individual off the employer's premises during non-working hours" does not generally constitute a "legitimate business reason" for discharge. Thus, an employer cannot fire an employee because he or she was seen drinking beer or smoking a cigarette on Saturday night at a local restaurant. About 30 states in the United States (in large measure at the behest of the so-called "tobacco lobby"!) have passed similar **off-duty conduct statutes**. These laws usually prohibit employers from firing or even refusing to hire an employee because he or she is a smoker. (Are there any justifiable reasons why an employer would not want a smoker in his or her employee?)

To date, a handful of states such as California, Colorado, New York, and North Dakota have taken this a step further by protecting not only off-duty use of lawful products (tobacco, alcohol, etc.) by employees, but also providing protection against employee discharge for "legal recreational activities" or "lawful activities" off the employer's premises during non-working hours. These broad statutes create a vast and somewhat muddled new exception to the doctrine of employment-at-will, and are only now being preliminarily interpreted by the state courts.

For example, the Wal-Mart Corporation traditionally had rather strict "anti-fraternization" policies, which prohibited certain types of co-worker dating. This policy, however, has been challenged under the State of New York's off-duty conduct statute, which prohibits the discharge of employees for legal off-hours, off-premises "recreational activities." While dating a co-worker is clearly "legal" under New York state law, the question before the courts has been whether it is a "recreational activity"!! One state court in New York has said it is not, and upheld Wal-Mart's decision to fire an employee for dating a co-worker. Another court though, has held that the New York off-duty law is meant to apply to any employee social activity, dating, or otherwise, so long as it occurs off work hours and away from the employer's premises. Obviously, this is a very interesting and developing area of the law, and one which has become even more important in the age of social media such as Facebook and the Internet. For example, can an employee be fired for material he or she discusses on his or her blog? In an earlier chapter, we learned that if an employee discusses "working conditions" in this manner such actions may be protected under the National Labor Relations Act (NLRA). But what about just general social media "posts"? Can, for example, an employer fire an employee for a purportedly "risqué" picture posted on his or her Facebook page?

IV. EMPLOYMENT DISCRIMINATION

A. Overview

Over the past five decades or so, a vast array of new laws have been enacted protecting employees from "discrimination." Employees today cannot be discriminated against in hiring, firing, or while on the job, on the basis of their sex, race, religion, age, national origin, and disability, among other things. One initial question is why would an employer ever logically discriminate? In a "free market" approach, won't employers always hire the *best* (potentially most productive) employee regardless of his or her race, sex, religion, age, etc? Moreover, won't a "rational" employer always promote and reward employees based on their "merit" without regard for things like their sex, national origin, etc.? What's the "market failure" here justifying the need for government intervention?

The above question is a complex one, but one possible answer might turn on a principal/agent problem (discussed in the chapter on corporate governance). An owner (principal) of a small entrepreneurial business may indeed always hire the "best" worker without regard to any of the aforementioned factors. The owner of a small computer company just starting out might care less if his or her employee is purple with white polka dots, so long as the employee is highly productive. However, not all companies are small owner-run entrepreneurial ventures. Hiring is frequently done by managers with strong input from other employees (agents) (and the evidence is that employees often want to hire people they like—generally people that are like them). Moreover, in many types of organizations employee "productivity" may be much harder to measure. Government agencies, for example, are non-profit in orientation, and it is sometimes very difficult to measure exactly how much a given employee is contributing to some sort of "bottom line." Moreover, in government entities the principal/agent distinction is at best very blurred.

In what types of organizations would you expect to find more discrimination? What types of hiring officials are most likely to discriminate? Can even highly aggressive government intervention ever really get rid of such "discrimination"?

B. Equal Pay Act/Comparable Worth

In 1963, the U.S. Congress enacted one of the first anti-discrimination laws, the **Equal Pay Act (EPA)**. This law prohibits employers from discriminating against employees by paying lower wages to employees of one sex versus the other sex for the same or equal work. The law was basically designed to eliminate discrimination against women whereby females regularly got paid less than males doing the same job. Under the EPA, men and women doing "substantially equal" work must be paid the same. The EPA thus represents an apples versus apples comparison—a large accounting firm hiring recent college graduate male and female accountants must pay these individuals the same pay; that is, it cannot discriminate and, for example, pay female entry-level accountants less (e.g., on the grounds that the female accountants may be more likely to start families and leave the firm). The law does allow, however, for some exceptions to this if the pay differentials are based on factors other than sex; for example, accountants are paid solely on a per-hour billed basis, and for some other reasons. In general, though, the EPA mandates that men and women doing essentially the exact same job must receive the same rate of pay.

Despite the EPA, however, a substantial gap between the average earnings of women and the average earnings of men working full time in the United States continues to exist. In general, women tend to earn about 75 percent of what men earn in full-time employment. A large part of the reason for this is that many relatively low-paying jobs; for example, social work, domestic service, elementary school teaching, clerical work, and nursing, tend to be female dominated. This has led to some observers advocating the concept of **comparable worth**. This concept says that jobs that are evaluated to be "comparable" should be paid the same. Thus, if a female-dominated job such as nursing is judged to be overall comparable to a male-dominated job such as accounting, then nurses and accountants should receive the same rate of pay. Advocates of comparable worth believe such a concept is the only way to overcome general societal wage bias against women. To date, the concept of comparable worth has *not* been adopted in the United States, although it has been adopted in some other countries.

Can you think of any arguments against the concept of comparable worth? Do you think the EPA represents good or bad public policy?

C. Civil Rights Act of 1964, Title VII

1. Overview

In 1964, the U.S. Congress enacted a major piece of civil rights legislation, Title VII of which deals with employment discrimination. Title VII prohibits discrimination in hiring, terms or conditions of employment, referral of applicants, etc. based on race, color, religion, sex, or national origin. Enforcement of Title VII is the responsibility of the **U.S. Equal Employment Opportunity Commission** (EEOC). In Texas, under a work-sharing arrangement with the EEOC, the Civic Rights Division of the Texas Workforce Commission, www .twc.state.tx.us, also has the authority to handle Title VII cases. Title VII generally applies to all United States employers with 15 or more employees (note that small, perhaps owner-operated businesses are exempted from the law's coverage). One interesting question that has arisen, however, is whether professional partnerships, such as accounting partnerships, are deemed to be "employers" for purposes of the Act. In general, the courts have held such partnerships to be **employers** under Title VII.

2. *Disparate Treatment versus Disparate Impact*

There are two major theories of enforcement under Title VII. The first is **disparate treatment**. This theory says that it is unlawful to treat employees disparately or differently on the basis of their race, sex, religion, etc. For example, it would be unlawful for a strict Baptist employer to never give raises or promotions to Catholic employees regardless of their job performance. In such a situation, the employer would clearly be discriminating on the basis of religion. Catholic employees would point to comparable Baptist employees in making their case; for example, my sales performance is as good as or better than Baptist employees doing the job, but they get raises and I do not. While there are different burdens of proof in disparate treatment cases, the basic concept is rather uncontroversial; that is, people of most all political stripes agree that it should be unlawful for employers to clearly treat employees differently based on their religion, sex, color, national origin, etc.

In contrast, the concept of **disparate impact** is far more controversial. This theory says that there may be some employer practices that although neutral on their face have an illegal discriminatory impact. For example, an employer policy that it will only hire employees 5 feet 8 inches tall or higher in no way directly discriminates against any protected class. However, what's the *impact* of such a requirement? (Hint: Are more women or men 5 feet 8 inches tall or taller?) Or, what if an employer refuses to hire employees with any prior "arrest records"? The classic case in this area, **Griggs v. Duke Power Co.**, is set forth below.

Griggs v. Duke Power Co.
Supreme Court of the United States
401 U.S. 424 (1971)

FACTS: Prior to the Civil Rights Act, Duke Power Company openly discriminated against African-Americans in hiring decisions at its Dan River Plant. African-American employees brought this action to challenge the company's requirement of a high school diploma or passing intelligence tests for employment in certain jobs.

HOLDING: The Supreme Court held that the employer had not shown the "business necessity" of having a high school diploma or passing an intelligence test for work as a janitor; that is, there was no demonstrable relationship between having a high school diploma/passing a test and doing this job. Consequently, the use of such criteria was held to have an unlawful "disparate impact" on a protected class.

CASE QUESTIONS:

1. After *Griggs*, are height and weight requirements unlawful? What permissible requirements could be substituted?
2. Comment on the proposition that the rule of law derived in *Griggs* can be summarized as: "[a]ny test used must measure the person for the job and not the person in the abstract."

3. Sex Discrimination

Title VII prohibits discrimination on the basis of sex. Thus, employers cannot treat employees differently in terms of hiring, promotions, firing, etc. because they are female or male. Also, under *Griggs*, employees must demonstrate a clear business necessity if they adopt policies such as minimum height requirements that have a disparate impact on one sex—females. The EEOC and the courts have uniformly held, however, that Title VII's protections against sex discrimination do not apply to homosexuals or transsexuals. Some state and local discrimination laws (which can be broader in nature than Title VII) do provide rights along these lines; that is, protection against discrimination on the basis of sexual orientation.

In recent years, the courts have interpreted Title VII's prohibition against sex discrimination to include protection against **sexual harassment**. Traditionally, the courts protected employees from **"quid pro quo sexual harassment"**; that is, unless you have sex with me I'm going to have you fired. In the famous 1986 U. S. Supreme Court case of **Meritor Savings Bank v. Vinson**[3] the nation's highest court held that employees can also have a cause of action for **environmental sexual harassment** where such harassment is pervasive enough in nature. Examples of environmental sexual harassment would include sexual comments, jokes and innuendoes, and the display of sexually oriented pictures (such as cutouts from *Playboy* magazine) in the office. One interesting question is to what extent can employers lawfully take certain steps to prevent situations that might lead to sexual harassment. For example, can employers outrightly prohibit all employee dating? (See earlier discussion on the New York off-duty privacy statute). Moreover, even if employers can lawfully prohibit all dating among co-workers, is such a policy good human resources management? Can such a policy really be enforced?

Another interesting issue that has arisen has been with respect to the workplace "reporting" of dating/sexual relation situations. For example, the University of Texas at Austin apparently permits professor/student and athletic coach/athlete dating so long as the relationship is "reported" to higher-level supervisors. Failure to report such relationships, though, can lead to employee discharge. Thus, in January of 2013, the University fired Bev Kearney, women's track and field coach, the University of Texas, Austin, because she failed to report a consensual relationship she had with one of the members of the team.

In certain situations, though, the courts have permitted employers to explicitly discriminate on the basis of sex. The case below involves one such situation.

EEOC v. Mercy Health Center
29 Fair Employment Practices Cases (BNA) 159
(D. C. W. D. Okla. 1982)

FACTS: Mercy Health Center in Oklahoma City, Oklahoma, maintained a policy whereby males were not hired for the position of staff nurse in the hospital's labor and delivery area. The EEOC challenged this policy.

---

3. **Meritor Savings Bank v. Vinson, 477 U.S. 57 (1986).**

HOLDING: The personal/sexual privacy rights of the patients permit the hospital to adopt a policy whereby gender (female) is a **bona fide occupational qualification**. Thus, the hospital's policy of hiring only female labor and delivery nurses was upheld.

CASE QUESTIONS:

1. Do you agree with the court's decision in this case?
2. Do you find it interesting (perhaps hypocritical) that the hospital involved permitted male doctors in the labor and delivery room, but not male nurses? What might be the justification for this policy difference?

4. Religious Discrimination

Title VII prohibits religious discrimination and, in general, employers are required to **reasonably accommodate** religious requirements of employees unless such accommodation constitutes an **undue hardship**. The following interesting case is illustrative of this concept.

EEOC v. Sambo's of Georgia, Inc.
530 F. Supp. 86 (N.D. Ga. 1981)

FACTS: Mr. Mohan S. Tucker applied for a job as a manager at Sambo's Restaurant. The restaurant has a grooming policy of no facial hair. Tucker, however, was a practicing Sikh, a religion that forbids the shaving of facial hair and requires the wearing of a turban. The restaurant told Tucker, though, that it could make no exceptions to its grooming policies and that he would not be hired. Tucker filed charges with the EEOC which filed suit against the employer for religious discrimination.

HOLDING: The court held that concerns for sanitation and adverse customer reaction permitted the restaurant to not accommodate Tucker. The restaurant was justified in wanting to have a "clean cut" image.

CASE QUESTIONS:

1. Do you think the EEOC was out of line in bringing this case to federal court in the first place?
2. What types of "reasonable accommodations" of employee religious beliefs make sense to you? Should a retail chain store "accommodate" an employee, who cannot work on Saturdays because it is her Sabbath, by having her work weekday evenings instead of Saturdays? How might other employees view such "accommodations"?

5. Racial Discrimination

Clearly the principal thrust of Title VII as enacted was to try and eliminate racial discrimination in employment. Over the past almost 50 years, the law has hopefully had at least some success in eliminating the most overt forms of racial discrimination in employment. In addition to Title VII, in 1965 President Lyndon B. Johnson issued presidential Executive

Order 11246 mandating **affirmative action** in employment by companies holding fairly significant federal government contracts. Given the breadth of the federal government's private contracting, today about 22 percent of the civilian labor force in the United States is covered by Executive Order 11246. In recent years, however, there has been considerable backlash against "affirmative action" plans in employment, with allegations of "reverse discrimination." Indeed, in various states, state referendums have been held regarding whether "affirmative action" should still be permissible in state employment. What are your thoughts on this very controversial issue?

D. Age Discrimination in Employment Act (ADEA)

In 1967, Congress passed the **Age Discrimination in Employment Act (ADEA)**. This law protects older workers, age 40 and above, from employment discrimination—such workers are deemed to be within the "protected age group." It is important to note that federal law does *not* protect younger employees who feel they are being discriminated against on the basis of their age. For example, a company can under the ADEA lawfully refuse to promote a 28-year-old executive to a top corporate staff position because he or she is too young. Some state laws, however, do provide broader protection against discrimination based on age. As part of various amendments to the ADEA, Congress has also adopted laws basically outlawing mandatory retirement for most employees in the United States. One important exception to this, though, is a provision that allows for mandatory retirement at age 65 for individuals employed in bona fide executive or high policy-making positions. The EEOC has recently held meetings where it has expressed concern about the impact of the current economic climate on older workers and their employment. The number of age discrimination charges filed with the EEOC have grown steadily in recent years.

E. Disabilities Discrimination

On July 26, 1990, President George Bush signed into law the **Americans with Disabilities Act (ADA)**. The ADA prohibits employers with 15 or more employees from discriminating against **disabled** individuals who with or without **reasonable accommodations** are qualified to perform the **essential functions of the job**. The law specifically excludes from its coverage employees or job applicants who are currently engaging in the illegal use of drugs. Alcoholics, however, are not excluded from the coverage of the ADA. Over the past decade or so, the federal courts and the EEOC have begun interpreting the various provisions of the ADA. Preliminary statistics from the EEOC show that the most "popular" types of charges brought under the ADA involve alleged discrimination based on back impairments and emotional or psychiatric impairments. One interesting issue in the psychiatric as well as other areas is whether employers can treat an employee as *no longer* being "disabled" if he or she takes medications which basically work to help the employee overcome the disability. Congressional amendments to the ADA in 2008 state that employees are still to be regarded as "disabled" even if they are taking corrective medications. Do you agree with this congressional action?

F. Employer Retaliation and Title VII

Another controversial issue under Title VII has been to what extent employees are protected from employer **retaliation** if they complain about employment discrimination to the EEOC or another entity (such as the Texas Workforce Commission). Some lower federal courts had held that only where very significant adverse employment action had been taken against an employee for bringing an EEOC charge; for example, the employee was fired or demoted, could the employee bring another charge for unlawful "retaliation." The U.S. Supreme Court, however, in the fairly recent case of **Burlington Northern & Santa Fe Railway v. White**[4] overruled these lower court decisions and adopted a far broader definition of retaliation under Title VII. Justice Stephen Breyer writing for the U.S. Supreme Court stated that Title VII protected employees not just from workplace retaliation such as discharge or demotion, but from any employer action that would dissuade a reasonable worker from making a charge of discrimination. Various corporate representatives, however, immediately attacked this new standard as being very unclear, and one that will lead to considerable new litigation.

V. ALTERNATIVE DISPUTE RESOLUTION (ADR) AND THE EEOC

Recent years have brought a sharp increase in employment discrimination charges brought to the EEOC and state agencies like the Texas Workforce Commission. Some of this increase has been related to increased societal awareness of employment discrimination issues (e.g., sexual harassment) but a good deal of the increase has been related to the plethora of new laws in the area—laws such as the ADA. In recent years, the EEOC and its commissioners began questioning whether the agency's traditional approach to handling charges was still viable. They found that the dispute resolution forum of last resort—that is, federal courts—had in many respects become the forum of "first resort." In short, the EEOC was taking cases or encouraging cases be taken to federal court without looking at any alternatives. To change things, the EEOC issued a policy statement encouraging the use of **ADR** to settle routine employment discrimination claims through *mediation* and *conciliation* in order to free up commission resources to address the more egregious cases in federal court. The EEOC then requested and received from Congress an additional $37 million per year to implement this and related programs. Today, a large percentage of the cases filed with the EEOC do not go to litigation but are settled through ADR. Moreover, a recent U.S. Supreme Court case involving Circuit City stores upheld employer "new hire agreements" whereby newly hired employees agree that any employment-related disputes they have are to go to ADR/arbitration rather than to court.

CHAPTER SUMMARY

In recent decades, the government has begun widely regulating employment relationship. Indeed, today, in many respects the doctrine of employment-at-will to some extent exists in

---

4. **Burlington Northern & Santa Fe Railway v. White 548 U.S. 53 (2006).**

name only. The underlying reason for this strong government intervention has been perceived market failures. Of particular importance in recent years has been the growth in government regulation of employment discrimination. Today, there is broad federal legislation prohibiting discrimination in employment on the basis of age, disability, sex, race, national origin, and religion among things. Moreover, under the EPA, men and women doing the same job must receive equal wages, and under President Johnson's Executive Order 11246 most federal contractors are required to develop affirmative action plans. Some state and local governments have enacted even more pervasive regulation of these and other employment areas; for example, state laws prohibiting employer interference with employee off-duty activities and discrimination based on sexual orientation.

13

DEBTOR-CREDITOR AND CONSUMER CREDIT LAW

PART ONE—DEBTOR-CREDITOR LAW

I. INTRODUCTION TO DEBTOR-CREDITOR LAW

In Chapter 3, we discussed the civil trial procedures and discussed how businesses could use the civil legal system. Often, collection of those civil judgments or of debts will become necessary. However, in some states it is very difficult to collect these judgments. Texas is one of those states and has earned the reputation for being a debtors' haven. In this chapter, we will first examine the legal means to collect judgments or civil debts.

Consider the situation where Riley Granger, Corp. sold 72,500 units of their product to the Texas business, "We Are the Champions," hereinafter called Champions, for a total of $183,209. Champions is not a very successful business and goes out of business owing Riley Granger, Corp. the amount of the last shipment, $183,209. Riley Granger wants to collect this debt. Champions is a general partnership owned by three individuals: Tom, Dick, and Harry. In this chapter, we will analyze how Riley Granger, Corp. legally can attempt to collect the debt from Champions. We will refer to this hypothetical as **Riley Granger, Corp. v. We Are the Champions**.

In this hypothetical, the Riley Granger, Corp. would be the **Creditor**, the party to whom the debt is owned and Champions, a general partnership, and the three individual owners would be the **Debtor**, the party who owes the debt. Another way of describing these terms is that the creditor is the party loaning the money and the debtor is the party who has borrowed the money.

In collecting a debt, it is very important to determine whether the creditor is a secured creditor or an unsecured creditor. An unsecured creditor does not have a right to seize any of the debtor's property and hold that property to secure the debt. On the other hand, a **secured creditor** is someone who has the benefit of having a **security interest** over some of the debtor's property, which gives the creditor the right to seize some of the debtor's property, hold that property, and even sell that property if the debtor does not pay the debt. Furthermore, the creditor who is not paid in full after the sale of the property can still sue the debtor for the remaining balance just like the unsecured creditor. However, in those rare situations where such a sale covers the costs of the sale and the debt, any remaining balance must be returned to the debtor.

A security interest can arise in several different legal means. One of the common ways to become a secured creditor is to have a security interest over some specific property of the debtor and there are several ways of creating a security interest. However, a creditor does not always have the luxury of being a secured creditor and in those situations must simply sue the debtor in civil court and attempt to collect the debt from the debtor. Remember, having a judgment against someone does NOT mean that you will be able to collect the debt.

II. SECURED CREDITORS

A. General Type of Secured Creditors

Obviously a creditor will want to have security over collateral and will therefore normally whenever possible enter into a **security agreement** with the debtor. A security agreement is normally a written agreement that gives the secured party, the creditor, the right to seize the **collateral**, the property that is specified in the security agreement to secure the debt. This allows the creditor to hold the collateral until the debtor pays the debt or if the debtor does not pay the debt, the creditor under certain rules and restrictions, is allowed to sell the collateral and apply the proceeds of the sale to the debt and the costs of sale. If there is any remaining balance then the creditor can sue the debtor for the remaining balance in civil court. As stated earlier, if the sale satisfies all of the creditor's claims against the debtor and the costs of the repossession, storage of the collateral and costs of the sale, the remaining balance must be returned to the debtor.

B. Real Estate

Probably the most well-known secured transaction deals with real estate. If you want to buy a house, you normally do not pay cash for the house. Instead, you go to a bank or other lending institution and they have you fill out an application for a loan, and a survey is done on the property and also a title search to make sure there are no unforeseen problems in the property transaction. An appraisal is also conducted to make sure there is sufficient value to the property. If everything is in order the bank or lending institution loans you the money to purchase the house, but takes a security interest in the real estate. If you do not pay for the house, then the bank or lending institution can foreclose on your house. We saw this happen in recent years in record numbers across the country due to some lending institutions being overly aggressive in making these types of loans and the debtors now with the current recession being unable to make their payments.

C. Purchase Money Security Interest (PMSI)

However, security interests are also taken by creditors in other types of transactions as well. For instance, when you go to purchase an automobile, furniture, or basically any other expensive property where the seller extends you credit, the seller will become the secured creditor and go through the proper legal steps to create a security interest in the property that they are selling to the debtor. Whether it is the actual seller of this type of property or the lending institution that loans you the money for this specific purchase, the creditor holds a **purchase money security interest (PMSI)** in the collateral. Holding a PMSI is important because it gives the PMSI holder priority over other secured creditors over the secured property.

In secured transactions, there are two important things for the secured party to maintain. First, there needs to be enough secured property to cover the debt. Therefore, often a security interest will also cover **after-acquired property**, the property that the debtor buys after the initial transaction. Second, the secured party wants to have **priority**, which means that their security interest will be paid before the other secured parties' interests and those of the unsecured creditors. Priority can become very complicated because normally the debtors have other debts that they are not paying as well.

D. Example of the Complexity of Secured Transactions

For instance, Joe Farmer and his wife Mary own their home which they purchased in 1999 on a 30-year note. Until January of 2009, they had made the monthly note of $1833 each and every month. They also as a family own three personal vehicles and have three individual car notes with the bank. All three car notes are secured by the automobiles that where purchased under those notes. All three car notes are also in default. The Farmers owe unsecured debt in the form of credit cards to 15 different credit card companies in the amount of $153,799. Joe and Mary also farm and own a farm with a mortgage to Farm Credit Association in the amount of $3.67 million. As last year's crop failed, Joe and Mary were unable to make the payment of $221,000 to Farm Credit Association and Farm Credit has begun foreclosure proceeding on the farm. Farm Credit Association's security interest was for the real estate as well as all for the farming equipment and implements that the Farmers owned at the time of loan. The Farm Credit security interest also included any after-acquired property. The automobiles were purchased after the Farm Credit loan was created. The Farmers also purchased a new tractor and a combine from John Deere after the Farm Credit loan. The Farmers owe John Deere $453,302. The Farmers also bought a planter and hay baler after the Farm Credit loan, which was purchased with cash. Since the Farmers are not paying their bills, who would be able to get what property? That would depend on who had priority in the situation. As for the house, the bank would have priority if they properly perfected their security interest in the house at the time of purchase and would be allowed to foreclose on the house. The same would be true for Farm Credit Association, in that if they had properly perfected their security interest on the farm, equipment and implements, and after-acquired property, Farm Credit would be allowed to foreclose on the farm and any equipment and implements the Farmers owned free and clear, at the time of the Farm Credit transaction. This would also include the planter and hay baler that the Farmers bought after the Farm Credit transaction as after-acquired property if no one else had a security interest in the planter or baler and since the Farmers paid cash, there would not be in this hypothetical. As for the lending institution's claim on the automobiles and John Deere's claim on the tractor and combine, they are PMSI and would belong to the lending institution and John Deere respectfully in spite of the after-acquired property clause in Farm Credit's security agreement. As for the credit card companies, they would have to look to the remaining assets, if any, that the Farmers would have left after all of the collateral **have** been taken by the secured parties.

The point of this hypothetical is to show you how complicated secured transactions can be but also the importance of being secured. The chances of the credit card companies recovering much or anything is slim. Likewise, the secured creditors, would also, like the credit card companies have to look to the remaining assets of the Farmers to satisfy any debt above the secured property's value. Hopefully, this illustration shows you how important it is to have a secured interest and to have priority over other secured interest holders. Hopefully, this will also serve to show you how complicated this area of the law can be.

In our hypothetical **Riley Granger, Corp. v. We Are the Champions** case, the Riley Granger Corp. could have a PMSI if they properly perfected their PMSI and if they did they would be allowed to foreclose on the last shipment before the other creditors of Champions. Therefore, the Riley Granger Corporation would have priority over the other creditors. However, if the value of the property had diminished and it was not enough to cover the costs of the foreclosure, the sale and the debt and the Riley Granger, Corp. was still owed $32,000, then they would become unsecured creditors of the $32,000 and would have to look to the remaining non-secured assets of Champions for their remaining debt collection.

III. LIEN HOLDERS

A. Introduction

Often, the creditor does not have the opportunity to enter into a written security interest and therefore, does not get the benefits of being a secured creditor as specified above. However, there are other ways of creating a **lien**, which will give you the right to possibly hold the debtor's property in certain situations to satisfy the debt giving you some priority over the other creditors of the debtor. Some of those situations are discussed below.

B. Artisan's Lien

An **artisan's lien** is a common law lien that is given to an **artisan**. An artisan is someone who provides services or labor to the debtor on the debtor's personal property. For instance, the cleaners has the right via the artisan's lien to hold your clothes that the cleaners has cleaned until the debtor pays for the services of cleaning the debtor's clothes. Texas specifically recognizes this type of artisan's lien in the Texas Property Code, Section 70.002.

An artisan lien is a **possessory lien** which means that the creditor must still have the property in their possession to execute on the lien. Therefore, when someone takes their personal property to be repaired, serviced, cleaned, etc., as long as the person providing the service still has possession of the debtor's property they can hold the property until the debtor pays for the property. However, once the owner has retrieved their property the lien is lost due to the fact that an artisan lien is a possessory lien and once the creditor has lost possession, they no longer have a lien. This is normally true even if the debtor pays for the debt with a check and the check turns out to be insufficient or the debtor stops the payment on the check. Ordinarily, the creditor is not allowed to repossess the property to restore the lien.

C. Worker's Lien

In Texas, there is a special type of artisan's lien found in the Texas Property Code Section 70.001 that allows the creditor to repossess the property to restore the lien. This is a statutory lien and is available to garages and repair shops, "mechanics" that work on vehicles, motorboats, vessels, or outboard motors. If the debtor takes possession of the vehicle, motorboat, vessel, or outboard motor, after payment of the work on the property, the mechanic that performed the labor on said property can repossess the subject property if they payment is insufficient, if the debtor stops payment on the form of payment given to the creditor, if the account has been closed, or if there is no such account upon with the payment was drawn, then the mechanic creditor has the right to repossess the property. In other words, the lien does not cease when possession ceases. However, under this law, the mechanic must have had the debtor sign a separate written notice agreeing that the debtor has been informed of the possible repossession. This lien is lost if the debtor has sold the subject property to a purchaser for full value who did not know of the possible lien, a **bona fide purchaser**. If the creditor does repossess the property, the debtor is also liable for all costs of repossession. Furthermore, the debtor can also be responsible for reasonable attorney's fees.

D. Landlord's Lien

Texas recognizes two different types of landlord's lien, one for farmers who lease farm land and another for building landlords. The first type for the farmers is found in the Texas Property Code Section 54.001 and following for landlords who lease land to a farmer for the purposes of growing a crop. This lien normally applies to the crop for that growing year. However, if the crop is harvested and sold to a bona fide purchaser, the lien is lost. The second type of landlord's lien applies to a building owner who leases all or part of the building to a tenant. This lien is found in the Texas Property Code Section 54.021 and following. If the tenant does not pay the rent when due, the lien applies only to property of the tenant that is non-exempt. Exempt property includes:

(1) wearing apparel; (2) tools, apparatus, and books of a trade or profession; (3) schoolbooks; (4) a family library; (5) family portraits and pictures; (6) one couch, two livingroom chairs, and a dining table and chairs; (7) beds and bedding; (8) kitchen furniture and utensils; (9) food and foodstuffs; (10) medicine and medical supplies; (11) one automobile and one truck; (12) agricultural implements; (13) children's toys not commonly used by adults; (14) goods that the landlord or the landlord's agent knows are owned by a person other than the tenant or an occupant of the residence; and (15) goods that the

landlord or the landlord's agent knows are subject to a recorded chattel mortgage or financing agreement. (Texas Property Code Section 54.042)

However, for this type of landlord's lien to be effective, the lien must be in a written lease and the provisions claiming the landlord's lien must be underlined and printed in a conspicuous manner. Furthermore, the landlord must seize the property in a manner that does not breach the peace. To receive compensation for the packing, moving, or storing of the seized property, the landlord must have stated the right to receive said reimbursement in the written lease.

E. Mechanic's, Contractor's, or Materialman's Lien

A mechanic's, contractor's, or materialman's lien is found in Chapter 53 of the Texas Property Code. This lien will apply to situations where repairs, improvements, labor or materials, or specially fabricated materials are provided on real estate such as existing houses or other buildings but also on such real estate as levees or railroads. The lien attaches only to the real estate where the specified service was provided and not to adjoining property. There are specific statutory requirements to perfect this lien (Texas Property Code Sections 53.051 to 53.058) and must be completely following or the lien is lost. However, if properly perfected, it attaches to the real estate upon which the service was performed, and the subcontractors, laborers, and materialmen who have properly perfected their liens have preference in payment over other creditors of the original contractor. These types of liens can prevent the property being sold or the priority taking effect upon the sale of the property.

If the mechanic's, contractor's, or materialman's lien is filed on a homestead it must be based on a written contract and the said contract must be executed prior to any of the work being performed or it is lost. Furthermore, the contract must be filed in the County Clerk's Office of the county in which the real estate is located.

F. Miscellaneous Texas Liens

1. Other Statutory Liens

Texas has many types of statutory liens. In Texas, there are many statutory liens for numerous situations. For instance, in the Texas Property Code Section 70.003, there are liens for people that care for animals, property owners who lease their property for animal grazing, and cotton ginners. Other various types of liens are found throughout Texas law. Assuming the debt is due and the debtor cannot pay the debt, what do you as the creditor do next? You try to execute on the lien. If you have any kind of security interest, you are allowed to foreclose on that collateral. However, usually it is not as easy as going over and going to the debtor's house or place of business and demanding the property and the debtor agrees and turns the property over to you. You normally will need to go through legal proceeding to foreclose on the property and take possession of said property. This can be complicated in a legal sense and often is made more difficult due to the reluctance of the state official who is required to go with you to take the property for the debtor. After all, people get to be very fond of their property and if they feel so strongly about the property that they will not turn it over to you, it can become a very difficult situation. So, how is this legally accomplished?

2. Attachment

In Texas, attachment is covered in the Civil Practice and Remedies Code, Chapter 61. A party is entitled to a **writ of attachment**, a court order that orders the attachment or seizure of the property, if the debtor is in fact indebted to the creditor and the debtor will probably otherwise dispose of the property prior to the satisfaction of the dispute between the creditor and debtor. Furthermore, this is only allowed if the debtor is about to leave the state or take the property out of the state, is hiding the property to defraud his creditors, the debtor has already disposed of some of his property to stop his creditors from attaching the property, is about to sell the property, the debtor obtained the property from the creditor under false pretenses, or the debtor is not a resident of Texas. Furthermore, a writ of attachment can only be issued if the creditor has filed a suit against the debtor in the appropriate civil court of Texas. An appropriate writ of attachment enables even an unsecured creditor to seize property but again, only in the above listed situation. The purpose of the writ of attachment is to prevent the debtor from disposing of the property during a civil lawsuit to prevent the creditor from obtaining the property to satisfy any judgment that the creditor might receive.

Only the appropriate court can issue a writ of attachment and again, only when the debtor is taking any of those steps listed above to deprive the creditor of the property. In order to have the court take this action, the creditor must have filed an affidavit with the court showing which of the general need for the writ and the specific grounds for issuance of the writ of attachment in the case, and the amount of demand. Furthermore, the creditor/ plaintiff must file a bond in an amount set by the court to cover the losses of the debtor/ defendant if the writ of attachment is issued when the debtor/defendant wins the lawsuit against him. Therefore, the creditor/plaintiff cannot simply file the lawsuit just to get the writ of attachment and once he or she has the property abandon the lawsuit. The creditor/plaintiff must complete the lawsuit and the resulting judgment must be for the creditor/plaintiff. Furthermore, a writ of attachment can only be levied against the non-exempt, appropriate property of the debtor/defendant. We will discuss exempt property later in this chapter.

Once the property is seized, it is held by the officer of the government until the lawsuit is finalized. Third parties, for instance a secured party, can file a claim on the seized property. After the lawsuit is finalized, the property is given to the appropriate party, the secured party if they had priority, the creditor/plaintiff if they win the lawsuit by proving that they are entitled to the property, or returned to the debtor/defendant if the creditor/ plaintiff does not prevail in the claim. If the property is given to the creditor/plaintiff, they can keep the property to satisfy the debt or sell the property to satisfy the debt.

3. Garnishment

Garnishment is found in Chapter 63 of the Texas Civil Practice and Remedies Code. A **writ of garnishment** is a court order to seize the money of the debtor. It is normally issued against a financial institution that has money of the debtor on deposit. However, it cannot be used in Texas against an employer of the debtor in an effort to collect current wages owed to the debtor. Some states do allow the garnishment of current wages but Texas does not.

A writ of garnishment can be issued if a writ of attachment has been issued or if the creditor/plaintiff has sued for a debt and the debtor/defendant does not have sufficient non-exempt property to satisfy the debt that is located within the state of Texas other than the money garnished. Only the appropriate court can issue a writ of garnishment.

If a bank receives a writ of garnishment on a depositor's (debtor/defendant) account, the **garnishee**, the bank, is allowed neither to pay any of the debts of the debtor/defendant nor release any money in the account to the debtor/defendant. The garnishee is allowed to charge an administrative fee for their costs incurred in any proceedings the garnishee is involved in during the conflict between the creditor and the defendant. If the lawsuit is resolved in the creditor's favor, the money is given to the creditor after the garnishees claimed, legal fees have been paid, and the amount is credited against the debt that the debtor/defendant owes the creditor/plaintiff. If there are not sufficient funds in the account to satisfy the debt, the creditor/plaintiff can proceed with other means of collection of the debt such as executing on the judgment.

4. Execution of Judgment/Judgment Liens

If the creditor/plaintiff wins the lawsuit and neither the writ of attachment nor writ of garnishment has satisfied their claim against the debtor/defendant, the creditor/plaintiff can execute on the judgment by requesting a **writ of execution** against the debtor/defendant. In Texas, this is handled by Chapter 34 of the Civil Practice and Remedies Code. A writ of execution is a court order to seize any non-exempt property of a judgment debtor/defendant for up to 10 years after the final judgment was issued by the court. A judgment becomes final 30 days after the court order if there is no appeal or after the court order on the final appeal. It can be extended for another 10-year period anytime during the initial 10-year period. In addition to the time period, the writ of execution remains in effect only up until the time of the death of the defendant. In other words, the death of the defendant stays the execution of the writ of execution.

The appropriate executing officer of the court, sheriff, constable, etc. upon receiving the writ is required to search for property belonging to the debtor/defendant being sure that that property belongs to the debtor/defendant. Furthermore, the writ of execution is only valid on property that the debtor owns that is not mortgaged, subject to other lien, or in trust. If property is seized the officer of the court must care for the property. The defendant/debtor has the rights to recover the property if they pay the judgment in full including interest and costs associated with the writ of execution.

If the defendant/debtor does not pay the judgment then the property is sold and the proceeds of the sale are credited to the judgment and the proceeds are paid to the plaintiff/creditor. The officer of the court is allowed to retain part of the sale proceeds as their costs of executing the writ, caring for the property and the sale of the property. The officer of the court is not allowed to purchase the property. A writ of execution can be utilized against real or personal property.

However, the above writs of attachment, garnishment, or execution can only be used against the proper property of the debtor/defendant. Under Texas law, any exempt property of the debtor/defendant cannot be seized.

IV. EXEMPT PROPERTY

The property that is exempt from seizure to satisfy the debt of the defendant when there is no valid, legal security interest on that property is the exempt property. This can vary drastically from state to state. Texas gives very broad interpretation to exempt property.

In Texas, exempt property is abundant. However, the general provisions for exempt property are found in the Texas Property Code and in the Texas Constitution. These include exemptions for real property and personal property. Texas also grants exemptions, as well, for several special exemptions covering a variety of types of property. We will only look at the general exempt property rules.

A. Real Property Exemptions—Homestead Exemptions

In Texas, a debtor can claim that some of his real property is exempt and the creditor cannot levy against that exempt real property. Real Property that is exempt from creditors is specified in the Texas Property Code, Chapter 41. Keep in mind that real property that is subject to purchase money claims (mortgage), taxes, or mechanic's and materialman's liens is not covered by these provisions and is available for foreclosure to the taxing authority or the mortgage holder or the holder of the mechanic's and materialman's lien. These exemptions for real estate apply to the owner's **homestead**. Texas law allows a debtor to have either a rural or urban homestead exemption. The debtor must choose one of the other but not both. Note, there is no limitation on the value of the real property homestead, either urban or rural, and often the exempt property can be worth thousands if not millions of dollars.

1. Urban Homestead
An urban homestead is defined as land used for the purposes of a home for a family or a single adult person or as both an urban home and a business location. Texas Property Code Section 41.002 The party claiming the urban homestead exemption can claim not more than 10 acres of land and all the improvements thereon. Furthermore, the land can be in one or more contiguous (touching each other) lots. The homestead is urban if at the time the homestead designation was made the property was located in the city limits or extraterritorial limits of the city as defined by state law and was given police protection, fire, and any three of the following city services: electric, natural gas, sewer, storm sewer, or water.

2. Rural Homestead
If the party chooses to claim a rural homestead, the family can choose not more than 200 acres of land. Furthermore, the 200 acres of land can be in one or more parcels. The rural exemption

also includes all the improvements thereon. If the party claiming the exemption is a single adult, the amount of the rural homestead is limited to 100 acres. If the party owns more than the exempt amount, the party can designate which 100 or 200 acres that they are claiming. However, that designation can still be in more than one parcel of land and it does not have to be contiguous. The appropriate state officer is allowed to seize and eventually sell any property above the exempt amount.

B. Personal Property Exemptions

Texas allows extensive personal property exemptions for debtors, which means that any personal property that is subject to the exemptions is not available for satisfaction of a debt unless of course it was collateral that was the subject of a secured transaction. The Texas Property Code, Chapter 42, sets forth the personal property exemptions. Texas law makes a difference for a single person and families. A family is defined as someone who is not a single adult. Therefore, the family unit can be a single parent as long as there is a child involved. The personal property exemption available to a family is for property that has an aggregate fair market value of not more than $60,000, exclusive of the amount of any liens, security interests, or other charges encumbering the property. If you are a single adult, the amount of the exemption is lowered to $30,000.

However, there is certain property that is not allowed to be seized at all under Chapter 42 of the Texas Property Code. This includes current wages as we discussed above when we were discussing garnishment. Furthermore, neither alimony nor child support payments can be seized either. However, there is an exception to this and current wages can be seized for court-ordered past-due child support payments that are the obligation of the debtor. Health aids that are professionally prescribed of the debtor or any of debtor's dependents are also exempt and do not count toward the $60,000 or $30,000 limit. Finally, a Bible or any other religious book that contains the sacred writings of the debtor's religion is also exempt from seizure and the value does not count when determining the $60,000 or $30,000 amount in the general exemption of personal property, but it can be seized in a landlord's lien or if it is secured collateral.

According to the Texas Property Code, Section 42.002, personal property that can be exempt from creditors and total either $60,000 or $30,000 can include any of the following types of property:

1. home furnishings, including family heirlooms;
2. provisions for consumption;
3. farming or ranching vehicles and implements;
4. tools, equipment, books, and apparatus, including boats and motor vehicles used in a trade or profession;
5. wearing apparel;
6. jewelry not to exceed 25 percent of the aggregate limitations prescribed by Section 42.001(a);
7. two firearms;

8. athletic and sporting equipment, including bicycles;
9. a two-wheeled, three-wheeled, or four-wheeled motor vehicle for each member of a family or single adult who holds a driver's license or who does not hold a driver's license but who relies on another person to operate the vehicle for the benefit of the non-licensed person;
10. the following animals and forage on hand for their consumption:
    A. two horses, mules, or donkeys and a saddle, blanket, and bridle for each;
    B. 12 head of cattle;
    C. 60 head of other types of livestock; and
    D. 120 fowl; and
11. household pets.

Furthermore, certain types of retirement accounts that are owned by the debtor can also be exempt and are not subject to any type of execution by the creditors. Texas Property Code Section 42.0021 Also, certain savings plans for college can also be exempted under Section 42.0022.

Keep in mind that if any of the personal property is pledged as collateral in any secured transaction, it cannot be exempted under these provisions. Also, remember that the debtor gets to specify what personal property that they are claiming as exempt.

Therefore, if the plaintiff, Granger Riley, Corp., filed a suit against Champions and the three individual partners and received a judgment for $35,000, the plaintiff could wait the required time period, request a writ of execution, and levy against any of the personal property of the partners that is eligible. However, Granger Riley, Corp. could not levy against the wages owed to the partners from their other jobs, certain retirement accounts, or college savings accounts, any of their health aids such as a hearing aids or a prosthetic leg, their family Bible, their child support payments from their children's other parent, alimony payments owed to a partner by a former spouse, etc.

However, they could levy against the rest of the personal property of the debtor/defendants but only the property that is not exempted by debtor worth more than above a total of $30,000 worth of property for a single debtor or $60,000 worth of property for a partner with a family. Therefore, the debtor would be allowed to set aside either $30,000 worth of personal property if the debtor is single or $60,000 worth of personal property if the debtor is a family and the debtor can choose the property he or she, if the debtor is single, or they (family) want to keep. Furthermore, remember this is actual value of the personal property minus the debt owed to another creditor on the property. Therefore, if you had a work of art, a family heirloom, it would be exempt up to the $30,000/$60,000 limit. If you owed the bank $100,000 on this $110,000 work of art, the value of the art would be $10,000 and you would still have $50,000 or $20,000 of property to still designate as exempt.

Therefore, if someone has planned properly can they in reality exempt much more property than property of a value of $60,000 or $30,000? For instance, could your $10,000 hunting dog suddenly become the family pet or could your "priceless" antiques suddenly become "old junk" with no value! There are often cases of security fraud involved in the designation of the exempt property by the debtor and it is sometimes very difficult to prove the fraud especially if you do not know a "priceless" antique from "old junk" or a prized, very valuable hunting dog from the family pet.

So how much property would the Granger Riley, Corp. actually be able to seize and sell and subsequently apply to the debt? Often it is nothing or very little due to the advanced planning of the debtor and the very generous Texas laws. Now, can you see why Texas is considered a debtor's haven?

V. GUARANTORS, SURETIES, AND CO-SIGNORS

Since it is so difficult, if not impossible to collect a debt, it would be better for the creditor to have more than one debtor that they could levy against. Therefore, often creditors will require someone to co-sign the debt obligation. For instance, if you wanted to lease an apartment and the landlord was worried that you would not pay the rent, the landlord could require your parents or another adult to co-sign, sign a suretyship or guaranty agreement.

If the landlord asks your parents of that other adult to co-sign the lease then your parents or other adult would become the **co-signor(s)** on that lease obligation, which would mean that any co-signors, like you the debtor, would have to pay the payments and be responsible for the total debt.

Another way to accomplish this goal if you are the creditor is to have someone guarantee the debt. A guarantee is a promise to pay the debts of someone else. This makes that person a **guarantor** and like the co-signor can obligate that person to pay the debt. Normally, under state law, the creditor must try to collect the debt from the debtor first and if they are unable to do so, then the creditor can collect the debt from the guarantor. Still another way to accomplish you goal of making someone else liable is to have someone serve as a **surety**. A surety, like a guarantor, promises to pay the debt of someone else but unlike the guarantor, when dealing with a surety, the creditor does not have to try to collect the debt from the debtor first. Therefore, a surety is primarily responsible for the debt just like the debtor. However, the guarantor is only secondarily liable, meaning that the creditor must try to collect from the primary debtor first and if unsuccessful, then try to collect the debt from the surety.

Obviously, you should NEVER serve as a co-signor, guarantor, or surety unless you intend to pay the debt because legally you just might have to pay the debt if the original signor of the lease, note, or other type of debt obligation does not pay that debt. Also, remember that for the co-signor, guarantor, or surety to be responsible, the obligation must be in writing due to the written requirement of contracts. An oral agreement to co-sign or serve as a guarantor or surety is not legally binding.

VI. BANKRUPTCY

Bankruptcy is the ultimate debtor's right. Bankruptcy should also be the avenue of last resort for the debtor. Bankruptcy is a Constitutional right of debtors. Article 1, Section 8 of the U. S. Constitution Bankruptcy is handled by the Federal Bankruptcy Code, which was largely overhauled in 2005 with the passage of the **Bankruptcy Abuse Prevention and Consumer Protection Act of 2005**. The 2005 law was primarily aimed at trying to curb the abuses that were being done by using the Bankruptcy Code in a way that probably was not intended when it had been "reformed" in the Bankruptcy Reform Act of 1978. Many criticized the Act as being too easy on the debtor and allowing them too many ways to discharge debts thereby being unfair to the creditors. The effect of these reforms is still undetermined for sure.

Under the Bankruptcy Code, there are several chapters under which a debtor can file bankruptcy. For instance, Chapter 7 allows liquidation of your property, payment of your debts, and a debt that not paid in full can be discharged, totally forgiven, by the bankruptcy judge. Chapter 11 is primarily used by businesses in financial trouble. For instance, the General Motors and Chrysler bankruptcies of 2009 were both under Chapter 11. This allows the bankruptcy court to review the debtor's and the creditor's plans for the reorganization of the debtor's debt obligations. Chapter 13 can be utilized by wage earners with a set income. Here, the debtor takes their wages and other income and similar to Chapter 11, formulates a plan and tries to live under that plan and work their way out of bankruptcy. The debtor pays a certain amount of their income into the bankruptcy court which in turn distributes that money to the creditors for up to five years. There are restrictions on the total amount of the debt and the required income of the wage earner debtor. There are also specialized chapters for farmers, railroads, etc.

PART TWO—CONSUMER CREDIT LAW

I. INTRODUCTION TO CONSUMER CREDIT LAW

As we have seen, debtors borrowing money and creditors extending credit or loaning money are very common occurrences in the case of both individuals and in the business world. Credit is what makes businesses able to operate and it seems the American way of life with Americans owing trillions of dollars in credit card debt and other forms of debt. In 2008, we saw the banks foreclosing on Americans houses in record numbers and in turn the banks needing huge government bailouts just to save themselves from having to close down, which, in turn, limited the available credit that slowed businesses' ability to operate. This is part led to two of the three major American automobile industries filing bankruptcy in 2009, largely due to of credit extension problems and debt obligations that they could not pay.

Creditors are going to charge interest for extending the credit or loaning money to the debtor. We have seen that charging too much money for the extension of credit is illegal when we discussed **usury** limits in contracts. Finally, we discussed the problems of being paid back the money that you have loaned to someone else in the preceding section. Now, we want to discuss some of the protections given to consumers who are debtors. Prior to the U.S. Government passing the federal laws to protect consumers in credit obligations, the creditors were largely left to state law, which often did not provide enough protection or information and therefore, left the consumer in the dark about the cost of the credit as well as other information on the credit transaction. Therefore, the U.S. Government entered into the consumer credit area.

II. CONSUMER CREDIT PROTECTION ACT 15 U.S.C. SECTIONS 1601 ET SEQ.

The Consumer Credit Protection Act was passed by Congress in May 1969 for the expressed purpose of:

(a) The Congress finds that economic stabilization would be enhanced and the competition among the various financial institutions and other firms engaged in the extension of consumer credit would be strengthened by the informed use of credit. The informed use of credit results from an awareness of the cost thereof by consumers. It is the purpose of this title to assure a meaningful disclosure of credit terms so that the consumer will be able to compare more readily the various credit terms available to him and avoid the uninformed use of credit, and to protect the consumer against inaccurate and unfair credit billing and credit card practices.

(b) The Congress also finds that there has been a recent trend toward leasing automobiles and other durable goods for consumer use as an alternative to installment credit sales and that these leases have been offered without adequate cost disclosures. It is the purpose of this title to assure a meaningful disclosure of the terms of leases of personal property for personal, family, or household purposes so as to enable the lessee to compare more readily the various lease terms available to him, limit balloon payments in consumer leasing, enable comparison of lease terms with credit terms where appropriate, and to assure meaningful and accurate disclosures of lease terms in advertisement. (Consumer Credit Protection Act 15 U.S.C. Section 1601)

In other words, Congress wanted to make the use of credit more uniform and to require disclosure to the consumers about the cost of the extension of credit in numerous different situations. The Consumer Credit Protection Act is an umbrella law that contains several sections such as Title I, Truth in Lending Act, pertaining to the cost of extension of credit and requiring the costs of the credit to be disclosed to the debtor, thereby, making it possible for the consumer to comparison shop by mandating uniform terms and standards.

A. Truth in Lending Act 15 U.S.C. Title I, Section 1601 et seq.

The **Truth in Lending Act (TILA)** is strictly a consumer law in that it only applies to loans for personal, family, or household purposes. It does not apply to businesses. Furthermore, it only covers loans of up to $25,000 but not over $25,000 except for a real estate transaction in the purchasing of a house with a mortgage that will be repaid in more than four installments. It also only applies to creditors who regularly extend credit such as financial institutions, credit card companies, stores who extend credit, etc. For instance, if you purchased a new Ford X150 pickup truck for your personal use and paid $2,000 down and financed

$23,750 with Ford Motor Credit, a company that regularly extends credit to consumers, on a 60-month note, this would be a **closed-ended credit transaction**. However, TILA would not apply if you were purchasing the exact same truck under the same terms but as the delivery truck for your business since this would be for business purposes.

The TILA is a disclosure law and is administered by the Federal Reserve Board, which has the authority to adopt rules and regulations for the interpretation and enforcement of the TILA. One of these regulations is **Regulation Z** that requires a series of disclosures from the creditor to the debtor. Basically all of the terms of the credit transaction must be included in the disclosure statement such as the cash price compared to the total cost of the item when it is financed, the finance charges including the interest, and other fees to be paid by the debtor for the credit. The **annual percentage rate** (APR), the starting date of the obligation, the number of payments, amount of the payment, a description of the collateral, and costs for late payments and/or prepayments. The APR is the effective annual cost of the interest being charged to the debtor stated in a yearly percentage, which also includes any fees or costs of the loan.

All of these disclosures must be made in a clear and easy-to-understand manner. The debtor can then take the amount of the APR and compare it to what other financial institutions offer. For instance, if you are thinking about buying that Ford X150, you can take the TILA disclosure statement from a number of financial institutions and compare it to the one from Ford Motor Credit Corporation and decide which one gives you the better deal.

TILA also applies to **open-ended credit transactions** where the creditor makes a series of loans over time, such as credit card accounts where the debtor has the option to pay the debt in full or by making minimum periodic payments until the loan is paid in full. The credit card company must disclose the credit terms in advertisements as well as at the beginning of the relationship when the card holder first receives the card. Furthermore, the credit card company must explain the finance charge, when it begins, how it is calculated, and how it can change. Furthermore, in each statement the credit card company is also required to disclose the previous balance, amounts and dates of all purchases or cash advances, all payments or credits to the account, finance charges, and the date that the payment is due.

The TILA also gives debtors the right of rescission in home loans with a mortgage covered under the TILA up to three days after the transaction if the proper disclosures were made under the TILA. If the home loan is rescinded, the financial institution has 20 days to return all the monies paid by the debtor. However, if the TILA is not followed properly by the financial institution, the debtor can cancel the loan for up to three years. However, the only type of violations that are covered are actual errors and minor clerical errors are not covered by these provision. Furthermore, any willful violations of the disclosure requirements of TILA and Regulation Z can result in criminal charges. This right of rescission only applies to TILA-required disclosures in home loans.

Penalties for failure to follow the TILA in other types of TILA loans are levied by the Federal Trade Commission (FTC) and seven other federal agencies. These penalties can include reimbursement of any amount overcharged and any billing errors by the creditor or their actual damages as well as twice the finance charges as a penalty, plus reasonable attorney's fees. However, if the creditor is shown to have a pattern of negligent acts or misleading provisions in the disclosure or intentionally failed to disclose, there can be criminal charges brought by the Department of Justice, which can lead to a fine of up to $5,000 or one-year imprisonment or both.

B. Fair Credit Billing Act 15 U.S.C. Sections 1666–1666j

Part D of the TILA deals with fair credit billing and is often referred to as the **Fair Credit Billing Act (FCBA)**. The TILA was amended in 1974 to help consumers have an opportunity to object to inaccurate billing and have a uniform means to correct credit card billing errors. Under the FCBA, if a consumer, also called a debtor or obligor, notices an error in his or her credit card bill, they have the right to notify the credit card company at the address provided on the statement in writing within 60 days. In the written notification, the consumer must provide his or her name, address, account number, and the claimed inaccuracy including the amount as well as the basis for the claim. The creditor must then notify the consumer of the receipt of the consumer's claim within 30 days. However, this notice is waived if the creditor resolves the dispute within the 30 days. The creditor then must investigate the claimed inaccuracy and notify the consumer of the outcome within two billing cycles, but not more than 90 days during which the creditor can take no steps to collect the debt other than to continue to send statements showing the debt but the debt must be shown as in dispute.

If the consumer's claim was found to be correct, the creditor must correct the billing error and notify the consumer in writing. However, if there is no error, the creditor must still notify the consumer and also give proof of the accuracy of the bill. If the creditor does not follow these steps, the consumer can file suit against the creditor, but the only penalty is that the creditor forfeits their right to collect the debt and a penalty of $50 for each item that was disputed.

Furthermore, the FCBA requires creditors to honor any and all claims other than tort claims. Therefore, if the consumer makes a good-faith effort to satisfy a claim with a seller of faulty products that the consumer purchased with a credit card, the consumer can refuse to pay the debt on that product if he or she notifies the creditor immediately after determining that the product is faulty. The creditor is then required to intervene between the debtor and the seller of the product in an effort to resolve the differences between the two (FCBA 15 U.S.C. Section 1666i).

Furthermore, in addition to requiring the credit card company to make prompt credit of any payments on the accounts (FCBA 15 U.S.C. Section 1666b) the FCBA makes provisions for returning items and in turn crediting the account when a credit card was used to purchase the items (FCBA 15 U.S.C Section 1666e) and returning a credit balance to the consumer when the consumer overpays his or her account (FCBA 15 U.S.C Section 1666d).

C. Consumer Leasing Act 15 U.S.C. Sections 1667–1667f

Part E of the TILA is a section devoted to consumer leasing and is normally referred to as the **Consumer Leasing Act.** The Consumer Leasing Act refers to a **consumer lease** as:

a contract in the form of a lease or bailment for the use of personal property by a natural person for a period of time exceeding four months, and for a total contractual obligation not exceeding $25,000, primarily for personal, family, or household purposes, whether or not the lessee has the option to purchase or otherwise become the owner of the property at the expiration of the lease, except that such term shall not include any credit sale … of this title. Such term does not include a lease for agricultural, business, or commercial purposes, or to a government or governmental agency or instrumentality, or to an organization. (15 U.S.C. Section 1667(1))

Therefore, a consumer lease is for personal property leased by a consumer for personal use where the total payments under the lease do not exceed $25,000. Furthermore, real estate is excluded as is any business, agricultural, or commercial property. The lessee must be a natural person, in other words, corporations are also excluded.

Every **lessor**, party offering the lease to a consumer **lessee**, must make the following disclosures accurately in a clear and conspicuous manner in a dated, written statement that must be given to the lessee prior to the execution of the lease. These disclosures include:

1. A brief description or identification of the leased property;
2. The amount of any payment by the lessee required at the inception of the lease;
3. The amount paid or payable by the lessee for official fees, registration, certificate of title, or license fees or taxes;
4. The amount of other charges payable by the lessee not included in the periodic payments, a description of the charges and that the lessee shall be liable for the differential, if any, between the anticipated fair market value of the leased property and its appraised actual value at the termination of the lease, if the lessee has such liability;
5. A statement of the amount or method of determining the amount of any liabilities the lease imposes upon the lessee at the end of the term and whether or not the lessee has the option to purchase the leased property and at what price and time;
6. A statement identifying all express warranties and guarantees made by the manufacturer or lessor with respect to the leased property, and identifying the party responsible for maintaining or servicing the leased property together with a description of the responsibility;
7. A brief description of insurance provided or paid for by the lessor or required of the lessee, including the types and amounts of the coverages and costs;
8. A description of any security interest held or to be retained by the lessor in connection with the lease and a clear identification of the property to which the security interest relates;
9. The number, amount, and due dates or periods of payments under the lease and the total amount of such periodic payments;
10. Where the lease provides that the lessee shall be liable for the anticipated fair market value of the property on expiration of the lease, the fair market value of the property at the inception of the lease, the aggregate cost of the lease on expiration, and the differential between them; and

11. A statement of the conditions under which the lessee or lessor may terminate the lease prior to the end of the term and the amount or method of determining any penalty or other charge for delinquency, default, late payments, or early termination. (15 U.S.C. Section 1667a)

Any lessor that fails to make these disclosures is subject to the penalties contained in 15 U.S.C. Sec 1640, the general penalties under TILA. These damages include actual damages of not less than $100, but not more than $1,000 for an individual debtor. Class action suits representing many debtors can be larger.

D. Fair Debt Collection Protection Act 15 U.S.C. Sections 1692a–1692p

The **Fair Debt Collection Practices Act (FDCPA)** was passed by Congress in 1978. It is directed at collection agencies and their perceived abusive, deceptive, and unfair techniques in collecting debts. Congress felt that:

Abusive debt collection practices contribute to the number of personal bankruptcies, to marital instability, to the loss of jobs, and to invasions of individual privacy. (15 U.S.C. Section 1962)

The FDCA provides guidelines for these collection agencies on how to properly collect debts. However, it also sets forth protections for the consumer/debtor. FDCPA applies to consumer loans meaning loans for personal transactions. In other words, it applies to loans entered into by individuals and families for household, consumer loans. The basis for the government's action in this area is its involvement in interstate commerce (15 U.S.C. Section1692(d)).

A debt collector is defined by the FDCPA as:

The term "debt collector" means any person who uses any instrumentality of interstate commerce or the mails in any business the principal purpose of which is the collection of any debts, or who regularly collects or attempts to collect, directly or indirectly, debts owed or due or asserted to be owed or due another. Notwithstanding the exclusion provided by clause (F) of the last sentence of this paragraph, the term includes any creditor who, in the process of collecting his own debts, uses any name other than his own which would indicate that a third person is collecting or attempting to collect such debts. For the purpose of section 1692f (6) of this title, such term also includes any person who uses any instrumentality of interstate commerce or the mails in any business the principal purpose of which is the enforcement of security interests. The term does not include:

(A) any officer or employee of a creditor while, in the name of the creditor, collecting debts for such creditor;
(B) any person while acting as a debt collector for another person, both of whom are related by common ownership or affiliated by corporate control, if the person acting

as a debt collector does so only for persons to whom it is so related or affiliated and if the principal business of such person is not the collection of debts;

(C) any officer or employee of the United States or any State to the extent that collecting or attempting to collect any debt is in the performance of his official duties;

(D) any person while serving or attempting to serve legal process on any other person in connection with the judicial enforcement of any debt;

(E) any nonprofit organization which, at the request of consumers, performs bona fide consumer credit counseling and assists consumers in the liquidation of their debts by receiving payments from such consumers and distributing such amounts to creditors; and

(F) any person collecting or attempting to collect any debt owed or due or asserted to be owed or due another to the extent such activity

　(i)　is incidental to a bona fide fiduciary obligation or a bona fide escrow arrangement;

　(ii)　concerns a debt which was originated by such person;

　(iii)　concerns a debt which was not in default at the time it was obtained by such person; or

　(iv)　concerns a debt obtained by such person as a secured party in a commercial credit transaction involving the creditor. (15 U.S.C. Section 1692a(6))

This means that anyone who regularly collects debts on behalf of someone else is a debt collector. This can include collection agencies but can also include an individual attorney who is trying to collect the debt of one of his or her clients. However, if Dillard's was trying to collect a debt "in house" that is owed to Dillard's, that collection effort would not be covered by the FDCPA. However, Dillard's needs to make it clear that it is in fact Dillard's that is trying to collect the debt and cannot represent that it is a third party or the collection effort will be covered by FDCPA. Of course, Dillard's actions even if not covered by the FDCPA might be covered by state law and the appropriate state regulatory agency.

The FDCPA puts limitations on the ability of the debt collector to contact third parties (Section 1692b) and the consumer/debtor himself or herself (Section 1692c). Unless the debt collector has the permission of the consumer/debtor or the appropriate court, the debt collector is not allowed to contact the consumer at unusual times or locations, including inconvenient times and places. Ordinarily this means that the debt collector is allowed to contact the consumer at the consumer's place of abode or business between 8 a.m. and 9 p.m. However, if the debt collector is notified that the consumer is represented by an attorney or that the consumer's employer prohibits the consumer getting personal calls at work, then the debt collector is not allowed to contact the consumer. Furthermore, if the consumer notifies the debt collector in writing that the consumer is not going to pay the debt, then the debt collector is not allowed to personally contact the consumer except in rare situations and must either cease collections efforts or file a lawsuit to collect the debt.

Section 1692d sets forth the conduct that a debt collector cannot do and is therefore, considered to be abusive or harassment. This includes the threat of violence or any other threat of criminal actions to physically harm the consumer, their reputation or property; the use of obscene or profane language meant to abuse the hearer or reader; publication of a list of consumers who will not pay their debts, except that these people can be reported to a consumer reporting agency; repeatedly calling the consumer and just letting the phone ring and ring or repeated phone calls simply meant to harass, abuse, or annoy the consumer or making phone calls and not identifying themselves; or advertising a sale of debts to coerce payment of the debt. Furthermore, Section 1692e prohibits the debt collector from claiming or representing themselves as being associated with the U.S. government or any state government; misrepresenting the amount of the character, debt or legal status of the debt; falsely representing the services rendered or payment that the debt collector is to receive; threatening to take any legal action that cannot legally be done; disgracing the consumer by alleging that the consumer committed a crime; alluding to the possibility of the arrest of the consumer; and claiming that they are an attorney when in fact the debt collector is not an attorney. Furthermore, there can be no allegations that the debt has been transferred to someone else, using any misrepresentation or deceptive means to collect or attempt to collect the debt or obtain information about the consumer, falsely representing that documents are part of the legal process, misrepresenting that they work for or are associated with consumer-reporting agencies as well as other listed practices by the debt collector.

Furthermore, the debt collector is not allowed to use any unfair means to collect or attempt to collect the debt. 15 U.S.C. Section 1692f The FDCPA gives several examples of unfair practices by the debt collector. These include collecting any amounts that are outside the agreement that created the debt, accepting post-dated checks unless the consumer/ debtor is notified in writing before the debt collector deposits the post-dated checks, soliciting a post-dated check for the purpose of threatening to institute criminal action, depositing the post-dated check prior to the date on the check, making collect calls to the consumer/ debtor or anything else that causes the consumer/debtor additional charges, threatening to take or attempting to take exempt property, and communicating with the consumer/debtor by post card or using any false address as that of the debt collector.

15 U.S.C. Section 1692g requires a written notice to be sent to the consumer/debtor within five days of the first communication with the debtor about the collection of debt. This notice must contain the following:

1. The amount of the debt.
2. The name of the creditor to whom the debt is owed.
3. A statement informing the debtor that he or she has 30 days from the date of the receipt of the notice to dispute the validity of the debt or absent any dispute that the debt collector will assume the debt is a valid debt owed to the creditor (however, this is not an admission of liability in court).
4. This statement also must inform the consumer/debtor that they have the right to dispute the debt and if they do, the debt collector will obtain proof of the debt or judgment.
5. That if the consumer/debtor requests in writing within the 30-day period that the name and address of the original creditor will be mailed to them.

If the consumer/debtor disputes any amount of the debt, the debt collector must stop any attempts to collect the debt until the dispute is resolved. If the dispute is only partial, the debt collector can continue to collect the remaining balance of the debt (15 U.S.C. Section 1692g). Venue is proper in a real estate debt where the real estate is located or if it is personal property proper venue is where the consumer/debtor signed the contract that is the subject of the debt or where the consumer/debtor resides (15 U.S.C. Section 1692i).

If the debt collector fails to follow the FDCPA, the debt collector is liable for actual damages plus $1,000 for the individual consumer/debtor, costs, and reasonable attorney's fees. Further damages can be added if the court finds that the debt collector acted in bad faith and with the intent to harass the consumer/debtor.

E. Fair Credit Reporting Act 15 U.S.C Sections 1681–1681x

The **Fair Credit Reporting Act (FCRA)** was created in 1970 and amended in 1996 to insure that banks and other lending institutions have accurate credit information, which is supplied to them by credit reporting agencies. The FCRA is intended to regulate the consumer credit reporting agencies or as the FCRA puts it there "is a need to insure that consumer reporting agencies exercise their grave responsibilities with fairness, impartiality, and a respect for the consumer's right to privacy" (15 U.S.C. Section 1681).

Consumer reporting agencies are defined as:

any person which means any individual, partnership, corporation, trust, estate, cooperative, association, government or governmental subdivision or agency, or other entity, that regularly engages in the practice of assembling or evaluating consumer credit to prepare a consumer report which is defined as any written, oral, or other communication of any information by a consumer reporting agency bearing on a consumer's credit worthiness, credit standing, credit capacity, character, general reputation, personal characteristics, or mode of living which is used or expected to be used or collected in whole or in part for the purpose of serving as a factor in establishing the consumer's eligibility for credit or insurance to be used primarily for personal, family, or household purposes; employment purposes; or any other purpose authorized under §1681b. (15 U.S.C. Section 1681a)

The other authorized purposes under Section 1681b include providing the credit report in response to a court order or subpoena, as per the written request of the consumer/debtor, for the purposes of information on a credit transaction of the consumer/debtor, for employment purposes of the consumer/debtor, insurance for the consumer/debtor, issuance of a license by the government that requires proof of financial responsibility or has other legitimate business purposes. Furthermore, the credit report can be provided to the appropriate state agency for proof of ability to pay child support as requested by the consumer/debtor.

However, the use of the credit reports by employers was amended by the 1996 amendments. Now, employers must notify the consumer/debtor prior to accessing the credit report and obtain their consent. Furthermore, if the credit report is going to serve as the basis for refusing to hire or promote the employee or in the termination of the employee, the employer prior to taking that action must make a pre-adverse action disclosure to the employee, which must contain their credit report as well as a copy of a brochure from the FTC on the FCRA.

Ordinarily, a consumer/debtor will apply for a loan or credit extension, and the lending institution or entity that is extending credit will request a credit report from the credit reporting agencies and subsequently review the report and either extend the credit or deny the application. If the application is denied, the credit reporting agency must notify the consumer/debtor of the adverse action due to the credit report. The consumer/debtor then has the right to request in writing a copy of the credit report and review the credit report for any inaccuracies. If an inaccuracy is found, the consumer/debtor must notify the credit reporting agency of the error in writing. The credit reporting agencies are required to keep their files up to date and accurate. If the credit reporting agency does not feel that the report is inaccurate and does not feel that any correction is necessary, then without proper proof, the correction is not required. However, if the consumer/debtor still feels that the report is inaccurate, the consumer/debtor has the right to file a written report limited to 100 words or less stating their side of the dispute. The credit reporting agency is required to include the objection with the credit report.

If a credit reporting agency violates the FCRA, the FTC can go to federal district court to obtain a cease and desist order or take the case to an FTC administrative law court. The credit reporting agency is liable for actual damages to the consumer/debtor and for additional damages not to exceed $1,000 and attorney's fees.

F. Equal Credit Opportunity Act 15 U.S.C. Sections 1691–1691f

Congress passed the **Equal Credit Opportunity Act (ECOA)** in 1974 in an attempt to stop discrimination. It has been amended several times and basically now attempts to stop discrimination in the issuance of credit based on race, color, religion, sex, national origin, marital status, and age. However, in some situations such as in community property states like Texas, the marital status can enter into the process due to community property laws. (Remember, when you get married, you marry your spouse's credit history. Therefore, if they have a bad credit history, then, you after the marriage, now have bad credit.) Furthermore, the creditor is not allowed to discriminate against the consumer/debtor when they apply due to the income of the applicant being due to public assistance benefits or due to the fact that the applicant has ever utilized any of their rights under the CCPA.

Section 1691b of the FCRA authorized the **Federal Reserve Board** to pass regulations to carry out the FCRA. The Federal Reserve Board has done so with **Regulation B.** The Federal Reserve Board amended Regulation B in 2003 and the changes went into effect from April 15, 2004. Regulation B implements the ECOA. Therefore, the regulation contains a general prohibition against discrimination but also contains rules about taking and evaluating credit applications, how credit history is reported on accounts used by spouses, what must be done in the event of a credit extension denial, and limitations on requiring signatures on the documents other than the signature of the applicant, and exempts certain types of credit applications.

FCRA applies to **applicants** and **creditors**. An applicant is defined as "any person who applies to a creditor directly for an extension, renewal, or continuation of credit, or applies to a creditor indirectly by use of an existing credit plan for an amount exceeding a previously established credit limit" (15 U.S.C. Section 1691a(b)). A Creditor is defined as "any person who regularly extends, renews, or continues credit; any person who regularly arranges for the continuation of credit; or any assignee of an original creditor who participates in the decision to extend, renew, or continue credit" (15 U.S.C. Section 1691a(e)). However, the FRB amended the definition to clarify that a creditor also includes those who make the decision to deny or extend credit, as well as those who negotiate and set the terms of the credit with the consumer.

Regulation B prohibits the creditor from asking the applicant for information in the application for the extension of credit about a spouse (except in some community property situations 15 U.S.C. Section 1691d(c)) or former spouse, their marital status, any alimony or child support payments received, gender, whether they plan to have more children, or any other information about their race, color, religion, sex, national origin, marital status, or age. A creditor has 30 days to make a decision on a credit application from the day the application is received and must notify the applicant of the decision on the application within that same 30 days in writing and must contain the decision on the application, either granting the credit or denying the credit application. If the creditor denies the application, the notice must contain a statement of why the application was denied or a notice of the applicant's rights to receive such a notice and state the applicant's basic rights under the ECOA and the name and address of the relevant administration that the creditor can contact about violations and compliance with the ECOA.

If the provisions of the ECOA are not followed, then the FTC and sometimes other agencies listed in 15 U.S.C. Section 1691c and including the Federal Deposit Insurance Corporation (national banks and savings and loans associations), National Credit Union Administration (credit unions), Department of Transportation (airlines), etc., can bring suit on behalf of the applicant in administrative court or seek an injunction in Federal District Court. In addition, an applicant can personally bring a lawsuit in Federal District Court. There is a two-year statute of limitations. If a creditor is found to have violated the ECOA the applicant can recover their actual damages 15 U.S.C. Section 1691e(a) and seek punitive damages 15 U.S.C. Section 1691e(b) as well. However, the punitive damages cannot exceed $10,000 for an individual applicant. Applicant can also seek equitable relief to prohibit further discrimination by the creditor (15 U.S.C. Section 1691e(c)). Furthermore, the successful applicant who brings a civil suit can also recover attorney's fees and court costs (15 U.S.C. Section 1691e(d)). Any of the governmental agencies that enforce the ECOA can also refer the case to the United States Attorney General and the Attorney General can bring the civil suit on behalf of the applicant (15 U.S.C. Section 1691e(g)(h)).

G. Credit Repair Organizations Act 15 U.S.C. Sections 1679–1679(j)

The **Credit Repair Organizations Act (CROA)** was added to the EEOC in 1996 to ensure truthful disclosure of all information about the services sold to consumers by credit repair organizations and that the credit repair organizations are not being unfair or deceptive either in their advertising of those services or in their business practices (15 U.S.C. Section 1679). A credit repair organization:

means any person who uses any instrumentality of interstate commerce or the mails to sell, provide, or perform (or represent that such person can or will sell, provide, or perform) any service, in return for the payment of money or other valuable consideration, for the express or implied purpose of—
   (i) improving any consumer's credit record, credit history, or credit rating; or
   (ii) providing advice or assistance to any consumer with regard to any activity or service described in clause (i). (15 U.S.C. Section 1679a(3)(A))

However, non-profit organizations which are exempt from taxation are excluded as are creditors who are attempting to help the consumer restructure a debt owed to the creditor. Actions that are prohibited by the credit repair organizations include:

1. No credit reporting agency can make any untrue or misleading statement nor encourage any consumer to make an untrue or misleading statement.
2. Make nay statement or encourage any consumer to change the consumer's identification to prevent the display of the consumer's credit record, history or credit rating.
3. Make or use any untrue or misleading representations about the services of the credit reporting organization.
4. Committing or attempting to commit any fraud or deception.
   Requiring any payment from the Consumer before all of the services have been rendered. (15 U.S.C. Section 1679b)

Furthermore, the credit repair organization must give a detailed written disclosure to the consumer as specified in 15 U.S.C. Section 1679c, which basically tells the consumer what their rights are under both federal and state laws. The required disclosure is as follows:

You have a right to dispute inaccurate information in your credit report by contacting the credit bureau directly. However, neither you nor any "credit repair" company or credit repair organization has the right to have accurate, current, and verifiable information removed from your credit report. The credit bureau must remove accurate, negative information from your report only if it is over 7 years old. Bankruptcy information can be reported for 10 years.
   You have a right to obtain a copy of your credit report from a credit bureau. You may be charged a reasonable fee. There is no fee, however, if you have been turned down for credit, employment, insurance, or a rental dwelling because of information in your credit report within the preceding 60 days. The credit bureau must provide someone to help you interpret the information in your credit file. You are entitled to receive a free copy of your credit report if you are unemployed and intend to apply for employment in the next 60 days, if you are a recipient of public welfare assistance, or if you have reason to believe that there is inaccurate information in your credit report due to fraud.

You have a right to sue a credit repair organization that violates the Credit Repair Organization Act. This law prohibits deceptive practices by credit repair organizations.

You have the right to cancel your contract with any credit repair organization for any reason within 3 business days from the date you signed it.

Credit bureaus are required to follow reasonable procedures to ensure that the information they report is accurate. However, mistakes may occur.

You may, on your own, notify a credit bureau in writing that you dispute the accuracy of information in your credit file. The credit bureau must then reinvestigate and modify or remove inaccurate or incomplete information. The credit bureau may not charge any fee for this service. Any pertinent information and copies of all documents you have concerning an error should be given to the credit bureau.

If the credit bureau's reinvestigation does not resolve the dispute to your satisfaction, you may send a brief statement to the credit bureau, to be kept in your file, explaining why you think the record is inaccurate. The credit bureau must include a summary of your statement about disputed information with any report it issues about you.

The FTC regulates credit bureaus and credit repair organizations. For more information, contact:

The Public Reference Branch Federal Trade Commission Washington, D.C. 20580.

If the consumer still chooses to enter into a contract with the credit repair organization, then the credit repair organization must provide the consumer with a written contract at least three days prior to rendering any services on behalf of the consumer. The credit repair organization must include in the written contact their name and principal business address as well as, all of the terms and conditions of the payment required by the consumer including the total amount of all payment that will be made to the credit reporting organization or any other person, and a full and detailed description of all of the services to be rendered by the credit reporting agency, including all guarantees of performance and an estimate of the date by which their services will be completed and how long it will take to perform said services. Furthermore, the credit repair organization must include a three-day right of termination in the written contract and must make this specified disclosure in a conspicuous manner in immediate proximity to the consumer's signature on the contract.

> You may cancel this contract without penalty or obligation at any time before midnight of the 3rd business day after the date on which you signed the contract. See the attached notice of cancellation form for an explanation of this right. (15 U.S.C. Section 1679d(b)(4)

Obviously the credit repair organization must also include the notice of cancellation form on the contract and this form must be in duplicate. It must be named "Notice of Cancellation." That form must contain the following disclosure in bold face type:

You may cancel this contract, without any penalty or obligation, at any time before midnight of the 3rd day which begins after the date the contract is signed by you.

> **To cancel this contract, mail or deliver a signed, dated name of copy of this cancellation notice, or any other written notice to [name of Credit Repair Organization] at [address of the Credit Repair Organization] before midnight on [date required].**
> **I hereby cancel this transaction,**
> **[Date]**
> **[purchaser's signature]**

This must be given to the consumer along with a signed copy of the contract with the Credit Repair Organization at the time the contract is signed (15 U.S.C. Section 1679e).

Furthermore, there can be no waiver, nor attempt at waiver of the consumer's rights under the CROA. Any attempt to obtain a waiver is a violation of the CROA and any contract that does contract containing any waivers of the consumer's rights under the CROA is void (15 U.S.C. Section 1679f).

The CROA is enforced by the FTC. If it is determined that a credit repair organization violated any of the terms of the CROA, then the credit repair organization is responsible for actual damages, which are defined as the greater of the actual damage suffered by the consumer or the amount paid to the credit repair organization. Furthermore, the consumer is entitled to punitive damages as determined by the court as well as reasonable attorney's fees and court costs. The court is instructed to consider the following factors when awarding punitive damages:

1. the frequency and persistence of noncompliance by the credit repair organization;
2. the nature of the noncompliance;
3. the extent to which such noncompliance was intentional; and
4. in the case of any class action, the number of consumers adversely affected (15 U.S.C. Section 1679g)

The statute of limitations is five years for the CROA and is in addition to any State Law provisions for control of credit repair organizations.

Of course, the question remains, how much can the credit repair organization actually do that the consumer cannot do on their own? The answer is very little or nothing, hence the disclosure requirements.

IV. ELECTRONIC FUNDS TRANSFER ACT 15 U.S.C. SECTIONS §1693–1693r

When Congress passed the **Electronic Funds Transfer Act (EFTA)** in 1978, they made it clear that the purpose was to "provide a basic framework establishing the rights, liabilities, and responsibilities of participants in the electronic transfer systems (15 U.S.C. Section 1693). However, Congress made it clear that the primary object of the EFTA is the provision of individual consumer rights. Therefore, the EFTA is a regulation of the financial institutions that provide electronic fund transfer services. The EFTA is administered by the Board of Governors of the Federal Reserve System and in that capacity the Federal Reserve Board has adopted Regulation E to carry out the purposes of the EFTA (15 U.S.C. Section 1693b)

An **electronic fund transfer** is defined as:

> any transfer of funds, other than a transaction originated by check, draft, or similar paper instrument, which is initiated through an electronic terminal, telephonic instrument, or computer or magnetic tape so as to order, instruct, or authorize a financial institution to debit or credit an account. Such term includes, but is not limited to, point-of-sale transfers, automated teller machine transactions, direct deposits or withdrawals of funds, and transfers initiated by telephone. (15 U.S.C. Section 1693a(6))

The EFTA applies to a **financial institution**, which is defined as:

> a State or National bank, a State or Federal savings and loan association, a mutual savings bank, a State or Federal credit union, or any other person who, directly or indirectly, holds an account belonging to a consumer. (15 U.S.C. Section 1693a(8))

There are five major types of electronic fund transfers covered by the EFTA. These are automated teller machines (ATMs), point-of-sale transactions, transfers initiated by telephone, debit card transactions, and direct deposits/withdrawals. Regulation E requires that the consumer must have applied for or somehow requested either orally or in writing the electronic fund access device unless it is a renewal of the device. However, a financial institution can also send a customer an unsolicited access device if the access device is not validated, which means that it will not work until activated by the financial institution at the customer's request and is accompanied by a clear explanation of the customer's rights, duties, and obligations and the right to be disposed of the access device if the customer does not want to activate the device.

Acts that constitute an error can include:

1. an unauthorized electronic fund transfer;
2. an incorrect electronic fund transfer from or to the consumer's account;
3. the omission from a periodic statement of an electronic fund transfer affecting the consumer's account, which should have been included;
4. a computational error by the financial institution;
5. the consumer's receipt of an incorrect amount of money from an electronic terminal;
6. a consumer's request for additional information or clarification concerning an electronic fund transfer or any documentation required by this subchapter; or
7. any other error described in regulations of the Board. (15 U.S.C. Section 1693f)

A customer's liability for an unauthorized transfer is predicated upon the financial institution having properly provided the necessary, required disclosures to the consumer. However, the amount of the consumer's liability depends on whether the consumer gave the financial institution timely notice of the unauthorized transfer. If the consumer notifies the financial institution of the unauthorized transfer within two business days after learning of the unauthorized transfer, then their liability is limited to the amount of the transfer(s) or $50, whichever is less. However, if that specified timely notice is not given and it is more than two business days after the consumer discovers the unauthorized transfer, then the consumer is liable for up to $500 if the notice is given outside the two-day timely notice period if the financial institution determines that the charges would not have been made but for the consumer not giving the timely notice. However, a consumer must notify the financial institution within an outside time period of 60 days of the time that the unauthorized charge first appears on a periodic statement sent by the financial institution to the consumer. If the consumer does not notify the financial institution within this 60-day notice period then the consumer is responsible for all of the charges made after the close of the 60-day time period until notice is given. These time periods can be extended by extenuating circumstances. Notice can be in person, in writing, or oral. Written notice is effective when it is mailed to the consumer or delivers it for transaction to the consumer, in other word, when dispatched.

The financial institution must make the proper disclosures to the consumer as required by the EFTA and Regulation E. Those disclosures occur on three separate occasions and all three disclosures must be made properly by the financial institution. The first disclosure is at the time the consumer first applies for the access device or before the first time the access device is used. This disclosure must include a notice of the liabilities of the consumer, the telephone and address of the person or office the consumer must contact in the event of an unauthorized use, the business days of the financial institution, types of transfers allowed and any limitations on the frequency or dollar amounts of those transfers, what fees will be imposed by the financial institution for the electronic fund transfers, a summary of the consumer' s rights to receive receipts and periodic statements, how to make a stop-payment request on preauthorized requests and the time periods in which to do so, a summary of the liability of the financial institution to the consumer, the steps the consumer needs to take to resolve errors, when the financial institution can make information about the consumer's electronic fund transfers to third parties, ATM fees, and if a new service is added to the consumer's account, that new disclosures will be made including the new service. If any changes are made by the financial institution in the electronic fund transfers allowed by that institution, then the financial institution must give written notice to the consumer at least 21 days before the proposed changes are to take effect. These changes can include increasing the fees charged to the consumer, increasing the liability of the consumer, cancellation of electronic fund service(s), and changing the dollar amount of the transfer(s) allowed.

The second type of notice required is at the time of the electronic fund transfer. This is commonly satisfied with a receipt provided to the consumer at the time of the transaction. The information required to be present in the receipt is the amount of the transfer including the fee assessed by the financial institution for the transfer, the date, the type of transfer, and the consumer's account from which the transfer occurred, the identification code to identify the consumer's account that is limited to four digits or letters, the location of the terminal by street address or name and the owner/operator of the location, and the name of the third party to whom a transfer is made if applicable.

The third and final disclosure comes in the form of a periodic statement, which is required to be sent to the consumer on a monthly cycle if a transfer is made or quarterly even if no transfers have been made. This statement must contain the following disclosures:

1. The amount of the transfer, the date the transfer was credited to or debited from the consumers account, the type of transfer and the type of account involved and the terminal location if an electronic terminal was used, and the name of any third party to whom the transfer was made, if any.
2. The number on the account.
3. The amount of all fees assessed for the electronic fund transfers during the statement period.
4. The account balance at the beginning and ending period of the statement.
5. The address and telephone number to be used in the event of an inquiry about the statement or notice of unauthorized transfer.
6. The telephone number to use to determine if preauthorized transfers have been made. (There are special rules for preauthorized transfers such as the financial institution must notify the consumer within two business days if an unauthorized transfer was not made and a consumer must request a stop payment of a preauthorized transfer 3 business days before the scheduled date of the transfer.)

If a consumer orally notifies the financial institution within the maximum 60-day time period of an error, specifying the account and consumer's name, then the financial institution can request from the consumer written notice of the error. The financial institution has 10 business days from the date of receipt of the oral error notice. Such a request must contain the address where the written notice from the consumer to the financial institution is to be sent. If the notice of error is sent in writing by the consumer, then the financial institution has 10 business days to investigate the alleged error to complete the investigation and must notify the consumer in writing within 3 business days and must make any necessary corrections within 1 business day. However, if the institution cannot complete its investigation within the 10-day time period, they can take up to 45 days if the financial institution provisionally credits the consumer's account plus interest if necessary during the 10-day period, gives the consumer full use of the funds during the 45-day period and notifies the consumer within 2 business days of the provisional credit to their account, except that the financial institution can withhold $50 if they reasonably believe that an unauthorized transfer has in fact occurred. The financial institution does not have to provisionally credit the account if the consumer did not provide written confirmation of the oral notice when requested by the financial institution. Even if the error claimed by the consumer was found to be groundless the financial institution must sent a written notice to the consumer within three days of the completion of the investigation and said notice must include findings of the investigation and shall give the consumer notice of findings relied on and how the consumer can obtain a copy of findings. If the claimed error was shown to in fact have been itself in error, the financial institution must notify the consumer of the date and amount of the debiting if the account had been provisionally credited. Remember, any errors must be corrected in 1 business day. However, the time periods of 10 days can be doubled if the error involves an electronic fund transfer to or from the account within 30 days after the first deposit to the account was made and the 45-day time period can be extended to a 90-day period if the electronic fund transfer was made out of state, resulted in a point-of-sale debit card transaction, or occurred within 30 days after the first deposit to the account was made.

Regulation E makes special provisions for ATMs where the operator changes a fee. If they so charge a fee the operator of the machine must prominently and in a conspicuous location on or at the machine display a notice that a fee will be charged and the amount of the fee imposed for providing electronic fund transfer services or a balance inquiry. This fee can be displayed on the window screen of the ATM or on the receipt given to the consumer.

A financial institution is liable for not making a properly requested electronic fund transfer unless the consumer's account does not have sufficient funds to cover the transaction, the consumer's account is subject to legal seizure such as in a garnishment action, such transfer would exceed the credit limit, the electronic terminal has insufficient funds to complete the transaction or any other exceptions provided by the Board (15 U.S.C. Section 1693h(1)). Furthermore, the financial institution is not liable for failing to make a transfer dues to acts of God and technical malfunctions (15 U.S.C. Section 1693h(2)).

Civil damages for failing to comply with the EFTA include actual damages sustained by the consumer, an amount neither less than $100 nor greater than $1,000. However, if an action was predicated upon a consumer's claim of an unauthorized transfer and the financial institution did not provisionally re-credit a consumer's account within the 10-day time period and was not handled properly by the financial institution with the financial institution not making a good-faith investigation or not having a reasonable basis for believing that the consumer's account was not in error or the financial institution knowingly and willfully conclude that the account was not in error when it was in fact in error, then the consumer is entitled to treble damages. However, criminal penalties can be assessed against anyone who gives false or inaccurate information or fails to provide information which is required to be disclosed under the EFTA and can be fined not more than $5,000 or imprisoned for not more than one year or both.

V. RECENT ADDITIONS TO CONSUMER CREDIT LAW

In 2007, the United States found itself in the worst financial shape since the Great Depression. Jobs were being eliminated, people were seeing their savings disappear, and people could not pay their bills. The housing market was crashing due to people owing so much on their house that they could not pay the mortgage and homes were being repossessed at a record rate. In short, Americans had too much debt and not enough income to service the debt they had incurred. Part of this was due to irresponsible lending by the financial institutions in the housing industry. These financial institutions had been making very complicated loans and the consumers did not fully understand what they were getting into in the housing loan. In other words, the financial institutions were luring consumers into loans that they could not repay with promises of low payments. These risky credit practices in part led to the financial crisis. Even Americans who did not participate in the risky credit practices saw the value of their homes plummet because with so many foreclosures on the market, it drove the price of everyone's home down. Credit card debt was at an all-time high and the default rate was high and when people missed a credit card payment the interest rates on the credit card debt would soar. A lot of people had resorted to pay their house payment with credit cards. So they were in essence robbing from Peter to pay Paul.

In 2009, President Obama called for the creation of a new regulatory agency to oversee lending practices and to protect consumers in credit transactions to focus on protecting the consumers and not the financial institutions by protecting families from unfair, deceptive, and abusive financial practices. In July 2010, Congress passed the **Dodd-Frank Wall Street Reform and Consumer Protection Act**, which created the **Consumer Financial Protection Bureau (CFPB)**.

The CFPB has three main goals:

1. Educate the consumer against the abusive practices of the financial institutions,
2. Enforce federal consumer financial laws against financial institutions
3. Study available information to help consumers and financial institutions.

To carry out these goals, the CFPB is headed by a director with a deputy director and a chief of staff to assist the director. There are also several assistant directors to assist the director in carrying out the goals of the CFPB. Remember this bureau is supposed to consolidate several of the other federal consumer agencies so it has a large, complicated structure.

According to the CFPB website, the CFPB will protect consumers by carrying out federal consumer financial laws such as:

- Write rules, supervise companies, and enforce federal consumer financial protection laws
- Restrict unfair, deceptive, or abusive acts or practices
- Take consumer complaints
- Promote financial education
- Research consumer behavior
- Monitor financial markets for new risks to consumers
- Enforce laws that outlaw discrimination and other unfair treatment in consumer finance

Remember, this bureau was created a mere 15 months ago at the time of this writing and there is not much to report on enforcement or how it is operating. Again, only time will tell.

CHAPTER SUMMARY

In this chapter, we have concentrated on two different areas, Debtor-Creditor Law and Consumer Credit Law. In the debtor-creditor area, we concentrated on Texas law and discussed the differences in being a secured creditor and liens that were both common law and statutory, including artisan's liens, worker's liens, landlord's liens, and mechanic's, contractor's, or materialman's liens. We wrapped up this discussion with how to execute liens. We then discussed exempt property of two different types, rural and urban. Lastly we discussed one way to extend the liability by requiring guarantors, sureties, and co-signors.

In Consumer Credit Law, we discussed the umbrella law of the Consumer Credit Protection Act and several areas contained therein. We discussed the Truth in Lending Act which contained both the Fair Credit Billing Act and the Consumer Leasing Act. We also discussed the Fair Debt Collection Practices Act, Fair Credit Reporting Act, the Equal Employment Opportunity Act, the Credit Repair Organizations Act, and the Electronic Fund Transfer Act.

Then, we have the recently created Consumer Financial Protection Bureau (CFPB) and the impact it will have is still at best, cloudy.

The student should be aware of all of these legal topics and the purposes thereof. You should also know the reasons why each was created, the requirement of each, and the penalties for each as well.

14

REGULATION OF THE ENVIRONMENT

I. MEANS OF REGULATION OF THE ENVIRONMENT

A. Introduction

Every manufacturing process creates waste of some form. It could be heat, light, smoke, chemical compounds, greenhouse gases, or radioactive materials. When these wastes are disposed of into the environment, they become **pollution**, which is basically something that is not where it is supposed to be.

Once the government has determined the optimal amount of pollution, it must use its power to achieve it by the most efficient means possible. The government has several methods to achieve optimality. First, courts enforce the property rights accompanying the ownership of land through a system of tort law discussed in an earlier chapter. Second, the government uses its considerable influence to seek voluntary compliance with emission standards by businesses. Thirdly, Congress passes broad legislations that mandate reduction of pollution.

B. Tort Law

Two tort theories are commonly used by property owners who are injured by emissions, trespass to land, and nuisance. A trespass to land is any unauthorized physical intrusion or entry upon the land of another. A trespass can occur when one causes the invasion of particulate matter such as dust or soot onto the property of another. Actual injury to the land need not be proved, only that the invasion interfered with the owners' exclusive possession. If the dust or soot remained on the land, the owner would be entitled to recover the cost of its removal. The landowner can only recover damages for past invasions. If the invasions are ongoing, as they often are with particulate emissions, the owner may obtain an injunction prohibiting future invasions. However, obtaining such injunctions is problematic, as will be discussed below.

The more common tort involved with pollution is nuisance, which is an unreasonable interference with one's peaceful enjoyment or use of land. The interference can be a result of sight, sound, odor, smoke, vibrations, or even the height of a building. Damages can be recovered for the past loss of use and enjoyment and a permanent injunction can be obtained to prevent future interference.

While it may seem that a permanent injunction is an ideal way to rid society of polluters, permanent injunctions against polluters are difficult to obtain. In the landmark case of **Boomer v. Atlantic Cement Company 287 N.Y.S. (1967)**, the defendant cement company was sued by neighboring property owners for the alleged interference caused by dirt, smoke, and vibrations emanating from the plant. At the time of the case, the rule of law in New York was that the plaintiffs were entitled to an injunction regardless of the cost of eliminating the nuisance. However, the court in *Boomer* stated that it could not ignore the great disparity, in this case, between the cost of eliminating the nuisance and the benefit to the neighbors. The investment in the plant was over $45 million and it employed 300 people. There was no available technology that could eliminate the nuisance; therefore, the plant would have to shut down. The court said it could no longer ignore the economic costs of injunctions and refused to issue one in this case.

Other states soon adopted this rule and rendered the use of nuisance suits ineffective for eliminating pollution. However, courts will now award what they call, permanent damages, which amounts to a one-time compensation for all future harm caused by the nuisance.

Permanent injunctions are more common in cases of public nuisance, which is an action that interferes with the health, safety, and property rights of a community. When the injury of an entire community is compared with the cost of abatement, there is less disparity than with private nuisance so the likelihood of obtaining an injunction is greater. However, only public officials have the standing to bring a suit for public nuisance, making the decision to sue a political one.

C. Voluntary Compliance

Over the past 50 years, increased waste production and population density has moved environmental concerns to the forefront. It began with serious problems that could be seen and smelled such as the Cuyahoga River that was so polluted that it once caught fire. Toxic waste dumps that leaked into groundwater tables and leached into the soil prompted the creation of the Superfund to clean up these dumpsites. The fund was once financed by businesses but now uses taxpayer funds.

It is difficult for environmental regulation to keep pace with the growth of industry. The Environmental Protection Agency (EPA) relies upon citizen groups such as the **National Resources Defense Council (NRDC)** to pressure polluters to reduce their emissions. The federal government provides information to the public through the **Toxics Release Inventory (TRI)**, which provides details on the emissions by 22,000 plants of over 300 chemicals believed to have health consequences. This information comes from the self-reporting of emissions by firms.

Health risks associated with the environment are high on the audience-intrinsic interest scale and are widely reported by the media. The EPA and citizen groups are adept at using the media to gain the cooperation of industry to set voluntary emission standards. This method is more efficient than legislation but often the threat of legislation is necessary to elicit cooperation.

D. Legislation

One way to legislate the optimal amount of pollution is by using command-and-control regulations. One such method is for Congress to place emission limits on the amount of certain wastes that may be disposed into the environment by each producer. The advantage of this method is that all producers are treated equally and the amount of emissions can be limited directly. A disadvantage of this method is that such limits are difficult to enforce because each firm must be constantly monitored. This is significant because no command-and-control plan is effective without proper enforcement, otherwise, polluters will accept the low risk of getting caught and fined, as opposed to spending tens of millions of dollars on abatement. Some legislation provides for criminal prosecution for certain violations as felonies.

Another disadvantage is that although each producer is treated equally, all producers are not equal. More recently constructed plants may have incorporated newer emission technology that would give them a cost advantage over older firms. The older firms could be under-priced by newer firms, and possibly forced out of business, with a consequent dislocation of labor and capital and a reduction in competition.

Another command-and-control method is to tax certain emissions and allow firms to decide whether to cut emissions by investing in emission control technology or to continue to pollute and pay the tax. The additional advantage of this method is that it encourages the development and use of new technology by rewarding, through lower taxes, those who use it. The disadvantages are the same as using emission limits with one additional problem. The tax must be set so that the market responds by producing the optimal amount of pollution. A great deal of information must be known about the cost structures of the firm, and the response of consumers to the subsequent increases in prices that result from the tax, in order to determine the optimal tax rate.

An alternative to command-and-control methods is the tradable permits system. Under this system, the government decides the optimal annual amount of environmental discharge of a particular emission. Usually, it is based on some fraction of the current amount of discharge and can be reduced over a period of years. Permits are then distributed to producers based upon a percentage of their production, or by auction. The permits allow the holder to discharge a certain unit, such as 1 ton, of an emission into the environment. Each producer can discharge only the amount of an emission for which it has permits. Otherwise, they must adopt emission control technology to eliminate its discharge. The permits can be freely traded, usually, through a broker.

The market price of the permits is determined by the laws of supply and demand and will be affected by, among other factors, the cost of emission control technology, the demand for the product that produces the emissions, and the number of permits issued by the government. Theoretically, the price of the last permit traded would be equal to the marginal cost of eliminating the last unit of emissions.

The major advantage of the permit system is that plants that can most efficiently reduce emissions have an incentive to do so because they can sell their permits. Plants that cannot reduce their emissions in a cost-effective manner will continue to pollute but will have an incentive to adopt emission control technology if and when it becomes cost effective. Society gets a reduction in emissions for the least expenditure of resources.

Another advantage of the permit system is that it produces a known amount of emissions. Other command-and-control systems have an indirect often unpredictable effect on abatement because they rely upon market forces to ultimately determine the amount of emissions. For instance, a tax on emissions relies, in part, upon the increase in the cost of production to increase the price of the product, which reduces the quantity demanded and the quantity produced of the product.

Like command-and-control methods, the permit system requires monitoring emissions to insure compliance. However, since producers have an alternative to adopting expensive control technology, they may be more likely to comply.

Some object to the permit system because permits are the equivalent to licenses to pollute. Permits for sulfur dioxide were renamed "allowances" in order to make them more acceptable to the public. Supporters of the permit system point out that those producers are allowed to pollute under command-and-control methods without the requirement of a permit. Many environmentalists favor the permit system because it enables environmental activist groups to purchase allowances and retire them.

One example of the tradable permit system is the way the Clean Air Act of 1990 dealt with sulfur dioxide, a major component of acid rain. In 1993, the EPA auctioned allowance permits to emit 150,010 tons of sulfur dioxide under rules that required more than 300 pages of fine print in the *Federal Register*. The permits were sold to bidders at prices ranging from $122 to $450 per ton. Although electricity-generating plants bought most of them, some were sold to environmental groups who promptly retired them. By 2002, the amount of permits will be reduced by half. Perhaps predicting that prices for permits would soar, most generating plants have invested in costly abatement equipment and are using less-polluting fuel.

II. THE POLITICS OF ENVIRONMENT

A. Reasons for Pollution

Businesses do not necessarily pollute because they are unethical. Businesses often pollute because competition forces them to do so. If competitors are keeping the prices of their product low by not treating their wastes, then other firms must follow suit or be priced out of the market. Furthermore, it is not just other members of the industry that concern businesses but producers of substitute products as well. Costs imposed on the airline industry to reduce pollution make travel by car, bus, or train more attractive to passengers. Hence, the effects of legislation are complex and affect many powerful interests, which, in turn, affect the interests of individual members of Congress.

B. Political Problems

Usually, the costs of pollution abatement have more of an impact on some states than others, which makes it difficult to achieve a consensus in Congress. For example, the 1977 Clean Air Act amendments required all new coal-fired power plants to have scrubbers that remove most of the sulfur dioxide from emissions. Older plants were not required to have scrubbers. Fifteen years later, still less than one quarter of coal-fired plants had scrubbers. One alternative to the use of scrubbers was to use western low-sulfur coal, which drastically reduced sulfur dioxide emissions. Western coal was cheaper to mine and contained less than 0.5 percent sulfur compared to most eastern coal, which had a sulfur content of 4–5 percent. Although transportation to the East was expensive, it was still more cost effective to use low-sulfur coal in older power plants than to retrofit them with scrubbers.

The political problem with requiring the use of low-sulfur coal was that it would put producers of eastern coal out of business. Thousands of miners in the Ohio River Valley and Appalachia would lose their jobs and the towns in which they lived would disappear. Members of Congress from coal-producing states sought a way out by proposing a 20 percent tax credit for the installation of scrubbers, which would cause fewer plants to switch to low-sulfur coal. The measure would save 3,000–5,000 miner jobs, but at an estimated cost of $3.3 billion. The number of states benefiting from the proposed tax credit was small, and they were forced into a compromise measure that provided $250 million to displaced coal miners for unemployment benefits and retraining. The price of each job saved by the tax credit for scrubbers, approximately $1 million, was more than the majority of Congress could swallow. However, the compromise was significant in that it was the first time funds were appropriated for an industry that was displaced by environmental legislation.

Another political complication with the reduction of pollution is what to do with the waste. No one wants to live near a waste disposal site, and as rural areas become more populated, there are fewer and fewer locations that are not subject to the Not in My Backyard (NIMBY) movement. Scrubbers use a system that sprays a mixture of water and limestone inside a smokestack causing a chemical reaction that removes the sulfur but produces sludge. A scrubber may use as much as 400 tons of limestone and thousands of gallons of water per day and produces hundreds of tons of sludge that must be put somewhere. As the costs of waste disposal sites increase, the optimal amount of pollution abatement, determined by cost-benefit analysis, decreases, which does not bode well for the environment.

III. HISTORY OF THE ENVIRONMENTAL MOVEMENT

American awareness of the environment became a popular movement and culminated in the first Earth Day on April 22, 1970. This movement was very peaceful in contrast to the other movements of the 1960s like the anti-war protests. Of course, environmentalism did not begin on Earth Day. For that you could go back as far as 1652 when Boston established a public water supply system.

However, pollution was still everywhere throughout the 1700s and 1800s with the people in the United States having very little concern for the environment. After all, you could always move to the West away from the pollution. However, by the mid-1800s, literary works started calling attention to pollution. Probably, the most influential of these was by Henry David Thoreau with his work *Walden, of Life in the Woods* in 1854. Yellowstone became the first national park in 1872.

By the end of the century, John Muir published *The Mountains of California* in 1894. It was Muir who took President Teddy Roosevelt on a western camping trip in 1903 and Roosevelt made conservation a theme of his administration and even after his administration. In fact, Roosevelt has been called the Conservation President. During his administration, he signed a legislation creating five national parks. It was also during his administration that the Antiquities Act was passed, which proclaims historic landmarks, historic structures, and other historic objects to be national monuments.

During the New Deal, President Franklin Roosevelt (FDR) took several steps to help the environment such as the Civilian Conservation Corps (CCC) that employed unemployed young men, up to 300,000 at one time at its height and a total of over 3 million totally, to plant trees and perform other conservation efforts. The CCC planted about 3 billion trees. The CCC, which was one of the most popular of all of the New Deal programs, lasted from 1933 to 1942 when most of the young men left for World War II. It also helped make the public aware of conservation. However, probably the most lasting thing that FDR did for the environment was the creation of the Tennessee Valley Authority (TVA), which helped control flooding in the Tennessee River by creating nine dams and also provided electricity to the Southeast, not to mention recreation areas as well as provision of drinking water. The TVA manages 293,000 acres of land and 11,000 miles of shoreline. FDR also created the Soil Conservation Service in 1935 that works to reduce erosion in agricultural/farming land.

After World War II, veterans started to move their new families to the suburbs and the concept of ecology, valuing natural real beauty and the environment over efficiency and commerce. After all, the growth of the cities had shown pollution at its worst with the publication of information about air pollution and deterioration of the cities. Again, the literary world had a large hand in public awareness of problems in the environment with the publication of *Silent Spring* by Rachel Carson in 1962, which was about widespread poisoning by pesticides and the impact on humans and the environment.

Presidents Kennedy and Johnson began discussing environment in their speeches in the early 1960s stressing protection of the wilderness and pushing to clean up the damage that had already been done to the environment. Richard Nixon also wanted to profit from supporting the environment and it became an issue in the 1968 Presidential campaign and when he got to be President, he began to study the need for one agency to be over the environment. Congress also got into the environment issue by passing the **National Environmental Policy Act (NEPA)** to change the role of the government from conservation to "create and maintain conditions under which man and nature can exist in productive harmony" and to "assure for all Americans safe, healthful, productive, esthetically and culturally pleasing surroundings" and required all federal agencies to submit Environmental Impact Statements (EISs). The NEPA also instructed President Nixon to create a Council on Environmental Quality. Three weeks after Nixon signed the bill, he told the nation in his State of the Union Address that the time for the environment had come. He followed this up with sending Congress an unprecedented environmental package and then created the United States EPA in 1970 by an executive order. Environmental law is mostly regulated by the EPA. The EPA is an independent agency. Its administrator is appointed by the President and confirmed by the Senate. The EPA administers most of the environmental laws and spends most of the federal budget for environmental regulation. Congress has been reluctant to give the power to set standards to the EPA because the potential compliance costs to businesses could be devastating to particular industries. Such affects could be far reaching, giving the EPA vast power to affect the economy. It has broad rule-making powers to adopt regulations to promote all of the environmental laws. It also has adjudicatory power to hold hearings and order remedies for violations of these environmental laws. The EPA can also file suit in federal court against suspected violators of federal environmental law.

IV. ENVIRONMENTAL PROTECTION AGENCY

The EPA has the power to enforce some statutes by issuing complaints and granting hearings before an administrative law judge. Rulings by the agency can be appealed to the administrator and then to the federal court system. Other statutes, particularly those providing criminal sanctions, require the EPA to forward cases to the Department of Justice, which may bring suit against alleged violators. Still other statutes grant standing to private citizens to sue the EPA for not enforcing the law or to sue polluters directly.

Although Congress was at one time concerned that the agency would be captured by the industries that it regulates, the EPA has been quite active in using its power to put pressure on polluters to reduce pollution. During the late 1990s, EPA administrator Carol Browner put on the Internet detailed records of environmental inspection and infraction reports for 653 industrial facilities. The goal was to inform citizens as how to best protect themselves and their families and where to place pressure for environmental reform. The EPA once attempted to reform emission standards without Congressional authority by taking into account the risks to children. In one instance, the EPA reduced the emission standards for small particles of dust and soot because of the susceptibility of asthmatic children. In 1999, the court of appeals overturned the new standards on the grounds that they were arbitrary and capricious and exceeded EPA authority. The Texas equivalent to the EPA is the Texas Commission on Environmental Quality (TCEQ).

V. FEDERAL AREAS RELATING TO ENVIRONMENTAL PROTECTION AND POLLUTION CONTROL

A. Clean Air Act

Congress originally passed the **Clean Air Act** in 1963, which focused on air pollution between states and gave the states federal assistance in fighting air pollution. It has been amended in 1970, 1977, and 1990. These amendments have strengthened the federal government's authority to regulate air pollution. The federal government regulates air from both mobile sources and statutory sources.

The EPA has developed air-quality standards for stationary sources of air pollution, which are called the **national ambient air quality standards (NAAQS)**. These standards are set at two different levels. The primary level is designed to protect human beings and the secondary level is to protect vegetation, climate, and visibility, property such as buildings, statutes and other matter, and economic values. Specific standards have also been set for known pollutants like lead, carbon monoxide, and ozone as well as nitrogen oxide and sulfur oxide, which collectively cause acid rain and particles of matter. Even though the EPA sets the standards, it is the responsibility of the state governments to enforce these standards. However, the federal government has the right to enforce these standards if the state chooses not to do so. The states are to enforce these standards by preparing a **state implementation plan (SIP)**, which sets out that state's plan to implement the EPA standards. The EPA has also subdivided each state into **air quality control regions (AQCRs)** and monitors each region to ensure compliance. Regions that do not meet the EPA standards are designated **non-attainment areas** and the state must develop a plan to bring that area into compliance within a set time period. If the state does not do this, it is subject to severe penalties including the loss of federal highway funds and limitation on new sources of pollution, which means that the EPA can forbid new pollution-controlling industries in non-attainment areas.

1. Mobile Sources of Pollution

The primary mobile source of pollution is automobiles. The Clean Air Act and its amendments govern air pollution from automobiles as well as other mobile sources by specifying pollution standards and the time schedules to meet those standards. However, often these time schedules are not met and have to be extended by the federal government.

Emission standards have been set by the EPA for automobiles, trucks, buses airplanes, and even motorcycles. The EPA also regulates the production of automobiles to ensure compliance with its emission standards. All new automobiles must meet air quality control standards. If they do not, the EPA can require the manufacturer of the automobiles to recall and repair or replace pollution control devices that do not meet these standards. The EPA is also authorized by the Clean Air Act to regulate fuel and fuel additives. Leaded gasoline was prohibited from being sold in 1995, just like the production of engines that use leaded fuel was prohibited after model year 1992. Service stations are also subject to environmental regulations. As of the 1990 amendments, in addition to not being able to sell leaded gasoline by 1995, some service stations were required to sell gasoline with higher oxygen content. These service stations were located in over 40 cities that had experienced carbon monoxide pollution in the past. Service stations in Los Angeles and other eight of the most polluted cities had to sell even cleaner-burning gasoline than that of the national requirements.

The EPA in enforcing the Clean Air Act as to mobile sources of pollution attempts to update its standards whenever new scientific information becomes available. One area where the EPA has been especially active is in decreasing the acceptable standard for ozone, which is formed when sunlight combines with pollutants from automobiles since ozone is one of the basic ingredients of smog and since there has been so much discussion about the ozone layer and its effects on the world.

2. Stationary Sources of Air Pollution

Mobile sources of air pollution are not the only area of concern expressed in the Clean Air Act. The other source of concern is stationary sources of air pollution. A good example of a stationary source of air pollution is a manufacturing plant that emits pollutants into the air. Substantial amounts of air pollution are emitted by stationary sources of air pollution. To combat that problem, the Clean Air Act requires states to identify the major stationary sources of air pollution and to develop plans to reduce their level of pollution. Stationary sources of air pollution are generally required to install pollution control devices to control air pollution as either: (1) **Reasonably Available Control Technology (RACT)** that is normally required of existing stationary air pollution sources and (2) **Best Available Control Technology (BACT)** that is normally required by the Clean Air Act of new stationary sources of air pollution. However, states can also require BACT and normally do if it is part of the state's plan to reduce the level of air pollution in that region. The factors to consider in requiring RACT or BACT, in addition to the severity of the pollution in that area, include the cost of the equipment and the size of the polluting company.

Another area of concern regarding air pollution is toxic air pollutants that cause serious illness or even death to human beings. It is the job of the EPA to identify these toxic air pollutants. So far, the EPA has identified over 180 chemicals that are designated toxic air pollutants. These include asbestos, mercury, benzene, radio-nuclides, etc. The Clean Air Act requires the EPA to establish standards for the emission of these chemicals and requires stationary sources emitting these chemicals to utilize the maximum achievable control technology (MACT) to control their emission. MACT for existing sources is normally less stringent than for new sources. Furthermore, EPA standards for toxic substances are set without regard to economic or technological feasibility.

3. Future of Air Pollution

A new area of concern for the EPA in air pollution might be indoor air pollution. The EPA estimates that the air inside a building is 100 times more polluted than the outside air. This is due to several factors including lack of ventilation, over insulation, the construction materials, and the presence of hazardous chemicals in the building. The result is that very little or no fresh air is allowed into the building leading to headaches, dizziness, and fatigue among workers. Radon gas is also a problem primarily in the homes, with some estimates saying that 4–10 million homes have excessive radon gas levels. Radon gas damages lung tissue and it is estimated that radon causes up to 20,000 deaths each year. Presently, the EPA has not adopted any regulations governing indoor air quality but if the estimates are correct, how long will it be before building owners and construction companies are being sued for this problem? The repair costs and the damages could be enormous. Is it only a matter of time before the EPA must get involved? Only time will tell.

B. Clean Water Act

1. History of Water Pollution

Water pollution is a major problem in the world and has resulted in severe ecological and environmental problems rendering rivers and harbors hazardous and unfit for drinking water or recreation. The first water pollution actually dates back to 1886 when Congress enacted the River and Harbor Act. This Act established a permit system for the discharge of refuse, wastes, and sewage into the navigable waterways of the United States. In 1972, the permit system was replaced by the National Pollutant Discharge Elimination System (NPDES), which still requires anyone who plans to discharge pollutants into the waterways to obtain a permit from the EPA. The EPA can deny or set severe restrictions on the permit. Navigable waterways today include not only intrastate lakes and streams used by interstate travelers and industries but also coastal and fresh-water wetlands.

The Federal Water Pollution Control Act was passed by Congress in 1948 to regulate water pollution and was amended several times before it was totally updated by the Clean Water Act of 1972, which has been amended by the Clean Water Act of 1977 and the Water Quality Act of 1987. Collectively, these laws are referred to as the Clean Water Act. and like the Clean Air Act, are administered by the EPA.

The EPA has established water quality standards that determine what bodies of water are safe to use for public drinking water, recreation, propagation of fish and wildlife as well as agricultural and industrial uses. The states are primarily responsible for the enforcement of these standards but if the state fails to do so, the EPA can step in and enforce the standards. The Clean Water Act has several areas of concern.

2. Point Sources

The first area of concern for the EPA in the Clean Water Act is point sources of water pollution. Point sources are simply the point from which the water pollution comes and can include private industry such as mines and manufacturing plants, government sources of water pollution such as municipal sewage plants as well as other sources of water pollution. Point sources are required to install pollution control equipment based on two standards, these standards are as follows: (1) **Best Practical Control Technology (BPCT)** and (2) **Best Available Control Technology (BACT).** All previously existing point sources were required to immediately install BPCT. However, cost, severity of the pollution, and time necessary to install the equipment were considered. New point sources of water pollution, on the other hand, are required to install BACT regardless of cost. However, the EPA also has issued timetables for the existing point sources to install BACT equipment. Furthermore, all dischargers of water pollutants are required to keep records, maintain monitoring equipment, and keep samples of water pollutant discharges, all of which are subject to EPA review and can lead to fines and penalties for violations.

3. Thermal Pollution

The Clean Water Act specifically forbids thermal pollution. Thermal pollution is the discharge of heated waters or materials into the navigable waters of the United States because the heated discharge decreases the oxygen content of the water and can result in harm to fish in the water as well as any bird or animals that use the water. One of the major sources of thermal pollution is electricity-generating plants that are highly regulated by the EPA.

4. Wetlands

The Clean Water Act also protects wetlands. Wetlands are defined as areas that are inundated or saturated by surface water or ground water that support vegetation typically adapted for life in saturated soil conditions. This includes swamps, marshes, bogs, and any other area that supports animals and birds that are typically associated with this type of area. The owner of any wetland is prohibited from filling, dredging, or draining the wetland until they have received a permit from the Army Corps of Engineers, which is empowered to adopt regulations and conduct administrative proceedings to protect wetlands.

5. Oceans

a. Marine Sanctuaries

The **Marine Protection, Research, and Sanctuaries Act of 1972** protects the oceans from water pollution. It established marine sanctuaries at sea and requires a permit to dump wastes into the ocean. This law is violated often by cruise ship lines, which do not want to get into the trouble or expense to obtain a permit and occasionally you will hear of these cruise liners getting caught and being forced to pay fines for violation of the Act. Each violation of the Ocean Dumping Act can result in a civil penalty of not more than $50,000 or revocation or suspension of the permit of the polluter. If the polluter knowingly violates this law the penalty may be a $50,000 fine, imprisonment for up to one year or both, and an injunction can also be imposed.

b. Oil Spills

The Clean Water Act also authorizes the United States Government to clean up oil spills within 12 miles of the U.S. shore and on the continental shelf and to recover the costs from those responsible for the spill. Furthermore, in 1990, Congress passed the **Oil Pollution Act (OPA)** in response to the devastation of the Alaskan shore due to the Exxon Valdez accident and the oil companies' lack of preparedness to handle such a catastrophe. The first cleanup barge did not reach the spill site for 14 hours and the oil contaminated 1,100 miles of shoreline killing tens of thousands of birds and animals and countless numbers of fish. The OPA contains strict requirements for constructing oil tankers requiring all ocean-going oil tankers to be double hulled by 2015. This has met with great opposition by the tanker industry that feels this is an overreaction and less costly solutions should be used. The OPA also requires that each tanker owner and operator establish an oil cleanup contingency plan.

The U.S. Coast Guard administers the OPA and has its own set of regulations for emergency response plans. The Coast Guard must issue a certificate to a tanker before it can enter U.S. waters and to obtain the permit the tanker owner-operator must prove that it is fully insured to cover any liability resulting from an accident. The OPA also set up a $1-billion oil clean-up and economic compensation fund. The OPA allows for compensation for the damage to natural resources, private property, and the local economy. Civil penalties of $1,000 per barrel of spilled oil or $25,000 per day of the violation are allowed.

6. Drinking Water

The Safe Drinking Water Act of 1974 authorizes the EPA to establish national drinking water standards for human consumption and forbids the dumping of wastes into wells used for drinking purposes. Operators of public water supply systems must use the best available technology that is economically and technologically feasible. Of primary concern to the EPA are underground sources of pollutants such as landfills and pesticides. There are more than 200 known pollutants that exist in groundwater used for drinking in more than 30 states. These pollutants are known to cause cancer, liver and kidney damage, and even damage to the central nervous system. This Act was amended in 1996 to give the EPA greater flexibility in establishing regulatory standards governing drinking water. This allows the EPA to move at its own pace in setting control over the pollutants that are of most concern to the public. The amendment also requires each supplier of drinking water to send to its customers on a yearly basis a statement describing the source of its water, the level of any contaminants in the water, and the possible health consequences associated with those contaminants. Again, the states are primarily responsible for the enforcement of this law, but the EPA can enforce the law if the states are not doing so.

C. Toxic Substances

1. Federal Insecticide, Fungicide, and Rodenticide Act

The **Federal Insecticide, Fungicide and Rodenticide Act (FIFRA)** gave the federal government regulatory power over pesticides and related chemicals. The Act was substantially amended in 1972 and is now administered by the EPA. Pesticides must be registered with the EPA before they can be sold. The EPA can deny the registration, certify its use, or set limits on the amount of the chemical residue permitted to be on crops sold for human or even animal consumption. If the pesticide is found to pose an imminent danger or emergency, the EPA can suspend the registration and thus stop the sale of the pesticide immediately. If the danger is not imminent or an emergency, then the EPA must have a hearing prior to the cancellation of the registration. FIFRA also allows the EPA or its state counterpart to inspect the plants where the pesticides are manufactured. Under the **Food, Drug, and Cosmetic Act of 1996**, for a pesticide to remain on the market there must be a reasonable certainty of no harm to people due to the exposure to the pesticide. The 1996 amendment also requires the EPA to distribute to grocery stores brochures on high-risk pesticides that are in food and the grocery stores must display and distribute these brochures to the public. Violations of FIFRA can include selling pesticides or herbicides that are unregistered, or if the registration has been canceled or suspended, or if the pesticide or herbicide has a false or misleading label. Penalties for registrants and producers of the pesticide or herbicide include imprisonment of up to one year and a fine of not more than $50,000. Penalties for commercial dealers include imprisonment for up to one year and a fine or $25,000 and penalties for farmers and other private users of the pesticides or herbicides can include a fine of up to $1,000 and up to 30 days' imprisonment.

2. *Toxic Substances Control Act of 1976*

The **Toxic Substances Control Act** requires manufacturers and processors to test new chemicals to determine their effect on human health and the environment. The results of these tests must be sent to the EPA, which is charged with the administration of the Toxic Substances Control Act. These results must be sent to the EPA before the product can be sold. The EPA in turn can limit or even prohibit the manufacture and sale of the toxic substances or require special labeling of toxic substances. Hundreds of new chemicals and their compounds that may be toxic are discovered each year.

D. Hazardous Solid Wastes

1. *Resource Conservation and Recovery Act of 1976*

The Resource Conservation and Recovery Act (RCRA) regulates the disposal of new hazardous wastes. The RCRA was amended in 1984 and 1986. Those amendments decreased the use of land containment in the disposal of hazardous wastes and expanded the coverage of the RCRA to include some types of hazardous waste that were not originally covered by the RCRA. The EPA is authorized to regulate the facilities that generate, treat, store, transport, and dispose of hazardous wastes. States have the primary responsibility of implementing the RCRA but if the states fail to do so, the EPA can enforce the RCRA. Hazardous wastes are solid wastes that might cause or significantly contribute to an increase in the mortality or serious illness or hazard to human health or the environment if managed improperly. The EPA designates what solids qualify as hazardous wastes and can continually add to the list. The EPA has implemented a tracking system from the creation to the disposal of the hazardous waste. Basically, anyone creating or handling a hazardous waste must obtain a permit to do so from the government. The EPA also regulates the underground storage facilities of hazardous wastes, which can include something as common as underground gasoline storage tanks. Penalties under the RCRA include a civil fine of up to $25,000 for each violation. Criminal penalties can include fines of up to $50,000 per day per violation and imprisonment for up to two years, or both. Furthermore, criminal fines and times of imprisonment can be doubled for repeat offenders.

2. *Comprehensive Environmental Response, Compensation, and Liability Act (CERCLA) of 1980, (the Superfund)*

Congress created **Superfund** in the **Comprehensive Environmental Response, Compensation, and Liability Act (CERCLA) of 1980** to regulate the cleanup of disposal sites where hazardous wastes were leaking into the environment. The Act was significantly amended in 1986 and is administered by the EPA. The Act gives the federal government a mandate to clean up hazardous wastes that had been spilled, stored, or abandoned. The first thing the EPA had to do was to identify the hazardous waste sites and then rank them in order of severity of the risk. Those sites with the greatest severity of risk were put on a National Priority List that receives first consideration for cleanup. However, before the cleanup can begin, studies must be done to determine the best way to cleanup the hazardous waste site. The Superfund creates a fund to finance the cleanup of these sites. Said fund is financed through taxes on products that have the potential to create a hazardous waste site. The Superfund is a tort law that imposes strict liability and joint and several liabilities. This means that you are liable if you did the act that results in the hazardous waste and you are potentially responsible for the entire cost of the cleanup even if you are only one party that contributed to the hazardous waste site. The law is also retroactive, so even if you legally disposed of the chemicals when you disposed of them, it might be illegal now and therefore, you are responsible for the cleanup. However, this retroactive part of CERCLA is being challenged as being unconstitutional.

Therefore, the issue becomes, just who is liable under CERCLA? Basically, the answer is any potentially responsible party (PRP) that can include the generator who deposited the waste, the transporter of the waste to the site, the owner of the land at the time of the disposal of the waste that contains the hazardous waste site, and the current owner and operator of the site. Whoever cleans up the hazardous waste site, whether it is a government entity, state or federal, or a private individual, can seek reimbursement from the Superfund. If an individual is forced to clean up the site, that individual can file a contribution action against any other PRPs for a percentage of the costs. The Act also contains a right-to-know provision that requires businesses to disclose the presence of certain chemicals to the community, annually disclose emissions of chemical substances that are released into the environment, and immediately notify the government of any spills, accidents, and other emergencies that involve hazardous chemicals.

The Texas equivalent to the Superfund is the **Texas Solid Waste Disposal Act, which is found in the Health and Safety Code, Title 5 Sanitation and Environmental Quality, Chapter 361**. Section 361.271(a)(1) of the Texas Act lists a responsible party as "any owner or operator of a solid waste facility."

E. Nuclear Waste

Nuclear-powered fuel plants create radioactive wastes that can cause injury and death to human beings and other life and cause severe damage to the environment. Radiation pollution can be caused by accidents, human error, or faulty construction. Regulation of nuclear energy in the United States is handled by two federal agencies: the **Nuclear Regulatory Commission (NRC)** and the EPA. The NRC was created by the **Energy Reorganization Act of 1977** and licenses the construction and opening of commercial nuclear power plants and continually monitors the operation of those nuclear power plants. The EPA is empowered to set standards for radioactivity in the environment and disposal of nuclear wastes as well as thermal pollution from nuclear power plants and emissions from uranium mines and mills. Nuclear wastes currently listed by the United States NRC are:

1. Low-level waste (LLW) and includes radioactively contaminated protective clothing, tools, filters, etc.
2. Waste incidental to reprocessing (WIR) refers to certain waste by products that result from reprocessing spent nuclear fuel
3. High-level waste (HLW) is used nuclear reactor fuel, irradiated
4. Uranium mill tailings are the residues remaining after the processing of natural ore to extract uranium and thorium

The **Nuclear Waste Policy Act of 1982** established that the federal government was responsible to provide a permanent site for the disposal of HLW and the spent nuclear fuel. Currently, the government is looking at Yucca Mountain, Nevada, as a possible site. As you might expect, no state wants to have a permanent nuclear waste site within its borders and the location of the permanent site or sites has been the topic of much political debate.

The **Low-Level Radioactive Waste Policy Amendments of 1985** gives the states the responsibility to dispose of the low-level radioactive waste generated within their own borders. Furthermore, those sites will be regulated by the NRC and/or the states under standards set by the NRC.

The **Uranium Mill Tailing Radiation Control Act of 1978** establishes programs to stabilize and control uranium mill tailings. The main concern here is to prevent or at least minimize the diffusion of radon in to the environment. This act gives the NRC regulatory authority in this area.

F. Noise Pollution

The **Noise Control Act of 1972, U.S.C. Chapter 66** requires the EPA to establish noise emission standards that are maximum noise levels below which no harmful effects occur from the interference with speech or other activities. These standards must be achievable by the best available technology and they must be economically within reason. The EPA regulates noise sources such as rail and motor carriers, low-noise emission products, construction equipment, trucks, motorcycles, and the labeling of hearing protection devices. Most other noise control activities as of 1981 are handled at the state and local levels.

Illegal, willful or knowing, production or distribution of products in violation of these standards or in violation of labeling requirements can result in penalties up to $25,000 per day and imprisonment for up to one year, or both. For second violation, the penalties double. Violations are also subject to civil penalties of not more than $10,000 per day. Furthermore, each day of violation constitutes a separate violation.

The EPA is currently revising its regulation of the labeling of hearing protection devices such as ear plugs and products that emit noise that may adversely affect public health and welfare. This is being done in conjunction with the National Institute for Occupational Safety and Health. The purpose is to update these standards due to technology since 1979 when the standards were first put into effect.

G. Endangered Species Act

The Endangered Species Act (ESA) 16 U.S.C. Section 1531 et seq. (1973) is one of the most powerful environmental laws that currently exists because it is the major environmental law that can stop a construction project dead in its tracks and prevent the owner from developing his or her property and there is no compensation required for the prohibition of the land use. Adding the fact that the endangered species does not have to be a species that is liked by the owner and the public in general just adds salt to the open wound. The ESA covers conservation of the threatened species; both plant and animal, and the habitats where they are located. Species include birds, insects, fish, reptiles, mammals, crustaceans, flowers, grasses, and trees.

The Secretary of Commerce via the U.S. Fish and Wildlife Service and the Secretary of the Interior via the National Atmospheric Administration (NOAA) through the National Marine Fisheries Service (NMF) are empowered to declare a form of wildlife to be endangered or threatened. The National Wildlife Federation defines an endangered species as one that is likely to become extinct throughout all of a large portion of their range and threatened as likely to become endangered in the foreseeable future.

Normally, species are listed if there is (1) present or threatened destruction of the species habitat or range; (2) overuse of the species for commerce, recreation, science, or education; (3) losses due to disease or predators; (4) current inadequate protection; or (5) other man-made or natural threats to the species.

This Act requires the immediate designation of critical habitats for each endangered and threatened species, and real estate development by the government is prohibited in these areas. Critical habitat is defined as the geographical area occupied by the listed species or even an area outside the occupied areas if that is deemed necessary for conservation. On private land, there may be no clear authority that citizens much comply with ESA but any issuance of permits, at least federal permits (and there are several that are required), would have to receive the permission through ESA. Therefore, on private lands the owners can be prohibited or severely limited. One such agreement for private landowners is Safe Harbor Agreements (SHA), which is a voluntary agreement involving owners of private property who attempt to help an endangered species. In exchange for the help of the private land owner who enrolls his or her property with the U.S. Fish and Wildlife Service, they get the assurance of the Service that if the private land owner fulfills the requirements of the SHA, then the Service will not require any additional or different management activities without the consent of the owner. Furthermore, at the end of the enrollment period the private land owner can return the enrolled property back to the way it was before the beginning of the SHA. The Endangered Species Act prohibits the harassment, harming pursuit, hunting, shooting, wounding, killing, trapping, capturing, or collecting of any endangered or threatened species.

One success story from the ESA is the America bald eagle. In the 1960s, there were only 500 bald eagles left in the Lower 48. Dangerous pesticides like DDT had almost wiped out the bald eagles. It is estimated that today there are over 7,000 breeding pairs of bald eagles. Other success stories are that of the Florida panther, gray wolf, grizzly bear, peregrine falcon, and the red-cockaded woodpecker.

V. PRIVATE PROTECTION OF THE ENVIRONMENT

A. Private Right of Action

Many of the federal environmental laws allow private individuals to either personally enforce the laws or petition the EPA of appropriate governmental agencies to proceed in their interest. For instance, the Superfund allowed private individuals to sue other individuals for contribution in the cleanup.

B. Tort Theories

As seen early in this chapter, private individuals can also protect their property through the use of tort law. In fact, prior to federal laws, the only way to protect your property was through tort law. Particularly useful in this area is nuisance law. An individual can sue another individual who creates a nuisance on their real property. Pollution can be a form of nuisance whether it is physical or intangible such as noise.

C. Other Legal Doctrines

Keep in mind that the states are supposed to enforce the federal environmental laws but some states are very active in passing their own environmental laws that can be more strenuous than the federal laws. The federal laws were patterned after California law to some extent. However, the New England states and the Pacific Northwest are now generally recognized as having the most strenuous environmental laws.

Furthermore, international pressure and law or the lack thereof, can effect the United States environment as well. One of the big oppositions to the North American Free Trade Agreement was that many businesses would move to Mexico where the environmental laws were not as tough. However, they could locate along the U.S./Mexico border and when the south wind blew, causing major problems for states along the Mexican border. Also, take the example of Canada's complaints about American factories producing sulfuric oxide and nitrogen oxide that combine with oxygen to become acid rain. Canada's complaint to the United States was that the U.S. pollutions greatly contributed to Canada's acid rain problem. Many people feel this was partially the reason for the Clean Air Act amendment in 1990.

Furthermore, the political pressure of environmentalists through interest groups such as the Sierra Club and Green Peace is growing. Environmentalists are beginning to get more political as seen in the emergence of the Green Party as a political force to be reckoned with in the 2000 Presidential race.

VI. TRENDS IN THE ENVIRONMENTAL REGULATION

Given the emergence of environmentalists as interest groups and political groups and the growing awareness of recycling and other environmental programs, one can expect the area of environmental regulation to grow in the next few years. However, there will always be the opposition to environmental controls because those controls cost businesses money and are therefore, looked upon with disfavor. So, the battle will continue between the environmentalists, on the one hand, and the big business, on the other. Which will win? Again, only time will tell.

CHAPTER SUMMARY

Wastes are produced in all production processes and the disposal of these wastes is a cost of production much like other inputs that must be used. If a market system could assign ownership of the environment to individuals, then producers would be forced to negotiate with such owners for the use of the environment to dispose of their wastes. However, the unique nature of environment prevents its ownership by individuals. Rather, the environment is owned in common by all members of society, and, thus, no member of society has the right to tell another how to use commonly owned property.

This problem results in the production of negative externalities that are costs borne by someone other than the producer. Since the producer does not bear the full cost of his actions, he will have little incentive to curtail his activity that results in an overproduction of negative externalities.

Pollution is a negative externality and unless producers of pollution can be held accountable for the discharge of wastes, they will dispose of them into the environment with impunity. This is a proper role for the government. It can act as the owner of the environment and hold producers accountable for its use.

The first step in environmental regulation is to determine the optimal amount of pollution. Some may believe that the optimal amount of pollution is zero, but pollution actually saves society a vast amount of resources. Society could not afford the cost of disposing of all waste in such a way that it had no impact on the environment. The most useful way to determine the optimal regulation of the environment is to compare the costs and benefits of pollution abatement. It would be inefficient for society to spend more on abatement than it received in benefits.

The government uses different ways of implementing the optimal amount of regulation. To a certain extent, courts enforce the property rights of landowners who are harmed by industrial waste. The Environmental Protection Agency (EPA) informs the public of polluters and encourages citizen groups to pressure producers to pollute less.

Congress passes legislations that control emissions in a number of ways. The most efficient method is the emissions permit system that entitles holders of permits to a certain amount of emissions. The permits can be freely traded.

The politics of environmental regulation is complex. Pollution abatement is costly and the industry is well represented in Washington.

The EPA is the federal agency with the power to administer most of the federal environmental laws. These laws include several laws that regulate air, water, hazardous wastes, noise, toxic substances, and endangered species.

15

THE GLOBAL ENVIRONMENT

I. OVERVIEW OF CONTEMPORARY GLOBAL MARKETPLACE

A. Introduction

It's hard to read a newspaper or magazine these days without hearing about the globalization of the U.S. economy. The reason for this attention is simple: Foreign markets, foreign governments, and policymakers in a variety of international organizations like the European Union, the International Monetary Fund, the World Trade Organization, and the World Bank increasingly are playing an important role in shaping the opportunities available to U.S. businesses. Understanding the impacts of this global environment on the day-to-day operations and the strategic choices facing firms is therefore an important facet of any businessperson's knowledge base. Providing this awareness is the task of this and the next chapter.

B. The World Economy Today

Let's begin by providing an overview of the contemporary global marketplace. The gross domestic product (GDP) of the world's economy reached an estimated $70 trillion in 2011, with the United States accounting for 21.4 percent of this total. Other large markets include China, with 10.4 percent of the world's GDP; Japan, 8.1 percent; and the 27 member nations of the European Union (25.2 percent).

Developed countries like the United States, Canada, Japan, Australia, and those of the European Union account for about 60 percent of the world's economic activity. The developed countries are a major source of highly skilled workers, innovative technology, and new capital. They are also the most important market for the goods produced by developing countries that wish to stimulate their economic growth through increased exports.

C. Emerging Markets

While the developed countries account for the lion share of the world's GDP, the so-called **BRIC countries** (**B**razil, **R**ussia, **I**ndia, and **C**hina) have attracted increasing attention because they account for much of the growth in the global economy. China and India, the world's two most populous nations, are home to nearly 40 percent of the world's population. The People's Republic of China (PRC) is one of the last remaining countries in the world controlled by a Communist Party. A series of free market reforms beginning in 1978 have made it one of the world's fastest growing economies. Half of China's GDP is produced by for-profit firms, although the Communist Party still exerts significant control over the economy and over the banking sector. Nonetheless, because of the large size of its domestic market and its enormous potential, virtually every significant multinational corporation in the world has staked a claim in China. Foreign direct investment (FDI) in its economy is enormous: in 2011 alone, it amounted to $124 billion. As a result, China's manufacturing sector has boomed, and its economy has grown at an annual rate of over 9 percent in the past decade. China's growth accelerated after it joined the World Trade Organization in 2001, as firms flocked there to take advantage of its then abundant supply of low-cost labor. However, China has become a victim of its own success. Labor costs have risen at double digit rates over the past 10 years, and China is no longer the obvious location for new manufacturing facilities producing labor-intensive goods destined for Western markets.

India, the world's second-most populous country (1.2 billion residents), presents a similar picture. After gaining its independence from the British in 1947, India favored import substitution policies similar to those used by many South American countries (which we will discuss below). India's economic growth lagged well behind many of its Asian neighbors, and its political leaders—India is the world's largest democracy—struggled for decades to find a solution to the country's economic ills. In 1991, India's government began to open its economy by reducing trade and investment barriers and lessening the regulatory burdens imposed on its private sector. These new policies are bearing fruit. For example, India is now the second largest computer software exporter in the world and is the home of several home-grown multinational corporations.

Brazil's rapid growth is attributable to its rich endowment of natural resources: fertile farmland, ample water supplies, and mineral resources such as iron ore, bauxite, and manganese. It is also the dominant economy in South America, accounting for almost half of that continent's GDP. Brazil has benefited from the boom in the price of commodities triggered by China's growth.

Russia (or, more formally, the Russian Federation) was formed after the collapse of the Soviet Union in 1991. The country struggled for the first decade of its existence, as the inability of its first president, Boris Yeltsin, to solve Russia's numerous crises cast an economic pall over the region. Key Russian institutions, like the police, the tax collection system, the judicial system, and the military, functioned inadequately under Yeltsin's leadership. Russia had difficulty attracting FDI and new loans in the last years of Yeltsin's regime, due in part to its mismanagement of previous foreign loans, its de facto default on its foreign debts in 1998, and the general level of political instability and uncertainty that permeated the country. His successor as Russia's president, Vladimir Putin, moved aggressively to reform the country's tax system and curb corruption. The country, a major oil exporter, has benefited handsomely from the rise in world oil prices; however, Russia is still plagued by a legal system that foreign investors put little faith in and high levels of corruption.

Other countries also play important and growing roles in the world economy. Four Southeast Asian countries—collectively known as the Four Tigers in light of the Chinese heritage that three of the four share—have become influential forces in the contemporary world economy. The **Four Tigers**—Hong Kong, the Republic of China (Taiwan), Singapore, and South Korea—are notable for having made the transition from being low-income countries (those with per-capita incomes of $1,025 or less) to high-income countries (those with per-capita incomes greater than $12,476) since the end of the Second World War. Because of their post-War successes, the Four Tigers are also known as the **Newly Industrialized Countries**, or **NICs**. However, Hong Kong was not a country—until 1997, it was a British Crown Colony; now it is a special administrative region of the PRC—and whether Taiwan is an independent country or a merely a rebellious breakaway province of the People's Republic is a sensitive diplomatic issue. Experts trying to be politically correct thus refer to the NICs as the **Newly Industrialized Economies**, or **NIEs**. Regardless of what they are called, these experts note that the Four Tigers have risen to rank among the richest economies in the world by relying on an export-promotion growth strategy. A country using an **export-promotion growth strategy** develops its economy by relying on exports as its source of growth. Accordingly, the Four Tigers are often used as examples of the wisdom of liberalizing international trade as a vehicle for promoting prosperity throughout the world.

During the 1970s, other Southeast Asian nations began to copy the export-promotion growth strategy adopted by the Four Tigers. Malaysia, Thailand, Indonesia, and the Philippines opened up their economies to foreign investment and created a business environment favoring trade. During the 1980s and much of the 1990s, these countries were among the fastest growing in the world.

The countries of Latin America adopted a very different economic development approach after the Second World War. They relied on an **import-substitution growth strategy**. Countries adopting this approach try to stimulate the development of domestic manufacturing by raising barriers to imported goods. By keeping out imports, they then hope that their local manufacturing industries will have the opportunity to develop and grow. Unfortunately, while this approach yielded some short-term benefits, it proved to be less than successful over the longer term. The domestic markets of these countries were often too small to generate much domestic competition or to allow manufacturers to capture economies of scale. As a result, costs of production were often high. High costs of production led to high prices, which hurt consumers and often encouraged local firms to lobby their governments to impose even higher trade barriers to protect them from lower-priced foreign goods. Unfortunately, the high prices of locally produced manufacturing goods often damaged other sectors of the economy and made them less competitive in foreign markets. For example, for many years Brazil barred the import of computers and computer accessories. Brazilian policymakers hoped to stimulate the development of a local computer industry by shutting out foreign competitors. Buoyed by their expected successes in the computer industry, the policymakers then believed Brazilian entrepreneurs would be encouraged to invest in other high technology areas, ultimately putting Brazil at the cutting-edge of numerous innovative and rapidly growing industries. Unfortunately, this ban on foreign computers proved to be a perfect example of the law of unintended consequences. The ban caused Brazilian users to pay two or three times as much for Brazilian-made computers that were half as good as those commonly available in other countries. By forcing Brazilians to use high-priced, technologically obsolete, domestically produced computers, this policy hindered the modernization of thousands of Brazilian firms and reduced their competitiveness in world markets. Rather than being a vehicle for re-orienting the Brazilian economy toward high-technology, the ban on foreign computers caused Brazilian firms to fall behind their foreign counterparts in integrating computers into the work place.

In the late 1980s, many Latin American countries came to the conclusion that their import-substitution policies were not working. Such countries as Chile, Mexico, Brazil, Argentina, Peru, and Bolivia began to open up their economies, encourage foreign investment, and lower their trade barriers. As a result of these policies, for most of the 1990s, Latin America was one of the hottest markets in the world. Unfortunately, its economic growth slowed substantially in the first years of the new millennium, partly as a result of the slowdown in the world economy and partly as a result of mismanagement of fiscal policies. Many Latin American countries are also plagued by large income inequalities, which have created political and policy instability in the region. Fortunately, the boom in commodity prices occurring in the mid-2000s boosted many Latin American economies, including those of Argentina (food products), Brazil (food products and iron ore), Bolivia (natural gas and tin), Chile (copper), Mexico (oil), and Venezuela (oil).

D. The Foreign Exchange Market

Most nations have their own currencies. International businesses thus constantly need to exchange one currency for another to pay for goods, services, and inputs or to repay loans denominated in foreign currencies. For example, if Japan Airlines wishes to purchase a Boeing 787 aircraft, it must convert its home currency, yen, into U.S. dollars, the home currency of the Boeing Corporation, to pay for the transaction. The international monetary system provides the framework for this exchange of one currency into another. When it is functioning efficiently, the international monetary system allows firms to do so at low cost and with little risk.

The current international monetary system relies on a blending of two different types of exchange rate systems. (An **exchange rate** is the price of one currency denominated in terms of a second currency. For example, one U.S. dollar could be purchased in April 2013 for 0.6518 British pounds; the inverse relationship also is true: one British pound could be purchased for $1.5342.) The first type of exchange rate system is called a flexible exchange rate system. Under a **flexible exchange rate** system, the value (price) of a currency fluctuates according to demand and supply for that currency in the foreign exchange market. Consider the foreign exchange market for British pounds. The demand for pounds is derived from foreigners' demands for British goods, services, and assets. A German student on a Study Abroad trip to England who wishes to buy a souvenir to bring back to his parents in Hamburg or a ticket to see *Les Miserables* in the London's West End theater district will need British pounds to do so. Similarly, a manager of a big U.S.-based pension fund like the Texas Teacher's Retirement Fund who wishes to purchase 10,000 shares of British Airways on the London Stock Exchange for her fund will need British pounds as well. The daily demand for British pounds is determined by the actions of thousands of foreigners like the German student and the U.S. pension fund manager who wish to buy British-made products or British-owned assets, but who need pounds to do so.

The supply of British pounds is determined by the British demand for foreign goods, services, and assets. A British pension fund manager who wishes to buy 10,000 shares of Southwest Airlines on the New York Stock Exchange will need dollars to do so; similarly, a British tourist in Paris who wishes to take an elevator ride to the top of the Eiffel Tower will need euros. To get the dollars and euros they need, these British citizens will sell (or supply) British pounds to the foreign exchange market. Like other commodities, the price of the British pound in the foreign exchange market will be determined by the intersection of the demand and supply curves of British pounds.

At the center of the foreign exchange market are dozens of large international banks like Barclays (U.K.), Deutsche Bank (Germany), Credit Suisse (Switzerland), and Citibank (U.S.). Currency traders at these banks sit at computer monitors and constantly buy and sell currencies among themselves, hoping to profit by selling a currency for slightly more than they paid for it. The foreign exchange market is dominated by traders located in London, New York, and Tokyo, although trading also occurs in several dozen other major cities such as Sydney, Hong Kong, Singapore, Frankfurt, Bahrain, and Zurich. Each day some $4.0 trillion of foreign currency is traded, with most of these trades occurring between big international banks. Trading between these big banks establishes the wholesale price of foreign exchange. This wholesale market is then linked to the retail market, which consists of hundreds of thousands of businesses, consumers, and travelers who need foreign currency to buy goods, pay off foreign loans, or travel to the foreign paradises they've always dreamed of.

1. The Flexible Exchange Rate System

Many countries, especially those with solid free market economic systems, have chosen to use a flexible exchange rate system for determining the value of their currencies, including the United States, Japan, Canada, the United Kingdom, Switzerland, and Australia. These countries believe that the values of their currencies are best determined by the marketplace. This makes them free to use fiscal and monetary policies to solve domestic macroeconomic problems like inflation and unemployment. Unfortunately, flexible exchange rate do create some difficulties for businesses because they can fluctuate wildly on an hourly, daily, weekly, monthly, and yearly basis. In December 2001, for example, the U.S. dollar was worth 131 Japanese yen. Twelve years later, it was worth only 88 yen, or 33 percent less. The decreased value of the dollar in 2013 meant that Japanese goods were more expensive for U.S. consumers, for it now takes more dollars to obtain a given amount of yen than it did in 2001. However, the decreased value of the dollar makes it easier for Japanese consumers to buy U.S. goods, for it takes fewer yen to acquire the same number of dollars. When the value of the yen falls (or the dollar's value rises), the opposite occurs. Because of their impact on consumers' purchase decisions and relative production costs between the two nations, fluctuations in the yen–dollar exchange rate also introduce uncertainties into firms' export sales and plant-location decisions. At an exchange rate of 131 yen to the dollar, Toyota, Toshiba, Caterpillar, General Electric, and other firms selling to Japanese and U.S. consumers might wish to build their new plants in Japan; at an exchange rate of 88 yen to the dollar, these same firms might be better off locating their factories in the United States. Since the value of the yen can rise or fall dramatically, firms must proceed very cautiously in deciding where to locate long-lived factories in the new era of globalized business.

2. *The Fixed Exchange Rate System*

The second type of exchange rate system is called a fixed exchange rate system. In a **fixed exchange rate system**, a government promises that it will hold the value of its currency fixed relative to some major currency. As long as the government is able to honor that pledge, companies can make their business decisions knowing the exchange rate will not change. However, if the government fails to live up to its promise, chaos can result.

Currently, Panama, The Bahamas, Barbados, and Oman (among others) peg the value of their currencies to the dollar, while many former French colonies in Africa fix the value of their currencies to the euro, which is the currency used by France.

II. FORMS OF INTERNATIONAL BUSINESS ACTIVITIES

A. Introduction

The rapid growth of world economy has encouraged more firms to participate in international business activities. Businesses can exploit the opportunities created by the huge international marketplace in many ways. The two most important forms of international commerce are trade (exporting and importing) and foreign investment. Alternatively, firms can also participate through franchising, licensing, contract manufacturing, and other specialized modes of entry.

B. Trade

Most firms' initial forays into the international marketplace take the form of exporting and/or importing. **Exporting** involves selling products made in one's home country for the use of or resale by a resident of a foreign country. **Importing** involves the purchase of products made in a foreign country for use or resale in one's home country. The world's exports are enormous: in 2011, exports of goods totaled $17.8 trillion, while exports of services reached $4.1 trillion. As Figure 15.1 demonstrates, exports of goods and services and world GDP have grown dramatically since the end of the Second World War. In 2011, the United States exported $2,103 billion of goods and services, or about 14 percent of that year's GDP of $15 trillion. U.S. imports in 2011 totaled $2,663 billion, or about 18 percent of its GDP. As a result, the United States had a trade deficit of $560 billion, meaning the country imported more goods and services than it exported. See Figure 15.1 below

Both exporting and importing are vital to the prosperity and profitability of citizens, nations, and firms. Exporting generates economic activity and employment in the home

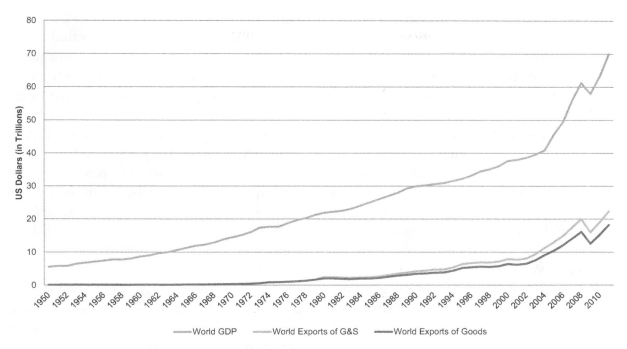

FIGURE 15.1 World Exports and GDP (1950–2011).

country, thereby increasing jobs, wages, profits, and tax revenues. Importing benefits consumers who have increased consumption choices as a result of the availability of foreign-made goods in their local malls and stores. By providing an alternative to domestically produced goods, imported goods also benefit consumers by driving down prices in the local market through increased competition and stimulating local manufacturers to improve the quality and price of domestically made goods.

Imports may also raise the competitiveness and productivity of domestic manufacturers. By purchasing parts and inputs where they are cheapest, domestic firms can lower their costs of production and devote their resources to those market niches where profit margins are highest. For example, West Virginia's Weirton Steel found it more profitable to close down some of its furnaces making slab steel and import that slab from overseas. By doing so, Weirton was able to focus its energies and capital expenditures on more profitable finished steel. Similarly, GM reduced its investment costs by $50 million by purchasing from Korean and Japanese manufacturers stamping dies needed for its Chinese and Mexican auto assembly plants.

B. International (Overseas) Investments

Firms may also participate in international business through overseas investments. **International investment** occurs when a resident of one country supplies capital to a resident of a second country. International investments can take two forms, foreign portfolio investments (FPI) and foreign direct investments (FDI). The distinction between the two forms of investments revolves around the issue of control: does the investor wish to (or expect to) actively manage the organization in which the investment is made? Conceptually, FDI occurs when the investor plans to actively manage the organization in which she has invested, while FPI occurs when the investor does not plan to manage that organization. Government statisticians are not mind readers, however, and do not ask international investors whether they seek to actively manage the organization in determining whether an international investment is FDI or FPI. Rather, the U.S. government classifies an international investment as being FDI when the investor owns 10 percent or more of the voting stock of the organization; if the investor owns less than 10 percent of the voting stock, the investment is classified as FPI. For example, if General Electric's pension fund buys 1,000 shares of Toyota stock, the investment is considered to be an FPI. If America's Kraft buys 100 percent of the common stock of Cadbury, Britain's leading chocolate company, that investment is classified as FDI. FDI can also take the form of new property, plant, or equipment, which is often owned by a local subsidiary of a foreign parent company. An example of this type of FDI would be Toyota (a Japanese company) building a truck assembly plant in San Antonio, Texas.

Both types of international investment are huge. FPI by Americans as of the end of 2011 are estimated to be $11.0 trillion; corresponding portfolio investments by foreigners in the U.S. economy are $12.4 trillion. Many of these portfolio investments involve purchases by residents of one country of stocks, bonds, and other securities issued by companies headquartered in other countries, or of securities issued by foreign governments. Foreign private citizens, for example, owned about $1.4 trillion of securities issued by the U.S. Treasury.

FDI made by U.S. residents totaled $4.7 trillion as of the end of 2011; corresponding direct investments in the U.S. economy made by foreign residents totaled $2.9 trillion. The primary destinations of U.S. FDI are the developed countries. The most important of these recipients (in descending order) are the United Kingdom, the Netherlands, Canada, Luxembourg, Japan, and Ireland. The primary sources of FDI in the U.S. economy are also developed countries. The most important providers of FDI to the United States (in descending order) are the United Kingdom, the Netherlands, Germany, Switzerland, and Canada.

It may seem a bit strange that the same countries are both the primary sources and the primary destinations of FDI involving the United States, for normally we think that capital flows to where it can receive the highest rates of return. Obviously, rates of return can't simultaneously be higher in the United States than in Canada (which would explain why Canadians would invest in the United States) and higher in Canada than in the United States (which would explain why Americans would invest in Canada).

This puzzle can be explained by the behavior of multinational corporations. A **multinational corporation** (MNC) is a firm with extensive international business involvement, typically owning or managing value-adding activities in several countries. Most MNCs engage in extensive FDI as a means of exploiting some competitive advantage that they possess, such as superior technology, a well-known brand name, or strong ties to an existing customer base. Caterpillar, for example, has built manufacturing facilities in North America, Japan, South America, Europe, and Asia to serve its customers throughout the world, all of whom recognize the strength of the company's technology and the excellent after-sales service support it offers purchasers of the company's equipment. Japanese archrival Komatsu has followed a similar FDI strategy. Each rival recognizes that a strong market presence in each of the world's market places is critical to its survival and prosperity. Accordingly, we observe Komatsu engaging in FDI in the United States, while Caterpillar engages in FDI in Japan. It is easy to understand the large two-way flows of FDI between each pair of developed countries when we realize that thousands of rival MNCs from the developed countries—GE/Philips/Toshiba/Samsung, Ford/Toyota/Daimler, and Canon/Xerox, to name just a few—copy the FDI strategies adopted by Caterpillar and Komatsu.

C. Other Forms of International Business between Komatsu and Firms

Firms may also participate in international commerce through other means, such as:

- *Licensing:* One firm may permit a firm in a foreign country to use all or some of its intellectual property in return for a royalty payment. (Intellectual property refers to such intangible assets as trademarks, brand names, copyrights, patents, trade secrets, etc.) For example, the NBA may license a Dutch sportswear manufacturer to produce and sell hats, sweatshirts, and other athletic clothing embroidered with the logos and colors of the Los Angeles Lakers, the Houston Rockets, and other teams in return for a percentage of the company's sales.
- *Franchising:* One firm may grant a firm in a foreign country the right to utilize its operating systems, brand names, and trademarks in return for a royalty payment. Many fast food companies, such as Pizza Hut, McDonalds, Wendy's, and Burger King, have used this technique to serve foreign markets.
- *Management contracts:* A firm in one country will contract to provide management services or operate facilities in a second country in return for a fee. Many upscale hotel chains use this approach. Marriott and Hilton, for example, operate and manage numerous hotels outside the United States that are owned by local business persons. This approach is beneficial to both parties. The local owners provide capital and knowledge of the local market; Marriott and Hilton provide their expertise in managing hotels.
- *Contract manufacturing:* A firm in one country will contract with a firm in another country to produce goods for it. Nike, for example, relies on contract manufacturing for most of its production. It contracts with shoe manufacturers in Indonesia, China, Malaysia, Vietnam, and other countries with low labor costs to produce athletic shoes according to its specifications.
- *Joint ventures:* One of the fastest growing forms of international business is the international joint venture, in which two or more firms from different countries agree to create a jointly owned, separate firm to promote their mutual business interests. The most successful joint ventures typically combine the strengths of the partner companies to address a specific business challenge each faces. For example, General Mills wished to enter the European breakfast cereal market. However, it lacked knowledge of the habits of European customers and a European distribution network. Nestle, a tough competitor in the European market, had well-established distribution systems, manufacturing

facilities, and brand name recognition in Europe, but no expertise in producing and marketing breakfast cereal. The two companies decided to create a new joint venture, Cereal Partners Worldwide, as a means of entering the European breakfast cereal market and overcoming the decades-long dominant position enjoyed by Kellogg's there.

Corporations can utilize any and all of these different approaches for engaging in international commerce. Ford Motor Company, for example, relies on FDI as its primary means of selling internationally. Most of the production of its North American plants is sold in North America; most of its European production is sold in Europe; most of its South American production is sold in South America. Relatively few Ford cars and trucks are exported from one region to another. Conversely, Boeing relies almost exclusively on exporting. Its commercial aircraft production is centered in Seattle, Washington area. Half of the aircraft manufactured in Seattle by Boeing are typically exported to foreign countries in any given year. Caterpillar has adopted a third approach: It relies on exporting and FDI for manufacturing and franchising for distribution. Half of its sales are made to foreigners. Of these foreign sales, two-thirds represent exports from U.S. factories and one-third from Caterpillar factories located outside North America. Caterpillar distributes its products through a franchise network of 65 U.S. and 127 foreign dealerships.

III. THE GROWTH OF INTERNATIONAL BUSINESS ACTIVITIES

One reason firms have been attracted to the international market place is its large size. A second attraction is its rapid growth. International business activity has been growing far more rapidly than economic activity in general. Growth in the two most important forms of international commerce, trade and FDI, has skyrocketed since the end of the Second World War. In the past decade alone, world trade has more than doubled. As Figure 15.1 indicates, trade in goods and services reached $22 trillion in 2011, accounting for 32 percent of the world's $70 trillion GDP. FDI has similarly grown by leaps and bounds. In 2011, FDI totaled $21.2 trillion, 10 times its 1990 level, as is shown in Table 15.1.

TABLE 15.1 Stock of Outward Foreign Direct Investment (billions of U.S. dollars)

	1980	1990	2000	2011
World	559	2,087	7,967	21,168
Developed countries	499	1,941	7,083	17,056
European Union	215	810	3,493	9,198
United States	215	732	2,694	4,499
Japan	20	201	278	963
China	0.0	4	28	366
Hong Kong	0.1	12	388	1,045
India	0.1	0.3	9	111

Source: *World Investment Report 2012* (United Nations).

Numerous factors have contributed to this enormous growth in international business activity. One important motivator of growth has been the desire of firms to expand the size of their customer bases. As the productive capacities of their factories increase and outgrow their domestic markets, firms often seek new customers outside their home markets to utilize their factories efficiently. It is not surprising that many of the world's first multinational corporations were headquartered in smaller countries like the Netherlands (Philips, Shell Oil, Unilever) or Switzerland (Nestle). Because of the small economic base of their home countries, such firms quickly faced the choice of internationalizing their operation or stagnating. Conversely, many U.S. companies were slow to internationalize because the large U.S. market provided them with a rich trove of customers.

Acquisition of resources is another important reason why firms participate in international commerce. Often, necessary inputs are unavailable in the home country; U.S. grocery chains like HEB and Kroger must import their bananas and other tropical fruits from countries like Costa Rica, Honduras, and Guatemala, for such produce is not grown commercially here. At other times, critical resources are available more cheaply in other countries. Many major U.S. software companies have established subsidiaries in India, particularly in the southern city of Bangalore, to take advantage of the thousands of highly skilled English-speaking computer programmers trained by local universities whose wages run a third of those paid to comparable U.S. programmers. Because of differences in time zones, many U.S. firms are able to work on software projects 24 hours a day: when U.S. programmers call it a day, their work effort is beamed via satellite to or accessed over the Internet by their Indian colleagues, who then work on the project. When the work day in India is finishing, it is beginning in North America. The additions to the software made by the Indian programmers are then bounced back via satellite or over the Internet to the U.S. programming team, and the project continues round the clock.

The need to keep up with rival firms also motivates firms to enter the international marketplace. Consider the two dominant earthmoving equipment manufacturers, Caterpillar and Komatsu. If Komatsu allows Caterpillar to monopolize the U.S. market, Komatsu knows that Caterpillar can use the lucrative flow of profits from that market to attack Komatsu's position elsewhere. Caterpillar similarly knows that if it gives Komatsu a free ride in the Japanese market, Komatsu will use its Japanese profits to fund a war chest to attack Caterpillar in other countries. Accordingly, when Caterpillar enters a new market or develops a new product niche, Komatsu is quick to follow (and vice versa). The changing definition of what constitutes a rival is also a factor. In the 1950s, GM considered its chief rivals to be its domestic competitors—Ford, Chrysler, and American Motors. The actions and products of foreign companies like Toyota, BMW, and Hyundai could be safely ignored. Today, GM recognizes that it competes on a global basis. GM's' executives know that should they ignore new products and innovations introduced by any of GM's foreign rivals anywhere, that decision will come back to haunt them. As a result, GM has built new factories in Poland, China, Thailand, and Brazil to make sure that it establishes a strong presence in all regions of the world and to try to keep its rivals from doing the same.

While market expansion, resource acquisition, and competitive forces are all important causes of international business growth, much of this growth could not have taken place without two other factors: technological changes and changes in government policies. Technological changes in such areas as telecommunications, transportation, and data processing have made it much easier to participate in international commerce. Beginning in the early nineteenth century, improvements in transportation—the steam engine, the railroad, the internal combustion engine, and the airplane—have lowered the costs of transportation and improved the speed and reliability of delivery. Lowering transportation costs alone would be a major stimulant to trade because of the **law of one price**. The law of one price says that the price of a good in the long run must be equal in all markets except for the cost of getting the good from one market to another. For example, if the price of wheat is $2 per bushel in country A and $7 per bushel in country B, and the costs of moving the wheat from A to B is $3, then entrepreneurs will ship wheat from A to B, making $2 profit in the process ($7 - $2 - $3). This activity will increase the price of wheat in country A and decrease its price in country B. The process will continue until the difference between the prices of wheat in the two countries equals $3, the costs of shipping the wheat from A to B. What improvements in transportation technology did was decrease the cost of shipping, meaning that it was profitable to ship even more wheat from A to B. Similarly, improvements in transportation reliability meant that firms were more willing to purchase inputs from more distant suppliers, which again is a boon to international trade. And transportation improvements make it easier for people to travel from one locale to another, which means they are more able to manage satellite factories and subsidiaries located far from company headquarters.

Similar stories also can be told of the benefits of improvements in telecommunications. Until the advent of the steam engine, the speed of communication was limited by the speed of a horse or a sailing vessel. Under these circumstances, it was extraordinarily expensive for firms to acquire timely information and thus difficult to manage overseas investments or exploit distant markets. The development of the telegraph was even more significant, for it decoupled the speed of communication from the speed of transportation. The continuing stream of innovations in communications that has characterized the nineteenth, twentieth, and twenty-first centuries has made it easier to learn about opportunities in foreign markets and to respond to threats from foreign rivals.

Innovations in data processing have also been critical to the growth of international commerce. Managing an elaborate worldwide network of suppliers and customers would be very difficult without modern computer networks. For example, Ford Motor Company relies on over 200 firms worldwide to supply the parts to build a typical Ford automobile. Other parts may be supplied by Ford factories in Belgium, England, Germany, Brazil, and Mexico. Plant managers must be able to monitor production levels, communicate changing inventory needs, and settle their financial obligations to each of their suppliers in timely fashion. Sophisticated modern data processing hardware and software helps Ford manage its overseas production and seek out domestic and international suppliers who can provide quality parts at low costs.

Finally, changes in government trade policies have also encouraged the growth of international commerce. While it is certainly true that barriers to trade exist in the world today— a point we take up later in this chapter—it is also true that barriers to international trade and investment are far lower today than they were in the 1930s. We will discuss at length the motivation for and effect of these changes in trade policy in the next chapter.

IV. TRADE AND PROSPERITY

We have noted the dramatic increase in international business activity since the Second World War. The growth in world trade is in fact the basis for much of the increase in wealth and prosperity that the world has enjoyed since that conflict.

A. What is Trade?

Trade can be defined as the voluntary exchange of goods, services, or assets owned by one individual for goods, services, or assets owned by another. International trade is fundamentally similar to domestic trade, except that the individuals party to the transaction happen to reside in different countries. The critical word in the definition of trade is that it is *voluntary*. The voluntary nature of trade implies that both parties to the trade must be better off with the trade than without it; if not, why would they trade? For example, when you go into McDonalds and buy a Big Mac for $3.59, you make the trade (your money for the restaurant's food) because you prefer the food to the money. Similarly, McDonalds is willing to make the trade (their food for your money) because they prefer the money to the food. Both sides are better off, because they prefer what the other guy has relative to what they have.

B. The Law of Comparative Advantage

Trade has the important advantage at the microeconomic level of making both parties to the transaction better off. At the macroeconomic level, it promotes the efficient allocation of resources and enhances the productivity of the nation through specialization. This comes about through the **theory of comparative advantage**, which states that a country should focus on producing and exporting goods and services for which it is relatively more productive than other countries; similarly, it should import goods and services for which other countries are relatively more productive than it is.

Essentially, the theory of comparative advantage boils down to an argument for specialization that is similar to the commonsense notions we use in our daily lives. Today, most of us buy almost everything we consume. We buy our food from grocery stores, our clothes from retailers at the mall, and our cars from automobile manufacturers. But this is a good thing, isn't it? After all, buying our clothes from a store rather than making them ourselves frees up the time it would have taken us to make our own clothes. Most of us use this time to specialize in our own productive specialty, whether it's carpentry or computer programming. We then trade our services in what we do best for those that others do better than us. By specializing and trading, rather than producing everything ourselves, we channel production to the most efficient producers, thereby ensuring more production overall and more goods and services for everyone to consume. This principle holds for nations just as it does for individuals. By specializing in what they do best and trading freely, countries are able to produce more of everything and, consequently, their citizens have more to consume than they would if trade were limited by tariffs, quotas, or other barriers.

Comparative advantage is one of the most important concepts in all of economics. International trade plays a larger role in the environment of business than ever before largely because more and more nations recognize the benefits of trading freely with one another. Despite this understanding, domestic political concerns often cause politicians and governments to ignore the lessons of comparative advantage, as we shall see in the next section.

V. NATIONAL POLICIES TOWARD INTERNATIONAL TRADE

A. Domestic Trade

Policymakers in most countries recognize the benefits of domestic trade. In the Western democracies, most governments impose relatively few constraints on the ability of their citizens to trade with one another. (Some notable exceptions include trade in prostitution, purchase of certain types of drugs, and the sale of body organs.) Yet this presumption in favor of unconstrained trade disappears when dealing with international trade. In most of these same Western democracies, bitter and continuing political debates occur as to whether the central government should take an active role in shaping the size and nature of trade between its residents and the residents of other countries.

B. International Trade

In the United States, this argument over the proper role of the government in international trade has been characterized as the **free trade-fair trade debate**. Some policymakers (known as free traders) believe that the government's role should be minimal; that is, reliance on the free market will lead to better outcomes than reliance on the cumulative wisdom of federal bureaucrats or the pleadings of special interest groups. In the opinion of free traders, any government intervention will reduce the benefits generated by international trade. Such intervention discourages the voluntary exchanges that constitute trade. By reducing the ability of citizens to trade, the government robs them of the opportunity to make themselves better off. Moreover, such intervention decreases the benefits that the national economy would otherwise gain through specialization of production generated by the theory of comparative advantage. In the free traders' view, free trade promotes the efficiency and productivity of the nation's resources and the wealth of its citizens; any government intervention reduces these advantages.

Other politicians (known as fair traders) believe that the national government should actively intervene in the international marketplace to ensure that the nation's businesses receive their "fair share" of domestic and foreign markets. To ensure that domestic firms receive their fair share of the local market, fair traders believe that the government is justified in protecting domestic firms from foreign competition by erecting barriers that discourage the sale of foreign-made goods. To ensure that domestic firms receive their fair share of foreign markets, fair traders believe that the government should promote the sale of domestically made goods in foreign markets through direct subsidies, tax incentives, cut-rate financing programs, government-to-government negotiations, and the like.

C. Barriers to Trade

Despite the benefits created by international trade, many nations erect barriers to trade for one reason or another. Over the centuries, nations have developed a variety of mechanisms to protect their domestic firms from foreign competitors. The three major types are tariffs, quotas, and non-quantitative non-tariff barriers. In this section, we will discuss these three types of barriers.

1. Tariffs

A tariff is a tax imposed on a good or service that is being traded internationally. Most tariffs are imposed on goods being imported into the country (an **import tariff**), although some countries impose tariffs on goods that are being exported from the country (an **export tariff**) or that are merely passing through the country on the way to another country (a **transit tariff**). Indonesia, for example, imposes a tariff on the export of logs from certain trees. By so doing, it protects jobs at Indonesian sawmills, for they have guaranteed access to cheap timber; it also promotes jobs in the Indonesian wood-working industry. Tariffs may be calculated on the basis of the good's value (an **ad valorem tariff**), on a per-unit basis (e.g., per pound) (a **specific tariff**), or on a combination of value and unit (a **compound tariff**).

Tariffs are imposed for two reasons. First, some nations—particularly less developed ones—rely on tariffs as a source of revenue for the central government. The government of Gambia, for example, obtains over 40 percent of its revenues from tariffs, while Ghana garners almost a quarter of its budget from them. Tariff revenues are a less important source of revenue for developed countries. Tariffs produce only 1.8 percent of Canada's federal budget and only 0.5 percent of that of the U.S. federal government.

Second, tariffs may be imposed as a barrier to imported goods. For example, suppose that the U.S. government imposes a $100 specific tariff on CD players used in motor vehicles. Foreign producers of such CD players will be forced to raise the price they charge for their goods in the United States, lowering the number of units they sell there. Because foreign-made and domestic-made CD players are substitute goods, the increase in the price of foreign-made CD players will increase the demand for U.S-made CD players, causing the sales of domestic-made CD players to increase and allowing domestic producers like Delphi to raise their prices. Domestic manufacturers of CD players, as well as firms and employees dependent on them, gain as more domestic units are sold. Such beneficiaries include workers in the domestic factories, communities where the factories are located, and suppliers to domestic CD manufacturers. Producers of alternative types of motor vehicle sound systems, like cassette players, DVD players, and satellite radio, will experience an increase in demand as consumers substitute away from higher-priced CD players. But other people lose from the higher tariff. Domestic consumers lose, for they must pay higher prices for CD players in their cars, vans, and pick-up trucks. Foreign producers also lose, as do people and organizations dependent on them, including their workers, suppliers, and communities where their factories are located, as well as their distributors in the United States.

2. Quotas

Another common form of trade barrier is the quota, which is a numerical limit on the amount of a good that can be imported into the country. There are two types of quotas. An **absolute quota** limits the amount of a good allowed into the country to some specific quantity: the United States, for example, utilized an elaborate system of absolute quotas by country and product on the importation of textiles. (These quotas were eliminated in the beginning of 2005.) The most binding absolute quota is one that imposes an absolute ban on the importation of an item: for example, the United States forbids the importation of drug paraphernalia, white and yellow phosphorus matches, and switchblade knives. The second type of quota is a tariff-rate quota. Under a **tariff-rate quota**, a specified amount of the good is allowed into the country at a zero or low tariff, but any amount above this threshold is subjected to an extremely high tariff that often blocks out any additional imports of the good. The United States imposes a tariff-rate quota on such goods as milk, ice cream, brooms, peanuts, and cotton, while Japan, South Korea, and Canada apply tariff-rate quotas on a variety of agricultural goods. Often such quotas are imposed on a country-by-country basis. The EU, for example, allows 46,000 metric tons of U.S. rice to enter the region using a tariff-rate quota.

The most well-known, and perhaps the most important tariff-rate quota imposed by the United States involves sugar. The United States annually allows about 2 million tons of sugar to be imported into the United States tariff free; all imports above this level must pay a 17-cent-per-pound tariff. (The total size of the U.S. market is about 10 million tons; domestic sugar growers produce about 8 million tons of sugar annually.) Because of this quota, the price received by domestic sugar producers soars above the world price. In April 2013, for example, the world price of sugar was 18 cents per pound, while the price received by domestic producers was 21 cents. In the absence of the quota, sugar would flow into the United States from the rest of the world, driving down the domestic price and driving up the world price until the two were equal, after taking into account transportation costs.

The impact of the quota is thus to maintain the price of U.S.-made sugar above the world price. Domestic sugar producers, such as sugar beet growers in North Dakota and Minnesota and sugar cane growers in Florida and Louisiana, benefit from the higher domestic price. U.S. farm implement dealers, pesticide and fertilizer companies, sugar processors, and other suppliers and customers to sugar beet and sugar cane farmers also gain from the increased U.S. sugar production.

The list of beneficiaries includes firms associated with the corn industry: As the price of sugar increases, the demand for corn-based fructose sweeteners, which can be substituted for sugar in many applications, such as for sweetening soft drinks or candy, also increases. Thus Archer-Daniels-Midland, the world's largest producer of fructose, benefits from the sugar quota, as do thousands of Midwest farmers who till the region's cornfields, as well as Midwestern farm implement dealers, pesticide and fertilizer companies, and the communities in which they reside.

Who loses from this quota? U.S. consumers are estimated to pay an additional $2 billion annually for sugar and sugar-based products. U.S. companies producing goods with high sugar content similarly find it more difficult to export their goods and discover that they are more vulnerable to foreign imports as a result of the sugar quota, for they must pay more for an important ingredient than their foreign competitors do. Corsicana's Collin Street Bakery's competitiveness in the world fruitcake market, for example, is hurt by the high price it must pay for the sugar it uses in its fruitcakes. U.S. candy manufacturers, fruit juice producers, and other firms who must use high-priced U.S.-grown sugar in their products similarly become less competitive in domestic and international markets vis-à-vis foreign rivals able to purchase sugar at the lower world price. Many small U.S. candy manufacturers have gone out of business as a result.

3. Non-Quantitative Non-Tariff Barriers

The impact of tariffs and quotas on a firm's ability to sell its goods in a foreign market are relatively easy to observe. Such is not the case for the third type of trade barrier, which we will label **non-quantitative non-tariff barriers** (i.e., not quotas and not tariffs), or NQNTBs. The effect of NQNTBs on trade is often difficult to assess. They are also often embedded in legal or bureaucratic procedures, making them difficult to change. Moreover, governments often implement economic, social, or cultural policies for what appear to be perfectly legitimate reasons, but the policies have the impact of acting as an NQNTB. As a result, NQNTBs are a frequent source of controversy and discord between otherwise friendly nations. NQNTBs can take a variety of forms, including product and testing standards, local-purchase requirements, regulatory controls, public sector procurement policies, and restricted access to local distribution networks.

Product and testing standards: Many nations impose testing and content standards on goods sold in their markets for health, safety, or public policy reasons. For example, the United States requires that food products contain labels that detail the nutritional value of the product to help consumers choose which one to buy. The label must list (in order of importance) the various ingredients used in the product, in part to help people avoid foods they are allergic to. Similarly, governments routinely regulate product definitions to help consumers make comparisons among competing brands. For example, fruit-flavored drinks may be sold as fruit juice in the United States only if they meet federal government standards for natural juice content. Products not meeting this threshold are sold as fruit drinks. Most consumers find such requirements beneficial, and most policymakers view the imposition of such standards as legitimate for a national government to undertake.

However, sometimes product and testing standards may be used as a barrier to trade. Japan discourages horticulture imports by requiring that potential exports be inspected by Japanese government officials in the exporting country, but oftentimes fails to provide an adequate supply of inspectors to do so. Japan managed to keep foreign-made skis out of its market by arguing that Japanese snow was different than the snow in other countries.

Since the foreign skis were not adequately tested on Japanese snow, to protect the safety of its skiers Japan banned the foreign skis from its slopes.

While most independent observers scoffed at this explanation, often the situation is not so clear cut. Sometimes a product or testing standard is imposed for what a country believes to be legitimate public policy reasons, yet appears to be a trade barrier in disguise in the eyes of foreign firms. For example, for the past decade the EU has banned beef produced with growth hormones from its markets on health and safety grounds. Such growth hormones are routinely utilized by the U.S. cattle industry. As a result, the productivity of U.S. beef producers is much higher than that of their European counterparts; in the absence of the ban on growth hormones, U.S. beef would likely dominate the European market. The U.S. beef industry has argued that the EU has failed to produce any evidence that cattle-fed growth hormones are unsafe and thus claims that the EU's policy is a trade barrier masquerading as a health regulation. The EU of course believes that it has the right to protect the health and safety of its residents.

Public procurement: Governments at all levels around the world often try to bias their procurement of goods and services to favor local residents and firms. Many large U.S. cities, for example, at one time or another have given preference to local citizens when filling civil service jobs or to local contractors when erecting public buildings in order to keep the money at home. Such public procurement policies often create trade conflicts in large industries where public ownership is common, such as telecommunications, electrical generation, and rail transportation. For example, much of the telecommunications industry in Europe was state owned, and these firms traditionally favored purchasing supplies and inputs from domestic firms, thereby harming the sales prospects of U.S. firms like AT&T, Cisco, and Motorola, or Korean firms like Samsung. Sometimes, governments have used public procurement policies to promote the development of new industries or cutting-edge technologies. For example, having dropped its outright ban on foreign computers, Brazil granted domestic producers of computer and telecommunications equipment a 12-percent bidding preference on public contracts. This bidding preference means that a Brazilian company would win the contract so long as its bid is no more than 12 percent above the lowest bid by a foreigner.

Local purchase requirements: Countries often impose requirements mandating that a product sold in the country must contain some minimum percentage of local content. Designed to protect local jobs and stimulate local economies, such local purchase requirements obviously serve as a barrier to the import of foreign goods and services. One area where local purchase requirements are widespread is the broadcasting industry; most of these requirements are directed against U.S. products, although other exporters of filmed entertainment, such as Mexico and the United Kingdom, are also harmed by some of them. For example, the EU's 1989 Broadcast Directive requires that a majority of radio and television airtime be reserved for European-origin programs. Some EU members have even tougher requirements. France demands that 60 percent of the programming on French TV and radio outlets originate in Europe and at least 40 percent be French or francophone in origin. Korea requires that no more than 20 percent of weekly broadcasting time can be devoted to imported television shows. Spain requires that its movie theaters devote at least

25 percent of their screen time to EU-produced features. Australia requires 55 percent of all TV programs broadcast be Australian-owned, and requires that 80 percent of all advertisements shown from 6 a.m. to midnight be Australian-produced.

Access to distribution systems: Modern businesses recognize the critical importance of marketing and distribution to the success of their endeavors. Blocking access to existing distribution systems within a country thus can be an important barrier to international trade. China limits the ability of foreign firms to operate and manage their own warehouses, distribution networks, wholesale outlets, or transport facilities, making it more difficult for them to penetrate Chinese markets. Similarly, the Japan Racing Association limits the number of races in which foreign horses can participate to nine a year, while Korea requires that domestic films be shown at each movie theater a minimum of 146 days a year, reducing the availability of screens to show foreign films and lessening the incentives for Western film companies to build new movie theaters there.

At other times, foreign firms may have difficulty accessing local distribution systems because existing distributors are locked into serving domestic firms. For example, U.S. auto manufacturers have difficulty in finding Japanese dealers to handle their products, for the dealers are often afraid that they will jeopardize their ongoing relationships with Japanese auto manufacturers. The U.S. is also concerned that its flat glass manufacturers are locked out of the Japanese market because the dominant Japanese flat glass manufacturers control flat glass wholesalers and retailers through exclusive dealing contracts, financial incentives, discriminatory pricing that punishes distributors who buy foreign-made glass, and punitive withholding of supply. Similar practices hurt Kodak's ability to compete against Fuji in the Japanese photographic film market.

Regulatory procedures: Governments around the world impose a variety of regulatory requirements on firms operating in their jurisdictions. Unfortunately, at times the process of establishing these rules seems to be biased against foreign firms. For example, unlike the U.S. regulatory process, which is transparent and open to all parties, the Japanese regulatory process lacks a public rule-making process, has no equivalent to freedom of information laws, and is influenced by informal "administrative guidance" by Japan's ministries. Foreigners thus have no understanding of how regulatory decisions are reached or how they might plead their case before appropriate authorities. Their suspicion is that regulatory outcomes are rigged to disadvantage them vis-à-vis local Japanese firms.

At other times, it is the outcomes of the regulatory proceedings that seem to be biased. For example, Japan and South Korea have discouraged consumption of foreign alcoholic beverages by imposing higher excise taxes on them than domestic products. By applying different standards for food additives than other countries—even ones generally regarded as safe—Japan makes it more difficult for other countries to export processed foods there. Korea's automobile taxes are based on engine size, thus raising a barrier to the sale of the larger cars produced by U.S. and German automobile manufacturers. South Korea discourages the import of agricultural goods by its slow customs clearance procedures. Most agricultural goods take two to four weeks to clear Korean customs, although perishable fruits and vegetables take five days on an average. (In contrast, most Asian nations take only three to four days to clear all types of foodstuffs.) Similarly, South Korea imposes different reimbursement procedures for imported pharmaceutical products than for domestically produced ones in a manner that encourages hospitals, doctors, and clinics to prescribe the domestic products. Indonesia encourages doctors to prescribe only generic drugs, but forbids foreigners from participating in the market for generic drugs. Canada has used its tax code to reduce the competition its publishing and broadcasting industries face from U.S. TV stations and magazines.

Investment controls: Many countries bar or limit FDI in order to avoid foreign domination of their economies or of key industries. These FDI controls often serve as a barrier to trade in these industries. For example, many countries limit foreign ownership of transportation, telecommunications, and broadcasting firms in the name of national security or protection of the national culture. Brazil, for example, requires that any provider of telecommunications services be at least 51 percent owned by Brazilians. The United States limits foreign ownership of its airlines to 25 percent, and imposes similar controls on foreign ownership of broadcasting outlets. China restricts FDI in a wide swath of industries, including insurance, advertising, tourism, construction, and education. Indonesia forbids foreigners from importing and distributing films and videotapes.

D. Public Choice Analysis

From this discussion, it is obvious that the world's nations have been very inventive in developing policies that promote the interests of their home industries. What is less obvious is that these policies inevitably make the domestic economy and the general public worse off. Simply put, the erection of trade barriers benefits the beneficiaries of these barriers to a lesser extent than the losses they impose on the rest of the economy. In the case of the sugar quota, for example, thousands of corn, sugar cane, and sugar beet farmers gain from the quota. However, 300 million American consumers pay more for their sugar as a result. Thousands of U.S. food processors pay more than their foreign competitors to sweeten their products, making their goods less competitive in international markets. Similarly, the United States bars foreign ships from transporting cargos from one U.S. port to another under the Jones Act. The Jones Act protects the jobs of thousands of members of U.S. maritime unions from foreign competition. However, it creates a variety of unintended and detrimental consequences. For example, during the summer months cruise ships busily ply the inside passage off the Pacific Coast to show thousands of travelers each year the beauties of Alaska and British Columbia. However, many of these ships go between Anchorage, Alaska, and Vancouver, British Columbia, rather than between Anchorage and Seattle, Washington, even though most of their customers are U.S. residents. Why? The Anchorage–Vancouver trip is an international route, not subject to the Jones Act. As a result, cruise ships save money by not needing to buy high-priced ships made in U.S. shipyards or to staff them with high-priced U.S. labor that the Jones Act would require. By creating an economic incentive to divert the cruise industry to Vancouver, the Jones Act hurts Seattle. Absent the Jones Act, more cruise ships would journey between Seattle and Anchorage, thus creating more jobs at Seattle's Sea-Tac Airport and among other sectors of Seattle's tourist industry, such as hotels, restaurants, taxis, and tourist attractions.

Why does country after country adopt trade barriers that damage their domestic economies? The answer lies in a branch of economics called public choice, which analyzes why governments make the decisions they do. **Public choice analysis** suggests that such outcomes rationally occur because special interest groups are more willing to work for the passage of laws that favor them than is the general public willing to work for the defeat of such laws. Florida sugar cane growers, for example, recognize that the sugar quota is vital to their economic survival. Accordingly, they are willing to fund Political Action Committees to pass along campaign contributions to persuade Congressmen and women of the righteousness of their position. (A major subplot of the 1996 Demi Moore–Burt Reynolds movie *Striptease* was this very issue.) Conversely, the existence of the sugar quota probably raises the cost that each American pays for sugar by $10 per year. Those individual American citizens quite rationally conclude that it is not worth their while to fly to Washington to lobby Congress to eliminate the sugar quota. Congresspersons know that if they support the sugar quota, they will be blessed by campaign contributions from sugar cane growers. They also know that if they vote against the sugar quota, the general public won't even notice. However, the sugar cane growers will notice, and are likely to support the Congressperson's opponent in the next election. Given this incentive structure, most Representatives and Senators quietly go along with the sugar quota.

This leads us to another point. The development of a nation's trade policy rarely is the result of some brilliant vision of the nation's role in the world economy. Rather, it is usually the result of the interplay of domestic political forces and domestic special interest groups. Former Speaker of the House Tip O'Neill summarized this point pithily: "All politics is local." When you try to make sense of the trade barriers erected by a country, you often need to study its domestic political situation. This approach also can be adopted to solve a company's problems in a foreign market. In the early 1980s, for example, Toyota's sales in the U.S. market were being hurt by "Buy American" advertising campaigns developed by GM, Ford, and Chrysler. Toyota's strategists decided to build new factories in the United States in order to make in the United States most of their cars sold there. Having done so, Toyota then ran a series of advertisements (some of which still run today), which demonstrated that Toyota has created an enormous number of jobs in numerous U.S. communities. Through this approach, Toyota defeated the "Buy American" movement; it also bought itself new political allies among the workers, communities, and Congressional delegations where its plants are located.

CHAPTER SUMMARY

The world's gross domestic product reached $70 trillion in 2011. The United States, Canada, Japan, the European Union, and other developed countries accounted for 60 percent of this total. Emerging markets, such as the BRIC countries and the Four Tigers of Southeast Asia, also play an important role in global commerce.

To conduct business internationally, one person—either the buyer or the seller—must convert his or her domestic currency into the currency of the other party. The foreign exchange market facilitates this currency conversion. Two major types of foreign exchange systems exist, flexible and fixed.

The most important form of international business activity is exporting and importing. In 2011, world exports of goods totaled $17.8 trillion, while exports of services amounted to $4.2 trillion. International investment is the second major form of international business activity. International investment is divided into two categories, foreign portfolio investment (FPI) and foreign direct investment (FDI). FPI by Americans reached $11.0 trillion at the end of 2011, while FDI surpassed $4.7 trillion. Other forms of international business activity include licensing, franchising, management contracts, contract manufacturing, and joint ventures.

Firms engage in international business for many reasons, including the desire to expand their customer bases, acquire resources, and match their competitors. Technological changes and changes in government policies have facilitated this growth in international business.

Many countries have erected barriers to restrict or control international business activities, such as by imposing tariffs, quotas, or other non-tariff barriers.

16

INTERNATIONAL COOPERATION TO PROMOTE GLOBAL PROSPERITY

The preceding chapter concluded with a discussion on the various barriers to trade that nations erect to protect special interest groups within their economies. However, the nations of the world also recognize that trade is beneficial to them and that everyone erecting trade barriers against each other makes everyone worse off. As a result, the post–World War II period has been characterized by a high degree of cooperation among the major trading nations. Some of this cooperation occurs through the efforts of three international institutions created for this purpose—the World Bank, the International Monetary Fund, and the GATT/WTO. The post-War period has also been marked by the growth of regional trading blocs such as the European Union and NAFTA.

I. A SHORT HISTORICAL DIGRESSION

The willingness of the world's nations to cooperate with one another after World War II to promote their mutual prosperity was heightened by what happened to them after World War I when they didn't choose a cooperative path. The causes of World War I were numerous and probably avoidable. Once the war started, however, a slaughter of unbelievable magnitude ensued. Millions of German, British, Canadian, French, Belgian, and (to a much lesser extent) American troops were killed or maimed in the trench warfare on the Western front. Similarly, Russia, Germany, Turkey, Italy, and Austria-Hungary lost millions of men in the fighting on the Eastern and Southern fronts.

World War I had profound consequences. The Czar was overthrown in Russia, leading to the Communist takeover of that country. Kaiser Wilhelm II abdicated his throne, creating a democracy in Germany that would soon prove to be unstable. The French government blamed Germany for starting the war. As a condition for accepting Germany's surrender, the French demanded that Germany pay France reparations to compensate France for the damage it suffered from the war.

The payment of reparations had severe repercussions, both economic and political. In order to repay France and the other victors, Germany resorted to printing more money.

A hyperinflation ensued, and newspapers were full of stories of German housewives needing wheelbarrows full of money to purchase a loaf of bread from the neighborhood bakery. The hyperinflation wiped out the savings of Germany's middle class; Germany's economy suffered and unemployment rose. Many historians of the day believed that the rise of Adolf Hitler was attributable to the economic chaos that resulted from the hyperinflation.

Much of the rest of Europe also suffered from unemployment as troops returning from the trenches were unable to find jobs. To improve their economic conditions, countries like the United Kingdom, France, Germany, Latvia, and Belgium devalued their currencies and raised their tariffs on imported goods. The purpose of these two measures was to stimulate exports and reduce imports, thereby boosting domestic employment. To see this, note the following:

- By devaluing its currency, the country effectively lowered the price of its goods to foreigners and raised the price of foreign goods to its consumers.
- By raising tariffs on imported goods, the country made foreign goods more expensive to its citizens and encouraged them to buy domestically made goods in place of the now more expensive foreign goods.

These two policies thus promoted employment at home and reduced the "export of jobs" to other countries. However, because they focused on the needs of the domestic economy but ignored the impact on other countries, such policies are often called **beggar-thy-neighbor** policies. Many experts believe that they worsened the economic problems of the European nations. Remember previously we discussed the benefits of trade: both parties to the trade are better off, and specialization promotes productivity gains. While the beggar-thy-neighbor policies may have kept jobs at home in the short run, over the longer run they discouraged trade. In so doing, they robbed those individuals who would like to trade of the benefits of exchange, and they forced nations to produce goods that they were not very efficient at producing. As a result, the productivity of labor and capital decreased. As labor productivity declined, downward pressure was put on wages. If wages are inflexible and are unable to fall to compensate for the lessened productivity of workers, then workers are laid off, thereby reducing their demand for goods produced by others. If the productivity of capital falls, then profits decline and firms are unable or unwilling to reinvest in new equipment and factories. Failure of firms to reinvest decreases the demand for capital goods, causing manufacturers of capital goods to lay off their workers and shut their factory gates. Moreover, failure to reinvest and improve a firm's property, plant, and equipment reduces its productivity and growth in the long run.

Many economists believe that these beggar-thy-neighbor policies prolonged and deepened the Great Depression that wracked the world in the 1930s. The economic chaos created by the Depression was transformed into political chaos, allowing fascist and communist dictators like Hitler, Mussolini, and Stalin to consolidate their political power. The Great Depression ended with the advent of World War II in September 1939. Needless to say, a high price was paid for ending the depression: tens of millions of people died in that war. Many contemporary leaders believed that the tensions that sparked World War II were directly attributable to the collective economic and political mismanagement of the world economy after World War I. The world's nations competed against one another, instead of cooperating with one another. They raised tariffs to discourage trade, instead of negotiating treaties to promote trade. They engaged in competitive exchange rate devaluations to gain temporary pricing advantages against their trade rivals, instead of cooperating with one another to promote stability and certainty in exchange rates.

II. THE BRETTON WOODS AGREEMENT

To avoid the mistakes they made after World War I, in late 1944 representatives of 44 Allied nations met in the small New Hampshire resort community of Bretton Woods. Their goal was to construct a post-war international economic environment that would promote peace and mutual prosperity. The Bretton Woods conference achieved this objective by creating two new international organizations to promote international economic and monetary cooperation and by agreeing to a new international monetary system. In particular, the Bretton Woods agreement created the following:

- **International Bank for Reconstruction and Development (IBRD)**. Its mission was to lend money to rebuild the infrastructure of war-torn Europe. Instead of punishing Germany (as was done at the end of World War I), the Allied nations recognized that the best way to ensure peace was to restore the economies of all European countries, victors (like France and the United Kingdom) and enemies (like Germany and Italy) alike. The **World Bank** (as the IBRD is more commonly known) was aided in its efforts by the **Marshall Plan**, a U.S.-sponsored aid program to restore the economies of U.S.-allied, non-Communist governments of Western Europe. The monies poured into the reconstruction of Western European railroads, highways, public buildings, and utilities created employment and revitalized the competitiveness and productivity of the recipient countries. After completing this mission, the World Bank took on a new objective: promoting economic growth and prosperity in less developed countries through the provision of low-interest rate, long-term loans.
- **International Monetary Fund (IMF)**. One of the IMF's goals was to discourage nations from pursuing competitive exchange rate devaluations, a beggar-thy-neighbor policy that had caused a decrease in world trade between the two world wars. The IMF also oversaw the functioning of the new international monetary system put in place by Bretton Woods, which created a dollar-based fixed exchange rate system. This system collapsed in August 1971, however.

These two institutions created by the Bretton Woods agreement continue to play major roles in promoting international economic cooperation. The World Bank makes on average $44 billion of new loans, loan guarantees, and other financing available to the world's less developed countries each year. The IMF stands ready to assist countries that face economic crisis. The IMF arranged over $100 billion of loans to help Indonesia, Thailand, the Philippines, and South Korea survive the Asian currency crisis of 1997–1998, for example. Similarly, it pledged $103 billion in loans and loan guarantees to help Ireland, Greece, and Portugal weather the banking crisis the Eurozone is currently experiencing.

III. GOVERNING WORLD TRADE

A. General Agreement on Tariffs and Trade (GATT)

Statesmen in the 1940s were also concerned about establishing a policy regime that would stimulate international trade. In 1947, most of the world's leading trading nations signed the **General Agreement on Tariffs and Trade (GATT)**. The GATT provided a cooperative environment in which nations could negotiate the reduction of trade barriers among themselves. During its 47-year life (1947–1994), the GATT sponsored eight rounds of trade negotiations that focused on reducing barriers to international trade. The GATT was particularly effective in reducing tariffs. In 1948, the average tariff imposed by the major trading nations was over 40 percent; by 1994, this figure had fallen to 3 percent.

The GATT sought to reduce trade barriers among its members on a non-discriminatory basis, so that trade would take place on the basis of comparative advantage. To do so, GATT members agreed to apply the **most favored nation (MFN)** principle in their dealings with one another. The MFN principle means that each GATT member agrees to treat every GATT member at least as well as it treats any other GATT member. Thus suppose Canada agreed to cut its tariff on furniture imported from Sweden by 25 percent. As Canada and Sweden were both GATT members, Canada would then be required by the MFN principle to grant a 25 percent tariff reduction on furniture imported from all other GATT members.

The use of the MFN principle encourages multilateral, rather than bilateral trade negotiations. Consider the bilateral negotiations between Canada and Sweden we just discussed. Canada is likely to be unwilling to cut its tariffs on Swedish furniture imports unless Sweden grants it some equivalent trade concession. If Canada is forced to give all other GATT members a 25 percent tariff reduction on furniture—even though they granted Canada nothing in return—Canadian trade officials will quickly decide that such bilateral negotiations make no sense. Accordingly, Canadian officials will decide that multilateral negotiations are a more appropriate policy to follow. Now comes the critical point: If your goal is to maximize the efficiency of the world economy, multilateral negotiations are far more beneficial than bilateral ones. Bilateral negotiations imply that international trade will be governed by nations that are the best bargainers. For example, Canada's furniture imports will be driven by which countries Canada has signed a trade agreement with. If Canada has a trade deal with Sweden, but not with Finland, then Swedish imports are favored regardless of whether Swedish manufacturers are more efficient than their Finnish counterparts. Conversely, multilateral negotiations, which lower the import barriers for all GATT members equally, encourage trade to take place on the basis of comparative advantage. To continue our example, if Canadian tariffs on Swedish furniture imports and Finnish furniture imports fall by an equal amount, then whether Canada imports Swedish or Finnish furniture depends on which country's furniture manufacturers are more efficient.

Thus, the MFN principle was critical to the GATT's success. However, GATT members agreed to allow members to ignore the MFN principle in two specific circumstances. First, members of regional trading blocs such as the European Union and NAFTA could grant trade preferences to their members without having to grant such preferences to all other GATT members. Second, GATT members could grant preferential treatment to less developed countries (LDCs) to aid in their development efforts. The U.S. tariff code, for example, contains the **Generalized System of Preferences**, which reduces the tariffs imposed on imports from certain LDCs. Most other nations have similar arrangements for the developing countries. Such preferential treatment is often granted to LDCs who are friendly with or politically aligned with the developed country granting the preference. France, for example, grants preferential treatment to many of its former colonies, as does the U.K. government to members of the British Commonwealth. The United States grants preferential treatment to most poor countries in the Western Hemisphere and to its military and political allies in Europe, Africa, and Asia. Not surprisingly, the U.S. has not granted such preferences to nations it views as particularly hostile to its interests, such as Cuba and North Korea.

The GATT has played a major role in reducing import tariffs that impede trade; its successes are evident from the steady increase in world trade. However, the GATT was not able to make much headway in reducing other barriers to trade, such as quotas and other non-tariff barriers. Accordingly, during the Uruguay Round (1986–1994), which was the last of the eight negotiating rounds sponsored by GATT, the GATT members agreed to create a new successor to the GATT, the World Trade Organization (WTO). The WTO's mandate is much broader than that of the GATT; moreover, the WTO has much stronger enforcement powers than the GATT.

B. World Trade Organization (WTO)

The **World Trade Organization** came into being on January 1, 1995. It currently has 157 members. As a successor organization to the GATT, the WTO has adopted the GATT's mission and many of its procedures. During its first decade of existence, the WTO has followed in the GATT's footsteps. It has continued to sponsor multilateral negotiations to reduce trade barriers. In 1996, its members signed the Information Technology Agreement, which eliminates trade barriers over time for such goods as telecommunications equipment, computers, software, and fax machines. In 1997, its members agreed to similar reductions to trade in financial services and telecommunications services. The **Doha Round**, which was initiated by WTO members in 2001 but is not yet completed, is focused on reducing agricultural subsidies and tariffs, liberalizing trade in services, and improving the access of LDCs to pharmaceutical products.

The WTO has four other important initiatives underway that, when completed, will increase international business opportunities dramatically.

- *The General Agreement on Trade in Services (GATS):* In 2011, international trade in services amounted to about $4.2 trillion. However, many nations impose barriers to such trade. In the international airline industry, for example, carriers must obtain landing rights from a foreign government before they can land in that country. Such landing rights are normally allocated on a bilateral basis. This means that the air services between the United States and the Philippines, for example, is reserved only for U.S. and Philippine carriers. The GATS' goal is to eliminate barriers to trade in this and other services as soon as possible.

- *Agreement on Trade Related Investment Measures (TRIMs):* Often, trade and investment are complementary in nature. In order to efficiently market its goods in a host country, for example, a firm may wish to establish a wholly owned distribution subsidiary in that country. Host country restrictions against such investments thus may discourage trade. WTO members are in the process of establishing a set of rules regarding such investments.

- *Trade-Related Aspects of Intellectual Property Rights (TRIPS):* Intellectual property rights comprise such things as patents, trademarks, brand names, copyrights, and trade secrets. The basis of many firms' international competitiveness is ownership of such intellectual property rights. The Walt Disney Company, for example, has thrived globally by exploiting its brand names and trademarks. Schoolchildren around the world skip off to school carrying lunch boxes and wearing T-shirts bearing the smiling faces of Mickey Mouse, Winnie-the-Pooh, Donald Duck, and other cartoon characters in the Disney family. Most MNCs are concerned that many countries fail to protect their intellectual property rights, a problem that a TRIPS agreement would address.

- *Agriculture:* Reducing barriers to trade in agricultural goods continues to be a major problem for the WTO, for import restrictions and export subsidies that distort international agricultural trade are wide spread. The United States and the European Union, for instance, have engaged in a long-term subsidy war over wheat. Japan has only begrudgingly begun to reduce its absolute ban on the importation of rice. Farmers represent a politically influential voting group in many countries, and resist reducing the subsidies they receive or eliminating barriers to the import of foreign foodstuffs. Freeing trade in agricultural goods and eliminating agricultural subsidies is a primary goal of the Doha Round negotiations.

All in all, the GATT/WTO have done a remarkable job in reducing barriers to trade since 1945. Tariffs in particular have fallen as a result of the efforts of GATT and WTO members. However, many barriers to trade still remain; clearly there is much work yet to be done by the WTO.

IV. REGIONAL TRADING BLOCS

A. Introduction

Another element of the post-war international business environment is the growth in the number and importance of regional trading blocs. Over 100 different regional economic integration arrangements have been created since the Second World War, although not all of them have had a major impact on their participants or on the world economy. Countries join regional trading blocs in order to promote economic prosperity and better the lives of their citizens. Trading blocs represent a middle position on a spectrum ranging from a perfectly open world economy, where every country's goods, services, labor, capital, and technology are free to locate where they choose, to a perfectly closed economy, where each country is completely self-sufficient and engages in no international trade whatsoever. Members of regional trading blocs agree to treat citizens and firms domiciled in member countries differently from citizens and firms from non-member countries. However, as we shall discuss, few regional trading blocs are perfect. All contain some exceptions or exemptions to protect politically important domestic special interest groups.

B. Forms and Benefits of Regional Trading Blocs

Experts distinguish between four types of trading blocs, which differ in terms of their breadth and depth:

1. *Free trade areas*: Members of free trade areas agree to reduce or eliminate barriers to trade among themselves. Accordingly, goods and services created in member states receive preferential treatment over goods and services produced by non-members. Each member is free to establish its own trade policies with non-members. One member may choose to erect high barriers to non-member goods, another member low barriers. This disparity of treatment of non-members can cause difficulties, however, for non-members will try to ship their goods to the member country with the lowest barriers. This problem is avoided with the next type of regional trading bloc, the customs union.
2. *Customs unions*: Members of customs unions create a free trade area, and then also adopt common trade policies toward non-members. Typically, customs union members agree to impose common external tariffs that are levied on all goods imported into the custom union.
3. *Common market*: Members of a common market create a customs union, and then also drop all barriers that hinder the free movement of labor, capital, and other factors of production among them. By allowing factor mobility, they hope that such factors of production as capital and labor will be used where they can be the most productively employed. Increased productivity, of course, is the primary means by which the standard of living of a country's citizens can be raised.
4. *Economic union*: Members of an economic union create a common market, and then deepen their economic integration by implementing similar macroeconomic (fiscal, monetary, taxation) and microeconomic (environmental, labor, etc.) policies. The close coordination necessary to implement an economic union suggests that each member must be willing to surrender a significant amount of its national sovereignty. As we discuss below, 17 members of the European Union are in the process of establishing an economic union through their joint usage of a single currency, the euro.

Policymakers around the world have been intrigued by regional economic integration because of its perceived benefits. The first obvious benefit of regional economic integration is that it expands trade among members. As we noted in the preceding chapter, increasing trade is an important mechanism for promoting prosperity and the creation of wealth. Another important benefit of regional economic integration is that it may increase the international competitiveness of domestic firms. By expanding the size of the barrier-free market available to domestic firms, it allows them to capture economies of scale by building larger, more efficient, sized factories to serve the entire market. They are also able to enjoy longer production runs of any given model of product they produce. Moreover, firms may benefit from easier access to newer technologies, lower-cost loans, or a larger pool of skilled workers as a result of membership in a regional trading bloc.

Consider the plight of a garden hose manufacturer in a country that is not a member of a regional trading bloc. If the firm is limited to serving its domestic market, it will build a small factory sized to meet the needs of that market. In order to produce different models of garden hoses—short ones, long ones, cheap ones, and heavy-duty ones—it will need to constantly start, stop, and retool its production line. These short production runs will raise its per-unit costs substantially. With such high costs, the garden hose manufacturer will be uncompetitive in foreign markets; indeed, it is likely to survive the onslaught of imports from larger countries only if it can convince the domestic legislature to assess high tariffs on imported hoses. Now, suppose the manufacturer's home country joins a regional trading bloc. The garden hose manufacturer then has tariff-free access to a much larger market. It can build a larger factory and benefit from economies of scale. It can schedule longer production runs of each type of hose, which reduces substantially its setup costs over time. As a result, the garden hose manufacturer will enjoy lower average costs of production. It will become more productive, thereby increasing its competitiveness inside and outside the trading bloc. Such reasoning lay behind the strong support Canada's manufacturing sector gave to the adoption of the NAFTA treaty. It also provides an explanation for the failure of the import substitution policies adopted by many Latin American countries that we discussed in the previous chapter.

Regional economic integration is a two-edged sword, however. While a firm from one member country has increased access to the markets of other members, firms from the other members also have improved access to its home market. In short, regional economic integration increases the competitiveness of the marketplace. Stagnant, low-productivity firms may find their very survival threatened by the establishment of a regional trading bloc. Conversely, innovative, dynamic firms can benefit enormously from the new opportunities created by the larger market. And consumers throughout the trading bloc gain from the increased level of competition.

Increased inflows of FDI is another benefit triggered by regional economic integration. Foreign MNCs often chose to locate new factories or assembly plants within the trading bloc in order to receive insider treatment. If Toyota builds a new automobile manufacturing facility in England, for example, the output of that factory is viewed as European in origin and can be sold within the European Union tariff free. These inflows of FDI increase competition within the trading bloc, again aiding consumers. Investment also has important long-run consequences for economic growth. In particular, increased capital investments raise the productivity of the work force. Increased labor productivity inevitably leads to higher wage rates, which raises per-capita incomes and standards of living, creating more demand for the products of numerous other firms throughout the economy.

Despite the advantages created by regional economic integration arrangements, not all economists and policymakers are convinced that their benefits outweigh their costs.

Regional integration arrangements clearly stimulate trade among their members, which creates a positive phenomenon known as **trade creation**. However, they may decrease trade between members and non-members. Of particular concern is the possible shifting of trade from low-cost non-member producers whose goods are subjected to tariffs to higher-cost member producers whose goods are not subject to the tariff, a phenomenon known as **trade diversion**. Whether a particular regional economic integration arrangement is of benefit to the world as a whole depends on whether its trade creation impacts are larger than its trade diversion effects.

To see this more clearly, consider the following example. Suppose the United States has a $2 per bushel tariff on tomatoes. It can produce tomatoes at a cost of $5 per bushel while Mexico can produce them at a cost of $4. Prior to the formation of NAFTA, resources will be allocated inefficiently. Because of the tariff, only U.S.-grown tomatoes will be sold in the U.S. market, for they are cheaper than Mexican tomatoes ($5 versus $6 (= $4 + $2)) even though Mexico is a more efficient producer of tomatoes. Now suppose NAFTA is formed, and the tariff is eliminated. Mexican tomatoes will dominate the U.S. market, for they now cost $4 per bushel, a dollar less than U.S.-grown ones. This shift of production from a higher-cost member to a lower-cost member is an example of trade creation and a benefit to the world economy, for resources are being used more efficiently.

However, let's change the story by assuming that Chile can produce tomatoes for only $2.50 per bushel. Prior to NAFTA's formation, Chilean tomatoes would dominate the U.S. market, for they can be sold for $4.50 ($2.50 plus the $2.00 tariff) and are thus cheaper than U.S. or Mexican-grown tomatoes. Now suppose NAFTA is formed, and U.S. tariffs are dropped against Mexican products but not Chilean ones. Mexican tomatoes will now dominate the U.S. market, selling for $4 per bushel as opposed to $4.50 for Chilean tomatoes and $5.00 for the U.S. ones. The shift of tomato production from more efficient Chile to less efficient Mexico constitutes trade diversion and a misallocation of resources.

Whether any regional economic integration arrangement is beneficial to the world economy depends on whether its trade creation or its trade diversion effects are larger. International policymakers, like those who staff the WTO, are thus ambivalent about regional trading blocs. They recognize political reality, however, and acknowledge that many nations will continue to support and develop regional economic integration arrangements regardless of their impact on the efficiency of the world economy. Let's now examine the most important of these trading blocs.

V. MAJOR REGIONAL TRADING BLOCS

A. The European Union

The European Union represents the most important example of a regional trading bloc in the world economy today. Its 28 members have a combined population of more than 500 million. All are democracies that have adopted free-market-oriented economic policies. One of the world's largest markets, the EU accounts for 25 percent of the world's GDP.

Like the World Bank, the IMF, and the GATT/WTO, the creation of the EU after the Second World War reflected the desire of its members to promote peace and prosperity through cooperation. Building upon a prior agreement in 1952 to restore their coal and steel industries to economic health, in 1957 six European nations—France, West Germany, Italy, and the *Benelux* nations (**Bel**gium, the **Net**herlands, and **Lux**embourg)—signed the Treaty of Rome. The **Treaty of Rome** created the European Economic Community (EEC). The members of the EEC agreed to create a common market among themselves, meaning that:

1. They agreed to allow free trade among themselves (what is necessary for a free trade area).
2. They agreed to develop common trade policies toward non-members (what is necessary to make a free trade area a customs union).
3. They agreed to allow free mobility of labor, capital, and technology among the members (which is necessary to make a customs union a common market).

Over time, the EEC expanded its membership and changed its name twice. In the 1970s, the European Economic Community added Denmark, Ireland, and the United Kingdom as members and changed its name to the European Community (EC). Greece, Spain, and Portugal joined in the 1980s. In 1993, the then 12 EC members amended the Treaty of Rome by signing the Treaty of Maastricht. The **Treaty of Maastricht** established a new goal of intensifying the EC's economic integration by establishing an economic union. As a result of the signing of the Treaty of Maastricht, the EC is now commonly called the European Union (EU). In 1995, three more countries joined the EU—Austria, Finland, and Sweden— bringing it to a total of 15 members. In May 2004, 10 additional countries, most of which were part of the former Soviet bloc, became EU members. The 10 are the Czech Republic, Cyprus, Estonia, Hungary, Latvia, Lithuania, Malta, Poland, the Slovak Republic, and Slovenia. Bulgaria and Romania joined in 2007. Croatia became a EU member in July, 2013. Today, every major Western European country except Norway and Switzerland are members of the EU. Norway and Switzerland were invited to join, but for domestic political reasons chose not to.

1. Governing the European Union

The EU is a unique institution in the world today, which is reflected in its governance structure. Its members are sovereign nations, yet they have agreed to surrender some of their powers to the EU. The EU is thus a "government of governments" and a "supranational government." It is a government of governments because the national governments retain their sovereignty. It is a supranational government because it exercises power above the national level.

The EU is governed by four primary institutions:

1. The *European Council of Ministers* (often referred to simply as the European Council), consisting of 28 representatives, each of which is selected by his or her home nation. Each Council member explicitly represents the interests of his or her home govern-

ment. The Irish representative, for example, fights for the interests and policies of Ireland, while the Dutch representative does the same for the Netherlands. A country's representative serving on the Council changes from issue to issue. When agricultural issues are being discussed, for instance, each country's Minister of Agriculture represents the country on the European Council; when transportation issues are on the agenda, the countries send their Ministers of Transport. On some issues, the Council requires unanimity before it approves a measure. On most issues, the Council requires a qualified majority of 255 votes (out of a maximum of 345) to pass a measure. In such cases, the four most populous EU members (Germany, France, Italy, and the United Kingdom) each have 29 votes. The other countries have lesser numbers of votes, ranging from Spain's and Poland's 27 votes to tiny Malta's 3 votes. However, reflecting the EU's status as a "government of governments," the Council is often unwilling to impose a decision on the minority. It often chooses to move slowly, stalling until it can develop a position that all the members will support. In one recent year, for example, 86 percent of all Council decisions were reached unanimously.

2. The *Commission of the European Union* consists of 28 members, one from each member country. Unlike the members of the Council, once named the 28 commissioners are supposed to shed their national identities and ignore the interests of their home country; all their loyalties are supposed to be given to "Europe" and to the promotion of the objectives of the Treaty of Rome. The Commission administers the EU's bureaucracy—some 33,000 people, popularly known as "Eurocrats"—and the EU's 134 billion annual budget (in April 2013, a euro ( ) was worth $1.30). Since the EU has 24 official languages into which all official documents must be translated, the EU spends 1 billion a year on translation services. Because the Council, the Commission, and many of the Eurocrats are headquartered in Brussels, Belgium, Europeans often use the term "Brussels" to refer to the EU government the way many Americans use the term "Washington" to refer to the U.S. federal government.

3. The *European Parliament* is composed of 736 individuals chosen in national elections once every five years to represent their local interests and philosophies. Seats in Parliament are allocated in rough proportion to population. Germany has the most seats (99), followed by France, Italy, and the United Kingdom (72 each); Malta has the smallest number of representatives, five.

4. The *European Court of Justice* is headed by 28 justices (one from each member state) serving six-year terms. The task of the Court of Justice is to interpret the meaning of EU law and to ensure that the various laws passed by each of the member states are compatible with their obligations under the Treaty of Rome. This latter task is growing in importance; by some estimates, 60 percent of the laws passed by the national governments of the 28 EU members are designed to implement EU laws, regulations, or procedures at the national level.

Decision-making in the EU is incredibly complicated, a reflection of the members' desires to build broad consensus before implementing new policies. Decisions are made slowly, and only with the assent of the Council, the Commission, and (in most cases) the Parliament. For example, seven years after the 1992 deadline for harmonizing EU regulations, the EU was still debating the definition of chocolate. (The Belgians, known for their high-quality chocolates, believe that chocolates can only be made with cocoa butter. The British and the Irish, home to many mass marketers of candy like Cadbury, argue that vegetable fats can be substituted for cocoa butter in producing chocolate.)

The European Council is generally acknowledged as the most powerful of the four institutions governing the EU. Ultimate decision-making power resides in the Council. The Council's power reflects the hesitancy of the member states to cede their sovereignty and control over their economic destinies to the eurocrats.

The European Commission has the sole power to propose legislation. As it controls the bureaucracy, new initiatives are difficult to implement without the cooperation of the Commission.

The Parliament was the weakest of the four governing institutions created by the Treaty of Rome. Each time the Treaty of Rome has been amended, however, the Parliament has received new powers. The most recent example of its new-found muscle was the mass resignation of all of the European Commissioners in 1999, which was triggered by a Parliamentary investigation into fraud, favoritism, inept management, and a lack of accountability in several programs administered by the Commission. As many Europeans are concerned about the lack of democracy in the EU (particularly the Danes and the Swedes) and about the lack of accountability in the EU's programs (an important concern of the British), the Parliament's powers are likely to continue to strengthen as the EU matures.

2. The Struggle to Create a Common Market

The goal of the Treaty of Rome to create a common market was indeed visionary. Unfortunately, it was also well ahead of its time. For many years, the EU members struggled to achieve this goal. To create a common market, the EU members had to come to an agreement to allow free movement of goods, services, and factors of production. To do so, literally thousands of regulations, product standards, and laws of the different member states had to be changed so that they were compatible with one another, which was necessary for one country's products to be sold in other member's markets. However, as our public choice discussion in the previous chapter indicated, a variety of special interest groups in each country resisted changing these rules because they did not wish to make it easier for potential foreign competitors to enter their domestic markets.

The EU originally relied on a process known as **harmonization** to create the common market. The EU encouraged its members to negotiate with one another to voluntarily adopt common or "harmonized" regulations and standards. Unfortunately, there were literally thousands of issues where the member states could not come to an agreement on what the harmonized regulations should look like, thereby frustrating the creation of a common market. In many cases, the positions taken by different states were reasonable, making it difficult for the members to come to an agreement. Consider, for example, the following issues that faced the EU in the early 1990s:

1. British tour companies sponsoring packaged ski vacations in the French Alps wished to hire British ski instructors, believing that neophyte British skiers would be more comfortable learning from some one whose attitudes and language skills were similar to their own. The French authorities insisted that only French-trained ski instructors who understood the local climate and snow conditions should be allowed to teach beginners in the French Alps. Essentially the British argued that the Treaty of Rome allowed any EU citizen to practice his or her trade or profession anywhere within the EU, while the French argued that such goals should not be at the expense of public safety.

2. The Spanish government insisted that any typewriters sold in Spain have a "tilde" key. (The tilde is an important accent mark in the Spanish language.) Typewriter manufacturers in other EU countries argued that such a restriction was contrary to the dictates of the Treaty of Rome. They believed that they should be allowed to sell typewriters without the tilde key in Spain, and that free market forces (and Spanish consumers) would decide whether the tilde key was important or not. The Spanish government replied that it had an obligation to protect the culture of the nation and the purity of its language; of course, Spanish typewriter manufacturers supported this decision, for it dramatically reduced the competitive threat of foreign typewriter imports.

3. When producing cherry yogurt, Belgium allowed its manufacturers to dye the yogurt with dyes made from beet root, but forbade them from using beet root to dye the cherries. German yogurt makers could use beet root to dye cherries, but not the yogurt. The effect was that German cherry yogurt could not be sold in Belgium, while Belgian cherry yogurt could not be sold in Germany.

Many such conflicts persisted for decades. In numerous cases, the EU members were hesitant to adopt harmonized national rules that would make it easy to sell the same product anywhere within the EU. Consider the cherry yogurt case. Belgian manufacturers lobbied their government to insist that any harmonized rule adopted by the EU follow Belgium's regulations. That way, Belgian manufacturers would not have to bear the costs of adapting their production techniques to meet the harmonized rule—their foreign rivals would. Similarly, German yogurt manufacturers lobbied their government to insist that any EU rule follow Germany's regulations. That way, German manufacturers would not bear the costs of adapting to the new rule—their foreign rivals would. In case after case, the national government preferred the status quo to any change that might hurt local firms. As a result, progress in creating the common market was slow. The costs of delay were high, however. EU experts estimated that if one set of rules governing product standards applied uniformly throughout the EU, EU manufacturers could lower their annual production costs by $260 billion, benefiting EU consumers and raising the competitiveness of EU manufacturers in world markets.

Progress toward harmonizing product standards and achieving the common market envisioned by the Treaty of Rome was so slow that some pessimists believed that the EU might collapse. However, in 1979, the *Cassis de Dijon* case came before the European Court of Justice. Cassis de Dijon is a liqueur made from blackcurrants in the Dijon region of France. A German wholesaler wanted to sell cassis in Germany but was unable to do so because of a German law that regulated the alcoholic content of liqueurs. Cassis de Dijon had too low an alcoholic content to qualify for sale in Germany. The German wholesaler sued the appropriate German regulatory authority, arguing that the German regulation violated the free movement of goods provisions of the Treaty of Rome. The case eventually reached the European Court of Justice. The Court found for the German wholesaler. In so doing, the Court developed the concept of **mutual recognition**: if one member state recognizes a product as appropriate for sale, then all other EU members are mutually bound to do the same. This, the Court determined, was an obligation that the members agreed to upon signing the Treaty of Rome. As France had deemed Cassis de Dijon to be a legitimate liqueur, Germany was therefore bound under the Treaty of Rome to allow it to be sold in Germany.

Although the court acknowledged some exceptions to the doctrine of mutual recognition in its decision, the implications of the *Cassis de Dijon* case were enormous. The pressure to harmonize product standards was reduced, because mutual recognition implied that goods legal under the laws of one member state could be sold throughout the EU. At the same time that the *Cassis de Dijon* case was being handed down by the Court of Justice, many Europeans were becoming concerned about the competitiveness of European firms in world markets. The EU renewed its efforts to create the common market called for by the Treaty of Rome. In 1987, the EU members agreed to implement the **Single European Act**, which amended the Treaty of Rome. The Single European Act called for the completion of the internal market (the term developed by the Eurocrats to mean common market) by the end of 1992. It required the adoption of some 279 regulatory changes by the EU and their implementation by all the member states. While not all of these 279 measures were completely implemented by the 1992 deadline, most were. Accordingly, it's fair to say that by the end of 1992 the common market (or internal market) called for by the Treaty of Rome had been put into place—but it took 35 years to do so! However, if you think about the magnitude of the challenge—getting a dozen independent countries (the EU's membership at that time) to cooperate peacefully on such a broad range of activities—perhaps 35 years is a remarkably short period of time.

3. The Treaty of Maastricht

As the Single European Act was taking effect, the Cold War ended. The Soviet Union dissolved, and the threat of nuclear war diminished substantially. The United States stood alone as the world's sole superpower. Some European politicians believed that Europe should free itself from geopolitical domination by the United States and reassert itself on the world's stage. European economists meanwhile believed that European firms were at a competitive disadvantage vis-à-vis their competitors in the other developed nations because of the costs and risks associated with the existence of so many European currencies. Addressing these concerns, in the early 1990s the then 12 EU members negotiated a new treaty that further amended the Treaty of Rome. This agreement, formally known as the **Treaty on European Union**, is more commonly referred to as the **Treaty of Maastricht**, after the small Dutch city where it was negotiated.

The Maastricht Treaty came into effect in November 1993. Besides changing the name of the EC to the EU, it has three primary provisions:

- Establishment of common defense and foreign policies in order to strengthen Europe's power in world politics
- Creation of the cohesion fund
- Creation of the Economic and Monetary Union

To date, the EU has not been very successful in achieving the first objective. EU members have had difficulty developing a consensus on knotty foreign policy questions ranging from Yugoslavia to Iraq to Syria. Their failure to do so has stalled development of common defense policies. The cohesion fund was established in order to promote regional development of countries whose per-capita GDP is less than 90 percent of the EU average, which at the time included Greece, Ireland, Portugal, and Spain. (The Irish economy boomed in the last decade, so Ireland no longer qualifies for additional cohesion funds.) The cohesion fund was designed to help bring the economies of the poorer member states up to the level of their richer brethren.

Creation of the Economic and Monetary Union (EMU) is by far the most important element of the Maastricht Treaty. The EMU calls for the creation of a single currency, called the euro, to serve participating members. In order to participate in the single currency bloc, members have to be in compliance with the **convergence criteria**, a set of requirements that forced their fiscal and monetary policies to converge. The convergence criteria included such elements as:

- The inflation rate of any EU member wishing to use the euro could be no higher that 1.5 percentage points above the average of the three members with the lowest inflation rates
- The long-term interest rates of any EU member wishing to use the euro as its currency could be no higher than 2 percentage points above the average of the three members with the lowest long-term interest rates
- A country's budget deficit could be no more than 3 percent of its GDP
- A government's outstanding debt had to be approaching a limit of no more than 60 percent of its GDP.

The United Kingdom, Denmark, and Sweden chose not to participate in the EMU. Greece initially was unable to meet the convergence criteria, and thus was not allowed to become a charter member of the EMU. However, Greece later met the convergence criteria and joined the single currency bloc in January 2001. Of the EU's 12 newest members, Cyprus, Estonia, Malta, Slovakia, and Slovenia have met the convergence criteria and have adopted the euro as their national currency.

Thus 17 members of the EU participate in the **euro zone**—the area where the euro is being used. The euro came into being on January 1, 1999. On that date the exchange rate between the euro and the national currencies of the participating members was fixed, and each member pledged never to change that exchange rate. However, no euro coins or notes were available on that date. For the next three years, the euro existed only as a bookkeeping currency to settle transactions among participating governments and their banking industries. Finally, on January 1, 2002 euro-denominated coins and bills became available for ordinary consumers to transact their daily business. After a short transition period, the national currencies were withdrawn from circulation and passed into history.

By creating the euro, the EU believed it would significantly reduce the currency conversion costs and exchange rate risks borne by European MNCs. Prior to the advent of the euro, firms conducting business within Europe were forced to pay fees to banks of anywhere from 0.4 to 2 percent of the transaction amount anytime they wished to convert French francs into Belgian francs, German marks into Dutch guilders, etc. Moreover, they bore exchange rate risk in many transactions. **Exchange rate risk** is the risk that an exchange rate may move adversely between the time a contract is entered into and the time that payment is made, thereby reducing the economic benefits derived from the transaction. For example, if the Netherlands-headquartered Philips agreed to sell light bulbs to a German lighting fixtures dealer for 100,000 German marks with payment to be made in 30 days, Philips ran the risk that the mark might fall in value between now and when it received payment. While the foreign exchange market has developed a variety of techniques to reduce this risk, they nonetheless entailed fees. EU officials estimated that Europeans would save $25 to $30 billion annually in currency conversion costs through the introduction of a single currency, making life easier for European travelers and chief financial officers. Many EU political leaders believed that the euro would become as important in world financial markets as the dollar currently is.

While the euro creates important benefits, it does have certain costs. Each of the countries using the euro as its national currency has to surrender control over a portion of its economic destiny. As you have learned (or will learn) in your macroeconomics class, countries have two primary policy tools for controlling inflation, unemployment levels, income growth, etc.: fiscal policy and monetary policy. Eurozone members no longer have any control over their monetary policy. Instead, the newly created **European Central Bank** (headquartered in Frankfurt, Germany) is now in charge of controlling the Eurozone's money supply, interest rates, and inflation. While the Maastricht Treaty says that the European Central Bank will focus on controlling inflation, many members of Eurozone believe that the European Central Bank should concentrate on solving the EU's chronic unemployment problems. Germany and the Netherlands are the primary supporters of the anti-inflation point of view, while France would prefer that the European Central Bank emphasize job growth. Fear that the French viewpoint would dominate the European Central Bank's decision making is one of the reasons that the United Kingdom chose not to be a charter member of the Eurozone.

4. The Future of the EU

The members of the European Union have done a remarkable job of implementing the goals of the Treaty of Rome. Nonetheless, the EU faces many challenges in the new millennium. The EU's voting rules and powers of its governing institutions may have to be altered. Some members felt that the EU's decision-making was too slow and unwieldy with 15 members. They fear that EU decision-making will crawl to a halt with 13 new members and no change in the existing voting rules. Other members believe that any change in the voting rules will shift power from the European Council of Ministers to the European Commission and inevitably lead to an unwarranted expansion of the EU's meddling in the national policies of its members. Addition of new members also has budgetary implications. The proposed entrants are much poorer and more agriculturally oriented than the existing members. Thus, many political leaders fear that their entry will inevitably result in future massive increases in the EU's budget and huge transfer payments from richer members like Germany, Luxembourg, and the Netherlands. Moreover, their entry will likely trigger major changes in the EU's Common Agricultural Policy, which subsidizes thousands of inefficient EU farmers at very high costs to the EU budget and to EU consumers. Existing beneficiaries of the EU's agricultural policies are not happy at the prospect of sharing their subsidies with hundreds of thousands of Czech, Hungarian, Polish, and other farmers.

Perhaps the most important challenge facing the members, however, is answering the fundamental question of what is the purpose of the EU. Is the EU primarily an economic entity or a political one? Some Europeans, led by the British, believe that the EU should focus on promoting the original goals of the Treaty of Rome, facilitating the free movement of goods, services, labor, capital, and technology among its members so that all may prosper from the benefits created by free trade and open markets. Other Europeans, led by some French politicians, believe that the creation of a strong, politically unified Europe should be the ultimate aspiration of the EU. Through the promotion of Europe-wide policies and initiatives, the French believe that Europe can re-establish its position as the world's premier geopolitical power. More importantly, the French believe that this approach will ensure that the nations of Europe avoid destroying each other as they did twice in the century that just ended.

B. NAFTA

The world's second largest trading bloc is located in North America. The North American Free Trade Agreement (NAFTA) is a free trade agreement among the three largest countries in North America—Canada, Mexico, and the United States. NAFTA builds upon strong pre-existing trading relationships between the United States and Canada and between the United States and Mexico. Even before the 1994 implementation of NAFTA, Canada and Mexico were the largest and third-largest trade partners of the United States, respectively. However, trade between Mexico and Canada was relatively minor. Access to the huge U.S. market is critical to both its NAFTA partners. Approximately 75 percent of export-dependent Canada's exports are to the United States; exports of Mexico's *maquiladoras* (plants along the U.S.–Mexico border that enjoyed preferential tariff status) were Mexico's second-largest source of foreign exchange.

1. The NAFTA Negotiations

NAFTA's primary goal is to promote economic prosperity of its members and further the economic integration of the North American economy. Many U.S. and Canadian MNCs believed that they could reduce their production costs substantially if they could build one factory that could serve all NAFTA consumers, rather than erect three smaller plants, one in each country, that would serve only local customers. NAFTA members agreed to eliminate tariffs on most goods shipped from one member to another over a period of 15 years, although some sectors were treated differently. For example, tariffs on automotive parts and products were phased out over a 10-year period. Many existing restrictions on FDI were eliminated. This provision primarily affected Mexico, which had more extensive restrictions on FDI than either Canada or the United States. Mexico promised, for example, to open up access to its financial services industry to Canadian and U.S. investors. However, certain politically powerful industries were exempted from NAFTA. Mexico refused to open its energy industry to FDI, believing its oil and gas reserves to be part of its "national patrimony" that should be developed only by Mexicans for the benefit of Mexicans. Canada protected its cultural industries—broadcasting, book and magazine publishing, and filmed entertainment—from FDI. Canada feared that without such protections these industries would be overwhelmed by their much larger U.S. counterparts, and Canada would lose its identity and heritage to its more populous Southern neighbor. Similarly, the United States refused to drop its prohibitions against foreigners holding majority stakes in U.S. broadcasting and air transportation firms.

The negotiations leading to the signing of the NAFTA were not easy. Labor unions in the United States and Canada were concerned that foreign companies might build so-called **screwdriver plants** to take advantage of the lowering of tariffs among NAFTA members. A screwdriver plant is one in which minimal value is added to the product. Metaphorically, in such factories the only equipment a worker needs is a screwdriver. Suppose, for example, that a Korean company manufactured automatic transmissions at a factory in Seoul and completely assembled them there except for one screw. The transmissions could then be shipped to Monterrey, where Mexican workers could twist in the final screw. Having received their final assembly in Mexico, the Korean firm could argue that the transmissions were "Mexican made" and hence qualified for NAFTA's low tariffs. To insure that foreign firms couldn't engage in such practices, the NAFTA contains **rules of origin** that determine whether a good is North-American-made and thus qualifies for preferential treatment under NAFTA. The general rule of origin is that products must undergo "substantial transformation" in order to qualify as North American. While what constitutes "substantial transformation" will largely be determined by court decisions, no doubt the Korean transmissions would fail this test. Some industries have their own rule of origin. In the automobile industry, for example, the rule of origin states that in order to qualify as a North American automobile, at least 62.5 percent of the value of the vehicle must have originated in Canada, Mexico, or the United States. The impact of this rule of origin has been significant. Volkswagen, for example, has had to increase its purchases of U.S.- and Canadian-made auto parts to ensure that vehicles coming off the assembly lines at its plant in Puebla, Mexico, qualify as North American in origin. The textile industry has a different type of rule of origin, called "yarn forward" or "fiber forward." To gain preferential tariff treatment under NAFTA, textiles or apparel must use fibers and yarn produced by Canadian, U.S., or Mexican mills.

Several other major issues arose in the public debate leading to the approval of NAFTA. The AFL-CIO and its affiliated unions, which are key elements of the Democratic Party's electoral base, were vocal opponents of the signing of NAFTA. The unions feared that many U.S. companies would take advantage of NAFTA to reduce their labor costs by shifting high-wage unionized jobs to Mexico. The AFL-CIO also raised concerns about the inadequacy of protection of human rights and workers' rights in Mexico. Environmental groups feared that U.S. companies would shut down their domestic factories and flee to Mexico in order to escape the costly environmental protection standards laid down by the Environmental Protection Agency and other environmental regulators in favor of less onerous regulations issued by their Mexican counterparts. As a result of pressures from the unions and the environmental groups, the NAFTA regulators agreed to two side agreements that protected workers' rights and the environment.

2. NAFTA's Impact

When the NAFTA was being debated in the U.S. Congress, proponents argued that it would be critical to the nation's future prosperity: approval would create hundreds of thousands of new jobs and happy times would soon arrive; its rejection, however, would lead to economic catastrophe. Opponents, no less apocalyptic in their language, argued the reverse. In reality, NAFTA has led neither to a brave new world nor to the end of the world. Most experts believe that NAFTA has a positive, though modest impact on Canada and the United States. Mexico, however, enjoyed substantial gains with the implementation of the treaty. Employment in its exporting sector doubled, from 600,000 prior to NAFTA to over 1.2 million workers. Mexico's importance as a manufacturing hub was temporarily diminished when China joined the World Trade Organization in 2001. In the early 2000s, many MNCs shifted their production facilities from Mexico to China to take advantage of the large supply of low-cost labor then available there. However, in the past decade wage rates have risen rapidly in China—an estimated 14 percent per year—so some MNCs have begun to shift production back to Mexico from China.

C. Mercosur and the Andean Pact

The preceding chapter discussed the evolution of economic policies adopted by many Latin American countries. During much of the Cold War, these countries had chosen to wall off their markets from foreign goods by adopting high tariffs, only to observe that their economic growth rates lagged behind those enjoyed by Southeast Asian countries that had adopted aggressive export-promotion policies. Numerous governments in the region elected in the late 1980s or early 1990s abandoned the policies of their predecessors and opened up their markets. Countries like Mexico, Brazil, Argentina, Bolivia, and Chile relaxed government regulations of their private sectors, encouraged FDI, privatized publicly-owned firms, and reduced trade barriers.

The signing of the **Mercosur Accord** in March 1991 furthered these policy initiatives. *Mercosur* refers to the geographic name in Spanish for the region where its four founding members—Argentina, Brazil, Paraguay, and Uruguay—are located. They agreed to establish a customs union and pledged to slash their tariffs on trade between themselves over a four-year period. In 1995, the members instituted a common external tariff on most goods imported into the Accord's domain, thereby implementing the customs union envisioned in 1991. Bolivia, Chile, Colombia, Ecuador, Peru, and Venezuela later joined Mercosur as associate members, agreeing to participate in its free trade area aspects but not its customs union elements.

Mercosur's performance to date has been impressive, although not without difficulties. During its first six years, trade among Mercosur members rose from $4 to $14 billion; in 2011 intra-Mercosur trade reached $54 billion. Foreign investors flocked to Mercosur, entranced by the opportunity to sell to a 380-million-person market with a combined GDP of $4.1 trillion. Of particular note was the $18 billion in FDI made by the world's leading motor vehicle manufacturers, including GM, Ford, Toyota, BMW, and Daimler. However, many of Latin America's emerging markets were hurt by the 1997–1998 Asian currency crisis. Brazil was particularly hard hit. Inflation soared, the Brazilian authorities devalued the Brazilian *real*, and investor confidence in the region deteriorated. Because Argentina competed with Brazil for export markets and FDI, it too was forced to devalue its currency in order to remain competitive with Brazil. Unfortunately, much of its foreign debt was denominated in U.S. dollars; Argentina then plunged into a fiscal crisis because of the difficulties of repaying the borrowed funds with its devalued currency.

South America is home to a second major trading bloc, the **Andean Pact**, which was formed in 1969. Its original members were Bolivia, Chile, Colombia, Ecuador, and Peru; Chile later dropped its membership but was replaced by Venezuela. For the first two decades of its existence, the Andean Pact was generally considered to be a failure. Trade among its members accounted for only 5 percent of their total trade. Part of the problem lay in geography: the Andes Mountains, after which the agreement is named, form a natural barrier to trade. The protectionist, import-substitution policies adopted by most of the Andean Pact countries also discouraged trade among its members.

In response to the signing of the Mercosur agreement, in 1991 the Andean Pact members recognized the need to rejuvenate their agreement. They agreed to establish a customs union, common regulations on capital movements, agriculture, and immigration, and a common external tariff. The new approach enjoyed modest success. By 2011, trade among members had risen to 6.9 percent of the members' total trade. In 2005, Mercosur and the Andean Pact agreed to a new cooperative agreement: the nations of the Andean Pact became associate members of Mercosur, while Mercosur members became associate members of the Andean Pact.

D. ASEAN and APEC

Asia is home to two important trading blocs. The **Association of Southeast Asian Nations (ASEAN)** was created in 1967 to promote economic and political cooperation in that region of the world. Founding members Thailand, Singapore, the Philippines, Malaysia, Indonesia, and Brunei were joined by Vietnam, Myanmar (the new name for Burma), Laos, and Cambodia in the 1990s. In 1993, ASEAN established a free trade area. Members pledged to eliminate tariffs on manufactured goods imported from other ASEAN countries by 2003, and on most other goods by the end of that decade. As is the case with other trading blocs, many MNCs have adopted ASEAN-wide strategies as internal barriers to trade and FDI have fallen.

The **Asia-Pacific Economic Cooperation** Forum (APEC) initiative has 21 members drawn from both coasts of the Pacific Ocean, including Canada, the United States, Mexico, Chile, Japan, Russia, China, the Four Tigers, Australia, New Zealand, and most of the members of ASEAN. APEC's members account for about 40 percent of world trade. APEC provides another forum for major trading powerhouses like the United States, Canada, Japan, South Korea, and China to lower trade and investment barriers.

CHAPTER SUMMARY

Representatives of 44 Allied nations met in Bretton Woods, New Hampshire, in 1944 to construct an international economic environment that would promote peace and prosperity after the Second World War ended. The Bretton Woods conference led to the creation of the World Bank and the International Monetary Fund.

The General Agreement on Tariffs and Trade (GATT) was responsible for slashing average tariffs from 40 to 3 percent over its lifetime (1947–1994). Its mission was taken over by the World Trade Organization, which was established in 1995 to reduce other impediments to trade in goods and services, protect intellectual property, and facilitate trade-related international investment.

Regional trading blocs play an important role in today's global economy. There are four different types of regional trading blocs: free trade area, customs union, common market, and economic union. Regional trading blocs expand trade among their members and raise the productivity and efficiency of firms and workers.

The most important regional trading bloc is the European Union, a 28-member association of European countries that account for 25 percent of the world's economy. The European Union is governed by four institutions: the Council of Ministers, the European Commission, the European Parliament, and the European Court of Justice. Seventeen of the EU members have abandoned their domestic currencies and adopted a common currency, the euro. Other important trading blocs include NAFTA, Mercosur, ASEAN, and APEC.

INDEX

Q

Quartering Act, 15
Quartering Act of 1765, 14
quasi contract, 85–86
quasi in rem jurisdiction, 66
quid pro quo sexual harassment, 316
quotas, 385–386

R

racial discrimination in employment,
    elimination of, 317–318
*Rahul K. Nath, M.D. v. Texas Children's Hospital
    and Baylor College of Medicine* 375 S.W.3d 403
    (Tex. App. Houston [14th District] 2012), 126
Railway Labor Act, 247
ratification, 95, 111
ratification, agency by, 111
ratification process, 18–19
rational basis test, 46
real property, 136
reasonable accommodations, 318
reasonable person of ordinary prudence, 158
reasonably accommodate religious
    requirements, 317
Reasonably Available Control Technology
    (RACT), 361
rebuttal witnesses, 74
reformation, 109
Refrigerator Safety Act (RSA), 214
Regents of University of California v. Bakke, 438
    U.S. 265 (1978), 61
regional trading blocs, 398–413
Regulation B, 342–343
Regulation E, 348–350
regulation of environment, Clean Air Act in
    1963, 359–361
regulation of environment, Clean Water Act of
    1972, 1977, 361–368
regulation of environment, command-and-
    control methods, 355–356
regulation of environment, environment
    movement, 357–359
regulation of environment, hazardous solid
    wastes, 364–366
regulation of environment, legislation, 355–356
regulation of environment, noise pollution, 367

regulation of environment, nuclear wastes, 366
regulation of environment, pollution issues,
    356–357
regulation of environment, private protection,
    368–369
regulation of environment, thermal pollution,
    362–364
regulation of environment, tort laws,
    353–354
regulation of environment, toxic substances,
    364
regulation of environment, trends in, 369
regulation of environment, voluntary
    compliance, 354–355
regulation of environment, Water Quality Act
    of 1987, 361–368
Regulation Z, 335
Regulatory Flexibility Act in 1980, 195
regulatory role, 1
Reichert v. State ex rel McCulloch 278 P.3d 455, 58
rejection, 90
rejoinder, 74
relevant market, 241
religious discrimination, elimination of, 317
Religious Freedom Restoration Act of 1993
    (RFRA), 41
remand, 75
Removal Doctrine, 65
repudiation, 105–106
request for admissions, 71
request for production, 71–72
resale price maintenance (RPM), 232
rescission, 108
rescission contract, 103
Reserve Powers Clause, 24
Resource Conservation and Recovery Act
    (RCRA), 364–365
respondeat superior, 113
restatement (third) of torts, 171
restitution, 95, 108–109
restraint of trade, 222
reverse the lower court, 75
revocation, 90
Revolutionary War, 15
Reynolds v. United States 98 U.S. 145 (1878), 39
right of privacy, 47